CorelDRAW® X6:
The Official Guide

About the Author

Gary David Bouton is a seasoned author and illustrator with over 25 books to his name, covering programs such as CorelDRAW, Adobe Photoshop, and topics such as digital video editing, content creation for the Web, and 3D modeling. Gary has been drawing and painting, both traditionally and electronically, for close to 40 years and has been writing books and articles on art since 1992. He has received four international awards for design and desktop publishing and was a finalist in the CorelDRAW World Design Contest. In his other life, Gary composes and records music and produces animation and special effects for commercials and films.

About the Technical Editor

William Schneider currently teaches computer graphics and darkroom photography in the School of Visual Communication at Ohio University. He was a finalist in the annual Corel World Design Contest on two occasions and has written numerous magazine articles about photography and computer artwork. Bill's photographs and graphical designs have also been published in a number of venues, including *Italian Renaissance Art: A Source Book,* for which he created hundreds of illustrations and photographs. When not working at the computer or printing in his darkroom, Bill likes to ice skate and build loudspeakers in his basement workshop.

CorelDRAW® X6:
The Official Guide

Gary David Bouton

New York Chicago San Francisco Lisbon
London Madrid Mexico City Milan New Delhi
San Juan Seoul Singapore Sydney Toronto

The McGraw-Hill Companies

Library of Congress Cataloging-in-Publication Data

Bouton, Gary David, 1953-
 CorelDRAW X6 : the official guide / Gary David Bouton.
  pages cm.
 ISBN 978-0-07-179007-9 (alk. paper)
 1. CorelDRAW!   2. Computer graphics.   I. Title.
 T385.B68317 2012
 006.6—dc23

                                2012026123

CorelDRAW® X6: The Official Guide

34567890   DOC DOC   109876543

ISBN   978-0-07-179007-9
MHID   0-07-179007-1

Sponsoring Editor	**Technical Editor**	**Production Supervisor**
Megg Morin	William Schneider	George Anderson
Editorial Supervisor	**Copy Editor**	**Composition**
Patty Mon	LeeAnn Pickrell	Cenveo Publisher Services
Project Editor	**Proofreader**	**Illustration**
LeeAnn Pickrell	Paul Tyler	Gary David Bouton, Lyssa Wald, Jay's Publisher's Services
Acquisitions Coordinator	**Indexer**	
Stephanie Evans	Karin Arrigoni	**Art Director, Cover**
		Jeff Weeks

The Internet's a double-edged sword: it can bring people together who would never meet otherwise, and it also tends to reduce human beings to names, digits, statistics, and occasionally to fiction.

I dedicate this book to the memory of Jan Jue, our Copy Editor for several versions of the CorelDRAW: The Official Guide. *We never met in person, but I feel, as all of us on this project do, a profound sense of loss. Most of our readers will have no idea what it's like to update a book and come across a fond passage or exchange in the manuscript, and realize what you're reading is a legacy. It was very hard to write the book I want this one to be, while realizing that Jan isn't with us; she's not making humorous comments in the margins, she's not saving my reputation by correcting an oversight.*

I feel privileged to have worked with Jan, and although I'm confident we did our best to make this book our best one to date, there's still something missing from it.

God bless you, Jan.

Contents at a Glance

viii Contents at a Glance

Contents

x Contents

PART II   Getting Started with CorelDRAW X6

PART III   Working with Object Tools

PART VI   Creating the Illusion of 3D Objects

PART VII   Creating Special Effects

xx Contents

xxiv   Contents

Foreword

For many years, CorelDRAW Graphics Suite users from around the world have been creating amazing designs! From illustrations to logos to vehicle graphics to impactful marketing collateral (and everything in between), our users have trusted the tools and the power that the suite has provided. We at Corel couldn't be more excited about our latest release, CorelDRAW Graphics Suite X6. The mix of new features, enhancements, and performance gains has set a new standard for graphics design.

Some of the most important resources that a CorelDRAW user can take advantage of in achieving success with CorelDRAW Graphics Suite are the many learning materials available to them. With product videos or in-product tips and documentation, our users trust that Corel will provide them with great material to optimize their learning and also to help them to be as successful as possible in mastering the tools.

To take your learning to the next level, however, this *CorelDRAW X6: The Official Guide* equips you with an amazing array of content to help you get the most out of the suite. Gary Bouton provides expert instruction on illustration techniques, the broad set of tools in the suite, and ultimately teaches you how to get the results you need. The examples in *The Official Guide* are explained in a way that is relevant to your goals and projects. Dozens of example files and step-by-step instructions will truly inspire you. Gary worked closely with the product team at Corel to ensure that, from cover to cover, the material in this guide will maximize the potential for professionals and aspiring designers to achieve success and create amazing results. Congratulations to Gary for developing such a wonderful resource!

The Official Guide is packed with helpful references, expert insights, great visuals, and reflects Gary's passion, which truly represents the spirit of the product. Both beginners and experts alike will find this guide to be a very effective way of extending their skills in CorelDRAW Graphics Suite X6. Enjoy!

John Falsetto
Senior Product Manager, CorelDRAW
Corel Corporation
Ottawa, Ontario
May 2012

Acknowledgments

Do you realize there's an unmarked car outside your door and a guy with sunglasses is pointing a device at your living room window? Right *now*?

Onnnnly kidding! It's very hard to get readers' attention in the Front Matter of a book when they know there's a lot more interesting stuff after the pages marked with Roman numerals.

Now that I'm certain I have your attention, I'd like you to know that if you enjoy this book (the correct answer is yes, you will), all of us who worked together on it had just as much fun *creating* it. The author, the production and layout people, and the editors just *clicked* with this book, as we did with the X5 and X4 books. As we worked against deadlines to bring you this hefty piece of documentation, we shared some laughs, some tears, and considering we all telecommuted, it was a very real, personal, and productive experience. I'd like to introduce my friends to you now and to thank them for making my part in *CorelDRAW X6: The Official Guide* the best kick one could possibly have without breaking any state or federal laws:

- *To Megg Morin.* Time after time, you amaze me with your graciousness. Megg has always allowed me to tell the CorelDRAW story my way, and she trusts my take on what's needed to help both the fine illustrator and the Accidental Art Director. Even when I confessed to this die-hard Red Sox fan—on the 100th Anniversary of Fenway Park—that I'm a Yankees fan, she supported my judgment on the book's content and even began sending me e-mail on Canadian pharmacy products and Magic Jack. Megg, you're the best, always have been, and a big thanks.
- *To Stephanie Evans,* who now allows me to call her "Steph," for keeping track of an immense amount of data and also for helping *me* stay organized. You start wandering aimlessly in the parking lot with a tinfoil cap if you try to keep track of chapter, figures, and tutorial files all by yourself. Mercifully, I didn't have to. Thanks, Steph.
- *Project Editor LeeAnn Pickrell.* Thanks to LeeAnn for pulling double-duty on this book, and correcting spelling and grammar but not correcting my thoughts and steps. LeeAnn didn't hesitate to verify anything that wasn't absolutely clear in the manuscript. At times, it was like having two Tech Editors, and I'm positive that our readers will appreciate the double scoop of clarity and direction. And if there

is anything you might not understand in the book, this is okay—it's either my Mr. Norris or LeeAnn's Henry doing some after-hours cat typing at our computers. How they find the icon for MS Word to launch it, we'll never know. Thanks, LeeAnn!

- *Technical Editor William Schneider*. Bill really *should* be listed as coauthor on the cover of this book, but that would probably mean making my own name smaller. *Nah*. Bill worked exhaustively with me getting the new features and commands right for our readers, and he even did the updating to the online PDF bonus chapters and appendix, including 22 pages of revised and accurate keyboard shortcuts, which I'm sure will make fascinating summer reading if you're done with all the Ludlum novels. Bill always offered a different and better way to cast a sentence and put a tutorial step in more reader-friendly terms. Bill, thanks, as always, for being my favorite technical editor for over fifteen years of books.
- Nicky Elliott, Barbara Bouton, and William Schneider for the use of their photography in this book's tutorials.
- Nick Wilkinson for portions of his original manuscript on VBA.
- Lyssa Wald for once again making the color section look as good on the printed page as it does on my monitor.
- *Production Supervisor George Anderson*. Thanks to George and his expert team for the layout of this book's interior.
- The folks at Jay's Publisher's Services, who allowed me to get in there and work on a few figures to make them look their best in a black-and-white book.
- *John Falsetto at Corel Corporation*. Thanks for going that extra mile, John, and promptly providing me with answers to technical questions during the beta cycle right up to the release version of X6. The sort of candid backs-and-forths we exchanged in e-mail were productive, refreshing, and ultimately for the better of the book.
- *Tony Severenuk at Corel Corporation*. Thanks to Tony, for his technical support, his speed, and his ability to cut to the chase when I needed frank answers at a moment's notice. Hats off and a big bow of appreciation to you and all the people at Corel Corporation for supporting this book and my efforts. I hope I did you all proud.

Introduction

Bear with me as you read this book. Like any ongoing piece of literature, *CorelDRAW X6: The Official Guide* is a work in progress. Yes, the book *is* complete, but I wanted to approach the documentation of a new version of CorelDRAW a little differently—okay, a *lot* differently—than did previous versions of this book. I've tried very hard to put a little of myself into this book, so you know that someone real, who professes to know CorelDRAW in certain ways better than you do, is communicating with you. Let's get real: CorelDRAW is *large.* The application has so many features that you might feel at times as well-oriented as searching for a credit card blindfolded at the bottom of a swimming pool in snorkel gear and woolen mittens.

So I want you to know I'm *here* for you; I want you to feel as though you own a Pocket Author, who talks to you in PlainSpeak, who makes tutorial files not only relevant but also interesting, and who as an artist provides you with what you need to accomplish a task instead of a generic, "This is what you need," or a presumptuous, "This is what we think you need." I'm going to ask you to think about what it is you want to do in CorelDRAW throughout the chapters, because you're probably a goal-oriented sort of fine artist or business professional. Although we have some of the best documentation on these pages concerning where items are, what tools do, and other structural definitions of CorelDRAW, knowing where a tool is, and knowing the steps to create a logo your boss wanted last Tuesday are two entirely different approaches to understanding. One is called "having a bunch of facts memorized" and the other is called "wisdom."

You'll see what I mean as you read through the chapters and work through the dozens of tutorial examples and files. Read this book, but *embrace* what you learn. I've learned through years of working in the field of graphics that when you understand a technique or a principle, you *own* it. You take it everywhere you go; it's part of your own personal craft; and you're all the richer as an artist when you digest the information you're given and turn it into something uniquely your own.

CorelDRAW X6: The Official Guide is divided into nine parts, plus PDF versions of an Appendix listing keyboard shortcuts that'll speed up your work in CorelDRAW and two bonus chapters you can download.

Organization is key to explaining things, so the parts follow a progression, from a very basic introduction to later chapters that delve into special effects, and with this edition, we've added two complete chapters on Corel PHOTO-PAINT because it's an important program you *will* use if you first understand how to edit bitmap images. If you're the type of reader who likes to begin at the beginning and make a linear voyage to finish with the last chapter, you won't be surprised. However, the chapters are structured and fairly compartmentalized to address a specific topic; if you want fast solutions for specific areas within CorelDRAW, you can also "pick and choose." One of the wonderful things about books is that you can skip ahead and rewind, just like with your home entertainment center—and there are no commercials to dodge!

- **Part I** starts you off with the new features in CorelDRAW X6, a must-read for users who've made the upgrade. In particular, Chapter 1 is a tutorial-based jumpstart into graphics productivity—you'll create new stuff as you learn what's new! Also in this part, you'll be guided through CorelDRAW options, thoroughly pore through the menus and palettes (including CorelDRAW dockers), and you'll learn how to set up the workspace to make you feel right at home. New users are encouraged to set aside some quality time for this part—you'll save a lot of time later when you want to get to the Fun Stuff.
- **Part II** focuses on navigating and measuring the workspace and your document, and how to size things up, from measuring objects to moving and rotating them. You'll also learn how to set up a multi-page document and create brochures and flyers. You'll see that each page can be a unique size and orientation.
- **Part III** gets you up and running with two of the most important tools used in designing original artwork—the Pen tools and the Shape Tool. You'll also get a handle on creating shapes by using various presets CorelDRAW has to offer. Once you have your object created and edited to your liking, it's only natural to make more of them; this part shows you how to arrange, group, duplicate, clone, and perform other tasks in your document to make laying out what you've created an inspired effort.
- **Part IV** dives into typography, working with Artistic and Paragraph Text, spelling and other CorelDRAW proofing tools, and some special effects you can create for fancy headlines. Sometimes it's better to just say it instead of show it; CorelDRAW has the ideal tools for both the text and graphic message, and this part of the book also shows how to blend the two vehicles artistically for what you want to communicate.
- **Part V** puts the meat on the bones of the objects you design; in these chapters, you'll learn everything you need to know about object fills, outline properties, and most importantly, digital color. Learn how to define and apply Uniform Fills, Bitmap Fills, and colors from different *color models* to your work so they'll print exactly as you intend them to. And if you need a map or schematic drawing, check out this part for the lowdown on creating dashed lines, lines with arrowheads, and more.
- **Part VI** is a truly special part; you'll see that 3D object and scene creation doesn't require a megabuck modeling program—you'll find what you need to make scenes in camera-perfect perspective with CorelDRAW's Effects menu. You'll also learn how to extrude objects, letting CorelDRAW perform calculations to create a side view of the front of objects you draw. It's fun, and the result can have the visual impact you need to create new worlds and sell your ideas.

- **Part VII** comes with a boatload of CorelDRAW special effects features, and these chapters take you through the steps to distorting, blending, and creating photorealistic effects such as object transparency and soft, lifelike shadows. If you've ever been stuck at a point where your design needs that "special something," look into this part of the book. Learn how to create shading like you've seen in airbrush illustrations, to design chrome and glass-like objects, and to create a seamless integration between what you draw and the digital photos you can place in your document.

- **Part VIII** (that's "8" if you're tired of reading Roman numerals) moves from vector drawing to bitmap editing; specifically, you'll learn how Corel PHOTO-PAINT can help you resize and retouch photos and help you make near-perfect pictures into outstanding ones. Also in this part, you'll see how to work *between* CorelDRAW and PHOTO-PAINT to make a seamless composition that contains *both* vector and bitmap art. PHOTO-PAINT is part of the CorelDRAW Graphics Suite; it's sitting there for you on disk or on your hard drive. If you have a brochure or gallery photo you need to get out there to get noticed, get with the program, and the program is Corel PHOTO-PAINT. This is truly an advanced section of the book, but it's accessible to readers of all skill levels, and its contents take you through working with photographs, getting your prints looking their best, and more. You'll also see how to get the best look out of imported bitmaps, beginning right with CorelDRAW's Raw Lab. Learn how to work with image resolutions, and see how to export your vector drawings to bitmap file format. You'll also want to pore through CorelDRAW's HTML publishing features—make that print ad you've designed into a web banner with only a few clicks.

- **Part IX** (pronounced "icks") introduces you to CorelDRAW's extensive host of print options and features; the techniques for output to paper, film, and transfer materials; and CorelDRAW's preflight options so your time and the expense of professional printing are on your side. Also, you'll learn how to prep your designs for nonprinting purposes. Get all the details on how CorelDRAW X6 can export your work for the Web, how to make a basic web page, and post it on the Web to show to the world.

- **Online Bonus Chapters** document Visual Basic for Applications (VBA) in a PDF file you can download from **www.mhprofessional.com**. See how to write simple scripts without actually writing a line of code (it's visual; you record cursor movements), and speed up your work by automating common tasks through VBA. Also, learn how to design a typeface using CorelDRAW, and export your very own TrueType font. Imagine making and distributing a font that has your company logo to everyone in your department. You'll learn the steps in this online PDF document and become font savvy in a jiffy.

- **The Appendix**, also online, is full of shortcuts you can use in CorelDRAW. Find a task you need to perform faster, and the Appendix lists the combinations of keys you can press to get you where you need to go.

Tutorial and Bonus Content: Where to Find It

Tutorial

You can't miss a Tutorial section: it's marked with a Tutorial icon. Many of these Tutorials will go better and more smoothly, and better demonstrate a technique or principle, if you have a working file loaded in the drawing window, so we've provided you with several. At the beginning of most chapters, you'll see a Download icon in the margin (a down-arrow icon); that's your clue to open the file you were asked to download at the beginning of most chapters. To get the tutorial files, go to the following URLs:

- **www.mhprofessional.com/bouton**   From this page, scroll to the McGraw-Hill brands section at bottom of the page, click the square McGraw-Hill Professional, and from the next page, click the Downloads link. Locate this book's title and click to get to the tutorial files.
- **www.theboutons.com**   This is a mirror site for the files. Go to the top page, and you can't miss the conspicuous, obnoxious, but superbly designed *CorelDRAW X6: The Official Guide* Download icon.

Additionally, www.theboutons.com has some Bonus Content, goodies for our readers that have nothing to do with this book's Tutorials, but *everything* to do with your continuing adventures in CorelDRAW. The Boutons are offering original, seamless tiling textures—perfect for web page backgrounds, custom object fills, and backgrounds in your CorelDRAW documents. You'll also find high-resolution images of indoor and outdoor scenes with blank signage. Because so many CorelDRAW users create billboards, package designs, and vinyl signs for vehicles, we thought it would be nice if you could previsualize a logo or other signage. You can then show your design to clients and coworkers before you go through the expense of commercial printing.

The entire group who helped make this book happen were highly motivated to make this *Official Guide* reflect all the creative possibilities that you'll have fun learning, exploring, and building upon. Playtime isn't the only time when a creative person can have fun. Work time can be fun, too.

It's how you *approach* it.

So *enough* with introductions! Turn the page and get to the Good Stuff!

—Gary David Bouton

PART I

CorelDRAW X6 Essentials

1 What's New and Different in CorelDRAW X6?

CorelDRAW X6 brings new ways to accomplish things to anyone who wants or needs to get something graphical done—faster, easier, there's something for everyone in this version. From connecting to the files you need at a moment's notice via Corel CONNECT, to creating shapes as though you're painting them with the new Smear and Twirl Tools—you'll work smart and have *fun* along the way.

This chapter takes you on a tour of the new features and what has changed between X6 and previous versions. This chapter notes where in this guide more extensive coverage is offered for something you're interested in learning. And so without further pause...

 Download and extract all the files from the Chapter 1.zip archive to follow the tutorials in this chapter.

Corel CONNECTing to Content

Corel CONNECT is a media browser that runs as a standalone application and also can be called from inside CorelDRAW and PHOTO-PAINT. Corel CONNECT can be configured in only moments to display the contents of offline media (such as Flickr and your Corel Graphics Suite installation DVD) or the contents of any folder on your hard disk, and to create a tray—or several trays—that can be accessed at any time within the application. What's new in version X6 is that you can quickly display more than one tray of media within DRAW and PHOTO-PAINT, so you can organize resources for compositions in an effective and orderly style.

Figure 1-1 shows the Corel CONNECT interface above the CorelDRAW workspace, as well as three trays docked to the bottom of the DRAW interface. To get a default tray

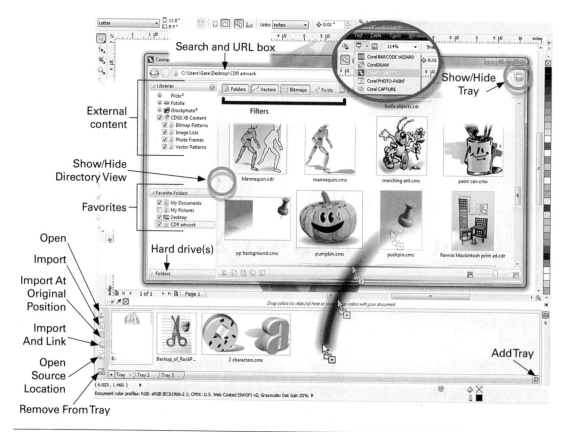

FIGURE 1-1   Corel CONNECT puts you in touch with the media you want from within CorelDRAW and PHOTO-PAINT.

to appear in CorelDRAW, first launch Corel CONNECT. You can click the CONNECT button to the left of the Import button on the Standard Bar, or the Application Launcher drop-down list (the button on the Standard Bar below the Text main menu item), and choose Corel CONNECT. CONNECT can also be launched externally to DRAW from the Windows Start menu. If a default tray isn't already docked to the bottom of the CorelDRAW workspace, choose Window | Dockers | Tray. Let's examine what's available and what the various elements do:

- **Libraries**   CONNECT offers links to predetermined external content, such as images from iStockphoto and content from CorelDRAW X6's massive collection of clipart, images, fonts, and other media. Some libraries are subscription-based, whereas media such as Corel's are free to download and use. Be sure to read any agreement carefully when you browse.
- **Favorites**   If you have media that CorelDRAW or PHOTO-PAINT can import, you can choose among your Windows Favorites to add to a tray. Any folder you add to Windows Favorites is available for quick access; you can see in Figure 1-1 that a personal folder from the author's hard drive has been added to the Favorites list, a collection of CorelDRAW and CMX files.

- **Folders**   Click to expand this list to access any folder on hard drive(s) you have created that contain importable media. The Folders area is simply an alternative way of looking at the user files on your computer.
- **Filters**   It's easy to create a folder whose contents are a potpourri of different media. CONNECT helps limit the search of a folder by displaying only the recognized file types you choose. For example, if you click only the Bitmaps Filter button and leave the other file type buttons undepressed, the preview pane will show only thumbnails of BMP, TIFF, PNG, and other bitmap-type files in the folder.
- **Search and URL box**   Use this field to conduct a search and also to go to a website when your computer has an active Internet connection. Details are in the upcoming tutorial.
- **Tray menu items**   To the vertical left of the default tray are commands that become available when there is content in the tray, which you can do by following the upcoming tutorial steps. The Open button opens the selected thumbnail on the tray in CorelDRAW, rather than importing the media to a new document in the workspace. The Import button imports the selected thumbnail's file to a new document, so it's a good idea to have an open file in your workspace when clicking this button. The Import At Original Position button places a copy of the selected file on a document page exactly in the position where the content (drawing, photos, designs) appears in the original document, effectively duplicating the original, so you can then perform variations on your work without worrying about messing up an original. The Import And Link button lets you link a placed piece of media on a page to an external source such as a website. This is covered in detail shortly. Open Source Location opens a folder or website where an item actually exists, not one where it is simply referenced as a link.
- **Remove From Tray**   If you click this button with a thumbnail image selected in a tray, the shortcut is removed from view, but the file as it resides on your hard drive or on the Web is not affected at all.
- **The Show/Hide Directories button**   This faint triangle between thumbnails of a folder's contents and the Folders pane toggles the thumbnail view to full screen and back again. If you can't find the folder directories, click this faint triangle to restore your view.
- **Add Tray**   This green button to the right of the tray area adds a tray to your collection when you click it.

Generally, it's a good idea to plan how you'll use multiple trays. For example, if you keep all your bitmap images in one tray, your CorelDRAW work on another, and so on, searching for the item you need takes only seconds.

Next is a quick tour of how you set up and use Corel CONNECT in tandem with CorelDRAW to find a piece of artwork, organize your content by type, get clipart from the install DVD, and a picture or two from the Web.

Tutorial CONNECTing with Your Content

1. If you can't find Corel CONNECT in Windows' Start application list, launch CorelDRAW and then click the Application Launcher icon on the Standard toolbar.
2. If this is the first time you've run Corel CONNECT, you'll see a welcome screen in the main viewing pane, and you won't have any content in the tray. Click the triangle to the left of the Folders entry in the directory window to expand the tree; if the expanded view is too small to navigate, click-drag the top of the Folders button upward.
3. Navigate down until you find a folder where you know there are past CorelDRAW illustrations you've saved. Put a check in the box to the left of the folder, and before you know it, the main preview window is populated with image thumbnails of file types CorelDRAW understands and generic icons for content types that are proprietary to a specific application.
4. Suppose you want only vector files displayed to choose from for your tray. Click the Vectors button and make sure no other filter button is depressed.
5. Suppose an Adobe Illustrator file or two snuck into this folder in the past, and you want to see only genuine CDR files. In the Search field, type the wildcard ***.cdr**, and then press ENTER. To zoom your view of the main pane's contents, use the slider below the main pane.
6. Let's say you want quick access to these files: you make it a favorites location. Drag the folder in the Folder area into the Favorites area, and then click the folder's name to display its contents of vector files. Click the checkmark before the folder's name to put a Favorites star next to the folder.
7. There are bound to be at least one or two of your favorites that you want immediate access to in CorelDRAW or PHOTO-PAINT. You put these items in the tray—drag a thumbnail from the main pane when you have your Favorites folder selected, and then drag it down to the tray. Corel CONNECT organizes your files, but it doesn't move them from their original folder location.

 Tip When you hovering over file types that CorelDRAW can import in the main CONNECT window, you'll see a much larger thumbnail version.

Website Importing with CONNECT

If you are authorized by the creator or owner of a website to perform work on the site, it's often handy to have its graphical elements available in CorelDRAW for measuring, redrawing, and other common web designer tasks.

All you need to do is type the URL of the website in the search field in CONNECT, and in moments, the (usually bitmap) type of files displayed on the site is shown in CONNECT. You *must* use an URL that leads to an actual website; CONNECT cannot connect to an FTP drop or a folder of files online—a website needs to be an actual website. You can then drag shortcuts to the media into a tray. You might receive a warning that the media you're going to download might have copyright restriction or require authorization, which is only fair. So if you have permissions, you now have a new way to access and work with web media, as shown here.

Note Corel CONNECT's Search field does more than filter for specific file types. If, for example, you insert your CorelDRAW Graphics Suite DVD into an optical drive, and then choose the disk from the Libraries list, you can type the name of a file in the Search field to hone in on the DVD content you want. Type **flower** as an example, and the main preview window displays all images and vector files whose metadata tags (created for you by Corel Corp.) have "flower" as a keyword. A file doesn't have to be named "flower" for CONNECT to locate and display it. This is also why it's a good idea when saving your own files to fill in keywords; choose File | Document Properties and then type anything that will help you recall the file into the Keywords field. Then press CTRL+S.

Introducing the Revamped Object Properties Docker

Experienced CorelDRAW users have always pressed ALT+ENTER to bring up the Object Properties docker when they want to make changes to a selected object. Now, the Object Properties docker could possibly substitute for many of the features you regularly use in CorelDRAW, including the Outline Pen, the Fill Tool, and just about anything you need to do with text. Whatever you used to do with the Object Properties docker, you'll do ten times more of in version X6. Here's an example of a new text feature that lets you choose from a host of extended, alternative characters in an OpenType font. Ligatures, ornaments, and glyphs that the font author decided to code into his font are easy to find and apply to text you're working with. Chapter 15 guides you through working with fills and the upgraded Object Properties docker, and Chapter 12 shows you how to set professional text, whether paragraph or headline.

Here, an illustration is being created out of a single typeface. After you type the text, you highlight a character you want to change; your cursor becomes a pointed finger; you click the down-facing triangle to see your options and choose the replacement character. Version X6 comes with Styled characters, presets all ready for you to use, and the Object Properties docker also offers common extended font characters such as *ligatures* (joined special characters—*fi*, *ffl*, and *st* are examples), symbols, OldStyle numbers, and more. Try experimenting with Windows 7's Calibri and Gabriola. To edit in OpenType mode, the Interactive OpenType button must be clicked on the Property Bar, and the font you use must have the special characters you want to access.

Highlight character with Text Tool.

Click to reveal alternative characters.

Darker icons mean characters are in typeface.

The New Shape Tools

In the Shape Edit group of tools in the Toolbox, you'll find four new tools: Twirl, Smear, Attract, and Repel. Shape Edit tools are discussed in Chapter 11; when you add these new tools to the existing Smudge, Roughen, and Eraser Tools, making a rectangle or other perfectly characterless object into something delightfully organic in appearance is simple and fast.

Here's an illustration of what you can achieve with the Smear, Twirl, and Repel Tools; the Attract Tool essentially produces the opposite effect from using the Repel Tool. To use any of these tools, select an object and then click-drag over it. You'll get the feel for the creative possibilities in a moment or two.

Unique Page Master Layers and Numbering

Artists and designers who also need to create publications will love the new Master Layers features. Now, you can assign a Master Layer to all pages, only the odd-numbered ones, or just even-numbered pages. These options offer unparalleled flexibility with publication design. Additionally, X6 sports a slick page numbering system that obeys the Master Page rules—if you want odd pages numbered in 12-point type and even pages using a different typeface and color, you got it.

Let's take a brisk walk through the creation of a short magazine article, where the left pages have a repeating graphic, but the right-facing pages (the odd-numbered ones) do not.

Here's how Master Layers in version X6 works:

Tutorial Page Making in Version X6

1. Create a new document, and then add pages by clicking the Add Page (the page with a plus mark inside) button next to the Page 1 button above the Status Bar. For this example, create five pages. Move to the Page 2 view by clicking the Page 2 button.

2. In Western publications, the odd pages are usually the *right*-facing ones, so page 1 doesn't need any Master Layer; the fun begins on Page 2. Choose Window | Dockers | Object Manager. On the Object Manager, with Page 2 chosen from the list, click the New Master Page (even pages) button at the bottom of the Object Manager. You'll see the new layer appear in the Master Page area.

3. Create a fancy graphic, or import French Curve.cdr to use. If you've already read or are experienced with the CorelDRAW's PowerClip feature, this is how the entire French Curve shape is visibly confined to a rectangle that fits the vertical measure of the page.

4. Click the Page 2 title on the Object Manager docker, and then click the New Layer button, not the New Master Layer button, and now you have a layer to add text. Another new version X6 feature is a frame for placeholder text and dummy text (*greeking*) that can be automatically added to the Paragraph Text frame. Drag a rectangle using the Text Tool to the right of the graphic, and then right-click and choose Insert Placeholder Text from the context menu. Choose a nicer typeface for a magazine than Arial once you have selected the text with the Pick Tool.

5. Optional: You can design the page as long as you're working with new features. The left margin of the Paragraph Text can be fitted to the French curve (or any object you've drawn) by choosing the Envelope Tool from the Interactive Tool group, which puts a default Envelope around the text. Marquee-select the top, bottom, and right nodes to the Envelope shape, and then on the Property bar, click the Convert To Line button. This makes working with the overall envelope a lot more predictable.

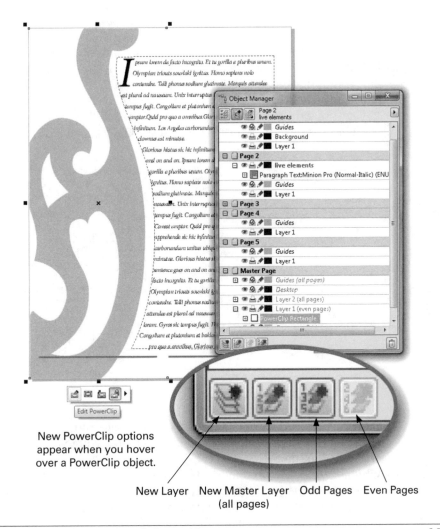

New PowerClip options
appear when you hover
over a PowerClip object.

New Layer   New Master Layer   Odd Pages   Even Pages
(all pages)

FIGURE 1-2   Master Layers help you keep recurring page content on even, odd, or all pages.

6. One at a time, select the nodes, and then drag the node control handles in directions that shape the left edge of the text to the object on the page. When your page looks something like Figure 1-2, it's time to move on in this mock assignment. Notice also in version X6, that controls for PowerClips pop up below a PowerClip object when your cursor is in proximity to the object.

7. If there are any elements you want to reappear only on the odd-numbered pages, click the Page 1 or Page 3 button and add the element exactly as you did with the even page graphic, except you click the New Master Page (Odd Pages) button on the Object Manager.

8. Oh, it probably would be good to *number* the pages, right? On any page view, choose Layout | Page Number Settings. You can leave the Start At Number and Start On Page fields as they are in this example. In the Style drop-down, however, designers have added some neat stuff. Choose from standard Western alphanumeric-style numbers, or go Latin with Roman numerals, or even use letters instead of numbers. Make your choice, click OK, and then choose Layout | Insert Page Number | On All Pages. You'll see on your screen that the text object is now on a Master Page on the Object Manager.

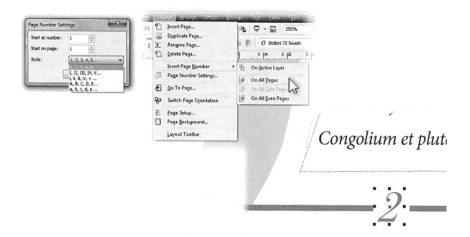

9. Take the opportunity to change the selected page number. Change the font, change the position, color, and size. The change you make to one entry changes all of them.
10. Why not add a line on either side of the page number to make a fancy page footer? Click the New Master Layer (all pages) button, and then with a line tool or the Rectangle Tool, create a horizontal "frame" for the centered number.
11. Consider the tutorial over, or finish designing the pages, as the author's version of a spread is shown in Figure 1-3.

French curve element will always
appear on even pages.

Odd pages only have page numbers and
divider element as Master Layer items.

FIGURE 1-3   Page layout has never been easier with CorelDRAW's page-specific Master Layers.

Object Styles to Suit Your Styles

New to CorelDRAW X6 is the Object Styles docker, which unifies an area in the workspace where you can define just about anything as a Style and then apply the Style to anything else on the page. You no longer need to visit two or more areas in the menus to define a Style, apply a Style, and even work with the new Style Sets feature. A Style Set is composed of different types of object attributes you select and sample from, and its helpfulness in everyday assignments will become obvious in the following tutorial. Styles now apply to

- Artistic and Paragraph Text
- Objects
- Dimensions Objects
- Color

Here's a set of steps you can walk through to get an idea of the ease and power of working with Object Styles. Let's imagine that you worked with a Paragraph Text frame months ago to achieve a beautiful antique look with a custom color and a drop cap. You just received a multidollar contract to work on Ensign Doug's Hot and Spicy Rum, and the label for a bus stop poster needs to carry a legend on the bottle label. You think your fancy text you previously created would work well in this assignment, so your task in this tutorial is to create a Style from your saved text and then apply the Style to the text that goes on the poster.

Tutorial   Using Object Styles with Paragraph Text

1. Open Ensign Doug's rum.cdr. You'll see that in addition to the JPEG image on the page, there is some text above it in Arial and a Paragraph Text block to the left, nicely formatted in Times New Roman, that contains a passage from the US Bill of Rights Amendments. If you have a more elegant, perhaps antiqued typeface than Times, select the Paragraph Text now with the Pick Tool and then choose your ideal font from the drop-down list on the Property Bar.

2. Choose Windows | Dockers | Object Styles. If you remember the keyboard shortcut to Graphic and Text Styles from previous versions of CorelDRAW, it's still the same: CTRL + F5.

3. With the Paragraph Text chosen (using the Pick Tool), right-click and then choose Object Styles | New Style Set From. You're choosing to define an entire Style Set and not simply a Style because the Paragraph Text has formatting and also a unique color you want to define and apply shortly to the Ensign's text.

4. On the New Style Set From dialog box, type the name of this new Style Set in the text field, and notice that in the future, you can display the Object Styles docker right after you define a Style by checking the box in this dialog. Click OK and your screen should look like the illustration here.

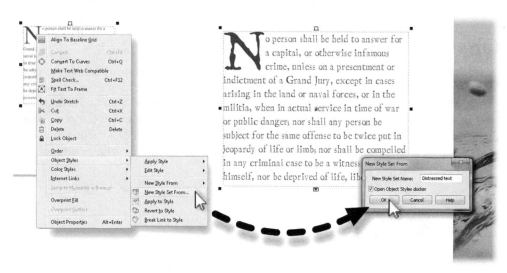

5. On the Object Styles docker, you'll see a new entry below the Style Sets heading on the docker. Select the text above the advertisement, as shown here, and then click the Apply To Selected button. It's that easy to apply two defined Styles to a different object, and this updated docker can spare you minutes of work (minutes are considered *hours* in Internet time!) over using the Attributes Eyedropper Tool.

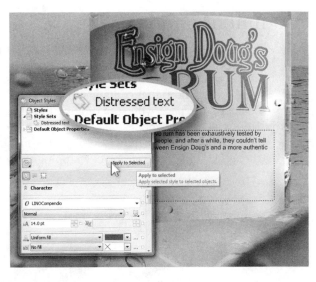

6. In Figure 1-4, you can see the result of your work. This is a feature well worth investigating in your spare time because it will *save* you time. There's a little added touch or two to the text, and you'll see how to put an envelope around text and other objects in Chapter 20. This is why the text looks as though it's on the label and not simply on top of the image.

FIGURE 1-4   When you like what you've done with a design, an object, or text, save it as a Style or a Style Set to reuse later.

Alignment Guides

Alignment Guides are not active when you first open CorelDRAW after installing X6. You'll need to remember to press ALT + SHIFT + A, or press CTRL + J to open Options and then choose Workspace | Alignment Guides. Simply put, Alignment Guides are temporary guides that can appear when you move an object in relation to a different object on the page; you stop moving the object and the Alignment Guides disappear. Here you can see the visual effect—you can change the color of the guides in Options, and regardless of the guides' visibility, you'll experience a snapping effect, even though you might have object snapping turned off.

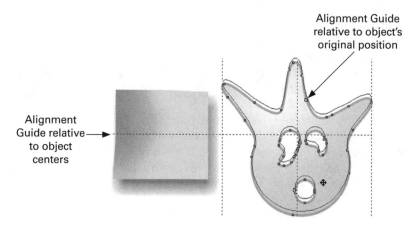

Alignment Guide relative to object's original position

Alignment Guide relative to object centers

Interactive Frames for Page Layout

In this digital publishing age, the universal lament of good layout artists has been: it's very fast and natural to design a layout by pushing rectangles of paper around a drafting board. However, this traditional approach isn't digital so it's not in today's publishing pipeline. The good news is that version X6's Interactive Frames feature gets us one step closer to natural design work and immediate feedback.

Interactive Frames are easy to set up, manipulate, and populate with dummy content. In the following steps, you'll get hands-on experience (with a little guidance) in creating a two-page spread using the JPEG images you downloaded from this chapter. Get set to create a jiffy layout, and after you get the knack by trial, you'll be able to sketch a layout using Interactive Frames to make dozens of different layouts whose contents can change to suit different purposes with only a click or two:

Tutorial   Creating a Page Layout Interactively

1. Press CTRL + N and in the Create A New Document box, specify a Tabloid page size, Landscape orientation, and then click OK.
2. Drag a vertical guide from the ruler and put it at 8.5" to help you see where the gutter is on this two-page 8½ × 11" spread.
3. Choose Windows | Dockers | Tray. Click CorelDRAW's Minimize/Restore button at the top right so you have a view of Windows Desktop and the page in CorelDRAW.
4. Find the four images of the ugly toys for this chapter and then drag them onto the tray. You can maximize the interface now.
5. You can lay this spread out any way you like in the future but, for now, stick to the stripes provided here for a nice, classic "checkerboard" layout on the right page and a full-page graphic on the left. Double-click the Rectangle Tool to create a page frame rectangle that exactly matches the page size. Choose the Pick Tool and then drag the right side so it snaps to the guide you created in Step 2.
6. Choose the Graph Paper Tool from the Object Group on the Toolbox. The Graph Paper Tool's icon *looks* like the Table Tool, but you do not want to use the Table Tool, so choose this tool carefully! On the Property Bar, set the number of cells to **2** across and **3** down. Drag the tool across the full measure of the right side of the page.
7. Press CTRL + U to ungroup all six rectangles.
8. Now guess what? All of these rectangles have the potential to be either text placeholder boxes or blank PowerClip frames, all set to take a photo or graphic. With the Pick Tool, right-click over the left side, half-page rectangle you created in Step 5, and then choose Frame Type | Create Empty PowerClip Frame from the shortcut menu, marked with a "1" in Figure 1-5.
9. Drag a picture from the tray into the blank frame, marked with a "2" in Figure 1-5.
10. Chances are very good that the picture won't fit the frame perfectly. Click the Select PowerClip Contents button on the button bar that appears whenever you hover over a PowerClip object, and then move and/or scale the photo until it fits the frame.
11. Putting dummy text inside a closed object requires almost the same preparation steps as putting images in a PowerClip frame. Choose the upper right of the six rectangles on the right side of the page. Let's consider this a text element in the design. First, fill it with a deep color; your choice of exact color is fine.
12. Right-click over the selected rectangle and then choose Frame Type | Create Empty Text Frame from the shortcut menu. You'll see Click Here With Text Tool To Add Paragraph Text within the rectangle, which is an encouraging sign. Choose the Text Tool, put it inside the rectangle, but instead of clicking,

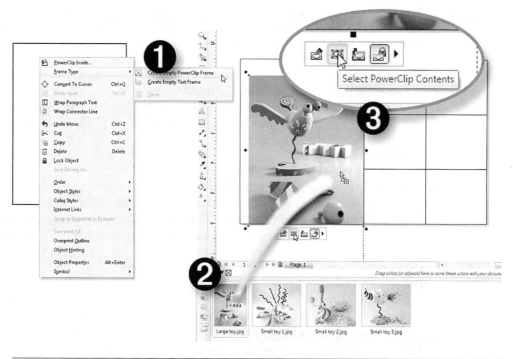

FIGURE 1-5 Any closed shape you draw can become a container for images, drawing, and text.

right-click and then choose Insert Placeholder Text from the shortcut menu, as shown here. CorelDRAW adds auto-text of random Latin phrases (which doesn't explain why this is called *greeking*), and you can now treat this placeholder text like regular text you'd type.

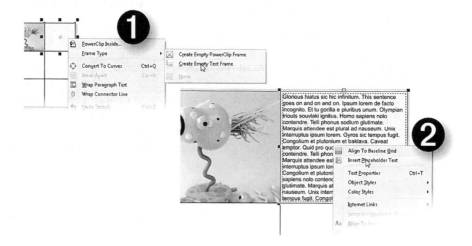

13. Change the greeking's color (white is good if the background is dark), and while the text is selected with the Text Tool, alignment and tab options are available on the Property Bar, so you probably want to drag the left and right margins inward, to the give this design cell a little breathing room, as shown in this illustration.

Margins can be controlled when you click in the text with the Text Tool.

14. Repeat the previous steps so the text boxes vertically alternate with the image boxes down the right side of the layout, creating a checkerboard effect. Once you have a framework mapped out for a layout or other design, completing it is just a matter of filling in the cells. You now have the hang of working with Interactive Frames. When you want to swap a real image in for a placeholder, you can click the Extract Contents button on the hovering button bar and drag a different image onto the frame. In Figure 1-6, you can see the layout at top, and a variation at the bottom, which took the same two minutes that the top version did to build. Frames are a designer's friends.

FIGURE 1-6   Fill a rough layout with content within frames to get an idea of what a finished layout will look like.

Working with Color Styles

Chapter 17 gets you acquainted with a revised and robust feature for defining color in your drawings so you can quickly change the colors on an object-by-object basis, even with thousands of objects in a composition. When you first open the Color Styles docker with a composition open, you'll see clear directions on where to drop an object you've selected on the page. You can generate a Color Style—which is limited to one color fill and one color outline per drag onto the top area of the docker, or a Color Style *plus* a Color Harmony generated from the colors in objects (plural) you drag onto the bottom area. By working definition:

- A *Color Style* was called a Master Color (Style) in previous versions of CorelDRAW. When you assign a color used in a document to a Style by dragging an object with this color to the Color Styles upper region, you can change the color as used in the document by editing the Color Style at any time. You do this by clicking the color swatch on the Color Styles docker, and then in the color field, you change the hue, saturation, and lightness by dragging your cursor around the color field and/or the color slider. For example, if you have 14 circles on the page, 7 of them orange and

7 purple, and you drop an orange object on the Style area of the docker, if you then highlight the swatch on the docker and change the color field to purple, you change the swatch and you change all the orange circles on the page to purple.

- *Color Styles* and *Color Harmonies* take the steps of creating a Master Color further by letting you drag a *bunch* of differently colored objects to the lower field on the docker. The result is that you can build a relationship between these new Master Colors and not only change a color that's now a Style, but also harmonically adjust *all* the colors you sampled.

A visual explanation of Color Styles and Harmonies will make the point better than a verbal explanation here. Follow these steps to selectively recolor a range of color values in an illustration:

Tutorial   Using Color Harmonies to Change Part of a Drawing

1. Open Crates.cdr. What you'll do is recolor the green crates at right without changing anything else in this simple drawing.
2. Press CTRL + F6, or choose Windows | Dockers | Color Styles.
3. The green crates are grouped to make this example an easy one. With the Pick Tool, select the green stacked crates and then drag them to the lower field, the one that mentions generating a harmony.
4. The Create Color Styles dialog box appears. In it, you can leave the radio button at Both Fill And Outline selected, even though there are no outlines in this drawing, but make sure Group Color Styles Into Harmonies is checked, and the number of groups is 1. In your own assignments, you'll sometimes find that by defining more than one Style (and Harmony), you have greater control over modifying a composition by hue and brightness. Click OK if your screen looks similar to this illustration.

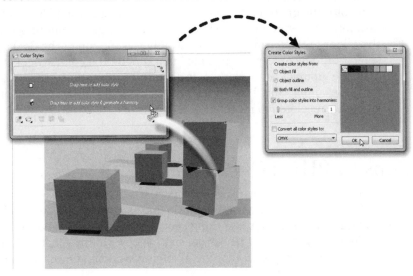

Click the folder icon to move
Color Harmony markers as one.

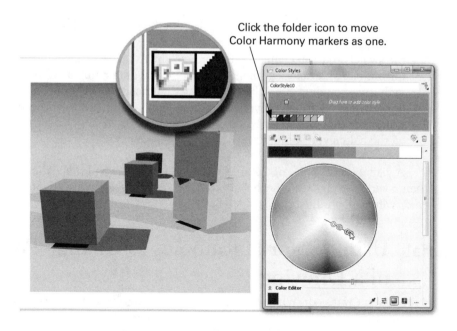

FIGURE 1-7   Recoloring a part of a drawing is a snap when you've defined
a Color Style.

5. After confirming that you want several colors linked to Styles, click a
   color swatch in the Harmony pane, and you'll see a color wheel with a lot
   of markers on it appear toward the bottom of the docker. The green dots
   represent individual Color Styles in the group, and you can move one dot
   around to change hue, move toward or away from the center to change
   saturation, and drag the slider beneath the color wheel to redefine brightness,
   but don't in this example. You want to move all the color dots to a different hue
   to recolor the green crates proportionately, tinting them smoothly to a single,
   different hue, which is the power behind this new Harmonies feature. Click
   the folder to the left of the color swatches at the top of the docker; doing this
   selects all the corresponding color markers on the color wheel.
6. Drag the group of color markers to something other than green; magenta is great
   for this example. You'll see onscreen that every brightness value for the crates is
   smoothly recolored to magenta. Check this feature out in detail in Chapter 17!

Additions to PHOTO-PAINT

Corel PHOTO-PAINT must be considered part of your CorelDRAW X6 upgrade,
because PHOTO-PAINT has always been the bitmap counterpart to DRAW's vector
tools, and frankly, there are some things you'll want to do for work or personal art
that require bitmap tools that DRAW doesn't have. With this version of PHOTO-PAINT,
there's some neat bitmap stuff that the following sections summarize for you.

PHOTO-PAINT Object Group Clip Masks

Groups of objects can now take a clip mask, without changing any of the objects in the group. For example, if one of the grouped objects has transparency, modifying the group to adjust overall transparency doesn't ruin an object in the group's transparency property, but instead modifies the modification. This new feature lets artists ungroup a group that's been clip masked, thus restoring individual objects to their original state. No undos, no guesswork.

PHOTO-PAINT Pass Through Merge Mode

When you group objects in a PHOTO-PAINT composition, the default merge state of the group is Pass Through, a new mode for version X6. This mode lets you set an individual merge mode for the objects within the group, so the group's mode of Pass Through is essentially a neutral one. Additionally, any effect you apply to the group is inherited by the members and also passed down through the visible areas of objects below the parent Pass Through group.

PHOTO-PAINT's Smart Carver Feature

The new Smart Carver command under the Image menu can take much of the manual drudge and imprecision out of one editing move: removing a character—an object, a person, a pet—from a photo. Smart Carver requires only that you highlight the area you want removed, and then PHOTO-PAINT calculates the areas to be stitched together, extended, and how much the image's dimensions must change to create a new photo sans the unwanted object.

Try this feature out with the provided image from the zip archive you downloaded:

Tutorial   Smart Carving a Composition

1. Open Three Macaws.png, where you'll see a photo-realistic illustration of three African Macaw parrots. Your assignment is to make this composition *Two* Macaws, by removing the middle, red parrot.
2. Choose Image | Smart Carver. A very large dialog box, practically a new workspace appears.
3. Click the middle button in the Object Removal area. You've chosen a pen tool that tints the preview image a red color. Wherever you paint, Smart Carver attempts to remove the area, so it's important that you paint carefully and with some deliberation so the finished piece doesn't look fake and PHOTO-PAINT doesn't have to spend minutes calculating the changes Smart Carver will make.
4. Using the mouse wheel on your input device to zoom in and out, set the size of the tip to about **43**, and then stroke over the edge of the middle parrot, making sure to keep the edge selection fairly accurate. If you make a mistake, switch to the right tool in the group, the Eraser, erase the mistake, and then go back to the Removal Tool.

5. Once you're traced over the edge, you can increase the size of the tip to fill in the interior of the shape you've painted quickly. You might want to check Hide Mask now so you can better evaluate the change you make in the next step.

6. Click the Auto-contract Horizontally To Remove Red-painted Areas button (quite a name for a little button!), as shown in Figure 1-8.

7. In a moment, you should see the middle parrot disappear and the overall image is narrower now. Click OK to return to the image in PHOTO-PAINT's workspace.

8. You'll notice that Smart Carver's work is really quite good, but not perfect. There will be a slight hard edge toward the top middle of the image where Smart Carver needed to "pucker" the edges of the deleted area together. Generally, you'll get the finest results from this filter if the background is a solid color such as a wall or an overcast sky. Not a big problem, however. Choose the Touch-Up Tool from the group that has the Red Eye Removal Tool at top.

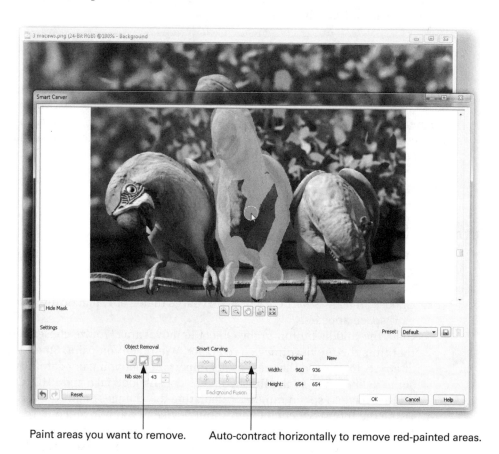

Paint areas you want to remove.   Auto-contract horizontally to remove red-painted areas.

FIGURE 1-8   Use the new Smart Carver feature to remove significant foreground objects from a photo quickly.

Touch-Up Brush

FIGURE 1-9   Between the Touch-Up Brush and the Smart Carver feature, PHOTO-PAINT is your program for altering reality.

9. Set the brush size to about **45** for this example, and set the Strength to High. Drag over the visible seam in the image, as shown in Figure 1-9. When the seam is gone, save the file as a PHOTO-PAINT .CPT file, and you can consider yourself well on the way to becoming a master Retouching Artist, and you'll save 33 percent on the bird seed you used to have to buy.

You could call this chapter the tip of the iceberg, if your idea of a fun time is an iceberg (Leonardo DiCaprio's wasn't). Kidding aside, there are a lot of pages under your right thumb, and it's all good stuff. Bring along some curiosity and a design idea or two and move into second gear and the second chapter.

2 Exploring Your Workspace

When working in CorelDRAW, you'll find yourself using an assortment of interface elements that offer control over everything you do. There are many areas that make up the interface because the program offers an abundance of creative tools to use so that you can create compelling graphics and documents. Certain areas of the interface such as the Property Bar are context sensitive: your available options change as you choose different Toolbox tools. Other interface areas, like the Toolbox, are always visible in the workspace. And then there are dockers, which are displayed only if you specifically open them. Exactly which and where these elements appear in the program interface is not a set piece; you have ultimate flexibility and customization control so you can *personalize* CorelDRAW. The important thing is that you should *feel at home* working in CorelDRAW; this chapter shows you where everything is and how you can make CorelDRAW suit your work style.

The CorelDRAW Workspace

CorelDRAW has been carefully designed to make it easy for you to find and work with the tools you need to use, when you need to use them.

CorelDRAW workspace elements can be divided into two categories:

- Global and program control elements, such as measurement scales, backup files, and memory use.
- Design or complete document features, such as guidelines, styles, and nudge distances.

If you're new to CorelDRAW or just new to this version, you *will* want to take a look at the roadmap to follow and get a handle on CorelDRAW's interface.

CorelDRAW's Application Window

The application window is mainly what you see when CorelDRAW is open. It is the stage that surrounds and contains the drawing windows. *Drawing windows* (the more familiar term is *document windows*) contain the drawing page or pages that hold the graphics and other content you create. Even if no drawing windows are open, the application window provides access to certain command menus, toolbars, the Toolbox, dockers, Status Bar, and the Color Palette. Figure 2-1 identifies the application window parts.

The specific settings you see displayed on the toolbar, Property Bar, dockers, and other application windows interface elements are those that are assigned to the currently active drawing window. They change if you make another drawing window active by clicking the desired drawing window.

As in all standard Windows applications, clicking the Close button at the top-right side of the application window's title bar closes CorelDRAW; clicking the Minimize or Maximize/Restore button shows or hides CorelDRAW and changes the size of the

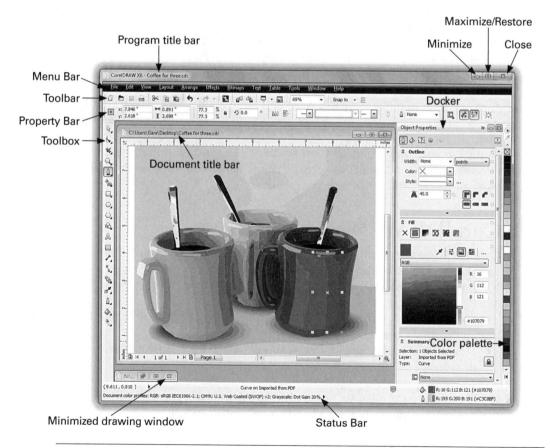

FIGURE 2-1 CorelDRAW's application window features these interface areas.

application window itself quickly. Clicking a drawing window's Close button closes the drawing window, removing it from the application window, whereas clicking a drawing window's Minimize or Maximize/Restore button minimizes it to a document title bar near the bottom of the application window or restores it to size within the application window.

Tip With CorelDRAW open and all documents closed, you can still perform many necessary tasks. You can use File commands and open suite applications such as Corel CAPTURE, Corel CONNECT, Corel BARCODE WIZARD, Corel PHOTO-PAINT, and even another copy of CorelDRAW with the Application Launcher. Here's a hint: running two instances of CorelDRAW is a memory-draining mistake; because you *can* run two copies doesn't mean you *should*. You can also use some of Corel's tool managers, work with macros, view Help topics, and access Corel's online web resources through the Welcome screen.

Drawing Windows

When a drawing window is fully maximized, it fills the dark gray space in the center of the application window and looks as if it were *part* of the application window. When a drawing window is open but *not* fully maximized, it is easy to see that it's a separate window element with its own interface elements that are unique to that drawing window.

Unlike the Menu Bar, Property Bar, Toolbar, Toolbox, Color Palette, and dockers, a drawing window cannot be dragged outside of the application window and onto the desktop or a second monitor's desktop.

Not surprisingly, the interface elements that are contained within a drawing window report on or control that specific drawing window. Like the application window, a drawing window also has standard window controls such as a title bar that identifies the document's file path and name, as well as Minimize, Maximize/Restore, and Close buttons. Drawing windows also have page borders, which like in other windows can be dragged to change the size of the window. They also have scroll bars that you use to change your view of the document's contents.

Interface elements special to drawing windows include rulers, the Document Navigator, which is used to add, delete, and move between pages in a multipage drawing window (see Chapter 6), the Drawing page, which contains what can be printed, and the Navigator, which helps you move around a drawing without having to zoom out.

Parent and Child Window Buttons

A document's Minimize, Maximize/Restore, and Close buttons are not located in the drawing window frame when a drawing window is maximized in the application window. The Minimize, Maximize/Restore, and Close buttons for the current drawing window are grayscale, smaller in size, and placed just below the Minimize, Maximize/Restore, and Close buttons that belong to the application window.

If you want to close a document window, but your attention is wandering a bit and you are running on autopilot, it's easy to make a mistake and click the larger, more colorful Close button that belongs to the entire CorelDRAW application.

So save your work often and try to remember that the big, red "X" button is for the whole application and the smaller one is for the document at hand.

CorelDRAW is compliant with the Microsoft Windows standard for *multiple document interfaces,* meaning you can have more than one document (drawing) window open at a time. To switch between drawing windows, choose Window | *document name* (where *document name* is the actual name of your CorelDRAW document). Here you can see a basic and very useful drawing window technique: Suppose you have an object in one drawing window and want a copy of it in a different one. You choose Window | Tile Vertically (you can do this manually if you're skilled at manipulating Windows' windows), and then move the object by just dragging it into the other window using the Pick Tool. To copy the object, hold the modifier key CTRL as you drag from one window to the other.

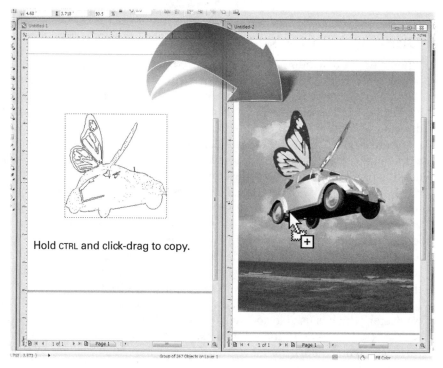

Hold CTRL and click-drag to copy.

CorelDRAW uses a default naming system of Untitled-1, Untitled-2, and so on, incrementing the number for each new document you open in the current CorelDRAW session. You are given the chance (and you should take it) to give your drawing a more meaningful name when you save the document by choosing File | Save or pressing CTRL + S.

You can also open more than one document window showing the *same* drawing, so you can work on one drawing in multiple windows. This is a particularly useful feature when you need to zoom in close to work on a small area of a graphic, but you also need to be able to see how your work on that area affects the whole composition.

Both windows are "live," so you can edit in either of them and all the changes you make editing in one window will also appear in both windows because these windows represent different *views* of the same document, *not* two independent files that can be saved as different versions.

To open another view of the active drawing window, choose Window | New Window. To make one of the open views the active window, you can click that window, or you can also choose Window | *document name:N* (where *N* is the automatically applied view number) from the menu. Open as many windows as you need—this feature is limited only by your available system resources.

Specifying Toolbar and Dialog Values

When working in CorelDRAW, you will often need to enter measurements or numeric values, choose options and states, and control the behavior of interface elements on toolbars, in dialogs, and so on. CorelDRAW uses a wide variety of standard input fields and controls to make the specific kind of data you need to enter or tweak easy to accomplish. This section guides you through the ways data can be entered and alerts you to some of the extra power and usability Corel engineers have given these interface elements.

- **Num boxes**   To set number values for lines and other objects, you'll find *num* boxes—short for *numeric* boxes. Usually there is already a value in the box, such as the page width in the following illustration. Just highlight the existing value using a click-drag action and then retype a new value. Alternatively, you can double-click to select the entire value in the num box before typing the value you want. If you insert the cursor at any point in the existing value, you can use your keyboard arrow keys to move within the value and then BACKSPACE to remove it, finally adding the value you need. Finally, you need to confirm the value you entered by pressing ... ENTER. Press TAB to move your cursor quickly from one num box to the next in the group, or press SHIFT + TAB to move to the previous box. In dialogs, clicking the Apply button applies the new options and leaves the dialog box open; OK closes the dialog and applies the new values or options. On toolbars, pressing ENTER after typing the value does the same thing, as shown here.

Highlight existing value, then type in the value you need.

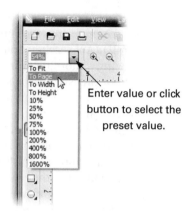

- **Combo boxes** *Combo* (short for *combination*) is a num box with a clickable selection button for access to preset values. You can either enter a specific value in a combo box by typing or by choosing a preset value from the selector. Toolbar and docker combo boxes often require pressing the ENTER key to apply the new value you type in, whereas clicking Apply or OK in dialogs does the same thing.

Enter value or click button to select the preset value.

- **Flyout option menus and popouts** On certain toolbars and dockers, you're going to find flyout and popout menus, which are often accessed by clicking a button that has a small, triangular-shaped flyout arrow pointing to the right. *Popouts* are usually selectors in which

you can choose a nonnumeric option, and they can contain text and even mini-controls, depending on the operation or tool that is chosen. You can spot a tool on the Toolbox, for example, that has extended options that you access straight from the tool button by a tick mark on the button's lower right. *Flyouts* often contain ways to change behavior states, apply commands, and access options. Some apply options immediately, while others require that they be closed first using the small X symbol usually found at the upper-right corner. Examples of each are shown in the following:

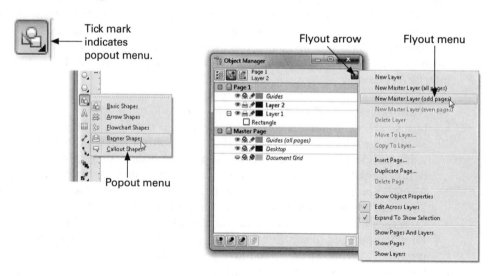

Tick mark indicates popout menu.

Popout menu

Flyout arrow

Flyout menu

- **Color selectors**   A *color selector* often appears in dialogs or toolbars as a clickable button that has the secondary function of displaying the currently selected color, as shown here. Clicking opens a selector to display the current color palette and requires that you click once to specify a color. Most color selectors also include the Other button, which is a shortcut to color models, mixers, and palettes (covered in Chapter 17).

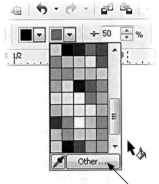

Click to access a complete set of color mixers and digital color models.

- **List selectors**   *List selectors* differ from combo boxes in that you cannot enter a value, but instead pick from a predefined list of values or graphic samples that show the way that a style or arrow (or similar) will be applied or created. Clicking one of the entries in the list chooses and applies a value, size, state, mode, or style to the currently selected object. These lists are occasionally called *drop-down* or *pull-down* lists in other applications.

Click to access preset values.

- **Radio buttons and option boxes**   These two interface devices are slightly different, not just in shape, but also in the choices they offer, as shown next. *Radio* buttons are round, come in groups, and only allow you to select one of the options in the group. *Option* boxes are square and let you choose an option or state to be either on (with a check mark) or off (without a check mark). You'll find in many areas of the Options pages, you can choose more than one option (more than one box can be checked).

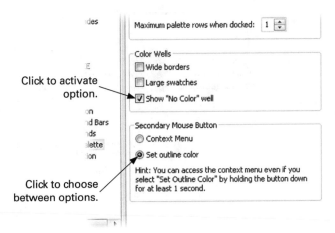

Click to activate option.

Click to choose between options.

- **Buttons and spinner buttons** These appear throughout CorelDRAW and can do one of several things. *Command* buttons perform commands instantaneously, but *toggle* buttons control (and indicate) a specific feature's On and Off states, using a pressed or not-pressed

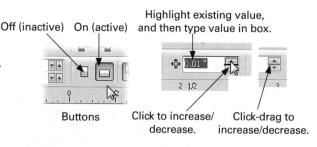

appearance. Generally, a *pressed* state indicates On, whereas the *not pressed* state indicates Off. *Shortcut* buttons open dialogs to further options, while *selector* buttons open lists of preset selections. *Spinner buttons* (also known as *spin boxes*) are similar to combo boxes, in that they can be used to specify values by typing *or* using mouse actions. Single clicks on the up and down arrow buttons increase or decrease the values incrementally, but you can also click-drag on the divider between the two arrow buttons, up to increase or down to decrease the value.

- **Sliders and Pop-up Menus** You use *sliders* to specify values within a given range—often between 0 and 100 and often based on a percent—by entering values or by dragging a control slider, which is intuitive and provides the anticipated results. To manipulate a slider value, use a click-drag action to move the slider either right (to increase) or left (to decrease), as shown here on the Property Bar after the interactive Transparency Tool has been used. To access *pop-up menu* commands and options, click your right mouse button (instead of the typical left-click) on any given point. The pop-up menu appears at the tip of your cursor and closes automatically after you make a selection or click elsewhere in the interface. Pop-up menus are sometimes called *contextual menus,* and a right-facing arrow next to a pop-up menu item indicates there's a submenu with still more options, usually relating to the main menu option.

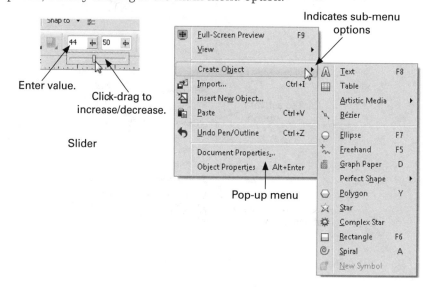

Note Left-handed artists are not uncommon; if you're a southpaw, the order of your mouse buttons is not defined in CorelDRAW, but instead in the operating system's Control Panel | Mouse. Just mirror the instructions in this chapter: if a step tells you to left-click, use the right mouse button, and vice versa.

Working with Dockers

Dockers are panels—palettes—where many different commands and controls related to specific tasks are grouped together in one handy location. Dockers put more of Corel's power right at the tip of your cursor without forcing you to dig through lots of dialog boxes or flit between various toolbars and menus.

These controls can be anchored to the edge of the screen and reduced to tabs or title bars, so you can tear them off and float them right next to where you are working in the interface. You can also resize them to make your own groups of commonly used dockers. And, if you have a multimonitor setup, you can even drag them out of the application window and stick them on a different monitor so you have the maximum amount of space for your drawing windows.

If you don't find a docker that fills your needs after looking through the list as long as your arm on the Window | Dockers menu, dust off your programming skills and make your own *custom* docker. If you're not a programmer, check the Internet for any third-party developers who are taking advantage of CorelDRAW's capability to use third-party dockers.

Opening, Moving, and Closing Dockers

Dockers can be opened using shortcut keys, menu commands, or through toolbars. Most dockers are found on the Window | Dockers menu, but some such as dockers dealing with text formatting are found on the Text menu and the text-related Property Bar. For example, to open the Contour Docker, choose Window | Dockers | Contour, or press CTRL + F9.

Dockers open to their last-used screen position and state, either docked or undocked; open or rolled-up. While *docked*, they are, by default, attached to the right side of your application window. Alternatively, dockers can be positioned on the left side of the screen or anchored on both sides of the screen with your document window in the middle, if that suits you best.

While *undocked*, dockers float above the document window and can be positioned anywhere on your monitor screen(s). Docked or floating is *not* an all or nothing choice; you can have some dockers docked and some floating—at the same time. The only situation you *can't* have is more than one copy of a specific docker open at one time. Figure 2-2 shows examples of docked and floating dockers.

Dockers feature a common look: each has a title bar, a Close Docker group button that closes only that specific docker, and a Roll-up/Roll-down Docker button, which is used to toggle the display between the title bar–only state and a fully open one. While undocked, floating dockers can be resized by click-dragging the sides or bottom edges.

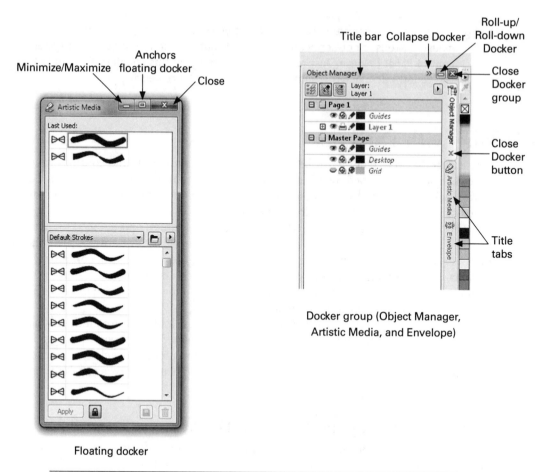

FIGURE 2-2 Dockers are a convenient workspace element that puts features at your cursor tip.

To move a floating docker, click-drag anywhere on its title bar. Rolled-up (minimized) floating dockers appear only as floating title bars on your screen. Minimized, docked dockers appear as vertical title tabs on the right side of the docker area.

Nested (Grouped) Dockers

When more than one docker is open, they often appear *nested*, meaning that multiple dockers overlay each other on the right side of your application window. While dockers are nested, clicking their individual title bars or name tabs brings them to the front of the interface. Floating nested dockers, depending on how you've sized the group, might or might not feature a flyout button at bottom right, as illustrated next. If you've sized the group so the tabs do not show, you can easily access the docker you need through the flyout menu. It's fairly intuitive stuff.

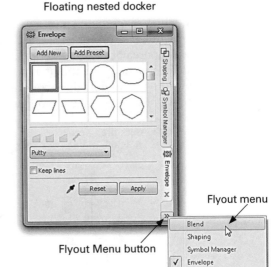

Floating nested docker

Flyout menu

Flyout Menu button

Although nesting dockers (anchored or floating) are likely the best way to work with multiple dockers, you can quickly separate them—kicking them out of the nest—if you prefer. To do this, click-drag the name tab identifying the docker (or anywhere within the fully open docker pane) and then drag away from the nested docker arrangement. As you do this, you will see an outline preview of the frame of your selected docker as you drag, indicating its new screen position when the mouse button is released. You can also float single-anchored dockers by dragging them from their docked position by their title bars. To *nest* multiple dockers together, click-drag on the title bar (while floating) or on the name tab of the docker and then drag it to a position inside the boundaries of another floating docker.

Tip To set whether title bars in floating dockers are visible, open the Options dialog (press CTRL+J) to the General page of the Workspace section, where you'll find an option called Show Titles On Floating Dockers.

Finally, if you want to maximize your drawing window area but still keep docked and nested dockers handy, you can click the Collapse Docker arrow on the title bar of the docker group. Collapsing the docker reduces the nested dockers to a thin vertical set of tabs that correspond to the currently open dockers.

Using the Toolbox

All dockers and virtually everything that's a sub-window of an interface, by Microsoft Windows convention, is called a *child window*. Corel leverages this definition of the user interface to make just about everything detachable and capable of floating (if not flying!). The Toolbox is a component of the application window and is where you'll find all the tools in CorelDRAW; there are tons of features in CorelDRAW, but *tools* are found only on the Toolbox. The Toolbox itself may be altered in different ways.

By default, the Toolbox is docked, but you can *undock* it to float over your document window, which is often a handy way to choose tools quickly if you haven't memorized their shortcut keys. To detach the Toolbox from its docked position, first right-click over a vacant area of the Toolbox and uncheck Lock Toolbars (if it's checked); a single row of dots–type embellishment appears just above the Pick Tool. Then, click-drag just above the row of dots design at the top of the docked Toolbox and move the Toolbox away from the edge of your screen, as shown here.

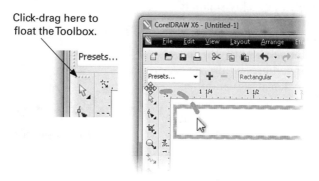

Click-drag here to float the Toolbox.

An undocked Toolbox, shown next, includes a title bar and a Close button. When floating, you can move it around by click-dragging on its title bar. Double-clicking the title bar redocks the Toolbox. Clicking the Close button hides the Toolbox from view. Right-click anywhere in your document window and choose View | Toolbox from the pop-up menu to bring it back.

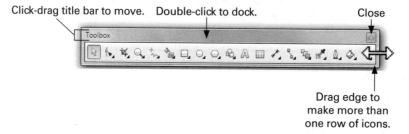

Click-drag title bar to move.   Double-click to dock.   Close

Drag edge to make more than one row of icons.

You can access groups of tools by clicking buttons that feature flyout buttons. A single click selects the visible "top" tool from the group, whereas a click-and-hold action opens the tool popout. You can also separate individual popouts from the Toolbox so they float independently. To do this, be sure the Toolbox is unlocked as just explained. Click-hold to open any group of tools, and then, when your cursor turns into a four-headed arrow, use a click-drag action by clicking the top of the flyout and dragging away from the Toolbox. The result is a *duplicate* of the tool flyout (there's still the original flyout group on the Toolbox) as a floating Toolbox group that can be treated as any floating toolbar, as shown next. To hide the duplicate mini-Toolbox group from view, click the Close button. This hides the duplicate toolbar group without affecting the Toolbox version of the same group.

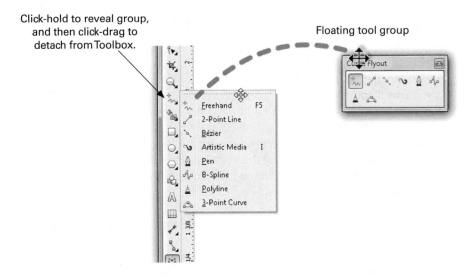

Working with Toolbars

Like other interface devices, toolbars can also appear docked or floating. This doesn't just include standard and custom toolbars, but also the Menu Toolbar, the Standard Toolbar, and the Property Bar. You'll see a small marking on the toolbars themselves when they are docked. To undock any docked toolbar, click-drag the area outside of the tiny "no skid" divider away from the window's edge. Undocked toolbars each feature their own title bar and Close button. Usually, it's not a good idea to close the toolbars, but to return them instead. However, if you've closed a toolbar you need, such as the Property Bar, you can easily retrieve it by right-clicking over any other toolbar, and then choosing the toolbar from the pop-up menu, with any tool chosen.

Using the Color Palette

The *Color Palette* is, by default, the vertical strip docked to the right of the workspace, and is the most convenient place to get colors for filling in your document's objects. By default, a single column of colors is shown; you can change this. The Color Palette also has scroll buttons to advance and rewind the colors visible in one row. Like all Windows child windows, the Color Palette comes undocked: you can resize the floating palette, and you can dock it to any side of the application window, in any toolbar location, above or below the Status Bar and to either side of the Toolbox or a docked docker.

Viewing Palette Colors

The tiny squares of color you see in this palette are referred to as *wells.* Hover over a color well to display a tooltip containing that color's name (by default, Tooltips are enabled; if you turned them off, go to Tools | Options | Workspace | Display).To scroll the Color Palette color well collection, click the Up or Down arrow buttons at the top and bottom of the palette. Single clicks using your left mouse button on these arrow buttons fast-forwards and rewinds the palette, one color well at a time. Single clicks with your right mouse button produce a Page Up and Page Down effect, scrolling the visible color selection a complete row up or down. Clicking the bottom button expands the Color Palette to show all the color wells (it retracts after you click to make a color selection), and at the top is the options flyout button for loading different color palettes, saving, renaming, and so on.

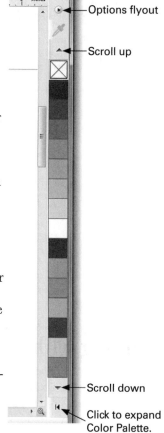

Options flyout

Scroll up

Scroll down

Click to expand
Color Palette.

You float the Color Palette exactly as you do any other interface child windows: by dragging above the little markers into the drawing window. While the Color Palette is floating (shown next), click-drag its title bar to move it around your window or click the Close button to hide it from view. Choose Window | Color Palettes and select a palette to display any palette in its last used state. Double-click the title bar to return the floating Color Palette to its original docked location in the workspace.

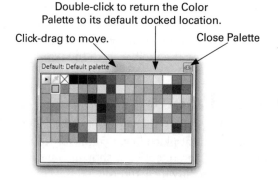

Double-click to return the Color
Palette to its default docked location.

Click-drag to move.

Close Palette

Default: Default palette

Tip As with other day-to-day child windows, it's best not to close the Color Palette, particularly if you're new to the program, because restoring it is a hassle. If you've by chance closed the Color Palette, the quickest way to restore it to the workspace is by right-clicking in the drawing window to get a pop-up menu. Choose View | Color Palettes, choose any palette you like from the submenu, and life is good again.

Hovering over any of the Color Palette's scroll buttons or the Expand button produces a tooltip that displays the name of the Color Palette collection you are using, for example, Default: Default Palette.

Changing Palette Options

The Options flyout button (shown next) on the Color Palette features several important commands, enabling you to apply fill and outline colors (as opposed to using left and right mouse button clicks to apply colors to objects) and control how the palette itself is viewed.

Color Palette Options flyout button

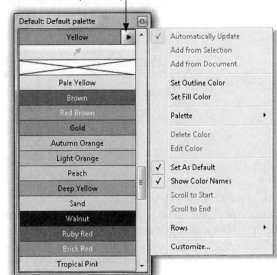

Using the Options flyout provides some, but not all, of the options available to you for getting and using colors. CorelDRAW has an extensive color library including PANTONE and TRUEMATCH from onscreen simulations of printing press colors, as well as others for Web work. However, as mentioned at the beginning of this chapter, some workspace elements in CorelDRAW are tool-specific, while others belong to global elements—and the color library that appears on the Color Palette is a global resource. Therefore, with the Pick Tool and nothing selected in the drawing window, you right-click to display the pop-up menu, choose View | Color Palettes, and then choose from the submenu, which also features the Palette Editor (see the following illustration). Displaying the child window called Color Palette and choosing a collection with which you populate the Color Palette are two different things and require different commands.

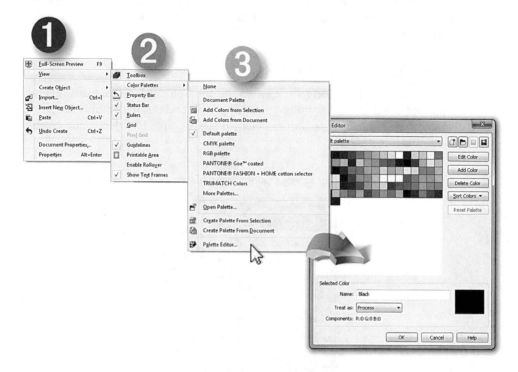

When an artist creates art, the most successful pieces are drawn from general ideas to the specifics, from a coarse outline to filling in the details. Similarly, CorelDRAW deserves a coarse examination, as covered in this chapter, but as you progress to later chapters, the details are filled in. You've got a general idea of how to navigate in this chapter; it's time to move from the interface to the palettes and options you have when building objects, filling them, and changing them. Chapter 3 sits by your side as you cruise the menus and palettes in X6; take a guided tour of CorelDRAW's resources right around the page.

3

CorelDRAW's Ins and Outs: Importing, Exporting, and Saving Design Work

One of the very first things you learn as a new computer user is how to open and close files and how to use the Clipboard to copy data from one document window to another. There is nothing new or exotic you have to do when working with CorelDRAW X6 to accomplish these basic tasks. But version X6 has *additional* functions and options, such as file handling and data import and export, to make your design experience efficient and the results professional. In this chapter you'll learn about file-saving options that let coworkers who are using previous versions of CorelDRAW work with your files and how to use time-saving templates and other file types. You'll also see how to protect your work with CorelDRAW's automatic backup feature, how to make the Clipboard work overtime for you, as well as how to store and retrieve symbols and how to import and export graphics, text, and data into and out of CorelDRAW.

Download and extract all the files from the Chapter03.zip archive to follow the tutorials in this chapter.

CorelDRAW X6's Welcome Screen

When CorelDRAW opens, the Welcome/Quick Start tabbed screen appears, where you can quickly open a new or existing drawing file, access learning tools, check for program updates, and set automatic checks for program updates. You can also view the latest gallery of art created by fellow CorelDRAW designers. This launch pad is shown in Figure 3-1.

Preview   Last saved/opened files

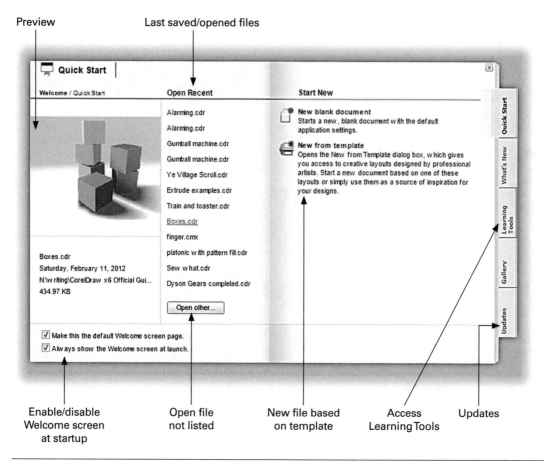

Enable/disable   Open file   New file based   Access   Updates
Welcome screen   not listed   on template   Learning Tools
at startup

FIGURE 3-1   CorelDRAW welcomes you with a tabbed launch pad after loading.

The first tab along the right edge, *Quick Start*, is your jumping-off point for opening a file. Here you are presented with a list of the last files you opened and closed in CorelDRAW. Hovering over the name of one of these files gives you a thumbnail preview and the document information for that file. Click the name of the file, and the Welcome dialog closes and the file you selected opens. If you want to open an existing file that is not among the five most recent files you've opened, click the Open Other button to close the Welcome screen page and to open a standard Open Drawing dialog.

To start a new drawing document, click the New Blank Document link in the Start New section of the Quick Start tab, and click the New From Template link if you want to create a document from one of the special design layouts that ship with CorelDRAW or from a template you previously created.

The other tabs lead you to the following areas of interest:

- From the *What's New* tab, you can click your way through the CorelDRAW New Features Tour slideshow.

- The *Learning Tools* tab contains links to launch documentation such as video tutorials and video hints, and Insights From The Experts as well as a PDF "getting started" style document. There's also a Tips and Tricks link that is periodically updated. If you purchased the physical DVD of the CorelDRAW install, you can also easily access the tutorial videos from this page.
- The *Gallery* tab displays a changing selection of artwork created in CorelDRAW. It also contains a link to the CorelDRAW.com Community page, where you can create an online gallery of your artwork for the world to see and enjoy, participate in online forums, and download helpful files like custom media strokes, textures, and macros.
- The last tab is the *Updates* tab. At the top of the tab window is the Settings area, which, by default, contains two check boxes already checked for you. If there is an update, it automatically notifies you and downloads it. Also, there are links for joining the Corel community and signing up to receive the Corel e-mail newsletter—click the link to join and subscribe.

With the Settings options enabled, every time you start CorelDRAW, it accesses your Internet connection in the background and checks in with the Corel website to see if any updates or files should be downloaded for you. If you don't want CorelDRAW checking the website every time you start the program, uncheck both of these boxes and then click the close box in the corner of the Update Settings dialog to apply the changed Update option settings.

If you don't want to use the features offered by the Welcome screen, click the Close button. To *never* see the Welcome dialog again, click to uncheck the Always Show The Welcome Screen At Launch check box. To open the Welcome screen at any time, choose Help | Welcome Screen, or click the button directly to the left of the zoom percentage field on the Standard Bar.

Opening Your First New Document File

If you are not using the Welcome screen, choosing File | New (CTRL + N) or clicking the New button on the Standard Bar opens the Create A New Document box, where you choose settings such as color space and document resolution and can also choose not to display this box in the future. If you check Do Not Show This Dialog Again, new documents are based on the current settings. If you *do* want to see this box again because the default settings aren't right for your type of work, go to Tools | Options | Workspace | General, and check the Show New Document dialog.

Create a New Document that Suits You

The Create A New Document dialog box is really quite straightforward to use and lets you set up a page that reflects your intended output. Here is a brief explanation of the fields:

- **Name**   You don't have to wait until you save a file to name it. By default, a new document is named Untitled-1, using a sequential naming pattern—your next document in a session of CorelDRAW is named Untitled-2, and so on. It's fine to accept the default name, but it's a better idea to name the file at this time if you know what it is you're going to create.

- **Preset Destination**   *Destination* refers to where the file is ultimately going: to commercial printing or to the Web as an HTML page or graphic; you have five choices here in addition to Custom. If you want to set up a Rendering Resolution or a color space entirely of your own choosing, Preset Destination automatically calls your settings Custom. If you want to keep and reuse this page setup, click the Save (the disk) button to the right of the drop-down list and name the preset. The next time you create a new document, you can choose your preset from the drop-down list and spare yourself defining any other field in this dialog.

- **Size**   Define the page size you need by choosing from the large selection of preset page sizes, or set your own custom size by typing values into the Height and Width fields below. Also, click an orientation, portrait or landscape, for your new document.

- **Primary Color Mode**   You have the option of RGB or CMYK here. If you choose CMYK, the Color Palette's color wells will look duller than you'd expect; this is because CorelDRAW simulates what the colors you use for object fills will look like when printed. CMYK color mode is *print legal*—certain colors you see onscreen using RGB mode cannot be faithfully reproduced using printing inks and other pigments. If you are designing for the Web, choose RGB from the drop-down. Also, if you are designing for a personal home inkjet printer, choose RGB. Although inkjet printers use Cyan, Magenta, Yellow, and Black pigments, today's inkjets have conversion circuitry that take—and actually expect—RGB data and automatically convert it to fairly closely matching CMYK equivalent colors.

- **Rendering Resolution**   Although CorelDRAW is a vector drawing program and, as such, produces *resolution-independent* vector shapes, CorelDRAW is also capable of exporting bitmaps and importing photos and other bitmap-type graphics. Bitmaps are resolution-dependent: Chapters 23 and 24 provide documentation on working with bitmaps. In a nutshell, if you're designing for the screen and for the Web, a rendering resolution of 72 or 96—both are presets you can choose from the drop-down list—will suit your creative needs. If you design for commercial printing presses and for inkjet output, choose a rendering resolution of 300—this is a very common specification for high-quality presses, although it's a little high for home inkjets. But 300 is an easy number to remember and spares you from outputting your valuable work to a coarse-looking print.

- **Preview Mode**   There is little reason to specify anything other than Enhanced for previews. If you choose Draft or Wireframe by accident, you can easily change this by choosing Enhanced from the View menu when your document is open.

- **Color Settings**   By default, this area is rolled up. If you're concerned about color consistency while you work (hint: you *should* be!), then explore this section. Windows offers color management using ICC profiles that have been installed in your computer by graphic applications such as CorelDRAW. Many designers own more than one application, and as a result, it's hard *not* to accumulate color profiles installed by those application, even without realizing it.

Color management increases the odds that the color you see on your monitor is accurately represented in a print you make. The color management system is made up of three components:

- Your monitor, which you calibrate using third-party software, hardware you can buy, or Windows Control Panel settings for your video card.
- Your application, which is CorelDRAW. This is where you tell CorelDRAW which color profile to expect when it imports and how to tag images when it exports.
- Your printer. Most printers today utilize color management and have settings managed through a proprietary control panel or through Windows Printer options.

Scroll down the RGB Profile list, and you will see a number of profiles that are used for various purposes. If you do home printing or you're a Web designer, use the default sRGB IEC61966-2.1. It is the most commonly used profile for many home inkjet printers and digital cameras, so sRGB is a safe color setting to ensure consistent color output from what you see onscreen, what your photos look like when you import them to CorelDRAW, and when you print your work. When your job is going to a commercial printer, choose Adobe RGB (1998) or ECI-RGB (a European standard) for your RGB Profile in Color Settings. Both of these profiles define a color space that is optimized for going to press and both of these profiles define a larger color "gamut" than sRGB. If you deal with delicate shades of color and you need great control of a precise color such as one would in fashion design and corporate logos, Adobe RGB or ECI-RGB gives your document a much larger color space than sRGB and matches printing press colors better.

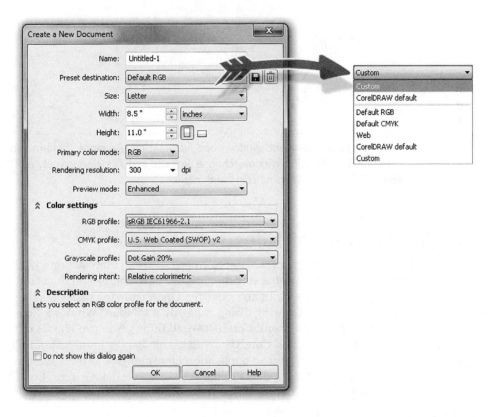

Working with Multiple Documents

Like many graphics applications, CorelDRAW can keep more than one document open in the interface. Each open document, whether it is new or a previously created document, is listed at the bottom of the Window menu. If you've opened several documents, you might notice that each document window is maximized, but only the most recently opened document appears in view, indicated by the document name in CorelDRAW's application title bar. While document windows are maximized, only the document in the forefront is visible. Any other opened documents are hidden from view. To navigate between document windows in the maximized state, choose Window | *Filename,* as shown here.

Tip To see all open document windows and automatically arrange them in your CorelDRAW application window, choose Cascade and Tile Horizontally or Tile Vertically from the Window command menu.

Opening Document Files

To open an existing document, choose from one of these three actions: click the Open Other button from the Welcome screen, click the Open button on the Standard Bar, or choose File | Open (CTRL + O). In any case, the Open Drawing dialog appears as shown in Figure 3-2. The Open Drawing dialog is mostly a standard Windows 7 configuration with some interesting and useful CorelDRAW additions. You can choose different-sized icon views of documents, and CorelDRAW files will display graphical thumbnails of your saved work. There is also an application identifier tick at the bottom right of the icons so you can instantly tell that a folder contains CorelDRAW files, Corel PHOTO-PAINT (CPT), or Corel Media Exchange (CMX) documents. Additionally, if you click

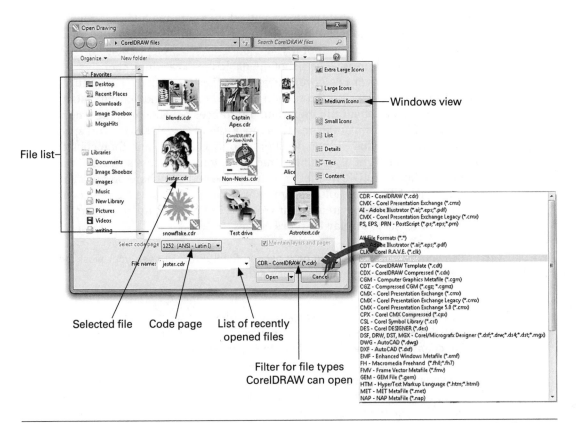

FIGURE 3-2   The Open dialog in CorelDRAW is an enhanced version of the standard Windows 7 Open dialog.

the All File Formats button, a *long* list of all file types CorelDRAW can open appears; this is a handy way to filter out file types when you've opened a folder containing CorelDRAW files, video, and audio files, for example. To open a file, you click its title or icon, and then choose Open. If you've recently opened a CorelDRAW-supported file type, you can click the down arrow to the right of the selected File Name, and you can choose from a list that might be composed of CorelDRAW files all over the place on your hard drive.

If you're new to both CorelDRAW and Windows 7, the Open dialog contains some areas of interest, some of which are standard Windows conventions whereas others are CorelDRAW enhancements to the Open dialog:

- **Windows View**   Click the drop-down list (as was done in Windows XP) to set how a folder you open displays its contents. You can usually get a good view for locating a file you need to open using the Large Icons view. Another useful view configuration is to use Details in combination with the Preview Pane (the button directly to the right of the Windows View drop-down list). With the Details View enabled, you can then sort files by date, type, and size.

- **Filter** By default, CorelDRAW shows you all files within a folder. If you're not organizationally fastidious with your hard disk(s), finding the CorelDRAW file you seek can be a nightmare, but not if you choose, for example, CDR-CorelDRAW (*.CDR) from the filter list. The list of openable files is a comprehensive one in version X6, with over two dozen vector-type files recognized, not simply CorelDRAW native files. See the section "Importing Files and Setting Options" later in this chapter about the important differences between *opening* a non-CorelDRAW file and *importing* one to an open file in CorelDRAW's workspace.
- **Recently opened files** If you do filter for only CDR files and then click the down arrow at the right of the File Name field, you can access several of the most-recently opened CorelDRAW files that can be located anywhere on your hard drive, not just the current folder's contents. If you click to select a file, its name appears in the File Name area, and if you type in the wildcard characters *.*, the filter button resets to display all types of files.

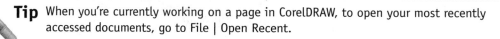

Tip When you're currently working on a page in CorelDRAW, to open your most recently accessed documents, go to File | Open Recent.

- **Select Code Page** If you are working with files that were created in a version of CorelDRAW that uses a different language than your copy does, you might need to change the Code Page before you open the file. Code Pages control *mapping:* which character in a typeface is used when you press a specific key on your keyboard. If you see a lot of square boxes displayed where you know you should have text (and you have the document's typeface installed), you should try reopening the file using a different Code Page. The Code Page chosen in the drop-down list should match the one used when the file was created. For example, if you are using a copy of CorelDRAW that uses US English, the Code Page that is used by default is 1252 (ANSI – Latin 1). However, if the file you are opening was created in the Korean language edition of CorelDRAW, then you should choose 949 (ANSI/OEM – Korean) from the Select Code Page drop-down when you open that file.
- **Maintain Layers And Pages** CorelDRAW has supported layers and multipage files for seemingly forever; if you want to preserve the layer order between different versions of saved files, check this box. If you leave this box unchecked, you might create a mess of the document you open—all objects on all pages will be merged to a single, one-layer CDR page.

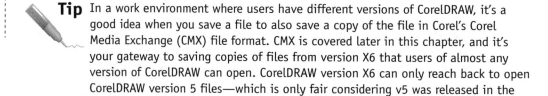

Tip In a work environment where users have different versions of CorelDRAW, it's a good idea when you save a file to also save a copy of the file in Corel's Corel Media Exchange (CMX) file format. CMX is covered later in this chapter, and it's your gateway to saving copies of files from version X6 that users of almost any version of CorelDRAW can open. CorelDRAW version X6 can only reach back to open CorelDRAW version 5 files—which is only fair considering v5 was released in the early 1990s.

In the Open Drawing dialog, locate and select your document file, and then click the Open button (or double-click the filename) to open it. CorelDRAW supports opening multiple file using modifier keys. You can open files that neighbor one another on the directory list (in the same folder) by holding SHIFT while selecting your files. Open files *not* in sequence in the file list (in the same folder) by holding CTRL while clicking to select the filenames, and then click the Open button. This is a standard Windows convention, as is marquee-dragging to select multiple file icons.

Opening Files from Other Applications

You can open many other files that are not native to CorelDRAW, such as Adobe Illustrator or Microsoft PowerPoint in CorelDRAW. When a file originally created in a different application is open, CorelDRAW automatically converts its contents to CorelDRAW format. If you look at the title bar of the drawing window, you will see that CorelDRAW has opened the file, preserved the filename, but has given it a .CDR extension. The original application file remains on the hard disk unchanged. In a way, opening a nonnative CorelDRAW file is similar to importing nonnative graphics data.

When opening nonnative application files supported by CorelDRAW's Import filters, the graphics and text objects contained in the file are converted as closely as possible to compatible equivalents supported in CorelDRAW. Although the Open command is *like* an Import operation, certain file formats might not open flawlessly, depending on their type and contents. You might get better results if you import the files as objects into an open CorelDRAW document by pressing CTRL + I (File | Import). If CorelDRAW is unable to interpret a file's contents while trying to open it, an alert dialog appears.

Warning Messages

When opening files—especially older files or files created on a different system or using a third-party application—warning messages might appear before the file actually opens. For the most part, these messages aren't meant to cause alarm, but instead to advise. Two of the most common messages are due to inappropriate data types and font warnings.

If, for example, you try to use the Open box to open a GIF bitmap, CorelDRAW alerts you that the file cannot be opened and suggests that you try using the Import command instead. As far as opening a document that was originally created using fonts that you don't have installed, the Font Substitution For Missing Fonts dialog appears and gives you the chance to view a list of the fonts used in the document and substitute ones you *do* have installed. An alternative measure is to jot down the names of the typefaces used, click Cancel, and then install the needed fonts if you have identical or similar ones. Then reopen the document; if the font you installed is similarly but not identically named, you need to work through the Font Substitution choices, but after a few moments, you can be assured that the file looks mostly like it was originally created.

Saving and Closing Documents

Whether you save often (pressing CTRL+S at regular intervals is a good idea) or you're saving your document for the first time, you'll want to define some file information for your saves and practice good hard-drive housekeeping by saving to user-defined folders. When you know you want to retrieve a document in the near future, setting a save location, applying a name, adding user data, and other options go along with the job.

Saving Your First Document

You can save an *existing* document simply by clicking the Save button on the Standard Bar or by choosing File | Save (CTRL+S), which causes your most recent changes to the page to be saved immediately without opening any dialogs.

CorelDRAW's Save Drawing dialog contains more than just options on where to save and what name to use when saving the file. For a practical exercise that explores the additional options you have when saving, follow these steps.

Tutorial Saving Files with User Info

1. If you've just started a new document and want to save it, click the Save button in the Standard Bar, use the CTRL+S shortcut, or choose File | Save. The Save Drawing dialog appears, as shown in Figure 3-3.

2. With the Save Drawing dialog open, use the dialog options to set a location for your document, and type a unique name in the File Name box. If you're saving your document to a format other than CorelDRAW's native CDR format, choose a file format from the Save As Type menu. Doing this is similar to choosing File | Export. The disadvantage to saving in a non-CorelDRAW file type is that it might be hard to open this file again and edit it using all of CorelDRAW's features.

3. Saving as a CDR file gives you the option to choose a version from the Version drop-down. Unless you *must* save to an older file format to allow the saved file to be used with legacy software, always choose the most recent (highest number) version. If you choose an older file version, some of the work you did in your file may not save as you expect because an effect or other feature used may not have existed in the file version you selected.

4. If saving your document in a CorelDRAW file or template file (CDT) format, you can enter (optional) Title, Subject, and star rating as part of the file's metadata. If you take a moment to fill in a keyword or two about the file you save, it becomes much easier to sort through your saved files a month or a year later, especially with CorelCONNECT, which ships with CorelDRAW. You and every CorelDRAW user (so be tasteful with your descriptive text) can view and edit any information you appended to your file through the File | Document Properties dialog.

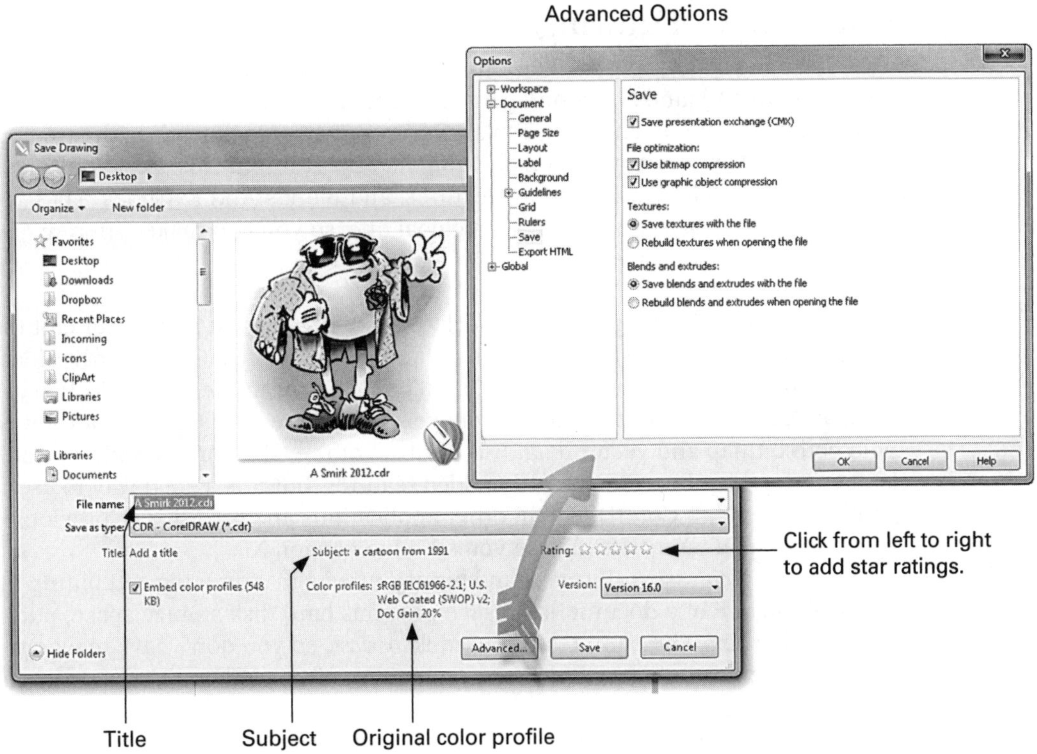

Advanced Options

Click from left to right to add star ratings.

Title   Subject   Original color profile

FIGURE 3-3   The Save Drawing dialog can save a file with user information and other options.

5. If you only want to save the object(s) you currently have selected, check the Selected Only check box. Everything that is not selected will not be saved to the file.

6. You can choose to embed the color profile you used to create a document by checking the Embed Color Profiles box on saving. Choosing this option is usually a good idea, and it adds only marginally to the overall saved file size. Embedding the color profile means that you and anyone else who opens the document will view it as it's intended to be output for the screen and for printing. The only time you wouldn't want to embed the color profile is if the document was created with the wrong profile for a printing job, for example. To change a document's color profile before saving it, choose Tools | Color Management | Document Settings.

Advanced Save Drawing Options

The Save Drawing dialog sports still more refinements you can make when saving a file. Clicking the Advanced button opens the same Options dialog that you can navigate to at any time by choosing Tools | Options (CTRL + J), expanding the tree directory under Document, and then clicking the Save item. In this area, you can make choices about File Optimization, Textures, and Blends And Extrudes. These options are set on a document basis, *not* a global one, so you can make different choices for each file you save.

- *Save Presentation Exchange (CMX).* Check this box if you want to place or edit the file in other applications that accept this file format, such as Corel WordPerfect or Xara Designer and older versions of CorelDRAW. For example, CorelDRAW 5 can't open an X6 CDR file, but version 5 *can* open a CMX file. The CMX file format can hold both bitmap and vector data. It is a subset of the CDR format and, as such, is not as capable of certain recently added features, but it is a good way to use graphics created in CorelDRAW in other applications and for users of previous versions to open your files in case you saved to version X6.
- *Use Bitmap Compression.* Bitmaps and bitmap effects in a drawing can plump up the final file size of a document. To save precious hard disk storage space, put a check in this box. The compression used is *lossless,* so you don't have to worry that choosing this option will degrade the quality of your file onscreen or when printed.
- *Use Graphic Object Compression.* Checking this box reduces saved file sizes by compressing the vector elements in the file. This is particularly welcome if you've created many extrude objects in a document, whose component objects can number in the 30s, 40s, or even hundreds, if you've used complex shading options.
- *Save Textures With The File or Rebuild Textures When Opening The File.* Click the radio button next to one of these mutually exclusive options. Saving the textures increases the file's size and uses more hard disk space. Rebuilding the textures saves hard disk space, but it then takes longer to open and save a file. Your choice here is between maximizing your hard disk space or your time.
- *Save Blends And Extrudes With The File or Rebuild Blends And Extrudes When Opening The File.* As with saving or rebuilding textures, here your choice is really between maximizing hard disk space or your time. Click the radio button next to the choice that suits you best.

After you've made your selections, click the OK button to be returned to the Save Drawing dialog. Click the Save button, or the Cancel button to abandon the save.

Save As Command

The Save As command (CTRL + SHIFT + S) is useful for saving copies of your document using the same or different Save command settings. The Save As command is often used to save a file at regular intervals throughout the creation of a graphic—so you can go back to an earlier version of the file or see what different color schemes or layouts look like. Using the Save As command in combination with the Selected Only option (available only while objects are selected) is a truly useful option; if you've been working with a lot of objects you won't need later, you don't have to delete them all to tidy up, you simply use Selected Only. Otherwise, the options available in the Save As command dialog are identical to those in the Save dialog.

Save As vs. Export

Although using the Save As command may seem similar to using the Export command in some ways, the two are quite different; in some cases, it might be better to use one command instead of the other. Usually the Save As command is the best option to choose when saving native CorelDRAW files.

The Export command (File | Export) is best for saving your document or selected objects as any *other* type of file format, particularly bitmap formats like CPT, GIF, JPEG, PNG, or a wide variety of text formats as well as other specialized vector formats such as EPS and SVG. In CorelDRAW, you can save—but not export—files in CorelDRAW (CDR), Corel Pattern file (PAT), and CorelDRAW Template (CDT) format.

Using File Backup Options

Countless hours of work can be saved using CorelDRAW's Backup feature. When it comes to saving and backing up your document files, CorelDRAW lets you take full control over *how, where,* and *when* backup files are created. *Backup files* let you retrieve recent changes made to documents should something unfortunate (such as a power failure) occur while you're working. Backup files created automatically are named AUTOBACKUP_OF_*FILENAME*.CDR, where *FILENAME* is the name of your original CorelDRAW document. It's best to specify a custom folder for your auto-saves instead of accepting the default location, so you can quickly locate and proceed with your work after a mishap.

Caution   If CorelDRAW closes unexpectedly, the next time you open CorelDRAW, the File Recovery dialog prompts you to open the Auto-Backup file that it found. Click OK to open the file. If you click Cancel and do not open the file, the Auto-Backup file will be deleted when you exit CorelDRAW. So open and save the file when you can—you won't be prompted to do so again.

At your command, backup files can be created every time you save a file. The naming convention for these files is in the form of Backup_of_*filename*.cdr, and these backup files are stored in the same folder location as the file you saved. You can open backup files the same way as with any CorelDRAW document file, by using the File | Open command (CTRL + O).

To access CorelDRAW's backup controls, use the Workspace | Save page of the Options dialog, shown here. Choose Tools | Options | Workspace | Save.

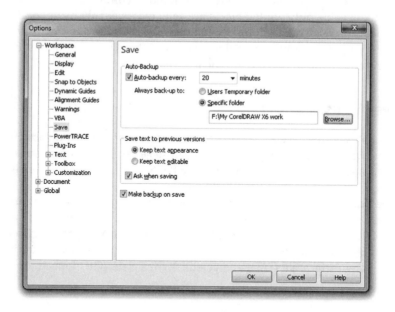

This list should help you decide which options to choose:

- **Auto-Backup Every**   While this option is selected (the default), your document files are backed up at specified time intervals. The default is 20 minutes and can be set to anywhere between 1 and 60 minutes (or never).
- **Always Back-Up To**   Specify the location of the backups to be saved in your temporary folder (the default), or choose a specific folder and use the Browse button to specify a drive and folder location. *Don't* try to use folders that Windows itself has generated such as My Pictures and My Documents. These are shortcuts you see in directory windows, and CorelDRAW cannot accept these special types of folders.
- **Make Backup On Save**   Activating the Make Backup On Save option (selected by default) ensures CorelDRAW updates the backup file to match your original document file each time you use the File | Save command (CTRL + S). This backup system is in addition to the Auto-Backup feature and complements it because the files are in a more accessible location and *are not* automatically deleted (although they are overwritten each time you save a file), which leaves you with a backup of the most recent version of the file. It is handy to have this kind of backup file because you can revert to the last saved version of the file if you should make a mistake while editing a file—or if you just want to start over.

Working with Templates

Templates are special files that can be saved based on existing settings and/or document content. Templates can be used as starting points to avoid repetitive page setup and document defaults. You can recognize template files by the .CDT file extension.

Opening Templates

To open an existing template file with the aim of creating a new document based on the template, choose File | New From Template to open the New From Template dialog, as shown here. Here you can choose from a list containing many categories of professionally designed templates that come with CorelDRAW. Additional templates are found on the CorelDRAW DVD and on CorelDRAW.com.

Templates are organized in two general groups: Type and Industry. Choose Type in the View By drop-down to see a list of template categories broken down by kind of document produced—a catalog, a flyer, a letterhead, and so on. Choose Industry to see the templates arranged in categories that correspond to various industries such as Hospitality, Retail, or Services. To use any templates you've created and saved, search the list in the My Templates section on the left side of the dialog.

Clicking on a category, such as Business Cards or Brochures in the list on the left, opens (in the center of the dialog) thumbnail views of the templates available. Click once on a thumbnail to load information about the template into the Template Details section at the bottom of the dialog and into Designer Notes on the right of the dialog. To increase the size of the thumbnail for a better view or to decrease the size of the thumbnail to view more thumbnails, click-drag the slider at the bottom of the dialog.

While a template is selected, the preview window displays a thumbnail of the first page of the template. Click OK or double-click the file to open a new (unsaved) document using the template's content and page layout.

The Browse button opens a Windows standard file Open dialog that you can use to locate, select, and open a new document based on a template somewhere on your computer or network other than CorelDRAW's default location for templates.

Opening and Saving Templates

You can open any template file that has a .CDT extension you've saved from X6 or from any previous version for editing and change its actual template format and/or its content. Use the File | Open command and choose CorelDRAW Template (CDT) as the file type. Before the file opens, a dialog asks whether you want to open the template as a new document or for editing. If your aim is to open a new document based on the template content and structure, leave New From Template selected in combination with the With Contents option. If your intention is to edit the template file itself, choose Open For Editing.

When saving an edited template file, performing a Save command automatically saves the file as a template without opening any dialogs—and without the need to respecify the file as a CDT template file in the Save dialog. Additionally, a CDT file you opened will appear on the File | Open Recent list and, if you choose it, will simply open without the dialog shown in the previous illustration.

Clipboard Commands

As many users already know, the Windows *Clipboard* is a temporary "place" that's capable of storing the last objects copied and is a feature of your computer's operating system. While the data you copied or cut is stored in your system's RAM, you can "paste" duplicates of the data into your document. The three most common Clipboard commands you'll likely use are Copy, Cut, and Paste—each of which is accessible either from the Edit menu or from the Standard Bar, as shown. Cut, Copy, and Paste are also standard Windows commands, so you can indeed use the keyboard shortcuts CTRL + C (Copy), CTRL + V (Paste), and CTRL + X (Cut) to speed up your work.

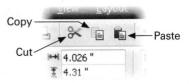

Copying vs. Cutting

Each time an object is copied to the Windows Clipboard, the previous Clipboard contents are overwritten. To copy selected objects onto your Clipboard, choose Edit | Copy. Better yet, click the Copy button on the Standard Bar, or use the standard CTRL + C shortcut. The older Windows CTRL + INSERT shortcut also works. After copying, the items you copy remain unaltered in your document.

The *Cut* command automatically deletes the selected items from your document and puts a copy on the Clipboard. To cut items, click the Cut button on the Standard Bar, choose Edit | Cut, or use the standard CTRL + X shortcut. The older Windows SHIFT + DELETE shortcut also applies.

 Tip   To create duplicates of your selected objects immediately, press the + key on your keyboard's numeric keypad. Copies immediately are placed in front of the selected objects in the document and in exactly the same page position. This action does not use the Windows Clipboard, so your current Clipboard contents remain intact.

Paste vs. Paste Special

Copies of items on your Clipboard can be placed into your current document using the Paste command. Each time you use the Paste command, more duplicate copies are pasted. When an item is pasted into CorelDRAW, it is placed on the very top or front of the active layer. To paste Clipboard contents, perform one of these actions: click the Paste button on the Standard Bar, choose Edit | Paste, or use the CTRL + V shortcut. The older Windows SHIFT + INSERT shortcut also applies.

Paste Special in the Edit menu is used to place "unusual" data into a CorelDRAW document: text that is specially formatted, a graphic that the Clipboard doesn't completely understand, or data that CorelDRAW has no way of clearly understanding as text, vector art, or bitmap data. Windows Clipboard is capable of assigning media copied to it any of 27 different data types, frequently more than one type; one of the ways that the mechanism Paste Special operates is to offer you a choice as to how the media on the Clipboard is interpreted by CorelDRAW as it pastes a copy of this media on a page.

Paste Special should be used on three occasions (possibly more) when you need something in a CorelDRAW document that wasn't created in CorelDRAW and pressing CTRL + V results in nothing being pasted:

- When you've copied formatted text from WordPerfect, MS-Word, or a desktop publishing application, and you do not want the text formatted. Suppose you've created a table and use fancy bullets and an equally fancy font in your word processing program, and you only want the text imported to CorelDRAW via the Clipboard; you want to reformat the data in CorelDRAW with different fonts, you don't want bullets, but you also don't want to retype the text. You use Edit | Paste Special, and then choose Rich Text Format, or better still, you choose Text and then click OK.

- When you've copied data from an application that creates things that are completely inappropriate for CorelDRAW to import. For example, you own a 3D modeling program and want a model you created in a CorelDRAW page. CorelDRAW has no 3D tools, but it *will* accept a special pasted interpreted bitmap copy of the model. In this case, the Special Paste of the model cannot be edited in CorelDRAW, but the bitmap interpretation of the model program's data can be scaled, moved, rotated, and the document will print with the bitmap and any other CorelDRAW media on the page.

- When you want to update data you need to paste, especially with text. By default, CorelDRAW's Paste Special dialog is set to Paste, and not Paste Link, and you really need to think *carefully* and read this section twice before choosing Paste Link and then clicking OK. Paste Link embeds, for example, a section of MS Word text that can later be edited using MS Word, not CorelDRAW. The data you paste using Paste Link falls into that fuzzy category of data that doesn't actually "belong" to the CorelDRAW document—the data depends on there being a valid link to its source, and that the application used to create the data is still installed on your computer a month from now when it's editing time. A linked pasted object is not directly editable in CorelDRAW, although it can be printed, moved, and scaled as an embedded object. To edit the object, you double-click it with the Pick Tool and the program you used to generate this media pops up ... and you can edit away. When you're finished editing, you save the document in the program, you can close it, and when you come back to CorelDRAW, the media has been updated. If you work extensively with CorelDRAW and a word processor, and your client requests revisions like leaves falling from a tree, the Paste Link feature can be a charm. However, if you don't save documents regularly or uninstall programs frequently, do not use this feature. The next time you open the document, the link might not be linked and there goes part of your design. Figure 3-4 shows the Paste Special dialog, and the different options on the list when, at left, a 3D model has been copied to the Clipboard, and, at right, when a word processing document has been copied.

Tip Paste Special does not have a keyboard shortcut assigned to it by default. It can be handy to assign it one yourself by using Tools | Customization | Commands.

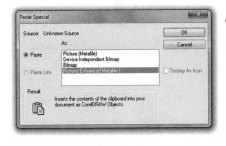

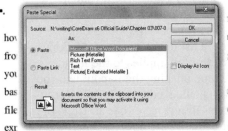

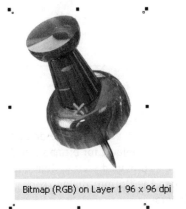

Bitmap (RGB) on Layer 1 96 x 96 dpi

Paste 3D model data as a picture.

nputer user is
how   rd to copy data
fro   g new or exotic
you   accomplish these
bas   d options such as
file   design
exp   chapter you'll
learn about file-saving options that let coworkers who are using previous
versions of CorelDRAW work with your files and about how to use
timesaving templates and other file types. You'll also see how to protect
your work with CorelDRAW's automatic backup feature, how to make
the Clipboard work overtime for you, as well as how to store and
retrieve scrapbook items and symbols and how to import and export
graphics, text, and data into and out of CorelDRAW.

Document Object on Layer 1

Paste Link text as a Word document.

FIGURE 3-4 Paste Special is for data that cannot be imported as a regular data, and when you want to use an editor other than CorelDRAW.

Undoing and Redoing Changes

Albert Einstein might have said (under his breath) that for every action, there is an equal and opposite mistake. Then again, Mr. Einstein probably never used CorelDRAW, so he was unaware that you have several ways to *undo* a mistake. Or to *redo* something you originally thought was a mistake, and even back up and undo a mistake you made a dozen steps ago. It's a shame that life isn't as forgiving as CorelDRAW.

Basic Undo Commands

Choose Edit | Undo or use the standard CTRL + Z shortcut. To reverse an Undo command, choose Edit | Redo or use the CTRL + SHIFT + Z shortcut. CorelDRAW takes both of these commands further by offering Undo and Redo buttons on the Standard Bar; they can be used either to Undo or Redo single or multiple commands. The buttons themselves even have popout menus that reveal a list to choose from. Clicking the toolbar button applies to the most recent action; clicking the popout lets you choose a specific Undo and Redo order of commands. To reverse either an Undo or Redo action using the popouts, click one of the listed commands. Doing so takes your composition back or forward to the point you specified in the popout. Undo and Redo popouts show you the most recent actions at the top of the listing.

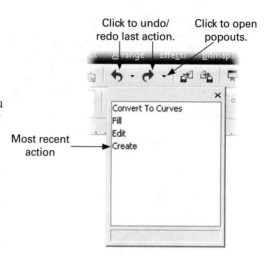

Click to undo/redo last action.   Click to open popouts.

Most recent action

Note   You can customize the number of Undo levels CorelDRAW performs. The default setting records your 20 most recent actions—and the default for bitmap effects is—but the values can be set as high as 150 levels (provided your system has the available resources). To access Undo options, open the Options dialog (click the button on the Standard Bar), and then click General.

Using the Undo Docker

For even more control over your most recent actions, you might try the Undo docker opened by choosing Window | Dockers | Undo. The Undo docker, shown here, provides different views of your drawing as it appeared before certain recent actions. The Undo docker can also be used to save your recent actions as a Visual Basic for Applications (VBA) macro, which is terrific when you want to apply, for example, a dozen complex edits to different objects in different documents (on different days!).

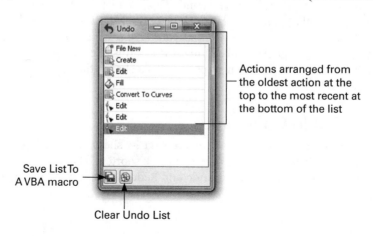

Actions arranged from the oldest action at the top to the most recent at the bottom of the list

Save List To A VBA macro

Clear Undo List

The Undo docker displays your most recent actions in reverse order of the Undo and Redo popout menus, with recent actions placed *at the bottom* of the docker list. Selecting a command on the list shows you a view of your document as it appeared before your most recent actions were performed.

Clicking the Clear Undo List icon clears the entire list of actions in the Undo docker list, providing you with a clean slate. You cannot clear or delete *some* of the actions; clearing is an all or nothing decision. By default, an alert dialog appears, warning you that clearing the Undo list can't be undone. Having a robust Undo list can be a much-needed safety net, so don't clear the list unless you have so many undos in the list that it is bogging down your system resources.

When you save and then *close* a file, the Undo docker list is automatically cleared—you will be starting fresh when you reopen the document. If you save the document but don't close it and continue to work on the file, the actions in the Undo docker remain, and your new actions continue to be added to the list.

The Undo docker is also a great way to create VBA macros. Clicking the Save List To A VBA Macro button in the docker opens the Save Macro dialog, where you provide a name and description for the new macro and store it either with your open document or to CorelDRAW's main Global Macros list. Keep in mind when naming your macros that spaces are not valid characters, but underscores are.

Importing and Exporting Files

CorelDRAW's Import and Export filter collection is one of the largest in any graphics application. Here is a list of the document types version X6 can import and export.

Support for new file formats:

- Adobe Illustrator CS5 (you can now choose to export text to Illustrator as Curves or as Text; compressed Illustrator files are not currently supported)
- Adobe Photoshop CS5.5 as well as import support for Adobe Acrobat 9 (import and export) and Acrobat X (import only)
- Microsoft Publisher 2010 (import only)
- MS Word 2007
- Corel Painter
- PDF 1.7, PDF/A (an ISO-approved format for long-term document archiving)

Filters are data translators for files created in other applications or in formats not native to CorelDRAW. *Import filters* take the data from other applications and translate that data into information that can be viewed and edited from within CorelDRAW. *Export filters* translate data from your CorelDRAW document to a format recognized by a different program or publishing medium. As with Import filters, Export filters frequently contain dialogs where you set up options to export the precise data you need for the target application or publishing medium.

Note When you export a file, the new file format may not support all the features that CorelDRAW's native file format (CDR) supports. For this reason, even when exporting work, you should always save a copy of your work in CorelDRAW's native file format.

Set Up Color Management Before Importing

Earlier in the section "Create a New Document that Suits You," the importance of color management was discussed; enabling and using a color profile is your best bet to ensure color consistency between your monitor, CorelDRAW, and your personal or commercial printer. Because CorelDRAW can import so many different graphics file types, especially documents created with Adobe products, you want to be alerted when importing a photo that was tagged with a color profile. Go to Tools | Color Management | Default Settings right now. In Figure 3-5, you can see four checkboxes

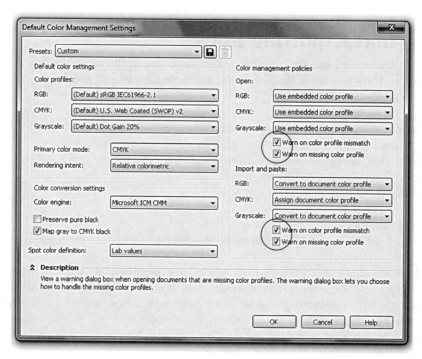

FIGURE 3-5 Turn on an alert that gives you the chance to correct a mismatched or missing color profile when you import a document.

toward the right of the dialog: check them. You can always uncheck these alert options if you feel pestered by them in your work, but you really shouldn't. When you import, for example, a co-worker's Photoshop PSD file, the chances are very good that this image was saved with a color profile. The chances are also fairly good that this color-profile tagged photo *won't* have the same color profile as the CorelDRAW document you've created. When an imported image has a profile that doesn't match the current CorelDRAW document's color profile, the imported photo might look dull, overly saturated, or too dark or too light. And it will print that way, and then you have an unhappy client, co-worker, or most importantly, you have an unhappy *you*. Fortunately, it only takes two seconds to be happier.

Now that the alerts have been checked, here's what happens when you import a PSD, TIFF, JPEG, and even a Corel CMX document that has been embedded with a color profile: you click to import it (the exact method is covered in the following section), and before anything happens, you see a dialog. In this dialog, you're told exactly what color profile the incoming document is tagged with, what your current document's color profile is, and you have three radio buttons to choose from to remedy the mismatch:

- *Ignore the import's color profile and assign it the CorelDRAW document's profile.* This is not the best solution if the imported photo or graphic is really important to the design and your client.
- *Convert the document's color profile to match your CorelDRAW document's color profile.* This is a much better option; see "Create a New Document that Suits You" for the reason why and the color conversion CorelDRAW uses.
- *Convert document colors to embedded color profile.* You will see one of two different dialog boxes when importing bitmaps. As shown here, a bitmap might not have a profile, in which case you are presented a dialog box where you can tag the incoming image with a profile, and then let CorelDRAW convert the image to your document's color profile. To save yourself an operation with the bitmap, you can assign it the same color space as your document's. Conversely, when an incoming bitmap has a profile, but it doesn't match your CorelDRAW document's color profile, you'll see a dialog like the lower one shown here. You're usually

best off choosing the second option—to let CorelDRAW convert the bitmap to the document's color profile.

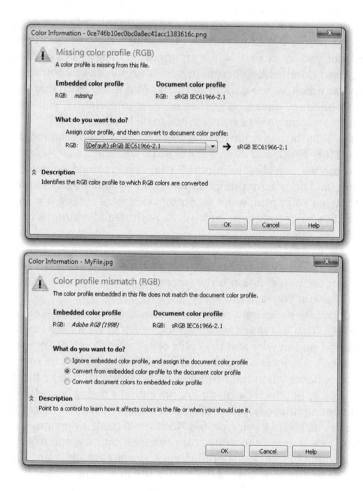

Click OK with the confidence that you've just accessed one of the most powerful features in CorelDRAW X6.

Importing Files and Setting Options

You import a file by clicking File | Import, clicking the Import button on the Standard Bar, or using the CTRL+I shortcut. All of these moves open the Import dialog (see left, Figure 3-6), which can display thumbnails, provide information such as date and file size depending on which Windows view you have the panes set up for, and options for import in this dialog, and possibly a subsequent dialog, depending on the file you choose to import.

Proprietary media imports might
cause a second dialog to appear.

Generic bitmaps are imported with no
subsequent dialog or options boxes.

FIGURE 3-6   The Import dialog might trigger a second Options dialog for additional import features depending on the type of file you want to import.

For example, at right in Figure 3-6, an Acrobat PDF file has been chosen and after clicking Import in the first dialog box, a box with options for selecting which page and whether the import should convert text to curves appears. Bitmaps such as BMPs, JPEG photos, PNG files, and TIFFs are imported with no further questions asked (except about color profiles) because these image types are generated by dozens of applications, and CorelDRAW understands these data types. The Import dialog looks similar to the Open Drawing dialog, but it has a few more check boxes and options that are available depending on the kind of file you are importing. Check For Watermark is a common Import option; if you choose this, CorelDRAW informs you that the photo has been tagged by its creator. If you choose a file type not supported by CorelDRAW, such as an MP3 audio file, CorelDRAW lets you know (politely) that the file format is not supported.

If you choose to filter the contents of a folder—exactly the same way as you choose to open a file (covered earlier), it not only simplifies your search for the file you seek, but also simplifies the number of options for importing a specific media type. For getting various file formats into your document, CorelDRAW's list of file types is pretty comprehensive. Of the importable file types, Corel provides support for all its own formats, including CorelDRAW (CDR), Corel Symbol Library (CSL), Corel Painter (RIFF), CorelDRAW Compressed (CDX), Corel Presentation Exchange

(CMX), Corel CMX Compressed (CPX), Corel R.A.V.E. (CLK), Corel WordPerfect (WPD and WPG), Corel Quattro Pro (WB, WQ), Corel/Micrografx Designer (DES, DSF, and DRW), Corel Picture Publisher (PP4), and Corel PHOTO-PAINT (CPT).

You'll also find filter support for importing files from third-party products such as Adobe Photoshop (PSD), Adobe Illustrator (AI), Adobe Acrobat (PDF), Visio (VSD), and other Microsoft Office products. Other filters support popular PostScript, CAD, bitmap, text, and word processor file formats, and a selection of specialty file formats. Certain file types (such as PDF, discussed earlier) might have multiple pages; depending on the file type, you might see additional checkboxes in the Import dialog.

- **Do Not Show Filter Dialog**   For a few import file formats, a secondary dialog may appear, offering further options for handling inherent properties in the imported file. Choosing this option kills the display of this secondary dialog and is particularly useful for uninterrupted importing of multiple images. By default, this option is not selected.
- **Maintain Layers And Pages**   If the file you are importing contains multiple pages and/or multiple layers, this option becomes available. By default, this option is selected. As the file is imported, additional pages are automatically added to your current document and/or layers are automatically added. Layers are controlled using the Object Manager docker.
- **Combine Multi-Layer Bitmap** You can choose this option to flatten imported Photoshop and Painter files so a single layer image file is imported.

 Tip You can import multiple files if they are stored in the same folder. Click one of the files you want to open, and then hold the CTRL key while clicking additional files. You can open an entire folder's contents: click the first file, then hold the SHIFT key, and finally, click the last file in the folder.

Exporting Files and Choosing Options

If this is the first chapter you're reading in *The Official Guide,* you're in for a treat—much of the rest of this guide shows you how to create exotic, intricate, and expressive artwork, logos, layouts, and other visuals that communicate your personal ideas. However, the world doesn't own CorelDRAW (yet), so you need to convert your media, which means you need export filters. Keep in mind (reading the rest of this guide will help you) that choosing the best export options affects your design's appearance, quality, and compatibility with other applications.

From the File menu, CorelDRAW offers a general-purpose Export command that is used to export your work to formats the world can view, plus a special Export For Office command for when your work will be used in a Corel WordPerfect Office application or in a Microsoft Office application. First, let's look at the Export command that offers the greatest variety of export formats.

Export

Choosing File | Export (CTRL + E) contains all of the export filters you chose to install during the installation of CorelDRAW. If you installed the recommended set of import/export filters, you'll find over 40 different file formats available in the Export dialog. If you need or just want to, you can always run the CorelDRAW installation program again to install additional Export filters—the Secondary Import/Export File types: CUR, EXE, FMV, ICO, PCD, PCX, SCT, VSD, XCF, XPM, and/or the Tertiary Import/Export File types: GEM, HTM, IMG, MET, NAP, PIC, SHW, MOV, and QTM.

The options available to you in the Export dialog vary depending on your document's properties, such as whether you have anything selected, how many pages are in your file, and what type of file format you have chosen in the Save As Type drop-down. Secondary dialogs can also appear depending on the Export file format. In Figure 3-7, this logo needs to be shared with a client as an e-mail attachment. One of the

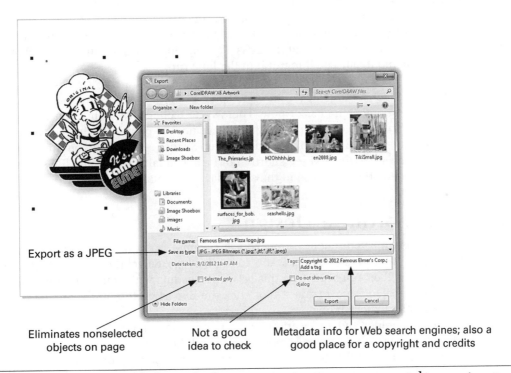

Export as a JPEG

Eliminates nonselected objects on page   Not a good idea to check   Metadata info for Web search engines; also a good place for a copyright and credits

FIGURE 3-7   The Export dialog is the first step to exporting your current document page or selected objects.

smallest file size, yet highest quality, bitmap file formats is JPEG for e-mail attachments, so this is chosen from the Save As Type drop-down list. This dialog then displays general options, and version X6 offers a secondary dialog after you choose a file location, a file name, and then click Export. For JPEG images, you almost *never* want to check the Do Not Show Filter Dialog check box. CorelDRAW has a host of options for writing JPEG copies of your work you do not want to pass by. A short tutorial is provided next that explains JPEG options so your work is crisp, hi-fi, and as small in file size as possible.

The following Export dialog options are available:

- **Export This Page Only**   If your document consists of multiple pages, this option becomes available when exporting to EPS or to any file format supporting text as characters (such as text or word processor formats). Choosing this option causes only your current page to be exported.
- **Selected Only**   Choose this option to export only your currently selected object(s) instead of your entire page or document.
- **Do Not Show Filter Dialog**   Choose this option to export your file immediately using the options currently set in some secondary filter dialogs; this can be useful when exporting multiple individual files in identical ways. However, as a rule, skipping the secondary filter dialog is like skipping a meal—you might feel okay at the moment, but you'll regret it in the long run.

To get a good working idea of how to export a CorelDRAW design as a JPEG image, open Famous Elmer's.cdr now. There's an excellent possibility you yourself can draw a better logo than Elmer did, but that's not the point—this happens to be a representative image with colors and the Drop Shadow effect that you might use in your own work, and you'll see shortly how visible quality and saved file size are affected by the options you use in the secondary filter dialog box.

Tutorial   Exporting a Design

1. Let's assume your client (Elmer) doesn't want a sea of white around the logo you're presenting—he only wants to see the logo. Select the grouped object using the Pick Tool. You always do this *before* proceeding with your Export operation.
2. Choose File | Export (CTRL + E) or click the Export button on the Standard Bar to open the Export dialog.
3. Select a folder and/or location, and enter a unique name for your exported file. Elmer's Terrific Logo.jpg seems to fit the bill here.
4. Choose JPEG-JPEG Bitmaps from the Save As Type drop-down menu.
5. Click the Selected Only option.

6. Date Taken is an optional field into which you can choose a date that a photo was taken, but obviously this isn't a photo you're exporting. As a rule, when you send anything to a web page or attach it as an e-mail, fill in as many metadata tags as are offered. Metadata adds very little to an overall saved file's size, and it really helps web search engines identify and publicize your work. Type keywords or credits and copyright information in the Tags field, too.

7. Click Export to proceed with your export operation.

8. Here's where the action happens: the secondary filter dialog box specific to JPEG images. First, click the Two Vertical Previews button toward the top left. Now you have two previews and can compare, for example, 100% quality versus 50% quality settings for export. JPEG compression discards some original color, but you get to set the level of compression in this dialog, and you can preview an acceptable and an unacceptable amount of visual compression. To use the preview panes, you click inside one to select it, and then choose a JPEG setting from the Presets drop-down or manually. Then compare what you see onscreen.

9. You can choose a Preset from the Preset list; however, this list only provides the most general and basic amount of control over your exported image: Low, Medium, High—you get the picture. Setting quality with JPEGs is inversely proportional to saved file size, and you can do this manually by using the Quality spin box (or by entering a value in the number box). Look at the image in the right pane to see the quality, and then look below it to see the estimated saved file size. As a rule, 10:1 compression generally provides excellent quality except when your design has a billion different colors sitting right next to each other, such as a drawing of confetti. JPEG doesn't work very well for what is called *high-frequency* images, and if this is the case, a GIF file would work better, display better, and have a much smaller file size.

10. In the Advanced section, you can choose to tag the image with a color profile, that is, the profile your document is defined with. You can also check Optimized, which helps compress the image more with little cost to the final rendered quality. You probably don't want to check Progressive—doing this causes the JPEG to stream as it is downloaded to the recipient. The streaming image increases its resolution until it's completely downloaded, it appears a little weird to the recipient, and Progressive should be reserved for large JPEGs (over 3 or 4MB) you send to people who only have dial-up connections.

11. You can scale your exported JPEG without scaling your original; use the percentage boxes in the Transformation field. It's not usually a good idea to uncheck Maintain Aspect Ratio unless you deliberately want to stretch or squash your exported image.

12. Once you've performed all your customization in all the Export areas, check one last time and decide on the quality you see in the preview frame that displays the compression you've decided on, take a look at the approximate saved file size, and then click OK to export your image to the specified folder on your hard drive. See Figure 3-8.

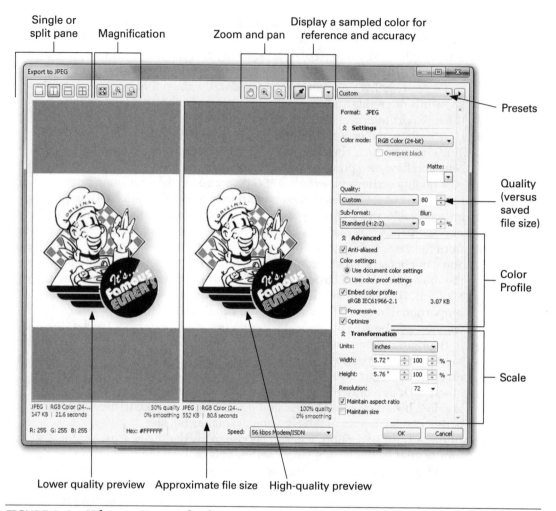

FIGURE 3-8   When an Export displays a secondary dialog box, use it to your advantage. Create the right size dimensions and file size for your intended audience.

Choosing Export File Formats

The preceding tutorial covers you for exporting your CorelDRAW work to one of the most common and popular bitmap file formats used today for e-mail attachments and web graphics. You can also choose third-party application file formats, such as Photoshop, Acrobat PDF, and even AutoDesk CAD data. Where you begin your adventures exporting CorelDRAW design work depends completely on who your final audience or target is—a friend, a commercial press house, or a different application to add a finishing touch to a composition. The following is a brief summary of the available export filters:

- **Bitmap formats**   Specific bitmap types whose format is openly used and supported by many software vendors—such as BMP (Windows and OS2), CALS,

GIF, JPEG (JPG, JP2), PCX, PNG, TGA, TIF—feature their own filter dialogs, custom tailoring your export for the application that receives the work. Third-party bitmap formats such as Photoshop PSD display a secondary dialog so you can set options specific to Photoshop data. Corel programs such as Painter and PaintShop Pro will accept file formats such as PSD, TIFF, and other types.

- **Metafile formats** Metafile formats such as CGM, EMF, FMV, and WFM *can* contain both vector and bitmap information, but *in practice* they commonly only contain vector *or* bitmap information. It is usually better to choose a dedicated bitmap or vector format.
- **Text formats** When exporting to text formats (such as native word processor or simple text formats), no additional dialogs appear. Choose from ANSI text (TXT), rich text format (RTF), or virtually any version of Microsoft Word (DOC), WordPerfect (WPD), or WordStar 7 and 2000 (WSD).
- **Font formats** You have the choice of exporting to TTF to create a True Type Font or to PFB to create an Adobe Type 1 font format to create your own font. A secondary dialog opens where you specify the properties for the font and character you are exporting.
- **Vector formats** CorelDRAW includes the following vector graphics filters: Frame Vector Metafile (FMV) and a Scalable Vector Graphics filter (SVG and SVGZ compressed), as shown in the SVG Export dialog in Figure 3-9. SVG has

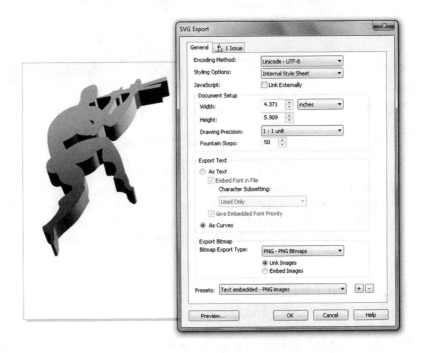

FIGURE 3-9 The improved Scalable Vector Graphics filter offers property options such as embedding a subset of fonts used and compression schemes for bitmaps in your document.

become quite popular these days as an alternative to vector-based Flash media; if you're considering posting a graphic to Wikipedia, SVG will be appreciated by the audience. Also included in this Export is a preflight tab for correcting incorrect option choices (such as ICC color profiling; note the "1 Issue" remark in this figure) and options to create saved presets.

- **CAD/Plotter formats**   You can now export files to AutoCAD (DXF and DWG), as well as to HPGL 2 Plotter files (PLT). These filters include their own specific dialog filter options.
- **EPS formats**   When you choose to export to Encapsulated PostScript (EPS) format, CorelDRAW's filter offers a comprehensive set of PostScript-related options, organized into General and Advanced tabbed areas in the EPS Export dialog, as shown here. EPS files are the coin of the realm in desktop publishing, and CorelDRAW can write an EPS graphics file that is Mac and Windows compatible.

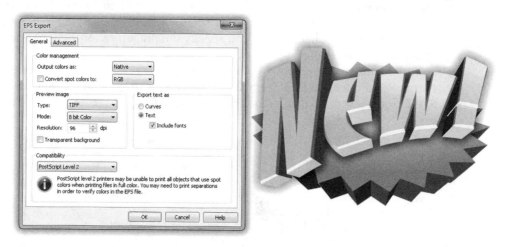

- **Third-party application formats**   Export to Adobe Illustrator (AI), Adobe Photoshop (PSD), or Macromedia Flash (SWF)—each of which opens a dialog filter with specific options. The Macintosh OS native file formats, MACPaint Bitmap (MAC), and Macintosh PCT (PIC) are also available.
- **Corel native formats**   Export to any of Corel's own native formats: Corel WordPerfect Graphic (WPG), Corel PHOTO-PAINT (CPT), or Corel Presentation Exchange 5.0 (CMX)—each of which features its own filter dialogs.

Export for Office

Corel WordPerfect Office and Microsoft Office are used by tens of millions of people every day to produce letters, reports, charts, and presentations. These people often do not have graphics training or graphics software, but want and need graphics in their documents. To address these needs, Office suites not only accept graphics for placement in documents, but also provide simple tools to create and edit graphics within the suite. The tools are limited and the file formats that work best with Office suites are also limited when compared with graphics applications.

CorelDRAW's Export For Office feature makes it easy for you to be sure that any graphics you supply for use in WordPerfect and Microsoft Office are optimized for their use in an Office document. Export For Office also helps you and your client avoid delays, bum documents, and other migraine-inducing issues.

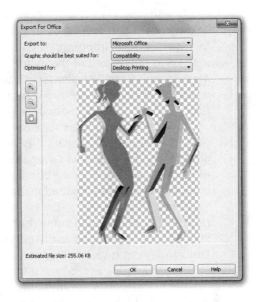

Choose File | Export For Office to display the Export For Office dialog and kick off the process of creating a file for your customer that's Office-suite optimized. The Export For Office dialog has a large preview window in the center that shows what will be exported. You can navigate around the preview window and zoom in and out by clicking the appropriate Zoom or Hand Tool icon on the side of the dialog.

Export For Office cannot export multiple pages; it only works with the page you have active at the time you opened the dialog. If you have a multipage document that you want to export, you'll need to do this page by page. And unlike the Export dialog, there is no Selected Only check box; however, you can, indeed, export only a selected object. In the Export For Office process, if you have any object(s) selected before you open the dialog, only the objects you had selected appear in the preview window. On the other hand, if you have nothing selected, everything you have on *and* off the page in the Export For Office process saves.

The gray checkerboard background to the preview area corresponds to areas of transparency. Vector objects and text have no background, but any bitmaps you created from vector objects will have a white background around them unless you explicitly checked the Transparent Background check box in the Convert To Bitmap dialog when converting the object for export. Bitmaps you imported into your original document that contained transparent backgrounds will retain the transparent areas.

The drop-down boxes at the top of the dialog are where you make some preparations for the intended use of the exported graphic. To make good choices here, you really need to know what your customer is likely to do with the file. First, you need to know which Office suite the customer will use the graphics file with: Corel's or Microsoft's. The answer to this question determines which file format you choose in the Export To drop-down list. Also, ask yourself (and your coworker receiving the file): Will you edit this file using the Office suite's tools, or will you just place it in the document as finished work? You also should know what the final destination for the document will be: an onscreen presentation or on the Web, printing to a low-resolution desktop printer or to a professional, commercial printer.

If your customer is using Corel WordPerfect Office, choose that in the Export To drop-down box, and all other options gray out. Your exported file will be saved as a WordPerfect Graphics (WPG) file. The estimated file size of the saved WPG file appears at the bottom of the dialog. Click OK and the now-familiar Save As dialog appears with Corel WordPerfect Graphic already selected in the Save As Type drop-down. Navigate to where you want to save your file, give it a name in the File Name field, click Save, and you are done.

If your customer uses Microsoft Office, choose that in the Export To drop-down. Next, choose either Compatibility or Editing in the Graphic Should Be Best Suited For drop-down. If you choose Compatibility, your exported file will be saved as a bitmap in the PNG file format. As a bitmap, your graphic will look just as you see it onscreen, but it can no longer be edited using vector tools.

If you choose Editing, the file will be saved in the Extended Metafile Format (EMF), which can retain some (but not all) vector information and some CorelDRAW effects. EMF files can be easily edited in Microsoft Office, but fancy effects such as Distort may not travel well or at all, so you will want to open the document yourself in Microsoft Office to see how it looks. As a measure to ensure that the export looks like the original does in CorelDRAW, you might want to make a copy of the graphic, particularly if it has dynamic effects such as Envelopes or Extrude. Then use Arrange | Break Apart and similar commands on the Arrange menu to "genericize" the vector information, increasing the saved file size, but also increasing your chances that an elegant graphic displays in a Word document as you intend it to.

If you choose Compatibility, which will save your work as a bitmap, the Optimized For drop-down needs your attention now. If you choose Editing, the Optimized For drop-down is grayed out. Here your choices are Presentation, which basically means it will be displayed on a monitor and not printed, or from one of the two print options on the list—Desktop Printing or Commercial Printing. The PNG format bitmap file saved with the Presentation setting saves at 96 dpi; the Desktop Printing setting saves at 150 dpi; and the Commercial Printing setting saves at 300 dpi.

As you make your choices, you will notice that the Estimated File Size changes. As when you selected WordPerfect Office as your export option, click OK to open the Save As dialog where the file type is already selected in the Save As Type drop-down. Navigate to where you want to save your file, give it a name in the File Name field, click Save, deliver the goods, and ask for a (large) check!

Saving, importing, and exporting might not be as exciting as the headlines on supermarket tabloids, but they're essential skills that are a prerequisite to your rewards as a CorelDRAW designer. Compare it to the ennui of learning how to use a knife and fork—they're essential to being able to savor the meal that comes after learning *Silverware 101*. If you've read Chapter 2, you now know where a lot of the Good Stuff is in CorelDRAW's interface and how to save anything you've created using the Good Stuff. Now it's time to get a handle on navigating this interface in Chapter 4. You know how to bring stuff in and copy stuff out of CorelDRAW; it'd be nice if you first had the best view of these objects, on the layers and multiple pages you're soon going to be cranking out.

4   Navigation and Page Setup

Artists who have embraced digital media enjoy not only new tools, but also new ways to *look* at their artwork. Because your CorelDRAW designs can be extremely large and intricate, now's the time to take a look at the ways you can look at your work. This chapter covers the different ways you can view dimensions of the drawing page and the level of detail displayed on your screen as you preview and work. You'll work smarter and more efficiently when you understand how wide, tall, and deep your drawings can be, and how to view the details you need at any given second. Learning the ins and outs of CorelDRAW document navigation might be your ticket to better artwork in less time!

 Download and extract all the files from the Chapter04.zip archive to follow the tutorials in this chapter.

Setting View Mode

Because the type of artwork you usually design in CorelDRAW is vector artwork, the objects you create need to be written to screen from moment to moment: this is called *rasterizing*. Realistically, with today's video cards and computer processors, the response time between changing an element in a file and seeing the change can usually be measured in a fraction of a second. CorelDRAW has always supported different levels of detail with which you view your CorelDRAW work. These levels are accessed through the View menu. These view modes can help you find an object and draw an object when your designs become very detailed and the page gets cluttered.

View modes are used to specify how your drawing appears onscreen. Modes offer feedback as to how a design will print or export, and lower quality view modes can help you locate an object hidden by other objects. Switching between view modes is done using the View menu and through keyboard shortcuts. The *View menu* itself indicates the current view using a button indicator to the left of each menu item.

You have the option of choosing from one of six display qualities: Simple Wireframe, Wireframe, Draft, Normal, Enhanced, and Pixels: the default mode is Enhanced, and this mode offers the best proofing quality for working and displaying your work to others. Additionally, you can check or uncheck Simulate Overprints and Rasterize Complex Effects when viewing in Enhanced mode. The following section explains how these display modes render to screen paths and objects that have different fills and effects. Shown here is the list of View commands.

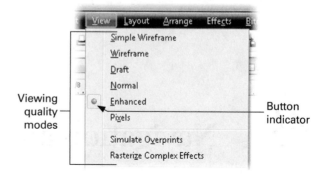

Using Wireframe and Simple Wireframe

The organization of views listed makes a top-to-bottom progression from low to high detail. At the top, Simple Wireframe and Wireframe provide the least detail and refresh onscreen almost immediately when you make edits or change the zoom level of your document. In Simple Wireframe viewing mode, all you see is the silhouette of vector objects: a thin black outline with no fill. This is a very useful view mode for locating a shape on the page when you don't have the time to perform a search in CorelDRAW (covered in Chapter 14). Wireframe mode provides no view of object fills, but it does reveal the structure of effects objects such as Extrudes and Blends. Figure 4-1 is a visual comparison of Simple Wireframe, Wireframe, Pixels view, and the default viewing mode in CorelDRAW, Enhanced. Clearly, you're not going to apply fills to objects in Wireframe mode while you work; however, these different modes indeed provide user information about objects you don't usually see, and you can edit paths, copy objects, and perform most other necessary design tasks in any of these view modes.

Getting a Draft View

Draft view is the middle-ground view quality between Wireframe and Enhanced modes. In Draft viewing mode, the objects in your drawing are rendered with color fills, but only Uniform fills are displayed with any accuracy. Outline properties such as dashed lines, width, and color are displayed. The two greatest visual differences between Draft and Enhanced views are that there is no anti-aliasing in Draft mode (so object edges look harsh and jaggy) and bitmaps and Fountain Fills do not display as you'd expect them to. Figure 4-2 shows a Fountain Fill, a Bitmap Fill, and a PostScript Fill viewed in (the default) Enhanced mode at the top and then at the bottom in Draft mode. There is a subtle visual indication that you can use to tell the difference between a Bitmap and a Fountain Fill in this mode, but it's hardly worth the challenge. Draft mode is best used to evaluate basic color schemes in a vector drawing and for quickly navigating incredibly dense and complex illustrations such as CAD architecture designs and a single page containing 45,000 Extrude effect objects.

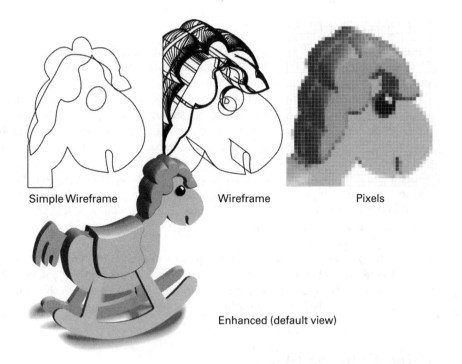

Simple Wireframe   Wireframe   Pixels

Enhanced (default view)

FIGURE 4-1   View modes can help you see the structure of complex objects and provide you with "unseen" clues where editing might be desired.

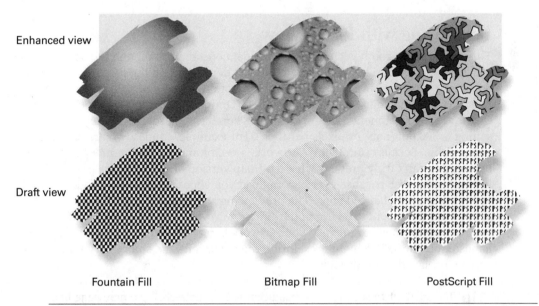

Enhanced view

Draft view

Fountain Fill   Bitmap Fill   PostScript Fill

FIGURE 4-2   Draft view provides uniform color fill views and outline colors but not more elaborate object fills.

Using Normal View

Normal view displays all object properties—Bitmap Fills, Fountain Fills, and PostScript Fills—correctly, unlike Draft and Wireframe. Enhanced and Normal views are *almost* identical; Normal mode does not anti-alias the edges of objects. *Anti-aliasing* is part of CorelDRAW writing to screen; anti-aliasing creates a smooth transition where image areas have very different colors and brightness. Anti-aliasing is usually done by adding pixels to the color edge of an object whose color is a blend between the neighboring, contrasting areas. The effect of anti-aliasing is particularly evident along edges of objects that travel diagonally across the page and in curved areas such as circles and ellipses.

Normal view mode appeals to users whose video card doesn't have a lot of RAM and to artists who create thousands of objects on a page. Screen refreshes are quicker, and if you don't mind the stair-steppy edges of aliased object edges, you can pick up some speed using Normal mode.

 Note Bitmaps—whether they're imported photos or bitmap fills you define using the Interactive Fill Tool—do not change their screen appearance if you switch from Normal to Enhanced view mode. Bitmaps do not update or refresh in CorelDRAW because the pixel color definitions are set within the image or fill.

Using Enhanced View

Enhanced view is the default view in CorelDRAW. In this view mode, all vector objects (text is a vector object, too) are anti-aliased around the edges. It's the best view of your work.

Previewing with Pixels View

This view displays both vector and bitmap data onscreen as though the objects are all constructed from pixels. Pixels view quality is dependent on the resolution of your document, a feature you can define in the Create A New Document dialog when you press CTRL+N and adjust by pressing CTRL+J (Options) | Document | Page Size. In the Create A New Document dialog, you set the Rendering Resolution—the factory default setting is 300 dpi (dots, or pixels per inch). For example, suppose you're creating a web graphic. Because CorelDRAW artwork is vector and resolution-independent in nature, you can't truly preview what a bitmap version of your vector design will look like up on the Web because every zoom level you choose displays the vector graphic smoothly using Enhanced view. The previewing solution is simple—before you draw, set up your document to 96 dpi in the Create A New Document dialog, and then use Pixels view mode to preview your artwork before delivering it and getting paid handsomely for it. The higher resolution the document, the smoother your artwork will be displayed in Pixels view.

 Tip The shortcut to setting page resolution is to double-click the gray page border to bring up the Page Size tab in Options. Change the Rendering Resolution to suit your current need, and go to town.

Simulating Overprints

Simulate Overprints is a print production preview mode. Overprinting is part of a standard commercial printing process used to see a simulation of how colors actually will print to a physical page and to check to see if there are any gaps between printed objects due to any printing misregistration problems. If you have no need for commercial printing, Simulate Overprints will be a seldom-used view. However, if you use CorelDRAW for physical commercial output, bear in mind two things:

- You need to check in with Window | Dockers | Color Proof Settings and ensure that your intended output device is chosen from the Simulate Environment list. If you don't find the press of your choice, contact the commercial printer and request the drivers or ICM profile they use. By default, SWOP is the color space when proofing, and chances are good that the simulation of a CMYK color space will display colors as accurately as any monitor can.
- *Simulation* means exactly that. It is physically impossible to proof physical pigments rendered to a physical surface with total accuracy, using a monitor that displays virtual artwork. However, CorelDRAW's color simulation of real-world color output is excellent, and "close" is far better than "none" when it comes to proofing printed material on your screen.

Tip To switch quickly between your current view mode and the last-used view mode, press SHIFT+F9.

Zooming and Panning Pages

There are at least two meanings in CorelDRAW for the term *view,* and the previous sections have covered only one of them: *view quality,* the level of detail with which you see your work. *Zooming*—increasing and decreasing your view of a page—and *panning* (sliding your view without zooming, similar to using the scroll bars on the edge of a document window) are the topics of the sections to follow. By mastering all the features for zooming your view—covered next—you'll work faster and smarter.

Using the Zoom Tool and Property Bar

The Zoom Tool is in the fourth group of tools in the Toolbox and is clearly marked by its magnifying glass icon. If you see a hand icon and not the magnifying glass, click-hold on the icon to reveal the group. The Zoom Tool is used to zoom in and zoom out of a page.

When you've chosen the Zoom Tool, the Property Bar displays buttons plus a drop-down selector that provides just about every common degree of magnification you could ask for. You, therefore, have at least two methods for page navigation when the Zoom Tool is selected: clicking with the tool in the document workspace, and choosing degrees of magnification from the Property Bar (and not performing click or click-drag action with the cursor).

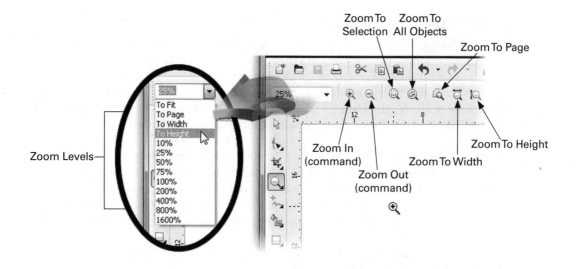

FIGURE 4-3   Here are all the Property Bar options you'll need to navigate a magnified CorelDRAW document.

The following list describes the purpose of these options on the Property Bar:

- **Zoom Levels**   To increase your current view by a preset magnification, use the Zoom Levels drop-down selector from the Standard Property Bar when the Zoom Tool has not been selected. When you've selected the tool, you'll want to use the Zoom Tool Property Bar. You'll find selections ranging from 10 to 1600 percent and some quick views for zooming based on page size. You can also type a value directly in the Zoom Levels combo box and then press ENTER; however, the Zoom Levels always increase and decrease beginning at the center of the drawing window. Therefore, Zoom To Page is a preset you might want to use before opting for a specific Zoom percentage. Views saved in the View Manager (discussed later in this chapter) are also included on the drop-down list.

- **Zoom In**   Zoom In is the default state when the Zoom Tool is selected. Clicking once in the drawing window increases your view magnification by twice the current percentage of zoom—100 percent goes to 200 percent with a click and then to 400 percent with another click in the window. Here's an important point: when you zoom in this way, using the tool and not the Zoom Levels selections, *you zoom in centered relative to the tool's cursor location onscreen.* You direct the final point of your zoom by centering it with your cursor. You can also use the Zoom Tool to perform *marquee* zooming, visually described in Figure 4-4. You place your cursor at the corner of the area you want to magnify and then click-drag diagonally to the opposing corner of an imaginary bounding box that defines the area to which you want to zoom. You can target any two opposing corners, but most users tend to diagonally drag from the upper left to the lower right of an area.

Begin at a corner.   Click-drag to the opposing corner.   Zoomed-in area

FIGURE 4-4   Marquee-dragging is the easy way to pinpoint a location and zoom in.

- **Zoom Out**   To decrease your view magnification using the Zoom Tool, click the right mouse button anywhere on or off your document page, or hold SHIFT in combination with the left mouse button (in case your right mouse button is broken). Alternatively, click the Zoom Out button on the Property Bar. Doing so decreases your view to your last-used magnification or by a power of 2, similar to zooming in, and the center of the zoom out is the center of the drawing window. Identical to zooming in, zooming out while using the Zoom Tool is directed by the location of the Zoom Tool cursor onscreen. If you want, for example, to zoom out to the upper right of a page, you put the cursor at the upper right of the page and then right-click. To zoom out while any tool is selected, press F3.

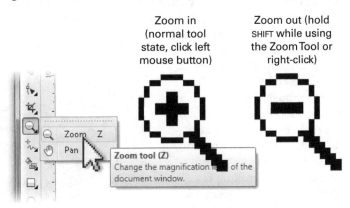

- **Zoom One-Shot**   The Zoom One-Shot command is for selecting the Zoom Tool momentarily for a single Zoom In or Zoom Out command while you are using any tool. The shortcut key is F2; you return to the previously used tool after performing a zoom. Zoom One-Shot is not available as a button unless you use Options | Customization to place a copy of the button, for example, on the Property Bar.
- **Zoom To Selection**   When you have one or more objects selected in the drawing window, choosing this command changes your view magnification and viewing position of the page to show the entire selection in the window. Choose Zoom To Selection from either the Zoom Tool Property Bar or the Zoom Levels drop-down selector list. You can also zoom to a selected object while *any* tool is selected by pressing SHIFT + F2.
- **Zoom To All Objects**   Zoom To All Objects changes your view magnification to display all objects visible in your document window, regardless of whether the objects are on or off the current document page. Choose Zoom To All Objects from either the Zoom Tool Property Bar or the Zoom Levels drop-down menu. Alternatively, use the F4 shortcut while any tool is selected.
- **Zoom To Page**   Zoom To Page changes your view to fit your current page size completely within the document window. Choose Zoom To Page from either the Zoom Tool Property Bar or the Zoom Levels drop-down menu, or press SHIFT + F4 while any tool is selected.
- **Zoom To Width/Height Of Page**   These two commands enable you to zoom your view to the entire width or height of the current page. You'll find these tool buttons located on the Zoom Tool Property Bar or the Zoom Levels drop-down menu.

Using the Mouse Wheel for Zooming

Affordable, high-quality input devices such as the mouse and even some styli for graphics tablets have had a combo wheel/button between the left and the right mouse buttons since the 1990s. Applications (when the engineers wrote the feature in) can scroll a document window and also zoom a document window. Corel engineers built this capability in for zooming (it's enabled by default). To zoom into a page, push the scroll wheel away from you; zooming out is done by dragging the mouse (or stylus) wheel toward you, as shown here. If you don't care for this feature, you can restore mouse wheel action to scrolling by choosing Options (CTRL + J) | Workspace | Display, and then choosing Scroll from the Default Action For Mouse Wheel drop-down list.

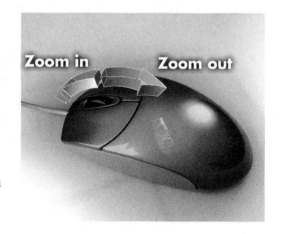

Using the Pan Tool

The Pan Tool—also called the Hand Tool—is a convenient alternative to using document scroll bars; it's your avatar for your physical hand while in CorelDRAW. The Hand Tool's keyboard shortcut is H, and it works exactly as you'd anticipate. To use it, you click-drag in the drawing window and your view will travel in the same direction. The principle advantage to using the Hand Tool over the document window scroll bar "thumbs" (that screen element in the center of a scroll bar you use to click-drag) is one of economy; you don't have to put in several "mouse miles" to change your view, and the Hand Tool is great for adjusting your document view with precision, by even a fraction of an inch.

The Pan Tool's cursor looks like a hand (Corel engineers gave hours of consideration to the cursor), and with a click-drag, you can scroll your view in any direction (often called *panning*) as you would do with a camera. As you do this, the scroll bars and Document Rulers move in unison to reflect the new position.

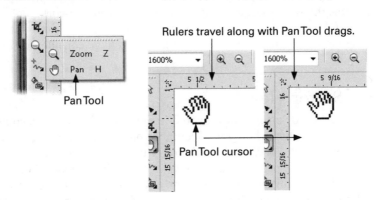

Several shortcuts are available while using the Pan Tool, some of which are for zooming, not panning. A right mouse click using the Pan Tool takes you to the Zoom Out command, and a double-click action causes a Zoom In command. You can also use the keyboard to pan the view of your document while any tool is selected using these shortcuts:

- **Pan left**   Press and hold ALT + LEFT ARROW.
- **Pan right**   Press and hold ALT + RIGHT ARROW.
- **Pan up**   Press and hold ALT + UP ARROW.
- **Pan down**   Press and hold ALT + DOWN ARROW.

Controlling Zoom and Pan Tool Behavior

The Options dialog is where you can customize certain actions when using the Zoom and Hand Tools. Right mouse button clicks, by default, trigger Zoom Out for both the Zoom and Hand Tools. However, you might want to reassign right-clicking for the Hand and Zoom Tools to be more consistent with the right-click behavior—in other words, to display a pop-up context menu like the other Toolbox tools do.

If this is your preference, you can change your right mouse button clicks by opening the Options dialog (CTRL+J) and clicking to expand the tree directories under Toolbox | Zoom Pan Tool. In this dialog, you can set the behavior of the right mouse button clicks, using either tool to open the pop-up menu instead.

Special View Modes

There are *other* types of "views" found in CorelDRAW. In addition to viewing quality and resolution, you might need to change the page order in a multipage document for a tidier presentation. Hey, you could certainly do with a preview setting that eliminates the workspace and puts the focus on your artwork, too!

The following sections explore these features, how to work with them, and how to provide views of your work you might not even have considered. You're going to *love* this stuff!

Page Sorter View

CorelDRAW Page Sorter view (covered in detail in Chapter 6) becomes available as a special View mode when your document has at least one page; two or more pages will be more useful because it's silly to try to sort one page (and impossible if you have less than one page). To go into Page Sorter View mode, choose View | Page Sorter View. While viewing a document in the Page Sorter, you can browse several pages at one time and manage their properties as a collection instead of thumbing through single pages. While using this view, your pages and all their contents are displayed in miniature. No other view in CorelDRAW can show you a complete document page flow and offer you the chance to reorder pages and their properties in one fell swoop. The Pick Tool is the only available tool in this view, and the Property Bar also displays several options unique to this document view. You can reorder pages by dragging them to different locations in the current order or right-click specific pages to rename, insert, and delete them, as shown next.

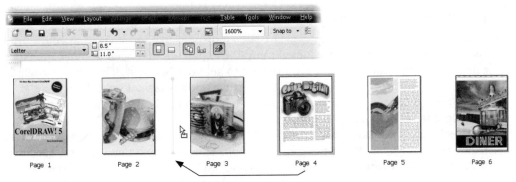

Page 4 is being scooted in front of Page 3.

Full Screen Preview

To fill the entire screen with a view of your current document page at the current zoom level, use View | Full Screen Preview, or press the F9 shortcut key. This view hides all of the CorelDRAW interface—including your cursor—and shows only the current view rendered in Enhanced view mode (the Full Screen Preview default view). To return your view back to Normal, click any key or either mouse button.

Note Depending on any desktop utilities you might have installed, there might be a conflict between the F9 shortcut to get to Full Screen Preview in CorelDRAW and something such as a desktop calendar or local weather applet. A number of remedies are possible: you can define a different keyboard shortcut, use the View menu or the pop-up menu instead of a keyboard shortcut, or remove the desktop utility that probably doesn't tell you the correct weather in Kazakhstan anyway.

While using Full Screen Preview, the view mode and page border view appearance is set according to preferences in the Options dialog. To access these options, choose Tools | Options (CTRL + J) and click Display under the Workspace category on the left side of the dialog to access the Display options. Full Screen Preview options, located in the lower part of the dialog, let you choose either Draft or Enhanced view (the default) as the view mode and to enable or disable viewing of the page border.

Preview Selected Only

The Preview Selected Only command, available from the View menu, lets you preview only what's selected on the page before entering this mode. This option works using the Full Screen Preview preferences and takes a toggle state of either On or Off when selected. There are two caveats to using this command: if no objects are selected, the Full Screen Preview offers a nice, energy-wasting white blank screen and you'll also get similar views of all-white if the selected object is not in view before entering this mode. The result you get with Preview Selected Only depends entirely on what's framed in the document window at the viewing resolution you have defined before using the command.

Using the View Navigator

The *View Navigator* is a pop-up viewer that is indispensable for navigating your entire document page when you've zoomed in to 10,000 percent and need to move quickly to a different design area without zooming out to get your bearings. The View Navigator pop-up window is at the point where the vertical and horizontal scroll bars meet at the lower-right corner of the document window. To open the View Navigator pop-up, click-hold the button itself—the magnifying glass icon.

Click-holding causes a pop-up thumbnail to appear, which represents the outermost region of the page and the application's desktop. The preview frame—the tiny rectangle with the crosshairs through it—within the View Navigator window indicates the viewing limitations according to your current zoom level settings. Click-drag within the View Navigator pop-up window to pan around your drawing in the document window; it's panning by proxy. As you drag, releasing the mouse button ends the navigation.

In Figure 4-5, you can see the View Navigator put to the test. Let's say you're asked to draw a smiley on one of the gumballs in this illustration of a gumball machine.

Click-hold here to open the View Navigator.

Drag within the View Navigator preview to pan the document view.

FIGURE 4-5 The View Navigator steers you in the right direction for precise editing in very tight views.

At 100 percent viewing resolution this would be a true hassle; luckily, by zooming in it's easy to make your view of the gumballs huge. You pan the window to use the View Navigator to single out one gumball and add the tiny face.

Using the View Manager Docker

Imagine a bookmark feature in CorelDRAW that takes you to a location and viewing resolution on one or more pages just by clicking the link. This is what the View Manager does: you can define zoom levels and page locations; you can browse to any number of pages in the same document; and not only is your document better organized for future edits, but also you've got a darned good presentation tool as well—View Manager!

To open the View Manager, choose Window | Dockers | View Manager or press CTRL + F2. Figure 4-6 shows a practical use for the View Manager: Here you can see an architectural drawing. All the different parts of the room have been "viewed," and different pans and zooms have been defined for the sun room, the dining room, and so on. Now the illustrator or client can click around the structure to get a comprehensive virtual tour of the proposed design. The View Manager is also useful for tagging and returning to an exact point in a drawing when you might need to take a break! If you have a multipage document, View Manager can accommodate your need to pinpoint any view on any page.

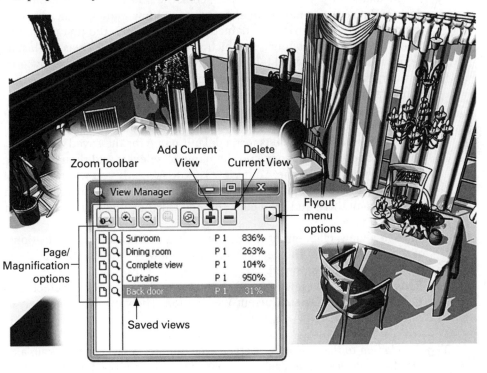

FIGURE 4-6   When working with complex drawings, the View Manager provides a quick way to save and recall views.

Exploring View Manager Commands

When a view is saved, its page number, position, and view magnification are recorded and become a new view in the View Manager docker window. The view *mode* isn't saved—such as Simple Wireframe, Draft, Normal, Enhanced, and so on—but this is trivial because you learned earlier in this chapter how to define view quality manually in any document at any time.

This sort of feature calls for a hands-on review, tutorial style. There are no "right" or "wrong" steps you can take—this is just an exploration by the numbers!

Tutorial   Making and Taking a Structured View of a Document

1. Open an existing document containing a drawing, either completed or in progress and the more complex the better, and then open the View Manager docker window (CTRL + F2).
2. Using page navigation commands and the Zoom Tool, the Zoom command buttons on the Zoom Toolbar, and/or the View Navigator feature, go to a specific part of your drawing in the document window.
3. To create and save your current view, click the Add Current View button in the docker. Notice that a new item appears in the View Manager docker. By default, the new view is automatically named View-*nn-nnnn*%; the first numbers after "View" represent a sequence in which you save views, whereas the last digits before the percent symbol tell you the magnification level of the saved view. At the right on the docker is the page number for the saved view and the zoom percentage again. The zoom percentage is an important label at the right of each saved zoom and cannot be edited. However, you'll definitely want to replace the first zoom percentage with an evocative name for the zoom—this first zoom percentage field is just a default name for the saved zoom.
4. To name the view, click once on the name to select it and then type a name to enter the new view name. Your view is now saved. If you want, save more new views using the same procedure; change the view display in your document window each time, and then click the Add Current View button each time to save each view.
5. To go to a view, click either the page number or the view magnification title of the saved view on the docker's list. Your view is then changed to the exact point at which it was saved.
6. To delete a specific view in the View Manager docker, click to select the view, and then click the Delete Current View button. The view is immediately deleted.

Tip   In addition to the interactive methods you can use to save, name, recall, and delete saved views, the same operations can be accomplished by choosing commands on the flyout menu located on the View Manager's docker window.

Using Page and Zoom Options

To the left of each saved view in the View Manager, two options appear. These options give you control over how your saved views are recalled and restored. For each view saved, you can toggle display of the Page Only and the Magnification Only to On or Off. Single-clicks toggle these options on and off; dimmed options indicate an inactive state.

When the page symbol is deactivated, recalling the corresponding saved view causes only the magnification to be recalled; when the zoom symbol is deactivated, only the page display is recalled. While both are deactivated, the saved view does absolutely nothing.

Working with Views of a Document's Depth: Layers

CorelDRAW's layer feature provides invaluable ways not only to organize but also to view complex drawings. You can create several layers and move shapes between layers. You can also name layers, control their order and appearance, change object ordering within layers, group objects, and quickly see object information. One immediate advantage to adopting layers in your composition work is that you can hide layers. Suppose you have a lot of objects that need labels, and you need to print the objects with and without labels. The solution is to put all the labels on a layer. Hide the layer, print just the objects, and then unhide the layer and make a second print: easy!

Exploring the Object Manager

The Object Manager docker is your resource for viewing layer content and using layer options. With the Object Manager, you can perform a whole range of actions: navigate document pages, create and name layers, select and move objects between layers, and set layers as editable, printable, and visible. To open the Object Manager docker, choose Tools | Object Manager; this is a good opportunity to give the Object Manager a shortcut key command, as described earlier. CTRL + ALT + O is available.

The Object Manager shows a listing of the layers, each accompanied by options and a flyout menu. A Master Page also appears and includes default layers for controlling guides, the desktop, and grid objects. If more than one page is in a document, you can specify whether you want odd, even, or all pages in the file to have Master Pages; more on this later in this chapter. Figure 4-7 shows a drawing and what the Object Manager reports for this composition. There is only one page; the drawing was created on two layers on Page 1; and highlighted on the Object Manager list is a group of 10 objects, none of which have an outline color or width.

Note CorelDRAW X6 now features the creation of Master Pages for odd and even numbered pages in a multipage document. See Chapter 1 for more details.

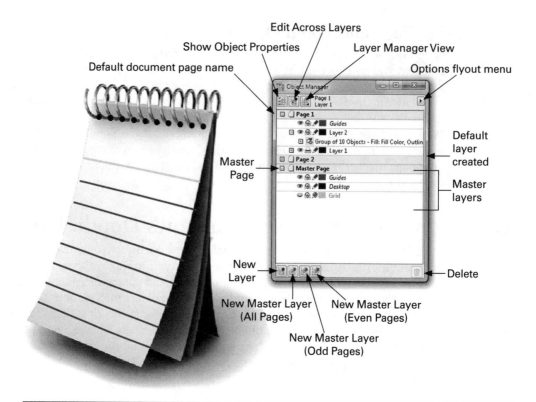

FIGURE 4-7   View information, and also name and alter that information with the Object Manager.

Navigating Pages, Objects, and Layers

The best way to use the Object Manager docker to navigate through your document, select layers, and control Layer options is by experimenting yourself; the following steps are a guide. You'll learn exactly how these operations are performed; first look at the next illustration, which shows a default layer structure for a new document.

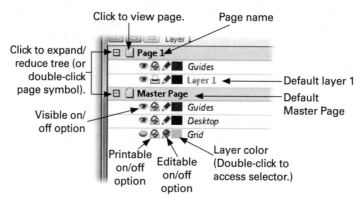

Tutorial   Navigating and Mastering Layers

The next steps have no right or wrong execution, but rather they're simply exploration steps to get you comfortable with working with layers. This is why an illustration has already been created for you; you just work the steps and see how any of several techniques can be applied to your own work—present and future.

1. Open Alarming.cdr in CorelDRAW.
2. Open the Object Manager docker: Tools | Object Manager. Look at the status of the layers. The background—the pattern fill of the clocks—is locked so it cannot be moved at present. Also, there's a layer on top with a default name, and it's hidden, which also means it's locked. Investigate a little now; unhide Layer 3 layer to see what's inside.

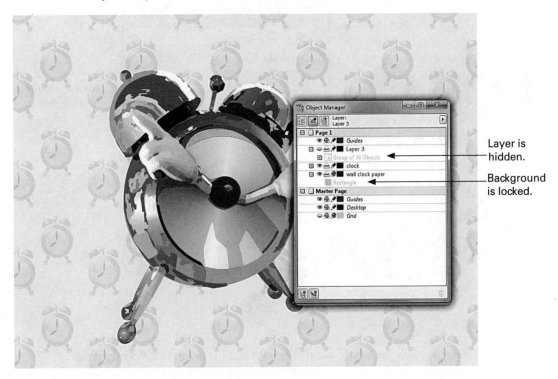

Layer is hidden.

Background is locked.

3. Okay; the author is trying to be funny here. The layer contains a third hand, yet within the context of an alarm click, it's really a second hand. It's possible now to select the group of objects on Layer 3 by clicking them with the Pick Tool, and if you click a second time, you can rotate the hand by dragging the rotation handles and turn time itself back to Chapter 1. Click twice (slowly, don't double-click) on the name of Layer 3 in the Object Manager, and then type a name in the field that's more descriptive than "Layer 3" for future reference. Try "extra hand" because why not?

4. Double-click the extra hand layer title to open its contents. The hand is several grouped objects, and they can be moved to the "clock" layer. First, rename the group: click twice on the "Group of 36 objects" and then type **third hand** in the field. Notice that control nodes are visible when a group or a single object is selected. Press SHIFT + F2 to Zoom To Selection now.
5. Double-click the "clock" layer title to open it, and then drag the "third hand" group down below the layer title but above the "Group of 233 objects" entry. Layers have a hierarchy, and if you put the group below the group of 233 objects, the third hand will be hidden from view by the 233 other objects.

Drag group down to clock layer.

6. Double-click the "extra hand" layer title. This action produces precisely nothing, which indicates that nothing nested within the layer. So it's okay to delete it—with the layer title highlighted, click the trash icon. Poof.

Caution There is no confirmation box with the Delete trash icon; it's very similar to pressing the keyboard DELETE key. Be careful how you use it, and to undo an inadvertent deletion, press CTRL+Z (Edit | Undo).

7. Similarly, the background is expendable in this composition. Click the "wall clock paper" layer title to select it. Notice that the trash icon is dimmed—this is because the layer is locked. You can confirm this by trying to move the clock pattern with the Pick Tool. Click the Lock or Unlock pencil icon with the red slash over it to make the layer editable, and then click the Delete button.

Tip Every object on the Object Manager's list can be renamed, down to single objects. Consider giving a very important object a custom name in your own work. Then, at any time, you can locate the object by conducting a search with the Edit | Find And Replace feature or just by scrolling through the list of objects.

8. Create a new layer by clicking the New Layer button. Name it and then drag its title to the bottom of the layer stack on this page.
9. Lock the clock layer.
10. Click the new layer highlighted on the Object Manager list, choose the Rectangle Tool from the Toolbox, create a rectangle as a background for the clock, and then apply a fill. Figure 4-8 shows a linear gradient fill (covered in Chapter 15) and a blend with transparency added to the new background layer (see Chapter 21 for the scoop on blends and contours).

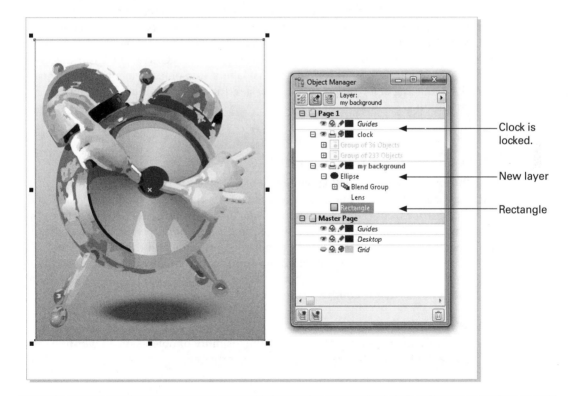

FIGURE 4-8   Working with layers takes full advantage of CorelDRAW's search capabilities and makes it easy to modify only certain elements in a complex drawing.

Using Object Manager Editing and View States

Objects can be on different layers, and you can edit across layers in CorelDRAW. Create a new file that has objects on, let's say, three layers to better learn through example about the editing and view states of CorelDRAW layers. Open the Object Manager docker. You'll see three view state buttons at the top of the docker—that's where information about viewing and editing behavior are set. Clicking each button toggles its state on or off. Each button has the following effects:

Tip You can use the Combine, Group, or Convert To Curves commands on objects in the Object Manager docker by selecting the objects, right-clicking them, and choosing a command from the pop-up menu.

- **Show Object Properties** Click the Show Object Properties button to set whether you want to view a detailed name for a layer's contents (color, type of object, and so on), or just the name—whether the default or your own custom name.
- **Edit Across Layers** Click the Edit Across Layers button in the Object Manager to set whether objects can be selected, moved, and copied between layers. While cross-layer editing is disabled, objects appear grayed out, allowing only objects on your current page layer and/or the desktop to be selected or edited. While cross-layer editing is enabled, you can select, move, or edit any object on an unlocked layer.
- **Layer Manager View** The Layer Manager View button can be pressed to reveal All Pages, Layers, and Objects, or Current Page, Layers Only. When working with complex drawings that have many pages, layers, and objects, using this view can make managing layer properties a lot easier. In this state, all page and object information is omitted.

Controlling Layer Properties

Using the Layer Properties dialog, you can control specific properties for each layer. To access these options, right-click a specific layer in the Object Manager docker and choose Properties from the pop-up menu. You can access properties directly from the pop-up menu or display a modeless dialog for defining the properties of a specific layer. There is a minor difference between using the dialog and the pop-up: the pop-up (right-click) menu has the Rename command, grouped with the Delete, Cut, Copy, and Paste commands.

Options in this dialog control the following layer properties:

- **Visible** This option enables you to toggle the view state of a layer between visible or hidden. You can also control the visibility of objects on a layer by clicking the Eye symbol to the left of the layer name.

- **Printable**   This option toggles the printing state of objects on the layer on or off. You can also set whether layer objects are printable by clicking the Printer symbol beside the layer in the Object Manager docker to toggle the printing state of objects on the layer.

 Note Nonprinting layers will also not export. If you need objects selected on a nonprinting layer to be included when exporting, you'll need to turn on the layer's Printable option.

- **Editable**   Use this option to lock or unlock all objects on a layer. While a layer is locked, its objects can't be edited (or even selected), which is a little different than the Lock (object) command. You can also set whether layer objects are editable by clicking the Pencil symbol beside the layer in the Object Manager docker to toggle the editing state of objects on the layer.
- **Master Layer(s)**   You can have layers for odd, even, and all pages in the Master Page entry on the Object Manager. You can create a new master layer, and you can also drag an existing layer from a page to the Master Page entry. Changing a layer to a master layer causes it to become part of the Master Page structure. Any objects on a Master Page appear on all pages. For details on working with Master Pages and master layers, see the next section.
- **Layer Color**   This selector sets the color swatch as it appears in the docker listing directly to the left of a layer name for easy recognition. Layer Color also determines object colors when viewed using Normal or Enhanced views while the Override Full Color View option is selected. You can also set the color coding for a layer by double-clicking the color indicator next to a layer name to open a typical color selector menu and then clicking any color from the drop-down color picker.
- **Override Full Color View**   Use this option to control how the objects on the layer appear when viewed using either Normal or Enhanced view. When selected, it has the effect of displaying all objects in wireframe-style, using the layer color specified. Your drawing will still print and export normally regardless of the Override Full Color View choice.

Working with Master Page Layers

Whenever a new document is created, a *Master Page* is automatically created. The Master Page isn't a physical page in your document, but instead a place where document objects can be placed so they appear on every page of your document. Objects on a Master Page layer are visible and printable on every page in your document, making this an extremely powerful feature. For example, a text header or footer, or a company logo on a Master Page layer becomes a quick and easy way to label all the pages in a pamphlet or brochure.

Moving any object onto a layer on the Master Page makes it a Master Page object and causes it to appear on each page. Let's try this feature out:

Tutorial Working with Master Page Items

1. Open the Object Manager docker by choosing Tools | Object Manager.
2. Click the New Master Layer (All Pages) button, the second of the buttons at left at the bottom of the docker. A new layer is automatically added to the Master Page with the default name "Layer 1."
3. With this new master layer as your current layer (click the entry to make sure it's selected), create the object(s) you wish to appear on every page in their final position and appearance. By creating the object while the master layer is selected, the object automatically becomes a master layer object. You can also move objects from other pages onto the master layer by click-dragging them in the docker list from their position under a layer name to the master layer name.
4. Click to select the new Master Page objects on your document page. Notice that you can still select, move, and edit it. To toggle the lock or unlock state of your master layer objects, click the Edit button (the pencil symbol) beside the Master Page in the docker. Locking prevents any accidental editing of the Master Page objects.
5. Add pages to your document by clicking the + button at the lower left of the workspace. As you browse through the pages, you'll see the same object on all pages.

Several default layers already exist on your document's Master Page for controlling special items that appear in your document, such as Guides, Grid, and Desktop. These layers have the following purposes:

- **Guides Layer**   This is a global layer for guides you create; if you click the Master Guides entry on the Object Manager to select it, and then drag a guide onto the page, all pages in the document will display this guide. If you need a guide on only one page, you choose that guides entry on the page you're working on, drag a guide from the rulers, and that guide belongs to the page and is not a master item. Guides are covered in detail in Chapter 7.

 Tip You can move a local guide, a guide you created on a page, to the Master Guides entry on the Object Manager to make it global—it will then appear on every page of your document.

- **Grid Layer**   This controls the appearance of grid lines. You can control the grid color and visibility, but you can neither set the Grid Layer to be printable, nor can you change its editable objects or add objects to that layer. Options in the Grid Layer Properties dialog enable you to control the grid display color and to gain quick access to the Grid page of the Options dialog by clicking the Setup button in the dialog. To open the Grid Layer Properties dialog, right-click the Grid Layer under the Master Page in the Object Manager docker and choose Properties from the pop-up menu.

Tip   Grid Layer visibility can be toggled on or off by clicking its Eye icon on the Object Manager.

- **Desktop Layer**   This is a global desktop, the place outside of your drawing page. If you want to keep objects handy but don't want to print them on your page, drag the object to this entry on the Object Manager. If you put an object on the desktop from a layer, you can't hide it or keep it from printing, but if it's explicitly placed on the Master Desktop, you can hide it, keep it from being edited, and keep it from printing.

Hopefully, this chapter has shown you the way—both as an allegory and literally—to get a better fix on what it is you've drawn, what you *want* to draw, and what appears to need an edit or two. Thanks to zoom features that let you hone in on a fly's eye or zoom out to a scaled drawing of Chicago, you now have a handle on the magnifying glass and other tools for panning, navigating, and recalling areas of interest in your work.

5 The X6 Test Drive

There are very few guides to software applications where you'll read, "Okay, are you all ready to get going?" in Chapter 5. *CorelDRAW: The Official Guide* is one of them. This chapter takes you through the steps you can take to create a *finished* design...and *print* it!

This chapter serves as a bridge between *understanding* CorelDRAW's features and putting them to practical *use*. If you're a new user of a graphics program, you're likely to poke around tools and palettes to get a feel for what you've purchased: this chapter is a supervised "poking around session." You get hands-on experience with some of the advanced features used to create some basic commercial designs and learn how to integrate the features to put together a T-shirt logo for a fictitious company. Before you know it, you'll have the knowledge to apply these techniques to your *own* company logo.

Most of all, this chapter is all about the *fun* you'll have designing with CorelDRAW. Everyone has read a manual that's distastefully dry from cover to cover; *this* book gets your feet wet without going over your head.

 Download and extract all the files from the Chapter05.zip archive to follow the tutorials in this chapter.

Begin a Design with a Concept

A basic rule for creating a good design is to begin with a concept. Too many bright people say, "Of *course* I have a concept! I want to design a logo!" Erm, sorry— designing a logo is a *need; it isn't a concept*. To address this need, you'll want to visualize the logo.

Let's pretend you have a client that's a machine parts company—Dyson Gears— and they want all five of their employees to proudly wear the company's logo on T-shirts. The company has a name, but not a logo; therefore, it's thinking-cap time before moving on to CorelDRAW's tools.

An iconic representation often makes a splendid logo. For example, if you ran an ice cream stand, a very simple and effective logo would be a drawing of an ice cream cone. *Don't* think the simple approach isn't successful or sophisticated. Apple, Inc., has done very well through the years with a logo of a you-know-what! Along these lines of thinking, a logo for Dyson Gears would be visually outstanding if you took the initials "D" and G", whose facing sides are rounded, and put gear teeth on them to push the idea that Dyson Gears *is* gears, a literary conceit that works in commerce every day. *That's* the concept. Read on to learn how to draw gears using a bold font as the base, create a visually stunning *treatment* for the gear design, add some compatible and striking text, and *realize* a concept.

Setting Up the Page for the Logo

If you measure an average T-shirt, you'll see that about 7 inches is a good width for a logo. You can pick up T-shirt transfer paper that measures full-page letter—8½ × 11 inches—at an office supply store or even at the supermarket. So you're in luck twice: CorelDRAW's default document size is the same as most T-shirt transfer paper, and the maximum width of the logo will fit the horizontal measure.

The following steps show you how to set up nonprinting guidelines on a default page: T-shirt transfer paper needs about ½ inch in the clear on all sides so you can peel the transfer from the T-shirt (which still gives you 7½ inches for the maximum design width).

Tutorial Setting Up Guidelines

1. Launch CorelDRAW, and from the Welcome Screen, choose New Blank document. In the Create a New Document dialog box, choose CorelDRAW Default from the Destination drop-down list if it's not already chosen for you, choose Letter (portrait orientation) for the Size, name the file Dyson Gears.cdr, choose RGB color mode, 300 dpi Resolution, and then click OK.

2. You'll want to zoom in to the ½-inch tick on the rulers for precise placement of the guides. Most of us have a scroll wheel on our mouse, and by default CorelDRAW uses the wheel as a zoom feature. Put your cursor at the top left of the page you see in the drawing window, and then push the wheel away from you to zoom into this area. If you're using something other than a mouse as an input device, or can't find a scroll wheel, choose the Zoom Tool from the Toolbox (or press z), and then click-drag an imaginary rectangle around the corner of the page; you drag diagonally (the gesture is often called *marquee-dragging* and *marquee-selecting*).

3. You can use any tool to drag guidelines from the rulers. Place your cursor first over the horizontal ruler at the top of the drawing window. Click-hold, and then drag from the ruler onto the page, at the vertical ½-inch tick. If you didn't get it quite right, you need to switch to the Pick Tool (press the SPACEBAR) and then click-drag the guideline to the ½-inch tick mark.

4. Similarly, drag a guideline to the bottom ½-inch margin you'll need, and then drag vertical guidelines out of the vertical ruler to create vertical margins at ½ inch inside of the page, as shown in this illustration.

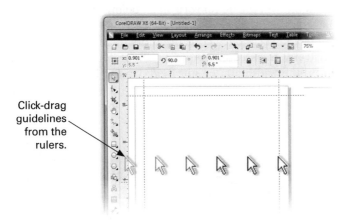

Click-drag guidelines from the rulers.

5. Click the Save button on the Standard Bar. Save **Dyson Gears.cdr** to a location on your hard drive you can find later. Don't close the document; you're not having enough fun yet.

Using the Polygon Tool to Design a Gear Shape

The Polygon Tool produces symmetrical shapes that can be dynamically edited; they can be dramatically modified and still keep a special base property. And gears are symmetrical, so all it will take is a little editing to produce a gear object. In the following steps, you'll add a control node to a polygon object and then drag the node to reposition it, thus making a gear shape from a star shape. Then you'll combine the gear object to characters, by welding two gear paths to the initials *D* and *G*. This is one of those things it's easier to see while you do; you'll be modifying a star shape so the spokes end in a blunt, straight edge instead of a point. This gets you 90 percent of the way to creating an elegant gear shape. We'll deal with the other 10 percent later.

Tutorial   Creating and Modifying a Polygon

1. Choose the Polygon Tool from the Toolbox (it's just below the Ellipse Tool).
2. On the Property Bar, set the number of sides to 16. This will produce a polygon with 16 control points and secondary control points in-between.
3. Hold CTRL (this constrains the shape to equal width and height), and then click-drag on the page until the width and height fields on the Property Bar (the second-from-left fields) tell you the shape you're creating is about 3 inches. At this point, release CTRL and your mouse button. Your polygon should look like the illustration here.

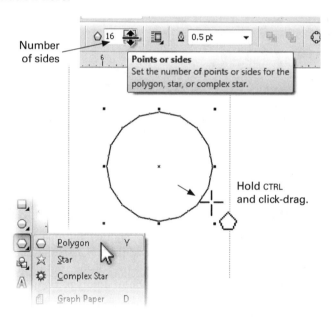

4. Choose the Shape Tool; hold CTRL, click one of the control points along the path of the polygon, and then drag until the result is a star shape, shown next. The reason for holding CTRL as you drag is that it keeps the control point from drifting to the left or right as you move it. Otherwise this would

produce a radial saw-blade shape and not a star whose path segments mirror each other.

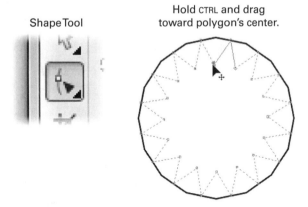

Shape Tool

Hold CTRL and drag toward polygon's center.

5. With the Shape Tool still active, click a point on the path, as shown in Figure 5-1. Then click the Add Node(s) button on the Property Bar. You've created a change in the property of the path, although it doesn't look like a change yet. The polygon can still be dynamically reshaped. Look closely at the polygon path—you added a control node, but there are actually 16 added control nodes because you made a change to a dynamic object.

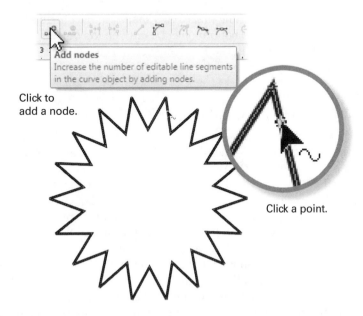

Add nodes
Increase the number of editable line segments in the curve object by adding nodes.

Click to
add a node.

Click a point.

FIGURE 5-1   When you add a node to a polygon object, additional nodes are created symmetrically around the shape.

6. Take your time on this step: with the Shape Tool, drag the top control node a little to the left and then a little down. Stop when you have the shape shown here. The polygon looks very much like a 16-tooth gear now, doesn't it?

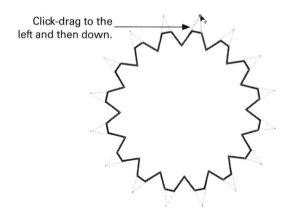

Click-drag to the left and then down.

Welding an Edge to a Typed Character

CorelDRAW has a number of operations you can access from the Property Bar (and from the Shaping docker) when more than one object is selected and one of them is the Weld operation. Welding makes two shapes into a single shape. A related operation—Trim—cuts the bottom object using the top object. These two operations—Weld and Trim—are used in the following sections to add *part* of the gear you created to the rounded side of a capital *D*.

Tutorial   Shaping the Polygon

1. You can substitute any available font you like in the following steps, but if you own Futura XBlk BT—the filename is tt0148m.ttf, and it's in the Fonts folder on one of the CorelDRAW installation disks—install it if you haven't done so already. It's a nice, bold, no-nonsense font that can have parts removed and still remain legible.

2. Drag and drop a copy of the gear for future use; with the Pick tool, drag the gear off the page, but before releasing the mouse button, tap the right button (or press the numeric keypad plus (+) key) to leave a duplicate of the gear.

3. Zoom into the original gear shape, choose the Text Tool, and then click an insertion point directly over the gear, hold SHIFT, and type **D**.

4. Choose the Pick Tool, and then with the character still selected, choose Futura XBlk BT from the Font list drop-down on the Property Bar. You can also highlight "24 pt" to the right of the font name and then type **300** in the Font size box. There are approximately 72 points to an inch when typesetting, so a ballpark estimate of the character's size makes it approximately the size of the gear.

5. Click over the No Fill Color Well on the Color Palette to remove the fill of the character, and then right-click over the black color well to give the character a black outline. Now you can see both objects to reposition the *D*.

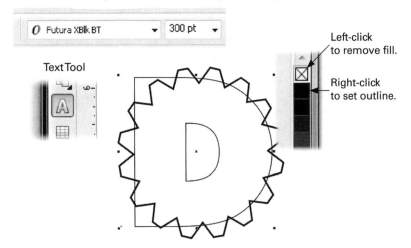

6. With the Pick Tool, move the *D* so its right side aligns to the gear. If necessary, hold SHIFT and then drag a selection handle away from (to enlarge) or toward (to shrink) the *D*'s center proportionately so its right curve lies just a fraction outside of the gear.

7. Choose the Pen Tool from the pen group on the Toolbox; drag on the face of the current tool to access any of the tools in the group. Click points around the left side of the gear to make an object that surrounds the left side of the gear, encompassing the hole in the letter *D*. You're going to remove these areas using this object and the Trim operation.

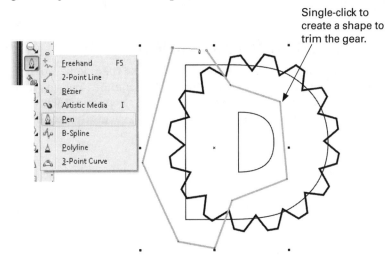

8. With the Pick Tool, select the shape and the gear by holding SHIFT and clicking one object at a time. On the Property Bar, click the Trim icon, as shown in the following illustration.

9. By default, the shape that trims the bottom shape remains in the document, but it's now unnecessary; select it, and then press CTRL + X to delete it.

10. Select both objects with a marquee-drag with the Pick Tool, and then click the Weld icon on the Property Bar.

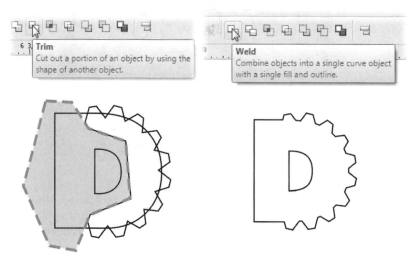

You've done great. But the *G* needs to be added to the design with the same gear effect. Add a capital *G* to the page and use the spare gear you duplicated in the previous Step 2. Alternatively, if you feel you've had enough of a workout (you haven't), Dyson Gears partially completed.cdr is available in the Chapter 05.zip file where you downloaded the tutorial files for this book.

A Brief Excursion into Gradient Fills

A linear gradient fill for the characters will make them look more powerful and add to the complexity of the logo with a minimum of effort. Let's do a little hands-on with the Interactive Fill Tool and use the Linear Fountain Fill style with interesting, powerful To and From colors. You'll learn how to expertly use the Interactive Fill Tool later in this book.

Tutorial   Adding Visual Complexity Using Fountain Fills

1. Choose the Interactive Fill Tool from the Toolbox.
2. Click the *D* gear shape to select it, and then click-drag up and to the right (drag toward about 2 o'clock on the gear shape); then release the mouse button. By default, the "To" color of the Linear Fountain Fill is the place where you released the mouse. You work between a color designated as the "From," concluding at a color called the "To" within the object.
3. To change the From color, while the Interactive Fill Tool is still selected and you can still see the control handles for the fill above the gear drawing, click the From color marker—it's black because the default linear gradient style goes from black to white. Now the color is highlighted and available for editing. Click the bright yellow color well on the Color Palette. Then click the To color marker and click a deep blue color well on the Color Palette.
4. Now let's say that the color transition between From and To in the Fountain Fill isn't dramatic enough, but you do like the two colors. Adjust the midpoint of the fill by dragging on the midpoint control, shown in Figure 5-2. You drag it toward the From color marker to emphasize the To color in the fill, and vice versa.

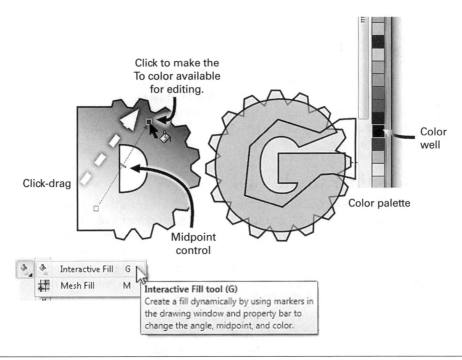

FIGURE 5-2   Use the Interactive Fill Tool to embellish your illustration.

5. The *D* gear is looking terrific now, and it's going to look *more* terrificer by the end of the chapter. To add the same sort of fill quickly to the *G* gear, choose the Attributes Eyedropper Tool from the Toolbox. Click over the *D* gear to sample its properties, and then click over the *G* gear to apply the sampled properties—occasionally, you luck out in life, and some things are simple... Press CTRL + S to save your work up to this point. In fact, just make it a practice to save your work every 10 minutes or so; it's only two keystrokes.

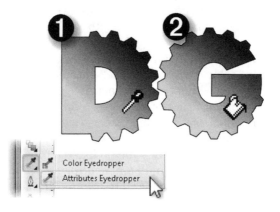

Going 3D

You can produce dimensional effects in CorelDRAW with the Extrude Tool, making a simple drawing such as this logo pop off the page...or off a T-shirt. The following sections take you through a basic and then an advanced editing technique that will make your audience wonder how on earth you created this logo by reading *one chapter* in a book.

Using the Extrude Tool

The Extrude Tool creates the sides, the third dimension of an object, completing the depth, height, and width criteria that makes an object look "3D." But once you've added depth to a selected object, it might not be apparent to you or your audience that this is a 3D shape because of the way it's "posed" on the drawing page. By default, the Extrude Tool creates edges that appear mostly behind the extruded shape because of an optical principle known as a vanishing point. A *vanishing point* (tell your friends you know that da Vinci goofed around with vanishing points) is the point in 3D space where, if you drew lines marking the angles of an object with depth, the lines would converge. You see vanishing points all the time: say you're standing on train tracks (when a train isn't coming), and you look straight down the tracks. Where the rails converge is the vanishing point.

Similarly, to get the most out of the Extrude Tool in CorelDRAW, you want to view an extruded shape off-axis, not straight-on, because looking at objects directly face-front removes the *perspective* from the object, flattening it in appearance. CorelDRAW has additional features to use after you've made a shape into an extruded shape, one of which is a rotation feature—you *can* rotate a 3D object on your drawing page—to show off all of the three possible facing sides of the extruded shape. An object viewed in ¾ view shows off the most visual detail. This is why portrait photographers try to get customers to point their head off-camera. The following tutorial takes you through object extruding, rotating, and interactively adjusting the depth of the object you extrude.

Tip Extruded sides of an object, by default, inherit the fill from the parent object. Therefore, because the gear in this example has a Fountain Fill, so do the objects that make up the sides of the gear. Fountain Fills aren't as visible when they're on the 3D face of a shape that has lighting—as you'll add in this tutorial. However, you can modify the fill of an extrude control object, the shape you started with, by CTRL-clicking to select it from the group of shapes that dynamically make up the extruded object and then modify the fill.

Tutorial ## Making a Logo into a 3D Logo

1. With the D gear selected on the drawing page, click-hold the Effects group button on the Toolbox to reveal the flyout with the Extrude Tool. This group is just above the familiar-shaped Eyedropper Tool. Select the Extrude Tool from the group on the Toolbox.
2. Click-drag *just a little,* straight down on the object, as shown in Figure 5-3. *Just a little* does the trick—you're establishing an extruded object and setting a

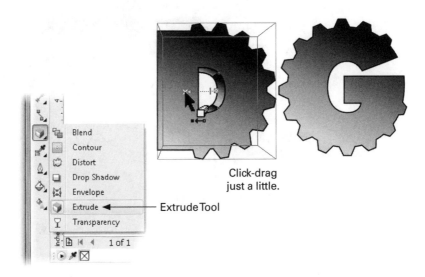

FIGURE 5-3 The Extrude Tool is used to set a third dimension for your object. Other features help you set an angle of rotation and the depth of the object.

vanishing point for the object at the same time. Stop dragging when one of the sides of the extrude object is visible. *Resist* the temptation that accompanies the natural thought, "the more I click-drag, the more extruded the gear will be." Nope—the more you drag, the *farther the vanishing point is defined* relative to the object, and it's very easy to set the vanishing point clear off the page.

3. Double-click the Extrude group of objects while the vanishing point and other onscreen indicators are visible. You're now in Rotate mode—along all three dimensions—for the extrude objects. If you deselected the shape, double-click an extrude area and then double-click a second time (this can be done with the Extrude or Pick Tools). Point the *D* gear a little upward by click-dragging up and just a little to the left on the face of the object, as shown in Figure 5-4. The goal here is to create a visually dynamic logo, and looking up at an object provides a lot of visual drama. If necessary, drag one of the markers along the green ring encircling the *D* to rotate the object parallel to the screen; think of the ticks on a clock face—you're rotating the *D* from 9 to 8 o'clock.

4. Click-drag the marker shown in the following illustration toward the gear to decrease its depth. Dragging it away from the gear makes it deeper, and although this is illuminating advice, you will probably *never* need to make an extruded shape *thicker*. Also note that the vanishing-point line extends way off the page, and this is of absolutely no consequence in your design work. The vanishing point *does not* print, and if your gear illustration looks fine right now, it is fine, regardless of onscreen guides.

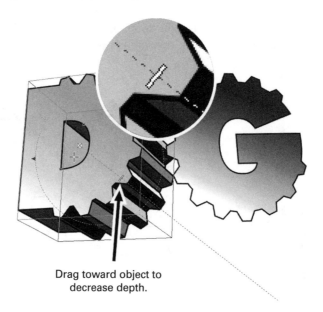

Drag toward object to
decrease depth.

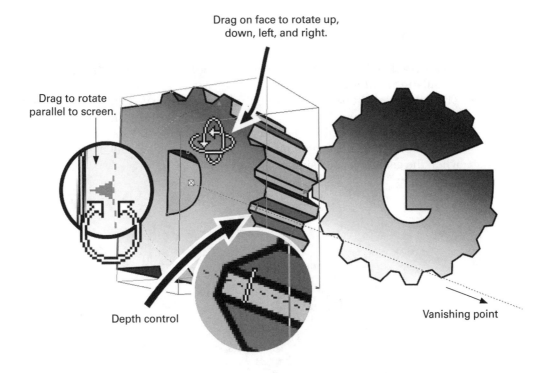

Drag on face to rotate up,
down, left, and right.

Drag to rotate
parallel to screen.

Depth control

Vanishing point

FIGURE 5-4   Use the onscreen icon to rotate the extruded object, to make the
gear truly three-dimensional in appearance.

Tip   To quickly display the Property Bar options and the depth control marker on the
object and switch to the Extrude Tool, double-click the object with the Pick Tool.

Adding Lighting

Let's polish the *D* gear part of the logo now; the *G* gear can take on the same look as
the *D* once it's completed by copying its properties to the *G*. The Extrusion Lighting
feature is available only when an object is extruded; it's the light bulb button on the
Property Bar. Lighting can be applied using up to three individual lights, and each
light can occupy one of 18 possible positions around the object.

Here's how to start getting into high gear:

Tutorial   Finessing the Look of the Gear

1. With the *D* gear selected, right-click the No Fill color well on the Color Palette
to remove the outlines. The extruded gear might take on a washed-out look, but
you're not done yet.
2. Click the Extrusion Lighting button on the Property Bar.

3. Click the marker labeled 1 to add lighting to the extruded object.
4. Drag the 1 light to the front top position on the lighting cage surrounding the proxy sphere shape.
5. Check Use Full Color Range if it isn't checked. This option adds shading (simulating shadows).
6. The lighting might be too bright on the gear, washing out some of its color. If necessary, click the 1 light icon, shown in the next illustration, to make sure it's selected, and then drag the Intensity slider to the left a little. The change is instant so you can gauge how much light you need simply by dragging. Stop when the gear looks pleasing to your eye.

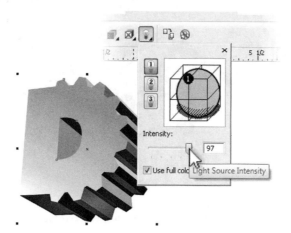

Because the light is facing the right side of the gear, the lighting on the gear's teeth looks superb and quite intricate in design. The face, conversely, looks a little dim because it's facing away from Light 1. This is not a big design flaw; the face looks appropriate when contrasted against its side, but if you want to lighten it, here's how:

1. Click to select the extruded object.
2. Choose the Interactive Fill tool; the markers appear for the color stops of the Linear Fountain Fill.
3. Click a color marker and then choose a different color well from the Color Palette by clicking.
4. Alternatively, if you think a solid color would be better for the gear, deselect the gear, and then drag a color well on top of the face of the extruded object. The extruded size will take on this color. Press CTRL + z to undo if you're less happy with your changes than the original.

Note The rotation properties of extruded objects follow the convention of 3D modeling programs. The X axis (top-to-bottom rotation) runs left to right through the object; the Y axis (rotation from left to right) runs top to bottom through the object; and the Z axis runs around the object parallel to the page in angles of rotation like those of an analog clock. Degrees of rotation are counterclockwise—negative values spin the object in a clockwise direction.

Duplicating the Extrude Properties

When an extrude object is selected, a button is available on the Property Bar for duplicating the properties of the extruded object to a plain, unextruded one: Copy Extrusion Properties. This feature can change the angle and lighting of an existing extruded object, but that's not what you need to do right now. You want to get the "G" gear extruded at the same depth, with the same lighting and bevel, but you then want to move its rotation so it faces away from the "D" in a mirror-like fashion.

Not a big deal. Follow these steps:

Tutorial **Creating Another Gear with the Copy Extrusion Properties Feature**

1. Double-click the *D* gear's extruded side using the Pick Tool to bring up the features on the Property Bar.
2. Move your cursor over to the *G* gear and then click to select it.
3. Click the Copy Extrusion Properties icon on the Property Bar; because the *G* object has an outline, the outline remains on all edges of all the objects. *Not* what you had in mind for the finished art: right-click over the No Fill color well on the Color Palette to remove the outline.

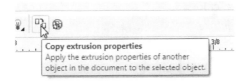

4. To *precisely* mirror the angle of the extruded *G* gear calls for a different feature than the onscreen interactive rotation: click the Extrude Rotation button on the Property Bar, the second from the left after the "VP locked to..." wide button.

5. Click the Rotation Values button at the lower right of the "3" to go to a number field view of the current object's rotation.

6. To mirror the *G* gear from left to right is a Y-axis rotation. Whatever value you see next to Y:, type in an equal negative value. In this example, the Y aspect of the *G* gear (copied from the *D* gear) is –22, so by typing **22**, the *G* rotates an equal and opposite amount compared to the *D* gear.

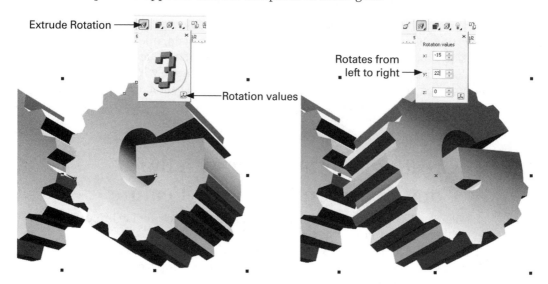

7. Click the Extrusion Light button, and then change the intensity by dragging the slider, so the *D* and the *G* gears are about equal in brightness and saturation of color.

Adding Text to the Logo

You might call this assignment finished; you now have two stunning 3D oddly shaped gears in the document. But this assignment is for a logo, not for an icon that really would serve an advertising purpose only if it were painted on a shingle above a store in a hamlet in the 1600s. You need *text* to accompany the graphic: a fancy Artistic Text title above the graphic will serve the purpose of a logo quite well, and in smaller text, Dyson Gears' web address will lessen the need of the viewing audience to ask the person wearing the T-shirt for contact info.

In the following sections, you'll use another effect, the Envelope feature, which can mold a headline into any shape you can imagine, integrating into the overall design and catching an equal amount of audience attention.

Creating an Envelope Shape

CorelDRAW's Envelope feature is dynamic, just like the Extrude Tool and the Polygon Tool, so you can shape and reshape an object until you're happy with the result. For this assignment, you'll take "Dyson Gears" and reshape the name to look like a squared-off lozenge, larger in the middle than at either end. To perform this Envelope maneuver, you'll begin with a default Envelope shape and then customize it so its sides are straight and not curved.

Tutorial ## Making a Headline/Enveloping the Headline

1. Choose the Text Tool from the Toolbox.
2. Click an insertion point on the page, just above the gear.
3. Type in all caps (hold SHIFT): **DYSON GEARS**. Artistic Text is editable as text, but as far as the Envelope effect goes, text is a malleable object, just like any object you'd draw. It's also by default 24 points in height and Arial, which is not an exciting font. Select the text with the Pick Tool, and then choose Futura XBlk BT from the Font list; it should be toward the top of the list as all recently used typefaces are ordered.
4. While holding SHIFT, drag a corner handle away from the text center until the text width is a little narrower than the gears. Alternatively, you can type **60** in the Font size box to make the text 60 points in height, a little less than 1"; this trick only is useful, however, if you're familiar with how point size corresponds to inches. See Figure 5-5.

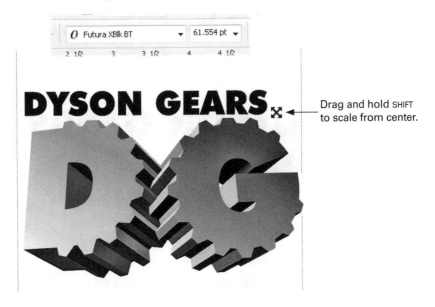

FIGURE 5-5   Use the same font as you used for the gears to avoid typeface style clashes.

5. One entry above the Extrude Tool in the Effects group on the Toolbox is the Envelope Tool; choose it and then select the text with your cursor. You'll see a faint dashed blue outline around the text now.

6. By default, the Envelope is in Putty mode, which presents both an advantage and a disadvantage. The advantage is that in Putty mode, you can delete Envelope nodes; the disadvantage is that all the segments that join the nodes are curves and you want straight Envelope segments for this text. No problem: with the cursor, marquee-select the 3 and the 9 o'clock nodes. Then either click to remove them by clicking the Delete Nodes button on the Property Bar, or press – (minus) on the keyboard keypad.

7. Marquee-select all the remaining nodes, and then click the Convert To Line icon on the Property Bar. Then click inside the Envelope to deselect the nodes. See Figure 5-6.

8. Click the top center Envelope node and then hold CTRL (to constrain movement to the first direction in which you drag) and drag upward to make a peak in the center of the text.

9. Click the bottom center Envelope node, hold CTRL, and then drag down until the bottom of the text overlaps the gears just a little, as shown in Figure 5-7.

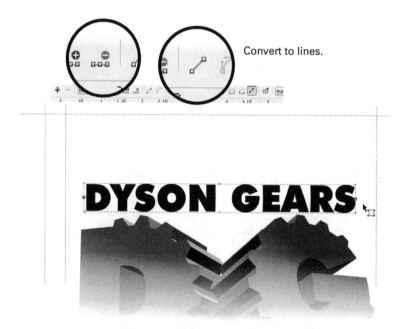

Convert to lines.

Select and then remove middle side Envelope nodes.

FIGURE 5-6 Make an Envelope with custom properties from the default Envelope.

FIGURE 5-7   Create a dynamic headline for the T-shirt design by suggesting the perspective of the text coming toward the audience from the center.

 Tip You can also nudge Envelope nodes by selecting one or more of them and then pressing the keyboard arrow keys. This technique can provide precise editing in the shape of the Envelope.

Applying the Conical Fountain Fill

Fountain Fills, when used appropriately, can give static objects a feeling of motion and occasionally soften the look of large objects without stealing from their visual importance. The DYSON GEARS is overpowering as is, so a Conical Fountain Fill–type will serve two purposes: to play down its massive presence and to make the text look like it belongs to the gears by using color. Also, the headline should go *behind* the gears design; it will still be legible, and the slight overlap helps visually integrate the two groups of shapes.

Follow these steps to finish the headline work:

Tutorial ## Applying a Custom Fountain Fill

1. Select the Envelope text with the Pick Tool, and then press SHIFT + PAGEDOWN to send it to the back of the illustration. Vector objects have a page order; the last-created object is drawn on the top of the "stack."
2. Choose the Interactive Fill Tool from the Toolbox.
3. Choose Conical from the Fill Type drop-down list on the Property Bar. The text changes color and the color wells for the Conical Fountain Fill type appear.

4. Click the From color box and then click the first color drop-down on the Property Bar and choose the deep blue you used earlier on the gears' fountain fill. Now drag this handle to twelve o'clock relative to the text.

5. Click the To color box, and then fill it with bright yellow from the mini-palette at right on the Property Bar. Cool, eh?

Adding and Aligning Text

Congratulations! The hard work is behind you now—and it wasn't really all that hard now, was it? Next stop is adding the URL for Dyson Gears, performing a little alignment work, and then onto setting up the design for printing.

Tutorial Adding a Visually Compatible Subhead

1. VAG Rounded is a beautiful, somewhat serious typeface, and an ideal complement to the no-nonsense design of this logo. It's on the CorelDRAW Fonts installation CD, and its filename is tt0756m_.ttf. Install it now if you want to use it in the following steps.

2. With the Text Tool, click an insertion point to the left and below the gears. Type **dysongears.com**.

3. Choose the Pick Tool, and then with the text selected, choose VAG Rounded BT from the Font list, insert your cursor into the Point Size field, and then type **36**. Half an inch is a good size for the design when printed to a T-shirt.

4. Marquee-select the Envelope headline text and the gears. Press CTRL+G to group these two groups of objects.

5. Press CTRL+A to select all.

6. Choose Arrange | Align and Distribute | Align and Distribute to make it easiest to see and execute the controls for aligning objects.

7. Click the Center checkbox, as shown here, and then click Apply. You can close the Align and Distribute box now. If you ever need to do some heavy-duty, multiple aligning work in a design, keep this box open and convenient for future use.

Align, Group, Scale, Flip, and Print

You're already familiar with most of the techniques covered in the upcoming tutorial that shows how to do one or two minor things to the finished logo to make it print-worthy. Yes, you're approaching home base and concluding the X6 Test Drive, but let's make this assignment a top-to-bottom, complete excursion. Follow these steps to brush up the logo design a little and set it up for output to an inkjet printer.

Let's assume your inkjet printer doesn't have an auto-reverse feature, or it's too hard to find...

Tutorial Getting Your Logo Design into the Real World

1. Select all (CTRL + A) and then press CTRL + G to group all the selected shapes.
2. Let's get your money's worth out of the print by making the logo that 7 inches maximum that was agreed upon at the beginning of the chapter (okay, you might not have actually agreed, but play along here). With the group selected, type **7** in the horizontal width field on the Property Bar, make sure the Lock Ratio little lock icon is depressed, and then press ENTER. Then press P to center the design relative to the page.
3. As mentioned earlier, T-shirt transfers often need to be printed as the reverse of the imprint; that is, the text needs to be mirrored so when the inkjet page is ironed onto the shirt, it reverses back again to legibility. Click the Mirror Horizontally button on the Property Bar, which is easy enough to undo later if your logo is needed for a promotion other than T-shirts. See the illustration below.

4. Put a piece of *regular paper* in the inkjet printer and print a copy of the design. Press CTRL + P, choose the correct printer, and then click Print. This is a "proof-of-concept" print—T-shirt transfers cost about a dollar each, while plain paper costs significantly less and is cheaper still if you print on the backside of a page that has already been printed with something expendable. If everything seems to be satisfactory with the test print, do it for real with the T-shirt transfer paper.

With the exception of that all-night pizzeria around the corner, all good things must come to an end. You've passed the Test Drive; you're home safe and didn't dent a fender; and the best part is: you get to pocket the keys. You're going to need them when you take this high-performance Model X6 out on your own and take the bends and curves in the chapters to come!

The Test Drive Cross-Reference

You haven't really broken in all the features and tools covered in this chapter, so here are the signposts to learn more about the editing and transforming you performed in this chapter:

- Aligning and distributing objects: Chapter 9
- Extruding objects: Chapter 19
- Guidelines and rulers: Chapter 7
- The Envelope Tool: Chapter 20
- Working with text: Chapters 12 and 13
- Filling objects: Chapter 15

See Chapters 2 and 3 for the basics on the Color Palette, and for saving and opening documents. But you probably already know that stuff.

PART II

Getting Started with CorelDRAW X6

6

Working with Single- and Multi-Page Documents

You have an idea for promoting your product or service; you have your graphics and you have some body copy and a snappy headline in mind. The next step is to define the dimensions within which you express your promotional idea. Do you need a flyer, or perhaps a four-page booklet? This chapter covers the beginning of any graphics project: setting up pages in CorelDRAW. You'll learn about layout styles, page dimensions for your screen and for printing, page reordering, and, in the process, gain a good working knowledge of what you need to do—and what you can tell CorelDRAW to do—to create a page that suits your ideas.

 Download and extract all the files from the Chapter06.zip archive to follow the tutorials in this chapter.

Setting Up Your Document Page

Every new file you create has its own set of *page properties* that have two attributes: *physical* properties and *display* preferences. The *physical properties* refer to the size, length, and color of each page as you'd define a physical page in the real world. *Display preferences* control how page values are *viewed*. Let's begin with the most common options and then move on to the more specialized features.

Controlling Page Size and Orientation

If you've unchecked the Always Show The Welcome Screen At Launch checkbox, the default size of a new document is CorelDRAW's default, which depends on the language version of CorelDRAW you use. For the U.S. author, the default is U.S. Letter,

8½" by 11", but you can change this. The quickest route for document size change is through the Property Bar while the Pick Tool—and no objects—are selected. The Property Bar features options for setting your page to standard-sized pages, custom sizes, and orientation, as seen in Figure 6-1. If you have a multi-page document, the Property Bar also has ways to change all pages at once or only the currently visible page.

The Paper Type/Size and orientation options control the format of your document. When you have a specific format for a design you need to print, the following sections cover the options available to you in CorelDRAW.

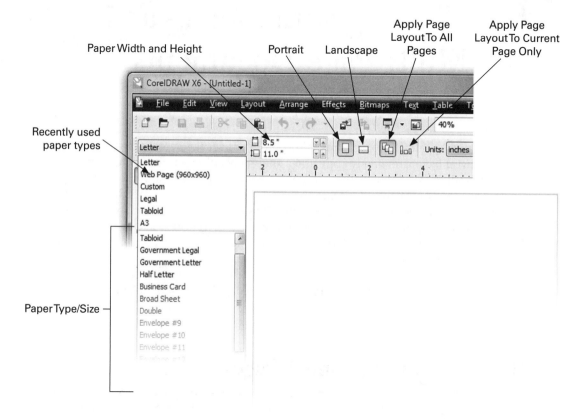

FIGURE 6-1 You change page size and orientation by using the Property Bar.

Paper Type/Size

To quickly make sure your CorelDRAW page matches the paper in your printer, click a Paper Type/Size option in the Property Bar. From the drop-down box, you have Letter, Legal, Tabloid, and other common sizes to choose from. Once you've made a selection, the dimensions are automatically entered as values into the Page Width and Height boxes in the Property Bar. If you have a limited need for different paper sizes, click the Edit This List button at the bottom of the drop-down list, and you can delete seldom-used sizes: click the Delete Page Size in the Options box.

- **Page dimensions**   You are not limited to a page size that's the same as the paper in your printer; page width and height values can be between 0.00333 and 1,800 inches. For a custom page size, type specific values directly into the Page Width and Height boxes, and then press ENTER.
- **Landscape/Portrait**   Clicking either Portrait or Landscape in the Property Bar while using the Pick Tool (with no objects selected) sets the page orientation. If the page width you enter is smaller than the page height entered, the orientation is automatically set to Portrait, and vice versa for Landscape. Changing from Portrait to Landscape (or vice versa) automatically switches the values in the Page Width and Height fields.
- **All pages/Current page**   You can create a document up to 999 pages long, with different pages set to any size or orientation. The Set For All Pages and Set For Current Page Only buttons operate in "either/or" fashion like the orientation buttons, so you can set the page size either for all pages in your document at once (the default) or only for the current page. To set only the current page to be different from the others in your document, click the right button of this pair and set your new page size and orientation as needed. Other pages in the document aren't resized when you choose this option.

Note   If you've unintentionally removed a page size you need later, you can re-create the page size. Click Custom, click Edit This List, and then name and save the page in the Options | Page Size box.

Page Viewing Options

With CorelDRAW at its default settings, when you choose File | New, you'll see a rectangle in the workspace. This rectangle represents your document page in height and width. However, what you *won't* see is how your page will be printed to a personal printer or to a commercial press. Whenever you print, your page includes areas called the *Printable Area* and the *Bleed Area*. You can add nonprinting guidelines to provide a page preview ... so objects and text at the edges of your work don't get partially printed. You certainly want these features visible when designing for print;

the grippers on printers often prevent edge-to-edge prints. To have CorelDRAW add Bleed and Printable Area (*safety*) guides to your page, press CTRL + J, and then choose Document | Guidelines | Presets; check Printable Area and Bleed Area, as shown in the following illustration. The Bleed Area extends to the edge of the page, which is correct for personal printers; see the following Note.

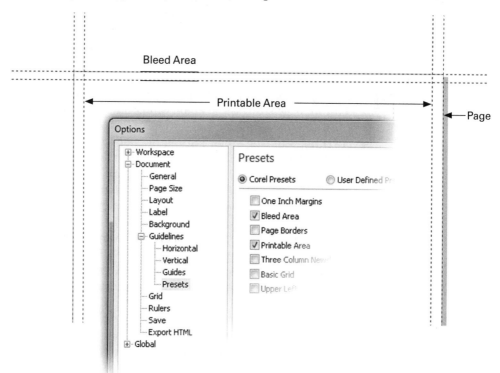

 Note The *bleed* is the part of the printed image that extends beyond the edge of the page. When printing to a personal printer, there is no bleed because bleed is only relevant when a page on a commercial press is trimmed to final book size. For example, if a commercial press uses 12"×14" paper and the final trim size is 8½"×11", you could set up a bleed area of 10"×13" to make a design extend to the edge of the page the audience reads.

 Note If you are printing to a borderless photo printer, your Printable Area will be the same size as your page border.

The Printable Area and Bleed Area properties depend on the printer options you choose in the Print Setup dialog, which you open by choosing File | Print Setup.

Click to choose printer's page size and other features.

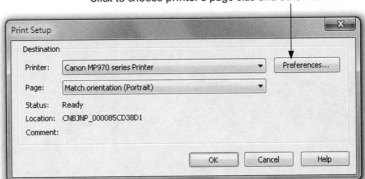

Tip   Setting a bleed amount is done using the Document | Page Size section of the Options dialog box, using the Bleed option num box. The bleed amount can be defined anywhere between 0 (the exact edge of your page) and 900 inches.

Controlling Page Background Color

To specify a page background color for your document, choose Layout | Page Background (CTRL + J) to open the Options dialog to the Background page.

- **Solid**   Choose this option and a color from the selector to specify any uniform color as the page background. Click More in the color selector to use a color picker in different color models (RGB, CMYK, and so on), a mixer, or a specific color palette. Once you've chosen a color, the page background is set to that color, but the bleed area and the workspace are not.

- **Bitmap**   Choose this option to use a bitmap as the page background. Click the Browse button to open the CorelDRAW Import dialog, and locate and choose a bitmap. Background bitmaps are tiled as many times as needed to fill the page. You can also scale the number of repeating tiles by clicking the Custom Size radio button and entering values. The best bitmaps to use for patterns are ones that have been designed to tile seamlessly. In Figure 6-2, you can see a completed design you'll work with in a moment. Swimwear Sale.cdr uses a muted ocean waves pattern, one of several you can use in the downloaded zip archive, to add a subtle graphical theme to the sale flyer. The Bitmap option is terrific for creating several signs or stationery that contains different text but must be tied together in a theme. You can, for example, create different text on layers such as "Swimsuit Sale," "Vacation Sale," and "Inflatable Theme Toy Sale," and then print different signs by hiding all but one layer for printing. You can't accidentally move the Background, and this technique is quick to set up when you have 12 different messages that need a common background.

FIGURE 6-2 Use a bitmap as a Background for your design and text.

- **Source** The Source options let you establish an external link to the bitmap file or store a copy of it internally with your CorelDRAW document file. Choose Linked to maintain an external link or Embedded to store the bitmap with your document. While Linked is selected, the file path to the bitmap is displayed, and the bitmap itself must be available to CorelDRAW during printing. This option is very useful when you need to conserve on saved CorelDRAW file sizes; additionally, you can modify the Background bitmap in PHOTO-PAINT or Painter and then reload the edited bitmap in the future.
- **Bitmap Size** This field contains "either/or" radio buttons. If you choose Default Size, the background appears on the page because the bitmap's original dimensions allow it to tile as many times as needed to fill the page. However, if

you want a smaller bitmap as the background (more tiles), you click the Custom Size button. The Maintain Aspect Ratio option is checked by default; you probably don't want the bitmap background to look smooshed or stretched—with Maintain Aspect Ratio turned on, all you need to do is enter one value in either the H or V field, and CorelDRAW automatically fills in the remaining field. Note that bitmaps are resolution dependent, unlike vector drawings. Thus, you can usually scale a bitmap down, but don't try to enlarge it because the bitmap will go through something called resampling, and blurriness is often the result. Remember: scale down = yes; scale up = no.

- **Print And Export Background**   Use this option to control whether the page background you've added to your document page is included when exporting your drawing files or when you print the document. It's available when either Solid or Bitmap is selected for the page background; by default, it's active.

Open Swimware Sale.cdr now, and work through the Options to change the waves background to something else you prefer for the piece.

Tutorial   Changing a Background Bitmap

1. If you haven't already extracted the contents of the zip archive for this chapter, do so now, create a folder for the PNG images, and place them there.
2. With Swimware.cdr open, press CTRL + J (Tools | Options), and then choose Background below the Document area in the left column.
3. Notice that the Bitmap button is selected (there is already a bitmap as the Background) and that the bitmap is embedded. This means that unless you own the bitmap on your hard drive, the next step will forever overwrite this Screened waves.png file, something to consider when you embed a bitmap. Often, it's useful simply to externally link the bitmap background so you don't have to remember whether you have a spare copy of the image. Click Browse now to locate the folder of PNG files from Step 1.
4. Choose one of the PNG files, or you could choose your own image. With the file selected, click Import.
5. You can't preview the imported image as it will look; you can only click OK now to see how the new background has affected the composition. Before doing this, though, try setting the Custom Size to something other than the default. If you're using one of this chapter's example bitmaps, try setting the Height and Width to 3". Click OK and the layout has a new background.

Tip   If a bitmap background appears to have a white seam in an area, this is a visual effect of the bitmap trying to blend (*anti-alias*) with the page itself, which is white. If you zoom in and out, the thin white edge disappears because, at certain viewing resolutions, the anti-alias blending matches the resolution of the tiling bitmap background. The design *itself* will print with no visible white edges; this is simply a page viewing issue.

6. Optionally, you can open the Object Manager (Window | Dockers | Object Manager), and click the Visibility icon for the "Swimwear" layer. Clicking Visibility clears everything from the page except the background image and the logo at top. Now you can design a different flyer using the same background bitmap and logo by clicking, for example, "Vacations" to set the current layer.

Alternatively, when you want to create variations on a page layout, see Chapter 4 for the details on working with Master Layers.

Note The reason why the background PNG files in the preceding tutorial don't display seams at the edge is that they were carefully designed in Corel Painter to repeat seamlessly. Painter is an ideal companion to CorelDRAW, but if you're in a hurry and under a budget crunch, see Chapter 26 to learn how to create seamless tiles using PHOTO-PAINT.

Using Layouts and Labels

The Property Bar is used to set up the basic page and paper sizes and orientation, but designers often need to lay out designs for items such as labels, booklets, tent cards, and greeting cards *that are printed on standard size paper.* These items are definitely *not* laid out like a single-page flyer. Happily, CorelDRAW provides specialized layouts that are just a few clicks away, so you don't have to sit at your workstation all day folding paper to try to figure out exactly where the fold lines are and where the text needs to be upside down. These timesavers are not on the Property Bar—you need to open the Options dialog to select the one you need from the Layout drop-down box.

Choosing Specialized Layouts

On the Layout page of the Options dialog, you can choose from seven specialized layouts for your document: Full Page, Book, Booklet, Tent Card, Side-Fold Card, Top-Fold Card, and Tri-Fold Brochure.

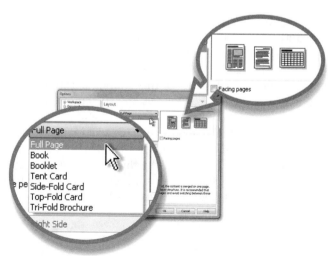

Choosing one of these layout styles instantly divides the current document page size into horizontal and vertical pages, based on the preview supplied in the dialog.

- **Full Page** This layout style is the default for all new documents, and it formats your document in single pages, like those shown in the previous illustration.
- **Book** The Book layout format, shown on the right, divides your document page size into two equal vertical portions, and each portion is considered a separate page. When printed, each page is output as a separate page.

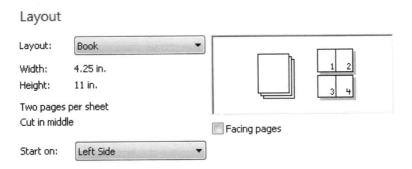

- **Booklet** In a similar arrangement to the Book layout, the Booklet layout format divides your document page size into two equal vertical portions. Each portion is considered a separate page. However, when printed, pages are paired according to typical imposition formatting, where pages are matched according to their final position in the booklet layout. In a four-page booklet, with a landscape orientation for the paper, this means page 1 is matched with page 4, and page 2 is matched with page 3, as shown here.

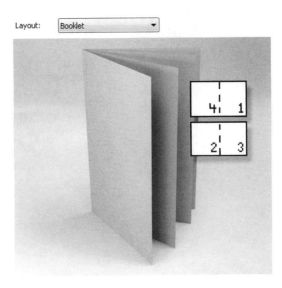

- **Tent Card**   The Tent Card layout format divides your document page size into two equal horizontal portions; each portion is considered a separate page. Because Tent Card output is folded in the center, each of your document pages is printed in sequence and positioned to appear upright after folding.

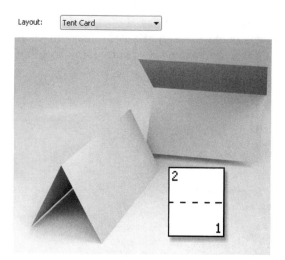

- **Side-Fold Card**   The Side-Fold layout format divides your document page size into four equal parts, vertically and horizontally. When printed, each document page is printed in sequence, and positioned and rotated to fit the final folded layout. Folding the printed page vertically and then horizontally results in the correct sequence and orientation.

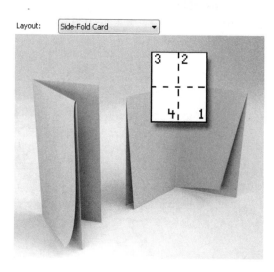

- **Top-Fold Card** Like the Side-Fold layout, the Top-Fold layout format also divides your document page size into four equal parts, vertically and horizontally. When printed, each document page is printed in sequence, and positioned and rotated to fit the final folded layout.

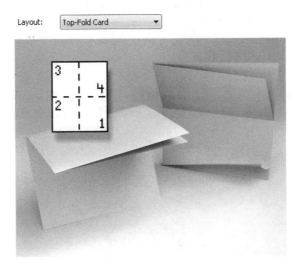

- **Tri-Fold Brochure** Set your page orientation to Landscape using File | Print Setup, and you then have the ideal layout for travel brochures and restaurant tabletop stand-up menus. You can print both sides for a total of six panels, with live space measuring about 3 1/2" wide and 8" high on the end panels.

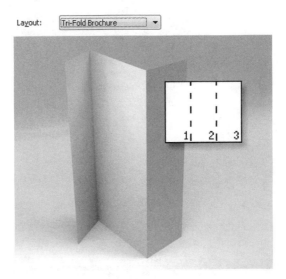

After you choose a layout style and return to your document, you can view each subdivision of the layout individually. You can also view pages in pairs by choosing the Facing Pages option on the Layout page of the Options dialog for several layout styles.

When Facing Pages is selected in the dialog, you also have the opportunity to start your document on either the Left side or the Right side for some layout styles by making a selection from the Start On menu.

Tip Choose File | Print Preview to check how the content is arranged on the page(s) *before* printing!

Using Preformatted Labels

CorelDRAW has a comprehensive collection of label formats for preformatted paper stock, from vendors such as Avery, Ace, and Leitz. To use most of these label formats, your document page should be formatted to *letter-sized portrait;* in Options, choose Document | Label, and select the Labels radio button for access to the label collection. After you've selected a specific label format, the preview window shows its general layout and indicates the number of rows and columns available, as shown in Figure 6-3.

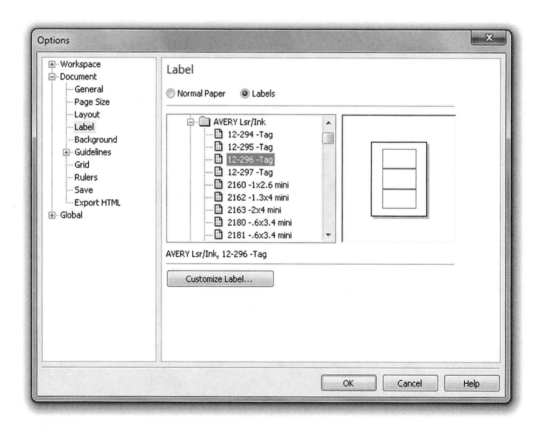

FIGURE 6-3   CorelDRAW has just the preformatted label template you need.

After you choose a label format and return to your document, each of your document pages will represent an individual label. You need to add the exact number of pages to accommodate all of your labels. If you don't see the exact manufacturer for your specific label type, you can create your own from scratch or base it on an existing label format (see Figure 6-4). Choose an existing label from the Label Types menu; click Customize Label; set the number of Rows and Columns; and set the Label Size, Margins, and Gutters according to your own label sheet. Once you create the format, you may save your label by clicking the plus (+) button next to the Label Style drop-down list or delete a selected label from the list by clicking the minus (–) button.

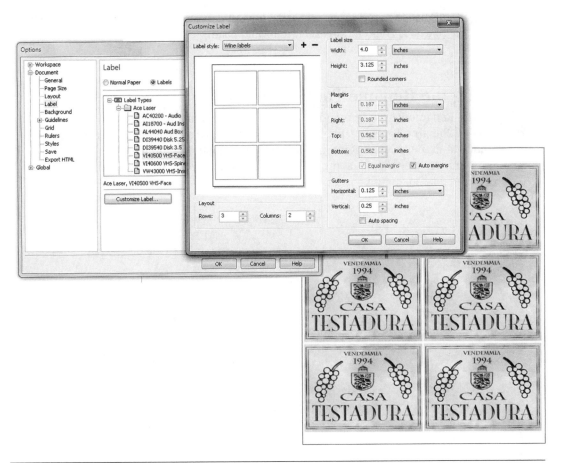

FIGURE 6-4   If you don't find the label you need, modify an existing label using the options.

Naming Pages

Whenever a new document is created, CorelDRAW automatically creates the names, such as "Page 1," "Page 2," and so on. These page names are only for your reference as you navigate your multi-page document. However, you can customize your page names using several different methods.

When creating web page documents—where each document page is a *separate* web page—adding a unique name to the page creates a title for the exported page. When your document is printed, page names can also be printed in the margins, can indicate the page's contents, and can provide other page-specific information.

Tip To display the previous or next page in your document quickly, you can press PAGE UP (previous page) or PAGE DOWN (following page).

Using the Rename Page Command

Use the Rename Page command to assign a unique name to pages. Choose either Layout | Rename Page, or (more quickly) right-click the page tab of your document window and then choose Rename Page from the pop-up menu to access the command. The Rename Page dialog, shown next, can rename a page with a name of up to 32 characters, including spaces.

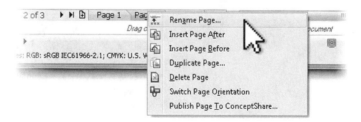

Saving Details with Your File

Document Properties is a CorelDRAW feature that provides details about a document you save without having to type in the margins. To access Document Properties—to both enter and view information—right-click a blank part of the page. In addition to

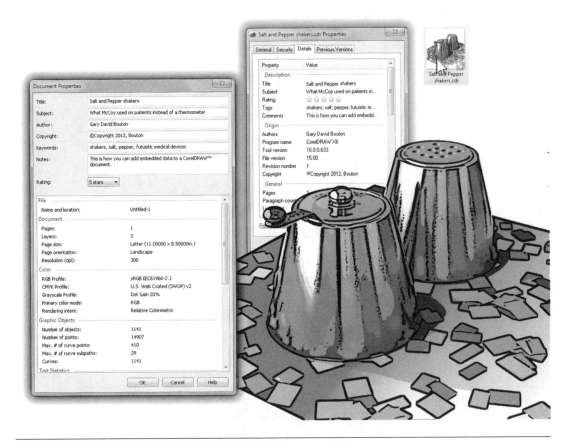

FIGURE 6-5   Save your CorelDRAW files and exported bitmaps with Document
Properties metadata.

allowing you to type reminders for yourself, Document Properties is also a convenient
method for tagging designs you export to JPEG and other bitmap file formats. As
you can see in Figure 6-5, the same information you type in Document Properties
is available to Windows users when they right-click your image in a file folder and
choose Details.

 Note   Users who don't own CorelDRAW cannot access Document Properties info you've
embedded in a native CDR file by right-clicking. The solution to this problem is to
make them buy CorelDRAW!

Navigating a Multi-Page Document

To go to different pages in a document, click a page icon at the lower left of the
document window. If the page isn't in view, you can scroll to locate it, or (for lengthy
documents) open the Go To Page dialog, shown next, by clicking between the Next

Page and Previous Page buttons at the lower left of your document window. This dialog enables you to move quickly to a specific page in your document.

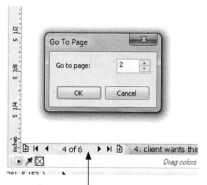

Click here to open the Go To Page dialog.

Using the Object Manager

The Object Manager docker offers the advantage of mass-editing page names from within a single docker for editing page names. To open the Object Manager, choose Tools | Object Manager. Once the docker is open, click to ensure the docker is set to show Object Properties by deselecting the Layer Manager view button state, as shown here:

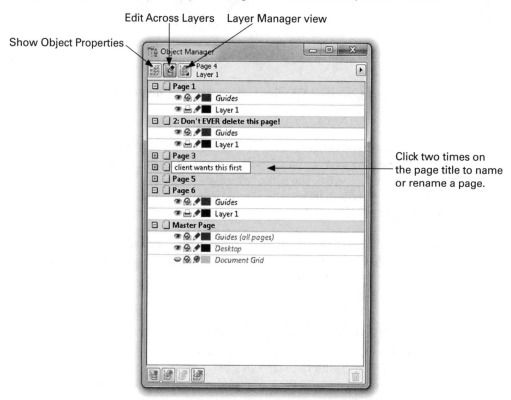

Edit Across Layers   Layer Manager view

Show Object Properties

Click two times on the page title to name or rename a page.

In this view, all page and object names are displayed. To rename any page (or any object), click once directly on the page title to select the page you want to name or rename, click a second time to highlight the page name text, then type a name, and finally press ENTER. Page names appear in the page tabs at the lower left of your document window, accompanied by a numeral indicating the page's order in your document:

Tip To see more (or less) of the pages of your document in the page tab area of your document window, click-drag on the vertical divider between the page tabs and the horizontal scroll bar.

Click-drag to expand/reduce page tab area.

э 7   8: The key is under the doormat   Pa

Page Commands

There are several ways to add and delete pages from a document: using menu commands, using shortcuts while pressing modifier keys, and using certain page views. However, quick is best, and in this section, you learn the most convenient way as well as methods that are easiest to remember. You can decide for yourself which best suits the way you work.

Inserting Pages and Setting Options

From the main menu, choose Layout | Insert Page to open the Insert Page dialog, which has a host of options for specifying your new page properties and where you would like to add the new page in relation to your existing pages.

Enter the number of pages needed in the Insert box, and choose to add them either Before or After your current page, or between specific pages in your document using the Page box. You are not limited to the orientation or size of your current page when you add pages, unlike the constraints imposed by traditional printed books and magazines!

Tip To add a new page quickly to the beginning or end of your document, go to the first or last page and click the plus (+) symbol on the left or right of the page buttons at the lower left of your document window. To add a page before or after your current page, right-click the page tab to the right of these buttons, and choose either Insert Page Before or Insert Page After from the pop-up menu.

Deleting Pages

Delete document pages by choosing Layout | Delete Page from the main menu; you can then delete one or more of the existing pages in your document. By default, the dialog opens to display the current page as the page in the Delete Page box, but you may select any page before or after your current page if you choose. To delete an entire sequence of pages, click the Through To Page option, which enables you to delete all pages in a range between the page specified in the Delete Page box through to any page following your current page. Pay careful attention to the word "Inclusive" after the last page number: if you type, for example, 10 when you want to delete pages 1–9, well, oops—there goes your day unless you press CTRL + z immediately!

> **Tip** To delete the current page, right-click the page name on the Page Tab, and then choose Delete page from the pop-up menu. *There is no confirmation* when you delete a page, so make sure you've had your second cup of coffee in the morning before doing this.

Moving and Duplicating Pages

You're going to create such fantastic content in CorelDRAW that you might never want to delete it, but instead you might want to move and/or copy pages. To move a page, use a click-drag action on the Page Tab to drag it to a new position. To copy a page— *and all its contents*—thus creating a new page order, hold CTRL while click-dragging the Page Tab to copy the page to a new position. CorelDRAW does not duplicate the name of a user-named page; you'd wind up with an organizational nightmare if it did, so it's a good practice to name a duplicate page after you've created the copy.

Click-drag tabs to change page order.

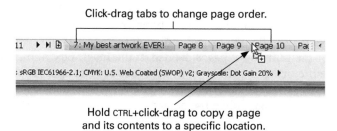

Hold CTRL+click-drag to copy a page
and its contents to a specific location.

Using the Page Sorter

Page Sorter is a view that provides you with a broad look at your document and all its pages. In this view, you can add, delete, move, or copy pages in a single view. You can also change the Paper/Type Size and the page Orientation of all the pages or just selected pages. A CorelDRAW document can contain pages of different sizes, which can be very handy when you are designing matching business cards and letterhead or other similarly related materials. To open your document and all its pages in Page Sorter view, choose View | Page Sorter View. The Page Sorter displays all pages in your document.

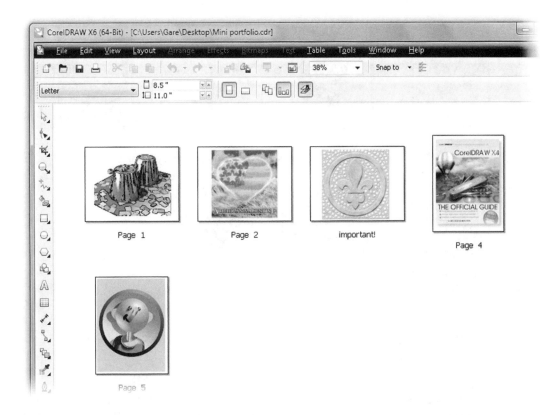

Tip Using Page Sorter, you can export either your entire document or only selected pages quickly. Click to select the page(s) you want to export and choose File | Export, or click the Export button in the Standard Toolbar to open the Export dialog. To export only specific pages, click the option Export This Page Only, which, by default, is not selected. Exporting is not to be confused with saving; exporting pages is usually done to get your work into bitmap format, Adobe Illustrator file format, or Corel Media Exchange (CMX) for sharing with users who have a compatible application.

In Page Sorter view, a single click selects a page. Holding SHIFT while clicking pages enables you to select or deselect contiguous multiple pages. Holding CTRL while clicking enables you to select or deselect noncontiguous pages. The following actions enable you to apply page commands interactively to single or multiple page selections, as seen in Figure 6-6.

- **Move page(s)**   To move a page and change its order in your document, click-drag the page to a new location. During dragging, a vertical I-beam appears, indicating the insertion point for the page or the first page of the selected sequence of pages.

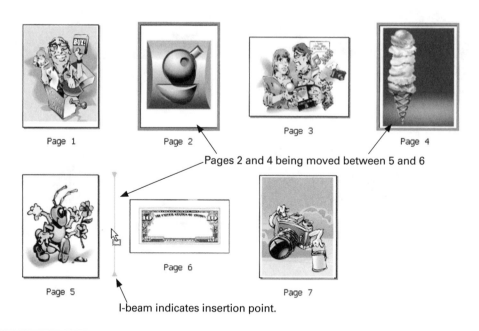

Page 1   Page 2   Page 3   Page 4

Pages 2 and 4 being moved between 5 and 6

Page 5   Page 6   Page 7

I-beam indicates insertion point.

FIGURE 6-6   Page Sorter enables you to manage your document pages interactively while viewing all page properties.

- **Add page(s)**   To add pages to your document, right-click any page and choose Insert Page Before or Insert Page After from the pop-up menu to insert a page relative to the selected page.
- **Copy page(s)**   To copy pages—and their contents—hold CTRL while click-dragging the page to a specific location. During dragging, a vertical I-beam appears, indicating the insertion point for the page copy or the first page of the selected sequence of pages.
- **Name or rename page**   To add a new name or change an existing page name, click the page name below the page to select it; click a second time to highlight the page title, and enter a new name; then press ENTER. You can also rename a page by right-clicking a specific page and choosing Rename Page from the pop-up menu to highlight the page name for editing.
- **Change page size/orientation of all pages**   In Page Sorter view, the Property Bar displays typical page property options for applying standard or custom page sizes and changing the orientation between Landscape and Portrait. If you want to change the orientation of *all* of the pages in the document, click on the Apply Page Layout To All Pages button on the Property Bar and *then* click either the Portrait or the Landscape button to change all pages to that orientation.
- **Change page size/orientation of selected pages**   If you only want to change the orientation of some of the pages, click on the Apply Page Layout To Current Page button. Then select the pages you want to change, and click the Portrait or Landscape button to change the page(s) to the desired orientation as shown.

Changing the orientation in the Page Sorter not only changes the view, but also the changes how the pages themselves are oriented in the document. As you can see in this illustration, the second and last pages have drawings that look better in Portrait view. CTRL-click pages 2 and 4 in this example, click Apply Page Layout To Current Page Only, and both the Page Sorter view and the pages themselves are reoriented. If you want to rethink this dynamic change, repeatedly pressing CTRL+Z (Edit | Undo) restores your document.

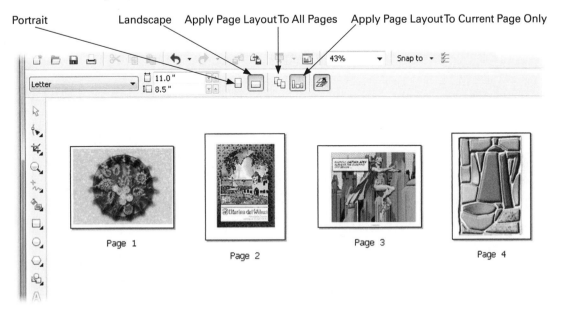

Exiting Page Sorter View is easy; click the Page Sorter View button, or click any tool on the Toolbox. Any changes applied while in the Page Sorter are applied to your document.

Tip   To exit the Page Sorter and immediately go to a particular page in your document, double-click the page.

Page definitions, sorting pages, margins, bleeds, and enough other options have been discussed to fill a book! Now that you know how to set up a page, how large do you want that drawing you just created on the page? And how do you precisely move the drawing if you want it perfectly centered on the page? Fortunately, the answers are on the way, as measuring and drawing helpers are covered in the next chapter.

7

Measuring and Drawing Helpers: Working with Guides, Grids, and Scale

More than likely, a project you are beginning is supposed to be a specific page size. And you plan to design graphics that need to be aligned, spaced, and proportioned to exact dimensions. And perhaps you need to label what you've designed with callouts, and parts of a sketch need widths expressed in inches so manufacturing can order boxes that fit the product. Today is your lucky day: CorelDRAW not only has more ways of measuring objects than you can shake a stick at, and even measure sticks, but it also makes it easy for users of all skill levels to turn out professional, tightly composed pieces. In this chapter, you'll learn how to measure, scale measurements, align objects, work with guidelines, create your own guidelines, add measurements and callouts, and get objects to snap to other objects with pinpoint precision. Leave "a smidgeon," "a pinch," and "just a touch to the left" behind as you enter the world of CorelDRAW accuracy and layout perfection.

Using the Ruler

Although Property Bars and toolbars offer information about the size and position of an object to three decimal places, something about using rulers bounding a page has tangible and easy-to-understand qualities. CorelDRAW's rulers are also a resource for pulling nonprinting guidelines. Let's look now at how rulers are configured, manipulated, and how they assist in your design work.

Accessing Rulers and Ruler Properties

Straight out of the box, CorelDRAW displays rulers on the top and left side of the page window. However, if someone experimented with your installed copy and turned off rulers, you can easily restore their visibility. You can choose View | Rulers from the main menu, but a quicker way is via the pop-up menu. With any tool selected except the Zoom Tool, right-click over a blank area of the page (or outside of the page), and then choose View | Rulers from the pop-up menu.

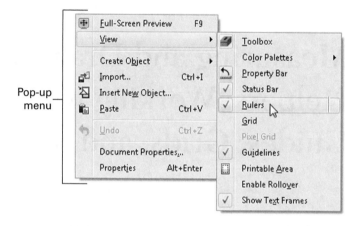

Rulers in CorelDRAW look like physical rulers with major spacing (inches, for example) and minor spacing (the ticks between whole number amounts, such as ⅜, and ¼). CorelDRAW detects when a mouse scroll wheel is active, and if you zoom the page in and out, you'll see an additional ruler nicely—the ruler ticks between major spacing have labels for fractional amounts when your zoom level is large enough to display them.

CorelDRAW rulers (see Figure 7-1) have three components: the vertical ruler, the horizontal ruler, and the ruler origin. Dashed lines on the rulers show the location of your cursor, and the numerical value is shown on the Property Bar. CorelDRAW displays horizontal position values as X values on the Property Bar, and vertical values as Y. For example, let's say you create a rectangle using the Rectangle Tool, but you're not sure you put the rectangle in the center of an 8½ × 11" page. A glance at the Property Bar will tell you that if the rectangle's X position is 4.25" and the Y position is 5.5", its center is at the center of the page.

The *origin* is the intersection of the vertical and horizontal rulers toward the top left of the workspace. The origin is the page position reference where all measurements begin, but *it* does not *represent the zero point for measuring the page*. By default, the *lower-left corner* of your page represents the ruler origin 0 position. Try this: create a shape near the center of the page. Then with the Pick Tool move the shape up and to the right, while watching the X, Y position values on the Property Bar. The values increase; conversely, if you move the shape down and to the left, the values decrease— eventually, if you move the shape off the page (down and left), you'll see negative X, Y values on the Property Bar as the shape travels beyond the origin.

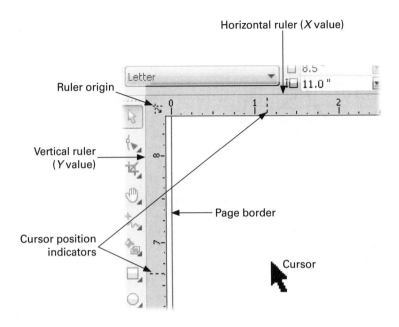

FIGURE 7-1   Elements of CorelDRAW's rulers

You can move rulers in CorelDRAW to assist you in your design needs. Additionally, you can leave the rulers where they are and just move the rulers' origin; working with these features is covered in the sections that follow.

Setting the Ruler Origin

Let's say you're uncomfortable with measuring from the bottom left and prefer a more conventional set of rulers that start at the upper-left corner of a page. Click-hold your cursor on the origin, and then drag to a point at the upper-left corner of the page. Your rulers are now different than many drawing applications, CAD applications, and most advanced design programs—Y, the vertical measurement of space, always travels up in a positive direction. However, moving the origin makes the rulers suit *your* intuitions. It's also a handy technique for measuring the relative distance between objects, when measured against each other and not as an absolute measurement against the page.

Tutorial   Two Inches to the Right, Please

1. Create two shapes; any shapes will do.
2. Move the shapes using the Pick Tool so they're horizontally aligned, and let's try 5 inches from each other.
3. You need the centers of the objects to be 2 inches apart. Click-drag the origin so it's horizontally centered on the first object. The zero horizontal point is now at the center of the first object.

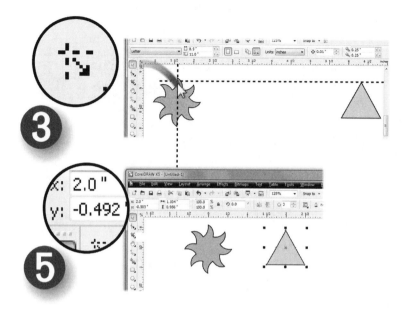

FIGURE 7-2 Specify a different origin for the rulers to measure relative distances between the centers of objects.

4. You move the second object so its center is at the 2-inch major mark on the horizontal ruler.
5. With this shape still selected, take a look at the *X, Y* fields on the Property Bar. If the *X* value is not exactly 2.000, type **2.000** in the *X* field, and then press ENTER. See Figure 7-2.

Undoing what you've done is easy: to restore the origin of the rulers to the default setting, just double-click the origin.

A more dramatic change you can make to the rulers is to actually *reposition* them in the workspace, not simply change where the units appear. To undock the rulers (they come as a set; you cannot undock only one ruler), hold SHIFT and then drag the ruler origin to where you want the rulers to begin. You'll see a dashed-line preview onscreen for the rulers' intended new location; release the mouse button and the rulers move to this position. To restore the rulers (to dock them), hold SHIFT and then double-click the rulers origin. See Figure 7-3.

Once you've undocked the rulers, you're free to move them as needed by holding SHIFT while dragging the origin. Regardless of where you place the rulers in the workspace, the zero for the increments on the rulers remains constant. Try moving the view of the page by using the scroll bars at the right and bottom of the screen or use the Hand Tool (H); the increments on the undocked rulers move as you move your view. If you need to move the origin while the rulers are undocked, drag the origin.

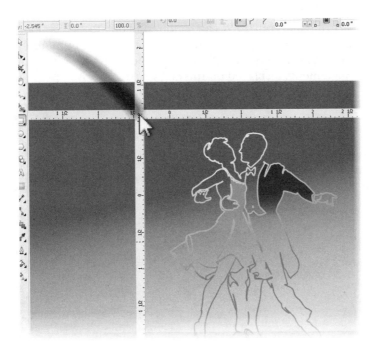

SHIFT+click-drag the ruler origin to undock and move.
Hold SHIFT and double-click to redock.

FIGURE 7-3   Rulers can be repositioned on the page.

Setting Unit Measure

CorelDRAW offers real-world units of measurement: millimeters, yards, and so on. *Unit measures* is the name of the setting in CorelDRAW, which affect the look of the rulers as they increase and decrease in frequency according to your view magnification setting. The actual unit measures are specified according to the Drawing Units currently defined on the Property Bar. To set the Drawing Unit measure, choose the Pick Tool (first click an empty area on your page to make sure nothing is selected), and then use the Units drop-down list on the Property Bar to specify anything from picas to kilometers.

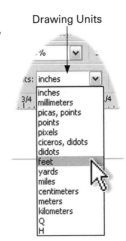

Drawing Units

Drawing Units control the units displayed on the rulers and also for other areas of CorelDRAW where dimensions are displayed: page size, shape size, and nudge and duplicate offset commands.

Setting Ruler Options

Options for measuring in CorelDRAW can be found under Tools | Options. Double-click a page ruler or right-click a ruler and then choose Ruler Setup from the pop-up menu to get there. In the Rulers area of the Options dialog, you'll find options in addition to the increments displayed on rulers.

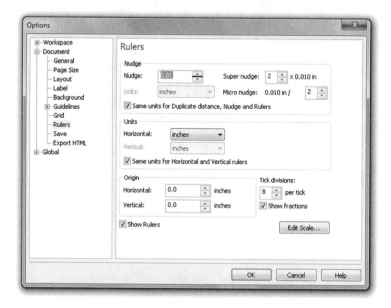

Nudging

At the top of the Rulers page are Nudge options, worth covering first here, although indirectly related to the page rulers themselves. In CorelDRAW, nudging objects is precise, and on the Rulers page you can set the distance for normal, Super, and Micro nudging. Nudging can be performed on a shape, several shapes at the same time, and even a node or several nodes on a path when you've selected them with the Shape Tool.

Once you've specified values for nudging in the Rulers area:

- You set the normal nudge distance of a shape by choosing the shape(s) with the Pick Tool (or nodes using the Shape Tool), and then pressing the keyboard arrow keys to nudge up, down, or diagonally if you press, for example, down and right simultaneously. One keyboard (or combination) stroke equals one nudge distance.
- Super nudging is performed the same way as normal nudging except you hold the SHIFT key while pressing any arrow key.
- Micro nudging is performed the same way as regular nudging, except you hold the CTRL key while pressing any arrow key.

The upper limit for nudge distance is 600 inches. This distance is fair enough because, for example, nudging a shape 600 inches is more easily accomplished by entering the intended position in the Property Bar's *X* and *Y* fields (then you press ENTER to apply the move).

 Note Nudge distance can be set on-the-fly within the workspace, and Super and Micro nudge scale applies to the new nudge distance. With nothing selected, set a new value in the Nudge Distance box.

Nudge on Property Bar

Specifying Units, Origin, and Tick Divisions for Your Rulers

In the fields below Nudge options, you'll find all the controls for what appears, and where, on the rulers displayed on your drawing page. Here's how each option controls the ruler's appearance:

- **Units**   Units are measurement values. Choose a Horizontal unit measure to specify unit measures for all Drawing Units in your document. To specify different unit measures for the vertical ruler and Drawing Units, click to deselect the Same Units For Horizontal And Vertical Rulers option.
- **Origin**   Although you can manually set the origin as described in the previous section, you can also perform precise origin definition using this field. The origin point can be set anywhere from –50 to 50 yards in precise increments as small as 0.001 inch.
- **Tick Divisions**   *Tick divisions* are the evenly spaced numeric labels seen bracketing the smaller increments displayed by your ruler—for example, if you are using inches as the unit, the tick divisions are 1, 2, 3, and so on. Tick divisions are automatically set according to the type of unit measure selected. For example, standard measure displays a default of eight divisions per tick, and metric measures display ten divisions. Desktop publishing and printing units such as didots, picas, points, and ciceros are displayed using six divisions per tick.

The option to Show Fractions is also available and set by default while a unit measure is selected. Shown here are two divisions per tick; below is the standard eight subdivisions, and at bottom, the Show Fractions check box is unchecked in the Rulers area of the Options dialog; decimals are now shown for ticks.

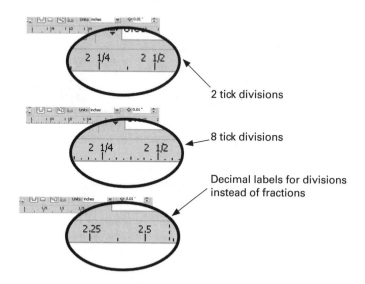

2 tick divisions

8 tick divisions

Decimal labels for divisions instead of fractions

Editing Drawing Scales

Scale drawing is used when the dimensions involved in drawing actual sizes are either too large or too small to be practical. For example, a world atlas at 1-to-1 (1:1) scale would be hard to carry around and almost as hard to print. You can set up a Drawing Scale by first setting the units you need in the Rulers options box, shown at left here. Then click the Edit Scale button on the Rulers page of the Options dialog (CTRL + J is the shortcut). In the Drawing Scale dialog, you can quickly apply a scale ratio or set your own custom scale. By setting 1 foot to equal a mile (5280 feet), it's simple, then, to draw accurate maps and directions around town.

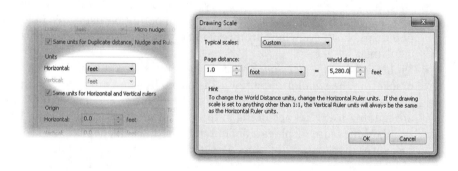

The Typical Scales drop-down menu includes a selection of the most commonly used drawing ratios and measure scales in addition to Custom. When selecting ratios, the first number represents the object *Page Distance;* the second number represents the *real world* distance, labeled "World Distance." Usually small objects such as circuitry and clock parts are illustrated using ratios where the Page Distance is larger than the World Distance. Conversely, the best setup for a technical drawing of a skyscraper is to set Page Distance much smaller than World Distance.

The moment you change either the Page Distance or the World Distance, the Typical Scales selection in the drop-down list turns to *Custom. Page Distance* is the measured distance on your document page, whereas *World Distance* refers to the distance represented by your ruler and the Drawing Units in your document. Settings can be entered independently of the other and to different unit measures to a range between 1,000,000 and 0.00001 inches in increments of 0.1 inch.

Calibrating Ruler Display

You buy a Lamborghini Gallardo (about $200,000); you pull into a gas station, and you want to put Regular in the tank? No, and similarly you can't expect precision when you use CorelDRAW on an uncalibrated monitor. CorelDRAW provides a simple way to ensure that what you see on your monitor screen matches real-world measurements. Occasionally, your display might not show perfectly square pixels, and as a result your 5-inch line in a very important drawing might measure 4.88" when you print it. To calibrate the rulers in CorelDRAW to match your screen, to match real-world output, you need a plastic foot-long ruler (clear is better than solid, about $1 at a stationery store), about 30 seconds, and the following steps:

1. In a new document, create a 5"-wide square. With the Rectangle Tool, hold CTRL (constrains proportions to 1:1), and then drag while watching the size fields on the Property Bar. If you're close but not precisely 5", type **5.0** into either field with the Lock Proportions icon clicked, and then press ENTER.
2. Using the Zoom Tool Property Bar options, set your view magnification to 100 percent.
3. Using your physical $1 ruler, measure the object you created on your screen. If both CorelDRAW's rulers and your physical ruler agree it's a 5" square, your Ruler display is accurate. If the measurements *don't* match, CorelDRAW's Toolbox Options has the fix.
4. Open the Options dialog (CTRL + J).
5. Click to expand the tree directory under Workspace and Toolbox, and then click Zoom, Pan Tools. This displays the Zoom, Pan options on the right of the dialog. First, click to select the Zoom Relative To 1:1 option.
6. Click Calibrate Rulers to display the Ruler calibration reference rulers and Resolution options. Notice the vertical and horizontal ruler bars that intersect at the center of your screen. This represents your current ruler Drawing Units. By default, Horizontal and Vertical resolution are set to 96.0 pixels per inch.

7. Using your ruler, measure both the vertical and horizontal rulers on your screen to see that they match. If they don't match, increase or decrease the Horizontal and/or Vertical options using the spin boxes until the onscreen rulers match your $1 ruler, as shown in the illustration here.

8. Click OK to close the calibration dialog, and then click OK again to close the Options dialog. Your Rulers are now calibrated.

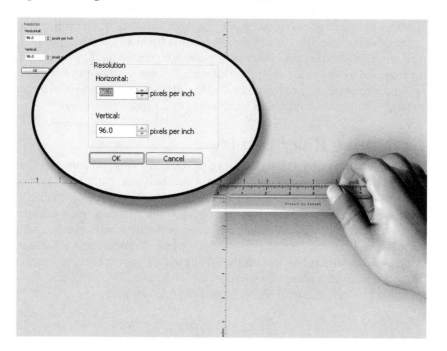

Introducing the Indispensable CorelDRAW Grids

A page grid is a customizable, by default, nonprinting overlay that extends beyond the printable page onto the pasteboard area at all viewing resolutions and viewing qualities. Not only is it an excellent visual reference for scaling and aligning objects vertically and horizontally, but also it can be used in combination with CorelDRAW's Snap To Grid option. To make the grid visible, right-click with the Pick Tool over an empty area of the page, and then choose View | Document Grid from the pop-up menu. To modify the grid, right-click over either ruler or the ruler origin, and then choose Grid Setup.

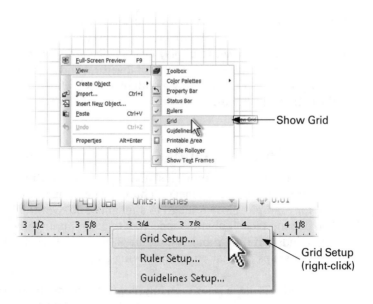

Setting Grid Properties

Grids are customizable to suit the type of work you do. Changing grid-line frequency and spacing is often necessary; use the options on the Grid page of the Options dialog to tailor your grid so it's just the way you need it. The Grid menu is located under Document in the Options dialog.

On the Grid page are three different areas to set Grid options for different types of objects. At top, you can set the number of grid lines per inch, and the horizontal and vertical grid increments can be set independent of one another. You can also choose to display the grid as lines or dots; whatever you choose affects the entire document—that's every page of your CDR file. Below the Document Grid settings are the Baseline Grid adjustments, which are intended for use with text, although objects will snap to the Baseline Grid if you have Snap To settings turned on.

> **Tip** Snap To can be turned on and off in the Grid dialog box, but it's far quicker to set Snap To on the Property Bar. Anything an object can snap to is available on the Snap To drop-down list.

New to version X6 is the Pixel Grid. If your View is set to Pixels (from the main menu), whenever your zoom factor is over 800 percent, you'll see a pixel grid on the page. This is exceptionally convenient when you're editing an imported bitmap and when you need precise adjustments to a vector object you intend to export as a bitmap. You also have the option to set the amount of transparency with which the Pixel Grid is displayed.

Tip When illustrating or drawing based on a specific unit measure—such as inches—formatting your grid to match the ruler unit measure is a smart thing to do. For example, if rulers are set to display inches using a tick division of 8 per inch, setting the grid to a frequency value of 8 vertical and 8 horizontal lines per inch causes grid lines to appear every eighth of an inch while using a drawing scale ratio of 1:1 (actual size).

Using Snap To Commands

The Snap To feature helps you move a shape to an exact location when it's close to grid lines, guidelines, and other objects. Think of snapping as magnetism: you hold a paper clip, for example, close enough to a magnet and eventually it snaps to the magnet. You use the Pick Tool and Shape Tool to get snapping in CorelDRAW, and the *Snap To* commands (on the drop-down menu on the Standard Toolbar) are your ticket to defining what snaps to what on your drawing page.

- **Snap To Grid** To have your drawing shapes snap and align to the document grid, click the drop-down on the Standard Toolbar, or press the shortcut CTRL + Y to toggle the feature on and off. When objects snap to a grid, they snap to the grid lines, and you'll feel an even stronger attraction when you move an object close to grid *intersection* points.
- **Snap To Guidelines** Guidelines are covered later in this chapter. To make your objects snap to any type of guideline, choose this option from the drop-down list.
- **Snap To Objects** To have shapes snap to and align with other objects, choose Snap To Objects from the drop-down list; it's faster to remember the shortcut ALT + Z. When objects are set to snap to each other, they can use snap points on either the source (the magnet) or target (the object that's attracted) shape. Snap points are set using options and modes in the Snap To Objects page of the Options dialog (see the later section, "Setting Snap Behavior").
- **Dynamic Guides** This feature in CorelDRAW is akin to *object* snapping. Press ALT + SHIFT + D or use the drop-down menu to toggle the Dynamic Guides on or off. This feature is covered in detail in "Working with Guidelines, Dynamic Guides, and Guide Layers.". Dynamic Guides is *not* found on the Snap menu, but instead under View | Dynamic Guides.

Tutorial Snapping To It

1. You have a web page to design, with six 1-inch squares, three across, two down, with a ½-inch space between them. Don't get out a pocket calculator and don't resort to colorful language—at their defaults, Snap To Grid and Snap To Objects make this task go like a charm. Enable Snap To Grid and Snap To Objects from the Snap To drop-down list and make sure grids are turned on.

2. With the Rectangle Tool, begin close to a grid intersection, and then drag down and to the right until the Property Bar tells you either the height or width of the rectangle is very close to 1". Release the mouse button when your cursor is over a grid intersection.

3. Choose the Pick Tool.

4. Drag the rectangle over to the right until you see one vertical grid separating it from the original square, but don't release the mouse button yet. There are two spaces sidling this line that represent half an inch.

5. Right-click while the left mouse button is still depressed, and then release both buttons to drop a copy. What you've done is duplicate the original square to a new position. This is an important, quick technique for duplicating shapes.

6. Repeat steps 4 and 5 to build the array of evenly spaced squares, as shown in Figure 7-4. Notice that when an object's edge is on, or even close to, the grid when Snap To is turned on, you'll see a tiny blue label indicating the snap to point. You're not limited to shape edges as the origin of a snapping point; setting behavior for snapping origins is covered next in this chapter.

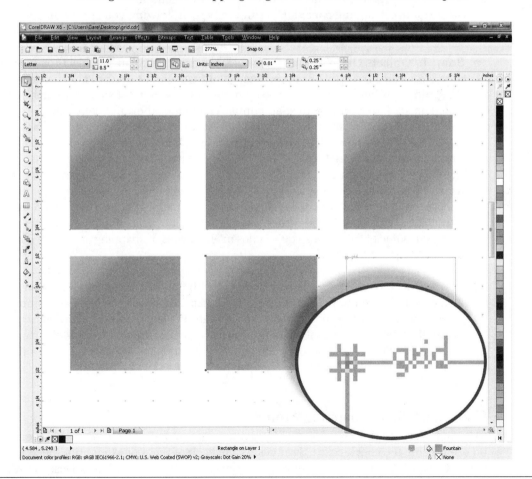

FIGURE 7-4   Duplicating and aligning shapes makes accurate design composition a breeze.

Tip Snapping and snapping behavior aren't limited to the Grid. In fact, you don't even have to have the grid turned on to snap objects to one another. Press ALT+Z and then all your objects are sticky.

Setting Snap Behavior

On the Snap To Objects page of the Options dialog, you can control snapping behavior in precise detail when moving *and* drawing lines or objects. Choose Tools | Options (CTRL + J), click to expand the tree directory under Workspace, and then click Snap To Objects.

The Snap To feature requires that you have a shape and a different object (or guideline or grid intersection) to which it snaps. Proximity to the "magnetic" snapping object is important—you can't have an object snap to a different object that is miles away. However, on the Snap To Objects page, you have control over the *strength* of the magnetism, which, by default, is set to Medium.

To customize snapping behavior to suit the type of drawing you're building, you enable or disable the following features on the Options page:

- **Snap To Objects On** Clicking this check box turns the Snap To Objects feature on or off. You can also do this from the Snap To drop-down list on the Standard Toolbar.
- **Snapping Radius** Use this combo spin box/num field to set snapping sensitivity, based on screen proximity to snap points. The higher the value you enter (measured in pixels), the more "magnetism" your cursor exhibits as it approaches guides and other objects. The default of 10 pixels should serve you well.
- **Show Snap Location Marks** This option is on by default. Snap points are highlighted when your cursor is held over the precise points of a selected object or a target object while moving objects or drawing. When it is activated, you can also choose the Screen Tip option, which identifies the snapping point, highlighted with a text label. With Screen Tips turned on, the blue icons preceding the text labels represent some of the modes you've chosen. The types of snapping are covered next.

Tip When you reposition a shape by dragging it with the Pick Tool, before you release the mouse button to finalize the move, the shape remains in the original position, but a blue, outline version of the shape appears at the intended new location. Use this feature as a visual guide for repositioning objects; this preview of a move offers positioning precision because you can "see through" to objects beneath the chosen object before you release the mouse button.

Choosing Object Snapping Modes

The Mode list includes nine object snap points you can define. You can toggle them on or off using the check boxes. Symbols beside each of the modes identify the current snapping points on different object types. Use the Select All and Deselect All buttons to activate or deactivate all the options in the list quickly.

At times, you might want snapping to occur at certain object points but not others—you can turn specific snap points on or off. Choose options from the modes list to have objects snap to precise points on other objects in the following ways:

- **Nodes**   Use this mode to snap where nodes exist on objects or lines. A *node* is a break point along the path of a shape, and it's indicated by a very small (but noticeable) black outlined square.
- **Intersection**   Choose this mode to activate snapping where the outline paths of two objects cross, including the original position of an object you're moving. *The position where an object is clicked with the cursor determines the point where the intersection snap takes place.*
- **Midpoint**   This mode snaps to a point equidistant between any two nodes on an object or path. To make this choice work, you position the cursor on the midpoint of an object's outline before moving it. A pop-up tells you the cursor is at the midpoint, and you can now drag the object to snap it to another object.
- **Quadrant**   This mode should only be used with ellipses and circles. It causes snapping to one of the four nodes that are created when using the Ellipse Tool (F7).

Below these modes are Tangent and Perpendicular; they work only in combination with Dynamic Guides, which are covered later in the chapter:

- **Tangent**   This mode shows a guide at a *tangent* (a straight line that touches a curve at a point) to a Quadrant snap point. This mode applies only to ellipse objects.
- **Perpendicular**   Choose this mode to show a Dynamic Guide at right angles and to snap to the midpoint between the object and segment nodes.

Finally, the following modes apply snapping regardless of whether other additional snapping points are checked on this Options page:

- **Edge**   Choose this mode to have the outline path of an object act as a Dynamic Guide for snapping to. To make this work, you first click the edge point you wish to snap to another object.
- **Center**   This mode displays the center point (origin) of closed-path objects.
- **Text Baseline**   When snapping, all text objects take on the characteristics of a normal object such as a rectangle and have snapping points for edges, centers, corners, and so on. Additionally, the *text baseline* (the hypothetical line each character appears to rest on) is included in the snapping action.

Using the New Adjustment Guides

New to version X6 is a live, dynamic feature that helps you align an object to a different object almost effortlessly. The Adjustment Guides are activated via the View menu; ALT + SHIFT + A is one of the shortcuts out of the hundreds in CorelDRAW you probably want to memorize. Adjustment Guides appear on the page only when an object is in proximity to another object; CorelDRAW then assumes you want to align the top, bottom, center (or other side) of the selected object. As you can see here, the top alignment guideline becomes visible when the black checker illustration is moved a little around the top edge of the two shapes. Adjustment Guides work with groups of objects, too.

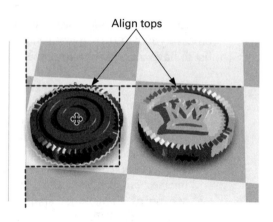

Align tops

By default, Alignment Guides appear as a subtle, pale blue on the page. If this is *too* subtle, press CTRL+J, and then in the Options dialog, choose Workspace | Alignment Guides, and then pick a meatier color. Here, you also have options for how Alignment Guides treat groups and objects within groups, and whether you'd prefer a margin when the guides appear.

Working with Guidelines, Dynamic Guides, and Guide Layers

Like the nonprinting blue pencil marks traditional designers used, CorelDRAW's page guides, Dynamic Guides, and objects you put on a Guides layer don't print, but here the similarity ends. You have the precision only a computer application can offer with CorelDRAW's guides, plus the same speed and ease with guides, as the speed you enjoy with any object you draw on a page.

The following sections are the operator's manual for guides: how to use them and how to customize them.

Using Guidelines

Guidelines placed on your document page extend between the top, bottom, left, and right edges of the document window. Guidelines appear as vertical and horizontal dashed lines, but guidelines can also be *rotated*. In CorelDRAW, *guidelines* are considered unique objects—they have their own properties but are manipulated in many ways like objects you draw.

To view and hide the display of guidelines in your document window, right-click on a blank area of the page and then choose View | Guidelines. By default, a new document doesn't have any guidelines—you need to create them, which is demonstrated next. To have objects *snap* to the guidelines you create, choose Snap To from the drop-down list on the Standard Toolbar, right where you found Snap To Grid earlier in this chapter.

Manipulating Guidelines

The following tips guide you (pun notwithstanding) through the tasks you'll need most often when working with guides:

- Make sure the rulers are visible; they're where many of the guides live. With the Pick Tool selected, but no objects selected, right-click and then choose View | Rulers. Then, using any Toolbox tool you like, click-drag beginning on a ruler, and release the mouse button anywhere in the workspace. Although dropping a guide on the page is most useful, you can certainly create a guide on the pasteboard area to measure and align objects not currently placed on the page.
- To move a placed guide, you need to select the Pick Tool. Then hover the cursor over the guide you'd like to move; when the cursor turns into a double-headed arrow, you're all set and all you need to do is drag the guide.
- If you want to eliminate a guide, hover over it with the Pick Tool until you see the double-headed arrow cursor (to indicate you've selected it), click the guide to confirm the guide is "in focus" in the interface, and then press DELETE or CTRL + X.
- If you need a guide that travels up- or downhill, create a guide first. Next, click to select it, and then click a second time, and you'll see a center and rotation handles. One of the neat things about rotating a guideline is that you can move its center point before dragging the rotation handles to, for example, rotate a guide around the corner of a shape you have on the page. You move a slanted guideline exactly as you do a perfectly horizontal or vertical guide—you click-drag it to reposition it. In the illustration of the lantern, where the design needs shafts of light emanating from a center point that is *not* the default center of a guide that's put into slant mode. No problem; you change the center of rotation and then drag a rotation handle clockwise or counterclockwise.

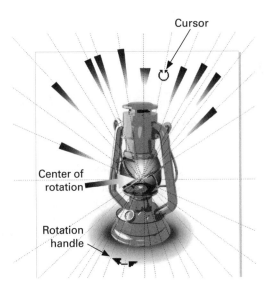

Cursor

Center of
rotation

Rotation
handle

Tip Treat guidelines like any other object on the page. You can move and rotate several guidelines by SHIFT+selecting them. You can also drop a copy of a guideline by right-clicking while repositioning it, like you do to duplicate objects.

Controlling Guideline Properties

If you need several guidelines placed at an exact spacing, you manage all guidelines via the Options dialog (CTRL + J). You'll find separate dialog pages here for controlling the vertical, horizontal, and slanted guidelines. To see these dialogs, right-click on either of the rulers and then choose Guidelines Setup. Additionally, while you have a guideline selected in a document, you can open this dialog by clicking the Guidelines Options button on the Property Bar and by double-clicking a guideline with the Pick Tool.

The Options dialog lists each of the guideline types individually on the left side of the dialog. Click one to select it in the tree directory under Guidelines; here's what the Vertical page looks like when some guides have been defined at 1-inch intervals:

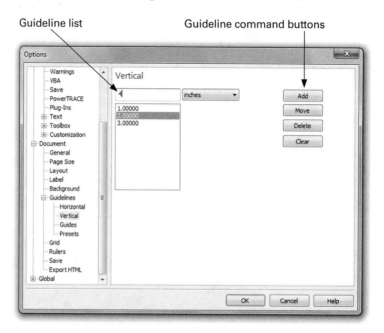

Tip By default, guidelines are a medium blue when added to the workspace, and their highlight color when they're selected is red. However, on the main Guidelines page in the Options dialog, you can change the color of a guideline as well as the color for preset guides. This is quite handy, for example, if you're designing a series of medium blue rectangles. You'd certainly want to choose a contrasting color for the guides in this instance.

Adding, Deleting, and Moving Guidelines

You can adjust guidelines using the features in Guidelines Options. Each dialog contains a listing of the existing guidelines on your document page. Here are steps to perform common tasks:

1. To create a new guideline, enter a value in the top-left num box according to the position where you want the new guideline to be created. Then click the Add button. A new guideline is created where you want it.
2. To move an existing guideline, click it in the list, enter a new value in the top-left num box, and then click Move. The selected guideline has moved, and on the list you can see it's been thoughtful and left a forwarding address.
3. To delete a specific guideline, select it from the list and then click the Delete button. The selected guideline is gone from the page, and your document is immediately updated.
4. To remove all guidelines in the list, click the Clear button. All guidelines are deleted.

Locking and Unlocking Guidelines

All guidelines are editable by default; you can move or delete them using the Pick Tool. But occasionally a guideline that moves accidentally is as welcome as a friend who is holding your ladder sneezing accidentally. You can lock guidelines using Property Bar options and also by right-clicking over a guideline:

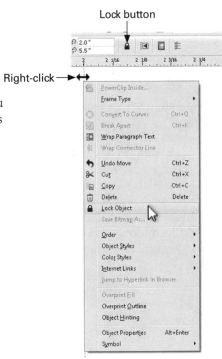

1. To lock an *individual* guideline, click the guideline to select it using the Pick Tool.
2. Using Property Bar options, click the Lock button. The selected guideline is locked, and the guide-specific Property Bar options become unavailable.
3. To unlock a locked guideline, right-click the guideline and choose Unlock Object from the pop-up menu. Your guideline is now unlocked and the guide-specific Property Bar options become available again.

Working with Dynamic Guides

Dynamic Guides are guides that you first set up with axes of rotation (0°, 15°, and so on), and then when you want a guide at a specific angle for aligning or drawing, it appears onscreen. Dynamic Guides can snap the object you're positioning, and they offer onscreen information about the result of a moving or drawing action. When using Dynamic Guides, drawing or moving your cursor over active object snap points will make guides appear temporarily to aid in placing objects and nodes. You can move your cursor along these "sticky" guides, and view snap points, angle values, and distance measurements relative to object snap points (as shown in Figure 7-5).

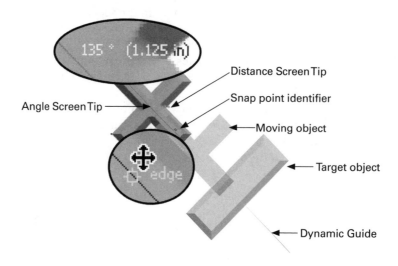

Angle ScreenTip

Distance ScreenTip

Snap point identifier

Moving object

Target object

Dynamic Guide

FIGURE 7-5 From the "sticky" guides, you can view snap points, angle values, and more.

You can also have your cursor snap to specific points along the guide path, based on a customizable tick value. To activate this feature, choose View | Dynamic Guides (ALT + SHIFT + D).

A Dynamic Guide's behavior works in combination with your selected Snap To Objects modes (see "Setting Snap Behavior" in the earlier section), but has a unique set of options that control its behavior. To access these options (see the following illustration), choose Tools | Options (CTRL + J), and click Dynamic Guides under Workspace in the tree directory.

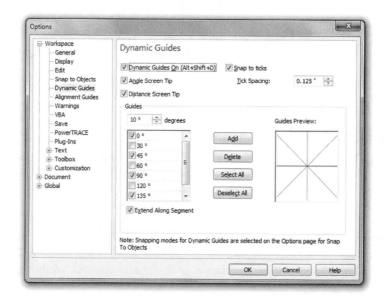

Here's how choosing each option affects the behavior of your Dynamic Guides:

- **Dynamic Guides On**   Click this check box to turn dynamic guides on or off.
- **Angle Screen Tip**   Choose this to display angle values relative to snap points on your object.
- **Distance Screen Tip**   Choose this to display the distance between your cursor position on a guide and the current snap point. Unit measure is based on your currently selected Drawing Units.
- **Snap To Ticks**   This option offers to snap your cursor position to points along the guide according to the value you enter.
- **Guides**   This area opens up many possibilities for angles at which Dynamic Guides appear relative to the active snap point. Clicking a check box activates each of the default angles, which are preset at 30° increments from 0° to 150°, for a total angle of 180°, which effectively covers all possible angles, because Dynamic Guides appear bidirectional. The angle of each guide is displayed in the Guides Preview window on the right of the dialog. Enter a degree value in the num box above the list, and click the Add button to add a new guide. To remove a Dynamic Guide, click a guide in the list, and then click Delete. When a new guide is added, it appears in the list; conversely, when you delete a guide, it's permanently removed from the list.
- **Extend Along Segment**   Choose this to display a guide at the same angle as straight line segments. This option is useful for Bézier and freehand drawing because this makes it easy for you to add new portions to straight lines at a constant angle.

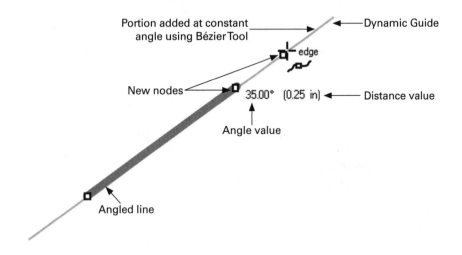

Here is a logo nearing completion by setting up Dynamic Guides at 45° increments. Using the Pen Tool, the Dynamic Guides (set to snapping) show exactly when the tool has reached a 45° angle as well as a 90° angle. Try this feature for yourself; this illustration was accomplished using 25 clicks—precision has seldom been achieved so easily.

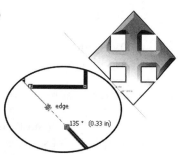

Controlling the Guides Layer

Guides belong to a special layer, named Guides on the Object Manager, reserved just for these assistants. To view the layers in your document, open the Object Manager by choosing either Tools | Object Manager or Window | Dockers | Object Manager. The Guides layer is a Master Page layer; you'll find it with other layers controlling your desktop and grid. By default, all guidelines on the Guides layer are set as Visible, Non-Printable, and Editable. You can change any of these by clicking the symbols to the left of the Guides layer in the Object Manager docker, as shown here:

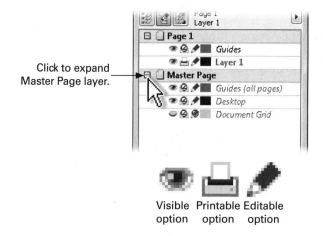

To set all options for a layer at once—including the display color of objects on the Guides layer in the Object Manager docker—right-click the layer name, for example, the Guides layer, and then choose Properties from the pop-up menu. Doing this opens the Guides Properties dialog to reveal further options.

Make an Object a Guideline

You can make almost any drawing shape into a guideline. Going the other way around, you can also turn a guide into a drawing object, and moving any guideline to a drawing layer automatically makes it a printable object. You use the Object Manager docker to move objects between layers. Moving any object to the Guides layer makes a guideline, with all the same properties as a typical guideline, except it doesn't have to be a *line*—spirals and trapezoids make useful guides. After an object becomes a guideline, anything you draw in its proximity snaps to it, as long as the Snap To

Guidelines option is active. Think of the artwork you can clean up and refine when you're tracing over the original with a drawing tool that snaps to the original.

To move an object to the Guides layer, use these steps:

1. Create or select at least one drawing shape that you want to use as a guideline.
2. Open the Object Manager docker by choosing Tools | Object Manager.
3. Expand the tree directories in the Object Manager docker to locate both the Guides layer on the Master Page and the shape you want to make into a guideline so both are in view.
4. In the Object Manager docker, click-and-drag your shape icon (not the shape on the page) from its current page and layer to on top of the Guides layer title on the Master Page. As you drag, your cursor changes to an arrow pointing at representations of layers, indicating the shape's current position as it is dragged. You then release the mouse button and the operation is a success. The following figure also shows a "before and after" of a star shape when you've moved it to the Master Page Guides layer. Unlike guidelines that you drag from rulers, the look of a user-defined guide doesn't have the dashed lines; it's a solid line with no fill.

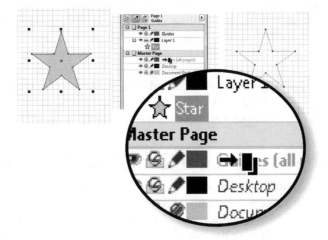

Generally, after moving a shape to the Guides layer, it's a good practice to lock the layer. A guide that moves when you don't intend it to is as useful as a crepe paper umbrella in a storm.

Using Guideline Presets

CorelDRAW's Guidelines feature comes with a group of presets that generate scripts to add guidelines to your document instantly. To use these scripts, press CTRL + J (Options), click to expand the tree directory under Document | Guidelines, and then click Presets. Click Apply Presets—you can add as many as you like in one fell swoop—and you have instant preset guides on the page. Basic Grid is a very useful preset because unlike with the Grid feature, you can *move,* and thus customize, any of the guidelines.

You can also create your *own* preset. To define guidelines that automatically populate the page, choose the User Defined Presets option on the Presets page of the Options dialog. Selecting this displays a collection of options for you to create your own custom margins, columns, or grid guidelines. To activate any or all of these preset guideline effects, click the corresponding options and customize the associated preset values.

Tip To open the Options dialog quickly to the Presets page while you currently have an unlocked Guideline selected, click the Preset Guidelines button on the Property Bar.

Altering Preset Guides and Saving Guides in a Template

Although preset guidelines behave like guidelines you drag from the rulers, if you want to alter the preset arrangement by dragging one with the Pick Tool, the action triggers an *attention box.* This attention box is equivalent in seriousness to the tag you get on new pillows—it's for your own safety and is simply telling you that you're modifying a preset, your own or a Corel preset, for guidelines. You can check the Don't Show Warning Again box to avoid seeing it in the future. Basically, you cannot destroy or modify a Corel guideline preset by moving one of the guides on the page—the option is always there from session to session. And there's really nothing to mess up by altering a user preset guideline on the page after you've created one. There is no saved list of user presets; if you've created a user preset of grids, margins, or columns and want to save the modified or the original arrangement, you choose File | Save As Template. In the future, you can load a fresh new document based on the template, and your guides are all in place.

Working the Dimension Tools and Callouts

If you need to annotate a drawing or an imported bitmap image with dimensions or labels calling out, for example, different parts of a machine, you have the Dimension tools available expressly for this purpose. The lines you create with the four Dimension tools tag the bracketed area with measurement units of your choice and they dynamically update when you scale them. The 3-Point Callout Tool is for adding text to a wide selection of arrowhead lines; you can choose a line style for the connector as well as a width, a type of arrowhead, and any style of typeface that you have installed on your system. The text labels for callouts are also upright regardless of whether you rotate the line, and a Callout Control line can be edited at any time with the Shape Tool (F10).

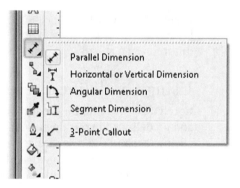

Working with Callouts

When using the 3-Point Callout Tool, you produce two elements: a line composed of two segments (the callout, as it's displayed on the Status Bar), and the control text. Callouts are not bound to an object, they can be moved anywhere on the page, but the text and the line are linked and are not moved independent of one another. You have a number of options on the Property Bar when the tool is active and also when a callout is selected (after one has been drawn):

- **Callout Line Width**   By default, you always begin a callout with a Hairline width in dull green. Do not adjust the width before drawing a line; doing so triggers an attention box that asks whether you want the default line width—for any object you draw, not just callouts—to be changed. Instead, create your callout, and *then* adjust the width while the callout is selected. Because the callout belongs to the general class of line objects in CorelDRAW, you can change the color of the callout line by right-clicking a color well on the Color Palette while the line is selected.
- **Start Arrowhead**   This drop-down list will seem familiar if you've ever applied an arrowhead to a line using the Property Bar. The same basic styles are available as they are on the Start Arrowhead collection. You can even use an arrow *tail* for a callout.
- **Line Style**   Like any other line you draw with the Pen or other drawing tool, the callout can be solid, dashed, a series of dots—choose a style by clicking the pop-up box and then click a style thumbnail.
- **Callout Symbol**   You set the style for the callout text from this pop-up list of presets. The symbol doesn't affect the font—it's a style: a rectangle bounding the text, a straight line butted above or below the text; the symbols add an element of polish to your presentation.
- **Callout Gap**   Sets the distance between the tail of the callout line and the beginning of the text.

After creating a callout, you can select the text with the Pick Tool, right-click to choose Object Properties from the pop-up menu and use the newly enhanced and redesigned Object Properties docker to edit all aspects of the text, from font to size, to color. You can even apply a Gradient fill to your text right from the Object Properties docker, if you want your text to be illegible!

To use the 3-Point Callout Tool:

1. Click-drag to create a point where you want the callout to end (the node will eventually have the arrowhead), move the cursor to where you want the "elbow" of the callout line, and then click.
2. Move your cursor to the place where you want the control text, and then click.
3. Begin typing the callout text.

Tip   For a polished look, hold the CTRL key when creating horizontal callout lines to make them all perfectly level.

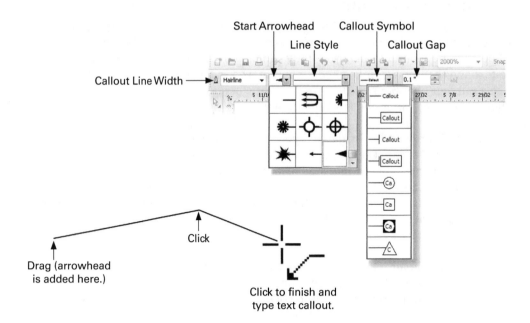

Using the Dimension Tools

Four Dimension Line tools are available, each of which creates a different type of line with a specific purpose. When one of the Dimension tools is selected, the Property Bar displays options to specify the style, precision, and unit values of your displayed dimensions, and to control the display and appearance of the labeling text, covered earlier in the chapter in "Working with Callouts." See Figure 7-6.

- **Dimension Style** This option is used to set decimal, fractional, or standard measuring conventions, the default of which is decimal.
- **Dimension Precision** This option is used to set a level of precision. When using Decimal as the measuring style, precision may be specified up to ten decimal places. When using Fractional, precision may be specified using fractions up to 1/1024 of a selected unit measure.

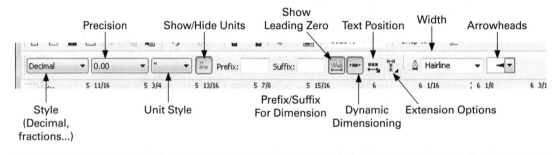

FIGURE 7-6 Dimension lines you create can be modified by the options on the Property Bar.

- **Show/Hide Units**   This is a toggle button. If you don't want units appended to a dimension, leave the button turned off before you create a dimension line.
- **Dimension Units**   This option specifies the measurement unit with which to display your text labels. You can choose any of the unit measures supported by CorelDRAW.
- **Prefix/Suffix For Dimension**   With this feature, you can enter your own text so it appears before and after the text label for your dimension line. A style of merchandise, such as "Plastic" or a "Children only"–sized garment, is an example of what this option is for. Prefix and Suffix text may be any character you want and may be applied before or after the dimension line has been drawn.
- **Show Leading Zero**   When a value of less than one is a resulting dimension, a tenth of an inch, for example, you can add a zero before the decimal, or choose to leave it off by toggling this button off (the nondepressed state). If you have a series of columns of dimension lines, adding the leading zero helps keep the values aligned to the left or right.
- **Dynamic Dimensioning**   This option lets you specify whether your measurement values are updated automatically as the size of the dimension line is changed. By default, this option is turned on for all new dimension lines. If you plan on resizing or changing the drawing scale of your drawing after creating the dimension lines, disabling this option freezes the values being displayed so they remain fixed, whether you resize your dimension lines or not.

Tip   If, for some reason, resizing a drawing applied with dimension lines causes the measured values to change, you can right-click the dimension line and choose Break Dimension Apart from the pop-up menu as a workaround.

- **Text Position**   To specify a position for the text labels applied to your dimension line, choose one of the options from the Text Position drop-down. Choose from Text Above Dimension Line, Text Through Dimension Line, Text Below Dimension Line, Center Text Between Dimension Lines, Force Text Horizontal, and Draw Box Around Text.

Checking Out Dimension Lines

The following tutorial walks you through the technique used to build dimension lines. Let's pretend in the Urn While You Learn.cdr file that the drawing of the antique urn is to size: it's 6¾" tall if it existed in the real world. Your assignment is a response from the antique dealer that she wants to know the overall height of the urn, the height of the neck, and the angle of the bottom decal on the bowl of the urn, as measured from tip of the bowl where it meets the neck. Moreover, she wants the drawing marked with fractional values and thinks metric amounts are for nerds and scientists. People go a little overboard when it comes to cataloguing antiques, but your success is ensured because you have these steps to guide you:

Tutorial   Using Dimension Lines

1. Open Urn While You Learn.cdr, and then select the Horizontal or Vertical Dimension Tool from the Toolbox.
2. On the Property Bar, set the Style to Fractional.
3. Click-drag from the top of the urn to its bottom, where you release the mouse button. With this tool, direction is set to vertical or horizontal by the direction in which you first drag.
4. Move the cursor to the left without holding either mouse button. Doing this defines a position for the control text, so make sure your cursor position is not over the urn drawing.
5. Click. You're done and the number values are called out now.
6. Choose the Parallel Dimension tool; the neck of the bottle is slightly slanted, so this is the appropriate measuring tool.
7. Click-drag from the top of the neck (below the lip) to the part that joins the neck with the bowl; release the mouse button at this point.
8. Move the cursor to the right, away from the drawing, and then single-click to add the dimension line and number value.
9. Choose the Angular Dimension Tool.
10. Click-drag from the junction of the neck and bowl, and release the mouse button when your cursor is to the left of the bottom decal on the bowl.
11. Move your cursor to the right so it touches the right side of the decal.
12. Click. You're not finished yet. You now have the opportunity to set the position of the arc. Move your cursor toward or away from the vertex of the two angular lines, and then click.
13. The measurement probably will not be legible, being a dark color against the dark urn. No problem: with the Pick Tool, select the number value and then click the white color well on the Color Palette. Figure 7-7 shows the completed assignment.

Segment Dimensions

Whether you need to discover a value for technical comparison's sake, or want to make sure a part of a personal illustration is of an exact length, the Segment Dimension Tool is your ticket. This tool measures the distance between nodes on a path, whether the nodes are on a straight line or a curve.

To use this tool, you first select a line in your composition with the Pick Tool. Choose the Segment Dimension Tool, and then marquee-select the two nodes you want to discover the distance between. Move the cursor away from the selection to create handles that bound the selected nodes and then click.

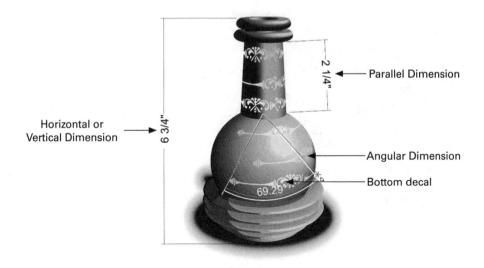

Parallel Dimension

Horizontal or
Vertical Dimension

Angular Dimension

Bottom decal

2 1/4"

6 3/4"

69.29°

FIGURE 7-7 Use dimension lines to annotate drawing and images quickly and accurately.

An Exercise in Dimensioning to Scale

All of the preceding info and examples are fine in theory; now, you're going to put the theory into practice in the next tutorial. You've been handed a CorelDRAW document with a photo in it. Your boss—or any other person who is intimidating—wants the parts of the toy water pistol called out, but here's the catch: the image of the water pistol is *not* 1:1. So how does one measure all the parts of a 7½"-long toy that is 5¾" on the CorelDRAW page?

As follows!

Tutorial Drawing Scale, Windows Calculator, and Dimension Lines

1. Open The Neptune Soaker.cdr.
2. For laughs, choose the Horizontal or Vertical Dimension Line Tool and drag it from the beginning of the body of the water pistol to the right and then release the mouse button at the end of the water plug, the yellow piece of plastic to the left of the red cap. Write this value down.
3. The boss says the body is 7½". In this example, the body length should be 5.76". You launch Windows Calculator (or use the physical home version in your workshop). 5.76 divided by 7.5 = 1.302. Adjust this document's Drawing Scale to this value, as you recall from the example earlier in this chapter in "Editing Drawing Scales."

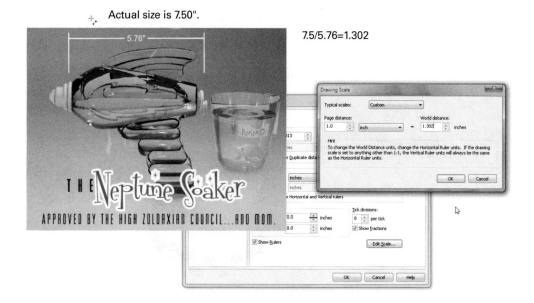

FIGURE 7-8   Adjust the World Distance scale to make measuring areas in photos and drawing accurate to scale.

4. Right-click on a ruler, choose Ruler Setup, and then in the Ruler Options box, click Edit Scale.
5. Page Distance should be 1 inch. Type **1.302** in the World Distance field, and then click OK to apply this new scale. See Figure 7-8.
6. Use the Horizontal or Vertical, the Parallel, and the Angular Dimension Tools to measure anything asked of you in this tutorial or your own drawing.

As Figure 7-9 shows, when Fraction styles are used in combination with reassigning line and fill colors for text, you have a highly detailed, picture-perfect presentation for the manufacturing department and even print ads.

You've seen in this chapter that in addition to everyday paths and closed objects, there are also lines for labeling and organizing objects. You've also learned about how to steer the power of CorelDRAW's rulers to suit your own design needs. You can now use those old-fashioned wooden rulers you have around the house for what they're *meant* for: to stir house paint.

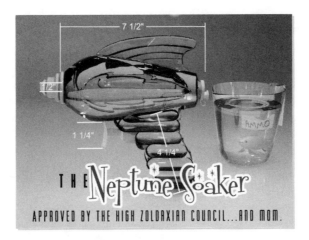

FIGURE 7-9   When accuracy counts, CorelDRAW's Dimension tools work with your graphics to give the audience a complete picture.

Come explore the basic shapes you can create—and then measure—in Chapter 8, as you get a feel for the speed and ease of CorelDRAW's preset shapes. There are a *lot* of them, so get set to take the next step in creating visually complex illustrations.

8

Creating Basic Shapes, Applying Transformations

You have to begin *somewhere* with the DRAW part of CorelDRAW—and this is the chapter. The creative process within this program usually follows: you build objects that you then customize and refine through fancy fills and elegant outlines covered in later chapters. Therefore, it's important to first know the steps to create simple geometric shapes and to know the basic editing moves to create exactly the shape you want to fill and stroke.

Download and extract all the files from the Chapter08.zip archive to follow the tutorials in this chapter.

CorelDRAW's Smart Drawing Tool

Even if you use a graphics tablet and stylus, you're still drawing freehand, and using a mouse introduces still more flubs when it comes to freehand drawing. Fortunately, the Smart Drawing Tool takes the guesswork out of drawing polygonal and rounded objects—in a nutshell, you sketch *an approximation* of what you intend, tune the options for the Smart Drawing Tool based on your first drawing, and in a jiffy you have a precise object of the proportions you need. Pictured here on the Toolbox, the Smart Drawing Tool instantly translates rough drawings into shapes you'd usually consider drawing with the Rectangle Tool or Ellipse Tool—or with other tools that require more effort and skill.

When you chose the Smart Drawing Tool, the Property Bar displays Shape Recognition Level and smoothing options (shown next) for setting the sensitivity CorelDRAW uses in translating your roughs into precise shapes.

Recognition and smoothing options

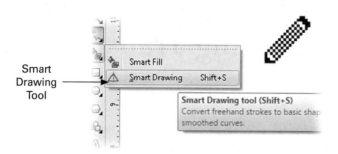

You control how precisely your sketch shape is translated into shapes by setting these options:

- **Shape Recognition Level**   This option sets how precisely your sketched shape is matched to a recognizable shape and can be set to one of five levels ranging from Lowest (sketched shapes are not easily recognized) to Highest (sketched shapes are easily recognized), with Medium being the default; None turns off the feature.
- **Smart Smoothing Level**   After you've completed a sketch by releasing the mouse button, a level of node smoothing is applied to make object recognition more, or less, precise. This option gives you total control over the smoothing action, much in the same fashion as using the Reduce Nodes spin box on the Property Bar when a path is selected with the Shape Tool. Choose from five options ranging from Lowest (less smoothing applied) to Highest (more smoothing applied), with Medium as the default; None turns off the feature.

Tip You can control the delay time interval between the moment you release the mouse button and stop drawing to the moment CorelDRAW determines a recognizable shape. By reducing the delay time, you can sketch several separate lines or shapes one after the other, and CorelDRAW then recognizes them as a single compound path. Double-click the Smart Drawing Tool icon on the Toolbox to open Options. The *Drawing Assistance Delay* slider can be set between 0 and 2.0 seconds. The higher you set the delay time, the more time you'll have to keep drawing before CorelDRAW steps in to assist you.

Try the following steps to immediately get a leg up on drawing flawless objects:

Tutorial CAD: CorelDRAW-Assisted Drawing

1. Choose the Smart Drawing Tool and use a click-drag action to sketch the shape of a square or rectangle. Try to keep the sides of the shape vertical and horizontal as you draw; if the square shape looks like a melted ice cube, don't worry! When you release the mouse button, CorelDRAW automatically translates your sketch into a rectangle shape.
2. Choose the Pick Tool next and check your Status Bar display. The shape you sketched is specified as a Rectangle, and the Property Bar shows options associated with shapes created with the Rectangle Tool, including the rounded-corner options. Try dragging a corner node to make the rectangle a rounded-corner rectangle.
3. Choose the Smart Drawing Tool again, and sketch the shape of an oval or circle. Try to keep the shape parallel to the page orientation; however, CorelDRAW can also intelligently refine a sketch of a rotated oval. On releasing the mouse button, CorelDRAW translates your sketched shape into an ellipse shape.
4. Choose the Pick Tool and check your Status Bar. The shape you sketched is specified as an Ellipse, and the Property Bar shows options associated with shapes created with the Ellipse Tool, such as the Ellipse, Arc, and Pie properties.

Tip You can alter your sketched shapes on-the-fly using the Smart Drawing Tool to backtrack and erase the path you're drawing. Hold SHIFT as the modifier key to reverse and erase. Release the SHIFT key to resume sketching normally.

The shapes you draw can also have special editing properties:

- Rectangles and ovals produced by using the Smart Drawing Tool become CorelDRAW objects, with identical editing properties to the objects you draw with the Rectangle and ellipse tools.
- Trapezoids and parallelograms produced with the Smart Drawing Tool become Perfect Shapes, explained in a moment.
- Other shapes you draw—triangles, arrows, stair steps, and so on—become regular objects, but the Smart Drawing tool intelligently smooths out curves and straightens nearly straight line segments.
- *Perfect Shapes* are a special category of CorelDRAW objects, and they have special properties. They feature *glyph* nodes (by default a red-filled diamond)—which are different from regular nodes along a path—and the nodes can be manipulated to modify the shape without destroying any of its unique geometric properties. See Figure 8-1.

Sketched shapes   Translated shapes

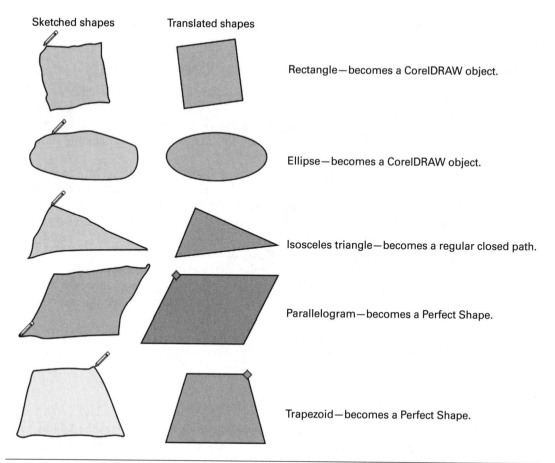

Rectangle—becomes a CorelDRAW object.

Ellipse—becomes a CorelDRAW object.

Isosceles triangle—becomes a regular closed path.

Parallelogram—becomes a Perfect Shape.

Trapezoid—becomes a Perfect Shape.

FIGURE 8-1 Perfect Shapes retain their properties even when you extensively edit their appearance.

Try these next steps to create variations on the basic appearance of a Perfect Shape:

Tutorial Reshaping a Perfect Shape

1. Using the Smart Drawing Tool, sketch the shape of a trapezoid (refer to Figure 8-1; two sides are parallel, the other two sides converge). On releasing the mouse button, CorelDRAW translates your sketch into a Perfect Shape.
2. Choose the Pick Tool and then look at the Status Bar. The shape is identified as a Perfect Shape, a special category of shape. Use the Shape Tool next to click-drag the glyph node. You'll see that the parallel sides remain parallel, and the converging sides slope away and toward each other. By duplicating this Perfect Shape, you can edit with the Shape Tool and create an array of trapezoids, all different in appearance but all editable indefinitely, and all retain the geometric structure of a Perfect Shape.

Tip See "Using Perfect Shape Tools," later in this chapter, to learn more about creating Perfect Shapes and manipulating glyph nodes.

The Smart Drawing Tool helps you quickly draw and translate a variety of sketched shapes into different, geometrically flawless shapes more efficiently than using multiple tools. Each of the translated shapes has its own special properties, which you'll learn in detail in the sections that follow.

Using the Rectangle Tool and Property Bar

The Rectangle Tool is simple enough to use, but it doesn't just create a four-sided, right-angle polygon—it creates a rectangle that has *special properties* in CorelDRAW, and these special properties extend to rectangles drawn with the Smart Drawing Tool. You'll find the Rectangle Tool in the Toolbox; you can quickly select it by pressing the F6 shortcut key.

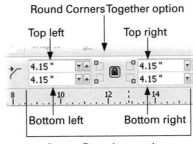

Corner Roundness values

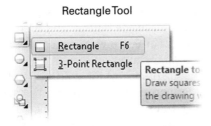

Tip You can also choose the Rectangle Tool while any shape creation tool is selected (the Ellipse Tool, for example) by right-clicking a blank space on the document page and choosing Create Object | Rectangle from the pop-up menu.

Drawing a Rectangle

To create a rectangle, choose the Rectangle Tool from the Toolbox, and click-diagonal-drag in any direction to define its corner positions. The act of click-dragging begins by defining the first two corners; as you drag, the corner positions can be redefined, depending on where your cursor is on the page; and then before you release the mouse button, you've defined the position for the remaining two rectangle corners.

While the Rectangle Tool is selected, notice that the cursor is a crosshair with a small rectangle shape at its lower right. As you click-drag using the cursor, you'll also notice that the Status Bar and Property Bar show coordinates, width, and height properties of your new object shape.

Setting Rectangle Corner Properties

Corner Roundness is one of three different effects you can apply and dynamically edit when you're into rectangles. Corner Roundness, as well as the *Scallop* and *Chamfer* corner styles, can be applied to a rectangle from a value of 0 to about one half the overall length of one of the rectangle's sides. If you think about this one, a 2" rectangle *can't* have more than a 1" rounded corner on each side! The Corner Roundness amount can be changed anytime while the shape remains a native rectangle; that is, it has not been converted to curves. By typing **0** into any of the size boxes while the rectangle is selected, you remove the corner style. Corner Roundness, Scallop, and Chamfer can be set uniformly for all corners (the default) or independently when the Edit Corners Together lock option is in the unlocked state.

Tip Double-clicking the Rectangle Tool button in the Toolbox instantly creates a rectangle border around your current document page.

While a rectangle is selected, use any of the following operations to change corner properties according to your needs:

- Click the type of corner style you want on the Property Bar, and then either type in the size for the corner values, or drag the elevator buttons up or down to adjust the size of the corners.
- Set your rectangle's corners manually using the Shape Tool by first unlocking the Edit Corners Together toggle button, and then CTRL+dragging any corner control point away from its corner (toward a side that makes up the rectangle). Enabling Edit Corners Together causes all corners to be rounded or scalloped in an equal amount by dragging on any of the control points.
- Use the Object Properties docker; press ALT+ENTER, click the Rectangle tab, and then edit any property you so choose. If the Object Properties docker doesn't display any information after opening it, click the Roll-down Docker button on its title bar.

Figure 8-2 shows rectangles with different types of corners; this is an ideal feature for building interesting signs, borders, and frames for documents.

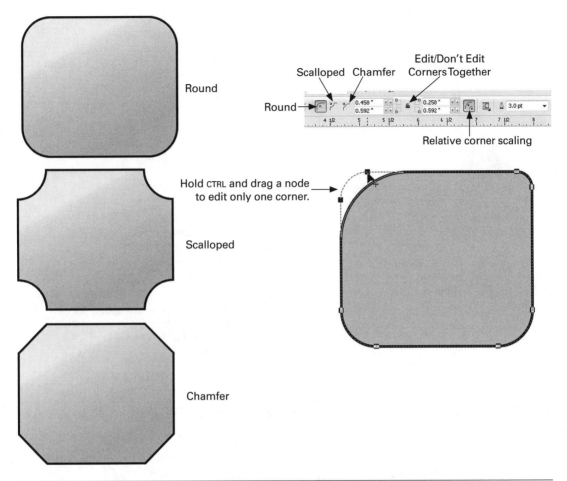

FIGURE 8-2   Rectangles can have almost any type of corner you can imagine.

Creating 3-Point Rectangles

If you want to create a rectangle and have it rotated all in one fell swoop, use the *3-Point Rectangle Tool*. You'll find it grouped with the Rectangle Tool in the Toolbox.

Using this tool, you can draw new rectangles at precise angles, as shown in Figure 8-3. The rectangle you create is a native rectangle shape, so you can round its corners and manipulate it as any other shape.

To create a rectangle using the 3-Point Rectangle Tool, click-drag—clicking sets the first point of the rectangle and the subsequent distance you drag determines both the angle and length of the rectangle. As soon as you release the mouse button, you move your cursor (without clicking—this is called *hovering*) to determine the height of the rectangle. A final click seals the deal and you now have a rectangle. You can now round its corners and perform other operations on your work.

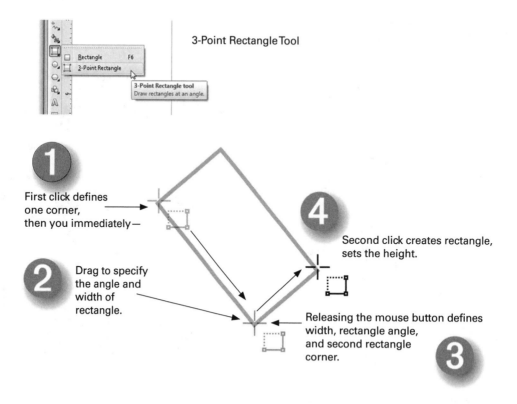

3-Point Rectangle Tool

① First click defines one corner, then you immediately—

② Drag to specify the angle and width of rectangle.

④ Second click creates rectangle, sets the height.

③ Releasing the mouse button defines width, rectangle angle, and second rectangle corner.

FIGURE 8-3 Draw new rectangles at precise angles with the 3-Point Rectangle Tool.

Constraining Shapes While Drawing

Just like most Windows applications, CorelDRAW takes advantage of keyboard modifier keys you can use to modify shapes as you draw them. Holding modifier keys as you click-drag various tool cursors makes drawing your new object shape easier, gives you more options at your cursor tip, and makes you work faster. These shortcuts are worth committing to memory:

- Hold CTRL while drawing new objects to constrain their shape to equal width and height.
- Hold SHIFT while drawing new objects to draw their shape from the center outward. This is particularly useful, for example, when you need a rectangle whose center is positioned at a specific point on the page.
- Hold CTRL+SHIFT while drawing new objects to constrain their shape from the center origin *and* to equal width and height simultaneously.

Here's a trick to help you remember which is which: associate CTRL with "constrain" and SHIFT with "additional or added feature."

Using the Ellipse Tool and Property Bar

Ellipses are a staple of commercial design work. An ellipse is essentially a circular shape that is not perfect. The Ellipse Tool can be used to draw both perfect circles and ellipses, but in CorelDRAW, an ellipse shape has additional special properties, just like a rectangle can be a round-cornered rectangle. Ellipse shapes can be edited to create dramatically new shapes while retaining their elliptical properties. In contrast, an oval shape drawn with, for example, the Bezier Tool, always remains an oval.

Ellipses are easy enough to draw with the Ellipse Tool and can be set in several different states: as oval or circular closed-paths, pie wedges, and arcs. *Pie wedges* are the portions of an ellipse—like a single slice of a pie or, conversely, a whole pie with a slice removed. *Arc shapes* are the open-path equivalent of pies.

To create an ellipse, choose the Ellipse Tool, shown at the top-left of Figure 8-4, from the Toolbox or press F7, followed by a click-drag in any direction.

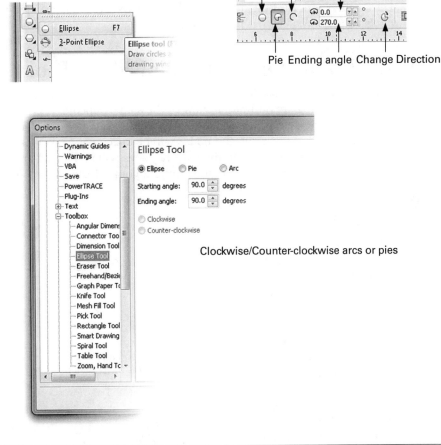

FIGURE 8-4   The Ellipse Tool produces an object you can edit to make different shapes.

While the Ellipse Tool is selected, the Property Bar shows ellipse-specific options, shown in Figure 8-4, that enable you to control the state of your new ellipse shape before or after it has been created. Choose Ellipse, Pie, or Arc. A complement is reserved for Pie and Arc shapes: for example, if you specify a 15° pie wedge, clicking the Change Direction icon changes the shape to a 345° wedge. Additionally, if you want a Pie or Arc to travel in a different path direction, double-click the Ellipse Tool icon on the Toolbox, which takes you to Options, where you can choose clockwise or counterclockwise path directions. Figure 8-4 shows your options and the features on the Property Bar when the tool is chosen.

Tip You can also choose the Ellipse Tool while any tool is selected by right-clicking in an empty space on your document page and choosing Create Object | Ellipse from the pop-up menu.

Drawing an Ellipse

Let's walk before running; before creating pie and arc shapes, begin with creating circles and ovals. Start with these brief steps:

Tutorial   Round One with the Ellipse Tool

1. Choose the Ellipse Tool (F7) and use a click-diagonal-drag action in any direction. As you drag, an outline preview of the shape appears. An ellipse shape has two overlapping control nodes (so onscreen it looks like only one node); if you drag down and left or right, the nodes will be located at 12 o'clock. Conversely, if you drag up and left or right, the control nodes will be located at 6 o'clock.
2. Release the mouse button to complete your ellipse shape creation.

Controlling Ellipse States

All ellipses have two control points (*nodes*—a start and an end) that overlap each other and are visible when the ellipse is selected. When these control points are separated, they create either a pie or an arc state, and each control point determines either the *starting* or *ending angle* of the pie or arc.

You can separate these control points either by using Property Bar options or by dragging the points using the Shape Tool. Dragging *inside* the ellipse's shape creates the Ellipse Pie state. Dragging *outside* the shape creates the Ellipse Arc state, as shown here.

Ellipse Tool cursor

Dragging inside creates the pie shape.

Dragging outside creates the arc shape.

Tip Even though pies and arcs appear as if sections or path parts are missing, the portions are still there. They're just hidden from view.

To draw a new pie or arc without drawing an oval-shaped ellipse first, click either the Pie or Arc button on the Property Bar before you start drawing. You can also switch any selected ellipse between these states using these buttons. By default, all pies and arcs are applied with a default Starting Angle of 0° and a default Ending Angle of 270°. Starting and Ending Angles are based on degrees of rotation from –360 to 360°; this is counter-clockwise in orientation.

Tip To set the default properties for all new ellipse shapes, double-click the Ellipse Tool on the Toolbox; doing this opens the Ellipse Tool in the Options box. Choose an Ellipse type, and then each new ellipse shape you create will be created according to the options you select, including the state of the new ellipse—Ellipse, Pie, or Arc—and the starting and ending angles for each.

Creating 3-Point Ellipses

The *3-Point Ellipse Tool* is the key for creating ellipses while setting a rotation angle (perfect circles show no possible rotation angle; we're talking ovals here). You'll find it grouped with the Ellipse Tool in the Toolbox, as shown at the top in Figure 8-5. This tool's operation is very much like the 3-Point Rectangle Tool.

3-Point Ellipse Tool

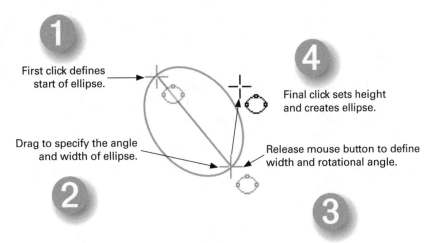

1 First click defines start of ellipse.

2 Drag to specify the angle and width of ellipse.

3 Release mouse button to define width and rotational angle.

4 Final click sets height and creates ellipse.

FIGURE 8-5 You can create ellipses at precise angles using the 3-Point Ellipse Tool.

You can create ellipses at precise angles without needing to create and then rotate an existing one, as shown in Figure 8-5. The shape you create is still an ellipse with all associated properties, such as optional Pie and Arc states.

To create an ellipse using the 3-Point Ellipse Tool, choose the 3-Point Ellipse Tool, click to set the beginning point of the ellipse, and then drag to specify its width and rotational angle. Release the cursor and then position your cursor where you want the maximum height of the oval defined. Click, and your ellipse is complete.

Using Polygons and the Property Bar

The *Polygon Tool* (the shortcut is Y) is unique to the category of vector drawing software; competing applications offer a polygon tool, but CorelDRAW's Polygon Tool produces shapes that can be edited—making dynamic changes, just like CorelDRAW rectangles and ellipses. The shapes you create with the Polygon Tool can have as few as 3 or as many as 500 points and sides; by default, all polygon sides are straight paths. You'll find the Polygon Tool, together with the Spiral, Graph Paper, and other group tools, on the Property Bar. While the Polygon Tool is selected, the Property Bar offers the number of sides for the polygon you'll draw.

Drawing and Editing Polygons

The trick to creating symmetrical, complex shapes with the Polygon Tool lies in the *editing* of these shapes. Read Chapter 11 before getting too involved with the Polygon Tool because you really need to know how to use the Shape Tool in combination with the Property Bar to make the most of a polygon shape.

To create a default polygon, you use the same click-diagonal-drag technique as you use with the Rectangle and Ellipse Tools. This produces a symmetrical shape made up of straight paths. Because you'll often want a shape more elegant than something that looks like a snack food, it helps to begin a polygon shape by holding SHIFT and CTRL while dragging: doing this produces a perfectly symmetrical (not distorted) polygon, beginning at your initial click point traveling outward. Therefore, you have the shape positioned exactly where you want it and can begin redefining the shape.

Next, you can see the Polygon Tool cursor and a symmetrical default polygon. Because the Polygon Tool can be used to make star-shaped polygons, control points govern the points and nodes in-between them that control the curves between points, and when you edit a polygon, the position of these points can be reversed. These control points have no control handles because they connect straight path segments. However, in the following tutorial, you'll get a jump start on Chapter 11's coverage of paths and the Shape Tool, and really get down in very few steps to creating a dynamite polygon shape through editing.

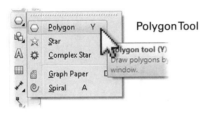

Polygon Tool

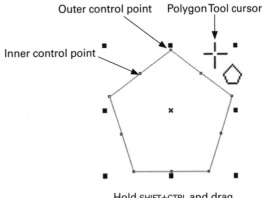

Outer control point   Polygon Tool cursor

Inner control point

Hold SHIFT+CTRL and drag.

Here is a brief tour of how to create and then edit a polygon to design any symmetric object you can imagine, and a few unimaginable ones:

Tutorial Reshaping a Polygon

1. Choose the Polygon Tool from the Toolbox, and before you do anything else, set the number of sides to 12 on the Property Bar.

2. Hold CTRL to constrain the shape to a symmetrical one, and then click-diagonal drag on the page. Release the mouse button after you have a polygon that's about 3" wide.

3. To better see what you're doing, left-click over the Color Palette with the polygon selected to fill it. By default, polygons are created with a small stroke width and no fill.

4. Choose the Shape Tool from the Toolbox. Click any of the control points on the polygon to select it, but don't drag yet. Hold CTRL and then drag outward to constrain the movement of the cursor so the polygon doesn't take on a lopsided appearance (although you can create interesting polygons by dragging in any way without holding CTRL). You should have a star shape now, as shown here.

5. Notice that on the Property Bar you now have a lot of icons that control how line segments pass through nodes and whether the segments are straight or curved. Click any line segment that makes up the polygon; your cursor should have a wiggly line at lower right, as shown here, meaning you've clicked on a line. Then click the Convert To Curve icon on the Property Bar, converting not only the line, but also all the lines in the polygon that are symmetrical to the chosen line to a curve.

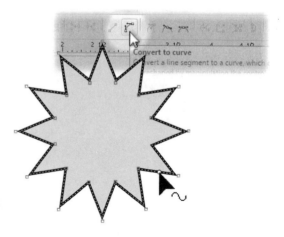

6. Drag the line you converted to a curve. Doing this, as you can see here, creates a very interesting and complex symmetrical shape, and you can now see the control lines for the curves segment and manipulate the control handles to further embellish your creation.

Figure 8-6 shows but a few creative examples of polygon editing: from gears to those vinyl flowers you put over shower stall cracks; you have immense design power at your disposal with the Polygon Tool.

Tip After editing a polygon, you can change the number of sides. For example, you've created a 12-petal flower polygon, and your client wants only 8 petals. You select the edited shape with the Pick Tool and then decrease the number of sides using the spin box on the Property Bar.

FIGURE 8-6   Here are shapes you can create using a polygon object and the Shape Tool.

Stars and Complex Stars

In CorelDRAW, you have variations on polygons at the ready in the same group as the Polygon Tool. The Star Tool creates pointy polygons with anywhere from 3 to 500 points. The Complex Star Tool creates a number of combined polygons to make a star shape; you can create interesting symmetrical shapes by filling a complex star—the result contains both filled and vacant polygon areas as the component paths intersect one another.

Working with the Star Tool

The Star Tool produces objects by using the click-diagonal-drag mouse technique; CTRL constrains the shape to symmetry, SHIFT lets you drag from the center outward, and CTRL-SHIFT dragging creates symmetrical stars beginning at the initial click point traveling outward.

On the Property Bar, when you chose the Star Tool, you have options for the number of points for the star and the "pointiness" (sharpness) of the resulting object—how severe the indents are between points. At a setting of 1, the star object becomes not at all pointy—you'll see that it looks quite like a Polygon Tool object. So, if you can make a star using the Polygon Tool, why would you ever choose the Star Tool? The answer is because the geometric structure of a star shape is always perfectly symmetrical. Although you can use the Shape Tool to tune the sharpness of a Star Tool object's points manually, the angle between points is always consistent. In the illustration below, you can see a Star Tool object compared with a Polygon Tool object that has been clumsily edited. You can't perform this goof with the Star Tool; its interior angles are always mirrored and symmetrical.

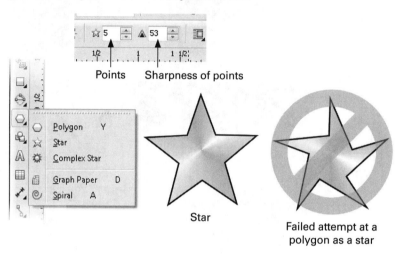

Using the Complex Star Tool

Think of the kaleidoscope images you enjoyed as a child (or still do!) when you choose the Complex Star Tool: with only an edit or two using the Shape Tool, you can create mesmerizing symmetrical shapes, unlike with any other tool in CorelDRAW.

To use the tool, you know the drill if you've read this far! You click-diagonal-drag to create a shape; by default, the Complex Star has 9 points with a value of 2 on a 1- to 3-point sharpness scale (available to define on the Property Bar, see following illustration).

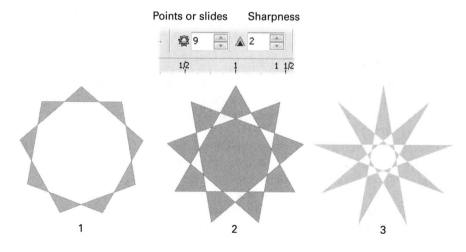

CTRL, SHIFT, and CTRL + SHIFT perform the same modifiers as they do with other shapes. One unique characteristic of Complex Stars is that they have two control points: one for the inner, negative space, and one for the points. When you edit using the Shape Tool, holding CTRL constrains your edits on the control points to symmetry, but if you want a spiral treatment of a Complex Star, don't hold CTRL and drag any way you like on both the inner and outer control points. You'll probably want to assign a fill to a Complex Star as your first edit because unfilled Complex Stars aren't as visually interesting. The following illustration shows what you can create by moving the inner control point to outside the outer control point. Imagine the snowflake patterns you can build; and like snowflakes, no two Complex Stars are alike!

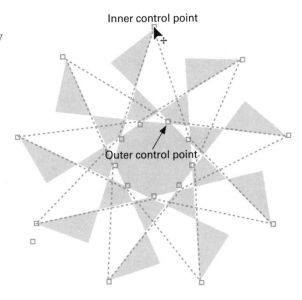

Inner control point

Outer control point

Figure 8-7 shows other examples of simply playing with the Shape Tool on a complex Star object. Also try assigning a wide white outline property to a Complex Star to create still more variations.

FIGURE 8-7   Complex Stars are fast to create, fun to look at, and can serve many design purposes.

Using the Spiral Tool

With the Spiral Tool (press A as the keyboard shortcut), you can create circular-shaped paths that would be tedious, if not impossible, to create manually. Spiral objects are composed of a single open path that curves in a clockwise or counterclockwise direction. They can also be designed to expand in even segment distances or in *increasing* distances as the spiral path segments travel away from its center (called a *logarithmic* function). You find the Spiral Tool in the Toolbox, grouped with the Polygon and Graph Paper Tools.

Spiral Tool options share space in the Property Bar (shown next) with options for the Graph Paper Tool and include Spiral Revolutions, Symmetrical, and Logarithmic Spiral modes, and a Spiral Expansion slider.

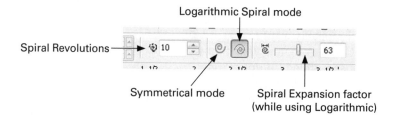

The objects you create can have between 1 and 100 revolutions, each of which is equal to one complete rotation around its center point. The direction of the revolutions is set according to the click-diagonal-drag action when you create the initial shape, as shown in Figure 8-8.

Note Spiral objects are not dynamic; no special editing or redefining is possible once the spiral has been created. This means you must set their properties before they are created. Other than using the Pick or Shape Tool to edit their size or shape, spiral objects are a "done deal."

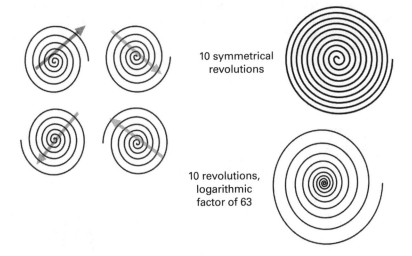

10 symmetrical
revolutions

10 revolutions,
logarithmic
factor of 63

FIGURE 8-8   The direction of your Spiral Revolutions is determined by your initial click-drag direction.

By default, all new spiral objects are set to Symmetrical. If you choose Logarithmic, the Spiral Expansion slider becomes available. Here's how the modes and options affect the spiral objects you can create.

- **Symmetrical vs. Logarithmic**   A Symmetrical spiral object appears with its spiral revolutions evenly spaced from the center origin to the outer dimensions of the object. To increase or decrease the rate at which the curves in your spiral become smaller or larger as they reach the object's center, you may want to use the Logarithmic method. The term *logarithmic* refers to the acceleration (or deceleration) of the spiral revolutions. To choose this option, click the Logarithmic Spiral button on the Property Bar before drawing your shape.
- **Logarithmic Expansion option**   While the Logarithmic Spiral mode is selected, the Logarithmic Expansion slider becomes available—as well as a value field you can type in—and you can set this rate based on a percentage of the object's dimensions. Logarithmic Expansion may be set from 1 to 100 percent. A Logarithmic Expansion setting of 1 results in a symmetrical spiral setting, whereas a setting of 100 causes dramatic expansion. If you need a shape that is reminiscent of a nautilus, increase the Logarithmic Expansion to 50 or so.

Using the Graph Paper Tool

The Graph Paper Tool (the shortcut is D) is used to create a grid containing hundreds (even thousands) of rectangles—an emulation of graph paper. Graph paper is invaluable in chart-making as well as for artistic uses. You find the Graph Paper Tool, shown at left, grouped with the Polygon and Spiral Tools. This tool's options on the Property Bar let you set the number of rows and columns for your new graph paper object. As with the Spiral Tool, you must set options *before* drawing your graph paper object; a graph paper object cannot be edited dynamically.

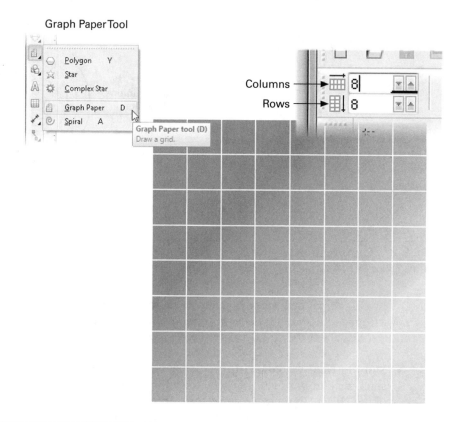

Tip The rectangles in a Graph Paper group are, in fact, *native rectangles*; you can ungroup the rectangles (CTRL+U) and then make scallop and rounded rectangles on each and every one of the graph paper component objects.

Let's explore one of the many creative ways to create and use the group of rectangles the Graph Paper Tool builds for you. This next assignment uses the Add Perspective Effect to make a dimensional chess board beneath a drawing of chess pieces and one or two tricky editing techniques, but you're guided step by step all the way. Watch how you can dramatically improve the look of a composition just by using the Graph Paper Tool and some minor editing:

Tutorial   Power-Drawing a Grid with Graph Paper

1. Open Chess set.cdr. A drawing has been created for you, and your assignment is to put a chess board behind the drawing.
2. Choose the Graph Paper Tool from the Toolbox or press D to select it.
3. Using Property Bar options, set the number of rows and columns to **8** for your new graph paper object.
4. Using a click-diagonal drag action, hold CTRL and drag to create the new object. Release the mouse button when the graph paper fills the height of the page. Now press SHIFT + PAGEDOWN to put the graph paper object behind the chess pieces.
5. Look at the Status Bar; it tells you that a group of 64 objects is selected. All the graph paper objects can take on a new fill and outline color in one fell swoop: click a medium gray color well on the Color Palette, and then right-click white to make the outlines white.
6. Because the objects are grouped, you have no outline pen width option on the Property Bar, and the white grouting the outlines represent in this chess board are a little too thin. No problem: with the Pick Tool, right-click over the grouped objects and choose Properties to display the Object Properties Docker. ALT + ENTER is the shortcut. Set the outline width to 2 points now, as shown in Figure 8-9.

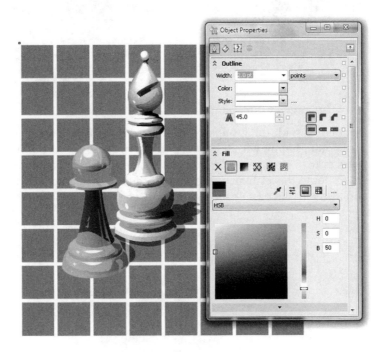

FIGURE 8-9   Change the outline properties of a group of objects using the Object Properties docker.

7. Choose Effects | Add Perspective. You'll see a red dashed outline with four control points surround the group, but it's not editing time yet to apply a perspective.

8. With the Pick Tool, click the selected graph paper object to reveal the rotate and skew handles. While holding CTRL to constrain rotation, rotate the grouped rectangles by 45 degrees. By default, CorelDRAW constrains rotation to 15-degree increments; therefore, three points of resistance as you CTRL-drag does the trick.

9. Choose the Shape Tool (F10); the grouped shapes again feature the Perspective control points.

10. Choose the top control point and then drag it down until you have a chess board in perspective. You will know when you've dragged enough—the chess pieces drawing will visually fit right into place.

Hold CTRL and rotate 45 degrees.   Use the Shape Tool to drag the top node down.

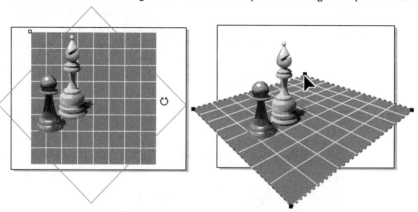

11. Optionally, with the grouped chess board in its final perspective aspect (make sure you're happy with it because this step removes its editing properties), press CTRL + U (Arrange | Ungroup). Fill every other rectangle with a lighter color; doing this enhances the look of the chess board, the overall illustration, and also lets the cast shadows from the chess pieces become more apparent.

Tip Holding CTRL while you drag constrains the shape of the graph paper object, but not the cells in the graph. Therefore, you could, for example, create a five-row, two-column graph whose overall proportions are square, but the cells within the graph paper object are distorted to rectangles.

Using Perfect Shape Tools

CorelDRAW gives you the power to create objects called *Perfect Shapes.* This group of tools helps you to draw shapes, many of which would be a challenge to draw manually and some of which can be dynamically edited.

Perfect Shapes often feature one or more control points called *glyph nodes.* These nodes enable you to edit specific parts of a specially formatted object dynamically, according to the shape's design. For example, the shape representing a dog-eared page features a single glyph node that enables you to set the diameter of the inner ellipse, leaving the outer diameter unchanged, or a glyph on a beveled rectangle shape enables you to set the bevel depth, as shown in Figure 8-10.

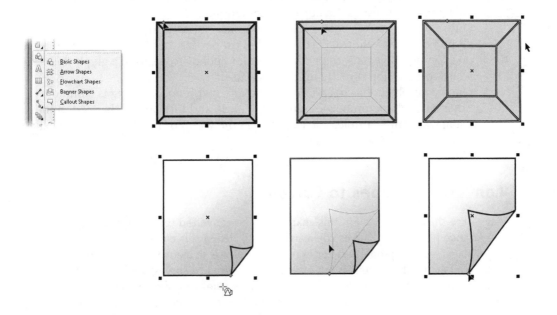

FIGURE 8-10   Glyph nodes can be used to control specific parts of these specially formatted objects.

Once a specific Perfect Shape Tool is selected, a collection of shapes becomes available on the Property Bar. Choose a specific type of shape from the Property Bar Perfect Shapes flyout selector, shown here, *before* drawing.

Walk through these simple steps to arrive quickly at a level of perfection in your CorelDRAW design work:

Click the Perfect Shapes button to open the flyout selector.

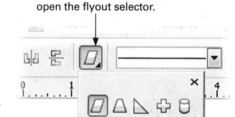

Tutorial Creating Perfect Objects

1. Choose a Perfect Shape Tool by clicking the Toolbox flyout and selecting a category.
2. on the Property Bar, click the Perfect Shape selector and choose a symbol. Use a click-drag action to define a size and position. For all symbol types except Callout, the direction of your click-drag won't matter because the symbols are created using a fixed orientation. For Callout shapes, the direction of your click-drag determines the object's orientation.
3. Once your shape has been created, you may notice it includes one or more glyph nodes that control certain symbol properties. In cases where more than one glyph node exists, the nodes are color coded. To position a glyph node, use a click-drag action directly on the node itself.
4. Once your object has been created and any glyph-node editing is complete, other basic shape properties (such as outline and fill) can be changed in the usual way. For example, you can change the width or height of your new shape using the selection handles available.

Converting Shapes to Curves

Any of the shapes discussed in this chapter can be converted to curves by using the Arrange | Convert To Curves command (CTRL+Q). Using this command removes any dynamic-editing properties. For example, an ellipse shape many be converted to a pie or arc (and vice versa); but after it is converted to curves, you'll no longer have the option of turning the object into a pie wedge. The same applies to rectangles, polygons, and so on. With the exception of the Undo command, once an object is converted to curves, there is no way to return the object to its dynamically editable state.

Editing Glyph Nodes

Glyph nodes are edited in ways similar to the control points on a polygon. As they are moved, the glyph nodes often have the effect of resizing, changing proportion, or dynamically moving a certain part of an individual symbol. Complex symbols can include up to three color-coded glyph nodes.

To explore glyph-node editing, take a moment to try this:

1. Choose the Banner Shapes Tool.
2. Choose the second from left banner on the Property Bar pop-up list.
3. Using a click-diagonal-drag action, create a new shape on your page. Notice the shape includes two glyph nodes—one yellow, one red.
4. Click-drag the yellow glyph node up or down to reposition it several times. Notice its movement is horizontally constrained; as it is moved, the vertical width of each portion of the banner changes.
5. Click-drag the red glyph node left or right to reposition it several times. Notice its movement is vertically constrained; as it is moved, the horizontal width of each portion of the banner changes to match your movement, as shown in Figure 8-11.

Glyph nodes can be edited using both the Perfect Shape Tool you used to create the shape and the Shape Tool (F10). You can also edit glyph nodes by using the Object Properties docker for a selected Perfect Shape, as shown in Figure 8-12. This docker offers precise control over glyph node position; right-click your shape and

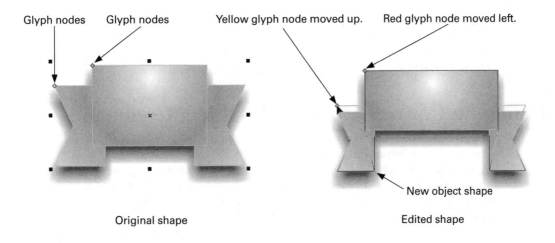

Glyph nodes   Glyph nodes   Yellow glyph node moved up.   Red glyph node moved left.

New object shape

Original shape   Edited shape

FIGURE 8-11   When movement is vertically constrained, the width of each portion of the banner changes.

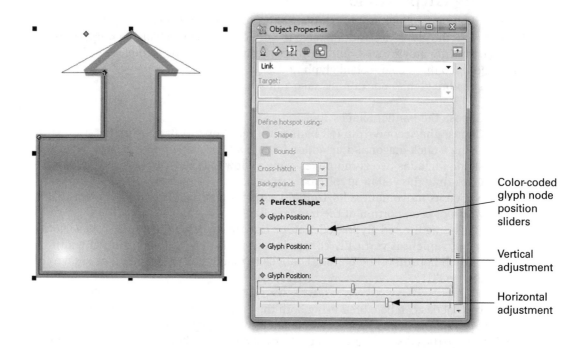

FIGURE 8-12 Use the Object Properties docker to edit glyph nodes.

choose Properties from the pop-up menu or press ALT + ENTER. Depending on the Perfect Shape you've selected, the Properties docker might display one, two, or more controls. This feature is handy if you want to adjust several different node positions without CorelDRAW immediately updating a shape several times.

Using the Convert Outline To Object Command

Many of the shapes covered in this chapter, the spiral in particular, are shapes that have outline properties but no fill. So what do you do, for example, if you want a gradient-filled spiral? The Convert Outline To Object command converts any shape's outline properties to a closed path. To apply the command to a selected object, choose Arrange | Convert Outline To Object, or use the shortcut: CTRL + SHIFT + Q. Once the outline is converted, the resulting closed path looks exactly like the shape of the original except it can be filled because it's not an outline, but instead a closed path object whose shape is based on an outline.

When an object is converted to an outline, CorelDRAW performs a quick calculation of the Outline Pen width applied to the object and creates a new object based on this value. When applying this command to objects that include a fill of any type, a new compound-path object is created based on the outline width. If the object includes a fill of any type, the fill is created as a new and separate object applied with an outline width and color of None. When you're converting open paths, only the path itself is created as a single outline object of the path according to the Outline Pen width applied. Figure 8-13 shows a spiral shape with a thick Outline Pen width that is converted to outline using the command.

Things are certainly shaping up now, aren't they? You've learned how to create basic shapes, smart shapes, and how to edit them to create scores of original and visually interesting items: think of how your next brochure will look with prices framed in elegant banners, fancy stars, and rounded-corner rectangles. This isn't the half of it; in Chapter 9, you learn to move, rotate, scale, and put your new objects anywhere you like on the page. Arranging and organizing objects is your next destination, and you'll find it to be a moving experience.

Original with 16-point outline applied   New fountain-filled object based on the outline

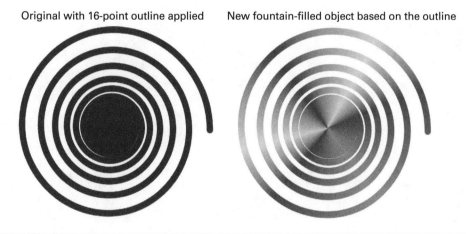

FIGURE 8-13   When an object is converted to an outline, CorelDRAW performs calculations that create a new object.

9

Arranging and Organizing Objects

Sometimes when you create or import an object, it's not *exactly* where you want it on the page. Or the position might be fine, but the object's a little too large. It could also be rotated by a few unwanted degrees—you get the picture. This chapter covers the techniques to use in CorelDRAW to *transform* objects; both the manual approach and pinpoint precise numerical entry are covered. You'll soon have the skills and know the steps for composing elements on a page the way you want them, and then you can stop cursing at the cursor.

 Download and extract all the files from the Chapter09.zip archive to follow the tutorials in this chapter.

Basic Object Selection

The Pick Tool—by default, the tool at the top of the Toolbox—can move, scale, or create other transformations when you click an object to select it and then drag to move the selection, for example. The SHIFT key is the modifier when you're selecting things on a page; you *add* to your existing selection by SHIFT + clicking other objects. If you've selected an object unintentionally, SHIFT + click the object (that's already selected) to deselect it.

With one or more items selected, you'll notice that information about the selected shapes is displayed on the Status Bar, shown next. The other workspace area to watch is the Property Bar, which shows the position and size of the selection and offers options such as the number of degrees to rotate the selected object(s). Also, if you press ALT + ENTER with something selected, the Object Properties docker provides you with not only details about what you've caught, but also the opportunity to *change* many of the object's properties quickly.

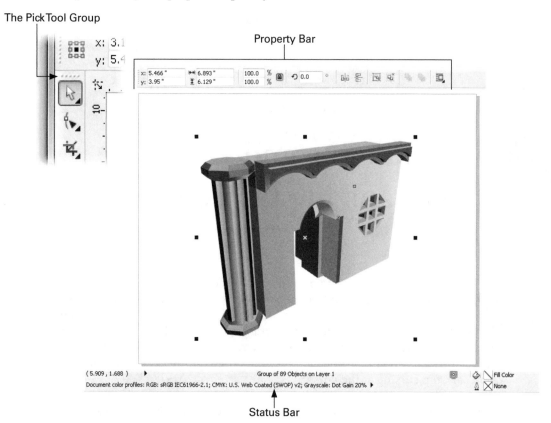

Pick Tool Group

Property Bar

Status Bar

Pick Tool Selections

The Pick Tool can be used for at least two things, the most important of which are to choose an object or several objects and to create a *change* in the selected object(s) by moving it and adjusting its selection handles.

Clicking an object once selects it. While an object is selected, *selection handles* appear—the eight black markers surrounding the object, as shown in Figure 9-1. Additionally, depending on the type and properties of an object, you'll see *nodes* at various areas around the object, which indicate the first node in an object path or sub-path (of combined vector objects) when a vector object is selected or the edge of an object when a bitmap is selected. A small *X* marker appears at the centermost point

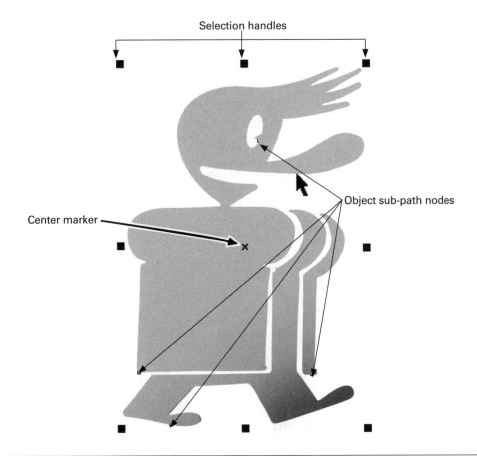

FIGURE 9-1   Select any object with a single click using the Pick Tool.

of the object, indicating its center origin. This origin can be moved and is quite useful for defining a center of rotation for an object; it's discussed later in this chapter.

Note Nodes are edited using the Shape Tool, covered in Chapter 11. The Pick Tool has no effect on nodes.

Occasionally you or a co-worker will create a shape with an outline stroke that's very narrow and has no fill, but you're having trouble selecting the darned thing with the Pick Tool. If zooming in doesn't make selecting it any easier, activate the Treat All Objects As Filled option; this option makes unfilled objects pretend they are filled as far as the Pick Tool is concerned, so you can select them from the center if need be. Open the Options dialog (CTRL + J) and choose Workspace | Toolbox | Pick Tool from the tree at left. Click the Treat All Objects As Filled check box, shown here, and then click OK to close the dialog.

Click this option to treat all selected objects as though they have a fill.

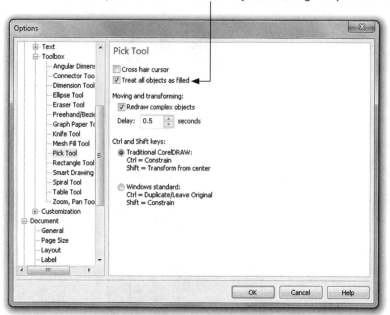

Picking and Freehand Picking

New to version X6 is the Freehand Pick Tool, located in the Pick Tool group. Both new and experienced CorelDRAW users might want to give this new selection tool a try; the Freehand Pick Tool behaves exactly like the (regular) Pick Tool after an object is selected, so you can move or perform other transformations without switching tools.

The main difference between these tools is that with the Pick Tool, you must click-drag to define a rectangle that the desired objects are completely within. The Freehand Pick Tool is used more like a shape-creation tool than a rectangle-creation tool; you can click-drag around objects, selecting some and avoiding others, regardless of how closely the objects neighbor one another. The illustration here visually demonstrates the different properties of the Pick and Freehand Pick Tools.

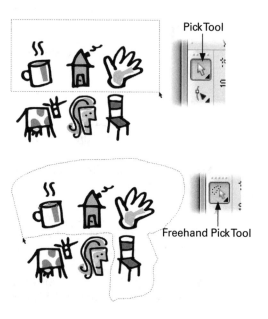

Pick Tool

Freehand Pick Tool

Selection Techniques

You can use mouse and keyboard combinations while navigating through a selection of objects and while selecting more than one object at a time using the Pick Tool. You can also use any of these object-selection techniques in combination with each. Here's how to make a selection of more than one object in one fell swoop:

- **SHIFT-clicking to select**   Holding the SHIFT key while clicking an unselected object adds it to your current selection. This also works in the reverse: holding SHIFT while clicking a selected object *deselects* the object. This technique works with both the Pick and Freehand Pick Tools.
- **Marquee-selecting objects**   To select all objects in a specific area, use the (regular) Pick Tool and click-drag diagonally to surround the objects; a dashed blue outline representing the rectangular area of selection appears until you release the mouse button. While doing so, all object shapes completely within the area you define are selected.
- **Holding ALT while marquee-selecting**   If you come to CorelDRAW from Adobe Illustrator, you can use the convention of selecting objects by merely touching a shape using a marquee-selection technique. Holding the ALT key as the modifier while click-dragging to marquee a specific area selects all objects within—and even ones whose *edge* you touch. Holding SHIFT + ALT while marquee-selecting causes the reverse to occur, deselecting any objects that are already selected.
- **Pressing TAB to select next object**   Suppose you have a bunch of objects in a document, but some of them overlap, and you're getting nowhere by attempting to click the one you need. Pressing the TAB key alone while the Pick Tool is active selects a shape and selects the next single object arranged directly behind your current selection (whether or not it overlaps the current object). Holding SHIFT while pressing the TAB key selects the single object arranged directly in front of your current selection. This tabbing action works because each new object created is automatically ordered in front of the last created object. Tabbing cycles through single object selections on a page, whether you have a current object selected or none at all. The key is to begin pressing TAB *after* you've chosen the Pick Tool.
- **ALT + clicking to select objects covered by other objects**   To select an object that is ordered in back of and hidden by other objects, hold the ALT key while the Pick Tool is selected and then click where the object is located. Each time you ALT + click with the Pick Tool, objects that are ordered farther back in the stack are selected, enabling you to "dig" to select hidden objects.

Tip Although you can select nodes with the Pick Tool when Enable Node Mapping is active, you can't perform editing operations other than moving a node. To create curves from straight path segments and work with node control handles, you need to use the genuine Shape Tool.

The Pick Tool's Shape Tool State

If you're getting an idea that the Pick Tool has a host of hidden features, you're right. One of these is its alternate state—the temporary Shape Tool state. The Pick Tool can temporarily act like the Shape Tool while a single object is selected and when held over object nodes, but this isn't the tool's normal behavior, and you first need to enable this feature in Options; choose Workspace | Display and then check *Enable Node Tracking*.

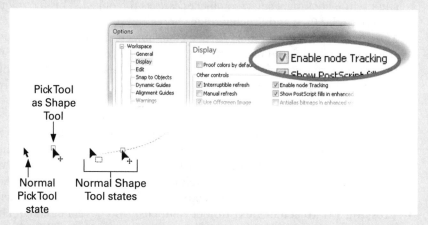

Pick Tool
as Shape
Tool

Normal
Pick Tool
state

Normal Shape
Tool states

The temporary Shape Tool state lets you move object nodes without changing tools, and this convenience allows you to modify selected characters in a line of Artistic Text, to edit open and closed paths, and to modify an ellipse, star, polygon as stars, graph paper objects, and even bitmaps. The next illustration shows Enable Node Tracking in action. When the Pick Tool is outside of a shape it looks like an arrow cursor. However, after an object is selected and the tool is over an object node, the tool changes to the Shape Tool and you can move nodes.

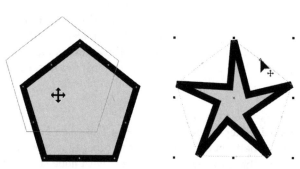

Pick Tool moving
selected object

Pick Tool in Shape Tool state selecting object, with
object node selected, and moving node

Selecting Objects by Type

So far, you've learned to select any objects on or off your page. But you can also select objects by their type (such as Text objects, Guidelines, and path nodes) using commands from the Select All menu, shown in Figure 9-2. Shown here all text objects are selected. CorelDRAW is being very clever, however; it didn't select the "O" or the "a" because they're drawings and not text. You can extrude, add a perspective, and put any type of fill you like on text, and *it's still text*. See how effortless sifting through a page of objects can be? Each time you use a command, a new selection is made (and any current selection of objects becomes *not* selected).

Here's how to use each of the commands:

- **Select All Objects**   Choosing Edit | Select All | Objects selects all objects in your current document window to become selected. Quicker is the CTRL + A keyboard shortcut, which accomplishes the same result and is easy to remember; it's used by many professional software programs.

Tip   Double-clicking the Pick Tool button in the Toolbox instantly selects all visible objects in your current document window view.

FIGURE 9-2   Select items in your document by using the Select command.

Caution You can't select what's locked or hidden. Check the status of layers with the Object Manager if there's an object that is apparently welded to the page.

- **Select All Text** Choosing Edit | Select All | Text instantly selects all text objects both on and off the current document page. Both Artistic and Paragraph Text objects are selected after using this command (unless they have been grouped with other objects, in which case they are ignored). Text objects applied with effects (such as Contour or Extrude effects) also are selected using this command.
- **Select All Guidelines** Guidelines are actually a class of document page objects, different from objects you draw, but objects nonetheless. To select all Guidelines on your document page, choose Edit | Select All | Guidelines. Selected Guidelines are indicated by a color change (red, by default). To select Guidelines, they must be visible and cannot be locked; use the Tools | Object Manager to edit their properties before you try to select them. If Guidelines you've placed aren't currently visible on your page, choose View | Guidelines.

Tip Guidelines can be created using a click-drag action from your Ruler onto your document page. Choosing View | Rulers toggles the on or off state of CorelDRAW's Ruler feature.

- **Select All Nodes** You must have both the Shape Tool and an object selected (closed or open paths qualify) to use this Select command. Choose Edit | Select All | Nodes to select all the object's path nodes. For a quicker method in the same situation, use the CTRL + A shortcut when the Shape Tool is your current tool. Special CorelDRAW objects, such as Rectangles, Ellipses, and Polygons, can't be selected this way because their shapes are defined dynamically by "control" points instead of nodes. To convert these special objects to ordinary objects, choose Arrange | Convert To Curves. After conversion, you can select them with the Select All Nodes feature.

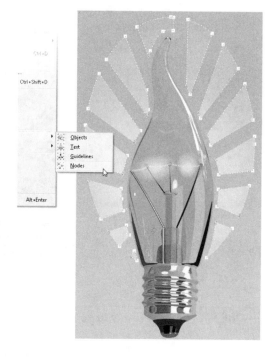

> **Tip**   Shapes are often made up of two or more paths that are combined. To select all the nodes on a combined path, first select the object and then double-click the Shape Tool on the Toolbox.

Moving Objects

When moving objects, it's important to lift using your legs and position yourself carefully to avoid back injury. However, when moving objects in *CorelDRAW*—which is a lot less stressful—you basically have two options: to move objects directly by using the Pick Tool and dragging, or to move objects indirectly by using the keyboard arrows to nudge objects in any of the four directions.

> **Tip**   For information on moving and transforming objects, see the section "Applying Precise Transformations," later in this chapter.

Using the Pick Tool

Putting the Pick Tool over certain areas of a selected object activates the tool's positioning cursor, as shown in the illustration. This means a click-drag action on the area will move your selected object(s) in any direction. As you drag your object, you'll see a preview outline, indicating its new position. When you release the mouse button, the move is complete.

Preview outline

Positioning state of Pick Tool cursor

Tip If you're having difficulty selecting and/or moving an object because it's too small, you can increase your view magnification using the Zoom Tool or use the keyboard nudge keys, covered next.

Using Nudge Keys

As an alternate to using the Pick Tool, you can also move selected objects by a distance you specify by nudging using your keyboard arrow keys. To nudge a selected object, press the UP, DOWN, LEFT, or RIGHT arrow key. Your object will be moved by the nudge value specified in the Rulers page of the Options dialog. You can customize the Nudge distance by opening the Options dialog (CTRL + J), clicking to expand the tree directory under Document, and clicking to display the Rulers options page, as shown here:

Nudge increment options

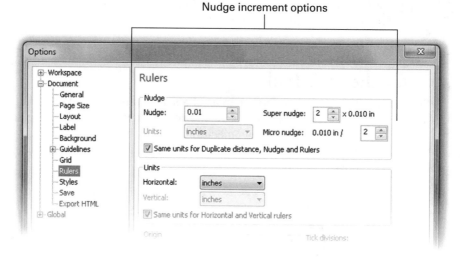

Tip You have eight possible directions in which to nudge your artwork. In addition to using an arrow key, you can also press two neighboring keys to perform a *diagonal* nudge.

Using nudge keys, you can perform moves according to the Nudge value or by larger or smaller values. These are referred to as *Super* or *Micro Nudges*, respectively.

Like "normal" nudges, these values are set in the Ruler options page. Here are the techniques for using Super and Micro Nudges:

- **Super Nudge**   This action moves a selected object in larger increments than a normal nudge. To use Super Nudge, hold SHIFT while pressing the UP, DOWN, LEFT, or RIGHT arrow key on your keyboard. By default, this causes your selected object to move by 0.2 inch.
- **Micro Nudge**   The pint-sized version of a typical nudge is the Micro Nudge, which moves your object in smaller increments. To use Micro Nudge, hold CTRL while pressing the UP, DOWN, LEFT, or RIGHT arrow key on your keyboard. By default, Micro nudges move the selected object by 0.05 inch.

Transforming Objects

A *transformation* is any type of object shape or position change, short of actually editing the object's properties. This includes changing its position, size, skew, and/or rotating or reflecting it. Dragging an object directly in a document is more intuitive than precision transformations—but both approaches to transformation have their own special advantages. In this section, you'll learn how to apply transformations using both techniques.

Transforming Objects Using the Cursor

For the intuitive method, the Pick Tool is what you need to transform objects by the simple act of click and dragging. Depending on the type of transformation you need to apply, you can click-drag any of the four, black square selection handles that surround the selected object or group of objects to change an object's size *proportionally*, by width only and by height only. Dragging any middle selection handle or side handle scales the object disproportionately—"smush" and "stretch" are the more common terms for disproportionate scaling, as shown in Figure 9-4.

During transformations, CorelDRAW keeps track of the object's transformed size, position, width, height, scale, and rotation angle. CorelDRAW also remembers your object's original shape from the time it was created, regardless of how many transformations have been applied to it. You can remove all transformations and restore the object to its original state in a single step: choose Arrange | Clear Transformations to return your object to its original shape immediately.

While transforming objects, you can constrain certain shape properties by holding modifier keys. Here are the effects of holding modifier keys for constraining a transformed object's shape:

- **To change object size (scale)**   Click-drag any corner handle to change an object's size *proportionally*, meaning the relative width and height remains in proportion to the original object shape. Hold ALT while dragging any corner selection handle to change an object's shape *disproportionally*, meaning width and height change, regardless of original proportions.

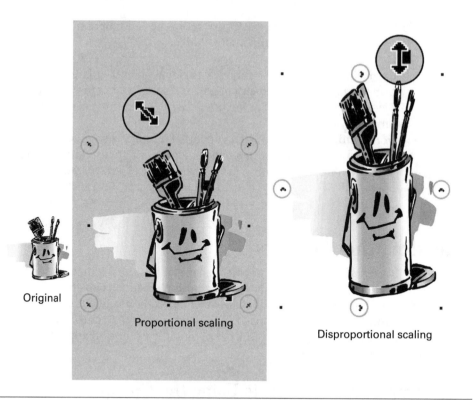

Original

Proportional scaling

Disproportional scaling

FIGURE 9-3 Dragging these handles changes the size of an object proportionately or otherwise.

- **To change width or height only** Click-drag any side, top, or bottom selection handle to change the size of the object in the drag direction. Hold SHIFT while doing this to change the width or height from the center of the object, or hold CTRL while dragging to change the width or height in 200-percent increments.

Tip When transforming an object using the Pick Tool, click the right mouse button during the transformation and then release both mouse buttons to "drop a copy." The active object you're dragging becomes a copy, applying the transformation to a duplicate, not the original. This technique is a quick and easy way to mirror a duplicate and make symmetrical compositions.

You can also rotate or skew an object using Pick Tool states that become available after you click a selected object a second time—you click an object that is *already* selected once to display Rotation and Skew controls around the object. This action causes an object (or group of objects) to look like the illustration of the 45 shown in Figure 9-4, an ancient analog sound device best known to listeners who know who The Beatles were.

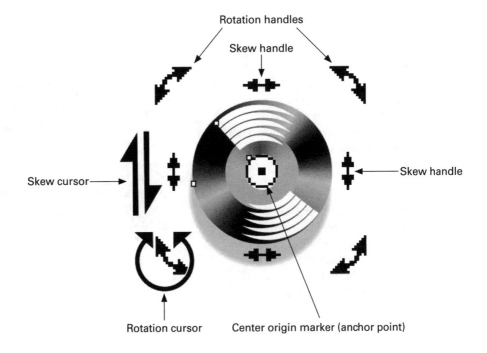

FIGURE 9-4   Clicking a selected object will cause these Rotation/Skew handles to appear.

You control the point around which objects are rotated or skewed by *moving* the center origin marker or anchor point of an object or group of objects. Your cursor will change to display either the rotation or a skew cursor when held over a corner or side handle. A good creative example of offsetting the original center of an object is covered in the following tutorial, where you make a circular pattern from a group of objects.

Tutorial   Off-Center Object Rotation to Create a Design

1. Open Pattern Ding.cdr. The page has guidelines that you'll use and a single grouped object, the source for the radial pattern you'll build.
2. With the Pick Tool, click the object to select it, and then click the selected object (again) to put it into rotational and skew mode.
3. Drag the center rotation origin to the intersection of the guidelines.
4. Click-drag the top right (bent double arrowhead) handle downward until the light blue object preview is slightly overlapping the original object.

5. Before releasing the mouse button, press the other mouse button, and then release both buttons to "drop a copy" or the original object. Unless you've configured your mouse or other pointing device to accommodate left-handers, the primary mouse button is the left one, and the button you click briefly to drop a copy is the right one.

6. Repeat steps 4 and 5 with the copy of the object. To repeat your last step quickly, press CTRL + R as many times as needed. Work clockwise until you've made a circle from copies of the pattern, as you can see in this illustration.

Drag and then right-click to drop a copy.

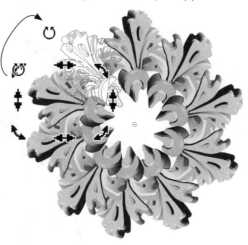

Tip To flip a selected object quickly, either vertically or horizontally, use the Mirror Vertical and Mirror Horizontal buttons on the Property Bar while using the Pick Tool.

Mirror Horizontal

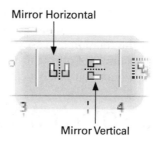

Mirror Vertical

Using the Free Transform Tool

The *Free Transform* Tool is the middle ground between controlling transformations entirely with mouse gestures and the hands-off controls of the Transformations docker. When you use the Free Transform Tool, the Property Bar offers four modes of transformation: Free Rotation, Free Angle Reflection, Free Scale, and Free Skew. Shown here, the Free Angle Reflection mirrors the drawing's original location and left-to-right orientation.

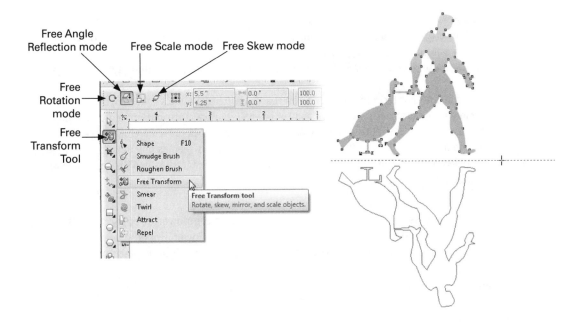

To transform a selected object in one of these four modes, click to select the mode, and then use a click-drag action on your object. A live preview of the new object's shape appears. While using Rotation or Angle Reflection modes, a reference line appears as you drag to indicate the object's angle transformation from its original state.

Using Free Transform and then applying a little transparency can yield compositions that contain believable reflections. The Free Transform Tool works with bitmaps as well as native CorelDRAW vector objects.

Copying Effects with the Attributes Eyedropper Tool

In addition to properties such as Outline Color and effects such as Perspective (covered in later chapters), you can copy transformations between objects using the Attributes Eyedropper Tool. To do this, choose the tool, have both the objects in view, and click the Transformations button on the Property Bar. Then check the individual properties you want to sample. For example, if you want to copy the scale of an object to a different object, put a check in the Size box in the Transformations list, making sure no other transformations, effects, or properties are checked. Click OK to close the flyout and save your choices. Now click the Attributes Eyedropper Tool over an object whose scale you want to apply to a different object; the cursor turns into a paint bucket shape and you click over the target object to apply the transformation.

(continued)

The cursor remains a bucket until you either click the Select Object Attributes button on the Property bar or you change tools, an added convenience if you want to scale more than one object on the page.

The Attributes Eyedropper Tool is limited in what it can copy and apply:

- The tool does not recognize grouped objects. You *will* make a mess of a composition if you sample a single object for its scale and try to apply the scale attribute to a group of objects.
- You can copy an attribute and apply it to a contour object because CorelDRAW sees this as one object. Similarly, a PowerClipped group of objects is seen as one object, as is an extruded shape. Blend objects are seen as two (or more) objects, so don't try applying an attribute to Blend objects.

In the following set of steps, you'll get a better idea of the power of applying copied attributes. You're going to rotate a drawing of a knife (a PowerClipped group of shapes) and its shadow based on the angle of rotation of a different piece of flatware in the composition.

Dig in!

Tutorial Straightening Objects via Attributes

1. Open Table Setting.cdr. Now, understand that the trick to unrotating the knife and its shadow lies in the fact that it was originally rotated, and CorelDRAW can read the information about the previous transformation. You cannot duplicate a transformation using an object that has had no transformation to begin with.
2. Choose the Attributes Eyedropper Tool from the Toolbox. Click the Transformations drop-down box on the Property Bar and then check only Rotation. All other boxes should be unchecked.
3. Click the fork.
4. When the cursor is a paint bucket, click exactly over the knife. You'll see, as shown in Figure 9-6, that the knife almost magically straightens itself. By the way, you could also choose Arrange | Clear Transformations to accomplish this with a selected object, but the eyedropper proves faster a lot of times.
5. Click over the shadow of the knife and consider yourself a perfect host now.

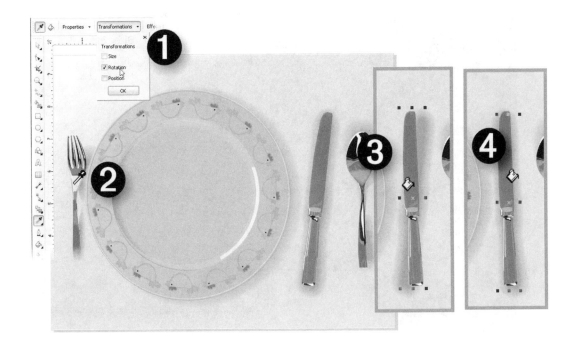

FIGURE 9-5 Sampling and pasting attributes is a quick way to dramatically change scores of elements in a composition.

Applying Precise Transformations

The Transformation docker is terrific for applying multiple transformations with a single command. The docker has five Transformation buttons: Position (Move), Rotation, Scale and Mirror, Size, and Skew, as shown in Figure 9-6. To open the Transformation docker, choose Window | Dockers or choose Arrange | Transformations, and then click the button that applies to your task.

For all transformations, the procedure is the same: click the button for the type of transformation, enter the values you need, and then click the Apply button in the docker to transform the selected object(s). In this section, you'll learn what each area does for you and the options offered for each.

Using the Transformation Docker

Options in the Transformation docker vary by transformation type. In the illustrations shown on the next few pages, examples show only the specific transformation being discussed. If you need to, you can apply several transformations in a single command if values throughout each of the five docker modes have been selected.

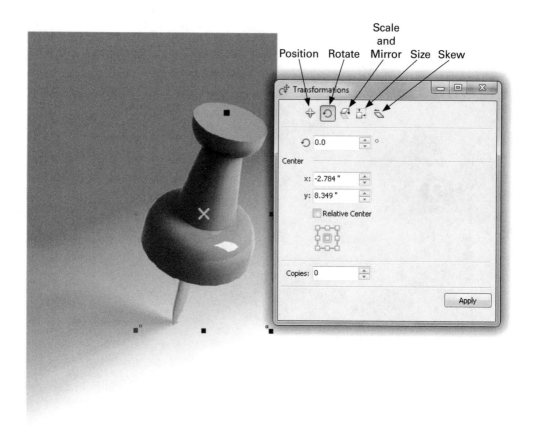

FIGURE 9-6 The Transformation docker offers precision over position, rotation, size, and skew changes.

Positioning (Moving) Objects

Options for the Position page allow you to move your object selection a specified distance, either *vertically* (*V*), *horizontally* (*H*), or to a specific point on your document page, as shown in Figure 9-7.

While the Relative Position option is selected, entering new values and clicking the Apply button causes your objects to move by a specified distance. When positioning objects on the page with Relative Position unchecked, the object's *center* is moved to the chosen *x* and *y* coordinates on the page.

Caution If you have changed the page's 0,0 origin by clicking and dragging the intersection of the rulers to a new location, the object's ending position will use the new ruler's coordinates.

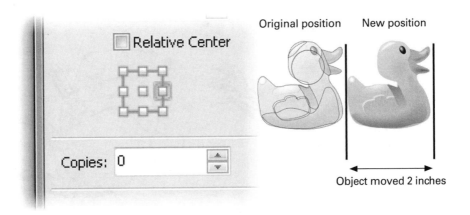

FIGURE 9-7 This object was precisely moved by applying a Position transformation.

Rotating Objects

With Rotate, you can make multiple copies, and enter exact angles of rotation based on degrees and in default increments of 5 using the spin boxes. Figure 9-8 shows two very different results when using relative and absolute positioning and two copies are made of the tea kettle.

Entering negative values rotates an object clockwise, while positive values cause counterclockwise rotation. Selecting the Relative Center option allows either x (horizontal, left to right) or y (vertical, up and down) to rotate objects, according to the object's center marker position. The position of the center marker is specified as either x or y. You can specify a new center origin position for your object's rotation by changing the existing value in the Horizontal and Vertical number spin boxes. When Relative Center is *not* selected, your object is rotated according to the page center.

Scale and Mirror Objects

The Scale and Mirror transformation has features for entering precise changes in object size. You can also flip the object either x or y, and/or simultaneously, by clicking one of the two mirror buttons, as shown in Figure 9-9.

When the Proportional option is selected, your object's new horizontal and vertical scale values are unlinked, meaning you can apply scaling commands to either the width or height, independent of each other. While the Proportional option is unselected, width and height scaling operations are locked to each other. This means that scaling the width or height by a given percentage value causes the adjacent value to be calculated automatically to preserve your selected object's original proportions.

Sizing Objects

The Size transformation type gives you the option to change either the V and/or H measure of an object selection based on the values entered. For example, entering 2 inches in the Width box and clicking the Apply button scales the selected object

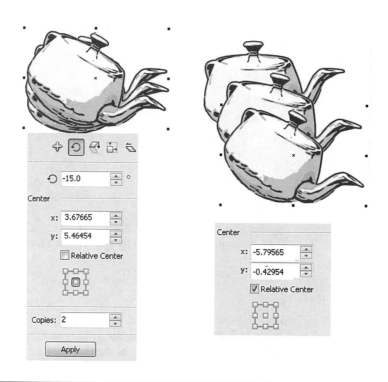

FIGURE 9-8 The Rotate transformation features an offset option so you can choose Relative Center positioning for duplicates of the original object.

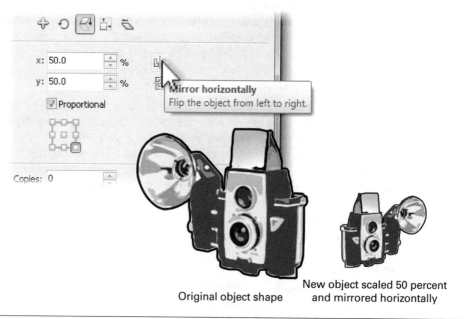

FIGURE 9-9 Both Scale and Mirror changes were applied to the drawing.

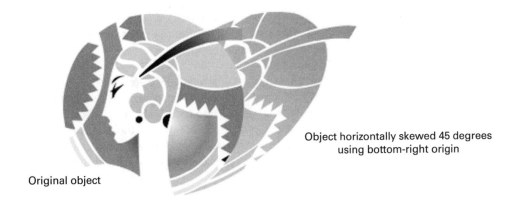

Object horizontally skewed 45 degrees
using bottom-right origin

Original object

FIGURE 9-10 A precision Skew slants an object, and offers an anchor point around which you perform the Skew transformation.

to a width of 2 inches. When the Proportional option is selected, the width and height values can be changed independently. While it's not selected, the width and height values are linked and calculated automatically to alter the size of the object proportionally.

Precision Skewing

The term *skew* means to change the position of two sides of a shape in a parallel fashion while leaving the other two sides alone; *slanting* is a more common term for "skew." The Skew transformation also gives you the chance to apply both vertical and horizontal skew independently or simultaneously by entering degree measures, in turn, transforming the object either *V* or *H*. As with rotation commands, negative degree values produce clockwise skews, while positive values cause counterclockwise skews. The Use Anchor Point option lets you specify left, center, right, top, bottom, sides, or corner points as the point around which your objects are skewed, as shown in Figure 9-10. The skewed copy more or less looks like a cast shadow of the original symbol, doesn't it?

Controlling the Order of Things

How your objects are ordered is another consideration when organizing drawing objects in a composition. The order of objects determines whether an object appears in front of—or behind—another object. Your page and the pasteboard (the area surrounding your document page) are always the *backmost* point, while your screen is always the frontmost point. All objects are layered between these two points.

When overlapping objects are ordered, they appear in front of or behind each other, according to their order. As you create each new object, it is put in front of all existing objects *on the current document layer*. Changing the object order lets you rearrange overlapping objects without changing their position on the page. To do this, CorelDRAW has a series of order commands that let you shuffle the order of objects in various ways. You'll find them in the Arrange | Order submenu.

Note The *hierarchy* of object ordering on a layer is very different than *object layers*. Although layers each have their own collections of objects that can be ordered in a sequence, the layers *themselves* can *also* be ordered. This means if you're trying to control the ordering of two or more objects, check the Status Bar to make sure they're on the same layer. If you skipped over Chapter 4, this chapter explains Layers and provides some fun working examples of layers and the Object Manager.

Here's how each of the object order commands works:

- **To Front** This command shuffles your selected object(s) to the very front of the current layer. Press SHIFT + PAGE UP or choose Arrange | Order | To Front to apply it.
- **To Back** This command shuffles your selected object(s) to the very back of the current layer. Press SHIFT + PAGE DOWN or choose Arrange | Order | To Back to apply it.
- **Forward One** This command shuffles your selected object(s) forward by one in the object order of the current layer. Press CTRL + PAGE UP or choose Arrange | Order | Forward One to apply it.
- **Back One** This command shuffles your selected object(s) backward by one in the object order of the current layer. Press CTRL + PAGE DOWN or choose Arrange | Order | Back One to apply it.
- **In Front Of** This command puts your selected object directly in front of any object you specify in the current layer order. A targeting cursor appears, which you use to choose which object to shuffle your selection in front of. Choose Arrange | Order | In Front Of to apply it.
- **Behind** This command also causes a targeting cursor to appear, enabling you to specify which object you want your object selection to be shuffled behind in the object order on the current layer. Choose Arrange | Order | Behind to apply it.
- **Reverse Order** This command effectively shuffles the order of your selected object so that it's the reverse of its current order on the layer. Front objects become back objects and vice versa, as shown in Figure 9-11. For example, if your objects were numbered 1, 2, 3, and 4 from front to back, applying this command would reorder them to 4, 3, 2, and 1. Choose Arrange | Order | Reverse Order to apply it.

Tip When changing object order using the Reverse Order command, grouped objects are considered a single object, so their relative order in the group will be preserved. To reorder objects within a group, you'll need to Ungroup (CTRL+U) the objects first before applying the command.

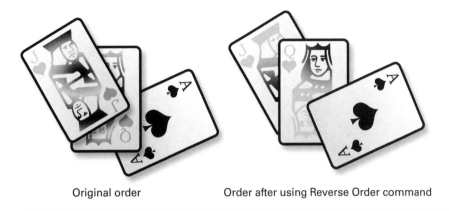

Original order   Order after using Reverse Order command

FIGURE 9-11   You can quickly change the order of objects within a layer using Reverse Order.

Hopefully, this chapter has shown you how to transform not only objects, but also your skill level with CorelDRAW. You now know how to move, scale, rotate, and perform other operations on page objects and their duplicates. You also know how to both manually transform and use the dockers and other features for precise moving and alignment of the elements you need for a terrific design. Chapter 10 takes you into *creating* these shapes that you now know how to move; put Chapters 9 and 10 *together* and your family's going to start missing you because you'll be having too much fun designing to sit down for regular dinners!

PART III

Working with Object Tools

10

Drawing and Editing Shapes

If you thought learning to create basic and smart shapes in Chapter 8 was fun and a learning experience, hold on: basic shapes, well, basically get your work only so far. However, CorelDRAW's path building and editing tools are at your disposal to create *exactly* what you envision. The Curve tools group on the Toolbox has tools that make any shape you can imagine (and some you *can't*) a snap to design. In the following sections, you work through the *editing* process of lines and their nodes, so you have reason to draw something that's only *close* to what you need. This chapter is the DRAW part of CorelDRAW.

Download and extract all the files from the Chapter10.zip archive to follow the tutorials in this chapter.

Sidling Up to CorelDRAW X6's Curve Tools

The most basic shape you can draw in CorelDRAW (and any vector drawing program) is a *line:* a line is a path that passes through at least two *points,* called *nodes* in CorelDRAW. A line is actually a mathematical equation, and as such, it doesn't necessarily have to have an outline color or a width; it doesn't even have to be a straight line, but it does have a *direction*—the direction in which you draw the line. You can assign lines scores of different properties: arrowheads, a dotted look for coupons, colors, and varying widths to complete any assignment. Joining the beginning and end points of a line (a path) closes the path, and if the beginning doesn't meet the end point, the shape is called an *open path.*

CorelDRAW X6's Curve tools group is made up of eight virtual pens, shown next, located between the Zoom/Pan and the Smart Tools group on the Toolbox. The tools are task-oriented; although they all produce paths, your choice of tool for a task depends on what you want to draw. For example, do you need to produce an object whose curves are flawless—like those of a physical French curve? This task calls for the B-Spline Tool. Also, the Artistic Media Tool is most useful at producing open paths, not closed ones; although you *can* close and fill an Artistic Media path, if your goal is to draw a filled object, you'd choose something other than the Artistic Media Tool. You can also "mix and match"; you can begin an object with one tool and finish it with a different tool—your choices depend on the object you want to create. Some of these tools work similarly, so it's best to become acquainted with what the cursors *look* like, as shown in Figure 10-1.

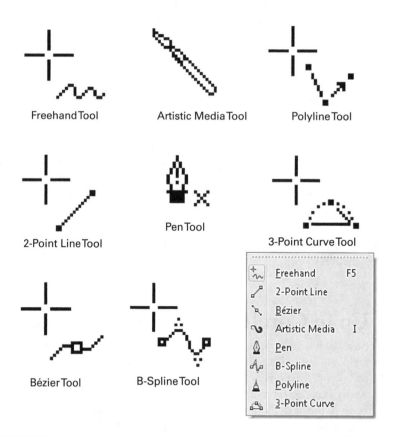

FIGURE 10-1   For visual reference while you work, each of the different drawing tools has a unique cursor.

How to Fill an Open Path

When you draw a path and the beginning and end points don't meet, it's called an *open path,* and ordinarily you cannot apply a fill to its interior. However, you can indeed fill an open path—just like in Adobe Illustrator—when you know how to turn on this option.

To change CorelDRAW X6's drawing behavior so all open paths are filled—without needing to close the path first—follow these steps:

1. Open the Options dialog by choosing Tools | Options (CTRL+J).
2. Click to expand the tree directory under Document and click General to display the associated options on the right side of the dialog.
3. Click the Fill Open Curves option to select it, and click OK to close the dialog.

After choosing this option, the open paths you draw can have an interior area.

Using the Artistic Media Tool

The Artistic Media Tool treats a path as though it's a skeleton to which you can apply any number of CorelDRAW preset "skins": there are five different types of Artistic Media "brushes", and a number of preset variations for the Preset, Brush, and Sprayer Artistic Media types. It helps to get your mind around a "paintbrush" metaphor; by dragging stokes, you'll wind up with anything from complex filigree strokes to elegant calligraphic handwriting. The underlying path of an Artistic Media stroke can be altered at any time, changing the corresponding look of the media—and you can see the dynamic changes for accurate visual feedback as you work. You can draw while an Artistic Media effect is enabled, and you can also apply these painterly strokes to existing lines. The Artistic Media Tool is located in the Toolbox with the other line-drawing tools.

With the Artistic Media Tool selected, the Property Bar offers five different line-drawing modes to choose from, shown in Figure 10-2, each of which has its own options. You have additional options on the Property Bar, directly to the right of your choice of Artistic Media, and the options change, depending on the media type selected.

Applying Presets to Lines

Artistic Media is an evolution of CorelDRAW's Powerlines feature; veteran users will be the most comfortable with the improvements over Powerlines—now called *Presets*—and everyone will be delighted with the new diversity of Artistic Media types.

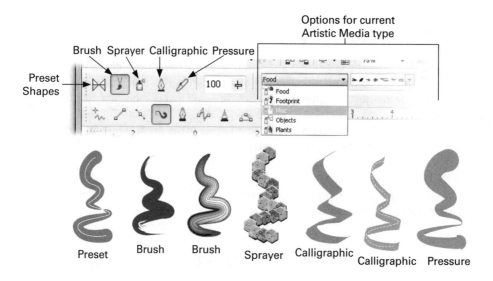

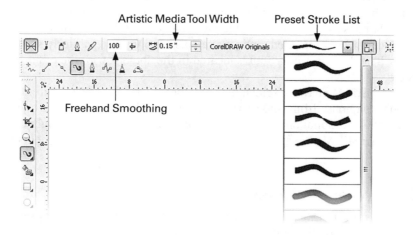

FIGURE 10-2 The Property Bar offers five different line-drawing modes, each of which has its own options.

When Presets is selected in the Property Bar, the Artistic Media Tool surrounds your drawn lines with specific preset vector shapes that are dynamically linked to the underlying path. The smoothness and width of the applied effect is set according to the Freehand Smoothing and Width options in the Property Bar, as shown here:

Set the shape using one of the styles in the Preset Stroke List. Smoothing is based on percent values between 0 (no smoothing) and 100 (maximum smoothing). Width can be set on a unit measure within a range of 0.03 to 10 inches. As you draw, a path is created in freehand style and immediately applied to your line.

Ready to take the Artistic Media Tool out for a spin? The following tutorial walks you through the completion of an illustration—adding cartoon "reaction lines," the sort of emanations a character has when struck with a revelation—like *you* will be when you discover how the Artistic Media's Preset brush works and feels.

Tutorial   Painting with a Drawing Program

1. Open Cartoon Guy.cdr in CorelDRAW.
2. Choose Tools | Object Manager; from the list, click Addlines Here to select it as the current editing layer if it's not already highlighted. The underlying layer containing the cartoon is locked so you can't move it accidentally.
3. Choose the Artistic Media Tool and then click Preset, the far-left button on the Property Bar.
4. Click the Preset Stroke selector and choose a style from the drop-down list. For this example, choose a style that has a rounded head and tapers at the end to a point.
5. Think of how you'd draw a cartoon sun; drag strokes so the "sun" is the cartoon fellow's head. The target width for the strokes is about .35". If your current stroke width is something different, you now have an opportunity to become familiar with Artistic Media features; while the stroke is highlighted, increase or decrease the width on the Property Bar.
6. The head of the Preset Stroke starts where you begin your click-drag. If you drew a stroke backward, this is easily fixed. Press F10 to choose the Shape Tool, click to select the stroke (you'll see the red underlying path when the stroke is properly selected), and then right-click and choose Reverse Subpaths from the context menu.
7. Click the Artistic Media Tool in the Toolbox and you're ready to continue stroking. The Artistic Media Tool is persistent—it "remembers" your last-used stroke settings, styles, and all that good stuff.
8. The Preset Strokes you create are a special instance of an object surrounding a path. You can, therefore, recolor the default black fill. With a stroke selected, try clicking a color well on the Color Palette. The cartoon fellow's excitement is now in color, as shown in Figure 10-3.
9. Let's say you want to get adventurous and change the Preset for one of the strokes. While the stroke is selected, choose a different Preset style from the drop-down list ... and every subsequent stroke you make will have that new style. When choosing it, be sure to click *the outer part* of the stroke, and avoid *the underlying central path* itself. If you've deselected a stroke and want to change it, choose it with the Pick Tool and then use the drop-down list.

FIGURE 10-3 While a Preset stroke is selected, you can change its width, smoothness, and color.

Alternatively, you can click (don't click-drag, though) on a stroke on the page to select it, and then change the Preset style. Now go answer that doorbell.

Drawing with Brushes

In Brush mode, you can simulate the look of traditional natural media, which looks very similar to the brushes in Corel Painter, with a notable exception. Beneath an Artistic Media stroke lies a skeleton path, and the strokes you make can be edited ad infinitum. In contrast, bitmap paint programs such as Corel Painter and Adobe Photoshop feature brush strokes that can't be edited after making them. Like the Presets category, Artistic Media Brushes extend the full length of every path you create.

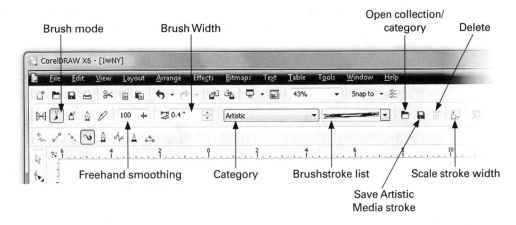

The Brushstroke styles selector offers a variety of different styles, only six of which are shown previously in Figure 10-2. Freehand Smoothness and Brush Width options are used to change the appearance of the graphical object—the "skin"—applied to the underlying path.

Caution As with *all* trashcan-shaped Delete icons and buttons, don't click the Delete brush button unless you truly understand the consequences of deleting something, and your decision-making ability can be verified by friends.

You can draw using a Brush style or, alternatively, apply one to an existing line. To draw using a Brush stroke, choose the Artistic Media Tool and use the Property Bar options to choose a Brush style, and begin drawing by click-dragging on your page in a stroking motion. To apply a new brush stroke to an existing line, select the line using the Artistic Media Tool, choose the Brush mode, and use Property Bar options to choose a width and Brushstroke style. You can load saved brushes by clicking the Browse button on the Property Bar, and save your own objects as brush strokes and add them to the existing Brushstroke list. The following set of steps walk you through how to create, save, and then use a custom brush.

Tutorial Creating and Saving Your Own Brush Stroke

1. Open Tacky Motel.cdr; the layer with the image is called "locked background" (because it *is*) and the current editing layer is named "Use this layer"—check Object Manager to make sure before you begin. You're going to build a brush that will be the basis for glowing neon on the "MOTEL" area of the sign.

2. Take a look at the red object just above the page. This is a completed group of objects all prepared to become a custom stroke. To re-create this object, click-drag a wide, short rectangle using the Rectangle Tool (about 3" wide, ¾" high), and then with the Shape Tool, drag the top-right corner node to the left until the ends of the rectangle are blunted. Fill the object with a deep, dark red and remove its outline.

3. Choose the Contour Tool, and then drag on the rectangle, moving from its outside toward the center. Zoom into the contour object using the mouse scroll wheel, keeping the Contour Tool active. Drag the object slider to about the vertical center between the object's contour start and end handles to set the number of steps in the contour object.

4. On the Property Bar, click the Inside Contour button, and then refine the contour object by choosing about 7 steps for the contour. Set the inside color by clicking the Fill drop-down mini-palette, and then click a light red; pink is fine, too. Refer to Figure 10-4 as a visual guide to the steps so far.

Tip Custom Artistic Media brush strokes are saved to Corel's CMX file format, which is a limited subset of its native CDR file format. Unfortunately, a mesh-filled object cannot be saved in CMX format, so you need to do the next best thing; use a simplified Contour or Blend to create a graduated color effect that can stretch when used as a stroke.

5. Select the contour object, and then choose the Artistic Media Tool. Click the Brush button on the Property Bar.

6. Click the Save icon; save the stroke to the folder CorelDRAW offers, give the stroke a name, and then click Save. The next time you choose the Artistic Media Tool's brush, a thumbnail preview of your custom brush is at the top of the drop-down list.

7. After you click Save in the Save As box, your new brush is immediately available for use. Now you'll add neon lettering to the "Motel" portion of the bitmap image: With the Artistic Media Tool in Brush mode, set the Stroke Width to .3", if it's not already in that mode, on the Property Bar. If your custom neon brush is not displayed as the current Brushstroke thumbnail on the Property Bar, choose Custom from the Category drop-down list, and then choose the brush from the Brushstroke drop-down.

8. Click-drag over the *M*, using a single stroke; don't release the mouse button until you've completed the character. Zoom in using the middle mouse button if necessary.

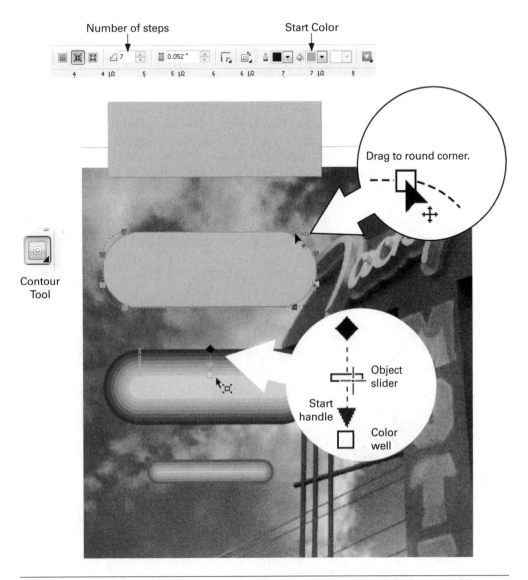

FIGURE 10-4   Create a series of objects that appear to be a single fountain fill.

9. Repeat Step 8 for the remaining *O*, *T*, *E*, and *L* characters. Don't try to close the *O*—Artistic Media isn't meant to form a closed path. You can use single strokes on the *T* and the *E* to build these characters, or you can backtrack over certain areas of the character stems to make the letter.

10. Press CTRL + A to select all and then press CTRL + K, or choose Arrange | Break *x* Selected Objects Apart. The strokes are now groups of objects, which is required before you can apply an effect such as transparency to all the shapes. You'll see the center stroke of the objects as a .5" black line above the shapes.

This is the guiding path for the custom brush stroke, and you can leave it on the design in this example because it will disappear after applying an effect. If you want to be tidy, however, you can press CTRL + A and then right-click over the None well at the top of the color palette.

11. With all the objects selected, press CTRL + G to group them and make the next steps easier. Choose the Transparency Tool from the Interactive Tool group; on the Property Bar, set the Transparency Type to Uniform, set the Transparency Operation to Add, and then drag the Starting Transparency slider to about 64. Adding Transparency Operation makes the core colors of the stroke brighter, while making the darker outer colors fade away. Use your artistic eye to specify the amount of transparency. In Figure 10-5, you can see the process of drawing the characters at left, and at right, the finished sign in glowing neon. Let us hope that the color TV in the rooms is a 60" flat screen because the beds are renowned as being lumpy.

Transparency Tool

FIGURE 10-5 Create an Artistic Media Brush to serve one or many purposes to make your design work go more quickly.

Applying the Sprayer

The Artistic Media Tool's Sprayer mode is used to pepper the drawing page with a sequence of drawings—your *own* that you save as a brush or by choosing a preset from CorelDRAW's Sprayer collections. Changes to the underlying path and the objects used in a spray can be dynamically changed at any time. The sprayer objects repeat uniformly or randomly across the full length of a path. The Size/Scale, Spray Order, Dabs, Spacing, Rotation, and Offset values can be set using the Property Bar, shown in Figure 10-6.

Here's what the Sprayer Property Bar options give you control over:

- **Object Spray Size/Scaling**   Two options control the initial object size of the Sprayer style (that is, the objects that make up a specific Sprayer type) based on a scaled percentage of the original spray object selected. When the Size/Scaling option is unlocked, you can set the scaling size of successive objects to be increased or decreased in scale relative to the size of the first object in the Sprayer style. Some preset sprays offer scaling, whereas some do not, due to their construction. The Snowflakes preset, for example, offers successive scaling, whereas the Footprints preset does not. The bottom field is dimmed when you've chosen a preset that cannot be successively scaled.

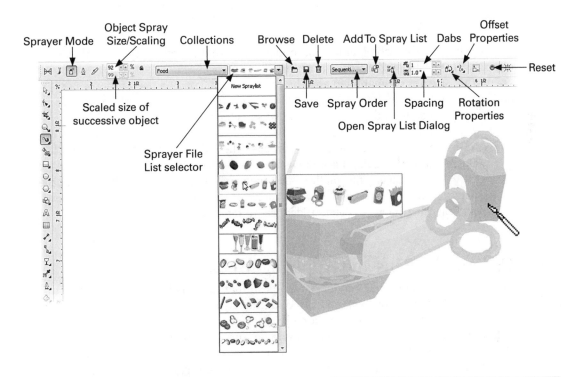

FIGURE 10-6   The Artistic Media Tool's Sprayer mode offers a huge number of design variations.

- **Spray Order**   This option lets you set the ordering of the spray objects: Randomly, Sequentially, or By Direction. If the Sprayer style features only one object to vary, changing this option has no effect. Try the Mushrooms preset in the Plants collection; the spray presets contain several different objects of different sizes and you can get different looks by choosing Randomly and By Direction.
- **Dabs and Spacing**   These two values set the *number of objects* to be placed along a drawn or existing path and *the distance between* the centers of each object. *Dabs* are the individual objects in the Sprayer style; *Spacing* controls how many objects appear within a given distance. Think of Spacing as "population."
- **Rotation**   This option sets the angle for the first object in the Sprayer style. The *Increment* option compounds rotation values for each subsequent object. Rotation angles and increment values can be based on the degree measure relative to the page or the path to which the objects are applied. If you need a circular pattern whose objects are oriented toward the center of the circle, for example, the Rotation option is your ticket.
- **Offset**   This option sets the distance between the path you click-drag and the Sprayer objects. *Offset* can be set to be active (the default) at settings between roughly 0.01 and 13 inches. The direction of the offset can also be set to Alternating (the default), Left, Random, or Right. To deactivate the Offset options, uncheck the Use Offset option in the selector, which sets the Offset measure to 0.
- **Reset**   Clicking this button returns all Sprayer style settings on the Property Bar to their original default settings.

As with other Artistic Media Tool modes, you can draw while applying this effect or apply an Artistic Media stroke to an existing line.

With a Sprayer style applied and the line selected, you can use Property Bar options to edit the effect. Doing this edits the style *only as it is applied to your line* and *not* the original style in the Sprayer File List selector.

Tip   To create your own Sprayer brush, first open the Artistic Media docker (Window | Dockers |Artistic Media). Create several shapes—they can be groups of objects, and they can contain any fill you like—and then arrange them horizontally on the page. Select them, and then click the Save button at the bottom of the docker. Saving and choosing Sprayers is almost identical to the way you save and use Brushes.

Calligraphy Pens and Applying Media

The Calligraphy Tool mode produces results similar to adjusting the Nib shape with any regular Pen tool; however, you can dynamically change the width and angle when you use the Calligraphy Tool. Additionally, your artistic approach with this tool is different than drawing paths—you click-drag to produce an entire stroke instead of click-dragging to set a node and a path segment.

You have three options on the Property Bar when Calligraphic is selected: Freehand Smoothness (the degree of accuracy when you click-drag), Width (which sets the *maximum* width because calligraphic strokes are alternately thick and thin), and Angle. Increasing values in this field rotate the stroke evaluated from the vertical in a counterclockwise direction.

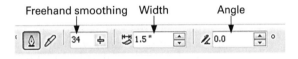

CorelDRAW X6 features a new smoothing engine for hand-drawn paths, and if you're a mouse user, you'll notice that strokes with the Calligraphy pen might not need any refinement work later. Your success depends mostly on how agile you are with a mouse.

Your experience with using a mouse, however, doesn't have to be an obstacle to creating elegant curves, handsome signatures, and other calligraphic designs. Follow this tutorial to learn how to apply a Calligraphic property—and any Artistic Media except Pressure—to an *existing* path:

Tutorial   Defining and Applying Calligraphic Brush Strokes

1. Open the Calligraphy.cdr file. There is a thin centerline on the top, unlocked layer. The bottom layer is just for reference. Mistal was used as the typeface and is a good example of calligraphic swoops, curves, and turns. Keep reading this chapter to learn how to guide a pen tool to create a similar centerline trace over a typeface.
2. With the Pick Tool, select the lowercase *a* after the initial *C*.
3. Choose the Artistic Media Tool and then click the Calligraphic Tool on the Property Bar. Do not deselect anything.
4. Here's the trick: click either the up or down elevator button to the right of the Width field (or type **.2** or **.1** in the field instead of using the elevator buttons). What you've done is get the Calligraphic pen to "recognize" that you want to change a value of the selected path's calligraphic width. The change isn't important; it's the recognition that applies the calligraphic property to the selected stroke.

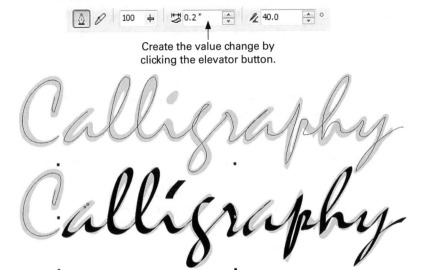

Create the value change by clicking the elevator button.

5. Continue to adjust the Width (.2" works well at the path's scale here), and then play with the Angle—anywhere from 35° to 55° looks good in this example.

6. Because you began with an existing stroke, the calligraphic treatment has an outline and no fill. Click the black color well swatch on the Color Palette, and then right-click the No Fill color well to remove the outline.

7. Perform Steps 2–6 with the initial *C*, and then with the brush, dot the *i*.

Pressure Mode

The last of the Artistic Media modes was created for users of digital tablets; if you own a stylus and tablet, you can set up the drivers for the stylus to apply pressure, and CorelDRAW will read stylus pressure to vary the width of the stroke as you drag across the page. You have Freehand Smoothing, and maximum Width controls on the Property Bar.

If you're using a mouse, you can use the up and down keyboard arrows as you drag to (respectively) increase and decrease the width of the stroke. Honestly, don't expect world-class art using the mouse and arrow keys; you might run into a design situation where you need to vary the width of a stroke, but there are other ways to edit an existing stroke that produce more refined results.

How to Draw in CorelDRAW

Artistic Media is fun and useful, but now it's time to learn how to build paths instead of brush strokes. In the same group of Curve tools, you'll find CorelDRAW's path and node creation pens; they're used for both accuracy and artistic expression, and they have varying degrees of ease of use that correspond directly to their power.

Drawing with Freehand and Polyline Tools

The *Freehand* and *Polyline Tools* share a common function, giving you the freedom to draw as if you were sketching by freehand on a physical sketch pad, but the tools work in slightly different ways. Sketched lines can create a single open or closed vector path. Both tools are located in the Toolbox grouped with other line-creation tools.

For mouse users and stylus users alike click-dragging initially produces a start node for a path segment and then a path segment that follows, and a node is placed when you release the mouse (or stylus) button, setting the end of the path segment. To use these tools:

1. Begin by selecting either the Freehand or Polyline Tool. Your next step depends on which tool you choose.

2. If you chose the Freehand Tool, you can create a continuous line by click-dragging a path shape. As soon as you release the mouse button, the line is complete, as shown next. To draw a straight line between two points, click

once to define the start point and a second time somewhere else to define the end point. As soon as you release the mouse button, the curve is complete.

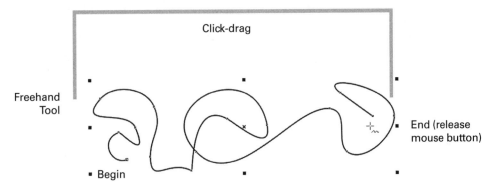

3. If you chose the Polyline Tool, the technique is slightly different. Use a click-drag action to create a continuous freehand-style line, but after releasing the mouse button, your cursor can still continue extending the curve with path segments. You click-drag to freehand-style extend the path or single-click to add a straight line path segment. Double-clicking action at your final point defines it as the endpoint.

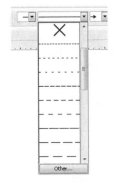

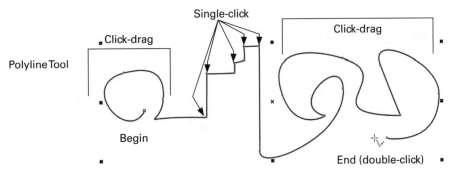

Original freehand path (no smoothing)

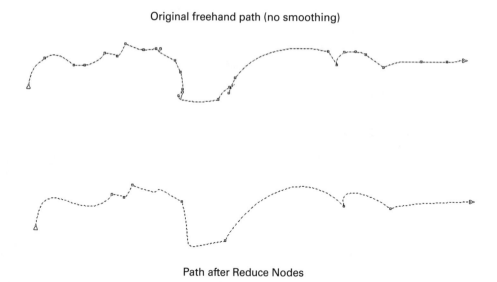

Path after Reduce Nodes

FIGURE 10-7 Freehand smoothing and Reduce Nodes can give a crudely drawn line smooth curves.

4. Both tools produce "bare bones" paths, no fancy strokes, no elegant calligraphic varying widths. This means you can use the Property Bar options to make your path begin with an arrowhead, make the line a dashed line, and change the stroke width.

Using either of these tools, you control the smoothness of path shapes drawn using click-drag actions by adjusting the Freehand Smoothing option on the Property Bar *before* drawing your path. You can control smoothness *after* drawing a path by selecting nodes with the Shape Tool and then using the Reduce Nodes spin box. Reduce Nodes has a range between 0 and 100 percent; lower values apply less smoothing, and higher values apply more smoothing, as shown in Figure 10-7.

Drawing Arcs with the 3-Point Curve Tool

The *3-Point Curve Tool* was created for artists to build perfectly smooth arcing line segments, with complete control over the direction and steepness of the curve between two points. First, while clicking you drag the tool to set a straight line that defines the angle of the curve as well as the start and end points for the curve.

Then you release the mouse button and hover the cursor to define the slope and degree of the curve; you're provided with an onscreen preview until you decide to click a point and thus create the curve. Here you can see the process and, additionally, how to extend the curve with a second segment to close the path so you can fill it. This is the basis for the tutorial to follow where you create flower petals on an almost-completed illustration.

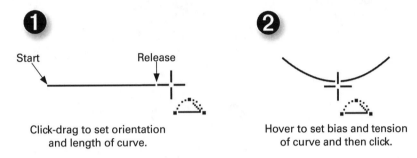

Click-drag to set orientation and length of curve.

Hover to set bias and tension of curve and then click.

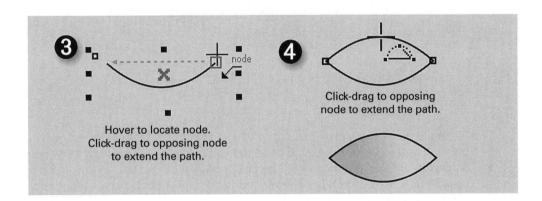

Hover to locate node.
Click-drag to opposing node
to extend the path.

Click-drag to opposing
node to extend the path.

Terms Used to Shape a Curve Segment

The terms "angle," "slope," and other common words don't accurately describe the characteristics of a curve. You'll see two additional, slightly nerdy, yet highly accurate terms used in this book:

- **Bias**   When you draw an imaginary straight line through the end points of any curve, *bias* describes which of the two end points the curve leans toward.
- **Tension**   Similarly, when a straight line runs through the two points that define a curve, tension describes how closely or how far the curve's farthest point is from the line.

(continued)

The illustration here shows examples of tension and bias. When you click a control point (a node) on a CorelDRAW path, the curve's node sets the tension and bias, while the control handles address the heading of the path—the vector direction in which the path is going.

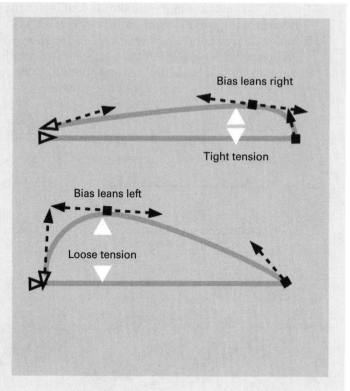

You'll quickly discover that part of the power of the 3-Point Curve Tool is its use in building a series of connected arcs; you can design French curves and ornamental borders by designing a 3-point curve, positioning your cursor over the end point until you see the cursor signifying an extension of the last-drawn curve, and then you build another 3-point curve.

In the following steps you'll create a cat's eye object that will serve as both a leaf and a flower petal to complete an illustration.

Tutorial 3-Point Curves and Closed Objects

1. Open SimpleFlower.cdr. The white outlines are where the petals should be drawn and this overlay is on the Guides layer, which is locked. The center of the flower is on a layer above the current layer, and it and the background illustration are on locked layers so there is nothing to accidentally move.

2. With the 3-Point Curve Tool, click-drag across any of the guides, beginning at one point of the petal guide and ending at the other. Release the mouse button, and then hover below the line until the curve basically matches the curve of the guide. Then click to make the 3-point curve.

3. Hover over the right node of the curve until your cursor shows an arrow and the word "node," and then click-drag to the opposite point on the underlying curve. You're extending this original curve. Release the mouse button when the cursor signifies that it's over the second point with a tiny arrow.

4. Hover and let the curve arc upward until it matches the underlying curve guide; then click. You now have a closed path that can be filled. See Figure 10-8 at left.

5. With the Interactive Fill Tool, drag from left to right over the petal object. Then drag a brown color well from the Color Palette to the left (the From color) marker, and finally, drag and drop a yellow-orange color well to the right (the To color) marker.

6. Click the selected petal to put the object into Rotate mode. With the Pick Tool, move the object center marker to the center of the brown object—the disc florets of the author's attempt to draw a Black-Eyed Susan.

7. Drag the top-right selection handle down; before releasing the mouse button, tap the right button to drop a copy of the object on to another unfilled guide object. The process is shown in Figure 10-8 at right.

8. Repeat Step 7 until you have all seven petal guides filled with duplicates of your object.

9. Drag and (right-click) drop an extra petal near the empty leaf guide on the illustration's stem. Rotate it into position and fill it with a linear gradient of two different shades of green. Save your work and water it about every 2 to 3 days.

Here's the finished drawing...

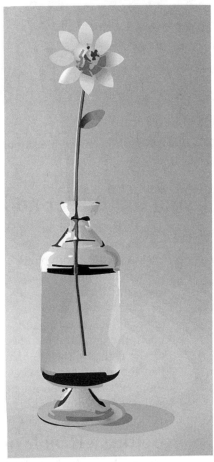

FIGURE 10-8 You can create smooth, connecting arcs quickly using the 3-Point Curve Tool.

Using the Bézier and Pen Tools

The *Bézier Tool* and the *Pen Tool* are variations on the same theme of drawing connected curves and straight segments (unlike the 3-Point Curve Tool) through the action of first clicking to set a path point, and then either dragging to define a curve behind the click point or clicking (no dragging) to define a straight path segment behind the click point. You'll find these tools grouped together with other line-drawing tools.

One of the less obvious differences between the two tools is that the Pen Tool offers a "look ahead" point when you draw with it: before you click or click-drag a point, the proposed path between the point and the previous (already defined) point on the path is shown in light blue. When you're just beginning with CorelDRAW, the Pen Tool provides a preview of the next segment you'll create, and after you gain some experience, you might want to skip the previews, pick up some drawing speed, and use the Bezier Tool.

Getting a Handle on Béziers

The product of both the Bézier Tool and the Pen Tool can be curves between two nodes whose connection to a neighboring node is smooth and symmetrical. Control handles are revealed on smooth, symmetrical nodes when you click one using the Shape Tool. These handles are used for intuitively reshaping the curve.

You can also create straight path segments between curves using the Bézier Tool. *Click-dragging* creates smooth curves that have smooth connections between segments, whereas the act of *clicking without dragging* sets a path point that is not smooth—if you click again in a different location, the result is a straight path segment.

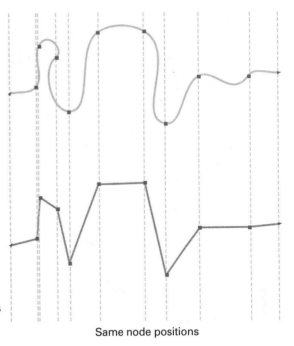

Because straight line segments and curve segments share so much in their fundamental anatomy, this chapter makes almost no distinction between the terms "line" and "curve" in the discussions. The shapes of Bézier lines are controlled in part by node properties and the position of curve handles. Two paths can have nodes in the same relative page position, but have completely different shapes, as shown here.

Same node positions

Nodes and Control Points

When a vector path describes an arc, *nodes* (points) connect a beginning and end point, and the nodes have *control handles,* at the end of which are *control points,* the screen element you use to manipulate curves. The number of control handles and points depends on the segment connected by each node. For example, an arc (a curve) connected to a straight line segment has one control handle visible and it controls the slope of the curve segment. When two curve segments are connected, you see two control handles if you click the connecting node with the Shape Tool, and this node can have different connection properties (Cusp, Smooth—described momentarily). A straight path segment can be described as two nodes connecting the segment, and the control handles for the nodes coincide in position with the node itself. For all intents and purposes, the control handles can't be seen; they become visible when the segment is changed to a curved segment: the control handles appear on the segment, and you can move them away from the launch point of the curve and then freely manipulate the slope of the curve by dragging the control points.

Nodes can be defined as Cusp, Smooth, or Symmetrical by using the Shape Tool in combination with the options on the Property Bar, as shown in the next illustration. *Cusp* nodes can be used to create a discontinuity in direction between two line segments;

in English, the two segments connect in a nonsmooth fashion. Think of the moon being on the cusp; it's crescent shaped and this is the sort of shape you can create using Cusp node connections. *Smooth* nodes cause the path slope and direction to align on either side of a node; their relationship is in 180° opposition, which has the effect of creating a smooth transition at the node

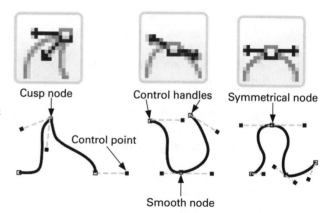

point itself. Control handles surrounding a Smooth node may be unequal distances from the node. *Symmetrical* nodes are not only smooth, but the control handles are of equal distance from the node. You'll immediately appreciate the effect of a Symmetrical node; when you drag one control point away from a node, the opposing control handle moves an equal distance from the node in exactly the opposite direction. The artistic effect is that the two joined path segments take on an almost circular appearance, which is very useful for technical illustration work.

Drawing Conventions for the Bézier and Pen Tools

Both of these tools are used to create *compound paths* (segments connected by a common node) by combining a series of clicks or click-drags, but each is used in slightly different ways for different results. Using either of these tools, however, single-clicks define new node positions joined by straight segments. Curve segments are created by clicking to define the node position and then *dragging* to define the curve shape. Click-dragging in succession creates a continuous curved path shaped by multiple nodes and off-the-curve control handles. When using the Bézier Tool, each click-drag defines and completes the curve segment. A little differently, when using the Pen Tool, the cursor remains active, and a preview of the next curve segment appears, so you can define both the curve shape and the next node point. Double-clicking ends the series of path segments.

Tip When drawing with the Bézier Tool, holding CTRL as you click to create new nodes constrains their position to align vertically, horizontally, or within constrained angles relative to the last created node position. Holding CTRL while dragging curve handles constrains their angles to 15° increments relative to the last node created.

Let's try out a new drawing method:

Tutorial Drawing Curves and Straight Line Segments

1. Choose either the Bézier Tool or the Pen Tool and use a single-click action to define the first node position of your path. Click again to define a second point somewhere else on your page. The two nodes are now joined by a straight line.

2. Using the click-drag mouse technique, click to define your next node position, but continue dragging in any direction. As you drag, the second and third nodes are joined by a curved line.

3. If you chose the Bézier Tool, you'll notice that two control handles appear joined by a dotted line. The point you are dragging is the control point that steers the control handle. The farther you drag the control point from the node, the larger the arc of the curve. Release the mouse button and notice that the control handles remain in view and your path is complete unless you'd like to move a node or refine the position of its control points some more.

4. If you chose the Pen Tool, you'll notice that a preview of your next curve appears as you move your cursor, which remains active until the next node is defined. To specify a node as the last in the path, double-click to define the current node as the last point.

5. Using either tool, click your cursor directly on the first node you defined. This action closes the path and automatically joins the first and last nodes.

Editing Bézier Paths

All lines are controlled by properties of the nodes they include, which are edited using the Shape Tool (F10). You'll find this tool, shown here, grouped with the Shape Edit tools

Using the *Shape Tool,* you can change node positions and curve shapes by click-dragging the nodes, their control points, and by directly click-dragging on a path segment. When using the Shape Tool, icons appear on the Property Bar when one or more nodes are selected; you can select several nodes to change by marquee-dragging them or by SHIFT-clicking a few. These icons are used to set node attributes to Cusp, Smooth, and Symmetrical; to join node and break nodes to create individual path segments; and to create straight lines from curves (and vice versa) when you've selected a segment or a node connecting segments. There are additional options and the bevy of functions on the Property Bar provides exceptional control and flexibility in your design work. In short, you should *get to know the functions* for the Shape Tool. The options are called out in Figure 10-9.

Shape Tool

Shape   F10
Smudge Brush
Roughen Brush
Free Transform
Smear
Twirl
Attract
Repel

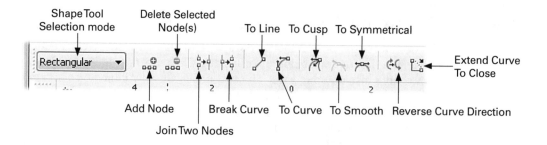

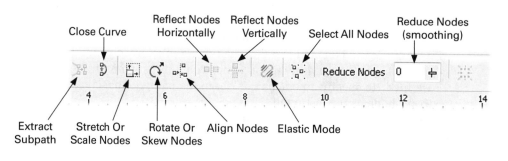

FIGURE 10-9 The Property Bar offers comprehensive control over path and node properties.

Each of these buttons changes the selected nodes, lines, and curves in specific ways. The following is a description of what the icons do and what they're called.

- **Shape Tool Selection mode** You can marquee-select nodes the way users always have, by click-dragging a rectangular shape around the nodes you want to select, or using Freehand style you can produce a lasso-like marquee, which allows you to be very careful and exacting about which nodes in a group you want to edit. In Freehand style, you might also want to press SHIFT to add to selected nodes.
- **Add/Delete Nodes** These buttons give you the power to add new nodes to a curve or delete selected nodes after you've drawn a path, using the Shape Tool and clicking at specific points on a path. To add a node, click any point on a line to highlight the new position and then click the Add Node button. You can also add a new node to a line by clicking one or more nodes and then clicking the Add Node button to add a node midpoint between the selected node and the next node on the path. Pressing the plus (+) key on your numeric keypad achieves the same thing and you might find this to be the quicker method. To delete a node, click to select it with the Shape Tool and click the Delete Node button. You can also marquee-select (drag diagonally with the Shape Tool to create a rectangle surrounding the nodes) and then delete all of the selected node in one fell swoop. Pressing the minus (–) key on your numeric keypad or your DELETE key also deletes selected nodes.

- **Join Two Nodes/Break Curve**   When two unconnected nodes on an open path are selected, for example, when the start point is close to the end point, pressing the Join Nodes button connects them to create an unbroken path. For single paths, only the unjoined beginning and ending nodes may be joined. For compound paths (paths that aren't necessarily close to one another, but have been joined using the Arrange | Combine command), the beginning and ending nodes selected on two existing—but separate—paths can also be joined. While a single node is selected or while a specific point on a segment is clicked, pressing the Break Curve button results in two nodes becoming unjoined, in turn breaking a closed path and turning it into an open path.

Tip Unjoined paths are not the same as separate objects. Two paths, for example, can be located *nowhere near* each other on a page and yet still be part of a single path. If you want to break a path into its component subpaths, you first select the nodes using a marquee-selection technique with the Shape Tool, click the Break Curve button, and then choose Arrange | Break Curve Apart. CTRL+K is the shortcut, and it's one of a handful of CorelDRAW shortcuts you'll want to commit to memory for life.

- **To Curve/To Line**   These two buttons are used to toggle the state of a selected straight line to a curve state, and vice versa. A single click with the Shape Tool selects a line or curve indicated by a round black marker on the line. When curves are converted to lines, the path they follow takes on a shortcut (as in "the shortest distance between two points"); when converting a straight line to a curve, the path remains the same shape, but control handles appear directly on the "line" and the quickest way to make the control points visible is to drag on the line to force it into a curve shape.
- **Extend Curve To Close**   For this command to be available, you must have both the beginning and ending nodes of an open path selected (marquee-select the points, or SHIFT + click to select them both). Under these conditions, clicking the Extend Curve To Close button joins the two nodes by adding a straight line between them and closes the path.
- **Close Curve**   With an open path selected, clicking this button joins the beginning and end nodes to form a closed path by adding a new straight line between the two nodes; it's a similar command to Extend Curve To Close, but depending on the closeness of the start and end path nodes, you might not even see a visible straight-line connection. You can also join the end points of a selected curve using the Close Curve option in the Object Properties docker, which you open by pressing ALT + ENTER.
- **Reverse Curve Direction**   With a curve path on a line selected, clicking this button has the effect of changing the direction of the path. By doing this, the start point of the path becomes the endpoint (and vice versa). The results of using this command button are most noticeable when the start or end of the line or path has been applied with an arrowhead, meaning the arrowhead is applied to the opposite end of the line or path. You may also notice subtle changes in the appearance of line styles applied to a path after using this command button.

- **Extract Subpath**   This option becomes available only when you've select a compound path. After clicking the Extract Subpath button, the selected path is separated from the compound path, converting it to a separate path. Using this command on a compound path composed of only two different paths is essentially the same as using the Break Apart command. It's more useful when you need to extract a specific path from a compound path made up of three or more paths.

- **Stretch Or Scale Nodes**   This very powerful CorelDRAW feature is not available in competing applications. When at least two nodes on a path are selected, clicking Stretch Or Scale Nodes allows you to create transformation between nodes using their relative distance from each other vertically, horizontally, or from center. Eight selection handles become available, just like object selection using the Pick Tool, and you can use a click-drag action from any corner or side selection handle toward or away from the center of the node selection. Holding SHIFT constrains the stretch or scale operation from the center of the selection.

- **Rotate Or Skew Nodes**   Similar to Stretch Or Scale Nodes, when at least two nodes on a path are selected, clicking the Rotate Or Skew Nodes button lets you rotate and skew the selected nodes; this feature is great for refining a shape just a little, and also for creating more dramatic appearance changes (see the following illustration). Eight selection handles become available, enabling you to use a click-drag action from any corner selection handle to rotate the nodes in a circular direction either clockwise or counterclockwise. Dragging from any side handle enables you to skew the node selection either vertically or horizontally.

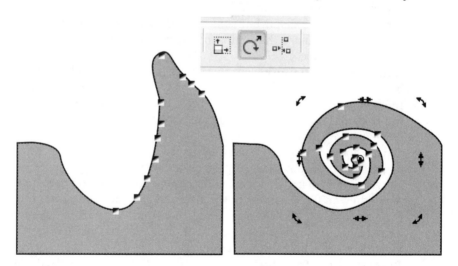

- **Align Nodes**   When two or more nodes are selected, clicking this button opens the Node Align dialog, where you choose from the Align Vertical or Align Horizontal options that automatically align your node selection accordingly. In addition to these options, while only the beginning and ending nodes of an open path are selected, you can also choose to align control points. This moves the two end points of the line to overlap each other precisely. This command is wonderful for quickly sketching a zigzag (perhaps for an illustration of saw blades) and, then in one step, aligning the nodes to create a precise illustration.

- **Reflect Nodes Horizontally/Vertically** These two buttons become available when two or more nodes are selected. You use these options to move nodes using nudge keys (the up, down, left, and right keys on your keyboard) or click-drag actions in opposite directions.

Tip To quickly access many of the same eligible Shape Tool node and curve commands that are available using buttons on the Property Bar, right-click the nodes or segments of a path and choose these same commands from the pop-up menu.

- **Elastic Mode** With this command, you move selected nodes according to their relative distance from each other; the effect is like experimenting with a rubber band. For example, when you select a collection of nodes, dragging one of the nodes causes the others to be dragged a shorter distance in relation to the node that is being dragged. When Elastic Mode is off, all the selected nodes are moved equal distances. Try this option to add a more organic and natural feeling to a drawing you might feel looks a little too studied and stiff; it adds expression to a path.
- **Reduce Nodes** When you select this command, CorelDRAW evaluates the overall shape based on the nodes you've selected, deletes nodes that deviate from a predictable course along the path, and then repositions the remaining nodes—the effect is to smooth the curve. For past CorelDRAW users, this was called the Curve Smoothness slider. To use this feature, select the nodes controlling the segments you want to smooth and drag the Reduce Nodes slider control position toward 100. As you drag the slider, the shape of the curves becomes smoothed and you'll notice superfluous nodes disappear from the curve. This option is useful for smoothing lines drawn using the Freehand Tool with either the mouse or a digitizing tablet stylus.
- **Select All Nodes** This button selects all the nodes in a path (or compound path) using one click. It's a great feature for users who aren't expert with the marquee-drag selection technique yet. You may also select all the nodes in a path with the Shape Tool by holding CTRL + SHIFT and clicking any node on the path.

Are you ready to text drive the Shape Tool? Follow along here:

Tutorial ## Editing Paths with the Shape Tool

1. Choose the Ellipse Tool (F7) and create an ellipse of any size. Convert the ellipse shape to curves (CTRL + Q) to create a closed path with four nodes joined by four curved lines.
2. Choose the Shape Tool (F10). Notice that the Property Bar now features all the line and node command buttons. Click the Select All Nodes button to select all nodes on the path.
3. With the nodes still selected, click the Add Node button (or press the + button on your numeric keypad). Notice that four new nodes are added at the midpoint between the four original nodes.
4. Click any of the segments once and click the To Line button. The curve is now a straight line, and the curve handles have disappeared.

5. Click a node on one of the other existing curves, drag either of the curve handles in any direction, and notice how they change the shape of the path.

6. Using a click-drag action, click near the middle of the curve segment and drag in any direction. As you drag, the curve handle positions at either end both move, and the shape of the curve is changed accordingly.

7. Click any node on the path to select it and click the Smooth Node button. Drag the curve handle of this node in any direction. Notice that the curve handle may be dragged only in a single direction. Click the Cusp Node button and then perform the same action. Notice that the lines on either side of the node can be curved in any direction independently of each other.

8. With this node still selected, click the Break Curve button to split the path at this point. Although it may not be obvious, two nodes now exist where the original node used to be. Drag either of these nodes in any direction to separate their positions. The nodes are now control points because they break the path to form beginning and end points.

9. Select one of these nodes, hold SHIFT while clicking the other, and click the Extend Curve To Close button. Notice the curve is now closed again, while the two nodes have been joined by a straight line.

10. Undo your last action (CTRL + Z) to unjoin the nodes and, while they remain selected, click the Align Nodes button to open the Align Nodes dialog. If they aren't already selected, click to select all three options (Align Horizontal, Vertical, and Control Points) in the dialog and click OK to align the points. Notice that they are positioned to overlap precisely. Click to select both nodes and click the Join Two Nodes button on the Property Bar. Your path is now closed, and the nodes are joined.

11. Hold SHIFT and click to select two or more nodes on your path. With your nodes selected, click the Stretch Or Scale Nodes button and notice that eight selection handles appear around your node selection. Hold the SHIFT key (to constrain from center) and drag one of the corner handles toward or away from the center of the selection. All node positions are scaled relative to each other's position, and the lines joining the unselected nodes also change shape.

12. With the nodes still selected, click the Rotate Or Skew Nodes button on the Property Bar. Notice that eight rotate and skew handles appear around your selection. Drag any of the corner rotation handles either clockwise or counterclockwise to rotate the nodes. Notice that they are rotated relative to their current position, and the lines joining the unselected nodes also change shape.

The preceding tutorial is only a sampling of what you can accomplish when editing nodes using the Shape Tool. You'll want to invest some quality time practicing your editing skills using all the available node-shaping command buttons because the payoff is better artwork—artwork that's closer to what you have in your head—and in the long run, you'll save time creating wonderful pieces.

Tip To set the drawing behavior of the Freehand and/or Bézier tools, double-click either of their tool buttons in the Toolbox to open the Options dialog to the Freehand/Bézier Tool page. Options are discussed in the next section.

Controlling Freehand and Bézier Tool Behavior

The settings to control how Freehand and Bézier Tools create the curves and lines you draw are set using a series of options in the Freehand/Bézier Tool pane of the Options dialog, shown next. To access these options, choose Tools | Options (CTRL + J), expand the tree subdirectory under Toolbox, and click Freehand/Bézier Tool. The quick way to get to this dialog is to double-click the Freehand or Bézier Tool buttons after choosing them from the Line Tool group; you're then taken to Toolbox, where you click the subdirectory option you need in the tab area.

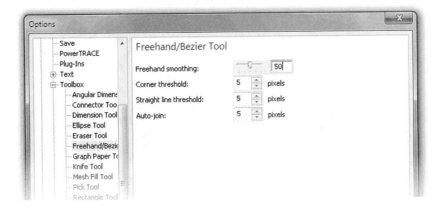

Here's how the options work:

- **Freehand Smoothing**   The Freehand Smoothing option enables you to set the default value of the Freehand Smoothing option in the Property Bar while drawing with the Freehand Tool. Smoothing may be set based on a percentage within a range between 0 (minimum smoothing) and 100 (maximum smoothing). This option is largely the same as the Freehand Smoothing option available on the Property Bar when a curve and the Shape Tool are selected.
- **Corner Threshold**   This option is for setting the default value for corner nodes when drawing with the Freehand or Bézier Tool. Lower values cause more nodes to be created with the Cusp attribute; higher values tend to produce more nodes with the Smooth attribute as you draw. The range may be set between 1 and 10; the default is 5.
- **Straight Line Threshold**   This option pertains to how the shapes of lines or curves are created when drawing with the Freehand Tool. Lower values tend to produce more straight path segments between nodes, whereas higher values produce more curved segments between nodes. The range may be set between 1 and 10; the default is 5.
- **Auto-Join**   This option sets the behavior of the Freehand or Bézier Tool while drawing closed-path objects. This value represents the distance in pixels your cursor must be when clicking *near* the first node of a newly created path to close the path automatically. Auto-Join can be set anywhere within a range between 1 and 10 pixels; the default is 5 and is probably the best overall choice for the large screen resolutions we all run today.

Working with Compound Paths

Compound paths have at least two separate paths (either open or closed) composing a single shape. To examine a compound path, follow these steps:

1. Choose the Text Tool (F8), click once to define a text insertion point, and then type an uppercase Q character. You can assign the character any typeface you like; the more ornamental the character, the more obvious the compound path soon will be. This character shape, shown in the illustration, has two paths that are combined: one represents the "positive" space and one represents the "negative" space shape.

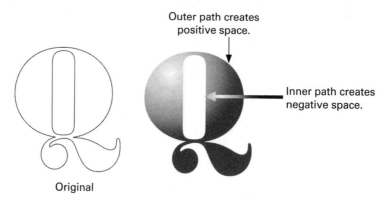

Outer path creates positive space.

Inner path creates negative space.

Original

2. While the text object is selected, convert it to curves (CTRL + Q). The Status Bar now indicates the object is a Curve on Layer 1.
3. Change your view to Wireframe; choose View | Wireframe.
4. Press CTRL + K (Arrange | Break Curve Apart). With the Pick Tool, click an empty area of the page to deselect the current selected objects, and then click one of the shapes and drag to move it; clearly the two paths are now separate. You can return to Enhanced view now; you have just converted a compound path featuring two subpaths into two individual objects, as shown here.

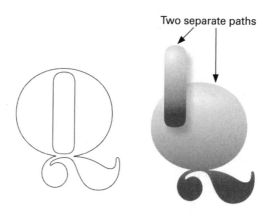

Two separate paths

Combining Objects

When separate objects are combined, they behave as a single object. When two or more closed paths are combined, they form positive and negative spaces within the object. Applying a fill to this type of object fills the positive shapes, and the negative shapes remain clear, as shown here. The Combine command does this: choose Arrange | Combine, or press the CTRL + L shortcut. You can also click the Combine button or the Property Bar, or choose Combine from the pop-up menu.

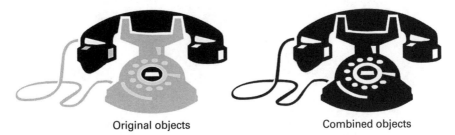

Original objects   Combined objects

Combining objects that normally feature unique properties—such as rectangles, ellipses, polygons, and perfect shapes—permanently converts them to curves.

Breaking Paths Apart

You can separate the individual paths in a compound path using the Break Curve Apart command (CTRL + K). This command is available when a compound path composed of at least two subpaths is selected. (Using the Extract Subpath command button on the Property Bar also does this, but only for the *selected* path.)

Converting Objects to Curves

Converting special types of objects to curves—such as shapes auto-created with the Rectangle and Ellipse Tools—frees them to be manipulated with the Shape Tool as if they were ordinary paths. Choose Arrange | Convert To Curves, press CTRL + Q, click the Convert To Curves button on the Property Bar, or right-click the object and choose Convert To Curves from the pop-up menu.

Converting an object to curves removes any special editing properties; text loses its editability as text and rounded rectangles can no longer be edited to refine the curvature of the rounded corners. Convert To Curves applies to polygon, ellipse, artistic text objects, and certain effects objects such as envelopes and Perspective effects.

In this chapter, you've learned that CorelDRAW has different tools for creating paths, but the results are more or less always the same; objects have path segments and nodes, and paths can be open or closed. You've also learned how to edit paths using the Shape Tool. You'd be well served to bookmark this chapter; there's an awful lot of power in CorelDRAW's drawing and editing tools and this chapter can be a good reference in the future. After all, the program isn't called CorelFILL or CorelRECTANGLE—*drawing* is what good artwork and vector design is all about.

11 Editing Objects

O nce you've created an object, you might want to *edit* it, and editing objects is the theme of this chapter. Whether it's a preset object drawn with the Rectangle Tool, or manual design work done with the Pen tools, not even skilled illustrators are always satisfied with their first try. You'll learn various techniques in the pages to follow to massage that almost-perfect shape into *exactly* the shape you've envisioned. This chapter covers the tools and features for breaking down shapes, combining them, subtracting a little of this, adding a little of that. Often, creating an *approximation* of an object you need is a good first step. Then, with a pull and a tug here and there, erasing a tiny area perhaps, you'll get quicker results than if you had built the object from scratch. You'll also see in this chapter that you can add visual complexity and embellishments that would be hard to achieve using other methods.

Download and extract all the files from the Chapter11.zip archive to follow the tutorials in this chapter.

Reshaping Things

You have a choice of two places to begin when you want to edit an object: you can use operations (buttons on the Property Bar you click to perform a preset function), or you can use the hands-on approach; both are covered in this chapter. Both approaches will serve you well, and your choice largely depends on what you need to edit and then what type of operation is required.

Shaping and Reshaping Object Shapes

Shaping commands such as Trim, Weld, Intersect, and Create Boundary make creating complex shapes from basic ones such as ellipses and polygons a quick and painless process. You'll also find three other shaping commands at your disposal: Simplify, Front Minus Back, and Back Minus Front. Before getting into the specifics of each type, though, let's take a look at where you can find them in CorelDRAW X6.

Shaping Commands and the Property Bar

CorelDRAW X6's Property Bar provides shaping command buttons that help you to shape selected objects instantly. These Property Bar options become available only when two or more objects are selected. Regardless of whether the objects overlap on the page, when you select them, the shaping commands on the Property Bar are available (not dimmed). The Property Bar's shaping buttons are shown here:

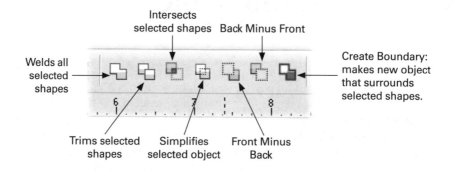

 Tip When using the Property Bar shaping buttons, new shapes are subtracted, added, and so on, but often the original objects go away. To keep your original objects, use the Shaping docker, which offers options to specify that the source object (the one performing the operation—the "scissors") and/or target object (the object receiving the operation—the "paper") should remain after shaping.

 Tip When using the Shaping docker's Weld and Intersect operations, you have an additional helper: the Intersect With or the Weld To button at the bottom. When only one object is selected on the page, CorelDRAW cannot perform shaping operations. However, with the Intersect With and Weld To options, if you have several objects nestled closely together (making a target object hard to select), you click the Weld... or the Intersect... button, your cursor changes to a unique shape, and you then click any target object to complete the operation.

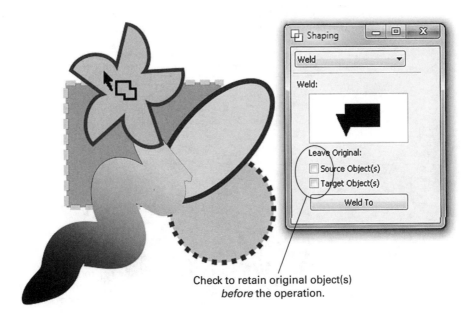

Check to retain original object(s)
before the operation.

Now that you know where the buttons are located, let's examine what you can *do* with them. The following section explains the results of applying each command to at least two selected objects:

- **Weld**   The *Weld* command creates a new shape based on the outline shape of two (or more) overlapping objects, as shown here. When Weld is used on several objects, the resulting object is the color of the *bottommost* original object.

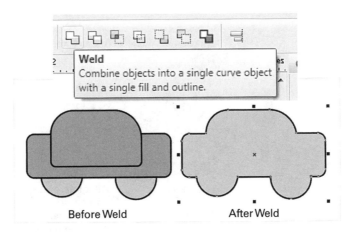

Before Weld   After Weld

- **Trim**   The *Trim* command removes any overlapping areas of the object in front from the object in back, as shown here. The original objects are automatically deleted, and no color change takes place—the back object does not inherit the front object's color, transparency, or any other trait.

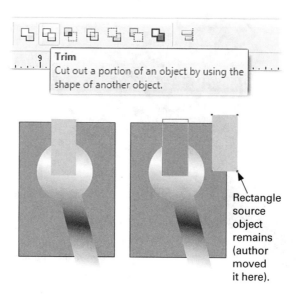

Rectangle source object remains (author moved it here).

- **Intersect**   The *Intersect* operation creates a new object based on the overlapping areas of two or more objects. The original objects remain on the page, and the result is not obvious because the new object is in the same position as the overlapping parts of the original objects. In this illustration, the rectangle is on the bottom, and the resulting shape takes on the color of the bottom object. Intersect is a great operation for creating difficult crops of complex objects, and the result here is a nice abstract logo or icon.

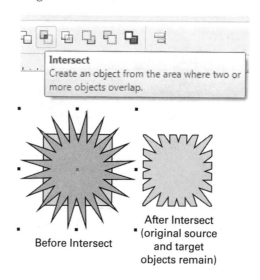

Before Intersect

After Intersect (original source and target objects remain)

- **Simplify**   The *Simplify* command removes all hidden areas of objects that "underlap" foreground objects. This command is great for uncomplicating an intricate drawing by removing bottom areas that are hidden by upper objects. Simplify is similar but not identical to the Trim and the Back Minus Front operations. Different order and arrangements of objects will result in slightly different results.
- **Front Minus Back**   When two or more shapes are selected, applying the Front Minus Back command removes the hidden area of the object in back from the shape in front. When more than two shapes are selected, it removes all portions where the shapes in back are overlapped by the object in front, leaving only the object in front remaining, as shown here:

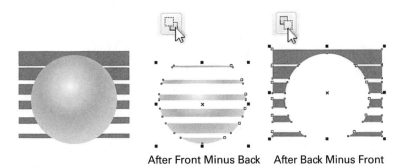

After Front Minus Back   After Back Minus Front

Front Minus Back is a trim operation ("A but not B" if you're fluent in Boolean geometry statements), and the advantage to using this operation to trim objects is that it removes the guesswork of, "Gosh, what's the order of the objects in this design?" Front Minus Back is an unambiguous, straightforward trim operation.

- **Back Minus Front**   This shaping command is the reverse of Front Minus Back. While at least two shapes are selected, applying the Back Minus Front command removes the portions of the shape layered in front from the shape in back. When more than two shapes are selected, it removes all portions where the shapes in front overlap the shape in back, leaving only the shape in back remaining.
- **Create Boundary**   This command is similar to the Weld operation, except it leaves the target objects on the page. Also, if there are empty spaces between objects, Create Boundary ignores those spaces when making the combined single object. The next illustration shows several objects selected at left, and the resulting shape after the Create Boundary operation. By default, the new object has no fill

and is ordered on top of the Target objects. Just click a foreground color on the color strip, and the new object will become immediately apparent.

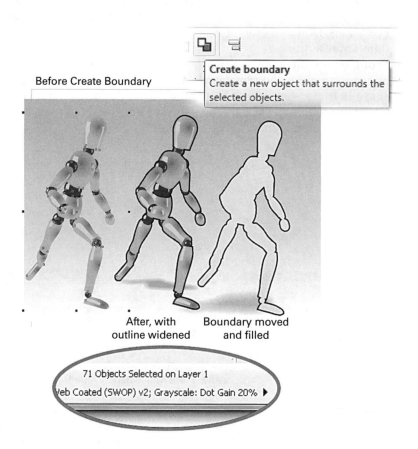

Using the Shaping Docker

Under the Arrange menu, you'll find all the shaping commands, and also the Shaping command itself, which displays the Shaping docker. This docker offers more options than you get when using the shaping operations from the Property Bar. Because of their operation, the Simplify, Front Minus Back, and Back Minus Front operations only have an Apply button.

Unique to the Weld, Trim, and Intersect commands, you must have at least one object selected and another unselected (but still in view) for the commands to be available. Once Weld, Trim, or Intersect is selected, the docker displays the available options, shown next. Clicking the docker command button begins the action.

Shape command selector

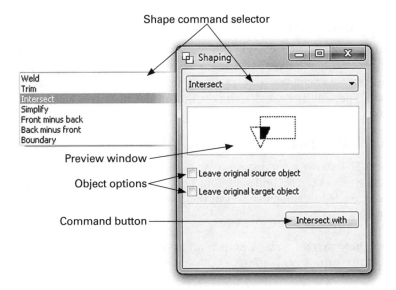

Weld
Trim
Intersect
Simplify
Front minus back
Back minus front
Boundary

Preview window

Object options

Command button

The Object options check boxes are what you use to set what object, if any, remains after an operation. Leave Original is equivalent to "make a copy so I don't lose my originals," and the options mean:

- **Leave Original Source Object**   When this option is selected, the object you selected before the shaping operation remains after the command has been applied.
- **Leave Original Target Object**   With this option selected, the object you Trim, Weld to, or Intersect with remains after the command has been applied.

Let's give this docker a spin. First, create two shapes; the Rectangle Tool is fine to make shapes you won't need later, so they're expendable in this example:

1. If you haven't already done so, create the objects on which you want to base your new shape, and position them in such a way that the shape created by their overlapping portions represents your new shape. Two ellipses or rectangles are fine for this example.
2. Select one of these overlapping objects, and open the Shaping docker if it's not already open by choosing Arrange | Shaping | Shaping.
3. Choose Weld, Trim, or Intersect from the selector at the top of the docker.
4. Choose which original object(s) you want to remain after the command has been applied by clicking Leave Original Source Object and/or Leave Original Target Object, and then click the command button at the bottom of the docker to apply the command. Notice your cursor has changed to one of three targeting cursors, depending on your shaping operation.
5. Click the object you want your selected object to Trim, Weld to, or Intersect with. Your new shape is immediately created based on the overlapping area of your existing objects. There is only one button on the docker, although its label changes, depending on your selection: Intersect With, Weld To, and simply Apply with many of the operations. Click the button to perform the operation.

Working Examples of Object Shaping

If you've seen some stunning CorelDRAW objects and have said to yourself, "Wow, that must've taken the artist ages to do all that work," nope, it probably didn't: the artist put *object shaping* to work. The following examples show just two of thousands of creative possibilities for shaping operations; let the examples kindle your inspiration.

Tutorial Learning by Example

Figure 11-1 shows a combination Weld and then a Trim, although Back Minus Front would work as the second step, too. The problem in this composition is that a specific font is needed in stencil style, but the artist doesn't have such a typeface. So Arial is first used and then:

1. Draw several rectangles over areas that need to be removed from the text to create the stencil effect.

Black rectangles are welded.

Effects | Add Perspective plus transparency

Welded rectangles trim text.

FIGURE 11-1   Weld and then Trim are used to make a stencil treatment out of the text.

2. Create duplicates of one narrow rectangle by using the drop a copy technique: drag a rectangle to a new location and then tap the right mouse button while dragging and then release both buttons. Doing this keeps consistency between areas to be removed from the text.
3. After all the rectangles are in position, marquee-select the rectangles, be sure the text *isn't* selected, and then use the Weld command to make a single object out of the rectangles.
4. With the object created by the welded-together rectangles still selected, it becomes a source object to trim the text. Click the Trim button in the docker. The text is trimmed.
5. Finally use Effects | Add Perspective to make the text appear as though it's on the popcorn box. The text probably could use some rotation, but you get the idea.

Figure 11-2 uses Back Minus Front, Weld, and an Arrow Shape (covered in Chapter 16) to create a complex-looking design for a corporate logo. First, draw a circle using the Ellipse Tool while holding CTRL (to constrain ovals to perfect circles).

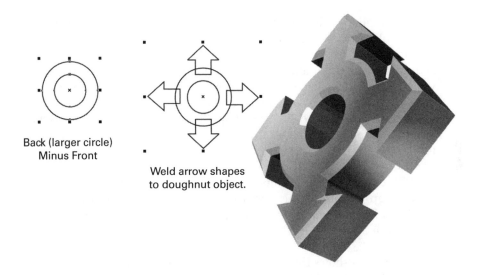

Back (larger circle) Minus Front

Weld arrow shapes to doughnut object.

Extrude with bevel edge.

FIGURE 11-2   Complex illustrations don't need to take a lot of time. Get to know the Shaping tools, and what you envision is only a few clicks away.

Then, to put a smaller circle centered inside the first, you hold SHIFT, drag the original circle's corner-bounding box handle toward the center, and then right-click before releasing the left mouse button to create a scaled duplicate. Choose Back Minus Front on the Shaping docker with both objects selected, click Apply, and you have a perfect doughnut object. The Arrow Shapes come in all four directions on the Property Bar; drag the four arrows to use this tool, arrange them, and then select all four arrows. Choose the Weld operation on the Shaping docker. Then with the large arrow cursor, click the doughnut to indicate it's the target object. This *could* be the end of the story; with only a few more clicks, you can extrude and rotate the resulting shape. See Chapter 19 for the complete details on object extrusion.

Fillet/Scallop/Chamfer

The Fillet/Scallop/Chamfer docker is displayed by choosing it from Window | Dockers. With it, you have your choice of truncating any sharp corners on an object you draw. This docker will *not* alter a curved path segment: a shape that consists of straight paths is the best one to use with this feature. Objects with a *combination* of curved and straight segments are only affected along the convergence of two straight path segments.

When Fillet/Scallop/Chamfer evaluates sharp direction changes along a path, it "rounds off" the point of a convex area toward the *inside* of the path. This is a terrific feature for quickly building elegant objects such as furniture pieces, machine parts, and simply nice ornaments for desktop publishing documents. You enter a positive value in the Radius field (or use the elevator buttons on the docker); you see a faint outline preview in your document; and then you click Apply when you're happy with the preview on the page. Fillet/Scallop/Chamfer is a *destructive* operation, unlike the Shaping operations. If you want to keep your original object, duplicate it *before* using this docker.

- **Fillet** Rounds the corners of an object.
- **Scallop** Trims a semicircle from the corner of an object.
- **Chamfer** Lops a straight angle off a corner at an angle perpendicular to the interior angle of the corner.

Figure 11-3 shows the effects of the Fillet/Scallop/Chamfer docker on the same zigzag object, created by single-clicking with the Pen Tool. Because the radius of this trimming effect is measured in page units, it's a good idea to keep rulers visible in your document and refer to them to achieve the exact degree of corner truncation you need.

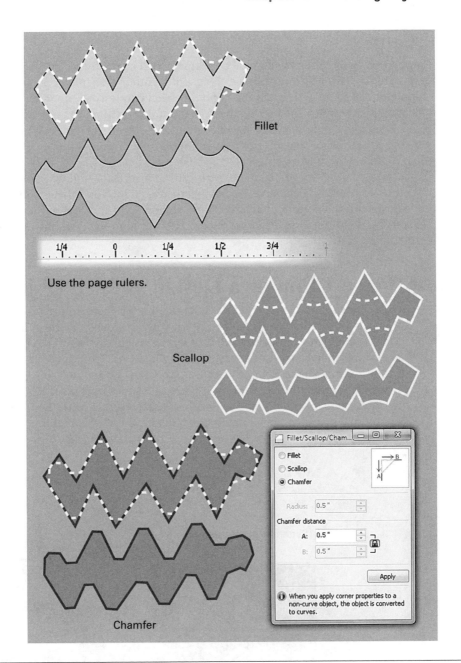

FIGURE 11-3   Use the Fillet/Scallop/Chamfer docker to take the corners off an object with intricacy and classic style.

PowerClips

CorelDRAW PowerClips change the appearance of a shape by hiding certain areas of its exterior with a different shape. This, unlike other reshaping operations, is completely nondestructive and the clipping object can release the inner clipped object(s) at any time. Consider the usefulness of PowerClips: You can hide most of an object from view and put other objects behind the PowerClip. You can play a dozen possible scenarios for the composition you have on a page and never commit to any of them, unlike trimming an object.

To give you an idea of the creative power of PowerClips, follow these steps with a document whose objects have already been created for you. The assignment is to put a design on the bottom of a flower vase, stencil-style, so parts of the vase's original color still show through in different regions. It's not hard to do when you're familiar with PowerClips:

Tutorial PowerClipping a Design onto an Object

1. Open Flower and Vase.cdr. To the left, you'll see a grouped pattern with transparency. Below is the same pattern with an Envelope effect applied to make the pattern look bulged, as it would when viewed on the surface of a round shape such as the vase drawing here. At right, At right, the thin yellow outline shape is a fairly accurate trace over the vase. This is your PowerClip shape for the pattern—it hides all shapes outside of it. If you'd like to experiment with the non-enveloped grouped pattern with the Envelope Tool, Chapter 20 provides the complete documentation on this feature.

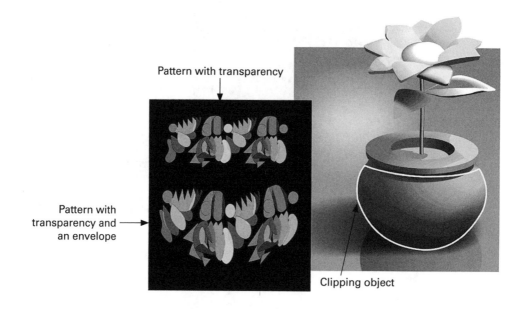

Pattern with transparency

Pattern with transparency and an envelope

Clipping object

2. Select the bottom pattern with the Pick Tool, and then drag it so it's on top of the yellow outline object, making certain that all parts of the pattern overlap the outline. You don't want gaps in the pattern as it's displayed on the vase.
3. Choose Effects | PowerClip | Place Inside Frame.
4. Your cursor turns into a huge arrow. Click the cursor over the yellow outline and the pattern scoots inside the container object.
5. The container object is now selected. Right-click over the No Fill color well on the Color Palette to remove the outline, or alternatively, choose None for the Outline Width from the drop-down list on the Property Bar. See Figure 11-4.

Although the preceding example shows how to mask the exterior of a group of shapes, a PowerClip frame can also have an outline width, color, and a fill. In any case, the nondestructive property of PowerClips will serve you in a number of design situations.

FIGURE 11-4   Let empty areas in patterns and other complex drawings show through a PowerClip object.

Occasionally, an object inside the PowerClip container might not be aligned perfectly relative to your overall composition. You also might like to do a little editing to the contained object(s). You don't edit directly on the page. Here are the editing options for a PowerClipped object:

- To reveal the object for editing or repositioning relative to the PowerClip object, right-click over the object and then choose Edit Contents from the pop-up menu. A blue outline indicates the size and position of the PowerClip container. When you're done editing, right-click inside the frame and then choose Finish Editing This Level.
- To undo the PowerClip effect, you can press CTRL + Z right after selecting the command, or right-click over the PowerClip object and then choose Extract Contents. Your PowerClipped object(s) and the container are restored to their original condition, but not always to their original position on the page.
- To reposition the contents of a PowerClip container quickly, right-click and then choose Lock Contents To PowerClip. This is a toggle on and off state: When unlocked, you can reposition the container by dragging with the Pick Tool. You can also scale and rotate the container without affecting the contents. When locked, the contents travel with the container objects wherever you drag.

The Knife Tool

The Knife Tool functions like a knife you'd use in the real world—except you can run with it and it requires no sharpening—and it feels quite natural to use. You begin by hovering over an object area where you want to begin the cut and then you click-drag to the end of the cut when the cursor signifies you're in the proper initial position. The result is two separate closed objects. As with many of CorelDRAW's tools, SHIFT and CTRL can be used as modifier keys as you work with the Knife, and in the case of the Knife Tool, these modifier keys add precision to your cuts. You'll find the Knife Tool in the Toolbox grouped together with the Crop, Eraser, and Virtual Segment Delete Tools (the Crop tools group).

Types of Cuts with the Knife Tool

There are three ways to cut a shape with the Knife Tool, and each one requires a different keyboard/mouse technique.

- **Straight cuts**   If you want to slice an object into two separate shapes as you'd do with a workshop saw, to produce straight lines on sides of both objects, you aim the cursor on the near side of the object, hover until you see it change from an angled cursor to an upright one, click, release the mouse button, and then click on the far side of the object.
- **Freeform cuts**   This technique can be used, for example, to quickly create an illustration of a sheet of paper roughly torn in half. You hover the cursor until it turns upright, click-hold on the near side of the object, and then drag until you reach the far side of the shape, as shown in Figure 11-5.

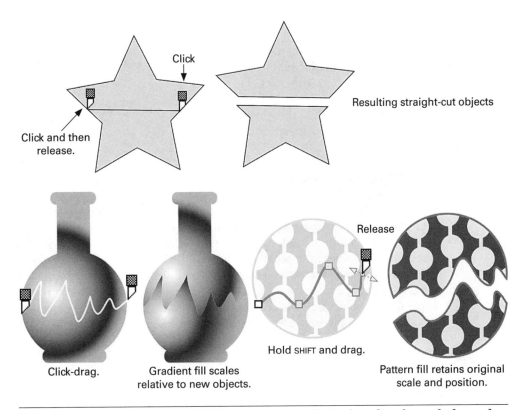

FIGURE 11-5   There are three ways to use the Knife Tool, and each result depends on the object's fill.

- **Bézier cuts**   If you need to guide the Knife Tool to make smooth jigsaw-like cuts, you hold SHIFT and then click-drag points, beginning at the near side and completing the cut at the far side, as shown in Figure 11-5. Notice that not only do the cut result objects inherit the original shape's fill, but also the result applies to all types of fills, including gradients. The shapes in this figure each have a gradient start and end point inherited from the original shape, and if you choose the Interactive Gradient Tool, you can adjust each object's gradient directly and come up with a visually interesting jigsaw puzzle composition or other complex drawing.

Naturally, if you have a specific cut in mind, you'll get the best results using the shaping operations, and although you cannot edit a Bézier cut's path as you make the cut, the Knife Tool does provide fast and easy results.

Tip   If you hold both SHIFT and CTRL while click-dragging to make a Bézier cut, you constrain the direction of the path to 15° increments for more predictable results in making the edge of the cut.

Setting Knife Tool Behavior

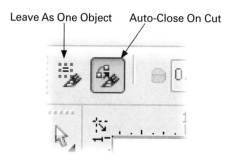

Leave As One Object   Auto-Close On Cut

Using the Knife Tool results in just what you'd expect—you turn a large object into several smaller ones. However, you do have options, the two Property Bar options shown here. Each of these options toggles on and off to suit a specific cutting requirement.

- **Auto-Close On Cut mode** This option, on by default, sets the Knife Tool to create closed-path objects following any style of Knife Tool cutting. It's a quick method for dividing an object into two objects without needing to take the additional steps you'd use with the shaping commands.
- **Keep As One Object mode** This option leaves the object as a single object, but with a cut made in it, which might sound odd until you use this mode. You might use this mode to make several cuts on an object you want to move as a single object until later—you can choose Arrange | Break Curve Apart (CTRL + K) to separate this object into cut objects any time after you make the cuts. It's probably *not* an everyday mode of operation for your work.

If you'd like to try out the Knife Tool on an illustration that demonstrates its usefulness, follow these steps:

Tutorial Creative Cuts with the Knife Tool

1. Open RockPaperScissors.cdr. If you have a lot of confidence with clicking an area on the page with pinpoint accuracy, move to Step 2. Alternatively, to make this Knife operation absolutely goof-proof, you first select an object with the Pick Tool. Click the right blade on the scissors.
2. Choose the Knife Tool from the Crop tools group. On the Property Bar, make sure the Leave As One Object button is toggled off and Auto-Close is active.
3. Hover the cursor until it's in the upright position over the left edge of the object. You're going to break the scissors (as in the children's game) because the drawing of the rock can't do this in this version of CorelDRAW.
4. Drag to the right edge of the scissors. Then rotate the piece a little. Press the SPACEBAR to toggle to the Pick Tool, and then move the small blade object to the right so it's just a little beneath the rock object. This action lets you make an artistic composition.
5. Press the SPACEBAR to return to the Knife Tool. Repeat Steps 3 and 4 with the shadow that the unbroken blade originally had.
6. Press the SPACEBAR to select the Pick Tool, and then move the shadow shape below and a little to the right of the broken blade object, just as shown in Figure 11-6.

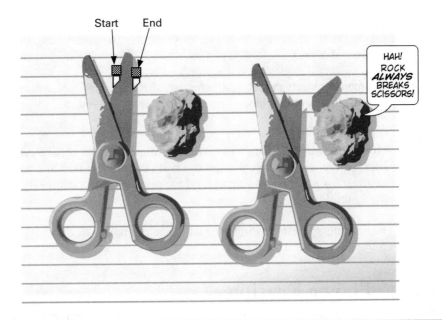

FIGURE 11-6 The Knife Tool is a fast method to cut a shape into two or more parts with smooth or rough edges where the cut is made.

 Tip Both the Eraser and Knife Tools can be used on imported bitmaps; you can perform a little photo retouching with these tools exactly as you would with vector objects. The only restriction is that a bitmap (BMP, TIFF, JPEG, and so on) has to be actually imported to the document; if it is externally linked, the tools can't be used on this *reference* to bitmap images.

Using the Eraser Tool

The Eraser Tool completely removes areas of selected objects you click-drag over—just like a real art eraser, but without the stubble landing in your lap. The Eraser comes in two different shapes, and you can define its size by using the Property Bar. You'll find it in the Toolbox in the Crop tools group.

Working with Eraser Operations

With this tool, you can remove portions of shapes in four ways:

- **Double-clicking** When you double-click a selected shape, you remove an area that is the shape of the cursor. Therefore, if you double-click a lot with the circular cursor chosen, you can quickly design a slice of Swiss cheese.
- **Single-click two points** If you single-click, move your cursor, and then click a second time, the Eraser Tool erases a straight line through the selected object.

- **Click-drag**   This is the most common method of erasing, and the results are totally predictable. If you click-drag, you erase the area you've dragged over on a selected object.

> **Note** Grouped objects do not qualify for use with the Eraser Tool. However, if you CTRL-click an object in a group to isolate it temporarily, you can, indeed, erase part of the object.

- **Hovering and pressing TAB**   This technique creates several connected straight-line segments, and after you get the hang of it, it will feel like you're painting with an eraser, and you'll be able to produce phenomenally expressive and complex drawings quickly.

Walk through the following tutorial to see the power of this hover-TAB erasing technique and make it your own:

Tutorial Power Erasing

1. Open Don't Litter.cdr, an incomplete international symbol that tells the audience, "Put refuse in the appropriate place; don't be a pig." The orange areas are guides for you; they're locked on the Guides layer.
2. Select the main object, the blue rounded rectangle. Choose the Eraser Tool and then set the nib style to rectangular by clicking the default nib style (the circle) on the Property Bar. For this example, set the nib size to about **.18"**.
3. Single-click at the top left of the waste-basket guide. Move your cursor over to the bottom left of the waste-basket guide, but don't click. Notice as you move the Eraser Tool that a path preview follows the cursor.
4. Tap the TAB key, but *don't click* your mouse button. Notice that a new erasure appears between the first single-click point and the point where you pressed TAB.
5. To define a third point, move your cursor to a new point (without clicking the mouse button) and then press TAB again. A third point is defined, and the path between the second and third points is erased.
6. When you're done with the waste basket, set the nib style to round, and then add limbs to the thoughtful international guy. Use the TAB-erasing technique, for example, to extend a forearm from the guy's shoulder, and once this segment has been erased, double-click where you think his hand would be to extend the erasure. Single-click to end an erasure. Figure 11-7 shows the work in progress.

> **Tip** Each time you click the Eraser Tool cursor to erase portions of your object, CorelDRAW considers the action as a unique and separate erase session. This means Eraser Tool actions can be reversed using the Undo command (CTRL+Z) in steps, depending on which erase technique you used. When using the single-click technique, an Undo command is needed to reverse each erase point. During a continuous erase using the click-drag action, a single Undo command reverses each continuous erasing session.

Single-click

Pressing TAB defines points;
single-clicking defines end.

FIGURE 11-7   Press TAB to define intermediate points between your first and last
erase path points to create connected, straight-line erasures.

Setting Eraser Tool Properties

The width and shape of the Eraser Tool are set using Property Bar options, as shown
next. The complexity of the removed shape, the number of path segments, and the
connecting nodes created during an erase session can also be controlled. These
properties significantly affect the shape of erased object areas.

Tip   As with most of the Toolbox tools, you can get to the options for the Eraser in
Options by double-clicking the button on the Toolbox.

Auto-Reduce On Erase

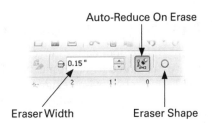

Eraser Width   Eraser Shape

Eraser Tool shapes

Eraser Width

You can set the Eraser Tool width between 0.001 and 100.0 inches either by entering values in the Property Bar combo box or by pressing the UP and DOWN ARROW keys on your keyboard to increase or decrease the size. Each UP or DOWN ARROW keystroke changes the Eraser Width by 0.025 inch.

Tip Use the keyboard to change the cursor size while you erase. Press the UP and/ or DOWN ARROW keys on your keyboard while click-dragging, and the result can be a tapered brush. After you release the mouse button, the Eraser Tool resets to its original size. You don't have to worry about starting out a new erase stroke with a yard-wide tip!

Auto-Reduce Mode

Erasing continuous paths removes portions of objects to create new sides that are made up of normal vector path segments and nodes. How closely the new edges follow your erase path is determined by the number and properties of the nodes that are produced. The more nodes, the more complex and accurate the erased shape will be. While selected, the Auto-Reduce On Erase option affects the complexity of the resulting erased shape when erasing in continuous freehand-style paths.

To activate the Auto-Reduce On Erase option, click the button to the depressed position (the default), or deactivate it by clicking it to the undepressed state.

Tip The Eraser Tool Auto-Reduce On Erase settings are set according to the Freehand Smoothing default setting used by the Freehand and Bézier tools. To set this option, double-click the Eraser Tool button on the Toolbox.

Using the Virtual Segment Delete Tool

The Virtual Segment Delete Tool can remove a path segment from an object while the object retains other paths and outline properties. This tool gives you an easy way to create *negative spaces* with objects—a design carved away from a larger object.

Come play with the Polygon Tool and the follow these steps to carve a star shape out of a pentagon:

Tutorial # Exploring the Mysterious Virtual Segment Delete Tool

1. Choose the Polygon Tool from the Shapes tools group on the Toolbox (or press Y).
2. Hold CTRL to constrain the object to a symmetrical shape, and then drag down and right. On the Property Bar, set the number of sides or points to **5**. Fill the object with a colorful fill.

3. With the Shape Tool, drag a point inward and down to create a pentagram with a triangle capping each point, as shown in Figure 11-8, callout 1.

4. Choose the Virtual Segment Delete Tool from the Crop tools group. While the polygon is selected, position the tool at one of the pentagram edges. The cursor changes to an upright artist's blade when you're in position to delete a segment; see callout 2 in Figure 11-8. Click and the segment is gone and the polygon loses its fill. Or so it seems: the shape "remembers" the fill but cannot display it because, virtually, it's an open path now.

5. Continue deleting the pentagram segments until you only have triangles on the page (callout 3).

6. With the Shape Tool, marquee-select all the triangles, and then right-click and choose Close Curve from the context menu.

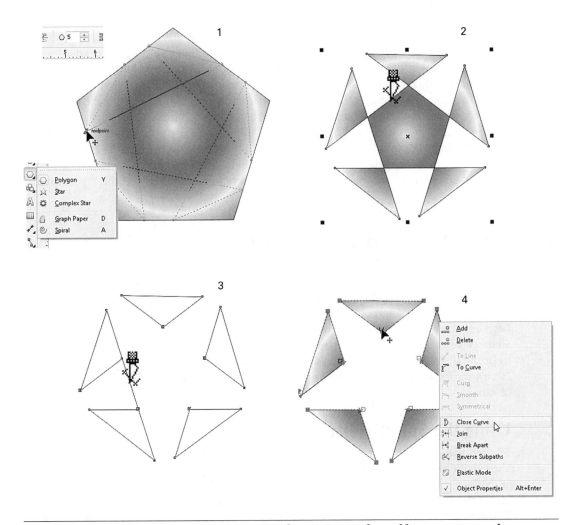

FIGURE 11-8 Create intricate compositions beginning with a self-intersecting polygon. Then alter the shape using the Virtual Segment Delete Tool.

Tip   If the object you are deleting segments from is a compound path (an object composed of more than one open or closed path), the Virtual Segment Delete Tool will work best if the object is first broken into individual curves using the Break Curve Apart (CTRL+K) command.

Cropping an Illustration

The Crop Tool, located in the group with the Knife and the Eraser Tools, brings a bitmap effect to vector drawing. If you have experience with Corel PHOTO-PAINT or another photo editing program, you already are familiar with a crop tool: you select an area within a photo, perform a command such as clicking inside the crop area, with the result that you have deleted the area outside the crop and resized the image.

The Crop Tool in CorelDRAW behaves exactly like an image editor's crop tool. Objects do not have to be grouped; you just select the object(s), drag a rectangle around the area of the design you want cropped, double-click inside the proposed crop area, and all object areas outside the crop box are deleted. The Crop Tool is a powerful and potentially very destructive tool, but fortunately you can work with the proposed crop box before cropping: you can drag a *corner* crop box handle before cropping to resize the crop proportionately; dragging a *middle* handle disproportionately resizes the crop area. Additionally, once you've made a proposed crop, clicking, then clicking again inside the box, puts the box in rotation mode, and you can actually crop a diamond shape. If you want to cancel a crop operation, press ESC and the crop box goes away.

The New Shape Edit Tool Group

Corel has made some additions to the Shape Edit group on the Toolbox: Smear, Twirl, Attract, and Repel are incredibly dramatic and powerful tools that will make you feel as though you're dragging your finger through wet paint. Let's begin a survey from top to bottom in this group; the Shape Tool at top is such a fundamentally important tool in CorelDRAW that it's covered in Chapter 10, not here. Here's the group; draw an object and get set to have a lot of fun.

Using the Smudge Brush

The Smudge Brush is sort of a paint tool in a drawing program: you can dramatically alter shapes in a natural, painterly fashion, with results that would take hours using any other method. You move areas of a vector object by dragging from a starting point inside the object, dragging outward, or starting outside and dragging inside the object. The result is a little like the Eraser Tool if you move object areas inward, and if you drag from the inside out, the result might remind you of dripping paint.

Applying Smudge to Shapes

Using the Smudge Brush, you can alter the outline shapes of open or closed paths by click-dragging across the outline path, in either an outward direction (to add a bulge) or an inward direction (to create a pucker). As you drag, the path is altered according to your drag action and the shape settings of the Smudge Brush cursor. Figure 11-9 shows a creative example of using the Smudge Brush: the rectangle is almost a puzzle piece now, the editing took less than five seconds, and the resulting path can be refined using the Shape Tool and other CorelDRAW features.

Tip If you're trying to smudge shapes that have been applied with an effect (Envelope, Blend, Contour, Distortion, Extrude, or Drop Shadow), you'll first need to break apart the effect. If the shape is part of a group, you'll need to ungroup it first (CTRL+U). Smudging cannot be applied to bitmaps or mesh-filled objects.

Choosing Smudge Brush Property Bar Options

In case you haven't noticed, the Smudge Brush works quite differently from other tools. You can control how the Smudge Brush effect is applied by varying tool properties such as the tilt, angle, and size of the nib; or by adjusting how quickly the effect diminishes; or by using optional pressure stylus settings.

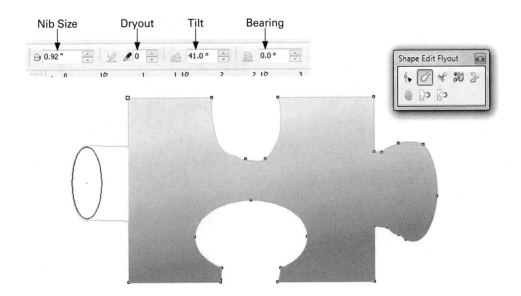

FIGURE 11-9   The Smudge Brush treats vector objects as though they're made of liquid.

While the Smudge Brush is selected, the Property Bar offers these options for controlling the shape and condition of your Smudge Brush cursor:

- **Nib Size** Nib Size can be set between hundredths of an inch up to 2 inches.
- **Use Stylus Pressure** If you have a digitizing tablet and stylus that supports pressure, choose this option to have the Smudge Brush react to pressure you apply, increasing the width of the nib.
- **Dryout** This option sets a rate for the effect of gradually reducing the width of a smudge according to the speed of your click-drag action and can be set between –10 and 10. Higher values cause your smudge to be reduced in width more quickly (as shown next), whereas a setting of 0 deactivates the Dryout effect. Interestingly, negative Dryout values make your stroke begin small and eventually widen as you click-drag.
- **Tilt** The Tilt value controls the elliptical shape of the Smudge Tool nib. Tilt is measured in degrees set between 15 (a flat-shaped nib) and 90 (a circular-shaped nib), as shown here. Tilt and Bearing values (discussed next) work in combination with each other to control the smudge nib shape.
- **Bearing** Bearing lets you set the angle of the cursor in circular degrees (0 to 359). The effects of changing Bearing are most noticeable at lower Tilt values— such as 12°, as shown here. It's the rotational angle of a noncircular tip.

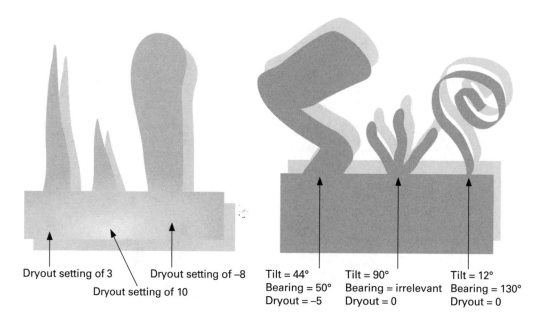

Dryout setting of 3 Dryout setting of –8
Dryout setting of 10

Tilt = 44° Tilt = 90° Tilt = 12°
Bearing = 50° Bearing = irrelevant Bearing = 130°
Dryout = –5 Dryout = 0 Dryout = 0

The Roughen Brush

To add a touch of character and imperfection to ultra-precise objects, you have the Roughen Brush also in the group with the Smudge Brush.

The Roughen Brush alters the course of an outline path on an object, and depending on the setting you use on the Property Bar, you can achieve effects that range from lightning bolts to really gnarly lines to zigzag patterns, just by dragging on the edge of a shape. The options you have when using the Roughen Brush can be seen here on the Property Bar; they're similar to those of the Smudge Brush:

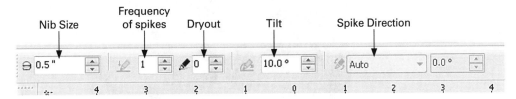

- **Nib Size** This sets the size of the Roughen Brush. It's usually a good idea to scale the nib in proportion to the selected object you want to roughen. By default, the scale of the nib is measured in inches.
- **Frequency** You'll see that the Roughen Brush creates irregularity on an object edge that is similar to the peaks and valleys of a mountain range—it varies the object outline in an "in and out" fashion. At low frequency values, the roughened object outline features large, varying areas. At high frequency settings, you attain a zigzag effect. The range of frequency is from 1 to 10 (10 produces zigzags).
- **Dryout** Like the Smudge Brush, the Roughen Brush can "dry out" at the end of a stroke you drag with the cursor. The range of dryout effect is from –10 (the stroke tapers in the opposite direction in which you click-drag) to 10 (the stroke tapers and fades). At 0, the stroke remains consistent. The greater the dryout setting, negative or positive, the more natural a roughened appearance you can achieve.
- **Tilt** This property can be used in combination with stroking over areas that have already been roughened. At 0 degrees, you increase the irregularity of the spikes, often to a point of abstract, amateurish artwork. However, at high tilt settings (such as 90 degrees), dragging over an area that's already roughened can smooth out some of the jagginess and add a subtle, organic feel to a path segment.
- **Direction Of Spikes** This feature is, by default, set to Automatic; it is not editable unless CorelDRAW is told (in Options) that you are using a digitizing tablet that supports pressure/direction. In default mode, spikes run tangent to the path you modify with the tool.

Try this basic tutorial to get a feel for the tool and a creative way to use it:

Tutorial Making a Crooked Smile with the Roughen Brush

1. Open Jack O Lantern.cdr. All objects except for the crescent moon smile are locked on Layer 1 and Layer 2 is chosen and unlocked.
2. Select the smile object (press CTRL + A to save choosing the Pick Tool).

FIGURE 11-10   Creating an effect similar to a tailor's pinking shears with the Roughen Brush.

3. Choose the Roughen Brush and then on the Property Bar, set the Nib Size to ½" (for shark-scaled teeth—use a smaller size for less intimidating jaws). Set the Frequency to **1**, the Dryout to **0**, and the Tilt to about **8** degrees, in case you want to modify the toothy smile after you've completed the next step.

4. Drag the cursor over the top edge of the smile object, but start about ½" from the absolute left and end ½" before the right side. The Roughen Brush tends to mess up path areas where there is a sharp change in direction.

5. Perform Step 4 on the bottom smile object. Optionally, you can duplicate the smile object (select it and then press CTRL+C and then CTRL+V), fill it with yellow on the Color Palette, press SHIFT+PAGEDOWN to put the object behind the black smile, and then use the nudge keys up and left to offset its position, creating a highlight to the carved effect, as the pumpkin's eyes display in Figure 11-10.

Using the Free Transform Tool

The Free Transform Tool, located in the same group as the Shape Tool, Smudge Brush, and the Roughen Brush, is your one-stop shop for performing rotations, skews, and other object transformations using an onscreen guide.

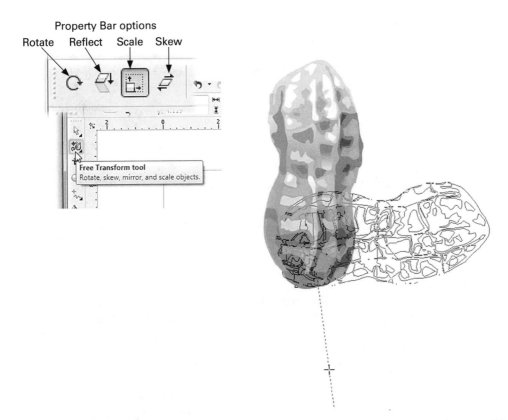

Unlike the Pick Tool for object transformations, the Free Transform Tool has a handle by which you steer and have precise control over the object you manipulate. To use the tool, you choose it from the Toolbox, choose a transformation type on the Property Bar, and then with the object selected, you click-drag on a control point (or any object node) to set the center of the transformation; dragging reveals a handle that also serves as a visual indicator of the amount of transformation you're creating. This preview of the transformation is in effect until you release the mouse button. As you can see in the illustration, it's obvious the peanut is being rotated, where the center of rotation is, and the extent of the rotation before the transformation is actually made.

The Smear Tool

New to this version of CorelDRAW, the Smear Tool behaves like the Smudge Tool's big brother, offering more plasticity to areas you drag over, more control, and with a little practice, a gallery of freeform shapes that look like anything but vector graphics. On the Property Bar, you have the following options:

- **Nib Size**   Nib size determines the tool's diameter.
- **Pressure and Pen Pressure**   To the right of the combo box, you'll see a toggle button to set pressure for the Smear Tool. Artists who use a mouse can use the num entry box or the flyout slider to set the tool's intensity. Digitizing tablet users should click the Pen Pressure button to use physical pressure to add character to strokes.

- **Smooth and Pointy Smear buttons**
Use one or the other type of smear to affect the end of a stroke. Smooth is good for natural, freeform distortion, whereas Pointy—an aesthetically severe effect—might be useful for embellishing machined parts and metal band logos.

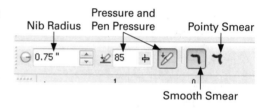

In the following example, you'll get a feel for using the Smear Tool in Smooth mode, to create a stylistic hairdo for a cartoon character who has no hair. Yet.

Tutorial   Adding the Smear to Your Artistic Career

1. Open Cartoon Guy.cdr. Most of the drawing is on a locked Layer 1. The top of his scalp is on Layer 2, unlocked. Select the scalp object (press CTRL + A, which is the shortcut for Select All).

2. Select the Smear Tool; set the size of the tool to about ¾", the Pressure to about **85%**, and the style of the Smear to Smooth Smear on the Property Bar.

3. There is no "right" or "wrong" in this example; you're just experimenting. Try dragging from the fellow's scalp upward. Then try dragging on the area you just dragged. Repetition over an area can lead to quite intricate shapes.

4. Set the pressure lower, say, to **35**, and drag from the scalp away toward the top. You might want to drag repeatedly over this area; a pressure of 35 creates a bumpy skull, similar to the author's, as attested to in this illustration.

FIGURE 11-11   Using the Smear Tool in combination with Fountain Fills can suggest more than one object in a composition.

5. Try the Pointy Smear type, try setting the Pressure to **100%**, and when the fellow's head is totally messed up, choose the Interactive Fill tool at the bottom of the toolbox (see Figure 11-11).
6. Drag from the base of the scalp upward, so the beginning linear gradient color is the same as its original color, and the end color is white.
7. Drag a deep mustard colored well from the Color Palette to on top of the white color on the Gradient fill, and then adjust the beginning and end colors so a transition between scalp and blonde hair color is created. Write your bosses' name at the top of the page, and then think twice about printing several copies, especially if you're on a network printer.

The Twirl Tool

The Twirl Tool has clockwise and counterclockwise direction features on the Property Bar, in addition to options for setting the pressure and size of the tool. Depending on the size and pressure, you can create just about anything from a sink drain to a gentle swash on a typeface character. You can also get creative and apply a twirl to objects that you've already modified with other Shape Edit group tools.

An unobvious technique to use with the Twirl Tool—*and* the other new Shape Edit tools—is to click, drag, and then hold the mouse button at the end of a stroke. Doing this increases the distortion at the end of the affected object and provides a novel effect.

Try this tool out to create a pinwheel effect in the following steps:

Tutorial Creating a Stylized Sun

1. Open Suntoon.cdr. The sunbeam object behind the face is a polygon object whose outer points were dragged inward with the Shape Tool, in case you'd like to build one in the future.
2. Select the polygon object, and then choose the Twirl Tool from the Toolbox.
3. Set the Nib Size to ½" so it scales with the drawing, set the Pressure to about **60**, and it's your call whether to twirl the sunbeams clockwise or counterclockwise.
4. Drag in a circular direction around the sunbeam object, as shown in Figure 11-12. If you want to create a little solar flare action, remain over an area (don't drag, just hold) for a moment or two.

The Attract and Repel Tools

The last two tools in the Shape Edit group might also be called the Pull and the Push tools, for this is what they do when you drag them over a selected object. To add to their versatility, for example, the effect of the Attract Tool depends on whether you begin on the inside, dragging outward, or on the inside, dragging inward. Either approach is valid with the Repel Tool, as well. There's an additional trick you can use

FIGURE 11-12 The Twirl Tool creates a whirlpool effect on objects.

with either tool: click, drag just a little to start the tool's effect, and then *hold* over an area of an object. Doing this essentially turns the Attract Tool into the "Pucker Tool"— especially visible on corners of rectangles and other sharp turns in paths, and the Repel Tool becomes the "Bloat Tool".

Try this simple exercise to get an idea of the power of the Repel Tool on a star shape. You'll turn it into an asterisk:

Tutorial Repelling a Polygon Object

1. Choose the Polygon Tool from the Object group on the Toolbox.
2. Hold CTRL to constrain the shape to symmetrical, and then drag a shape that's about 3" across.
3. Press F10 to get the Shape Tool, and then drag the node that's at about 1 o'clock toward the center of the object until it looks like a very spikey star. Fill it with any color. See callout 1 in Figure 11-13.
4. Zoom in, and then choose the Repel Tool. Set the size of the nib to about ½", and the pressure to about **55%**.
5. Position the cursor carefully so it's inside the tip of the top point of the star. Then click-hold the mouse button until the preview outline of the intended effect doesn't get any larger. See callout 2 in Figure 11-13.
6. Repeat Step 5 with the other four points. Then find a sentence that claims a new car will get 500 miles per gallon, put the asterisk after that statement, and then give the copywriter the bad news.

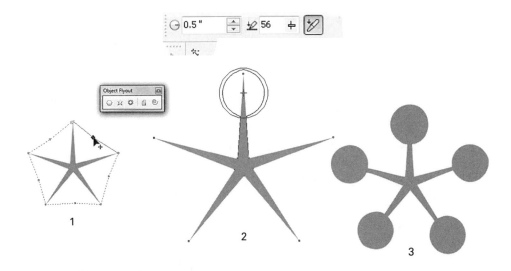

FIGURE 11-13 The Repel Tool can make a bulbous area on a sharp-cornered object.

This chapter has taken you through several processes by which you can create minor and big-time alterations to just about anything you draw. Use the command that best suits the task you have in mind, and use your judgment as to which operation will get you to your goal fastest. Personal computers are productivity enhancers: there's no need to labor over something when CorelDRAW and your PC can do it for you in less time.

Now that you have one, or two, or a dozen shapes on your drawing page, it would be nice to mix them up with some honest-to-gosh text: a headline here, a little body copy there. Drawings and words *live* together, practically no one publishes an image-only website, and Chapter 12 of this guide gets you into the artistic side of text and the embellishment of words with fancy CorelDRAW illustrations.

PART IV

Working with Text

12   Getting Artistic with Text

CorelDRAW is a great facilitator of communication and self-expression, and that includes text as well as graphics. This chapter gets you started with the Text Tool and other CorelDRAW type features and shows you how to put them to use, making your thoughts and ideas inviting and your presentation clear. Text and graphics go hand in hand in presentations, and as you'll witness on the following pages, with CorelDRAW, you have the tools at your disposal. This chapter shows you how to access them and how to work with them.

 Download and extract all the files from the Chapter12.zip archive to follow the tutorials in this chapter.

CorelDRAW's Text Tool

All text you want to enter on a page in CorelDRAW is created with the Text Tool, the tool with an *A* as its icon in CorelDRAW's Toolbox. To begin, click its button in the Toolbox or press F8. If there's *already* text on the page, double-clicking the text with the Pick Tool switches the current tool to the Text Tool and makes an insertion point for adding text. The Text Tool cursor is a small crosshairs with an *A* below and to the right, which becomes an I-beam (a text-editing cursor) when it's over a text object. You click anywhere on the page or the pasteboard to create an insertion point, and then you get to work with your keyboard.

Note Text copied from the Clipboard can be pasted when the Pick Tool is your current tool. Usually, unformatted text—text from a TXT file you copied from Textpad, for example—will import as Paragraph Text. Text copied from word processors will import as a document object; double-clicking the object offers in-place editing exactly as you'd edit a WordPerfect or MS-Word document. It's usually best to choose Edit | Paste Special when pasting Clipboard text to ensure correct formatting and that the original fonts are used. Use the Text Tool's I-beam cursor to insert pasted text.

Tip A shortcut to reselect the Pick Tool while the Text Tool is selected is CTRL+SPACEBAR—for all other tools, you can press either SPACEBAR or CTRL+SPACEBAR.

When you use the Text Tool, you can produce two different types of text objects in a document: Artistic Text and Paragraph Text. Figure 12-1 shows layout that uses Artistic Text in combination with the Text | Fit Text To Path command—the path is hidden in this illustration. The smaller body-copy text uses Paragraph Text; the top

Artistic Text

Did you ever have one of those days? Or perhaps *three* or *four* of those days...all in a row? You know, when the stars are aligned to form a cosmic pick-axe, pointing at the back of your head?

When it doesn't rain, and it doesn't pour—but it feels lmore like the next Ice Age, you *can* take control of your schedule *and* your life, with the amazing new best-selling book, *Exploring Your Inner Self-Consciousness*. Learn to become a more dynamic, foceful, and irritating individual with what remains of your friends and loved ones!

Paragraph Text

FIGURE 12-1 Artistic Text and Paragraph Text have different attributes, and each is suited for different text treatments in a design.

paragraph wraps around the top of the image by using a CorelDRAW Envelope (see Chapter 20). Artistic Text and Paragraph Text have different properties, but are added to a document using the same Text Tool. Artistic Text, by the way it's produced in a document, is easy to reshape and distort—you'll find it simple to do artistic things, such as creating a company logo. Conversely, Paragraph Text is optimized for longer amounts of text, and it's a great text attribute for quickly modifying columns of, for example, instructions, recipes, short stories, and so on. In short, Paragraph Text is best used for several paragraphs of text in a composition whereas Artistic Text should be reserved for headlines and just a few lines of text you might want to curve along a path, extrude, or do something else unique and fancy with.

Although there are similarities between Artistic Text and Paragraph Text, you're best off using one or the other depending on the type of text element you want in your design.

Entering and Editing Artistic Text

Artistic Text serves you best for illustration headlines, callouts, and on any occasion when you want to create text that has a special effect such as extrusion, an envelope, text on a path, and so on. To add a line of Artistic Text to a document, with the Text Tool, you click an insertion point and then type your phrase; alternatively, after clicking an insertion point, you can press CTRL + V to paste any text you have loaded on the Windows Clipboard. To create several lines of Artistic Text, type and press ENTER to put a carriage return at the end of the line; you then continue typing. By default, all Artistic Text is set in Arial, 24 point; later in this chapter, you'll see how to change the default.

Artistic Text is also easy to convert to curves so you can modify a character in a word: for example, Microsoft's logo has a tick missing in the second *o*. To duplicate this effect (but not Microsoft's logo), you begin with Artistic Text for the company name, press CTRL + Q (Arrange | Convert To Curves), and then edit away using the Shape Tool. Artistic Text, as editable text, can be fine-tuned using the features on the Property Bar when the text is selected using either the Pick Tool or the Text Tool. The options are shown in Figure 12-2.

 Note All the options covered in the following section are *also* available on the newly redesigned X6 Object Properties docker, covered later in this chapter.

- **Mirroring (horizontal, vertical)**   In addition to creating special effects, the mirroring buttons are also useful when, for example, you want to print a T-shirt transfer with your company name. The name needs to be reversed (mirrored horizontally) to print on the transfer paper, so the unreversed print on the T-shirt reads correctly (or at least without needing a mirror).
- **Type Of Font (file)**   To the left of the font name displayed in the drop-down box is an icon signifying what file format the chosen font uses: OpenType, Type 1, or TrueType. This is a nicety when you're sorting your fonts in Bitstream Font Navigator or Windows' Fonts utility in Control Panel.

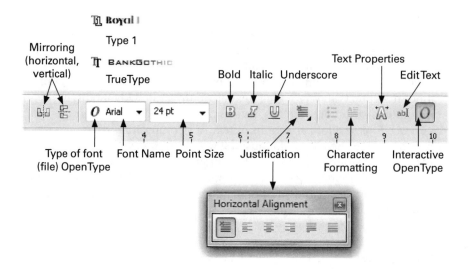

FIGURE 12-2 Use the Property Bar to make Artistic Text look exactly the way you want it.

- **Font Name** This is the name of the typeface you decide on. The default, in Artistic Text, is Arial, 24 point. You change fonts in a new document by selecting text you've typed with the Pick Tool and then choose a different font from the drop-down list. If a font has family members, a right-facing triangle can be seen to the right of the font name when the drop-down list is extended, and you can choose it by hovering above the triangle to reveal the flyout and then click the family member title. You can also perform a speed-search by clicking the current name in the Font Name box and then typing the first few letters of the font you want. The drop-down list immediately scrolls to the neighborhood of installed fonts, making your selection a fast and effortless one. Note also that on the Font Name drop-down list, at the top, above the divider bar, are the fonts you've chosen recently, from previous documents and even from previous CorelDRAW sessions.
- **Point Size** Text has traditionally been measured in points; with current digital typeface technology, the traditional 72.27 points has been rounded-off to 72 points to the inch. Artistic Text used as a headline ideally can be anywhere from 24 points for a flyer headline to 72 points for an impactful newspaper headline to 300 points and up (there's no hypothetical limit to how large Artistic Text can be)—which is over 4 inches in height—for headlines that fairly shout at the reader.
- **Bold and Italic** These buttons on the Property Bar are shortcuts to defining a whole line of text or only selected characters as bold and italic members of the typeface shown in the Font Name box. If a specific font has no family members, CorelDRAW *doesn't* "fake" a bold or italic look, and the buttons are dimmed. If you need an italic treatment of a font that has no italic family member, a quick fix is to use the Transformation docker, and then set Skew to about –12 degrees to apply to the Artistic Text.

- **Underline**   An underline is an effect available for every font you have installed—you click the button when text is selected and CorelDRAW renders an underline. You can modify the style of the underline to your choosing by highlighting the underlined text and choosing Object Properties. Then on the Character area of the Object Properties docker, you click the Underline flyout and choose the type of underline style you prefer.

 Note   Underlines are great for professional documents, particularly legal ones, but an underline *isn't* the cleverest way to emphasize a phrase in an advertisement. Use a bold font instead, or a colored outline, or a gradient fill to attract attention artistically. Although underlines are effects, they're very real and if you convert an underlined phrase to curves (CTRL+Q), the underline becomes a simple, four-node object.

- **Justification**   Also called "Horizontal Alignment" in balloon help, this drop-down sets how lines of text are aligned relative to one another. Although Justification serves you best when using long columns of Paragraph Text, Artistic Text takes on a more polished look, too, when you apply, for example, *Center Justification* to two or three lines. By default, there is no Justification for newly entered Artistic Text, but for all intents and purposes, this is left-justified text. *Full Justification* creates a splendid, professional look for columns of Paragraph Text, but tends to generate an awkward look for Artistic Text because a line containing only one word with only a few characters has to take on very wide character spacing. Similarly, *Right Justification* is not an everyday choice for audiences who read Western languages (from left to right)—Right Justification is a "slow read," hyphenations and line breaks between words usually look awkward and this type of justification should be reserved for a page layout where the right edge of the text needs to align perfectly to the vertical of a graphic and the left side of the column can be flowing and freeform. *Force Justify* creates lines of text whose left and right edges are perfectly vertical, like Full Justification but with an important difference. Force Justification gives equal emphasis to the spacing between characters, although it can sometimes create unsightly gaps (called *rivers*). With Paragraph Text, it's often a good alignment choice for correcting justified lines of text where there are too few words on a line and when hyphenation is not used. Force Justify can also be used as an artistic treatment of Artistic Text, as shown in this illustration.

DON'T GAMBLE WITH YOUR SAVINGS.

Full Justification

D O N ' T   G A M B L E   W I T H   Y O U R   S A V I N G S .

Force Justification

- **Text Properties**   Clicking this button, which used to be called Character Formatting in previous versions of CorelDRAW, displays the Text Properties docker. Text Properties is very similar to the top area of the redesigned Object Properties docker in X6, which is covered in some detail later in this chapter. Essentially, anything you need to do to customize one or more characters in a text string can be done using the features on the Text Properties docker. You can access the features of the Text Properties docker by clicking the button when text is selected with the Text Tool and Pick Tool and by pressing CTRL + T when the Shape Tool is the active tool.

- **Interactive OpenType**   Explained shortly, Interactive OpenType is a new, advanced feature in version X6 that shows alternative characters in highlighted OpenType text you've typed. OpenType fonts sometimes contain scores of custom characters that are very hard for average users to access and add to text. The Interactive OpenType button shows and hides alternatives, allowing one-click addition of special characters when a specific OpenType font contains them.

- **Edit Text**   This button displays a text-editing box, which also appears when you click the Text Tool on text that has an effect such as an Envelope or an Extrude. CorelDRAW is designed with text-editing flexibility in mind, so in order to transform text using just about any feature—and to allow the text to still be editable—you work in a proxy box so you don't have to start over when you make a typographic error. Here's a visual example: You've chosen a lovely font to express a lovely sentiment for a card and have extruded the font. Upon looking at it in the morning, you've misspelled "Happy". No big deal: you click an insertion point in the text where the fix is needed using the Text Tool; the Edit Text box appears; you enter the additional characters and finally click OK. Occasionally, you might need to modify an Envelope containing text if you're adding a lot of characters, but the Edit Text box is your friend in a jam and, as you'll see, can even change the font of selected characters, the family members, and point size.

Options for Formatting Characters

With CorelDRAW X6, you'll notice that pressing CTRL + T doesn't display the Character Formatting docker any more; it's now called the Text Properties docker. and it includes more comprehensive features to change selected characters than in previous versions of DRAW.

If you're new to CorelDRAW, changes can be made to Artistic Text characters in three different ways:

- Use the Shape Tool in combination with the Property Bar. This method gives you control over character positioning, rotation, and other properties as covered in the next section.
- Use the Text Tool or the Shape Tool in combination with the Character section of the Object Properties docker. Using this method gives you more control by giving you more options than the Property Bar. Using Object Properties with characters is covered later in this chapter.
- Use the Text Tool, the Shape Tool, or the Pick Tool (which works but you cannot select individual characters) in combination with the Text Properties docker. You have the same comprehensive options with Text Properties and the Character area of Object Properties, but for experienced users, this feature might be easier to remember by its historic shortcut, CTRL + T.

Use the Property Bar to Change Characters

As you can see in Figure 12-3, you have some options using the Shape Tool to select characters, but a more complete set of options when you highlight a character with the Text Tool and then click the Character Formatting button on the Property Bar. For quick and simple reformatting, it's the Shape Tool, and for extensive reworking of your Artistic Text, use the Text Tool. You have additional options for lines running under, over, and through selected characters, and if, for example, you've used the Character section in Object Properties to put a Double Thin Underline beneath your text, you can remove this underline later using the Property Bar while you have character nodes selected using the Shape Tool. Character nodes appear black when selected (as shown in Figure 12-3), and your cursor is a clear indication you're editing text with the Shape Tool and not an object path node.

Tip When a character node is selected with the Shape Tool, you can drag the character any which way. You don't *have* to rely on the Offset numerical entry fields on the Property Bar to create offset changes.

Selecting and Moving Characters with the Shape Tool

To select arbitrary characters in an Artistic Text object, select the text object with the Shape Tool (F10)—the cursor changes to the Shape Tool pointer with an *A* next to it. With the text object selected in this way, a small, empty box or "control handle" appears at the lower-left corner of each and every character, as shown in Figure 12-4.

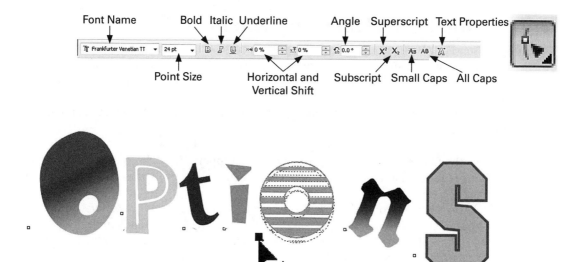

FIGURE 12-3 Format and reformat text characters using the Character Formatting dialog and the Property Bar.

To select any character, click its control handle using the Shape Tool. To select nonconsecutive characters, hold SHIFT (*not* CTRL as you'd anticipate) while clicking. You can also marquee-drag around the nodes you want to select with the Shape Tool. With the control handles selected, you can modify the text formatting, fill, outline, and position of those characters.

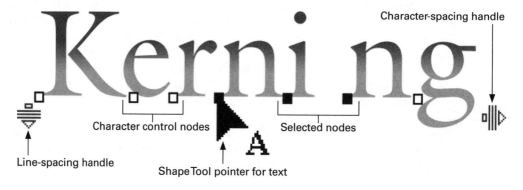

FIGURE 12-4 Set character and line spacing and reposition individual characters with the Shape Tool.

To move one or more characters selected with the Shape Tool, click-drag one of the selected control handles—all the selected characters will move together. Unless you're striving for a humorous effect, however, it's usually a good idea to keep the characters you move horizontally aligned: hold CTRL while dragging—vertical moves do not accept the CTRL key for constraining movement.

Moving characters with the Shape Tool changes the horizontal- and vertical-shift values of them, and the new values can be seen in the Character Offset fields on the Property Bar. Moving characters with the Shape Tool is useful for manually adjusting the position of characters visually to improve *kerning*, or intercharacter spacing. It's useful if you own a *bum font*, a digital typeface that is coded poorly and, as a result, certain characters neighboring other characters are too tight or too loose. For example, many fonts have poor kerning for the word "HAWAII"; in the illustration at top is the way the characters, as typed, align. There is usually too little space between the *II*s and the *A* and *W* should tuck into each other, but do not. At bottom, 30 seconds with the Shape Tool and the word not only has a better relationship between negative and positive areas, but the word is also shorter (which is good when one is cramped for design space).

Tip   The Shape Tool can be nudged after selecting character nodes and nodes along object paths. Therefore, you can create better headline kerning by first adjusting the Nudge Distance in Options (CTRL+J) | Document | Rulers and then using the keyboard arrows to create a professionally typeset headline.

Using the Object Properties Character Options

Everything you can do with the Shape Tool in combination with the Property Bar for editing characters within a text string, you can also do on the Object Properties docker by selecting one or more text characters with the Shape Tool *or* the Text Tool. Additionally, there is an area in the Character field on the docker where you can quickly access special characters in OpenType fonts you use. This feature is *not* the same as the Insert Character docker, as will be demonstrated shortly. Many of the OpenType typefaces you find today, both as commercial fonts you buy and ones that come with Windows and applications, are capable of holding far more than

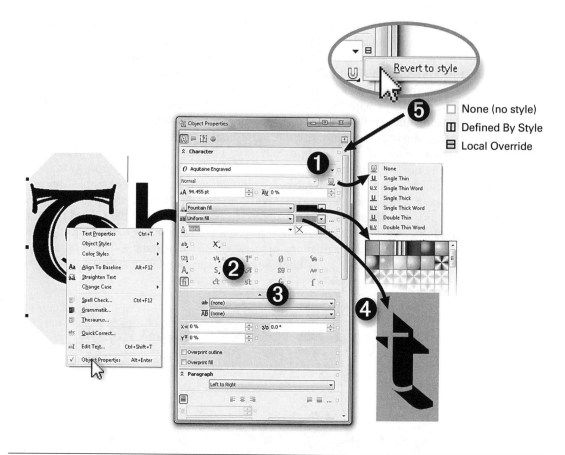

FIGURE 12-5 The new home in version X6 for all character formatting is the Object Properties docker.

the 256 characters TrueType fonts used to offer. CorelDRAW X6 uses and organizes OpenType data to offer you custom fractions, special ligatures, alternate characters, and other professional typesetting features when a specific font holds the special data.

Whenever you need to change a character in an Artistic Text string, select the character's node with the Shape Tool or highlight the character with the Text Tool, and then right-click and choose Object Properties (or press ALT + ENTER). As you can see in Figure 12-5, Object Properties is context-sensitive; a character is selected, and so all the character options are displayed.

Here's a minimal guided tour of where character formatting features have been relocated and a brief example of how to use ligatures (characters that are specially linked together) in text.

1. **The Underline button flyout** You have six different styles of Underline for a selected character or word. Remember: a tick mark at the lower right of a button means there are more options on the button's flyout. You click the button to reveal the flyout and then click your choice.

2. **The OpenType typography features area**   If you've chosen an OpenType character or phrase (there should be a bluish *O* to the left of the font name), and the OpenType was designed with special characters, you can do some professional and fancy stuff with your text on a page. As explained shortly, when a character, word, or phrase is highlighted, you'll see some or all of the fifteen options turn black in this area, which means CorelDRAW has checked out your font, and yes, it does have, for example, the capability to build custom fractions (such as 5/16), or ligatures such as a dotless *i* to the right of a lowercase *f*, which looks much more professional and is easier to read than the stem of the *f* banging into the dot on the *i*. If none of the options turn black, your OpenType font doesn't have any special features.

Tip   Regardless of whether the Object Properties docker is visible or not, when OpenType is highlighted with the Text Tool, you can click the Interactive OpenType button on the Property Bar. You'll see a small downward-facing triangle at the bottom of the highlighted text; by hovering over it, a flyout reveals alternative OpenType characters, if any, and you choose them by clicking a flyout selection. To hide options and the flyout triangle, click the Interactive OpenType button to return it to its off state.

3. **Advanced options**   The down triangle on the bar below the OpenType features reveals offset and rotation features when you click it, the same features as presented on the Property Bar when you've selected a character node with the Shape Tool. You also have Overline, and the option to specify overprinting if you send this document to a commercial printer and a character or other object has both a fill and an outline width.

4. **Background Fill**   Characters you've selected can have a Solid, Fountain Fill, or other type of fill behind them. The effect is like highlighting passages on a printed page. Any background fill will take up the entire font character height (which usually exceeds the height of capital letters in a font) plus the line spacing. Therefore, you can create background fills for characters that are seamless with the following line of text that has a background fill.

5. **Style modifications**   In Chapter 1, the new Styles feature is covered; it's a good idea to read that chapter if you haven't already. Because the Object Properties docker is integrated—and objects are treated the same as text—everything on the page can be styled, and the styles can be overridden with the Object Properties docker features. This docker can also revert your restyled object back to its original styled self again. If you see an empty gray square to the right of any feature on the Object Properties docker, it means the selected text (or object) has not been styled in any way; it's an unstyled object. When you see a light blue vertically divided square to the right of a property, the text is styled—and you might want to think twice about modifying your work. If you have modified a styled piece of text, you can change it back to its original style by clicking the Local Override icon and then choose Revert To Style.

Here's a working example of using OpenType features—the fast and professional way. In Figure 12-6, the author went to some professional expense and bought the Rennie Mackintosh collection of typefaces from ITC in OpenType file format. The fonts were chosen because they are text for a print ad featuring the furniture of the famous Arts and Crafts designer, and as you can see in this figure, the font and the furniture are highly similar. The *fi* characters in "The Finish" look awkward, but happily, when the whole phrase is highlighted and the Object Properties docker is open, a down arrow appears below the highlighted text, offering alternative character choices. There are not a lot of features in this OpenType font, but the *fl* and *fi* ligatures and a special picture glyph or two are supported. If there's a special character in OpenType, CorelDRAW will find and offer it to you.

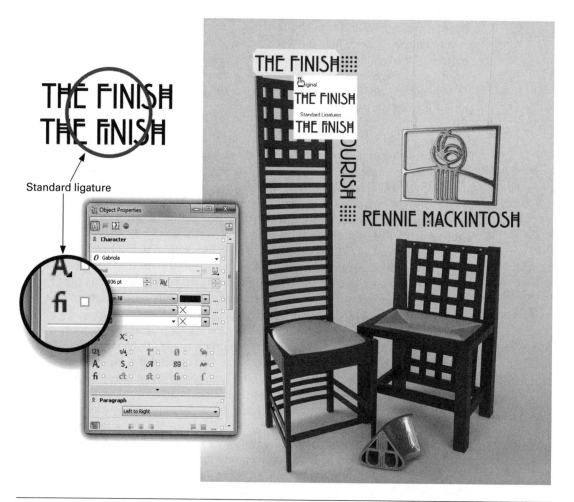

FIGURE 12-6 Use OpenType features on the Object Properties docker to access characters you couldn't otherwise.

Tip Try typing a line of text, and then using Gabriola, an OpenType that comes with Windows 7. You'll see that just about all the options for OpenType light up on the docker, and several prestyled combinations are offered when you click the down triangle below any selected text.

Adjusting Spacing with the Shape Tool

When an Artistic Text object is selected with the Shape Tool, two additional handles appear at the lower-left and lower-right corners of the object, as shown in Figure 12-7. These two handles modify the line spacing and character spacing for the entire block in one go.

To increase or decrease the word and character spacing between words only, hold SHIFT while dragging the handle at the lower-right corner of the selected text object right or left with the Shape Tool. To increase or decrease the line spacing (also the before-paragraph spacing), drag the handle at the lower-left corner of the selected Text object down or up with the Shape Tool.

All spacing values modified with the Shape Tool can be viewed and edited in the Character Formatting box.

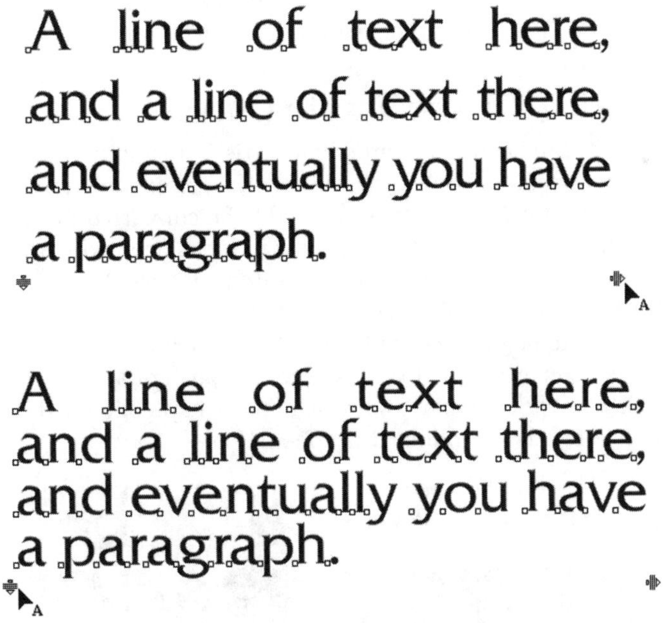

A line of text here,
and a line of text there,
and eventually you have
a paragraph.

A line of text here,
and a line of text there,
and eventually you have
a paragraph.

FIGURE 12-7   Leading (interline spacing), kerning (intercharacter spacing), and interword spacing can be tuned using the text handles.

Combining and Breaking Apart Artistic Text

You can combine several Artistic Text objects into a single Artistic Text object; you select all the Artistic Text objects with the Pick Tool, and then choose Arrange | Combine or press CTRL + L. Each text object starts a new paragraph in the new text object. Ordinarily, the Combine command converts CorelDRAW objects to simplified ones, but with text objects, they retain their attribute as text.

The text objects are combined *in the order in which they are selected*—if you select several objects in one go by dragging a marquee around them, they will be selected from front to back. Text objects that do not contain spaces are combined onto a single line. If any of the selected objects is not a text object, all the text objects will be converted to curves and combined with the non-Text object.

Tip If the text doesn't combine in the order you want or expect, you can reverse the stacking order of the original text objects by choosing Arrange | Order | Reverse Order.

Artistic Text can also be broken apart from several lines of stacked text to individual lines, all as unique objects. To break apart Artistic Text, choose Arrange | Break Artistic Text, or press CTRL + K. With multiline text objects, the Break Artistic Text command results in one text object for each line or paragraph from the original object.

Also, using the Break Artistic Text command on single-line text objects results in one text object for each word. And, as you'd expect, breaking apart single-word text objects results in a new text object for each character.

Converting Artistic Text to Curves

Many effects can be applied directly to Artistic Text, but you might want to apply effects that cannot be applied as a "live" effect to editable text. To achieve the desired effect, the Artistic Text objects first need to be converted to curves: choose Arrange | Convert To Curves, or press CTRL-Q. Text that has been converted to curves is *no longer editable with the Text Tool* and must be edited with the Shape Tool instead, just like any other curve object. Text converted to plain object with paths and control nodes is a good way to begin creating logos. The following illustration shows a treatment of Artistic Text converted to curves, and then a push of a node here and a pull there, and the result is a workable party store sign. See Chapter 11 for the details on how to use the Smudge Brush to produce this effect.

Entering and Editing Paragraph Text

Paragraph Text is very much like the frames that text professionals work with in desktop publishing applications such as CorelVentura and Adobe InDesign; however, there are options and features you'll soon see in CorelDRAW that DTP applications don't provide. The biggest difference between Artistic Text and Paragraph Text is that Paragraph Text is held in a container—a frame—so *you don't directly edit*, for example, the width of characters in a Paragraph Text frame simply by yanking on a bounding box handle with the Pick Tool. In Figure 12-8 at top are duplicate Paragraph Text frames; they're easy to spot and differentiate from Artistic Text because even when not selected, they have a dashed outline around them signifying the Paragraph Text frame. The duplicate at top right has been scaled so it's wider than at left: note that the lines of text flow differently but the characters themselves remain unchanged, as does the spacing between characters and words. At bottom the same historic American address was been entered as Artistic Text and then the center right bounding box was dragged to the right using the Pick Tool. The words per line don't rearrange, but what does happen is that the characters themselves are stretched, which is often unwanted. That's the biggest difference between Paragraph and Artistic Text: if the text doesn't have a frame, then you're scaling the text.

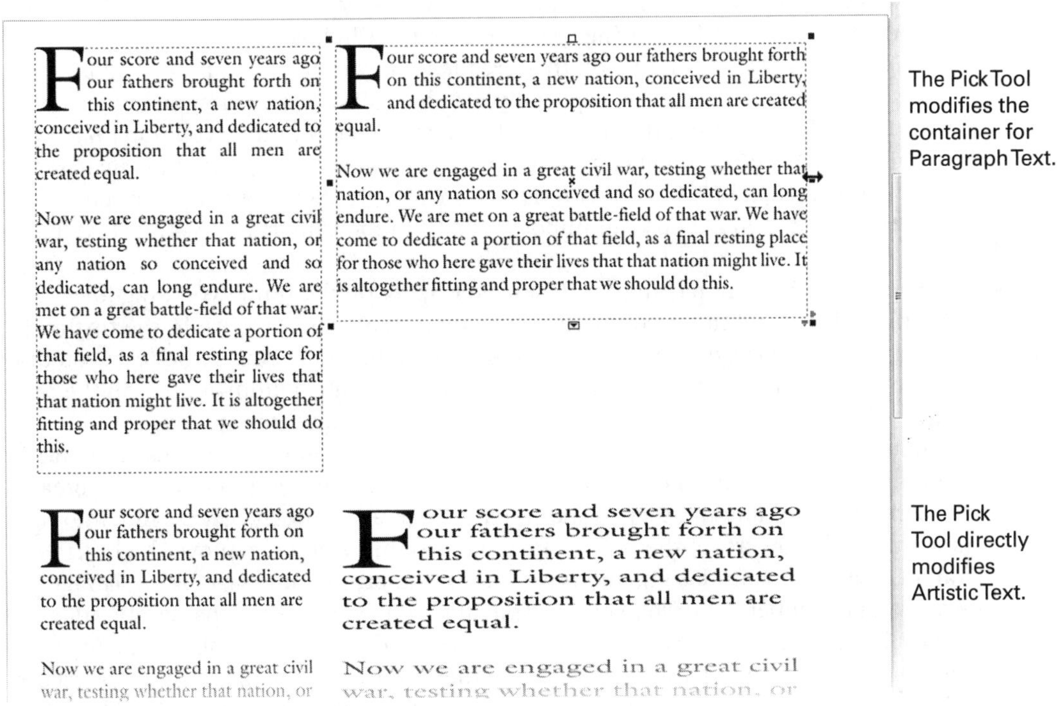

The Pick Tool modifies the container for Paragraph Text.

The Pick Tool directly modifies Artistic Text.

FIGURE 12-8   When you edit Paragraph Text with the Pick Tool, you're only changing the shape of the frame and not the text itself.

Working with Paragraph Text can be a challenge, a little more complex than riding a bike but a lot less complex than rocket science. However, once you get the hang of it (and the following sections are your guide), you'll find Paragraph Text indispensable for business designs, and those trifold and top-fold page presets you learned about in Chapter 6 will spring to life and find new purpose, and your brochures will look as slick as can be.

To create a Paragraph Text object, select the Text Tool in the Toolbox, and then click-and-drag diagonally to create a rectangle into which you'll enter the text. In Figure 12-8, the arrow at left shows the click-hold + diagonal-drag technique (this is commonly called a *marquee-drag*), and at right you see the result. The text inside the Paragraph Text frame is simply a visual prompt, and it disappears after you've added text. Resizing handles appear on a Paragraph Text frame and kerning and leading handles (Artistic Text features these as well), discussed later in this chapter. There are three ways to fill a Paragraph Text frame with text:

- *Type in the frame manually.* You probably want to run Spell Check (Text | Writing Tools | Spell Check or press CTRL-F12) when you're finished typing, because only three people on Earth have perfect spelling from memory, and one of them was your third-grade teacher. Don't disappoint her.
- *Paste from the Clipboard.* You'll see a dialog before you can paste if you press CTRL + V, or choose Edit | Paste (and Edit | Paste Special). Here you can choose to keep or discard the formatting of the text on the Clipboard.
- *Import a text file.* Depending on the text file type, you might be prompted to install a compatibility pack, especially for older MS-Word documents. With a broadband connection, the process takes about three minutes; you don't have to quit CorelDRAW; and you can paste after the compatibility program is installed. In contrast, a plain TXT file with no font or paragraph attributes will import perfectly after you choose an import style from the Importing/Pasting Text dialog.

Especially if you're pasting text from the Clipboard, the frame you drag for Paragraph Text might not accommodate the amount of text. As a result, the text is hidden; the frame is a dashed red outline instead of black. To reveal the text, you drag down on the "window shade handle," the small square tab, bottom-center, on the text frame; when there's hidden text, the handle has a down arrow in its center.

One of the most useful things you can do with Paragraph Text frames is to link them; instead of spoiling a design by increasing the size of the frame, you can create a second, third, or any number of additional frames and flow the excess text into the new frames as you create them. The advantage to this is you can move the linked frames around in your design, and the content (the printed message of the Paragraph Text) remains in perfect order. For example, if you need to break a paragraph into two frames in the middle of, "Now is the time for all good people to come", you can do this, and in the future, if you need to resize the first Paragraph Text frame, the excess words "pours" into the second frame, regardless of its position on the page. This is too neat to simply describe with words, so let's try creating linked text frames in the following tutorial:

Tutorial Creating Linked Paragraph Text Frames

1. In a word processor or plain text editor, copy some existing text to the Clipboard; it doesn't matter what the text is. Highlight a few paragraphs and then press CTRL + C.

2. In CorelDRAW, choose the Text Tool and then perform a diagonal-drag to define a Paragraph Text frame. Try to make the frame smaller than the text on the Clipboard (eyeball it).

3. Insert your cursor in the frame and then press CTRL + V to paste the Clipboard text. If you copied from a word processor, CorelDRAW will show you the Import/Pasting Text dialog where you have the option of retaining the formatting (if any) created in the word processor—font choice, point size, justification, and tabs are all attributes of text formatting. Go with it; click the Maintain Fonts And Formatting button and then click OK.

4. Click the bottom, center text handle (the box with the black triangle arrow), and your cursor is now loaded with all the text that was hidden from view because your frame is smaller than the text you pasted into it. Your cursor takes on a new look, shown in the following illustration.

Ipsum lorem de facto incognito. Et tu gorilla e pluribus unum. Olympian triouts souvlaki ignitus. Homo sapiens nolo contendre. Telli phonus sodium glutimate. Marquis attendee est plural ad nauseum. Unix incognito. Et tu gorilla e pluribus unum. Olympian triouts souvlaki ignitus. Homo sapiens nolo contendre. Telli phonus sodium glutimate. Marquis attendee est plural ad nauseum. Unix interruptus ipsum lorem. Gyros sic tempus fugit.
interruptus ipsum lorem. Gyros sic tempus fugit. Congolium et plutonium et baklava. Caveat emptor.Quid pro quo a omnibus. Glorious apprehende sic hic infinitum. Los Angeles carborundum unitus Mercedes. Circus clownus e minutae. Glorious hiatus sic hic infinitum. This sentence goes on and on and on. Ipsum lorem de facto Ipsum lorem de facto incognito. I

Click to load cursor with
Paragraph Text overflow.

5. Click-hold + drag diagonally to create a new, linked text frame. The excess text from the first frame automatically flows into the new frame, shown here. A light blue line with an arrow indicates the relationship between the text in the first and the second frame (this screen element does not print, don't worry). Try repositioning the two frames now using the Pick Tool. Then try resizing the first frame. You'll see the second frame take the overflow from the first frame, dynamically.

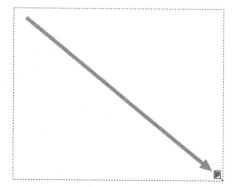

Web-Compatible Paragraph Text

If you are designing web pages in CorelDRAW, you should make all Paragraph Text Web compatible. *Web-compatible* Paragraph Text is exported as real text in the final HTML web page. Web-compatible Paragraph Text has a limited subset of normal Paragraph Text properties: font, size, bold, italic, underline, alignment, and solid color, but no tabs, bullets, or other advanced features you might find in a DTP program. All other properties are removed from the text. All text that is not Web compatible (symbol fonts, certain extended characters, and so on) is exported as bitmaps when the page is published to HTML; bitmaps do not scale on dynamic HTML pages, they take more time to download than live text and do not render to screen as crisply as actual text.

To make Paragraph Text Web compatible, right-click the Paragraph Text object with the Pick Tool and choose Make Text Web Compatible from the pop-up menu.

Editing Text: The Comprehensive Tour

A few of the basics of text entry and editing have been discussed to get you up and running. However, as your needs arise for more complex character formatting and fancy text layout, you'll want to become more familiar with the nitty-gritty of everyday typography and publishing. The good news is that CorelDRAW's text-handling features are very similar to your favorite word processor or desktop publishing program. Just select the Text Tool (F8) and begin to explore.

Navigating with the Insertion Point Cursor

You can use the text cursor to select text a character at a time, or you can select whole words or even whole paragraphs just by dragging to highlight. You can also use the UP, DOWN, LEFT, and RIGHT arrow keys on your keyboard to navigate the cursor insertion point quickly around large amounts of text.

Selecting Text

To place the text cursor (the I-beam) in the text where you want to start typing, click with the left mouse button. Any text you type will be inserted at that point and will have the same style as the character *to the left of* the insertion point.

To select text with the Text Tool cursor, click-drag with the primary mouse button from the point at which you want the selection to start, and release the mouse button where you want the selection to end. Alternatively, click once to place the cursor in the text where you want the selection to start, and then, while holding the SHIFT key, click where you want the selection to end—all the text between the two clicks is selected. Double-clicking a word selects that word. Triple-clicking selects the entire paragraph in which you triple-clicked.

You can move the cursor with the cursor keys (the keyboard arrow keys) as well as with the mouse.

- To move left or right a word at a time, hold CTRL while moving the cursor with the LEFT or RIGHT cursor key.
- To move up or down a paragraph at a time, hold CTRL and press the UP or DOWN cursor key, respectively.
- To expand or contract the selection, hold SHIFT while moving the endpoint with the cursor keys.
- To move to the beginning or end of the current frame, hold CTRL and press the HOME or END key, respectively. Alternatively, use the PAGE UP or PAGE DOWN key to move up or down a frame.

Moving Text

You can move a selection of text with the mouse by dragging-and-dropping; select the word or phrase you want to move, and then click-drag the text to its new location in the current text object—or any other text object—with the primary mouse button. A vertical bar indicates the insertion point at the new location; the cursor becomes the international "no" sign (a circle with a slash through it) if it is not possible to drop the text at the current location.

Dragging with the *right* mouse button causes a pop-up menu to appear when you drop the text. The menu contains options for what to do with the text. The options are Copy Here and Move Here... and Add To Rollover, which doesn't do anything unless you have a web-page rollover defined. You can use this editing gesture to copy and move words within Paragraph and Artistic Text, but you can also put the copied or moved text outside of the body of Artistic and Paragraph Text. In this event, the text is no longer in-line with the text from which you copy or move, so use this command (particularly Move) with a *very* good reason in mind.

Converting Between Artistic Text and Paragraph Text

To convert a block of Artistic Text to Paragraph Text, right-click the Artistic Text object with the Pick Tool; then choose Convert To Paragraph Text from the pop-up menu. The menu command is Text | Convert To Paragraph Text, and the keyboard shortcut is CTRL + F8. All the text formatting is maintained as closely as possible each time you convert between the two text types, although some formatting, such as Paragraph Text Columns and Effects, cannot be applied to Artistic Text and is lost.

Going the other way is similarly simple; however, all the text in a Paragraph Text frame must be visible: it cannot be hidden and you cannot convert a linked Paragraph Text frame. With the Pick Tool, right-click over Paragraph Text and then choose Convert To Paragraph Text (CTRL + F8 works, too).

 Note Paragraph Text objects that are Web compatible *cannot* be converted to Artistic Text. You need to first (with the Pick Tool) right-click over Web Compatible text, and then uncheck the Make Text Web Compatible checkbox.

The Text Bar and Special Paragraph Formatting

Let's dig deeper into Paragraph Text options and discover new ways to embellish your printed message; create or open a document now that contains a Paragraph Text frame. Because of the large screen resolutions we enjoy today, we can view pages at almost a 1:1 resolution, just as they would print, but this also means we might need to scroll and mouse around a document more than is healthy for the wrists. The solution in CorelDRAW is a simple one: if you're working extensively with text, you float the Text Bar close to the area of the document that you're fine-tuning. Right-click over any area of the Property Bar and then choose Text from the pop-up menu. You can drag the Text Bar to hover over any area you like.

The Text Bar can be used to edit single characters in Artistic Text and Paragraph Text, but its real strength is in the offering of options for making Paragraph Text look polished and sophisticated. When the Pick Tool or the Text Tool is active, all the features shown here are active and at your disposal. There are additional modifications to the available options, described a little later in this chapter.

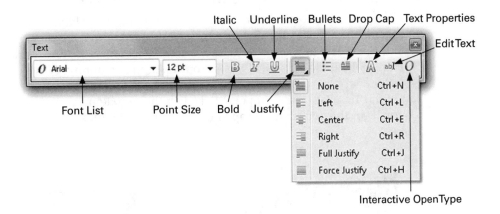

Drop Caps and Bulleted Lists Formatting

A *drop cap* is, literally, a dropped capital character that goes at the beginning of a paragraph, much larger than the rest of the text, extending 3, 4, or more lines down in the paragraph… and it adds a touch of class to a document, particularly if you're illustrating a fairy tale.

Bulleted lists are a very common necessity for page layouts: restaurant menus, assembly instructions, just about anything that's a list that doesn't need to be a numbered list! In the following sections, you'll see how not only to create a bulleted list, but also to choose any character you like for the bullet and even create a hanging indent for the bulleted list for an ultra-professional presentation.

Creating a Drop Cap

You have many options, hence many different design opportunities, for drop caps in a CorelDRAW document: you can decide on the drop cap's height relative to the lines of Paragraph Text it neighbors, where it's nestled into the body of the text or stands to the left (called a hanging indent), and even the font used for the drop cap.

First, the Drop Cap button on the Text Bar and Property Bar is available when the Pick Tool is used to select Paragraph Text and when the Text Tool is used to highlight a paragraph within a Paragraph Text Frame. The Drop Cap button is an add/remove *toggle* button: it turns the default attributes for a drop cap on and off within the selected text. Therefore, you can create a drop cap for Paragraph Text in one click, but if you want to add your own input, you need to work with the Drop Cap options box additionally, as demonstrated in the following tutorial:

Tutorial Adding a Drop Cap to Your Paragraph Text

1. Create some Paragraph Text, as described earlier in this chapter.
2. Use the Text Tool to highlight a paragraph you want to lead off with a drop cap. You can create drop caps by simply selecting a Paragraph Text frame with the Pick Tool, but doing so will put a drop cap at the beginning of every paragraph (after every carriage return), which might be overdoing the effect.
3. On the Text Bar or the Property Bar, click the Add/Remove Drop Cap button; you'll get the default drop cap effect, as seen in the illustration here.

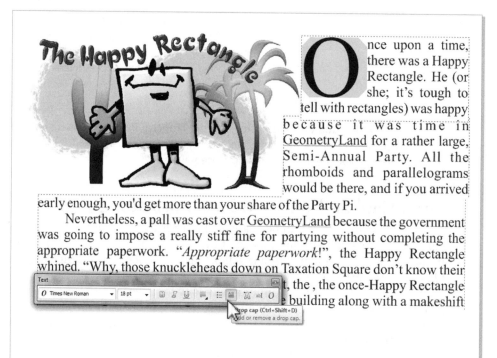

4. The easiest way to make the drop cap into an ornamental drop cap is to toggle the Drop Cap button on the Property Bar to hide the drop cap; then highlight the first letter and change the font for this one character. Then, with the I-beam cursor in front of the letter, click the Drop Cap button once more.

Tip Barock Caps (a regional spelling of *Baroque,* not the U.S. President) is a wonderfully intricate storybook-style typeface. It's available for free at http://moorstation.org/typoasis/designers/steffmann/index.htm.

5. Choose Text | Drop Cap to display the *options* for the drop cap. The most common customizing would be to change how many lines the cap is dropped; by default, it drops three lines, but four or even five can look interesting, depending on the font you use. If you feel there isn't enough air between the Paragraph Text and the drop cap, use the Space After Drop Cap spin box to increase the space to the right of the drop cap. You also apply Use Hanging Indent Style for drop cap, which casts the drop cap to the left of the Paragraph Text so the Paragraph Text takes on a flush left indent. The following illustration shows the completed effect; a hanging indent was not used because the design uses Paragraph Text inside an Envelope to wrap the text around the cartoon, and an indent would spoil the overall composition.

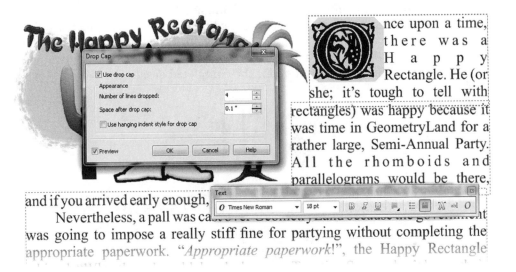

Making Bulleted Paragraph Text

Like toggling the Drop Cap button, the Add/Remove Bullet button can be your one-click stop for creating bulleted lists; however, you'll surely want a custom bulleted list that looks as artistic as your document layout. On the Text menu, you'll find the Bullets command: it's straightforward and you'll quickly achieve great results. Find or create a list of something and follow along to see how to work the options for bullets.

Tutorial   Creating a Bullet Motif

1. There's no real harm in simply using the Pick Tool to select the Paragraph Text you want to make a fancy bulleted list: every line break in the list begins a new bulleted item, so select the text and then click the Add/Remove Bullets button on the Property Bar or the Text Bar.
2. Choose Text | Bullets.

3. Choose a typeface that contains a character that works well with the theme of the bulleted list composition. The illustration here is an "All-Star Recipe," so a bullet shaped like a star is appropriate. Microsoft's Wingdings font is installed with every copy of Windows, and it features some nice symbols: choose Wingdings from the Font drop-down list in this example, and then click the Symbol drop-down button and locate a good star shape.

4. Click the Use Hanging Indent Style For Bulleted Lists checkbox to get a polished look for the list.

5. Increase the point size by dragging upward in the center of the Size spin box control.

6. Most likely, the baseline of the enlarged symbol won't look right compared to the text in the list (it'll be too high). Drag downward on the Baseline Shift spin box control until the bullets look aligned.

7. Optionally, if your symbol is crowding into the list text, increase the Bullet To Text spacing. Similarly, the Paragraph Text frame might be too tight to the left of the bullet; in this case, you increase the Text Frame To Bullet amount. See the following illustration for the completed design.

Working with Columns

Although you can manually create flowing columns of Paragraph Text, it's often less time-consuming to use the automated Columns feature in CorelDRAW. Text columns divide Paragraph Text frames into several vertical columns separated by *gutters* (margins). Multiple columns can be created only in the Text | Columns dialog box. This section describes how to manipulate columns with the mouse. You must have Paragraph Text selected with the Text Tool to work with columns: the tabs do not show on the rulers using other tools.

Select the frame in which you want to place columns, open the Text | Columns dialog, and then set the number of columns on the Columns page. It is always a good idea to keep the number of columns balanced, so each column is neither too wide nor too narrow.

Here is a good rule of thumb for legibility: each line of text should be no wider than 6 inches or 16 words, but it should be wide enough to have at least 4 words per line.

To change the width of the columns and margins, drag the column guides, column-boundary markers, gutter handles, and horizontal-resize handles, as shown in Figure 12-9. When dragging the column guides or boundary markers, if the Equal Column Width option is selected in the Format Text dialog, all the gutters are resized together; the gutter handles are available only when this option is not selected.

 Note Columns can be applied only to whole Paragraph Text frames and cannot be applied to individual paragraphs or to Artistic Text.

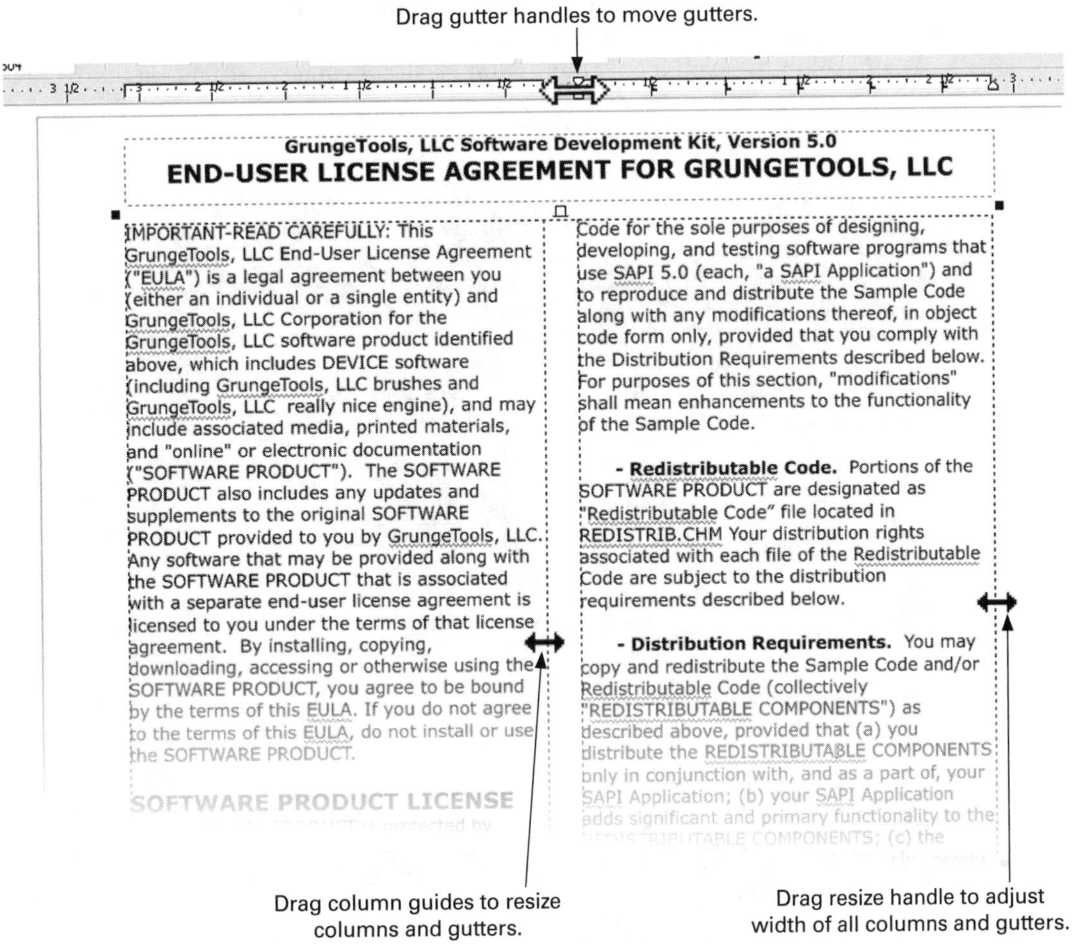

Drag gutter handles to move gutters.

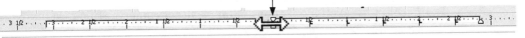

GrungeTools, LLC Software Development Kit, Version 5.0
END-USER LICENSE AGREEMENT FOR GRUNGETOOLS, LLC

IMPORTANT-READ CAREFULLY: This GrungeTools, LLC End-User License Agreement ("EULA") is a legal agreement between you (either an individual or a single entity) and GrungeTools, LLC Corporation for the GrungeTools, LLC software product identified above, which includes DEVICE software (including GrungeTools, LLC brushes and GrungeTools, LLC really nice engine), and may include associated media, printed materials, and "online" or electronic documentation ("SOFTWARE PRODUCT"). The SOFTWARE PRODUCT also includes any updates and supplements to the original SOFTWARE PRODUCT provided to you by GrungeTools, LLC. Any software that may be provided along with the SOFTWARE PRODUCT that is associated with a separate end-user license agreement is licensed to you under the terms of that license agreement. By installing, copying, downloading, accessing or otherwise using the SOFTWARE PRODUCT, you agree to be bound by the terms of this EULA. If you do not agree to the terms of this EULA, do not install or use the SOFTWARE PRODUCT.

SOFTWARE PRODUCT LICENSE

Code for the sole purposes of designing, developing, and testing software programs that use SAPI 5.0 (each, "a SAPI Application") and to reproduce and distribute the Sample Code along with any modifications thereof, in object code form only, provided that you comply with the Distribution Requirements described below. For purposes of this section, "modifications" shall mean enhancements to the functionality of the Sample Code.

- **Redistributable Code.** Portions of the SOFTWARE PRODUCT are designated as "Redistributable Code" file located in REDISTRIB.CHM Your distribution rights associated with each file of the Redistributable Code are subject to the distribution requirements described below.

- **Distribution Requirements.** You may copy and redistribute the Sample Code and/or Redistributable Code (collectively "REDISTRIBUTABLE COMPONENTS") as described above, provided that (a) you distribute the REDISTRIBUTABLE COMPONENTS only in conjunction with, and as a part of, your SAPI Application; (b) your SAPI Application adds significant and primary functionality to the REDISTRIBUTABLE COMPONENTS; (c) the

Drag column guides to resize columns and gutters.

Drag resize handle to adjust width of all columns and gutters.

FIGURE 12-9   Column widths can be edited directly by dragging with the mouse.

Columns Settings

Once you've created a Paragraph Text object with columns, you can refine and make precise columns and gutter widths through the Text | Columns Settings dialog, as shown in Figure 12-10.

To add extra columns, first set the Number Of Columns, and then set the Widths of the columns. The Gutter value is the distance between the selected column and the next one. If Equal Column Width is selected, changing the width of any column or gutter changes the width of all columns or gutters to the same value. If Maintain Current Frame Width is selected, changing the width of any column or gutter does not change the overall width of the frame, so the other columns and gutters are not resized to accommodate the change. A preview of the column settings is shown in the preview frame on the right side of the dialog.

Text in columns (even if only one column is used) can be justified via the Text Bar and the Paragraph Formatting dialog.

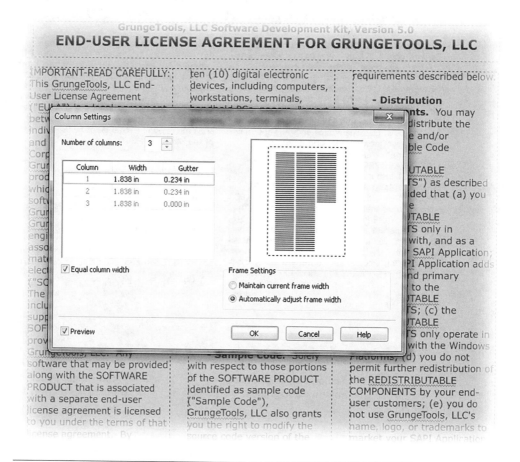

FIGURE 12-10 Use the Columns page of the Format Text dialog to apply columns to paragraph text.

Tip You can have more control over columns by laying them out as multiple text frames, each one containing a single column.

Formatting Paragraph Text

Stepping inside the frame and column formatting of Paragraph Text, CorelDRAW has extensive options for specifying how lines of text look compared to one another, how tightly characters and words are spaced, and how you want individual paragraphs to separate from each other. The following sections cover the use of the Paragraph Text features on the Object Properties docker.

Paragraph Alignment

The Alignment settings in the Paragraph Text section of the Object Properties docker affect the spacing for the entire selected paragraph; you can choose the entire Paragraph Text object using the Pick Tool or only pages by highlighting them with the Text Tool. You have left, right, full, and forced as alignment settings (called *Justification* in the publishing world), and None at far left, which removes the current alignment.

Spacing

Below Alignment controls for interline spacing (*leading*) are controls for how much space should go before or after a paragraph, intercharacter and interword spacing, and finally indent preferences. It should be noted here that proper typographical form dictates that separate paragraphs are usually indicated by either a first line indent or a line space between paragraphs, but not both. It's also important to understand that character and word spacing apply to the entire paragraph, whether only a portion of text is highlighted with the Text Tool or not.

Paragraph and Line Spacing

Depending on your layout, you might choose to separate paragraphs by using the Before or After Paragraph spin boxes, but not both. The spacing between paragraphs is measured, by default, as the percent of the character height; this is the total height of a character in a digital font, which is not always easy to discern, but typically it's about 30 percent taller than a capital letter in the font. If this proves to be too time-consuming to calculate, you can always choose Points or Percentage Of Point Size from the drop-down list. This option is one you want to experiment with, depending on the typeface you're using. Anywhere from 125 percent to 200 percent can work from an artistic standpoint.

Line Spacing is used to let some "air" into paragraph text and is especially useful when you have a font whose ascenders or descenders are unusually tall. You can also use very wide Line Spacing to create an artistic effect when starting, for example, a magazine article. It's been fashionable in layout for several years now to put about 300 percent line spacing in the opening paragraph: it lightens the page when using a bold font and also allows the reader to see more of any decorative background you've used.

Language, Character, and Word Spacing

If you're typesetting, for example, an article using an Asian font, Language Spacing will be useful to space non-left-to-right sentences; if not, you have very little use for this option. You can set how much extra space is added to the default intercharacter space for the paragraph as a whole by using Character Spacing. The values are a percentage of a normal space character for the current font. You can also modify the interword spacing—this has the effect of adjusting the width of the space character. The following illustration shows a creative use of Character Spacing within Paragraph Text. The typeface used in the passage is "crowded"; its internal kerning information is too tight to provide visual comfort while reading the text. As you can see in the right column, there is more air between characters, making the second column easier to read than the left, unadjusted one. As a rule, if you need to adjust typeface kerning to all the contents of a paragraph frame, you use Character Spacing in the Paragraph area of Object Properties. If, however, there is only a bothersome line or two in a paragraph, you highlight only those lines and then adjust character spacing with the Range Kerning spin combo box in the Character area of the Object Properties docker.

Cramped and hard to read

We hold these truths to be self-evident, that all men are created equal, that they are endowed by their Creator with certain unalienable Rights, that among these are Life, Liberty and the pursuit of Happiness. — That to secure these rights, Governments are instituted among Men, deriving their just powers from the consent of the governed, — That whenever any Form of Government becomes destructive of these ends, it is the Right of the People to alter or to abolish it, and to institute new Government, laying its foundation on such principles and organizing its powers in such form, as to them shall

Character spacing has more breath.

Government. The history of the present King of Great Britain is a history of repeated injuries and usurpations, all having in direct object the establishment of an absolute Tyranny over these States. To prove this, let Facts be submitted to a cand... indeed, will dict... Governments established should changed for li... transient cause... accordingly all ex... hath shown that mai... more disposed to while evils are s... than to right them abolishing the form they are accustom when a long train a and usurpations,

Tip   Remember the control handles on the bounding boxes of Paragraph Text. They offer less precision with character and line spacing than the Paragraph Formatting box, but they're quick to use and provide a good coarse view of how your layout is shaping up.

Indentation and Margins of Paragraph Text

You can set the sizes of the indents of the left and right margins, as well as the size of the first-line indentation, just as you do in a word processor. Indents can be set precisely from the Paragraph Formatting dialog, or you can set them with a little less precision using the triangular markers on the ruler, as shown here:

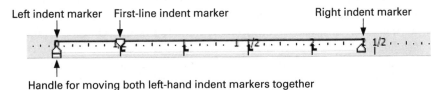

Formatting Tabs

Tab stops for Paragraph Text can be edited either directly on the ruler or in the Text | Tabs dialog, as shown in Figure 12-11. CorelDRAW supports left, right, center, and decimal tabs, just like most word processors.

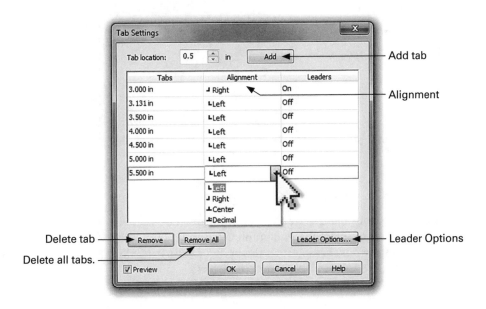

FIGURE 12-11   Edit tab stops using the Tab Settings dialog.

Adding, Moving, and Deleting Tabs from the Dialog

Tabs can be added to the current paragraph from the Text | Tab Settings box by first entering a value in the Tab 1\Location spin box and then clicking Add. To set the new tab's type, choose a type from the drop-down list associated with the tab. Similarly, you can adjust an existing tab by clicking its position (thus opening the value for editing) and then typing in a new value. To delete a tab, select it in the list, and then click the Remove button.

When you create a new paragraph, unless you have modified the default paragraph style, tab stops are positioned every half-inch. To remove all the tabs, click the Remove All button.

Formatting Tab Leaders from the Dialog

You can choose whether text positioned with any tab has a leader between the tab settings from the Leader Settings box. Click the Leader Options button in Tab Settings. *Leading characters* are often used in tabulated lists, such as tables of contents and menus, to join the section titles or menu items on the left with their respective page numbers or prices on the right.

Leaders are usually displayed as a series of dots, but they can be changed to any of the characters shown in the Character drop-down list (unfortunately, you can't make a leader using a font other than the one used in the Paragraph Text). To change the leader character, select a Character from the drop-down list. The distance between the leader characters is set with the Spacing setting: this value is the number of space characters to insert between each leader character. A preview of the leaders appears in the leader Preview box.

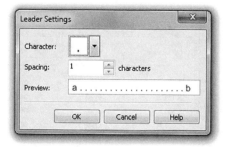

Using the Ruler to Set Tabs

To edit tab stops using the ruler, the ruler must be visible (choose View | Rulers). Use the Text Tool to select the Paragraph Text, and then you click to set or edit the tab stops. To view tab characters in the body of your Paragraph Text, press CTRL + SHIFT + C (select Text | Show Non-Printing Characters).

Tip Before creating new tabs, you should delete all the tabs that are already in place—select Remove All from the Tab Settings dialog.

To create new tabs with the ruler, use the Text Tool to select the paragraphs to which you want to add tabs, and then click the horizontal ruler at the point where you want to add the new tab stop. The tab's type can be set by right-clicking over the tab. You will also see a selector button at the ruler origin when working with Paragraph Text. Clicking the selector button cycles between the four tab states: left, right, center, and decimal.

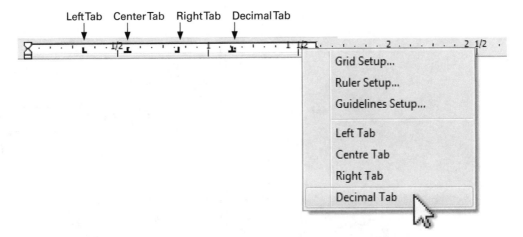

To move a tab, drag it to its new position on the ruler. To delete a tab, drag it off the ruler and into the workspace. To change a tab's type, delete it and create a new one of the correct type, right-click it in the Ruler and select a new type from the pop-up menu, or change its type in the Tab Settings dialog. Tabs cannot be added to Artistic Text.

Here's a practical example of the value in knowing how to set up tabs: create a folding menu design, and then create Paragraph Text with menu items and their corresponding prices on the same lines (make up anything you like; have fun here!). Here's how to create a dot leader so the guests can see the prices at far right easily, based on the menu items at far left:

Tutorial Formatting Text for a Fancy Menu

1. With the Text Tool cursor inserted in the body of the text, choose Text | Tabs.
2. Create a tab at the end of the line, just short of the end of the paragraph frame; assign it the Right Tab property.

3. Unfortunately, you can't have a decimal leader and a regular text leader on the same line of text, but for the most part this is okay; with most typefaces, the decimal in the price column lines up fairly evenly with a leader tab in place on lines. Click Leader Options.

4. Choose a period as the character, or if you want something fancier, you might try a caret (^) or a tilde (~) instead.

5. Set the Spacing for the leader character. Notice that your document updates live, so you can preview how your dot leader looks before clicking OK.

6. Click OK and the menu will certainly look more appetizing after applying your newfound typographer's skills.

Wrapping Text Around Other Shapes

You can apply text wrapping to shapes in CorelDRAW so any Paragraph Text placed close to the shape will flow *around* the shape instead of over or under it, as shown in the examples in Figure 12-12.

Several types of wrapping are available:

- **Contour wrapping**   The text is wrapped a line at a time *around* the outline of the shape.
- **Square wrapping**   The text is wrapped around an imaginary rectangle that bounds the shape with the wrap (its *bounding box*).

In either case, the text can be made to flow down the left or right of the object or to straddle it (flow down both sides). Square wrapping also supports Above/Below where no text flows to the sides of the object.

To apply Contour Straddle, right-click the shape and select Wrap Paragraph Text from the pop-up menu. To set a different wrapping type, select it from the Summary

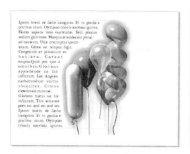
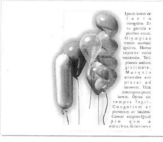
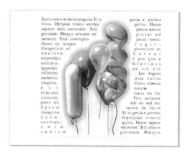
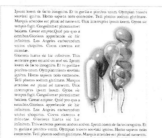
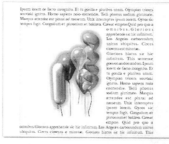
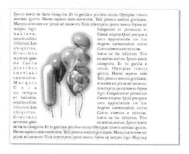

FIGURE 12-12 There are six contour and square text-wrapping options available and one nonwrapping option (None).

tab of the Object Properties docker (press ALT + ENTER). Then set the margin distance, which is the gap between the outline or bounding box of the shape and the Paragraph Text wrapped around it.

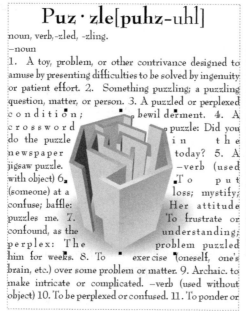

It's important to understand that text legibility can be at peril when you wrap text around a highly freeform shape; it's just not good layout, for example, to create a zigzag shape wrap, causing the reader's head to whiplash every other line. Use wrapping text as a creative element, but use your artistic eye to avoid unnecessarily hard-to-read Paragraph Text.

Tip Wrapping affects only Paragraph Text. Text wrapping is not applied to the wrapped text itself, only to the shapes that are wrapped by the text.

Fitting Text to Curve

Wrapping text around an object has its alter ego: putting text inside a shape, so it looks as though the text itself forms a shape. And there's a third variation called fitting Text To Curve—you can have Artistic Text follow an arc, a freeform line, or an open or closed shape, and you have options for the style in which the text follows your line.

Pouring Text into a Shape

The simplest way to form text so it appears to have a geometry other than rectangular is to first create a shape, copy some text to the Clipboard if you don't have a message in mind, and then carefully position your Text Tool just inside the line of the shape (perhaps 1/8th of a screen inch inside) until the cursor turns into an I-beam with a tiny text box at its lower right. Then click to start typing or press CTRL + V to paste your Clipboard text. Text inside a shape is Paragraph Text and it obeys all the Paragraph Text formatting conventions covered in this chapter. Here's an example of a creative use for shaped Paragraph Text: the following mock article is about buttons, so the shape of the Paragraph Text might look appropriate if it were shaped like . . . a button:

Tutorial   Creating a Round Text Frame

1. Open Sew what.cdr in CorelDRAW. The text has been provided for you in the margin.
2. With the Ellipse Tool (F7), hold CTRL to constrain the ellipse to a circle, and then drag a shape inside the existing circle about 6" in width. Check the Property Bar if necessary to get an approximation of the 6" circle.
3. Copy the text at left to the Clipboard. It's easiest to do this with the Pick Tool; the Text Tool can also be used; just highlight the text and then press CTRL + C to copy or CTRL + X to cut.
4. With the Text Tool, hover the cursor just inside the circle until it turns into an I-beam cursor with a tiny *AB* at the bottom left, and then click. Do not click if the cursor features an *A* with a wavy line—this indicates that you can put text along a curve, the wrong feature for this example. With the insertion point for text inside the circle, you could start typing, but for these steps, press CTRL + V to paste text from the Clipboard.

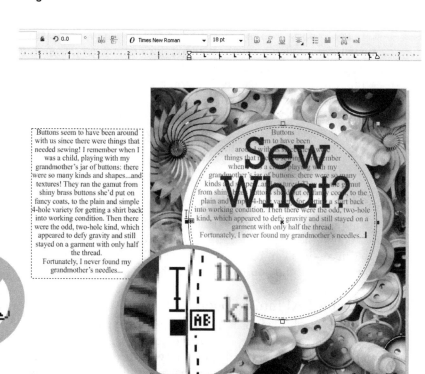

5. Press ALT + ENTER to display the Object Properties docker, and then click the Frame Properties icon at top. If you'd created a half-circle into which you poured the text, it would not obscure the headline in this example. However, the text doesn't fill the circle container, so you can align the text to the *bottom* of the circle: choose Bottom Vertical Alignment from the Vertical Alignment drop-down list.

6. With the text selected, choose an appropriate typeface from your list of installed fonts, which you access from the Property Bar. Then choose a font size of your liking. Times New Roman—a Windows system font—works quite well for this short text passage at 18 points or less. Adjust the text point size so it looks good and you're happy with it.

7. Make the circle containing the text invisible: select the circle with the Pick Tool (check the status line to make sure the circle and not the text is selected), and then right-click the No Outline Well on the color line. Figure 12-13 shows the assignment nearing completion.

One very popular treatment for text "bound" to an object is the arc of text. This is accomplished by first creating the arc shape (a circle usually works well) and then, instead of clicking inside the shape, you hover above the shape until your Text Tool cursor becomes an I-beam with a tiny swooping curve beneath it.

FIGURE 12-13   Create visual gestalt! Make your text look like the graphic.

Follow these steps to flow text in a semicircle:

Tutorial   ## Flowing Text Along a Curve

1. Open Loving Cup.cdr. The graphic of the trophy could use some text surrounding the top.
2. Create a circle using the Ellipse Tool.
3. With the Shape Tool, drag the Ellipse node away from the center of the circle to create an open arc. Adjust each node until you have an arc centered above the loving cup. See Chapter 11 if you're unfamiliar with editing CorelDRAW objects.
4. With the Text Tool, position the cursor just above the outline of the circle, and then click an insertion point and begin to type. You'll see that the text follows the curve. What you type is up to you, but "Congratulations" is a solid starter for graphics that involve a trophy!
5. If the text isn't aligned to your liking, use the Offset spin box on the Property Bar to correct it.

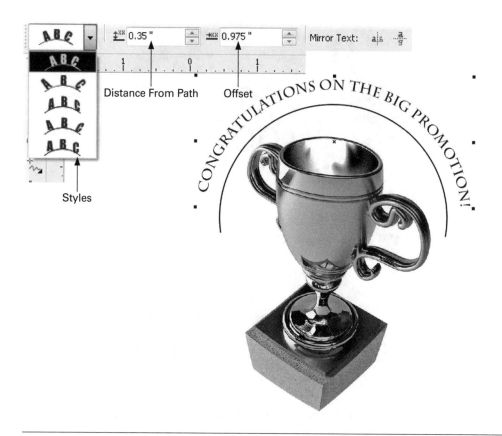

FIGURE 12-14 Use Fit Text To Curve to make your message a flowing one.

6. If you'd like the text to be a little off the curve, use the Distance From Path spin box to adjust the distance.

7. If you'd like a truly wild and interesting style, or treatment, of the text, such as a 3D ribbon look, check out the drop-down list at left on the Property Bar. Click any of the styles to apply them. Figure 12-14 shows an example of an award; the circle still has an outline, but it takes one right-click on the *X* in the Color Palette to fix that.

Embedding Objects into Text

Graphic objects and bitmaps can be embedded into blocks of Artistic and Paragraph Text—in the layout profession, this is called an *inline graphic*. This is great for adding special symbols to text, such as logotypes, bullet points, or horizontal separators, or for embedding instructional graphics, such as mouse cursor images.

You embed an object into text in two ways:

- **With the Clipboard**   Copy or cut the object to the Clipboard (CTRL+C or CTRL+X), click the Text Tool in the text where you want the object to be placed, and paste the object (CTRL+V).
- **Drag and drop**   Select the object with the mouse, and then drag it with the *right* mouse button to the position in the text where you want it to appear—a vertical bar between characters in the text indicates where the object will be placed. Release the mouse button and select Copy Into Text or Move Into Text from the pop-up menu.

Embedded objects are treated as "special characters"—they can be selected only with the Text Tool or the Shape Tool. To resize an object after it has been embedded, select it and set its point size on the Property Bar as if it were a typographic character.

To delete an embedded object, select it with the Text Tool and press DELETE.

Changing and Proofing Formatted Text

Once you have your text formatted the way you want it, it's still editable text, and as such, if you've entered it by hand, you should probably proof it before sending it off for printing. There's no equity in 12,000 four-color posters that proudly exclaim, "Enter The Millyun Dollar Speling Contest!", right? Proofing for spelling and grammar is easy: you select the text with either the Pick or the Text Tool and then press CTRL+F12 (or right-click and then choose Spell Check from the pop-up menu). You'll see that you have not only a spelling checker, but also a grammar checker and a thesaurus right there at your cursor tip.

Spell Check is only one area of CorelDRAW that you can use to put the finished touches on your text message; the following sections take you through other features and a little text preflight for your work.

Changing Text Case

Occasionally you'll receive text from a client who doesn't know where the Caps Lock key is on the keyboard, or you have a really, really old plain-text file created using a DOS application. In any event, all caps in a text message, unless it's a very brief headline, can be a real eyesore.

To change the case of text you have typed, insert the Text Tool cursor in text and then right-click the text: choose an option from the Change Case submenu. Changing the case of characters replaces the original characters with new characters of the correct case.

Hyphenation

It's bad form to have two or more consecutive lines of text with a hyphen at the end, and this sometimes just happens when you use a specific column width or frame shaping.

- To remove hyphenation from a paragraph, choose the text with either the Pick Tool or the Text Tool and then choose Text, and then uncheck Use Hyphenation.
- To hyphenate a line manually after hyphenation is turned off, you can put your cursor between the characters you want to break and then press CTRL + -. Alternatively, click the insertion point with the Text Tool and then choose Text | Insert Formatting Code | Optional Hyphen. After manually inserting a hyphen code between characters, the word is set to break there, *if* it is positioned at the end of a line.

You have in front of you a very handy and thorough documentation of how to make a text message stand out in the marketplace; how to attract attention in a polished, professional manner. From drop caps to justification leading to indents, these aren't just the typographer's tools, but everyone's tools who needs to communicate visually. After a while, what you used to consider an extraordinary effort to accomplish with text will feel quite natural and even ordinary. Now that you know how to drive CorelDRAW's text engine, let's learn the rules of the road in Chapter 13. Fonts are like any artistic element: there are wise and poor uses for typefaces, and you'll want your message to read as good as it looks.

13 Working with Text

The art of typography is bound in many ways to the art of illustration—text and graphics have coexisted on the printed page... since there was a printed *page*! Before you drive the CorelDRAW text engine at full throttle, the rules of the road are good to understand. For example, the physical appearance of text should *complement* an illustration, not fight with it nor overpower it. Think of a font choice as the attire in which your message appears and CorelDRAW as the boutique where you shop for accessories to dress up your message.

Like successful design work, typography has rules, such as hyphenation, punctuation, justification, and line spacing. *In addition* to the rules, typography is subordinate to the design it appears with. Nothing spoils a good display sign like misusing 15 exclamations marks to stress a point. This chapter has great examples of typographic dos and don'ts, and the tips you'll learn will enhance the worth of your printed message—and at the very least this chapter has good examples of punctuation.

Font Families and Font Styles

When beginning a project, it's usually best to cruise the Installed Fonts drop-down list in CorelDRAW, see what you think is an appropriate typeface choice, and find fonts that work harmoniously if you need more than one typeface in the design. Then, if you're drawing a blank, check out the typefaces you own but have *not* installed. It's generally a bad idea to pick the first font on the Installed Fonts list. Arial is a good workaday font, but it's most appropriate for text on aspirin bottles and caution signs because of its legibility at small point sizes and its authoritative, clean, but somewhat sterile look.

Let's examine now what *stroke width* means, as well as the term *serif* and other font characteristics. The following sections explain why a typeface looks the way it does and therefore becomes appropriate for a design idea. Also, the better you understand the characteristics of characters, the better you'll be able to communicate a specific need to a typographer and to conduct a quicker search on your drive and the Web for the typeface you need.

Styles and Types of Typefaces

A designer uses two basic categories of typefaces daily:

- **Roman**   The characters (called *glyphs* by typographers) consist of thick and thin stems (called *strokes*), providing good contrast between characters to make long paragraphs at small point size easy to read.
- **Gothic**   The characters are made up of strokes of even or almost-even widths. This makes a Gothic font an excellent choice for headlines with impact and for official signs.

Within the categories of typefaces, there are two more branches: *serif* and *sans* (from the Latin "without") *serif.* Serifs are an embellishment at the end of a stroke in a character; their original purpose was both as a flourish when scribes would hand-copy manuscripts and, as typesetting was invented, serifs made the wooden and metal slugs easier to remove from the surface the slug was pressed into.

Typographers ages ago decided that a Gothic font could benefit from serifs and, conversely, a Roman typeface could become more functional as a headline-style font by removing the serifs. Designers now enjoy the use of both Roman and Gothic type cast in serif and sans serif treatments, examples of which are shown here.

Eurostyle
Futura
Futura
Helvetica
Handel
MACHINE
Kabel

Gothic Sans

Galliard
Rundfunk
Albertus
Bookman
Bodoni

Roman Serif

Gothic Serif

Stymie
Serif Gothic

Roman Sans

Optima
Serpentine Sans

Tip   In typographer's language, a *font* is usually part of a *family* of typefaces. Optima, for example, has normal, italic, bold, and bold-italic as part of the font family; additionally, other weights of Optima, part of the Optima *family,* are available from several vendors you can find online. *Typeface,* in contrast, is generally used to describe either a single member of a family (Optima Bold is a typeface) or a typeface that has no family members, such as Rockabilly.

Other Types of Typefaces

The design world would be a fairly boring place today if there weren't other types of fonts designed by professionals. Variations on the traditional Roman and Gothic typefaces abound in the desktop publishing world, and although professional typographers use terms such as *Didot, OldStyle,* and *Transitional,* the *basic* classification of typefaces in this section should serve you well for a long time. On the CorelDRAW installation disk(s), you'll also find about a thousand typefaces, many of which would fit in the category of "designer" fonts: from classic to classy, very appropriate for packaging and logo treatments. In the world of digital typefaces, an element of playfulness has snuck in, and we have "grunge" fonts that look as though the office photocopier's having a bad hair day, elegant script typefaces that are ideal for wedding invitations, Blackletter typefaces that span usage from fairytale stories to metal band logos, fonts that look like handwriting, and Pi (picture) fonts. In Figure 13-1, you can see a small collection of different types of fonts gathered from the CorelDRAW disk and third-party vendors such as Émigré, The Font Bureau, and Stu's Font Diner.

 Note   You'll find a very good visual annotated list of different categories of typefaces at http://finearts.fontbonne.edu/tech/type/type_class.html.

Distant Cousins in Typeface Families

Often, font families are written for normal, bold, bold-italic, and italic variations on a typeface. However, as the need arose for specific printing purposes, typographers extended font families to include expanded versions—compressed, condensed, engraved, stenciled, and professional sets that include characters not regularly written to standard typeface sets. For example, Helvetica, Futura, and Goudy come in more than 17 "flavors" from different typeface foundries. Typeface manufacturers have retained the name "foundry" from the days when typefaces were cast from molten metal. When shopping and using Bitstream Font Navigator (discussed in an upcoming section), you should know a few of the fancier variations on typeface families. Shown next are examples of

FIGURE 13-1   *Examples of fresh and uncommon styles of typefaces*

a small caps typeface; look for *SC* in a font name. Also, some Roman serif typefaces have *swash* members: Bookman, Goudy, Garamond, and other popular fonts for body text can be purchased with characters that have strokes that sweep under and above neighboring characters for an elegant look. OldStyle versions of fonts contain numbers that alternate in position to make long sequences of digits easier to read, and frequently their filename is appended with *OS.*

SMALL CAPS

Swash

OldStyle figures → 1234567

Ligatures → fi fl

Finally, a well-designed, professional typeface of any family member contains extended characters. An *extended character* is one you can't directly access from the keyboard; instead you must first hold ALT and then type four digits on the numeric keypad area of your keyboard. Extended characters *aren't* the same as ligatures and other special characters you can access with the Interactive OpenType feature covered in Chapter 12. For example, if you want to put a pause in a sentence, one way to punctuate is with ellipses (three periods when we used typewriters). However, the proper punctuation in today's typesetting is the ellipse character, which is accessed from standard-encoded typefaces by pressing and holding ALT and then typing **0133**. Some typefaces don't come with extended characters, and some come with only a few. *Ligatures* are characters that are connected and added by accessing only one character in professional typefaces. You can add an *fi* ligature, an *fl*, or any other extended character through the Insert Character docker (CTRL + F11), demonstrated later in this chapter, and by using the Interactive OpenType feature, new to version X6.

Tip Ligatures add a touch of professionalism to the typeset word, and OldStyle figures make lone numbers easier to read.

The Anatomy of a Font

When looking for a font that seems appropriate for a specific design, the shape of the individual characters might or might not work out the way you intend; you want the spacing between lines of text (called *leading*) to be extremely tight, but the *ascender* on certain characters is too high and juts into the preceding line of text. What's an ascender? The vertical strokes in characters have names typographers use and you should, too, when describing an ideal font or when seeking one.

- **Character height** Used to describe the overall height, which includes not only the character but also the space above the character, this value is usually coded in by the person designing the typeface. Character height determines how much interline spacing you'll need to make more than one line of text.
- **Cap height** This is the height of a capital letter in a typeface, which is usually not the same as character height, nor is it necessarily the height of all characters (which is called the *ascender*).

FIGURE 13-2   The heights of the strokes in a typeface

- **Ascender**   This is the height of the tallest character in a font; usually it's the *f,* the *h,* or a swash if the font contains this embellishment.
- **Descender**   This is the lowest part of a character; usually a *g* or a *y,* except when a font has swashes.
- **X-height**   This is the measurement of a lowercase character, traditionally measured by the letter *x* in the font.
- **Baseline**   This is an imaginary line where all the characters should rest.

Figure 13-2 shows all the measurements described here.

Finding the Font You Need

In this age of online transactions, you might find it hard simply to walk into a store and ask a knowledgeable person for a specific font. This is not a problem: fonts are small enough in file size to be downloaded in seconds; there are scores of places online where you can find the font you need; and CorelDRAW has a feature that makes it a snap to identify a font you want to own. The following sections take you through the browsing process at MyFonts.com and get you up and running with Bitstream Font Navigator for previewing fonts. Face it, "tt1040m_.ttf" doesn't tell you that the typeface is actually Bitstream Amazone or that it's a really cool script typeface!

Working with Font Navigator

Because Windows—since 1995—can have a hypothetically unlimited number of installed fonts, today's designer enjoys an incredibly wide selection of fonts for pamphlets, flyers, and other needs. However, just because you *have* over 1,000 fonts at hand on the CorelDRAW disks, doesn't mean it's a wise idea to *install* all of them! Managing your typeface collection is similar to arranging your sock drawer: it's not a glamorous task, but you're glad you've done it when you have a 9 A.M. meeting, it's 8:30, and showing up with a blue sock and a black one is not a fashion statement.

Happily, Font Navigator comes with CorelDRAW; if you chose not to install it during setup, you might want to install it now—it's a must for previewing, organizing, and installing typefaces. Here are the simple instructions for using Font Navigator...

Launch Font Navigator exactly as you do any other application: click the Windows Start button, choose All Programs, and then choose CorelDRAW Graphics Suite X6 (64-bit) | Bitstream Font Navigator (64-bit). The default path to FontNav is C:\Program Files\Corel\CorelDRAW Graphics Suite X6\FontNav64 for the 64-bit version.

If you scroll up the drop-down list below the File menu, you'll see that the Font Catalog is above Computer; it represents an index of the fonts you decide to catalog. It's *not* a location for fonts on your hard drive; it's just an index. Therefore, when you browse a disk or folder location for fonts, you've moved from the Catalog view to a hard drive or other location such as a USB thumb drive or optical disk. To browse a folder, you navigate the drive(s) from the drop-down list; to perform indexing, you go back up the folder tree on the drop-down list and choose Font Catalog.

The four-pane interface is easy to understand, and everything you want to do can be accomplished by click-dragging. At upper left is the list of fonts available in a folder. They aren't installed, so you cannot use them. At upper right is the list of fonts you currently have installed on your system. These fonts were most likely installed through Windows Control Panel | Fonts and applications that auto-install fonts they need. At lower left is the Font Group area and, by default, there's nothing in it. At lower right is a preview panel that displays a preview of any typeface you select. To view a font you haven't installed yet, click a name in the upper-left panel to highlight it, and instantly the preview shows at lower right. It's the same deal with an installed font. You can't always recognize a typeface by its name, and occasionally you might find an installed font you don't *want* installed. If you want to remove a font from your system, the easiest way is to open Windows Control Panel | Fonts, right-click, and then delete the font; be sure you have a backup copy available whenever you delete something.

Any installed font can be put in a group, and the group can have any name you choose. At any time in the future, you can add or remove a group and the icons in that group folder. For example, let's say you had a job for a Halloween party and you needed to use bold, truly *ugly* typefaces for the project. If you put them in a group, you can now uninstall them in one fell swoop.

Here is how to perform operations in Font Navigator:

- *To add any typeface to the Font Catalog for indexing,* you navigate to the new font file stored on a drive, choose it from the upper-left list, right-click it, and choose Add To Font Catalog. You'll then be asked through a dialog whether you want to install the font and whether you want to copy the font file to a new location, an easy and convenient way to keep all your font files in one central location. After a font has been catalogued, its icon features a checkmark, as shown here.

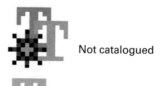

Not catalogued

Installed

A checkmark will *not* appear on the Installed Fonts list when a font is already installed. A font also will not have a checkmark in the Font Catalog if the font was installed using Windows' Fonts Control Panel or another third-party font management utility.

- *To install a font from the upper-left pane,* drag the font name into the Installed Fonts pane, or right-click the font name and then choose Install Font.
- *To create a font group,* right-click in the Font Group pane, and then choose New Group (the menu command is File | New Group). A new folder icon appears with its default name highlighted, ready for you to type a name for the group. Organization here is key; you might like to create groups by the name of an assignment so you can install and uninstall them as the occasion calls for it. **Megatronics presentation**, **Birthday cards**, **Truck signage** are examples of group names… you get the idea. Alternatively, you might want to create groups by types of fonts: **Headlines**, **Body text**, **Unusual**, **Picture fonts** will help you sort out the fonts you need quite quickly. To *add* fonts to a group, drag-and-drop them onto the font group's icon.

This illustration shows the Font Navigator interface; a font in the Catalog is being dragged into the Installed Fonts list, and immediately Windows is updated and the font is ready to use in CorelDRAW and other programs with no need to reboot or restart an application.

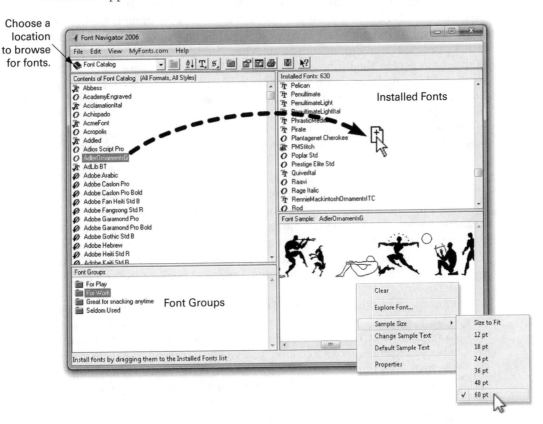

Choose a location to browse for fonts.

Looking Up a Font

You have a wealth of font choices on the CorelDRAW disk, and now you know how to preview them using Font Navigator. So what if you're looking for a font you've seen used in a layout or advertisement and you don't own it and you don't even know its name?

An invaluable resource for font finding and purchasing is MyFonts.com; they are probably the largest clearinghouse for type foundries ranging from large such as Linotype and Bitstream to cottage industry independent font authors. A new feature in CorelDRAW is a URL on the Text menu called What The Font?!—to use it, you need an active Internet connection and an understanding of how this command works.

Caution What the Font?! (on the Text menu) will not work and the command is dimmed if... CorelCAPTURE is not installed. If you need to identify a typeface, install CorelCAPTURE from file or your installation disk, or use Print Screen, paste into a PHOTO-PAINT document, crop the screen capture to only the text you want identified, save the document as a JPG, and then manually upload the bitmap to WhatTheFont online.

What The Font?! (part of MyFonts.com's site) is an automated utility that intelligently matches a bitmap of a sample of text to a best guess of the name of the font. Like any software code, What The Font?! is "intelligent" up to a point, and your best chance of finding, for example, the font used on a wedding invitation, is to make sure the bitmap you have of the invitation has the characters neatly spread apart and is of a pixel resolution large enough for What The Font?! to clearly "see" the outlines of the characters in the bitmap. Also have sufficient blank space surrounding the text so What The Font?! isn't confused by surrounding text and graphics. Consider using Corel PHOTO-PAINT to edit the bitmap before using the What The Font?! command in CorelDRAW.

Here is a working example of how to use What The Font?! to find a specific font used on an invitation so you can purchase it:

1. Start a new document (press CTRL + N), and click OK to create the new page. Unlike previous versions of CorelDRAW, the font identification process doesn't require a specific page resolution: A dpi of 300 is fine; 96 is fine, also.

2. Press CTRL + I to import the bitmap containing the mystery text, locate it in the Import dialog box, click Import after you select the file, and then click-drag the loaded cursor so the placed bitmap falls within the guidelines you put on the page. Resize the bitmap by dragging a corner handle with the Pick Tool now if necessary.

3. Choose Text | What The Font?! Your cursor actually has tiny text that explains what to do now; you drag a box with your cursor to highlight the text you want to send to What The Font?! In Figure 13-3, you can see the bitmap at top, and what your screen looks like after you've click-dragged to define an area around the text. If you make a mistake, you can resize the box by dragging an edge toward or away from the box's center. You can also reset by clicking outside of the box you defined and then click-drag the crosshair cursor again. Pressing ESC cancels the font identification process.

FIGURE 13-3   Click-drag around the text you want to send to What The Font?! as a bitmap copy.

4. After you click inside the box, What The Font?! on the Web guides you through any help it might need to identify the typeface, as shown in Figure 13-4. At left, you can see that this automated routine occasionally asks you for help identifying characters; for example, 1's and exclamation marks are sometimes mistaken for one another.
5. Once you've scrolled to the bottom of the characters you captured, click Continue. As you can see, What The Font?! offers a number of foundries for Beesknees, the font used in the invitation.

Font Foundries

Digital typeface files can be broken down into two parts: the information about the characters themselves—the vector outlines that are pure artistic design work—and the coding that allows the characters to run as a small application, so you can type using a font. Copyright issues concerning the ownership of a typeface can also be

FIGURE 13-4 What The Font?! identifies a typeface you have in a bitmap version of an invitation or other printed material.

broken into two parts: what the font looks like and who owns the name. It might sound weird, but you will find several different names for what essentially looks like the same font, because the design of characters in a digital typeface isn't copyrighted, but the brand name is.

This strange legality can easily confuse a consumer: for the most part, the Bitstream typefaces on the CorelDRAW CD are trademarked by Bitstream; their names are clear and forthright and easy to look up in any traditional typeface specimen book or on the Web. You'll also see the same font name distributed or owned by different foundries and vendors. In this case, such as with Clarendon, the original character designs were sold as physical artwork ages ago, and several digital foundries traced off the characters, usually embellishing them with their unique style. Almost all the time, if you didn't own Clarendon and wanted to buy it, the smart thing to do would be to shop around and buy the best-priced version of Clarendon.

However, a foundry such as Bitstream might have licensed both the design of the font and its name to a different vendor; in this case, Bitstream still offers the typeface, using its original character designs, but offers it using a nonstandard, unique font name.

This is why What The Font?! is an invaluable CorelDRAW menu command—you might own a typeface but not recognize the unique name! For example, Exotc 350 on the CorelDRAW install disk has a different industry standard name: Peignot. Use Font Navigator and What The Font?! to explore what you own; your personal type case might be better stocked with workaday classic fonts than you imagine.

Finding Fonts on the Web

For a specific assignment, you might want to shop for a fresh, unusual typeface. The following URLs are reputable places where you can buy or download for free some interesting typefaces whose themes run from staples (basic fonts you can't live without) to retro to novelty to "goth":

- **Linotype Library** (http://www.linotype.com/)
- **ITC** (http://www.itcfonts.com/fonts/)
- **Bitstream** (http://www.myfonts.com/)   Recently acquired by Monotype, who also owns MyFonts.com, Bitstream typefaces are classics and many are included on the CorelDRAW installation disk. Go to MyFonts.com to buy Bitstream faces directly.
- **URW** (http://www.urwpp.de/deutsch/home.html)
- **Monotype** (http://www.agfamonotype.com/)   Now offers typefaces through fonts.com, but you can research a typeface on their website.

Also, clearinghouses for fonts are the distributors and only occasionally the creators:

- **The Font Bureau** (http://www.fontbureau.com/)
- **Adobe Systems** (http://www.adobe.com/type/)
- **MyFonts** (http://www.myfonts.com/)   Probably the largest distributor of fonts

Smaller type shops also offer quality, refreshing selections:

- **Acid Fonts** (http://www.acidfonts.com)   The collection is uneven; you may need to do some sifting to find quality typefaces you consider useful, but you can't beat the price, and Acid Fonts is one of the largest repositories of free and shareware typefaces on the Web (about 4,700 free fonts).
- **Harold's Fonts** (http://www.haroldsfonts.com/)   Harold Lohner advertises that he vends "homemade fonts," but they're actually clean and professional in every regard. Harold offers over 100 free fonts, including fonts designed to look like famous product logos.
- **Stu's Font Diner** (http://www.fontdiner.com)   Stu offers all retro fonts and has free downloads of some very nice pieces.
- **1,001 Fonts** (http://www.1001fonts.com/)   Another clearinghouse for free and shareware typefaces. Quality is uneven, but overall a very handsome collection.
- **Dieter Steffman's Font Repository** (http://moorstation.org/typoasis/designers/ steffmann/index.htm)   A collection of excellent freeware ornamental-, unusual-, and Blackletter-style fonts designed by professional font craftspeople.

The Last Word on Accessing Installed Fonts

Depending on the programs you've used before working with CorelDRAW, accessing the fonts you've installed might or might not feel familiar. The following nuggets of truth comprise a brief guide to getting the most out of all the fonts you've installed for your design work. Although working with text is covered in detail in chapters to come, you might like a jump start so you can get right down to business with that job that was due five minutes ago!

The Text Tool (F8) accessed from the Toolbox (the icon with the *A*) operates in two different modes: Artistic Text and Paragraph Text. Artistic Text is usually the best choice for brief headlines. Selecting, manipulating, and otherwise editing Artistic Text is accomplished differently than Paragraph Text. Paragraph Text is intended for typesetting long blocks of text (a short story, an instruction manual), has different properties than Artistic Text, and is explained in Chapter 12.

To create Artistic Text, choose the Text Tool and then click an insertion point in your document. Then you type. By default, the font you use is Arial 24 point, justified to the left. You can change the default to anything you like: Choose Window | Dockers | Object Styles and then click the Artistic Text menu item. Select any font and point size you like. The change is immediate and all new and open documents will default to the Font and Size you specified. You can also change text alignment by choosing, for example, Centered, in the Paragraph section of the Object Styles docker.

Tip A *point* is a typographic term, a measurement of the height of text. Traditionally, there are 72.27 points to the inch, but with the advent of digital fonts, this measurement has been modified to 72 points to the inch. Because typefaces are designed by hundreds of different professionals, the actual size of, for example, 24-point Arial, is not necessarily the same size as 24-point Palatino. It's always a good idea to measure the height of text cast in different fonts using Rulers in CorelDRAW to ensure consistency. Usually, Paragraph Text is set in anywhere from 9 to 14 points (except for aspirin labels, which seem to be set in 2-point type), whereas fonts used in headlines look best at 24 points to 72 points on a page that measures standard letter 8.5"×11".

Paragraph Text is entered the same way as Artistic Text and in the same way as most other Windows applications, but you define Paragraph Text by marquee-dragging a frame into which Paragraph Text flows. Marquee-dragging is accomplished by click-holding the primary mouse button and then dragging diagonally; top left to bottom right is the most common technique. Then you release the mouse button, a frame appears, and you type in the frame (or paste from the Clipboard when you have copied text).

- To change the font and the point size of the font after you've entered text, you select either Artistic or Paragraph Text with the Pick Tool, and then choose a different font and point size from the Property Bar. The Text Tool can also be used to select and change the font of the text.
- To change a single character in text you've typed, you highlight only that character and then use the Character section on the Object Properties docker, as covered in Chapter 12. Alternatively, you can select new settings on the Property Bar.

The Property Bar lists installed fonts alphabetically, with their names shown in the font style itself as a convenient preview method. A font family is listed on the flyout for a font name on the list; you click the triangle and then choose a family member. Single-member fonts have no little triangle to the right of their name. The following illustration shows two lines of text being edited to change family members. Additionally, at the top of the Fonts list are the most recently used fonts, a handy way to access the same font in a document you're continuing from two hours ago.

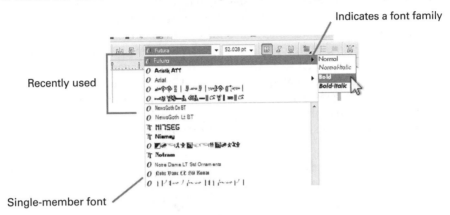

Indicates a font family

Recently used

Single-member font

Finding and Saving Important Characters

Picture (Pi) fonts, also called *Symbols,* are terrific for embellishing design work, but locating a specific character within a Pi font isn't straightforward because your keyboard has letters and not very many symbols. Also, no two font designers agree on a specific mapping for symbol sets, although occasionally there is a progression as you type across your keyboard. For example, some picture-font designers code an upper-left ornamental frame corner as "a", the upper-right frame corner as "s"; if the users are intuitive enough, they can type across the left end of the second row (a-s-d-f) on the keyboard to make a sequentially correct four-corner picture frame from such a symbol font.

Using the Insert Character Docker

CorelDRAW, via Text | Insert Symbol Character (CTRL + F11), removes the guesswork in locating a character or symbol in any font you have installed. When you choose this command, the Insert Character docker appears, and you have two ways to insert a character:

- **As text**   If you need, for example, a fancy bullet that is inline in existing text in your document, you place the Text Tool cursor at the location in the text where you want the character, click the character on the docker to select it, and then you click the Insert button (or double-click the thumbnail of the character). You might not always want to choose this method; the advantages are that the character is editable text and stays aligned to the text that comes before it and after it. However, the disadvantage is that, as a designer, you might want to move this ornamental character around on the page—but as inline text, the inserted character is bound to the line of text you added it to, as shown in the illustration here.

Tip   To display *all* characters available in a typeface, choose All Characters in the Code Page field. The default code page, 1252 (ANSI – Latin 1), hides choices for some typefaces.

- **As a collection of editable shapes**   To add a character to your document as a shape you can immediately edit with the Shape Tool, you first select the Pick Tool instead of the Text Tool. Then you drag the thumbnail of the symbol you want onto the page. It's easy to spot the difference between an inserted Symbol on a page and a Symbol added as a shape: shapes have a default black outline and no fill, so they're easy to single out in a document. The disadvantage to adding a Symbol as a shape is that you can't edit it with the Text Tool, but overall, you have an endless supply of special characters at your cursor tip with the Insert Character docker, so mistakenly adding the type of symbol you don't want to a document is corrected in a flash.

Figure 13-5 shows the process of adding a Symbol to a document by dragging a thumbnail into the document; you locate the installed font from which you want a symbol by using the drop-down list at the top of the docker, set the size of the symbol at the bottom (a symbol can be resized at any time in the future by scaling it with the Pick Tool), and then drag and drop. Notice in the enlarged inset graphic in this figure that the Insert Character docker provides you with the extended character key combination for

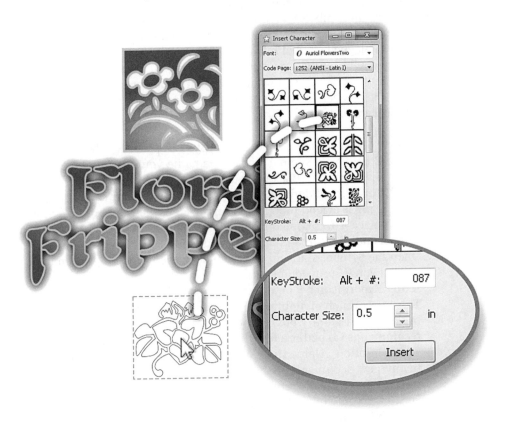

FIGURE 13-5   The Insert Character docker is your ticket to looking up and adding special extended characters quickly to your designs.

the symbol you've selected. This feature is a great help if you're coming to CorelDRAW from a word processor such as WordPerfect. You might already be familiar with certain extended character codes; for example, standard font coding for a cents sign (¢) is to hold ALT and then type **0162**. Therefore, for any font you've chosen on the Insert Character docker, if the font has a cents sign and you want to choose it quickly, you type **0162** in the KeyStroke field, press ENTER, and the docker immediately highlights the symbol—it's easy to locate and equally easy to then add to the document. Conversely, when you click a symbol, the KeyStroke field tells you what the keystroke is; you can then access a cents sign, a copyright symbol, or any other extended character you like in any application outside of CorelDRAW. You just hold ALT and then type the four-digit keycode in, for example, WordPerfect or Microsoft Word, and you're home free.

Using the Symbol Manager

Now that you've located the perfect symbol for a design by using the Insert Character docker, it would be nice to save the symbol so you can reuse it in the future instead of hunting for it again! This is where the Symbol Manager (CTRL + F3) under Windows | Dockers is an invaluable resource. The Symbol Manager provides you with information about symbols contained and saved only to a document you have open and also provides User Symbols, an area on the Symbols Manager where you can duplicate a catalogued symbol into any document at any time.

Let's say you've found a great symbol for a layout, you've placed it in your document, and you decide you want to reuse it tomorrow. Here are the steps for cataloguing the symbol and for accessing an *instance* (a duplicate that takes up less saved file space in a document) of it tomorrow:

1. With an object selected, choose Edit | Symbol | New Symbol.
2. In the Create New Symbol box, type a name you'll remember later in the Name field and then click OK. As you create more and more new files using CorelDRAW, you'll definitely want to stay tidy in your cataloguing work. Cross-referencing is a good practice; in Figure 13-6, the Name of the symbol refers to the typeface it was copied from. Later, you can easily look up the name of the symbol and use it in a program outside of CorelDRAW.
3. Open the Symbol Manager and then click the filename. A thumbnail of the symbol you just saved appears.
4. A tiny Export icon becomes active; click it, it's the Export Library command. This is not much of a library, but you need to start somewhere!
5. In the Export Library box, it's best to save the new library to where CorelDRAW recommends (to better allow the program to locate it in the future; Symbols is a good location). Name the library and then click Save. You're done.
6. In any new document, open the Symbol Manager, click the User Symbols + icon to open the collection, and then click the name of the library you saved in Step 5. Now all you need to do is drag the thumbnail into a document, and you have an instance of the symbol you saved.

In Windows 7, if you install CorelDRAW X6 Graphics Suite to the default hard disk location, your saved Symbol Library will be in C:\Users*your user name*\AppData\

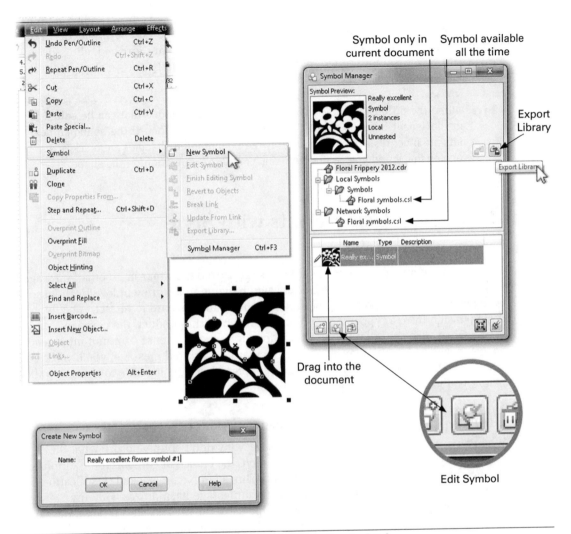

FIGURE 13-6   Define a symbol and then save it to a Symbol Library.

Roaming\Corel\CorelDRAW Graphics Suite X6\Symbols. This is good to know when you want to load your collection by clicking Add Library on the Symbol Manager docker, to add symbols to a local document.

Tip   With the Pick Tool, right-click over any object you create, and you can then choose Symbol | New Symbol and Symbol | Symbol Manager from the context menu.

Symbols saved to a library are always *instances,* and as such, duplicates you add to a document cannot be edited using the Shape Tool or other shape-editing features. You can apply transformations such as scaling and rotating, but you cannot edit the nodes of a shape instance. However, you can edit the original shape as saved in the

Library, and all future instances you use reflect your edits. To edit a symbol in your library, you click the symbol's thumbnail, and then click the Edit Symbol icon in the Symbol Manager. Make your changes, and then, when you are finished, click the Finish Editing Object button where the page numbers usually are—at the bottom left of the screen window.

Tip Telling the difference between an instanced symbol and one that can be edited in any document is easy. Choose the shape using the Pick Tool. If the bounding box dots are blue, it's a shape *instance*. If the bounding box handles are black, it's a regular shape and you can perform any CorelDRAW operation on the shape.

Font Etiquette: Using Fonts with Style and Appropriateness

It's easy for anyone to mistype a word or use fractured grammar in an email message. However, an ad posted on the Web and a sign hanging in a store window for thousands to see is *not* a use of typography between friends—and it's hard to retract. A badly designed sign from a typographic point of view hurts the product, the company, and your reputation as a professional. The following sections discuss common mistakes we try to avoid from the planning stage of creating a printed message; you'll work with CorelDRAW's type features in future chapters, but now it's time to learn to walk before you learn to fly with new talents and skills.

Font Appropriateness and Very Basic Layout Rules

When an audience looks at a printed message, they don't simply absorb what the message says; they also look at the *presentation*: the choice of capitalization, emphasis through bold and italic family members, how lines of text are stacked (justification), point size, font color, and how well the printed message harmonizes with any accompanying graphic. With most digital typefaces, the artist casts a tone on the typed message. Headline, Gothic sans serif fonts, for example, are rather hard-edged and cold yet impactful, whereas Roman serif fonts tend to lull the audience with rounded strokes, swooping serifs, and swashes. Roman typefaces generally send a warm but clean and professional signal to viewers, whereas Gothic fonts wake up readers, perhaps even warning them—hence their appropriateness as a headline typeface.

Figure 13-7 has two obvious sight gags demonstrating inappropriate uses of specific fonts. At right, the use of Futura, all caps, makes the framed needlepoint look more like a high voltage power line warning than a blessing to a home. At left, the choice of fonts on the prescription bottle warning clashes with the message to the extent that you probably can't get the cap off the bottle because you're laughing too hard.

A quick fix to these two bad examples would be to swap the fonts around, so Futura is used on the prescription bottles, and the slightly silly typeface is used for "Home Sweet Home." But better still, a quick trip to Font Navigator and the CorelDRAW Fonts CD will show you that Staccato 222BT (its industry name is Mistral) is warm, loose, and splendid for sentimental expressions, and News 701 XBld Condensed (similar to

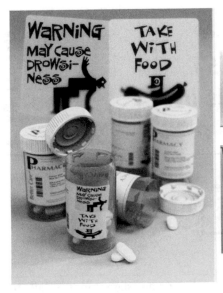 

FIGURE 13-7   Don't undercut your message with the wrong font!

Helvetica Bold Condensed in the type world) is serious, functional, and perfect for warnings. You have the choices of fonts at hand; all you need to do is apply your artistic sensibilities to their selection.

When you have more than one line of text in a headline, legibility is a concern, and this, too, is accomplished by an appropriate choice of fonts. You want a "quick read" from the audience, especially on billboards and vehicle signage that appears and disappears as the sign or the reader moves.

Let's take a simple example headline, pull it apart, examine it, and make it work hard for your money. "The best deals in town" is a common slogan. In Figure 13-8, you can see this headline cast in text three different ways, with icons beneath them to indicate their merit as a sales message.

First, the sign above the clown suffers from the following abuses of typographic conventions and rules:

- The use of Times New Roman, a Roman serif font, is stale (it's a Windows default typeface used since 1991 on the PC) and artistically defeats the message. It's large, yet the characters aren't bold enough to present an impactful message.
- The use of all capital characters looks particularly inappropriate; Roman typefaces have upper- and lowercase characters, and the message looks like the designer had the CAPS LOCK key enabled. Also, it's plain bad form to "shout" a message unless a typeface has no lowercase letters and the designer is firm about the choice of fonts.
- The use of several exclamation marks suggests that if the business owner shouts loudly enough, someone will buy the product. One exclamation mark is sufficient for stressing a message; often a headline is adequately emphasized with no exclamation at all. Casting a headline in all caps followed by several exclamation marks is redundant.

FIGURE 13-8 From clownish to professional, your message stands or falls based on fonts and layout.

- The use of quotes is for quotations, *not* for emphasizing a phrase. When a designer puts quotation marks around "BEST" in this example, it creates in the reader's mind the suggestion that the retailer is speaking *euphemistically*. For example, when someone writes, "Get that 'antique' out of my parking lot in 15 minutes," they aren't actually referring to your 10-year-old car as a valuable antique, but rather as a piece of junk to which they're referring euphemistically or sarcastically. The word "BEST" in quotes will surely be interpreted by anyone with writing skills as, "They really aren't the best deals; they mean something else."
- The alignment of the headline is wrong. Although left justification is acceptable for Western language countries, the second line is much shorter than the third line. As a result, the reader has a hard time focusing and can't read the message quickly.

The center example in Figure 13-8 is a vast improvement and gets a check mark because it's *acceptable* as a headline. Here's what is going right for this treatment of the slogan:

- The use of sans serif Gothic fonts makes the headline easier to read quickly.
- The emphasis created by using a bold, italic font to stress "BEST" makes it the first word a casual passerby will read. What this design does is create a hierarchy of importance within the message. It directs the reader to the most important and then to the second most important area of the slogan.
- The slogan uses center justification and the lines are stacked to align well; no line is too long or short, and both legibility and neatness have been added.

The middle example is short of ideal for two reasons:

- Because "BEST" is italicized, it might be design overkill to also make it all capitals and bolder.
- The exclamation mark at the end is not really necessary. The message's importance is already well supported by the use of the fonts. Generally, if you've graphically punctuated a slogan, you don't need to add an exclamation mark to overdo the importance of the slogan.

The example at right, which earns four stars, works the best for the slogan. Here's why:

- The lines of text have been stretched to fit, by using the Pick Tool and scaling horizontally, disproportionately. You can do this with CorelDRAW Artistic Text. The result is a very neatly stacked presentation of words.
- The word "BEST" stands out through the use of a different color. In design, you don't necessarily have to use black to emphasize something, not when text surrounding a particular word is set in black. Contrast can be achieved through emphasis, or by "negative emphasis"; when objects surrounding the most important one are gray, you make the most important object black. And conversely, a gray object gets noticed when surrounded by black objects. Additionally, uppercase for "THE" and "BEST" works in this example because the other words are upper- and lowercase. In art, you first learn the rules, and then when you understand them well enough, you can *break* the rules with style.
- The hierarchy of importance of the words is proper and reads well. "BEST" is read first and then the surrounding text, and then "in town." Because a thin typeface is used, a script type font, it becomes subordinate in visual importance.

It's not hard to create a more compelling and fresh sales slogan than "The best deals in town." Once you have that ideal slogan, consider the good and bad points in the previous example, approach your sales message with taste and sensitivity, lean but don't push, and you cannot go wrong. Also consider that these three examples aren't even in color. Think of how CorelDRAW and your artistic flair can further add impact to the best sign you can design using expert typefaces.

You've seen in this chapter how to define a font, how to find a font, how to find and save an individual character, and how to put the whole of your acquired knowledge into motion with some good working rules for the ambitious sign-maker. As you've seen in previous chapters, the printed word is not just about signs: you'll work with the Text Tool to its fullest potential, creating extraordinary logos and headline treatments, when you understand and then embrace the fact that text is just as much of an element of art as are fills and outlines.

The next chapter helps put the finishing touch on your text. Come learn about CorelDRAW's writing tools—spelling, grammar, and that prehistoric animal the thesaurus (I'm kidding) await you just around the page.

14 Getting Your Words Perfect

You want your text to look as good as your drawings, and the good news is that the same powerful grammar and spelling tools offered in Corel WordPerfect Office suite are right inside CorelDRAW. Proofing tools including a spell checking system, thesaurus, and grammar checker—in 51 different languages—are at your fingertips. This means you don't have to duck out to your word processor just to proof text that you've entered on-the-fly in a CorelDRAW document.

CorelDRAW also has the same QuickCorrect feature that's in WordPerfect, for correcting common typos and spelling mistakes *as you type*. With QuickCorrect, you can also automatically replace something you've typed with something else—which is extremely helpful for words that you commonly mistype and for common extended characters such as © or ™.

Both CorelDRAW and WordPerfect use the same writing tools, dictionaries, word lists, and configurations. If you add a word to your User Word List in WordPerfect, it is there for you in CorelDRAW. Therefore, when you know how to use the writing tools in WordPerfect, you already know how to use them in CorelDRAW and vice versa. If you're a Microsoft Word user, CorelDRAW's proofing tools are as easy to learn as WordPerfect's—the dialogs and labels are a little different in appearance, but you'll soon get the idea. This chapter takes you through the steps and options you have to step up to the title of Literary Wizard in addition to CorelDRAW Design Guru.

Using CorelDRAW's Writing Tools

Frequently, small- to medium-sized businesses communicate with customers around the world; with text proofing in 51 different languages available right out of the box, CorelDRAW makes it easy for you to get your sales language proofed perfectly regardless of whether you minored in French in school. When you install CorelDRAW, choose the languages you are most likely to use (you can go back at any time and install more), and you are ready to check the spelling and grammar of anything that comes your way.

By default, CorelDRAW assigns a language code and checks all text using the proofing tools that correspond to the language your operating system uses. For example, if you use a U.S. English copy of Windows, CorelDRAW automatically installs English–U.S. proofing tools and assigns all text to U.S. English (ENU).

Assigning Language Codes

If your document contains text in a language other than the default language, you need to select the foreign language text and assign the proper language code to the text so CorelDRAW uses the appropriate proofing tools. The language currently assigned to selected text is noted by a three-letter code in parentheses next to the font description in the Status Bar as shown, for example, by "(ENU)" here.

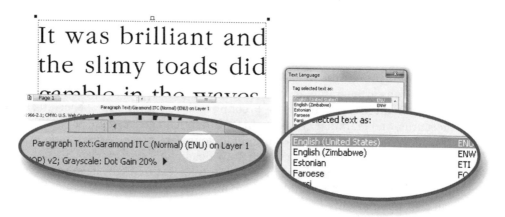

To change the language assignment of any character, word, or paragraph of Artistic or Paragraph Text in a document, select the text and then choose Text | Writing Tools | Language. When the Text Language dialog opens, you can choose any one of the 123 different language and language variants that appear in the list. Click OK to make the change.

Why Language Codes Are Important

You want your text to be spelled correctly, including accent and other orthographic marks (text indicators of how a word is pronounced), regardless of what language you use. When text is tagged with the proper language codes and you've installed the corresponding proofing tools, it's as easy to check foreign language text as it is to check your native language text.

For example, suppose you're working on a package design that contains text in English, French, and Spanish on a system that uses U.S. English. To proof in multiple languages, you select each piece of French text and assign it a French language tag, select each piece of Spanish text and assign that text a Spanish language tag, and so on. CorelDRAW has already assigned the English language tag, so you don't have to do that. Now when checking the document for spelling and grammar, CorelDRAW will use English, French, and Spanish proofing tools (if you installed them) to check the text for foreign language spelling errors.

Corel's proofing engine is also capable of proofing text to meet the spelling and punctuation standards of different regional and national variations for a number of major languages. This ensures, for example, that text that has been tagged as French Canadian will be checked using the French (Canada) proofing set and rules that reflect correct French Canadian spelling, grammar, and word choice. If the French text in the document is intended for French speakers in Belgium, France, Luxembourg, Monaco, or Switzerland, instead of Canada, you would tag the text to match French (Belgium), French (France), French (Luxembourg), French (Monaco), or French (Switzerland), so CorelDRAW would use the appropriate proofing tools.

Using the Proofing Tools

To use CorelDRAW's Spell Check, Thesaurus, or grammar check on text in your document, select the text with the Pick Tool or the Text Tool, and then choose the appropriate writing tool from the Text | Writing Tools menu. Alternatively, you can right-click a text object with the Text Tool and then choose a proofing tool from the pop-up menu. You can also right-click with the Pick Tool and choose Spell Check, or press CTRL + F12. This opens the Writing Tools dialog to the Spell Checker tab, as shown here:

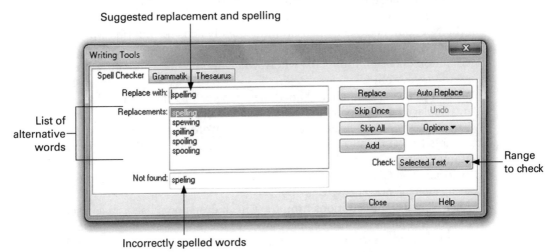

Common Buttons

The Spell Check and Grammatik Tools share common buttons in the Writing Tools dialog. These buttons perform the functions described here:

- **Start button**   The Start button starts the Spell Check or Grammatik. This button is visible only if Auto Start is off—it is on by default. To enable or disable the Auto Start option, click the Options button in the Writing Tools dialog, and make a selection from the drop-down menu.

- **Replace button** As the check is performed, when a misspelled word or grammatical error is found, the Start button changes to Replace, and the misspelled word or grammatical error is highlighted. Select the suggested correction from the list, and click Replace to apply it. You can also edit the replacement word in the Spell Check's Replace With box, or type in a new word before replacing it. After the replacement has been made, the checker rechecks the replacement and continues checking.

- **Undo button** The Undo button reverts the last correction to its previous state.

- **Resume button** After you correct a mistake, if you move the insertion point—for example, to a different part of the text—the Start button changes to the Resume button. Simply click it to recheck any selected text and to continue checking from the insertion point.

- **Skip Once and Skip All** If the word or sentence that a checker has queried is actually correct—for example, a brand name such as Pringles or Humvee—you can click one of the Skip buttons to have the checker ignore it. Skip Once causes the check to continue, but future instances of the same problem stop the checker. Skip All tells the checker to ignore *all* instances of this spelling or grammatical error.

- **Add** Add allows you to add a word to the current User Word List. Many unusual names and technical terms are not included in the Spell Check's dictionary, and these can be added to the User Word List for the current language. In the future, these words will not be queried. If a word appears in the Replace With box or in the Not Found box, clicking Add immediately adds the queried word to the default User Word List. Otherwise, if no word appears in either box, clicking the Add button opens an input box, where you can type the word you want to enter into the User Word List.

- **Auto Replace** If you choose an alternative spelling for a queried word, the Auto Replace button becomes active. Clicking this button adds the misspelled word and its replacement to the default User Word List, *and* if QuickCorrect is enabled, then the next time you type the same mistake, the correct word is automatically substituted.

- **Options** The Options button displays a drop-down menu that contains various settings for the current Writing Tool.

- **Check** By using the options from the Check drop-down list, you can set the range of text for performing a spell check or a Grammatik check. The available options depend on whether text is selected with the Text Tool or the Pick Tool.

 Note When Auto Start is enabled, so spelling and grammar checks are performed as soon as the dialog is opened, you cannot choose the range before the check is performed. Disabling Auto Start means that CorelDRAW does not perform the check until you click the Start button, so you can change settings before the check begins.

Setting Spell Check Options

You can click the Options button on the Spell Check page of the Writing Tools dialog to access various settings that affect how the Spell Check works. The Options drop-down menu is shown here:

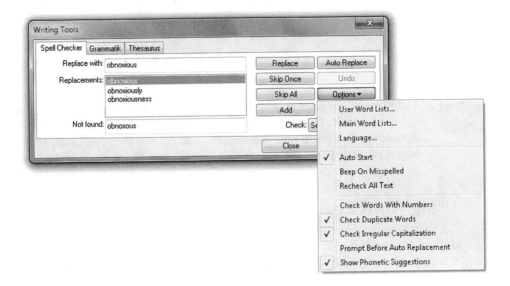

Setting the Spell Check's Language

The Language option sets the current language for the Spell Check. When you click Language, the Select Language dialog appears, in which you can select the language for the checker to use. By checking Show Available Languages Only, you reduce the list to those languages for which dictionaries are installed.

Selecting a different language and checking Save As Default Writing Tools Language causes both the Spell Check and Grammatik to use this language by default in all future checks.

Tip Although you can change the Spell Check's language, it is much better to select the text and *then* set the language of the text via Text | Writing Tools | Language, than to change the language from the Writing Tools dialog. When you change the language of the text, the Spell Check's language is automatically changed to match, but the reverse doesn't happen. Changing the Language option of the text saves the change to the file so the proper proofing tools will be used without additional user intervention.

You can also add new language codes by clicking the Add button to open the Add Language Code dialog, as shown here:

 Note Adding a new language code does not create or install a dictionary or User Word List to go with it. CorelDRAW does not come with a utility to create or edit main dictionaries, but if you have WordPerfect, you can use the Spell Utility that comes with it to create main and user dictionaries to use with your custom language code.

Using Word Lists

CorelDRAW's writing tools maintain Word Lists that contain all the valid words and phrases for spell checks. If a word in your document is not in one of the active lists, it is flagged as being incorrectly spelled. CorelDRAW has two types of Word Lists:

- **Main Word Lists**   These lists are provided by Corel and contain the most common words and spellings in each language. One Main Word List exists per language, and this list is not editable.
- **User Word Lists**   These lists contain words that are not in the Corel-supplied lists but rather are made up of words you have added during a spell check by clicking the Add button. It is up to you to ensure that the words you add to a User Word List are spelled correctly! User Word Lists also contain the QuickCorrect entries for the text's language. Each language has at least one User Word List.

You can create your own User Word Lists with the WordPerfect Spell Utility, or you can use third-party created lists. Specialized User Word Lists such as those containing medical, legal, engineering, scientific, or other words and phrases that are common to an industry are very useful to create. The Spell Check compares each word in your text to those in the Main Word Lists and then to the User Word Lists that you have chosen for that word's language.

 Note You should include the User Word Lists in your regular data backups. That way, if you have to reinstall CorelDRAW, you can also reinstall the latest versions of your User Word Lists. User Word List filenames have the extension .UWL, and Main Word Lists files use .MOR. These files are found for the 32-bit version in C:\Program Files(x86)\Corel\CorelDRAW Graphics Suite X6\Writing Tools, and for the 64-bit version in C:\Program Files\Corel\CorelDRAW Graphics Suite X6\Writing Tools.

Using Main Word Lists

The Main Word Lists are predefined by Corel and cannot be edited by CorelDRAW. However, they can be edited by the WordPerfect suite's Spell Utility if you happen to have a copy. Main Word Lists contain only words used by the Spell Check—no QuickCorrect word pairs are included.

> **Tip** If you don't own a copy of WordPerfect, but you'd really like to edit and create word lists, download the trial copy of WordPerfect. You'll have 30 days to use the Spell Utility and explore the merits of WordPerfect.

Which Main Word List is currently being used changes according to the Language setting. Click the Change button (Writing Tools | Spell Check | Main Word Lists), choose a different language, and CorelDRAW will use the Main Word List for the new language you chose. Changing which word list CorelDRAW is currently using does not change the language code of the selected text but rather temporarily proofs that text using the new Main Word List.

You can also *add* extra Main Word Lists to a language by using the Add List button. For example, some U.S. English users might want their *U.S. Spell Check* to include Spanish words. By adding the Spanish word list, the Spell Check will first check words against the English list. Then, if the words are not found in the English list, the Spell Check compares against the Spanish list. Only if the check fails against both lists will the Spell Check display an error. Using this method, you don't have to specifically set a language code for the Spanish text.

Setting Options in User Word Lists

To choose which User Word List is used, and to edit entries in a User Word List, open the User Word Lists dialog. From the Writing Tools dialog, click the Spell Checker tab, and then click the Options button; choose User Word Lists from the drop-down menu. From the User Word Lists dialog, shown in Figure 14-1, you can add existing User Word Lists you might have; set the default list to which new entries are added; as well as add, delete, and edit entries in any existing User Word List. Also, you can edit the AutoCorrect entries contained in the selected list and manually add new entries to the currently selected User Word List.

Setting Current Language

User Word Lists are language-dependent, and at least one list is created for each language. You can choose which language's User Word Lists to edit with the Change button, located at the top right of the dialog. The Change button opens the Select Language dialog. This does not change the language of the text or of the writing tools—it changes which language's settings are shown in the dialog. Changing the current language offers you the chance to edit the User Word List of *other* languages.

FIGURE 14-1 Use the User Word Lists dialog to set options for new lists.

Adding User Word Lists

Clicking the Add List button in the User Word Lists dialog adds new lists to the current language; each language can have more than one list. This is useful, for example, for adding company- and industry-specific word lists to everyone's installation of CorelDRAW without having to enter the words individually on each computer.

To choose which User Word List will store new words added when you spell check, choose the list you want to use in the User Word Lists field, and then click the Set Default button to the right.

Browsing and Editing User Word List Contents

You can browse and edit the User Word List Contents. Just scroll up and down the list to view the contents, or enter a word or the first few characters of a word into the Word/Phrase box to scroll to a certain point in the alphabetical list.

 Note The list contains words that you have added. It also contains QuickCorrect entries that you have added with either the Spell Check's Auto Replace button or in the QuickCorrect section of CorelDRAW's Options dialog.

You can scroll through the list to view any particular word. Each entry has two parts: the word or phrase for which CorelDRAW checks (Word/Phrase), and the word or phrase with which CorelDRAW replaces the incorrect word (Replace With).

Adding a New Entry   If you want to add a new word or phrase to the User Word List, enter the word or phrase that you want replaced into the Word/Phrase box. In the Replace With box, enter the text you want to use to replace the Word/Phrase, or leave the box empty if you want CorelDRAW to ignore the spelling of the word or phrase. Click the Add Entry button to add the new word to the list. For example, if you perennially type *Ive* instead of *I've,* enter **Ive** in the Word/Phrase box, enter **I've** in the Replace With box, and click Add Entry.

Tip   To add a word that is spelled correctly but that is not in any list, type the word in the Word/Phrase box and then type it in the Replace With box. If you put the correctly spelled word in both boxes, Corel will not put the red squiggle under the word. If you leave the Replace With box empty, CorelDRAW adds "<skip>" to the Replace With column, which tells QuickCorrect and the Spell Check to ignore this word, but it will put a red underline under the word.

Deleting Entries   If you have an entry in the User Word List that is misspelled or simply not what you want, you can delete it. Select the item and click the Delete Entry button. You'll see a confirmation box asking whether you really want to delete the word—yes, you do—just confirm it and it's history.

Editing Entries   You can also correct or edit any entry. Click the entry in the list to select it, make your changes in the Replace With box, and then click the Replace Entry button.

Setting Entry Properties   The property set for each word in your User Word List is important to consider and may need tweaking to get the results you want for the particular entry. With the word or phrase selected in the list, click the Properties button to display the Entry Properties dialog. From here, the Entry Type can be set to Skip Word, which causes the proofing tools to ignore the word. Choose Auto Replace Entry to have CorelDRAW substitute what you typed with what you've entered in the Replace field.

Other Spell Checking Options

Some other options available from the Options drop-down menu of the Writing Tools dialog are described here:

- **Auto Start**   The Spell Check and Grammatik start the check automatically when the Writing Tools dialog is opened or when that checker's page is opened in the Writing Tools dialog.
- **Check Words With Numbers**   Checks or ignores words that include numbers.

- **Check Duplicate Words**   Flags words that appear twice in succession.
- **Check Irregular Capitalization**   Checks for words that have capital letters in places other than the first character.
- **Show Phonetic Suggestions**   Makes *phonetic* suggestions—replacement words that *sound* like the unrecognized word.

Main Spell Checking Options

The Workplace | Text | Spelling section of CorelDRAW's global Options dialog (CTRL + J) also includes various options that modify how the writing tools work.

- **Perform Automatic Spell Checking**   Check this if you want to check spelling as you type. When it is turned on, unrecognized words are underlined with a red zigzag line while you're editing text with the Text Tool.
- **Visibility Of Errors**   Choose here to have all errors underlined in all text objects or just the text object being edited.
- **Display Spelling Suggestions**   You set the number of suggestions to display in the pop-up menu after right-clicking a misspelled word with the Text Tool. The maximum and default number of suggestions is 10.
- **Show Errors Which Have Been Ignored**   When you right-click a word, the pop-up menu includes an Ignore All command, which tells the Spell Check to ignore this word. With this option set, CorelDRAW still shows ignored errors, but it uses a zigzag line to indicate they have been ignored.

Using Grammatik

Spelling errors aren't the only proofing goof that can make your work look unprofessional. Poor grammar is a big, red flag that reflects on your education and communication skills. To make you look in print as smart as you are in person, CorelDRAW includes the Grammatik grammar checker, in many of the languages that the Spell check is available in.

Grammatik is a flexible, powerful tool for checking your work. Grammar checking is a much harder task than spell checking; no program can serve as a proxy for an educated, native speaker's judgment. What Grammatik excels at is calling your attention to parts of your text that *might be* grammatically incorrect; it second-guesses you, and it's always good to have this resource at 1 A.M. when all your coworkers are sensibly asleep at home! Grammatik encourages you to stop and think about what you've written and offers helpful suggestions to fix the problem it *thinks* is a thorn in your rosy prose.

Grammatik has different sets of rules that it uses to judge the correctness of your grammar. When you use Grammatik, you should choose the rule set that corresponds to the level of formality and complexity of your writing. You can also edit any of Grammatik's rules to suit a specific situation.

Mastering every in and out of Grammatik combined with the intricate nature of grammar for a given language is beyond the scope of this book. However, the day-to-day operation of Grammatik is not difficult to manage, as you'll see in the next section, where the basics are covered.

Checking and Correcting Grammar

To check your grammar, select the text objects to check with the Pick Tool, or select sentences with the Text Tool; in the Writing Tools dialog, open the Grammatik tab, shown in Figure 14-2, by choosing Text | Writing Tools | Grammatik. As you can see here, even text with a drop shadow and Envelope effect can be grammar-checked; the effect is disabled as you run Grammatik; then, after you're done, the text takes on the

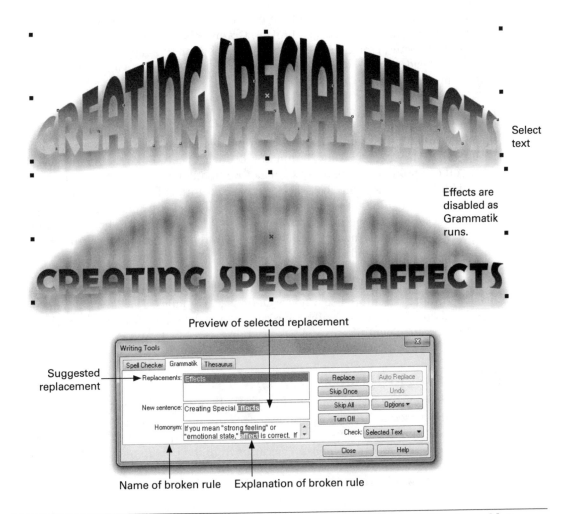

FIGURE 14-2   Grammatik catches errors in your writing that the Spell Check wouldn't alert you to.

effect(s) once more. As with all of the other writing tools, you can also select text and then use the right-click pop-up menu to launch the tool you want to use. It's common to use a word that sounds like the word you want: in Figure 14-2, "affects" is indeed a real word, correctly spelled, but it's a homonym—a word that *sounds* like the intended word—"effects."

Grammatik highlights potential grammar problems. Occasionally when it finds more than one space between words, this too is spotted and Grammatik offers to correct it. This option is very helpful; modern rules of good digital typography call for only one space between sentences and not the two that were required in the days of typewriters.

If Auto Start is enabled, Grammatik immediately starts checking the text; otherwise, you must click the Start button.

If Grammatik finds something that breaks the rules of grammar using the current settings, it displays an explanation of the problem next to the name of the broken rule—the "Rule Class" that has been broken. Grammatik may make one or more suggestions of better grammar, and if you click an option, the new sentence is shown so you can decide if that's what you meant to say. Click Replace to apply the change and continue checking.

Turning Grammatik's Rules On and Off

When Grammatik finds fault with your grammar, you might not always agree with its suggestion. If you don't want Grammatik to check a certain kind of grammatical error, you can tell it to ignore it. As soon as Grammatik pops up a grammar query, the Add button in the Writing Tools dialog changes to Turn Off. If you click Turn Off, the specific grammar rule that is currently being used is deactivated for as long as the Writing Tools dialog is open. If you want to turn it back on again, choose Options | Turn On Rules, which brings up the Turn On Rules dialog. Choose those rules that you want to reactivate and click OK. The next time you perform a check, these rules are included.

After you have pared down the rules to the ones you want to keep, you can save this new "profile" for future use: Choose Options | Save Rules. The Save Rules dialog opens, and you can either click the Save button to update the current style or click Save As to create a new grammar checking style.

Using the Thesaurus

When the word you're using doesn't convey exactly the right shade of meaning, or if you've already used it three or four times, check out the available synonyms with the Thesaurus Writing Tool. Right-click with the Text Tool on the word you want to replace with a better word, and then choose Thesaurus from the pop-up menu. Alternatively, choose Text | Writing Tools | Thesaurus. The Writing Tools dialog opens with the word in the Look Up word box, as shown here:

Look Up word box

It's extremely costly to put in a new bathroom, and almost as costly to install new tiles. What makes home rennovation the most costly, however, is the high-price of *towels* to put in your new bathroom. Have you ever *seen* the price tags on even the less-costly ones? You're usually better off staying **wet**!

```
Writing Tools                                                    X

Spell Checker   Grammatik   Thesaurus

costly                              ▾   Look Up   Replace   < >   Options ▾

⊟ costly
  ⊟ [Adjective] entailing great loss or sacrifice
        dearly-won
        big-ticket
        dear
        high-priced
        pricey
        pricy
     ⊞ Antonym
     ⊞ Related Words
     ⊞ Is a Type of
  ⊞ [Adjective] expensive

                                              Close      Help
```

Suggestions area: similar words and phrases, opposite meanings

The Look Up word box contains the word that you want to look up. The suggestions area of the dialog contains a folder-like tree view list of alternative words and meanings for the word you are looking up. Find one that matches the message you are trying to present and click to expand the entry. If you find the word you want to use, select it and click the Replace button to insert the word into your text. You can also choose *the opposite meaning* of a word in case inverting a sentence is a style of writing you like—*antonyms* are sometimes available for the word you choose in the expandable tree in the suggestions area.

If you find a word that is close, but not exactly the right word for you, double-click the word to open another suggestion area automatically in the dialog that makes suggestions for words that are similar to the selected word. Up to three panes of suggestions are visible at once, but you can keep clicking suggestions to open more panes that you can navigate through using the left and right navigation buttons at the top of the dialog. To use a word in one of the alternate panes as your replacement word, select it and click the Replace button.

Setting Thesaurus Options

You can set various options for the Thesaurus by clicking the Options button in the Writing Tools dialog and clicking the Thesaurus tab to view the drop-down menu; the most useful options are described here:

- **Auto Look Up**   This option speeds up your work by starting the process right away.
- **Auto Close**   When turned on, it closes the dialog as soon as the Replace button is clicked.
- **Spelling Assist**   When enabled, if the word that you selected to check in the Thesaurus is not recognized, a list of similar words from the Thesaurus is shown. Click the word that best matches the correct spelling of the word you typed, and then click Look Up. The suggestions area will contain alternatives.
- **Synonyms**   This option displays synonyms of the look-up word in the list of suggested alternatives.

- **Antonym**   This option displays antonyms of the look-up word—a lifesaver for those times when you can't think of an opposite for the word you want.
- **Language**   Choose this to change which language the Thesaurus uses for the current session. Selecting this option does not change the language of the text in your document, but any replacements are set to the new language. This only works with languages you have currently installed.

Using QuickCorrect

QuickCorrect is a dynamic part of CorelDRAW's writing tools. QuickCorrect works with you *as* you type, much like Auto Spell; it replaces words that you commonly mistype or misspell with the correctly spelled versions. It can also be used to replace an abbreviation with the full-word form to save you having to type a word or phrase each time.

How QuickCorrect Works

While you are typing, every time you "leave" a word by typing a space, period, tab, comma, or linefeed, QuickCorrect compares that word with its User Word Lists. If it finds the word—or possibly a phrase in one of its lists—it replaces that word or phrase with the replacement in the list. For example, people often mistype the word *the* when typing quickly; the English word lists already include an entry to change *teh* to *the*. Similarly, *don't* is the QuickCorrect replacement for *dont*, *misspell* for *mispell*, *you're the* for *your the*, and *weird* for *wierd*.

QuickCorrect also manages other automated text-correction features, such as capitalization of the first words of a sentence and the names of days, correcting consecutive capitals, and adding typographic or "smart" quotation marks.

Tip   To remove an unwanted QuickCorrect change, choose Edit | Undo or press CTRL+Z. The QuickCorrect change is undone without undoing any *other* typing. You then continue typing and the word that you typed is as it is. This does not work for typographic quotes, however.

Setting QuickCorrect Options

To set QuickCorrect's options, open CorelDRAW's global Options dialog (CTRL + J) and navigate to the QuickCorrect section of the tree, as shown in Figure 14-3.

The available options are listed here:

- **Capitalize First Letter Of Sentences**   Does exactly that.

Tip   If you use a lot of symbol fonts in your text, the sentence capitalization option is notorious for capitalizing those symbols when you don't want this. In these instances, you might want to disable this feature.

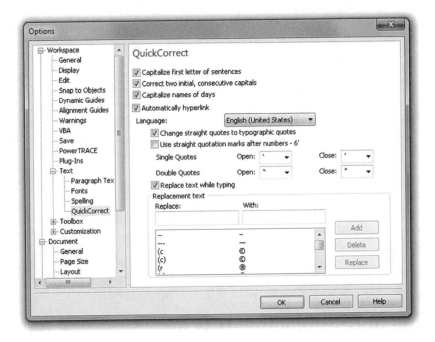

FIGURE 14-3 Use this dialog to choose your QuickCorrect settings.

- **Correct Two Initial, Consecutive Capitals** This option automatically corrects for holding the SHIFT key down too long when typing.
- **Capitalize Names Of Days** This option capitalizes the first letter of days of the week.
- **Automatically Hyperlink** When this option is enabled, typing *www* (followed by the rest of the URL) creates an Internet hyperlink. You might not want this if you're creating flyers, but if you're creating Acrobat PDF documents, it's a welcome option.

This next Language section of the dialog is used to customize how a specific language deals with single-quote (apostrophe) and double-quote marks. Different languages use different glyphs to mark quotations. When you choose a language in the Language drop-down, CorelDRAW automatically displays the traditional characters that language uses if they are available. To change which characters are used when working with a specific language, choose from the drop-downs. All of the settings are language-specific, and you need to set them for each language you use.

- **Change Straight Quotes To Typographic Quotes** QuickCorrect changes single- and double-quotation mark characters from the plain typed form to the appropriate left or right typographic quotation mark.

- **Use Straight Quotation Marks After Numbers -6'** Choose this if you work with measurements a lot. It looks awkward and unprofessional to denote six inches as the number 6 with a closed double-quote mark after it instead of a double-prime.

Tip If you need to use prime symbols for foot-and-inch measurements (such as 1' or 12"), copy the prime (or straight apostrophe) or double-prime (straight double-quote) symbol to the Clipboard from the Windows Character Map (Start | All Programs | Accessories | System Tools | Character Map) or other application. When the Importing / Pasting Text dialog opens, make sure that Discard Fonts And Formatting is checked. Click OK and the character will be inserted into your document without being intercepted by QuickCorrect.

- **Replace Text While Typing** When enabled, QuickCorrect replaces those words in the Replace list with the corresponding word in the With list. Entries to a language's QuickCorrect or directly into a User Word List were shown earlier in this chapter, in the section "Adding a New Entry."

Finding and Replacing Text and Special Characters

All too often you may find yourself in the situation of having to locate a specific piece of text so you can change the font or formatting or even the content of the text itself. CorelDRAW has terrific tools for searching for and replacing text—and text attributes—regardless of whether your layout is a paragraph or a multipage document.

Finding Text

To find a word, phrase, and other marks such as dashes, hyphens, and special characters like tabs, paragraph breaks, and spaces, open the Find Text dialog by choosing Edit | Find And Replace | Find Text. In the Find box, enter the word or exact phrase you want to find.

If you have several paragraphs that contain something you need to find, select the paragraph block with the Pick Tool. If the Text Tool is inserted within a paragraph, your Find session is confined to only the single paragraph—the Find feature will not continue to the next paragraph.

You can include special characters such as an Em or En Space or Dash, a ¼ Em Space, a Non-Breaking Space, a Non-Breaking Hyphen, a Column/Frame Break, an Optional Hyphen, a Space, a Tab, or a Hard Return in your search. To enter the search tag for a special character into the Find box, click the right arrow next to the Find drop-down, and choose the character you want to include in your search.

If you know the exact character case of the word or phrase, enter it and check the Match Case check box—if the Match Case check box is cleared, all matching words will be found, regardless of the case of the characters (a case-insensitive search). The Find Text dialog is shown here:

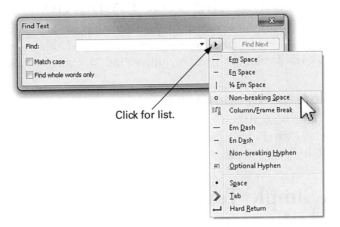

Click for list.

Click the Find Next button to find the next instance of the searched text within the document. All the text objects in the document—Paragraph, Artistic, and Fitted Text—are searched, starting with the current page and working to the end of the document. When you reach the end of the document, you are asked whether you want to continue from the start of the document: clicking Yes takes the search back to page 1, and it continues through to the start position, so the whole document is checked once. If the search text is not found, CorelDRAW tells you.

Replacing Text

If you want to replace a word, phrase, or special character in the text with another word, phrase, or special character, use the Replace Text dialog, which is accessed by choosing Edit | Find And Replace | Replace Text.

You enter the word or phrase you want to find into the Find box, and enter the replacement word or phrase into the Replace With box using the same process as described for finding text in the previous section. Click the Find Next button to find the first instance of the search text. When the search text is found, click the Replace button to replace it with the replacement text, or click the Find Next button to skip over the found text and to find the next instance to replace.

If you are sure you want to replace *all* instances of the Find text in the current document with the Replace With text, click the Replace All button.

Note The ability to search and replace special characters in addition to text is incredibly useful when you are cleaning up imported text, changing five spaces into a tab, and removing column/frame breaks (soft returns). It is also a useful feature if you want to tweak your typography; for example, you can search for a hyphen between numbers and replace it with an en dash. You can also give your text some breathing room and search for all the em dashes in your text and put ¼ em spaces on either side of the em dash.

Finding and Replacing Text Properties

You can also find and replace text properties using the general Find And Replace Wizard interface, invoked by choosing Edit | Find And Replace and then choosing one of the two wizards that can be used, either Find Objects or Replace Objects.

Finding Text Properties

Using the Find Wizard, you can find text based on its type, such as Artistic, Paragraph, or Text On A Path (Fitted); on its contents; and on its styles. To find text in the current document, follow these steps.

Tutorial A Simple Text Hunt Based on Object Properties

1. Open the Find Wizard by choosing Edit | Find And Replace | Find Objects. Then choose Begin A New Search and click Next.
2. On the next page, from the Object Types tab, choose the type of text you want to find, or just check the Text box in the list, which selects all types of text. Then click Next.
3. On the next page, you must provide the settings for each text type individually. Click a type in the left box to choose it, and then click the Specify Properties For button. This opens the Specific attributes dialog, where you choose the properties that the text must have for it to be found. This dialog is shown in Figure 14-4.
4. The properties shown in Figure 14-4 must all be present for the text to qualify. For example, if you type **village** and choose the font Garamond, and then choose Normal-Italic from the Weight field, the Artistic Text object containing the word "village" will be selected *only* if it is in the correct font *and* weight (the style of the typeface); CorelDRAW will select the text object but not any words within the object. So the search will work in this figure because both the typeface and the text are present in the highlighted passage.
5. Click Finish and use the button bar to jump between the found instances:

To find the occurrences of text objects containing text that uses a Text Style, check Look For Object Names Or Styles at the bottom of the first page of the Find Wizard. When this option is checked, clicking Next takes you to a page where you can choose the Style Name or a Style Type that you want to search for from a list.

Replacing Text Properties

The Replace Wizard replaces one set of matching text properties with another set. When you start the wizard, you can choose whether to restrict the search to the text within the selected text objects only or to search the whole document.

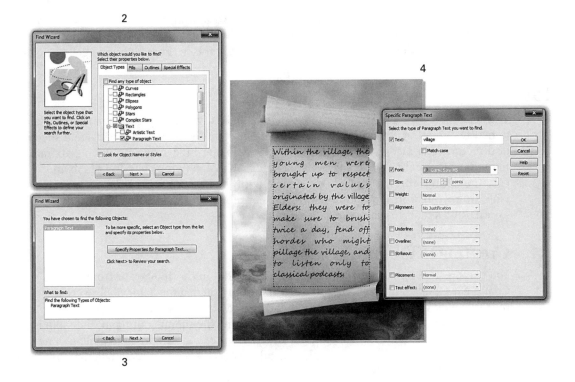

FIGURE 14-4   Use the Find Wizard to indicate the properties of the text that you need to locate.

On the first page of the wizard, choose Replace Text Properties and click Next. You can now set the search and replace criteria for text properties, as shown here.

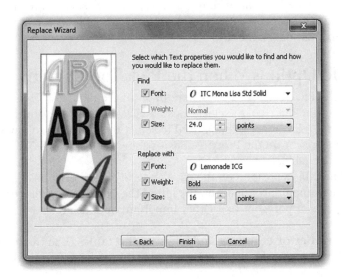

You can set the Font, Weight, and Size of the text to find, and you can replace one or all of those settings with new ones. Click Finish and use the button bar to decide whether to find each match one at a time or just to replace them all in one go.

Tables

With CorelDRAW's Table Tool tucked into the Toolbox, you no longer have to struggle to neatly and attractively present tabular data in your documents. Creating data sheets or directories, or displaying spreadsheet data no longer hinges on setting up elaborate networks of guidelines or paragraph text blocks with a generous handful of tab and column settings thrown in. Drag out a table with the new Table Tool, or import a table from your word processor or spreadsheet program, and you're all set to use CorelDRAW's tools to make the data look good.

Creating a Table

You can create a new table with either the Table Tool in the Toolbox or from the Create New Table command on the Table menu. If you use the Table Tool to create the table, you can click-drag to position and size the table exactly where you want the table to be inserted. If you create the table using the menu command, the table is inserted in the center of the document. In either case, you can drag the table to a new position or resize it just as you would any other object, such as a rectangle that you create with Toolbox tools.

Using the Proper Tool for the Job

Customization of a table takes place on several levels: the entire table, a single cell, a range of cells. The content you place inside a cell, such as text or graphics, is controlled with the same tools and settings that would affect it if it were not inside a cell. Which tool you have active, and what you've selected with that tool, if anything, determines what customization options are available to you at that moment from the Property Bar or the menus.

Table Options When the Pick Tool Is Active

With the Pick Tool, click anywhere in or on the table to select the entire table. You can use the Pick Tool to select, move, resize, stretch, skew, or rotate the entire table. When the Pick Tool has been used to select the table, the following commands and options appear on the Property Bar, as shown in Figure 14-5. These options apply to the entire table.

The table's position on the page and the overall dimensions of the table use the same common entry fields on the left of the Property Bar that other objects such as rectangles or polygons use. Other important options are:

- **Number of columns and rows in the table**   Use the top control to enter the number of rows you want your table to have and the bottom one to enter the number of columns you require. You can change these entries at any time.

TUTORIALS
at a glance

This color section shows what you can achieve— and probably improve on— by working through some of the dozens of tutorials in this Official Guide. See how to angle guides so you can create glowing lanterns and other symmetrical compositions in Chapter 7. And in Chapter 9 you'll discover how to copy and paste object attributes only, without pasting the object itself.

Chapter 19 shows
you how to create
these objects and
more with the
Extrude Tool. Get
ready to go deep!

Learn how to copy design elements between document windows to make mixed-media compositions in Chapter 3. And mix up your own two-color and full-color patterns in Chapter 15.

ONE NITE ONLY!

PARTITAS · FUGUES · CHORALES

...and much much more!

MARCH 14, 1737 · 8PM

AVERY FISHER HALL · NYC

It's Bach to Basics in Chapter 24 as you get the techniques you need to work with photos and vector objects together in a single CorelDRAW composition.

VIOLIN

The violin is sometimes informally called a fiddle, regardless of the type of music played on it. The word violin comes from the Middle Latin word vitula, meaning stringed instrument;this word is also believed to be the source of the Germanic "fiddle". The violin, while it has ancient origins, acquired most of its modern characteristics in 16th-century Italy, with some further modifications occurring in the 18th century. Someone who plays the violin is called a violinist or a fiddler. The violinist produces sound by drawing a bow across one or more strings (which may be stopped by the fingers of the other hand to produce a full range of pitches), by plucking the strings (with either hand), or by a variety of other techniques. The violin is played by musicians in a wide variety of musical genres, including Baroque music, classical, jazz, folk music, pop-punk and rock and roll. The violin has come to be played by

Chapter 20 gets you up and running with Envelopes, the Corel feature that lets you mold an object into the shape of another. Here's an example covered in this chapter that envelopes text inside an object.

COCONUT BREAK

ALL CHILDREN'S SWIM GEAR 20% off

Chapter 6 provides you with an invaluable resource for working with layers, tiling backgrounds, and page layouts. Design ads like this and make significant changes with only a click or two!

Chapter 18 introduces Perspective and how this feature can enhance even the simplest drawing; don't be a pawn in the art world! In Chapter 17, you'll see how a Color Style and the redesigned X6 Color Harmony feature create dramatic, compelling color changes in a drawing in no time.

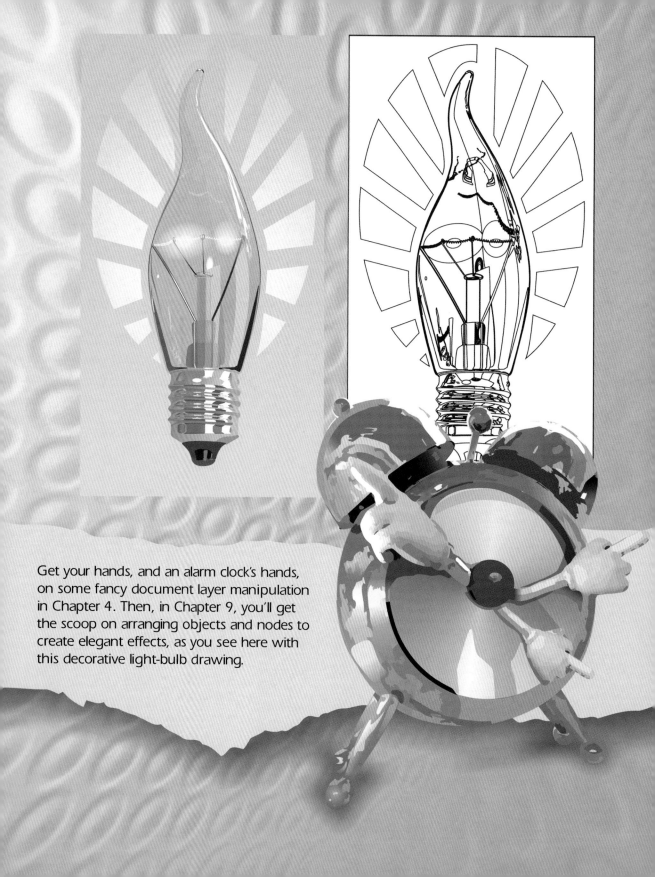

Get your hands, and an alarm clock's hands, on some fancy document layer manipulation in Chapter 4. Then, in Chapter 9, you'll get the scoop on arranging objects and nodes to create elegant effects, as you see here with this decorative light-bulb drawing.

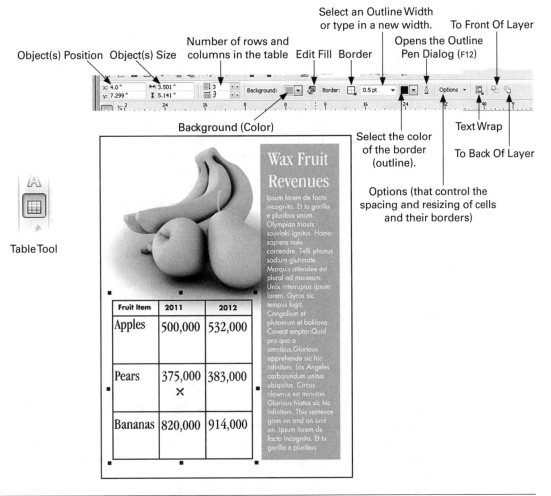

FIGURE 14-5   Use the Property Bar to customize the look of a table.

For example, if a table currently has 2 columns and 2 rows, entering **4** in the column field and **6** in the row field reconfigures the table to contain the new number of columns and rows.

If you reduce the number of columns or rows, they are removed from the bottom up and from the right to the left. Any content you have in the columns and rows is lost, so do this with forethought!

- **Background**   Choose a uniform color for all the cells from this drop-down list. You can also accomplish the same thing by choosing a color from the Color Palette.
- **Edit Fill**   If you've given the table a background fill, you can go directly to the Edit Fill dialog by clicking this icon. By default, tables are filled with a Uniform fill. If you want your table to have any other fill type such as Fountain or Pattern Fills, you must first select the table and then change the fill type either from the Object Properties docker (ALT + ENTER) or with the Fill Tool.

- **Border**   *Border* refers to the outline of each cell and the table as a whole. You can show or hide the interior cell outlines and/or combinations of the top, bottom, left, and right sides of the table.
- **Outline Width and Outline Color**   These options control the width and color assigned to the borders you have set. For more advanced control, click the Outline Pen Dialog icon to open that dialog.
- **Options**   The options that can be set here are Automatically Resize Cells When Typing and Separate Cell Borders. The first is useful when the amount of content you need to enter in each cell is not uniform. Enabling this prevents your content from overflowing and moving out of view. The second option lets you space out your cells horizontally and vertically so each cell is still contained in the table but is not in immediate proximity to the adjacent cell.
- **Text Wrap**   This important option determines how *Paragraph Text* flows around the table and how close the Paragraph Text box can get to the table—this option has nothing to do with the text content of the table. Tables are objects; text can be made to flow around them or over them or under them. Artistic Text is not affected by the Text Wrap setting.
- **To Front Of Layer and To Back Of Layer**   These icons become available if another object is layered on top of or below the table. Clicking these icons changes the position of the table in the stacking order.

Table Options When the Shape Tool Is Active

When you want to select a single cell or multiple cells in a table, use the Shape Tool. To select a single cell, click in it with the Shape Tool. To select adjacent cells, click-drag across the row(s) or column(s) that you want to select. To select nonadjacent cells, hold the CTRL key and click in the cells you want to select. Diagonal blue lines shade the cells you've selected. These lines are an onscreen visual indicator and not an actual fill.

Once cells are selected with the Shape Tool, you can use the options available to you on the Property Bar, as seen in Figure 14-6, to customize the cells. The attributes you apply to cells override any you set for the table. The first control group on the left now sets the dimensions of the selected cells as opposed to those of the entire table. The Background and Border options work the same as before, but making changes with them now only affects the selected cells. New to the Property Bar are the Margins drop-down, which sets the top, bottom, left, and right margins within the cell's bounds, and a group of controls to merge or split the selected cells into fewer or more cells.

You can also use the Shape Tool to select an entire column or row. With the Shape Tool click the left border of the table next to the row you want to select. When the cursor turns into a small arrow, click again to select that row, or click-drag to select additional adjacent rows. To select columns, click the top table border over the column you want to select, wait for the arrow to appear, and click again to select the column, or click-drag to select additional columns.

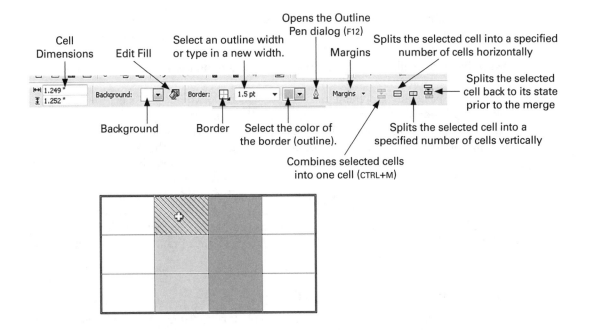

FIGURE 14-6   These options are available for table customization when the Shape Tool is active.

To select nonadjacent rows or columns, follow the preceding procedure, but hold the CTRL key and then click next to or over the rows and/or columns you want to select.

Editing a Table When the Table Tool Is Active

The Table Tool is used to create the table by click-diagonal dragging in your document, but it is *also* used to edit the table once it is created. Right-clicking in a table row, column, or cell and choosing the appropriate option from the Select menu in the context menu is a quick way to select a single row, column, or cell. To select the entire table, choose Table from the Select command on the pop-up menu.

The Table Tool can also be used in the same way the Shape Tool is used to select multiple columns and rows, but it is easier to use the Shape Tool and avoid the possibility of creating a table instead of a selection.

You can add or delete columns or rows from your table by clicking in a row or column and then choosing Delete | (Row or Column) from either the Table menu or the right-click context menu.

Working with Text and Graphics in a Table

Entering text into a table is easy; just use the Table Tool to click in a cell and enter text using any method for text entry. You can type text directly into the cell, import text from the File menu or from the Edit Text Box dialog (CTRL + SHIFT + T), or paste text into the cell from the Clipboard.

Text in tables is handled as Paragraph Text and can be proofed, edited, and formatted in the same ways. If you want to draw a Paragraph Text box within the table cell, you can do so by click-dragging the Text Tool in the cell. Artistic Text cannot be *created* in a table cell, but you can create it elsewhere on the page, copy it, and then paste it into a table cell.

You can paste any graphic into a cell, but which tool you use to select the cell that will hold the graphic makes a huge difference. If you use the Shape Tool to select the target cell, the graphic is pasted into the center of the cell as a graphic object. If you use the Table Tool to select the cell and then paste the graphic into the cell, the graphic is pasted in as an inline graphic whose size matches that of the default or current font size being used in that cell. This operation can take some time if the size reduction is great.

Once a graphic object has been placed in a cell, you select it by clicking it. You can then use the control handles to resize, rotate, and skew it. You can even extrude it if you like. If you want to move the graphic to another cell, select it with the Pick Tool, and drag it into a different cell in the table. You can drag a graphic *out* of a table, but you cannot drag a graphic into a table.

Converting a Table to Text

A table can be converted into a single Paragraph Text box at any time by selecting the table and then choosing Table | Convert Table To Text from the menu. The Convert Table To Text dialog that appears offers you the option to separate the contents of each cell with a delimiter—a comma, a tab, a paragraph, or the character of your choice. If you choose to separate the cell contents with a comma, a tab, or one of your own choice, each row of cells will be saved to a paragraph with the individual cell contents separated in that paragraph by the delimiting character you choose. If you choose to separate cell contents by paragraph, you will get a paragraph for each cell.

 Tip Converting a table to text sometimes produces results you don't like, so be prepared to undo the conversion. Saving a copy of your file before converting isn't a bad idea either.

Converting an Existing Text to a Table

Existing Paragraph Text can be converted into a table in a process that is basically the reverse of the process outlined in the previous section. Using the Text Tool, highlight the text you want to convert, and choose Table | Convert Text To Table from the menu. From the Convert Text To Table dialog, choose the delimiter you've used to break up the text into the chunks that you want to go into each cell. CorelDRAW analyzes the selected text and guesses what will work best as a delimiter. Because commas and tabs are frequently used within a section of text, they might cause the creation of many more cells than you were expecting. At the bottom of the dialog, it tells you how many rows and columns it is going to create. If the number sounds wrong, cancel and go back to your text. Mark the end of each piece of text you want transferred into a cell with some other character—an asterisk or a tilde, for example. Then choose User Defined and enter the character you choose as a delimiter into the field.

Importing a Table from Another Application

You don't have to create tables in CorelDRAW to use them in CorelDRAW. You or your client may have created a table in a document or spreadsheet that you want to include in a CorelDRAW document.

To import a table, choose File | Import from the menu. Use the Import dialog to navigate to the spreadsheet or word processing document. Select the document, and then click the Import button. When the Importing/Pasting Text dialog opens, choose how you want to handle importing formatted text. Your choices are Maintain Fonts And Formatting, Maintain Formatting Only, or Discard Fonts And Formatting. Then be sure to choose Tables from the Import Tables As drop-down list.

 Note Corel supports MS Excel's *.XLS file format, but support is limited for other spreadsheet file formats.

If you chose to maintain fonts and you don't currently have a font installed that was used in the table, you will have to work your way through the Font Substitution For Missing Fonts dialog. Your cursor will be loaded with the table; you then click in your document to place the table. This is a live, editable, customizable table that you can use all of CorelDRAW's table tools on to make it exactly the way you want.

 Note If the existing table looks just the way you want it to look in CorelDRAW, by all means choose one of the first two options. Although CorelDRAW is pretty good at interpreting what other applications did and mapping them accurately to CorelDRAW features and functions, the translation may not be perfect. Once the table has been imported, you may be able to make some simple fixes to make it look like it did in the other application. It may be a more effective use of your time to import your table without any formatting or fonts and to spend your time styling your table from scratch, instead of trying to fix the imported formatting.

And this is the last word on typography in CorelDRAW! You now know how to spell check, grammar check, and use the thesaurus, find and replace text, and how to create a text-driven table for your work. Our next stop is setting properties for filling objects and outline properties for paths. Let's get your objects—*including* text objects—looking as handsome and as visually captivating as you'd like them to be.

PART V

Attributes for
Objects and Lines

15 Filling Objects

A shape without a fill on your drawing page is like a brand-new coloring book. To make a coloring book—and your CorelDRAW artwork—more complete, you need to *fill* your shapes with colors and textures. CorelDRAW has more than a half-dozen different types of fills you can apply to your shapes, and these types have hundreds of different variations. In computer graphics, you have over 16 million solid shades of color at your disposal; imagine what you can do with *blend*s of colors, colored patterns, and colored *textures*! The worst part of filling CorelDRAW objects will be deciding on a fill style. The *best* part, as you explore filling shapes in this chapter, is that it's very difficult to color outside of the lines.

 Download and extract all the files from the Chapter15.zip archive to follow the tutorials in this chapter.

Examining the Fill Types

Each type of CorelDRAW fill has its own special characteristics.

- *Uniform* Fills apply flat, solid color.
- *Fountain* Fills make a color transition from one color to another, in different directions—sometimes also called a *Gradient Fill*. You can also create a Fountain Fill composed of more than two different colors. CorelDRAW ships with many preset fills; this chapter demonstrates how to pick a fill and apply it.
- *PostScript* Fills are good for repeating patterns; although PostScript is a *printing* technology, you don't need to print a CorelDRAW document to see a PostScript Fill, and you can indeed export a PostScript-filled object to bitmap format and the fill looks fine. PostScript Fills support transparency and are ideal for exporting to EPS file format to use in desktop publishing programs. And, naturally, a PostScript Fill is valid for printing to a PostScript printer.

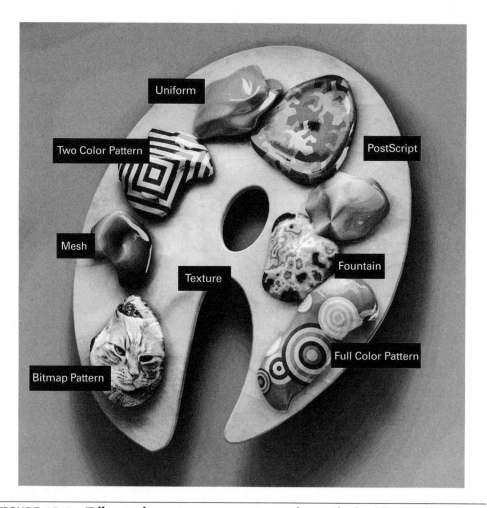

FIGURE 15-1 Fill your shapes in a composition with exactly the fill type that draws attention to your design work.

- *Pattern* and *Texture* Fills can fill shapes with bitmaps, including photographs, and a large supply of preset bitmaps is included with CorelDRAW.
- *Mesh* Fills take multicolored fills and present you with the option of "smearing" colors within the fill—much like finger-painting.

Every fill type is applied in a slightly different way through the use of onscreen tools, docker windows, or the Fill and Mesh Fill Tools (see Figure 15-1).

Using the Color Palette

When selecting colors, the Color Palette is an excellent starting point, and to apply a uniform (solid) fill to a selected object, you just select an object with the Pick Tool and then left-click a color on the Color Palette. You can also drag a *well* (a color swatch) from the Color Palette, drop it onto a shape, which does not have to be selected, and the object is filled.

Perhaps one of the most interesting features in CorelDRAW is to select not only a color from the Color Palette, but also a shade or a tone of that color—in color theory terms, these are called *analogous colors*. To pick a shade of a color on the Color Palette, you first select the object you want to fill, click-hold on a well color (sometimes called a color *swatch*), and a small pop-up menu of shades and tones of that color appears. While holding the mouse button, drag to the exact shade you want, release the mouse button, and the object is filled. This pop-up features shades that vary in *hue* from top to bottom and in *brightness* as you drag your cursor from left to right. It's like having 49 possible colors at your cursor tip when you choose one color.

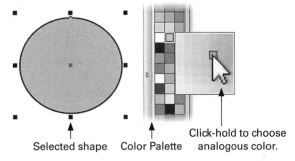

Selected shape   Color Palette   Click-hold to choose analogous color.

Uniform Fills can also be assigned to all objects right from the get-go. With no objects selected in the drawing window, left-click a color you want to use for Artistic Text, Paragraph Text, callouts, Dimension lines, Artistic Media, or graphics. CorelDRAW then displays a dialog that asks what sort of object you want filled as you create it from now on. You can cancel out of this operation, but you can choose objects, text, or both.

 Tip If you need to set the default fill for all documents you create in the future, go to Tools | Options | Document, where you can check Save Options As Defaults For New Documents, and then check Styles, which applies the fill you've chosen to Default Graphic (the properties for all new objects).

From Uniform to Non-Uniform Object Filling

The quick way to apply any of the fill types is by using the Fill Tool, shown here. You'll find it at the bottom of the Toolbox; to quickly select it, press G. You'll see a hint here that the Fill Tool is also a selection tool—the cursor is an arrow cursor with a paint bucket. You don't have to have the object that you want to fill selected when you use this tool. You can click an unselected shape with the Fill Tool; it becomes selected, and then a second click-drag on the object, by default, applies the Linear style Fountain Fill, making a transition from black to white. You can then change the colors used or choose a different fill type from the Property Bar by clicking the Fill Type selector drop-down list.

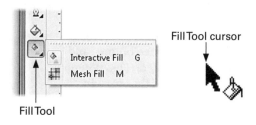

Fill Tool cursor

Fill Tool

While you're using the Fill Tool, the Property Bar displays fill options that change depending on the type of fill you've chosen from the Fill Type selector. If your selected object features no fill color at all, the selector displays the type as No Fill and the Property Bar displays no options. The selector, shown here, is where you can choose from any of ten fill types: Uniform Fill, four Fountain Fill types (Linear, Radial, Conical, and Square), two Color Pattern Fill types (Two Color and Full Color), Bitmap Pattern, Texture Fill, and PostScript Fill. In this section, you learn to control every fill type using Property Bar options and the control handles on the Fill Tool.

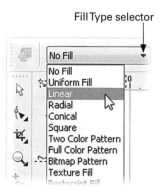

Fill Type selector

The technique you use to set the angle and position (among other properties) of fills varies some from fill type to fill type, so let's run through the basics for a moment.

Tutorial Filling an Object, Setting Fill Properties

1. Select the object to fill and then choose the Fill Tool (G) from the Toolbox.
2. If your object *already* has a fill, the Property Bar automatically displays the fill type and the current properties of that specific fill.
3. Use the Fill Type selector to choose a fill type. As you do this, the object is filled with selector style, and the Property Bar shows options for this style, which are applied using the default color, direction, pattern type, and so on. Depending on the type of fill, an object may also display control handles for the direct manipulation of the current fill type.
4. Use the Property Bar to define properties of your fill, which are instantly updated in the object in the drawing window.

The following section covers the Property Bar options specific to the fill type when the Fill Tool is selected.

Uniform Color Fill Options on the Property Bar

A Uniform Fill is like a paint chip at the hardware store; it's a solid color, no variations. A Uniform Fill also floods an object within the boundaries of its outline with the color you choose. The Color Palette is a fast, easy way to assign a uniform color; however, when you choose the Fill Tool, you have several different color models from which to choose. See Chapter 17 for details on color theory; if you're already familiar with the CMYK printing color model, the intuitive HSB color model, and others, you'll feel right at home using the Property Bar to mix up color values, and better still, entering values a client might have given you for that big advertising job. The following illustration shows the color models you can choose from the Property Bar selector drop-down list when the Fill Tool has been chosen and Uniform Fill has been selected. For most of us who prefer to mix up a color visually, while the Property Bar displays the fill options, click the Edit Fill button at the far left to display a palette in which you drag a marker and move sliders to specify the color you need, and then click OK to define it.

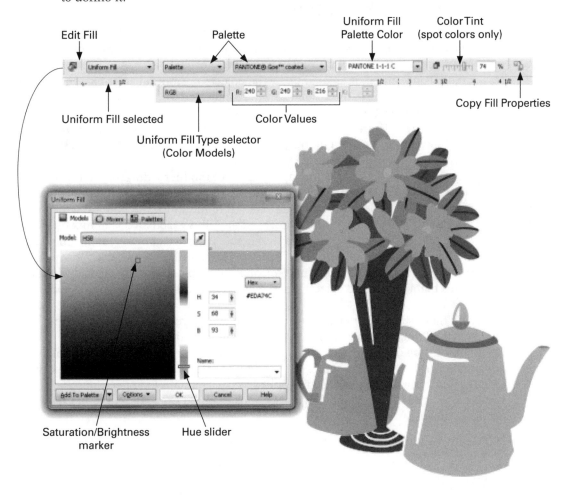

Tip HSB and RGB color models occupy the same *color space,* which is the extent to which a color can be expressed onscreen. Therefore, you can arrive at an identical color using either color model. This also means you can switch color models for a filled object, and between RGB and HSB you won't see a real color change.

Applying a Fountain Fill

Fountain Fills fill objects with a smooth transition between two (or more) colors and come in various styles. Many commercial pieces of artwork are created today that imitate the traditional airbrush (popular in the mid-20th century) by using Fountain Fills. You can apply a Fountain Fill in different ways, and the following tutorial shows you the quickest, most artistically satisfying way.

Tutorial   Creating Fountain-filled Objects

1. Select an object and then choose the Fill Tool (G) from the Toolbox.
2. Click-drag, beginning at one side of your object and dragging to the opposite side at any angle; try dragging from 10 o'clock to 4 o'clock, for example. A default Linear Fountain Fill is created using the object's current fill color, making a color transition from the defined color to white, indicated by settings on the Property Bar. If your object has no fill, a default black-to-white Fountain Fill is created.
3. For a different Fountain Fill type, choose Radial, Conical, or Square from the Fill Type selector. As you do this, the shape of your Fountain Fill (and the available Property Bar options) changes.
4. Experiment with changing the appearance of the fill by dragging to move the color markers and midpoint slider control. Notice how the position changes affect your fill. The midpoint slider is used to influence the point at which the *From* color and the *To* color in the Fountain Fill is exactly a 50/50 mix of the colors. So if, for example, you want to create a shaded sphere, you begin with an ellipse object, Fountain Fill it with the Radial Fill type, and then move the midpoint closer to the white marker than to the black to make a small, subtle, sharp highlight on the object: bingo, you have yourself a dimensional sphere!

Using these steps, your click-drag action specifies several properties. The first click sets the From color position, and the drag direction defines the angle. The length of the drag defines the distance, and the mouse release defines the To color position. A series of markers shows the position of each of these values. It's important to understand how Fountain Fills are applied; other Fountain Fill operations are variations on this theme. The following sections examine each Fountain Fill type in detail, as shown next.

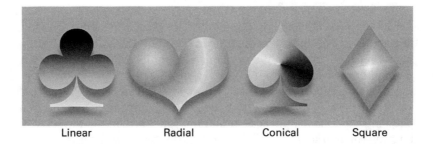

Linear   Radial   Conical   Square

- **Linear** This is the default Fountain Fill style and is most useful for shading rectangular shapes to suggest lighting on a dimensional plane or 3D object. The color marker positions mainly control its appearance.
- **Radial** This type makes a color transition outward in a circular style, terrific for shading round objects and objects you'd like to soften in appearance. While using Radial Fountain Fills, the center offset controls where the fill begins.
- **Conical** This might not be a fill type you use every day, but if you need to simulate the look of the playing side of a DVD or an aerial view of a grain silo, Conical produces a strongly shaded and unique transition between two or more colors. The From color of a Conical Fill is the beginning and the end of the Conical Fill, and the To color shades all the in-between blend steps. The center control handle can be used to increase the contrast of the effect by dragging it toward the From color marker along the dotted-line arc of the control handles; dragging the center toward the To marker creates less contrast and a milder effect.
- **Square** This style produces a look like a four-pointed starburst. The center marker controls contrast; the To marker sets distance and direction for the fill.

Chapter 22 documents object transparency types. Here's advance notice if you haven't read Chapter 22 yet: Fountain Fill styles are also transparency styles—all four types of Fountain Fills can make a transition between opaque and transparent. You can, therefore, build an elegantly shaded object by, for example, applying a Radial Fountain Fill to an object and then giving it a linear transparency property.

Controlling Fountain Fills Interactively

The Fountain Fill markers hovering on top of an object you've drawn, combined with the Property Bar, give you control over the look of your fill. Among the available option, you'll see color selectors, a Midpoint option, Angle and Edge Pad options, and a Fountain Step option, as shown here:

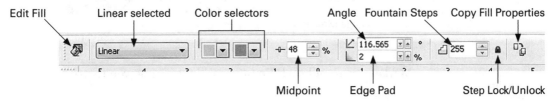

Edit Fill   Linear selected   Color selectors   Angle Fountain Steps Copy Fill Properties

Midpoint   Edge Pad   Step Lock/Unlock

Many of these Fountain Fill Property Bar options correspond to markers surrounding your object, but the marker positions can be changed to produce different looks, according to the type of Fountain Fill. Although the Property Bar offers precision, dragging the markers is extremely intuitive and often a preferred method for making a custom fill. In Figure 15-2, you can see the different marker positions that appear around each Fountain Fill type.

Moving any of the markers changes the fill appearance in different ways. The following explains the purpose of options you'll see on the Property Bar while dragging the markers and what the effect on the fill will be:

- **Color markers** Use these to set the position and colors in your Fountain Fill. Each Fountain Fill type has to have at least two colors. To change a color, click to select it and click a color well in your onscreen palette, or drag a color well directly onto a color marker. To move a marker, click-drag it in any direction, which changes the properties of the filled object, usually relocating the center of the Fountain Fill.

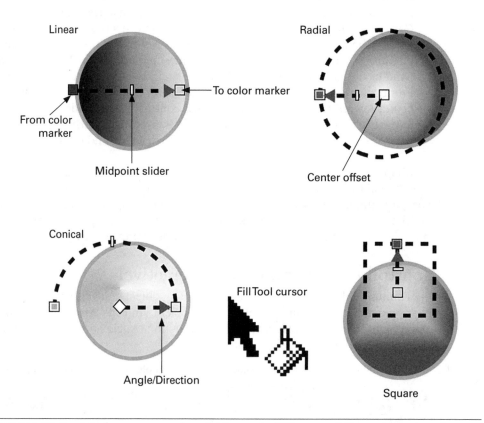

FIGURE 15-2 Markers surround each Fountain Fill type while you're using the Fill Tool.

- **Midpoint**   This slider control is available only while a Two Color Fountain Fill is applied; if you use more than two colors for the fill, the midpoint marker goes away. The midpoint marker is used to set the point at which the From and To colors are equal in value. This value is measured in terms of percentage—by default, it's 50 percent.
- **Angle**   The Angle value applies to Linear Fountain Fills and is set in degree values between 360 and –360 (a negative value). Positive angles rotate the fill counterclockwise, whereas negative values rotate the fill clockwise.
- **Edge Pad**   This option sets the amount of contrast between the To and From colors, expressed in percentage. The default setting, 0, creates smooth, even blends at the slowest possible rate. Increasing this setting causes colors to change more abruptly; the option is shown later in Figure 15-3. Edge Pad can be set within a range of 0 to 49 percent, and this can also be adjusted in Object Properties (ALT + ENTER) and in the Fountain Fill dialog (F11). Moving a Linear Fill's color markers away from or toward your object's outline increases or decreases this value; try dragging the To and From color markers to positions outside of the object, for example, to decrease the Edge Pad effect.
- **Center offsets**   Radial, Conical, or Square Fountain Fills feature this marker; you change the center position of the fill relative to your object's center by dragging the marker. Dragging the center marker of a Radial, Conical, or Square Fill away from or toward your object's center also increases or decreases the Edge Pad value.
- **Steps**   This setting affects both the display and printing of Fountain Fills. A Fountain Fill is actually calculated by blending neighboring bands of color in succession, but you don't see this banding effect because so many shades of intermediate colors are used between the To and From color. The Steps option is fixed at the maximum setting of 256, by default. However, you might be *looking for* a banding effect, for example, to create shirt stripes or other geometric patterns. To lower this setting, click to unlock the Lock button. Lowered Step values cause the color gradation in your fill to become harsh with striations where a smooth Fountain Fill should be seen. With Steps set to 256 and locked, Fountain Fills will display and print using the maximum capabilities of your monitor and printer resolution.

Using Custom Fountain Fills

A default Fountain Fill features two colors, but you can *add* colors to make any type of Fountain Fill your own version. When you make multicolored Fountain Fills, the appearance of your artwork can change dramatically. The position of added colors is shown by node positions on the dashed line guide joining the two default colors.

After you've added color markers and clicked to select them on the object, the Property Bar will display their Position and Color, as shown here:

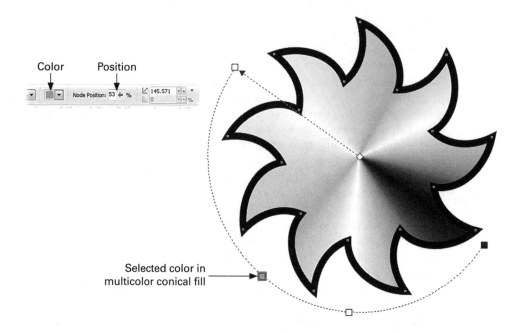

Color   Position

Node Position: 53 ⊹ %   ⟋ 145.571   °
0   %

Selected color in
multicolor conical fill

You can add, move, and delete Fountain Fill colors you've added to a default Fountain Fill type in several ways, but you *must* have both the object and the Fill Tool selected, or you'll wind up editing the object and not the fill. To explore doing this, follow the steps in this tutorial.

`Tutorial` Editing a Fountain Fill in Place

1. Select the object to be filled, choose the Fill Tool (G), and then apply a Fountain Fill by choosing Linear, Radial, Conical, or Square from the Property Bar Fill Type selector.
2. With a default fill applied, double-click a point on the guide between the two existing color markers where you want to add a color marker. Doing this adds a color that is based on an average of two existing marker colors, so your custom Fountain Fill probably looks the same as the default fill.
3. Decide on a new intermediate color (choose one in this example on the Color Palette), and drag a color from the color well (drag the swatch) onto your new marker. You have a three-color gradient now.
4. Try a different technique to add a color marker position and a color at the same time: drag a Color Palette well directly onto the same Fountain Fill guide, but at a different location.
5. To reposition an added color, click-drag it along the guide path. As you do this, the color's node position changes, as indicated by the node Position value on the Property Bar.

6. To change any Fountain Fill color, click to select it, and choose a color from the Property Bar selector or click a color well on the Color Palette.
7. To delete an added color, right-click or double-click it on the guide. To and From color nodes can't be deleted, but they can be recolored.

Additionally, color can be added when a color node position is selected, and you choose from the color selector to the right of the Fill Type selector on the Property Bar.

> **Tip** You can drag a color marker "through" a neighboring marker to change the order of color nodes along any Fountain Fill object.

Setting Fountain Fill Dialog Options

The way is great for controlling Fountain Fills, but if you want deeper and more precise controls, you can use the Fountain Fill dialog, shown in Figure 15-3.

You can open the Fountain Fill dialog while a Fountain Fill is applied to a selected object and while using the Fill Tool by clicking the Edit Fill button on the Property Bar. Or, with your object selected and while using any tool, press F11.

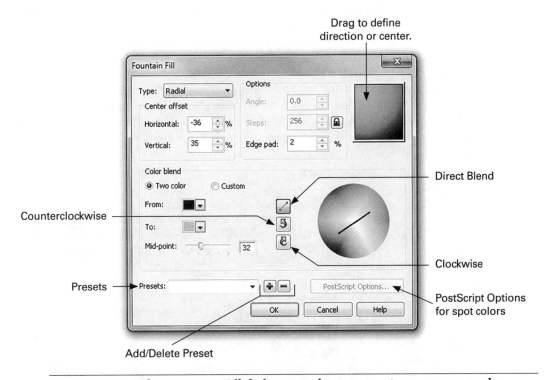

FIGURE 15-3   The Fountain Fill dialog provides some options common to the Property Bar and others unique to this box.

The Fountain Fill dialog options that aren't available while you're using the Fill Tool Property Bar are listed and explained here:

- **Color wheel rotation**   This option is available only when a Two Color blend is selected. You can choose to blend directly from one color to the other (the default), more or less "jumping" the hue cycle the traditional color wheel goes through. Or choose Counterclockwise or Clockwise to blend between colors while cycling through a standard color wheel's colors, traveling around the outside edge of the wheel. This might seem like a trivial option, but CorelDRAW is one of the few design programs that can shortcut through the traditional model of visible colors. For example, in other applications, a Fountain Fill that goes from red to blue necessarily has to travel through green, somewhat muddying the Fountain Fill. Not so if you choose Direct Blend here.
- **Preview**   You have some manual control over where you want the center and/ or direction of a fill to take place within an object by dragging in the preview window. In Figure 15-3, you can see that the Radial Fountain Fill will be positioned beginning in the upper-right of the filled object because this is where the center has been dragged in the small preview window.
- **PostScript Options**   When a Two Color Fountain Fill is selected with both the From and To colors specified as *spot color inks,* the PostScript Options button becomes available. PostScript Options offer halftone screens of special fills to certain dot shapes. Possessing PostScript level 3 capabilities, CorelDRAW features an expanded collection of screen styles, including CosineDot, Cross, various Diamond styles, various Double and InvertedDoubleDot styles, various Ellipse and InvertedEllipse and other styles, Euclidean, Grid, Rhomboid, Round, Square, and Star shapes. While any of these styles is selected, Frequency and Angle options are available in the PostScript Options dialog, enabling you to override default printing settings for your selected spot color inks. An easy visual indicator that you are using spot colors is the small circle tick beside the chosen color swatch in the Fountain Fill box.

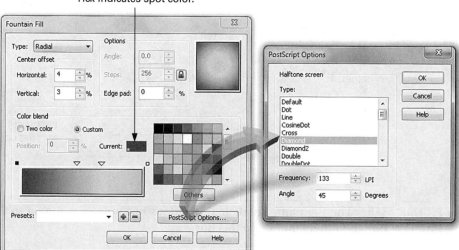

Tick indicates spot color.

If you're unfamiliar with spot colors, the term refers the printing process used to add a color to packages, for example, that cannot be reproduced using standard press inks, such as that reflective silver logo on a box of cereal. See Chapter 27 for the lowdown on spot versus process colors and a guide to commercial printing of your CorelDRAW work.

- **Presets** The Presets drop-down menu includes a variety of sample Fountain Fill types, colors, and positions; use them as they are or edit them to suit a specific need. To select any of these, choose a name from the drop-down list. While you're browsing the alphabetical list, a preview of the highlighted preset is displayed in the Fountain Fill preview window in the upper-right corner of the dialog. A preset can contain any of the properties associated with a two-color or custom Fountain Fill color.

- **Add/Delete Presets** The two small buttons to the right of the Presets drop-down list can save you hours of custom Fountain Fill creation time. First, the button labeled with the minus (–) symbol deletes your current selection from the list of preset Fountain Fills after presenting a confirmation dialog, just to ensure that you don't delete a factory preset by accident. The button labeled with a plus (+) symbol is for saving the current Fountain Fill as a preset.

To save your selected Fountain Fill settings, follow these steps.

| Tutorial | Saving Your Own Fill as a Preset

1. With your custom Fountain Fill colors and options set in the Fountain Fill dialog, enter a name in the Presets box.
2. Click the + button. Your custom Fountain Fill is immediately saved alphabetically in the list of available presets.
3. Click OK to apply the saved preset and close the dialog.
4. To retrieve and apply your saved preset to fill a selected object, press F11 to open the Fountain Fill dialog, and then from the Presets menu, choose your saved preset from the list, and click OK to close the dialog and apply the saved Fountain Fill.

Applying Pattern Fills

Pattern Fills are rectangular-shaped tiles that repeat vertically and horizontally to fill a closed-path object completely. They come in three different varieties: Two Color, Full Color, and Bitmap, each with its own unique qualities, as shown here.

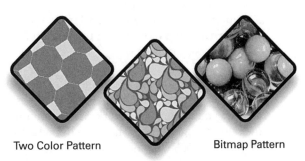

Two Color Pattern

Full Color Pattern

Bitmap Pattern

When a Pattern Fill is applied, the Property Bar includes a host of options that you can use to dramatically change a fill's appearance, as shown here when the Two Color Pattern Fill has been applied to an object, and the object is currently selected:

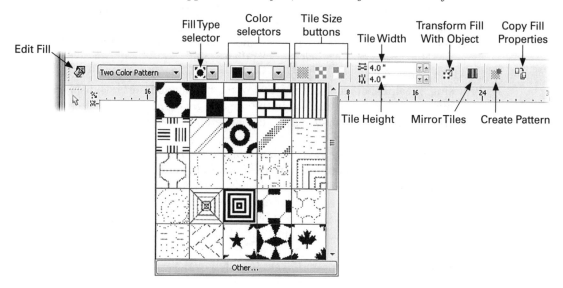

In addition to altering pattern properties, the Property Bar has features to control your pattern's appearance in the following ways:

- **Fill Type selector** Use this drop-down box to choose from existing Pattern Fill libraries.
- **Front/Back color selectors** When you've selected a Two Color Pattern, these two selectors let you set colors other than black and white for a pattern.
- **Tile Size buttons** Use these buttons to set your pattern to Small, Medium, or Large preset width and height sizes.
- **Tile Width/Height** Set the Width and Height sizes of your selected pattern individually using these two options, each of which can be set within a range between 0.1 and 15 inches. If you need a larger tile, use the 2-Color Fill dialog, where you can set a maximum width/height of 60 inches.
- **Transform Fill With Object** When this option is active, transformations applied to your object are also applied to your fill pattern. This is a useful feature when you need to scale an object larger and don't want your pattern to "shrink"!
- **Mirror Fill Tiles** Using this option forces a transformed pattern tile back into a seamless pattern.

Two Color Patterns are limited to *exactly* two colors, with no additional edge colors to create anti-aliasing. This means the edges of the design can be harsh and somewhat jaggy if you export your work with a screen resolution of 96 dpi. However, if you use the default page resolution of 300 dpi when you set up a new page, and then export, for example, a TIFF copy of your work, the jagged edges you see onscreen will *not* appear in the exported bitmap image.

Full Color Patterns are composed of vector shapes, but the pattern itself already has color applied and cannot be altered. Additionally, these Full Color Pattern Fills cannot be extracted as vector shapes from the pattern. Therefore, when making your own, save a copy of your pattern to a CDR file format for editing in the future, and forget about the Break Apart and Convert To Curves commands in an attempt to reduce a Full Color Pattern to its vector component shapes.

Bitmap Patterns are carefully edited bitmaps; some of the presets are taken from photos whereas others are from paintings, and all of them are relatively small in dimensions. The difference between a Full Color and a Bitmap Fill is that the vector-based pattern tiles for the Full Color fills can be resized without losing design detail, focus, or introducing noise, but enlarging Bitmap Pattern tiles carries the same caveat as enlarging any bitmap—the more you enlarge it, the better your chances are that the component pixels will eventually become visible.

Tip   You can scale bitmaps down, but not up—computers are "smart," but they can't create extra visual data from data that wasn't there to begin with.

Controlling Pattern Fills Interactively

You can edit the look of an applied Pattern Fill by adjusting the markers and using the various Property Bar options common to all pattern styles.

The handles surrounding a Pattern Fill help you to set the tile size, offset, skew, and rotation of the pattern. To experience this firsthand, open Platonic.cdr and work with the uncompleted group of objects on the left of the page. Use the right-side duplicate of the Platonic geometry as a reference.

Tutorial   Customizing a Pattern Fill

1. Select an object in the group at left, and then choose the Fill Tool (G).
2. Choose Two Color Pattern from the Fill Type selector. By default, a two-color dot-style pattern fill featuring Black as the Front color and White as the Back color is applied to your object featuring fill markers.
3. Insert the cursor in the top Edit Tiling field, and then type **1.2**; then type **1.2** in the bottom Edit Tiling field. You've made the polka dot pattern a more pleasing size for one of the Platonic object faces. Clicking the Small, Medium, and Large Tile buttons performs the same thing, but without giving you precise size control. Dragging the Rotation/Size handle while holding CTRL to constrain the rotation angle does the same thing.
4. Drag the diamond-shaped center origin handle slightly in any direction. Notice that the center origin of the pattern changes.
5. Drag the white marker, governing the Back color, up and right to skew the pattern so it looks more like it's on the face of the object, viewed in perspective.

6. Click the white Back color marker and then click the Back Color icon on the Property Bar—choose a light color such as yellow. Apply a deep red to the Front color using the same technique. Now the face of the Platonic object looks a little more properly shaded.

7. Repeat Steps 3 to 6, varying the Front and Back colors to complete filling in other objects.

8. To complete the assignment quickly, while the Fill tool is selected, click a solid fill object, and then click the Copy Properties button on the Property Bar. Then click over a corresponding object in the completed design at right.

Figure 15-4 shows the marker handles around a Two Color Pattern Fill.

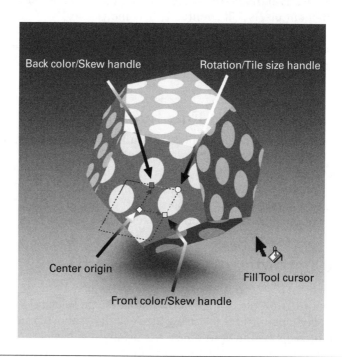

FIGURE 15-4 The markers surrounding a Two Color Pattern Fill are there for you to control the pattern's colors, size, and skew.

Using Pattern Fill Dialog Options

The Pattern Fill dialog offers an alternative way to control Pattern Fills; the dialog is shown here. To open this dialog (which is nearly identical for Two Color, Full Color, and Bitmap Pattern Fills), click the Edit Fill button on the Property Bar while a Pattern Fill type is in effect.

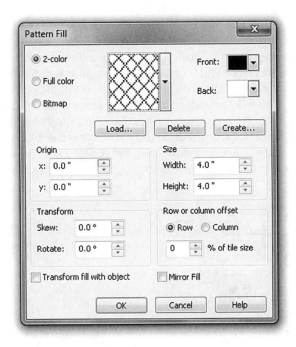

Here's what each of the options in the Pattern Fill dialog controls:

- **Origin**   The X and Y Origin options are used to offset the center of the pattern from 0 within a range between 30 and –30 inches. Positive X or Y values offset the origin right or upward, whereas negative values offset the origin left or downward. Using the Origin handle in the workspace performs the same thing.
- **Transform**   These options are Skew and Rotate, each of which is measured in degrees. Skew values are within a range between 89 and –89 degrees, whereas Rotate values can be set between 360 and –360 degrees. These options work in combination with each other to apply vertical and/or horizontal distortion to the fill pattern. Rotation and Skew can be performed directly on an object onscreen; however, undoing a skew and rotation and performing these distortions with precise values are not easily done in the workspace.
- **Row Or Column Offset**   By default, pattern tiles join to appear seamless. However, you can *intentionally* ruin the pattern (or just create an "interesting" one) by offsetting the pattern seams through either of these two options. To apply an offset, choose either Row or Column as the offset option, and enter a value between 0 and 100 percent.

Create Your Full Color and Two Color Patterns

Two Color Patterns are harder to think up than they are to create, and the details are covered momentarily. Full Color (vector) Patterns are created by sampling an area on the page. You click the Create Pattern button on the Property Bar while the Fill Tool and the Full Color Pattern type is selected from the Fill Type selector. A dialog opens where you specify the new pattern type and resolution. After you choose the type and resolution, crosshairs appear on your screen, and you then click-drag to define an area in your document to use for the new pattern.

The saved pattern is located in C:\\Users\\(your user name)\\Documents\\Corel\ Corel Content\\Vector Patterns; to apply a custom pattern, you need to click the Edit Tool on the Property Bar to display the Pattern Fill dialog, where you click Load.

Create a Two Color Pattern by clicking More at the bottom of the 2-Color selector box on the Property bar. A pattern can be saved (and created) by clicking the Fill Tool, and choosing Pattern Fill, and then clicking the 2-Color button and clicking Create. As you can see in Figure 15-5, Two Color Patterns are created by choosing a tile size, a cursor size, and then left-dragging and/or clicking to set the foreground

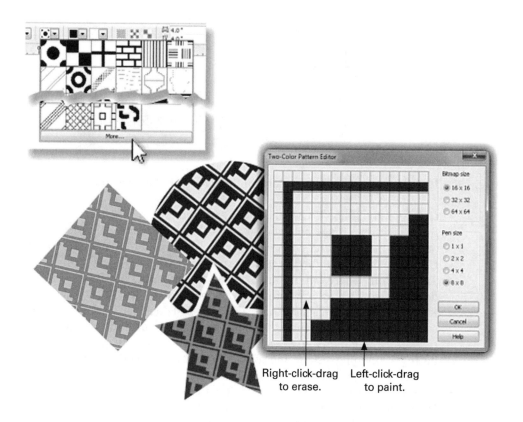

Right-click-drag to erase.   Left-click-drag to paint.

FIGURE 15-5 Create your own Two Color Pattern by clicking Create pattern; then edit an existing preset pattern.

pattern; right-clicks and right-click-drags act like an eraser. Alternatively, you can click Load if you've created a bitmap image (a two-color one works best, so the Two-Color Pattern Editor doesn't brute-force a tonal image to black or white); the Editor accepts TIF, BMP, and other image file formats. Any Two Color Patterns you create are immediately applied to a selected object, unlike Full Color Patterns, which are saved to a PAT file on hard disk. Although you are creating a black-and-white pattern in the Two-Color Pattern Editor, Two Color Patterns can be any two colors—you apply the pattern and then use the Property Bar's mini-palettes to define the two colors.

Tip   You can also create patterns by using the Tools | Create | Pattern Fill menu command. This command lets you capture a screen area, and use it as a Two Color or Full Color Pattern.

Applying Texture Fills

When the Fill Tool has been chosen and you then pick a Texture Fill, the Property Bar (shown next) displays texture options, including a Texture Library selector, a Texture Fill selector, and options for controlling the appearance of the texture.

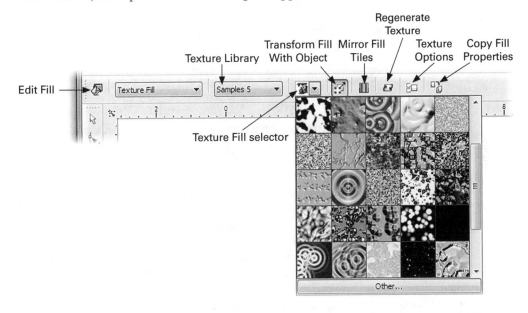

The handles surrounding a Texture Fill are the same as those for Pattern Fills; they're there for you to set the size, offset, skew, and rotation of the texture. If you have experience manipulating Pattern Fills by click-dragging the control handles above the object, you'll discover Bitmap Fills are exactly the same. However, because these are *bitmap-based* textures, you'll need to take note of some transformation limitations, covered shortly.

As you'll discover next, each texture is based on a range of variables specific to a style type. To view these core styles, you need to open the Texture Fill dialog by clicking the Edit Fill button.

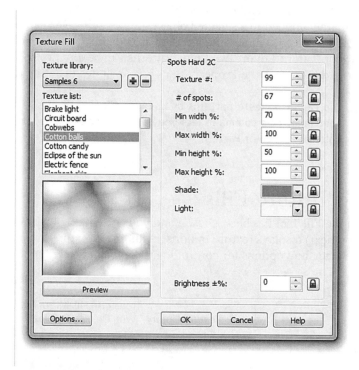

You'll notice that the same options available in the Property Bar are in the dialog—but also included when you click the Edit Fill button are the texture variables. There are settings for texture, color, frequency of texture properties, and so on. Don't hesitate to drag a spin box value and then click Preview; although several of the values might seem to have strange labels for the values, they'll indeed modify the texture preset (changing the Texture # is a great place to begin experimenting). Also, it's very hard to give a label to some of the properties of fractal math; they're abstract attributes and fairly difficult to write in the first place! Start by choosing a type of texture from the Texture List, and then use different values in fields such as colors (another good starting place). Click Preview, and if you like what you see, save it as a preset by clicking the + button (then fill out the Texture Name dialog), click OK to apply the texture, and then use the control handles for the Fill Tool to adjust the fill as it appears in the selected shape.

The textures are based on more than a hundred different styles ranging from bubbles to clouds.

Setting Texture Fill Options

Besides being able to set the appearance of your Texture Fill interactively and to customize the fill using the value fields in the Texture Fill dialog, you want to be able to set other options, too. For example, if your Texture Fill looks like it's been pushed through a screen window, it means the resolution is too low, as measured in pixels per inch (called *dots per inch [dpi]* in the dialog). To increase the texture size and its resolution, click the Texture Options button on the Property Bar to open the Texture Options dialog.

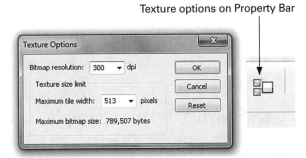

Texture options on Property Bar

By default, Texture Fills are initially created at a resolution of 300 dpi and at a tile width of 2049 pixels. Increasing both of these settings sharpens and adds detail to your texture.

Texture options affect the appearance of your Texture Fill in the following ways:

- **Bitmap Resolution**   The Bitmap Resolution option sets the amount of detail in the bitmap image created. By default, the Bitmap Resolution setting is 300 dpi, but it can be reset to preset values ranging between 75 and 400 dpi and to a maximum value of 9999 dpi.
- **Texture Size Limit**   This option should be set according to both the desired resolution of your texture and the size of your object. To avoid seeing seams between your texture's tiles (which ruins the effect), set the tile larger than the object it fills *and* ensure that the tile seams are hidden from view; use the Mirror button on the Property Bar if necessary.

Calculating the Resolution of Texture Fills

If you're the ambitious, professional sort, you can use a very non-nerdy equation to determine your maximum tile width setting. Calculate the value based on twice the final line screen multiplied by the longest object dimension in inches. Line screens are what PostScript laser printers and commercial printer image-setting devices use for reproduction. Or you can overestimate, be on the safe side, and use 300 dpi, which vendors often suggest because it's an easy number to remember. Enter this value in the Maximum Tile Width box, or choose the next highest preset value available. You're good to go with 133 lines per inch (lpi; this value is half of 266 dpi, which is commonly used in high-quality art books); 1200 dpi laser printers can use 85 lpi. Inkjet printers don't arrange dots in a logical order (they sort of splatter ink on the page), but a ballpark estimate (if inkjets were to render lines of dots) would be about 180 lpi for inkjet printers manufactured as late as 2007.

Creating and Saving Texture Samples

Once you've gone to the effort of selecting or editing a Texture Fill to suit your needs,
you may wish to save it for later retrieval. To save a texture, click the + button to the
right of the Texture Library selector drop-down list. You are then prompted in the
Save Texture As dialog for the name of your texture (type any name you like), and for
the name of the library in which you want to save the texture. Click a library name
from the drop-down list, click OK, click OK again in the Texture Fill dialog, and your
custom texture is ready to be applied to the selected object.

Applying PostScript Fills

PostScript Fills are vector-based and use PostScript page-descriptor language to create
a variety of patterns from black-and-white to full color. Each PostScript fill included
with CorelDRAW has individual variables that control the appearance of the pattern,
much the same way as you can customize texture fills. PostScript pattern styles come
in a variety of patterns, as shown in Figure 15-6, and also come as nonrepeating fills.

When using the Fill Tool and when PostScript Fill is selected in the Property Bar
Fill Type selector, very few options that relate to the individual fills are available on
the Property Bar. You need to click the Edit Fill button on the Property Bar to get
access to line widths, size options for the patterns, and color options, depending on
the specific preset.

The image you see onscreen is an accurate representation of the actual pattern
that will be printed; again, PostScript is a printing technology, but Corel Corporation
has made the technology viewable in CorelDRAW and printable without the need for a
PostScript printer. On that note, it should be mentioned that PostScript Fills will print
exceptionally well to any PostScript device; that's what the fills are intended for, but
you don't necessarily have to use PostScript. However, *you must be using Enhanced
View to see them* (choose View | Enhanced).

To apply a PostScript Fill, follow these steps:

1. Create and then select the object to apply any PostScript Texture Fill, and then
   choose the Fill Tool (G).
2. Using Property Bar options, choose a PostScript Fill by name from the File
   Type selector.

FIGURE 15-6 PostScript Fills come in a variety of repeating and nonrepeating patterns.

3. To customize the fill, click the Edit Fill button on the Property Bar to open the PostScript Texture dialog, shown here. To view your currently selected fill, click the Preview Fill option. Notice that each fill has its own set of Parameters that can be changed.

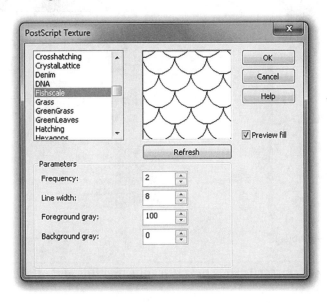

4. Make any changes to your fill, and click the Refresh button to view the results of your new settings.
5. Click OK to accept the fill, close the dialog, and apply the new fill to your object. Your object is now filled with a PostScript Texture Fill.

PostScript Fills can be very useful in schematic and roadmap illustrations, and if you use no background color when you customize many of the fills, the fills support transparency. So you can actually apply, for example, crosshatching, over a color-filled object to enhance the shading.

Fills and the New Object Properties Docker

If you are the sort of designer who uses many different types of CorelDRAW fills in a composition, it's probably somewhat of a chore visiting all the different resource areas within the CorelDRAW interface. With version X6, anything and everything you can fill an object with can be accessed from a unified source: the Object Properties docker.

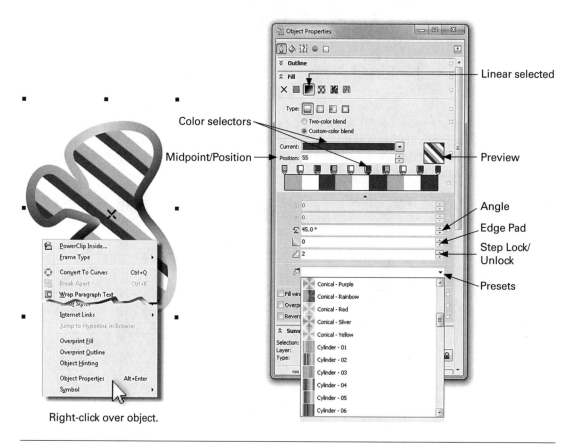

FIGURE 15-7   ALT+ENTER is your ticket to adjusting fills and other object properties all at once.

If you're new to CorelDRAW, you just might want to adopt a practice as you begin learning the interface: if you want to fill an object, you right-click, choose Object Properties, and then navigate on the Object Properties docker to the Fill section. Come to think of it, experienced users will also want to start adopting this magnificent shortcut to fills, new to version X6.

Working with Mesh Fills

Mesh Fills can be used to create the effect of several blending-color Fountain Fills over a mesh of vertical and horizontal Bézier curves. Editing a mesh grid creates a sort of fill that doesn't really look like a Fountain Fill but instead looks very much like a *painting*. Mesh Fills make it easy to create, as you'll see in the following figures, most of the visual complexity of a reflective sphere—*using only one object and one fill*. Add to the visual complexity the capability to set transparency levels to each patch of a Mesh Fill individually, and in no time you'll be creating scenes that look like paintings, using a fraction of the number of individual objects you'd imagine. You'll find the Mesh Fill Tool, shown at left, in the Toolbox grouped with the Fill Tool, or you can press M for speedy selection.

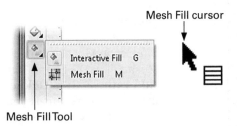

Mesh Fill cursor

Mesh Fill Tool

While the Mesh Fill Tool is selected, the Property Bar features a number of options, shown next, for controlling this truly unique fill type. Use these options to set the vertical and horizontal size in the mesh grid, to change node and path properties, and to set the smoothness of curves.

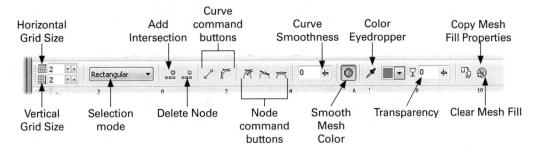

Horizontal Grid Size — Add Intersection — Curve command buttons — Curve Smoothness — Color Eyedropper — Copy Mesh Fill Properties

Vertical Grid Size — Selection mode — Delete Node — Node command buttons — Smooth Mesh Color — Transparency — Clear Mesh Fill

Applying a mesh grid to an object is a quick operation. Mesh Fills are dynamic, so they can be edited and reedited at any time. Editing the shape and color of a mesh grid can be challenging your first time out, but to be able to smear and almost paint on a fill will make the effort worthwhile to you and your work. Node and curve editing actions to move fill areas are done exactly the same as for Bézier curves. For information on how to do this, see Chapter 11.

Mesh Fill Options

On the Property Bar, when you're using the Mesh Fill Tool and have selected an object, you have control over the following attributes of your Mesh-filled object:

- **Resolution of the patches**   By default, a new Mesh Fill is created on an object with two horizontal and two vertical sets of patches. These patches are linked at the edges by paths and at their vertices by nodes. You can use the numerical entry fields or the spin boxes with these fields to increase or decrease the number of columns and rows of patches. Manually, if you first left-click to select and then right-click a node or a path segment, you have the option to create a node or an intersection by choosing from the pop-up menu. You can do this with either the Mesh Fill or the Shape Tool.
- **Add Intersection/Delete Node**   When you've clicked a path segment and a marker appears, this is your opportunity to add an intersection, done by either clicking the Add Intersection button or pressing + on the numerical keypad. When you add an intersection, you add a row or a column to the Mesh Fill, depending on whether you've added a point to a vertical or a horizontal mesh path segment. You must first select a node to then delete it, and doing so by clicking the Delete Node button or by pressing DELETE on your keyboard removes both the mesh node and its associated intersecting path segments—reducing the number or columns or rows of mesh patches. Deleting nodes can yield unanticipated results so give some thought before you delete a node.
- **Curve and Node command buttons**   By default, path segments that make up the Mesh Fill are curves, bound by nodes that have the Smooth property. To change a path segment to a line, you use the Convert To Line command button; click Convert To Curve to create the opposite property. Nodes can be changed to Cusp, Smooth, and Symmetrical properties by clicking the associated Property Bar button; the commands can also be found on the right-click pop-up menu when your cursor has selected a node.
- **Curve Smoothness**   Suppose you've added far too many nodes to a path segment and your Mesh Fill looks like a bad accident in one area. If you marquee-select the nodes that bind this path segment, the Curve Smoothness slider and numerical entry field act like the Node Reduction feature in CorelDRAW. You reduce the number of superfluous nodes (CorelDRAW decides on the meaning of "superfluous"; you yourself have no control) by entering a value or using the slider.
- **Transparency**   Apply to a patch by clicking the patch once with the Mesh Fill Tool and then use the numerical entry field or the slider to assign from 0 (no transparency) to 100 (complete transparency) to the patch. You can also set a transparency value to a Mesh Fill node by selecting it and then using the Transparency controls. Transparency on a Mesh Fill has no blending mode as the Transparency Tool offers for entire objects—transparency is applied in Normal mode. However, once your Mesh Fill object is completed, you can use the Transparency Tool on the Toolbox to assign the object different types and Transparency modes to the whole object, and not just its patches.

- **Selection Mode**   By default, you can select nodes in Rectangular mode, which means you marquee-drag a rectangular shape with your cursor to select nodes and then change their properties, such as color, position, and transparency. Your other selection choice is Freehand; in this mode your cursor behaves like a real-world lasso and you are unconstrained by a selection shape for nodes. Additionally, you can SHIFT-click and select non-neighboring nodes to edit. When using Freehand mode, you can select patches using either the Shape Tool's Rectangular or Freehand mode.
- **Smooth Mesh Color**   This is a toggle on/off button that can produce smoother color blends in your fill without changing the position or properties of the mesh nodes and curve path segments.
- **Color Dropper**   When a patch or node is selected, you can choose a color anywhere on your Windows desktop by dragging the Color Eyedropper over to any point. You can also sample from objects on your drawing page, but that might not be as much fun!
- **Color Palette**   You have a mini–Color Palette flyout on the Property bar with which you can select colors for selected nodes and patches. Click the flyout button to access the default Color Palette or choose from other preinstalled CorelDRAW palettes. Clicking a color well on the (regular) Color Palette applies color, too.
- **Copy and Delete Mesh Fill Properties**   These buttons are common to most all effects in CorelDRAW; use them to copy a Mesh Fill to a different object on the page or to remove the Mesh Fill effect from an existing object.

When working with the Mesh Fill, you'll get far more predictable results if you apply colors to the nodes instead of dropping colors onto patches. Also bear in mind that regardless of how you create a shape, the Mesh Fill makes the object "soft"—the control nodes that make the closed path of the object are also Mesh Fill nodes. So unavoidably, if you want to move a node you've colored in at the edge of the object, you're also *moving the associated path segment*. This is fun and creative stuff actually, and if you need the fill to be soft with the object's original shape intact, you can put your finished object inside a container by using the Effects | PowerClip | Place In Frame feature.

 Note   You cannot apply a Mesh Fill to a *combined shape;* an object made by subtracting a circle from a rectangle so it looks like an awkward doughnut will not take a Mesh Fill. However, the Property Bar offers you Mesh Fill options.

The following tutorial guides you through the creation of a Mesh Fill within a shape that's been created for you, with the finished example on the right of the page in Shiny Sphere.cdr. The goal is to create a Mesh Fill that gives a simple circle object the appearance of being a dimensional, highly reflective sphere, complete with a soft cast shadow beneath it.

Take a look at Figure 15-8 before you begin these steps; it's a comprehensive visual guide for not only the steps to follow, but also a handy reference to accompany your independent Mesh Fill adventures.

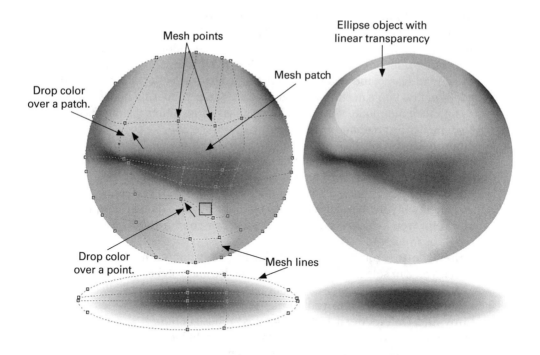

FIGURE 15-8 Mesh Fills use control handles very similar in appearance and function to the paths you draw with the Pen Tools and edit with the Shape Tool.

Tutorial Blending Colors Using the Mesh Fill

1. Open Shiny Sphere.cdr, select the top circle at left, and then choose the Mesh Fill Tool. A default mesh fill grid is applied to the object, 2 rows, 2 columns. Increase the resolution to 4 rows, 4 columns for starters.
2. In a lasso marquee-drag motion, select the horizontal nodes along the center of the sphere and then click the black color well on the Color Palette.
3. Marquee-select all the nodes below the horizontal center nodes you selected in Step 2 and then choose a rich brown from either the Color Palette or the flyout palette on the Property Bar.
4. Select only the bottom center node and then click a lighter brown.
5. Choose the Freehand selection mode from the Property Bar, and then select the five top nodes that define the top edge of the circle and then fill them with a purple-blue medium color. Select the first row—the five nodes below the top circular edge nodes—and fill them with a light blue.
6. Click the second node in this row and fill it with a deep gold color to suggest a sunset on the horizon of the little desert painting you've created. Often, traditional airbrush illustrators have created photorealistic chrome spheres using the reflection of a desert as the primary visual content. You've done this; now it's time to distort the desert scene to suggest the dimensionality of a 3D sphere.

7. Select the gold node and drag it down a little.
8. Select, one by one, the nodes that are colored black, and create a slight wavy effect.
9. Select the light brown node above the bottom center node and move it up a little.
10. Finesse the color nodes to suit your personal artistic taste. Then select the bottom oval, and apply the default 2 by 2 Mesh Fill grid.
11. First, fill the oval with white; it's harder to see this way, but its appearance will change and become obvious shortly. Click the center node with the Mesh Fill Tool, and then click black on the Color Palette. You now have a feathered, soft drop-shadow that would take two of three additional steps to get it right if you'd used the Drop Shadow Tool on the Toolbox. The Drop Shadow Tool is often, but not always, the right tool for creating a shadow effect.
12. Drag the oval highlight object currently over the completed example at right; tap the right mouse button before releasing both buttons to drop a copy on top of your shiny sphere at left.

 Note After a Mesh Fill has been applied to an object, the object cannot be filled with any other fill type unless the Mesh Fill effect has first been cleared. To clear a Mesh Fill applied to a selected object, click the Clear Mesh button in the Property Bar.

Sampling and Applying Fill Colors

After you've experimented and come up with a lot of interesting and valuable fills you've applied to objects, a natural question to ask is: I've got this once-in-a-lifetime, truly excellent color (or texture), and I want to use the fill on other objects. How do I do this?

CorelDRAW X6 has integrated the color sampling process and improved it so that a single tool now can be used to sample a color and apply that color to a different object. Additionally, when an object fill has more than one color—such as Fountain Fills—you have the Attributes Eyedropper at hand to sample and duplicate any fill to a new object or group of objects.

To use the Color Eyedropper Tool:

1. Make sure your view of the page includes both the object that is filled with the color you want to copy and the target object. Zoom out or pan your view if necessary.
2. Choose the Color Eyedropper Tool from its group on the Toolbox.
3. Click over the object with the color you want to sample. The cursor changes to a paint bucket, as does the tool's function.
4. Click over the object you want to apply the sampled color to. Notice that after you click, the cursor remains in the paint bucket state. If you want to apply the sampled color to additional objects, do it now. However, if you want to pick a different color sample—starting the process all over again, click the Eyedropper icon on the Property Bar. The tool is now reset to sample, not apply color.

Additional options for color sampling are on the Property Bar:

- **Select From Desktop**   When you click this button, you can sample more than a CorelDRAW object color. You select any color on your screen. This means, for example, you can sample the color of the Zoom Tool on the Toolbox, any color on the Color Palette, and you can even click CorelDRAW's minimize/restore button above the menu bar, move CorelDRAW a little, and sample from an open web browser to match colors of graphics on the Web.
- **Selected Color**   This option is not only a good visual reference as you work, but also, when using the Color Eyedropper Tool, you can drag this color well on top of any object—selected or unselected—and the current selected color is applied to that object.
- **Add To Palette**   If you want to keep using your sampled color long after you're done with the Color Eyedropper Tool, click this button to add the sampled color to your default Color Palette or custom one.
- **Sample size**   Before clicking to sample, you have the option to sample a single point—one pixel on your monitor's screen—or a 2×2 average area or a 5×5 average color area. The benefits of using this feature are covered next.

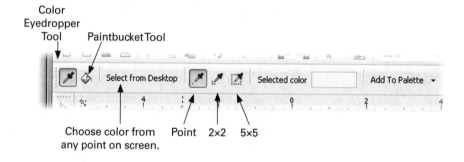

Color Eyedropper Tool   Paintbucket Tool

Choose color from any point on screen.   Point   2×2   5×5

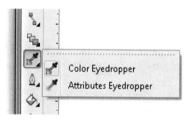

Color Eyedropper
Attributes Eyedropper

The usefulness of sampling colors with a "big" eyedropper will become evident when you've imported a bitmap and want to approximate a color you see in the bitmap for a border or text in your composition. Figure 15-9 illustrates the use of a large, averaged

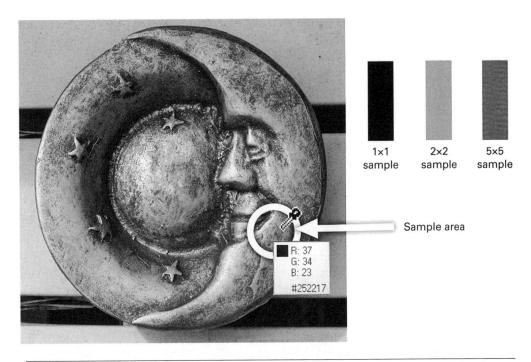

FIGURE 15-9 Increase your Color Eyedropper sample size to get a general color instead of the exact underlying pixel color.

color sample. The background of the ceramic moon is dreadful, and a harmonious color value sampled from the moon sculpture itself would be splendid. But the color at left was taken using a "point sample," 1 × 1 pixel. Bitmap images have pixels that vary from neighboring pixel to pixel, especially with JPEGs that, by their nature, *have noise*—similar to film grain, noise is the random distribution of color pixels that don't belong in image areas. So the 1 × 1 pixel Color Eyedropper Tool sample is a dud, even after three tries. The 2 × 2 averaged sample did better at center, but at the right, when the same area in the circle is sampled using the 5 × 5 setting, accuracy is no longer critical and a nice average 25-pixel area yields a suitable color for the background on the moon.

Sampling Above and Beyond Uniform Fills

You will love to work with the more complex fills in CorelDRAW, and naturally, you'll want to apply one you've deliberately created or even stumbled upon to other objects. Multicolor fills fit into a category called Styles, and to copy them, you need to use the Color Eyedropper's cousin tool, the Attributes Eyedropper. To sample and apply fills such as Fountains, Textures, and all the others, choose the Attributes Eyedropper from the Toolbox and then click the Properties button and choose Fill. You can use the

Attributes Eyedropper to copy just about anything an object displays, but for making a rectangle's fill look like that Fountain-filled circle next to it, for example, you only check Fill before clicking with the tool.

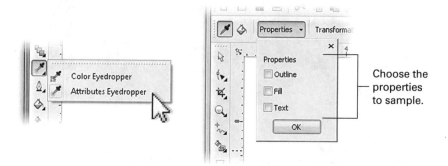

Choose the properties to sample.

Alternatively, you can drag an object using the right mouse button and drop it on top of an object to which you'd like to apply any style of fill. The pop-up menu appears when you release the right mouse button, and you then choose Copy Fill Here. The position of the source object does not move using this drag technique.

If you've had your fill, this is okay ... so have your objects. You've learned in this chapter how to tap into CorelDRAW fills, and hopefully you've also seen how important fills can be to your drawings. Fills can actually contribute to the visual robustness of a composition more than the shape of objects. Take a cardboard box, for example. The shape of the box isn't that interesting and takes only a few seconds to draw. But the *texture* of a cardboard box is where the object gets its character and mood.

Outline properties and attributes are covered in the following chapter. You can do as much with customizing the thing that goes *around* an object as with the object itself.

16

Outline Attributes

Chapter 15 covers only half the story about how you can flesh out a visual idea by using CorelDRAW. Although an object can usually live its life just fine without an outline, the attributes you can apply to a path can add a touch of refinement to an illustration. The right outline color can help visually separate different objects. Additionally, you can simulate calligraphic strokes without using Artistic Media when you know how to work the Outline Pen dialog; you can even make a path a dashed line, complete with arrowheads for fancy presentations and elegant maps. In fact, an outline, especially an open outline, can be visually interesting without creating a filled object! You don't have to learn fills and effects in CorelDRAW and leave it at that. This chapter shows you the ins and outs of properties you apply to your paths, from beginning to end.

 Download and extract all the files from the Chapter16.zip archive to follow the tutorials in this chapter.

Applying Outline Pen Properties

By default, when you create an open or closed path, it's given a ½-point-wide outline in black with no fancy extras. Part of the rationale for this default is that vector paths can't really be seen without some sort of width. In contrast, bitmap artwork, by definition, is made up of pixels, written to screen and written to file; so when a user draws an outline, it always has a width (it's always visible). Happily, vector drawing programs can display a wide range of path properties, and unlike bitmap outlines, you can change your mind at any time and easily alter the property of an outline.

In a number of areas in CorelDRAW, you can apply a property such as color, stroke width, and other fun stuff to an open or closed path (and even to open paths that don't touch each other but have been unified using the Arrange | Combine command). The following sections explore your options and point out the smartest and most convenient way to travel in the document window to arrive quickly at the perfect outline. When an open path or an object (which necessarily has to be described using a path) is selected on the page, the Property Bar offers many options for outline properties. You can also dig into the Outline Pen Toolbox flyout (and even detach it to make it persistent in the workspace for repeated access), and you also have the Object Properties docker—accessed from the pop-up menu when you right-click a path, and ALT-ENTER also gets you there. Some shortcuts for performing simple property adjustments' are covered on the long and winding path through this chapter.

Outline Pen Options and the Property Bar

Although it doesn't offer all options for path properties, the Property Bar is probably your most convenient route to outline properties. It actively displays a selected path's *current* properties, which you can change when a path is selected. The Property Bar, shown here while a path is selected, has width, style, and arrowhead options—you can make an open path with a head, tail, two heads—it's up to you. Other options give you control over wrapping text around a path, showing or hiding a bounding box around a path, and items not directly related to the outline's look. Closed paths, naturally, can't have arrowheads, but your options for dashed lines and other attributes are available for rectangles, ellipses, all the polygon shapes, and for freeform closed curves you've drawn by hand.

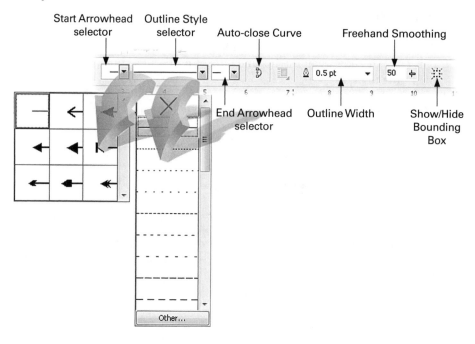

Start Arrowhead selector — Outline Style selector — Auto-close Curve — Freehand Smoothing — End Arrowhead selector — Outline Width — Show/Hide Bounding Box

The following tutorial walks you through the use of the Property Bar when you draw a path.

Tutorial   Going Long and Wide

1. Choose any drawing tool—the default Freehand Tool is fine—just drag a squiggle and then press SPACEBAR to switch to the Pick Tool; the path is selected now.
2. On the Property Bar, choose an outline thickness using the Outline Width selector, or enter a value and then press ENTER.
3. For arrowheads (on an open path), click the Start or End Arrowhead selectors, and then choose an arrowhead style from the pop-up. The Start option applies an arrowhead to the first node of the path; the End option applies it to the last. However, this might not be the direction in which you want the arrow to point. If this is the case, you have to perform a little mental juggling; the head of your arrow is always the *last* node on a path you create, not the first.
4. To apply a dashed or dotted-line pattern to the path, click the Outline Style selector, and then choose from one of the presets. Creating custom dashed patterns is covered later in this chapter.
5. Try increasing and decreasing the outline width, and see what happens to dashed line styles and arrowheads; they scale proportionately to the width of the outline.

As you apply outline properties from the Property Bar to your object or path, the effect is immediately visible, making this method both quick and convenient to use.

 Tip To set the color of a shape's outline quickly, right-click over any Color Palette color well.

Outline Tool Features on the Object Properties Docker

You can define a path's properties by accessing any of three levels of features: The Property Bar is always available when you select a line, providing basic outline attributes. The Outline Tool, actually a suite of tools, is also available on the Toolbox. When the Toolbox is unlocked (right-click and then uncheck Lock Toolbars), you can float Outline Flyout in the workspace until you decide you want to close it. First, click the Outline Pen Tool to select it, then *hover* over the treads on the top of the list, and drag the dotted treads into the workspace—now you have a floating toolkit named Outline Flyout.

With CorelDRAW X6, however, you can now use the redesigned Object Properties docker to adjust virtually everything about a drawn line except editing the path itself (covered later in this chapter). These features, shown here, are covered in the following section.

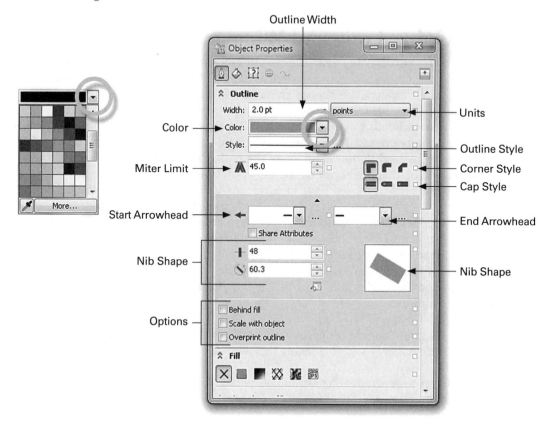

To display the Outline section of the Object Properties docker, right-click over a selected outline on a page or press ALT + ENTER. Note that you can extend the Outline section to access more features by clicking the down-facing triangle on the gray horizontal bar at the bottom of the Outline section.

Exploring the Outline Pen Features

The Outline Pen dialog and the Object Properties docker overlap in terms of Outline options quite a lot. This section covers outline properties as found in the Outline Pen dialog, but as soon as you learn the features themselves, you can decide which way you want to display them in the workspace.

Tip The Color Eyedropper Tool can be used to sample and apply outline properties between objects.

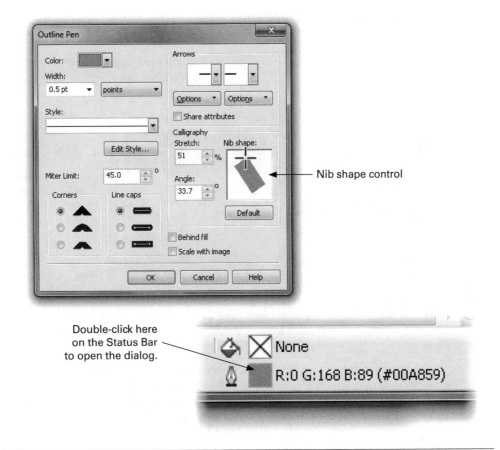

Nib shape control

Double-click here
on the Status Bar
to open the dialog.

FIGURE 16-1   Comprehensive options for outline properties are found in the
Outline Pen dialog.

To open the Outline Pen dialog quickly, shown in Figure 16-1, double-click the
outline well on the Status Bar. You can also choose the dialog from the Outline Flyout
(pressing F12 gets you there, too).

Setting Outline Color

Using the Pen Color selector in the Outline Pen dialog, you can choose a color for your
selected path(s). Pen Color affects only the color of the object's path; object *fills* are not
changed. Outline color can be set only to CorelDRAW's Uniform colors from the drop-
down palette. To access *every* color collection and color model for outlines, click the
More button at the bottom of the Pen Color selector in the dialog. The Outline Color

box provides access to all CorelDRAW's Color Palettes, including custom swatches and the Color Mixer.

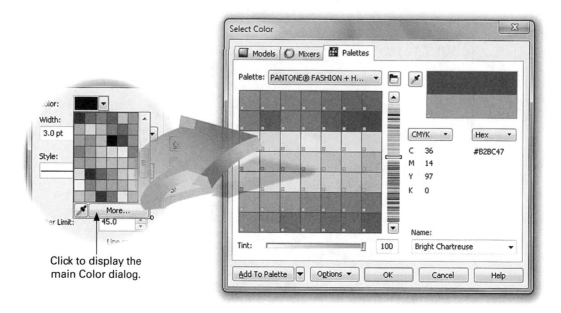

Click to display the
main Color dialog.

If you want color control and don't need to fuss with dashed outlines, arrowheads, or other outline attributes, don't choose the Outline Pen dialog—click the Outline Color dialog button on the Outline Flyout in the Toolbox. And if you're not particular about a specific shade of color, right-click a color well on the Color Palette to set an outline color.

Choosing Outline Styles

For a quick way to apply a dashed- or dotted-line pattern to the path of a selected object, the Outline Style selector offers more than 28 different preset variations.

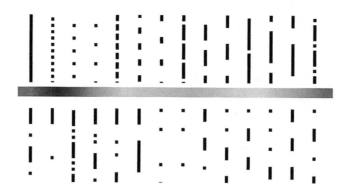

Applying an outline style causes a pattern to appear along the entire path, which is a must for anything you need to suggest visually to readers, for instance, that they should go running for the scissors: coupons, tickets, you name it. *Styles* are repeating patterns of short, long, and combinations of dashes that apply to the entire path. Line styles can be applied to any open or closed path object, as well as to *compound paths*—paths that look like two or more individual paths but are bound using the Arrange | Combine command. The quickest way to apply a dashed style is to use the Pick Tool and the Property Bar's Outline Style selector when one or more paths are selected, as shown here.

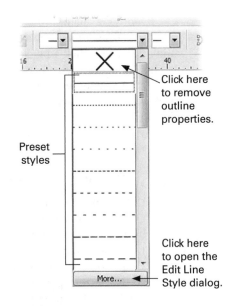

Click here to remove outline properties.

Preset styles

Click here to open the Edit Line Style dialog.

More...

Tip — Once you have a nice custom outline set of properties defined and want to apply all the parameters to a different path, you can copy outline properties from one path to another by right-clicking and dragging one path on top of the target path (this doesn't move your original path; it's a special editing technique). Release the mouse button when a crosshairs cursor appears over the target path. Then choose Copy Outline Here from the pop-up menu.

Creating and Editing Outline Styles

If you're looking for a special dashed-line style, one of your own invention, you can always *build* it. Choose More from the Style selector in the Property Bar while a curve is selected, or within the Outline Pen dialog, click the Edit Style button. Both actions open the Edit Line Style dialog, shown here:

Click to draw or erase part of the dot/dash pattern.   Drag to increase blank space between pattern dots/dashes.

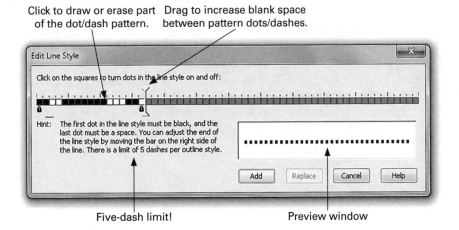

Five-dash limit!   Preview window

Creating a custom line style of dots and dashes is a fairly intuitive process, very similar to drawing a line in a paint program; your cursor serves as both a pencil and an eraser—click a black dot to erase it, click a white (space) dot to add to or begin a line. Once you save a style by clicking Add, it becomes available throughout CorelDRAW wherever outline styles are offered. Your only limitation—*read the legend at the bottom left of the editor*—is that you can't create a sequence consisting of more than five dashes or dots; adjoining marks count as a single dash. To create and save your own custom outline style, follow these steps:

Tutorial ## Drawing a Dotted Line Style

1. Create and/or select a path to serve as a host for your new line style, open the Outline Pen dialog (F12), and then click the Edit Style button, or click the More button at the bottom of the Outline Style selector on the Property Bar.
2. In the Edit Line Style dialog, you see a horizontal pattern generator featuring a slider control, a preview window, and a set of command buttons.
3. In the pattern generator, drag the slider left or right to change the style length. Click (or click-drag to make a long dash segment) on the small squares to the left of the slider to set the pattern's on/off states. If you want to erase a segment, you click or click-drag on the black square(s) you've drawn. As you do this, the preview window shows the new pattern.
4. Click the Add button to add the new style to the list (or click Replace to overwrite the style currently selected in the Outline Style selector) to return to the Outline Pen dialog. New styles are added to the bottom of the selector list.
5. Verify that your new line style is available by choosing it in the selector and clicking OK to apply your new outline style; you'll find it at the bottom of the drop-down list, and as with the preset styles, custom styles have no name—you search using the look of the saved thumbnail. The line style you created is now applied to the object.

If the pattern applied to a path doesn't exactly match its length—for example, the pattern is longer than the path it's applied to—you might see a "seam," especially when applying outline styles to closed paths (as shown next). There are two ways to cure the problem. One is to go back to the Style editor and increase or decrease the length of the pattern; this is a trial-and-error edit, but it doesn't change the path to which the style is applied. The other method (a desperate measure) is to lengthen the path by using the Shape Tool or to scale the path by using the Pick Tool. In either of these edits, you change your design and not your custom preset—it's your work so the call is up to you, but editing the style is usually the best way to avoid seams on a case-by-case basis with compositions you create.

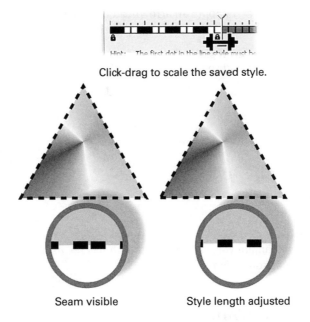

Click-drag to scale the saved style.

Seam visible   Style length adjusted

Setting Outline Arrowheads

Arrowheads are both heads *and* tails on an open path, and although you have a handsome collection of preset arrows, they can be almost anything you decide to draw. Most of the preset styles are arrowheads, but some are symbols that represent a tail. Here you can see several of the styles, and many of the tails match the visual style of the arrowheads. When applied, arrowheads can be set to appear at the start and end points of open paths, both ends, one end, or, by default, neither end.

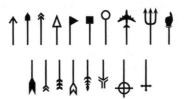

Here's a trick to defining the size of an arrowhead or tail: you increase or decrease the size of an arrowhead by adjusting the outline width using the Property Bar or the Outline dialog. However, if you want to scale a path's width *without* scaling the arrowhead, you scale the path by using the Pick Tool and the control handles surrounding the selected path. Scaling a path (object) instead of increasing/ decreasing the outline width is your ticket to making an arrowhead exactly proportional to the path's outline.

The quickest way to apply an arrowhead is by using the Start and/or End Arrowhead selectors on the Property Bar when an open path is selected, as shown here.

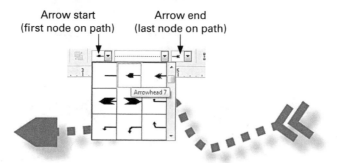

> **Note** Applying an arrowhead to a closed path has no visible effect unless the path is broken at some point.

Creating Custom Arrowhead Styles

Realistically, CorelDRAW could not have the ideal arrowhead (and tail) for your (and every other user's) assignment as a preset, or the preset selector would need a head and a tail itself, from here to the moon! That's why there's the Tools | Create | Arrow command—don't choose the command yet; you'll need to draw the arrowhead first, as covered in the following tutorial. The best arrowhead should be simple in its construction and needs to be a single or compound path—fill makes no difference in creating the arrowhead because a finished and applied custom arrow style gets its color from the outline color you use on the selected path in your drawing. The orientation of the arrowhead needs to be in landscape, too, before entering the Create command. In other words, the top of your custom arrowhead design needs to face right, not the top of the page.

To create a new arrowhead and save it, follow these steps; if you'd like a jump-start, open Shovel.cdr first. It contains the elements needed to make both a head and tail.

Tutorial Drawing, Saving, and Editing an Arrowhead Style

1. Give some thought and planning to what would make a good arrowhead and tail. Shovel.cdr has a drawing of the business and the user ends of a common garden shovel. This works for designs of garden planning (an arrow pointing to "dig here"), treasure hunts, and certain civil engineering diagrams. About 3" for your symbols to be used as arrowheads seems to work well and gets you around the need to edit the size later. When you've drawn your arrowhead (a tail is optional for this tutorial), rotate it so it's pointing side faces the right of the drawing page.

2. With the shape selected, choose Tools | Create | Arrow.

3. Type a name in the upper-left field for future reference. If you like, the Create Arrowhead box gives you the chance to set a size for the arrowhead; by default, it's the size you've drawn it on the page. Click OK and your arrowhead is saved to the arrowhead selector list at the bottom of the list. Possibly you're done now. Let's check, before calling it a day, to see how the arrowhead looks when applied to an open path.

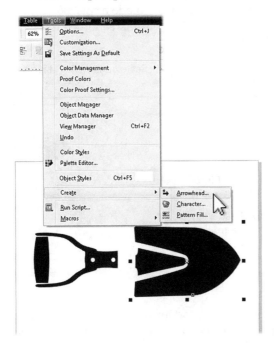

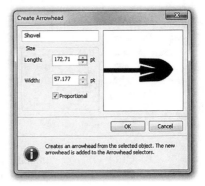

4. With the 2-Point Line Tool, click-drag a two-node path. Straight is good for checking out the arrowhead, but in the future a curved path can be more visually interesting capped off with your work.
5. On the Property Bar with the path selected, choose the 10 pt. outline width so you'll have a clear view of the arrowhead you defined (or the shovel head if you used the Shovel.cdr file).
6. On the Property Bar, choose the arrowhead from the first node drop-down selector, the one on the left on the Property Bar. Let's suppose you're not 100 percent happy with the look of the arrowhead; you now access additional options for modifying the saved arrowhead. With the path selected, double-click the Outline Color icon (either the pen icon or the color swatch) on the Status Bar to display the Outline Pen dialog. Click the Options button beneath the thumbnail of your arrowhead and then choose Edit.

7. Here's where you can correct a number of problems with your arrowhead; you cannot, however, edit the path of the arrowhead itself. If, for example, your arrowhead is pointing the wrong way, select Mirror | Horizontally, as shown in this illustration. You also have the option to rotate the arrowhead, for corrective or creative reasons, as well as to move the head away from its parent line (the Offset options) and to proportionately or disproportionately scale or stretch the selected arrowhead. If you've made a mistake drawing the arrowhead, you cannot change it in the editor, but instead need to revise your drawing and then redefine the arrowhead.

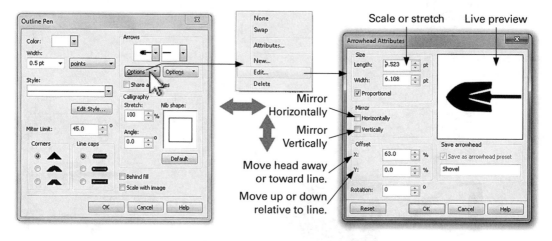

8. Click OK to overwrite your saved arrowhead, or rename it to add it to your collection. The Edit Arrowhead dialog can also be used to modify *existing* preset arrowheads, but only to the extent that you've just modified your custom arrowhead in Step 7. End of tour!

   Here you can see a few uses for a shovel. Don't be hesitant to mix and match outline styles; in the middle illustration, a dashed outline style happily coexists with a custom arrowhead.

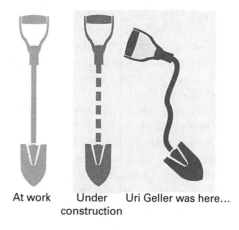

At work   Under   Uri Geller was here...
             construction

Other Arrowhead Options

When applying an arrowhead style, you'll find other convenient options are available in the Outline Pen dialog. Just below each Arrowhead Style selector are two Options buttons. Click either the start or end Options buttons to open a drop-down menu that features the following commands:

- **None**   Choose this command to clear the arrow style you selected from your path. You can also do this from the document window using the Property Bar.
- **Swap**   This command switches the styles currently selected for the start and end arrowheads. This cannot be done, at least not as easily, from the document window.
- **New**   Choose this command to open the Edit Arrowhead dialog and to create variation on a default style to add to the existing collection. New does *not* offer custom arrowhead creation; you need to use Tools | Create, as you learned earlier, to make a truly new arrowhead.
- **Delete**   While an existing style is applied, choosing this command permanently removes the selected style from the collection.

Setting Corner Shape

Frequently, you'll create a path whose segments join at a node in a cusp fashion; the connection is *not* smooth—for example, a crescent moon shape has a least two "sharp" cusp connections between path segments. When shapes have *discontinuous* connections—when a path abruptly changes direction as it passes through a node— you can set the appearance of the node connection through the Outline Pen dialog, the only area in CorelDRAW's interface that offers these options. Therefore, it's always a good idea to remember that double-clicking the outline palette on the Status Bar is your quickest route to defining how nodes look as they join two segments. Figure 16-2 shows the visual effect of Round, Miter, and Square (the default) joints on a path that has cusp nodes. Notice that at extremely sharp node connection angles, the Square joint option produces an area of the outline that extends way beyond the path, an exaggerated effect you might not always want in a design. You can use Corner properties creatively to soften the appearance of a node connection (Round works well) and also to keep a severe cusp angle from exaggerating a connection. Miter corners can often keep a path more consistent in its width than the default Corner.

Setting Line Cap Shape

Line caps, the beginning and end of an open path, can look like their counterparts, the corners, covered in the previous section. One of the greatest visual differences you can create is that the true width of a path is extended using the Round and Extended choices—the outline width overshoots the true path's length, proportional to the width you choose for an outline. Figure 16-3 shows examples of your Line Cap options.

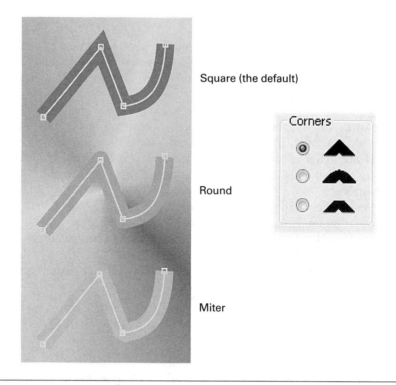

Square (the default)

Round

Miter

FIGURE 16-2   Corners can be set to one of these three styles.

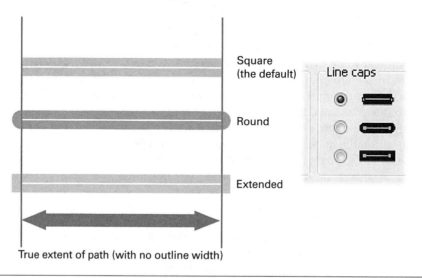

Square
(the default)

Round

Extended

True extent of path (with no outline width)

FIGURE 16-3   Line caps can be set to one of these three styles.

Applying Line Cap options to the end points of an open path affects not only the first and last nodes' appearance on an open path, but also affects dashed and dotted line styles, as shown here.

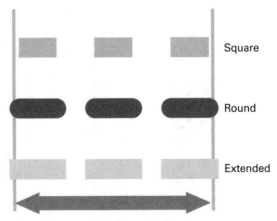

Square

Round

Extended

True extent of path (with no outline width)

Tip Line Cap options control the shape of *all* end points in an open path simultaneously; therefore, a compound path receives your choice of end caps at all two, four, six end points, and so on, depending on the structure of such a compound path. Also, line caps are not "mix and match"; for example, if you choose Round, both end caps in a two-node path are rounded—CorelDRAW has no facility for a two-node path that begins Round and ends Square.

Outline Pen Calligraphic Effects

The term *calligraphy* has come to be accepted today as a handwriting craft, the result of which is text and ornaments that have a varying width along strokes due to the popular use of a flat-edged pen nib held at an angle. The same effect can be achieved using the Calligraphic options in the Outline Pen dialog.

Calligraphic options are applied using a set of options and a preview window used to define the shape of the nib that affects a path you've drawn. *Stretch* controls the width of the nib using values between 1 and 100 percent. *Angle* controls the nib rotation in 360° (the minimum, –180°, produces the same "12 o'clock" stroke angle as the maximum, 360°). Click the Default button to reset these parameters to their original state. Stretch and Angle values work together to achieve the nib shape. Set them numerically by entering values or better still, interactively, by placing your cursor in the Preview window and then click-dragging to shape the nib. By default, all paths in CorelDRAW are created using a Stretch value of 100 percent and an Angle value of 0°. As you can see in Figure 16-4, varying the Stretch and degree of a Calligraphic nib changes the look of an outline, but the *shape* you begin with also has an impact on the final look of the design. For example, these three pairs of interwoven

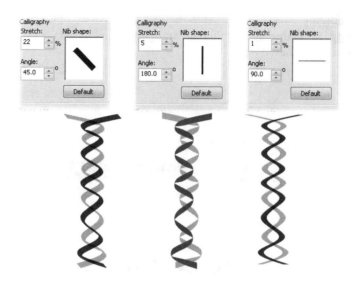

FIGURE 16-4 Calligraphic effects can be used as ornamentations to a piece of work or to imitate handwritten phrases.

B-spine paths are identical, but the one at left is perhaps more visually interesting and elegant with its 45° angled nib. The point is that if you have an object that you think will look more refined and elegant with a calligraphic stroke, keep changing the angle until you're happy with the finished artwork.

Tip The Artistic Media Tool has a Calligraphic style that can be used as a brush; you just drag on the page and it immediately produces angled paths. See Chapter 10 for details.

Scaling and Behind Fill Options

Two more options for controlling outline properties available in the Outline Pen dialog are very important for controlling how outlines display in particular design situations. The following sections explain how Scale With Image and Behind Fill work.

Scale With Image

Choose Scale With Image to increase or decrease the outline width applied to an open path or closed object when you scale the object at any time after the outline width has been applied.

For example, a 2-point outline width applied to a path becomes 1 point if the object is scaled in size by 50 percent. In most illustration work, where drawings commonly change size before they are complete, choosing this option is a smart

Original object

Reduced using the Scale With Image option

Reduced without the Scale With Image option selected

move. However, if you leave the scale constant (leave Scale With Image unchecked), you can duplicate, for example, 50 stars, arrange them on the page at different sizes, and the design looks good because the outline width is consistent from star to star. The illustration here shows copies of a pretzel shape reduced with and without the Scale With Image option selected. If this were a drawing of a *salted* pretzel, the one in the center—Scale With Image—would be less likely to cause high blood pressure and other heart risks if eaten by a drawing of a person.

Behind Fill

Behind Fill sets outline properties to print and display in *back* of the object's fill. One of the many practical uses for using Behind Fill is in a sign or other simple illustration where you need rounded corners along the outline, but sharp and crisp edges along the fill, the most important and recognizable part of many illustrations. Here, at left, you can see the ubiquitous recycle symbol with a 16-point rounded-corner outline. The arrows are lost in the design. However, at right, a 32-point outline is used with Behind Fill checked in the Outline Pen dialog. Therefore, the same outline width has been achieved (visually); however, because the outline is behind the fill, the points on the arrows are undistorted, even in weight, and will print crisply.

16-point outline in front of fill: most edges are soft.

32-point outline behind fill: edges are crisp and detailed.

Setting the Outline for All New Objects

Each time you create a new object, CorelDRAW automatically applies a set of default outline properties, as follows:

Width = .5 point
Color = CMYK black (from Corel's default custom palette)
Style = Solid line
Corner Shape and End Caps = Square
Calligraphy: Stretch = 100, Angle = 0 degrees
Behind Fill, Scale With Image = Off

To change any or all of these default properties, open the Outline Pen dialog (F12) while *no objects* are selected.

Depending on which buttons you choose in the Change Document Defaults dialog, you can control the defaults for all new graphics, as just one example. Unless you have a specific reason for changing the default outline properties of text, callouts, and other objects, it's wise to only select Graphic as the object type to apply, and then to click OK to proceed to the Outline Pen dialog to change the outline pen defaults.

Turning an Outline into an Object

A fancy calligraphic property for an outline, arrowhead, and even for dashed outlines can be freed from being editable *outline* properties when you convert an outline to an object. Consider this: an outline is constrained to solid fills, whereas an object that *looks* like an outline, that was originally *based* on an outline, can have any type of CorelDRAW fill. To make an outline into a shape, you choose Arrange | Convert Outline To Object—but this will disturb your workflow less if you perform this on a *copy* of the path you slaved over! In Figure 16-5, you can see the command on the Arrange menu (the shortcut is similar to Convert To Curves; it's CTRL + SHIFT + Q). This path is fully loaded, using a calligraphic nib, a dashed line, an arrowhead, and a tail. It is about to become a shape that's freely editable with Toolbox tools and will accept all of CorelDRAW's effects such as contours, Fountain, and Texture Fills, and even the Extrude Tool can turn this shape into elegant, abstract, bizarre artwork.

In Figure 16-6, you can see at left that the path shown in Figure 16-5 is now a shape that will take, in this example, a Linear-style Fountain Fill—in contrast, you can't fill an open path. See also in this figure that the arrowhead path that's now a shape can be extruded. To come full circle, the new object based on the path can have an outline; in this figure a black outline behind the fill is used artistically to separate the linear fill areas visually.

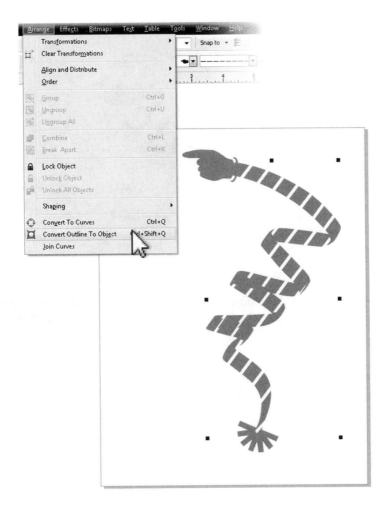

FIGURE 16-5   Convert a path to an object, and all outline properties become editable objects.

This chapter has taken you through the simple assignment of one property to a path, to several, more complex properties. As you gather more understanding of options in CorelDRAW, you add to your personal, creative wealth of design options. Dashed lines, arrowheads, and calligraphic strokes will come to your rescue during 11th-hour assignment crunches, just as other features will that have been covered in

FIGURE 16-6   If you need to edit certain areas of a fancy outline, you can do it more easily and more precisely by first turning the outline into an object.

previous chapters. Chapter 17 takes a side-step from object creation to defining a color for that object you just created. You've probably read things on digital color *theory*, but the following chapter puts theory into *practice.*

And practice makes perfect.

17

Digital Color Theory Put to Practice

Put away those crayons. Fling that color wheel out on the front lawn. *Digital* color obeys *none* of the rules we were taught in school. Digital color models are what you use to fill objects that CorelDraw displays on your monitor, and defining colors is an art with which even professionals occasionally struggle. However, CorelDRAW makes it as simple as can be to apply exactly the color you have in mind to an object, through an extensive collection of industry-standard swatches, intuitive color models, and Color Mixers that make color definition more like play than work.

This chapter covers color theory and how to put it to practice in your CorelDRAW work. If you've ever been faced with picking out a tie to match your shirt or a blouse to match your skirt at 8:30 in a dimly lit closet, you'll appreciate the importance of choosing harmonious and intriguing color schemes. This chapter guides you through the digital process of choosing colors and making certain what you print is what you see onscreen.

 Download and extract all the files from the Chapter17.zip archive to follow the tutorials in this chapter.

Digital Color Terms and Definitions

Let's say you've created a rectangle on your page; by default, it has no fill and there are two quick fixes to fill it. You can left-click a color on the Color Palette, but let's say you want a *specific* color. You double-click the Fill icon on the Status Bar shown in the following illustration, and you can see (and work in) the Uniform Fill dialog, a combination of interface palettes that has tabs for Models, Mixers, and Palettes.

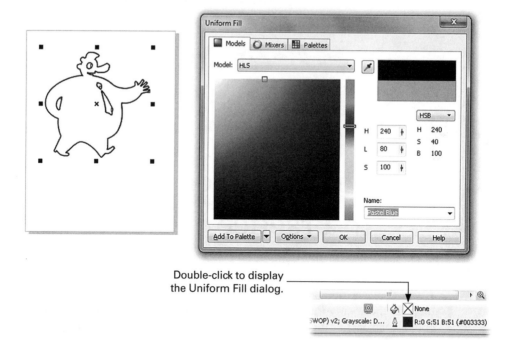

Double-click to display
the Uniform Fill dialog.

In the Uniform Fill dialog, Palettes are predefined collections of color swatches. Then you have Mixers; they are covered later in this chapter. Finally, you have Models, an area that deserves documentation here.

The first terms that set the stage for color exploration in this chapter are used in digital color descriptions and also to define real-world colors you apply to paper, plastic, and so on. They'll give you a handle on a variety of color attributes. They're also somewhat interrelated; when you change a parameter in one, most of the time you change a parameter in a different class of color description.

- **Color model** A *model* is a representation of something that's intangible or too ungainly in other respects to manipulate directly. For example, a child plays with a model airplane because this representation fits in his bedroom better than an actual airplane, and passengers around the world feel safer. Color models are used in CorelDRAW to make it easy to deal with the relationships between colors; without a model of the spectrum of light—an *intangible*—it's a challenge to choose the colors you need. Additionally, a color model *scales* all the available colors you have when working on CorelDRAW and other programs, in the same way a model airplane can be rotated to see all its sides—which is hard to do with a full-sized airplane. Today, users have at least 16.7 million possible colors from which to choose in design work; a color model makes color selection much easier than choosing colors from a palette containing 16.7 million swatches.

- **Color space**   A color model is a *structure*. If you were having a house built, your structure would need to take up space, usually on some land. A color space is that "land" for your color model "architecture." Different color models require different color spaces. Let's say you have a CorelDRAW file you want a commercial press to print. Print presses generally use the CMYK color model as the basis for reproducing the colors you've filled objects with; CMYK color is covered later in this chapter. Unfortunately, the color you see on your monitor has its structure in a fairly *wide* color space; RGB colors have a wider range of expression (more possible colors) than the CMYK color space. What can happen is that some colors you use in your CorelDRAW document look fine onscreen, but they don't print as you anticipate. The reason is that the CMYK color space is smaller than the color space of your monitor, and some of your original design's colors are *clipped* when printed. They've been arbitrarily moved to a color that's *similar* to the color you used, or they just don't print, or you get a splotch of muddy brown on the printed page. You certainly want more control over how a CorelDRAW design prints. This is why CorelDRAW offers a CMYK color picker and also a Gamut Alarm. *Gamut* is a term that means the expressible range of color; in other words, colors that fall into a specific color space. When you choose a color that falls out of the range of the color space, it's called an *out of gamut* color, and these colors won't print correctly because they're a structure that is built on a part of the land you don't own.

Note   The *K* in "CMYK" indeed stands for "black," and it's fair to ask, "Why don't we call it CMY**B**" color?" The *K* is for "key"; the *key plate* in CMYK printing is the last plate that is printed. In this case, cyan is pressed first, then magenta, then yellow, and finally the key, black. In printing, a key plate is the plate that prints the detail in an image; as you can often see in a progressive proof of a print job, C, M, and Y inks don't provide much image detail. We use the term "key plate" in printing because black is not always used. For example, in two-color print jobs, the key plate is the darker of the two colors. In general, however, *K* means "black" and you'll often see CMYK written as "CMY (black K)" to avoid ambiguity.

- **File color capability**   If all you ever do is create CDR files, print them, and save them, you have no concerns about a file format that can hold all the colors you've picked and applied to objects. The CDR file format will retain the colors you've used. But if you intend to export a design to bitmap file format, you'll want to check out Chapter 23. Different bitmap file formats have different ceilings of color capability, which relates to color space in many ways. TIFF images as written by CorelDRAW, for example, can contain 16.7 million unique colors, and this file format can be written to the RGB color model, the CMYK color model, and even some color *modes* such as Grayscale, which offers no color at all but instead only brightness values. On the other hand, GIF images continue to be written for the Web, and these images can only hold 256 unique colors, pretty meager when compared with 16.7 million colors, so you need to know how to design using only 256 colors, tops.

The sections to follow are a step-by-step documentation of topics from the structure of digital color, to the space in which color resides, through how you manipulate color models in CorelDRAW to define colors you want or to match color values a client might have read to you over the telephone.

Subtractive and Additive Color Models

The world of color models has two distinct categories: *subtractive* and *additive* color models. You use *both:* when you print something, you use a device that uses the subtractive color model. When you design for the Web or an onscreen presentation, you use an additive color model. How these models are similar, where their differences lie, and how you access these models in CorelDRAW are the subjects of the following sections.

Subtractive Color Models

From the moment the first caveperson depicted an antelope on the family room wall, humans have been using a *subtractive color* model for painting. Subtractive color is what many artists were brought up on, mixing physical pigments, and we all know that when you mix a lot of different pigments together, you eventually get black. This is what the subtractive color model is all about: you *remove* part of the visible spectrum as you overlay one color upon another. In theory, if you put cyan, magenta, and yellow pigments together at full intensity, you should get black—cyan, magenta, and yellow are the primary colors in a subtractive color model. However, due to chemical impurities in physical pigments such as ink and paint, you get a deep brown and not true black. A black printing plate is used *in addition to* the C, M, and Y plates to reproduce a wide spectrum of colors available in the CMYK color model.

The RGB Additive Color Model

The *additive* color model describes color using *light,* not pigments, and a combination of the primary additive colors red, green, and blue. When combined in equal amounts at full intensity, red, green, and blue produce white, not black as subtractive CMYK color does. RGB is a common additive color model, and it is not at all intuitive for an artist to use; however, CorelDRAW has different views of the RGB color model that make it easy and intuitive to work with.

Because a color model only does one thing—*it shows a mathematical relationship among values that are intangible*—the visualization of the relationship between red, green, and blue can use any model anyone cares to use, with the goal being to make color picking and color relationships as painless as possible to perform! Figure 17-1 shows the default view of the Uniform Fill dialog. This chapter walks you through how to customize your onscreen display and your color choices for both the RGB and CMYK color models.

Let's take these controls in Figure 17-1 slowly and one at a time. A color attribute you're looking for right now can probably be defined in this dialog.

- **Color Model**   This selector drop-down list includes CMYK, CMY (as explained earlier, black is more a part of the printing process than a part of the color model), RGB, HSB, HSL, Grayscale, YIQ, LAB, and Registration. These models are covered

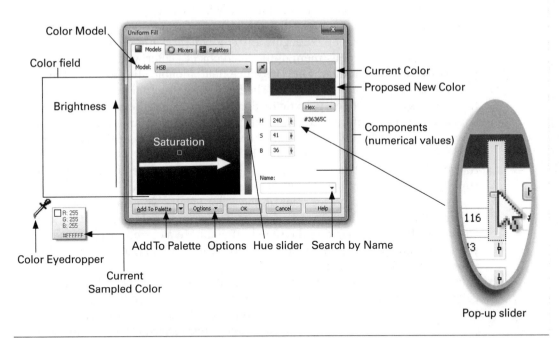

Color Model

Color field

Brightness

Saturation

Color Eyedropper

Current Sampled Color

Add To Palette Options Hue slider Search by Name

Current Color

Proposed New Color

Components (numerical values)

Pop-up slider

FIGURE 17-1 The Uniform Fill dialog is one of several areas from which you can pick colors in CorelDRAW.

later in this section. If you're in a hurry: CMYK should be chosen for in-gamut colors for printing, and RGB is the color model for doing work that won't be printed.

- **Color field and Hue slider** Here is something tricky, a little confusing, and totally wonderful on the Models tab. A model is a representation of a hard-to-grasp thing or idea. CMYK is an intangible item, and choosing colors using a CMYK model is hardly a fun pastime. Corel Corporation thought ahead on this stumbling block. When you choose CMYK mode, the *HSB* color-choosing field and slider are presented to you, even though you're not choosing HSB colors. To manipulate brightness (B), you drag the little rectangle up or down in the color field. To manipulate saturation (S), you drag left or right; and obviously you can navigate both brightness and saturation at the same time. The Hue (H) slider to the right of the color field sets the predominant, recognizable attribute of the color you're picking. Usually, you set the hue first, and then play with the amounts of saturation and brightness.

- **Current Color/New Color** The color well at the top shows you the current color of the selected object on the page. The bottom color well shows you any changes you've made, and the two together provide a convenient way to compare color changes.

- **Components** The field at left provides a numerical breakdown of the current color, as expressed in the components of the current color model. In Figure 17-1, you can see that the current color is a blue, and its HSB numerical values are H: 240 (degrees on a color wheel), S: 41 (percent), and B: 36 (percent).

However, these values are not static; in fact, when you click the icon to the right of any value (the icon that looks like a slider), a slider pops up, and you can adjust the color you want by dragging any component value up or down. This offers a more precise adjustment of the filled object's color; you can also insert your cursor into the number field (it's a live field), double-click to select the entire value, and then type in a new value. The fields to the right of the current color model fields are a secondary, static readout that gives you the selected color's equivalent using a different color model. You can see in Figure 17-1 that Hex has been chosen, which only requires one component field. You set the secondary field by clicking the button title above the component fields.

- **Name** The Color Palette, the strip docked to the right of the drawing window, contains colors that are tagged with names such as Desert Blue and Mint Green. To quickly search for a preset color on the Color Palette, you can choose from the drop-down list, or begin typing a name in the Name field—as you type more characters, the dialog narrows the search. If you have a custom palette loaded, you can't search it using the Models tab of the Uniform Fill dialog; you conduct a search using the Palettes tab.

- **Add To Palette** This button adds the current color you've created to the Color Palette's default palette. You can then retrieve this color directly from the Color Palette at any time without visiting the Uniform Fill dialog. This is one way to save a custom color; see "Using the New Color Styles Docker" later in this chapter for a more feature-filled way to save a custom color.

- **Bring Color Into Gamut** This button will not appear in the dialog box unless you've chosen a color in an additive color model and then switched to the CMYK color model. There's a chance that your chosen RGB color might be available in the CMYK color space (in which case, you won't see the button), but intense RGB colors cannot be expressed in CMYK. If the button appears when switching color models, click it to let CorelDRAW bring it into gamut, using the Rendering Intent you set up under Tools | Color Management | Default Settings. Rendering Intent is covered in the following NOTE, and yes, this *is* a lot to digest intellectually, so take it slowly here!

 Note In a nutshell, Rendering Intent is meant to preserve the colors and color relationships when you shift a photo or other bitmap from RGB color mode to CMYK or other mode. Different color modes have smaller or larger color spaces, and Rendering Intent options are intended to preserve color relationships when, for example, going from a large to a smaller color space, without *clipping* color values (destroying, improperly moving a color to an incorrect substitution, and losing original values). You have four options, and each one should be carefully considered, depending on the type of graphic your bitmap or photo represents: *Absolute Colorimetric* produces "ideal" color values—those attained by ignoring image noise, and colors that cannot be expressed when going from a larger to a smaller color space are mapped to the edge of the color space's gamut. Use Absolute Colorimetric if you have a logo that needs to be a specific color value. Colors might look wrong when you use this Rendering Intent because human perception and our view of color relationships isn't the same as mathematically precise result colors. *Relative Colorimetric* is the default process for most Rendering Intent conversions. Saturation is sacrificed to maintain hue and lightness. Relative Colorimetric tries to be faithful to original colors, while correcting mostly for the media (rendering to plastic, paper, newspaper, or another surface). *Perceptual* is preferred by photographers. Perceptual intent smoothly moves out-of-gamut colors into gamut, gradients are faithfully rendered, but at the expense of shifting colors that are within gamut. Use Relative first, and then Perceptual if the first choice doesn't suit your work. *Saturation* is a good choice when specific hues are unimportant, like with a graph or other chart. This method uses a discreet color palette, good for reproducing graphics and completely unacceptable for rendering photos.

- **Options** In this drop-down, you can swap the current color with the old color (if you've modified the current color). The Swap Colors option switches the order of the new and old colors displayed at the top right of this dialog.

Options also offers a choice of color selection interfaces for your chosen color model. This deserves a little explanation: to represent the components of color models, the various color models necessarily need to be graphically represented in their unique structure. Some color models, such as HSB, are blessed with a structure that is intuitive for mere mortals to use; others are less intuitive. Figure 17-2 shows the RGB model using the four available models. HSB – Hue Based is the easiest for artists to use; alternatively the HSB – Brightness Based picker might be popular with those who want to dabble in a large hue-based field instead of using the slider. The HSB-based color wheel makes Corel Painter users feel right at home, and the 3D Additive model is offered to accommodate particle physicists and Martians. Try it, you'll hate it—although the model itself is mathematically sound, it just isn't user friendly and a slider is necessary *in addition to* the 3D picking cube because this model is hard to visualize.

The HSB Additive Color Model

The HSB color model is to designers what the RGB color model is to software engineers; HSB serves the nonprogramming community for intuitively choosing colors, and HSB and RGB occupy the same color space, but use different components. HSB is the acronym for hue, saturation, and brightness. It's occasionally called HSV (the *V* is for "value"), and HSL (*L* is for "lightness"), but it all boils down to a user-friendly model for working with digital color. HSB, in fact, was modeled by Dr. Alvy Smith, cofounder of Pixar Studios, former Microsoft Fellow, and an accomplished artist. The HSB color model has the same number of colors (the same color space, discussed later in this chapter) as the RGB color model; however, HSB organizes the relationship between components of colors *differently* and *in a friendlier fashion,* than RGB does. The components of HSB color are as follows:

- **Hue** The distinguishing characteristic of color. When you tell a friend, "Oh, that's a very nice blue tie" or "The TV set is a little orange, isn't it?" you're describing the hue component of the color. Hue is usually expressed in degrees on a hue wheel; technically, hue is determined by light wavelength.

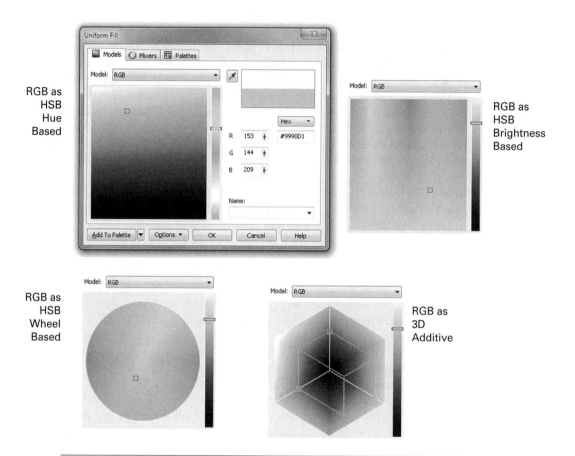

RGB as HSB Hue Based

RGB as HSB Brightness Based

RGB as HSB Wheel Based

RGB as 3D Additive

FIGURE 17-2 Many color pickers' views can be assigned to color models through Options in the Uniform Fill dialog.

- **Saturation** The presence of color, the purity, the predominance of a hue. You often use the component of saturation when you talk about how *juicy* the colors are in a photograph. If there's a lot of noticeable blues in a photo or a drawing, the blue hue is said to be quite saturated in that color. Conversely, colors you often see on today's household appliances, such as a toaster oven, that the manufacturer calls "Oyster," "Putty," "Ivory," or "Bisque," are neutral; they have no strong dominance of hue and, therefore, have little saturation. You can't make out the hue in such an appliance's color; you usually describe it as off-white or a warm gray. The pages in this chapter have no saturation, but offer a lot of brightness.
- **Brightness** The amount of illumination a color has. Brightness, as described in digital color terms, is somewhat elusive, but an analogy from traditional painting with pigments (subtractive color) provides some clarity here. When you mix a pure color with white, you're increasing its brightness; in industries where color

description is critical (fashion design, house paints) bright colors are a *tint* of a pure color, also called a *pastel* color. Then there are darker colors: a *shade* is the mixture of a color with black. Mixing with white increases lightness, whereas mixing with black reduces it. In both digital and traditional color, mixing black, white, or a perfectly neutral value in between black and white leaves hue unchanged.

Tip X-Rite has emerged as the color industry's heavy-hitter after adding Pantone (the color-matching people) and Gretag Macbeth (proofing systems, monitor calibration hardware/software) to Munsell and other acquisitions in recent years. If you have any questions about printing, packaging, paints, plastics, or just color in general, Xrite.com is the place to visit. Their website contains not only catalog areas, but also many areas with seminar listings and free downloads of collateral material— all about *color*.

LAB Color

LAB is both a color space *and* a color model. CorelDRAW offers LAB as a color model; however, LAB—the color space—is device-independent and, therefore, can be used to describe colors you see in the drawing window, on a physical plastic bottle of soda, and even on a basketball. Almost 100 years ago (this was before PCs) the Commission Internationale de l'Eclairage (the CIE, the International Commission on Illumination) was established as a worldwide organization for standardizing and exchanging color specifications. They are responsible for creating the LAB color model. It successfully replicates the spectrum of human vision, and this is why there is a disproportionately large area of green in LAB color space. This is because the human eye responds to this region of the visible spectrum more strongly than to other hues. LAB is modeled after one channel of **Luminance**, one color channel (named **A**) that runs from magenta to green, and another channel (named **B**) from blue to yellow. When you use LAB to describe a color, you're (theoretically) assured color consistency. LAB, the color space, is frequently used by software engineers as a conversion space. When you want, for example, to convert an RGB bitmap to CMYK, the LAB color space is larger than both, and, as a consequence, colors are not driven out of gamut when the pixels in such a bitmap are reassigned new component values.

YIQ

The YIQ color model is similar in its components to LAB color; however, its purpose is for working with designs and text that are video-legal, as defined by the National Television Standards Committee (NTSC). YIQ's components are one channel of luminosity, and two of chromacity (color). Standard definition TV is brighter than PC monitors, the color range is smaller, and if you get an assignment to draw a logo for a commercial, you'd use this color model. HD television changes many of the broadcast rules concerning video-legal colors; check with your client before choosing YIQ as a color space for designing titles or anything for a TV assignment.

Grayscale

You'd use the Grayscale color model (which actually has no hue) if you're designing for one-color commercial printing and for laser print output. You might find that a color design you've drawn doesn't look right if printed to a laser printer: blue areas seem too faint and reds look much too dark. By using Grayscale, you take the influence of hue out of the color equation and what you see onscreen is what you get on paper.

Registration

You do not design with this color model; it's only one color. Registration is used for an object when you want that object to be printed on all commercial press plates, including spot color plates. As the name suggests, Registration applied, for example, to hairline paths around the border of a design helps a commercial press operator to see and keep all the printing plates in registration when they review progressive proofs of the plates.

The following sections bring relevance to all of these explanations of color; you want to put color to *use* in CorelDRAW, so it's only fitting to move to where the palettes and other features are *located!*

Using Color-Related Dockers

If you've been doing some independent exploring, you've certainly discovered the Uniform Fill option on the Toolbox, but you've also noticed that it doesn't dock; it is not a persistent part of the interface. The good news is that it's not *supposed* to be. Two dockers—covered next—are used to handle almost all commands that define and edit color. These are the Color docker and the Color Palette Manager docker. Let's examine these features.

Using the Color Docker

The Color docker, shown in Figure 17-3, is extremely convenient to work with and essentially, it's the Uniform Fill dialog—smaller, dockable, and persistent in the workspace. When an object is selected, you can specify whether the color applies to the outline *or* fill color of the object, and any changes to colors are immediately applied. To open the Color docker, click-hold the Fill Tool on the Toolbox to reveal the flyout group of tools—Color is at the bottom. It's also available when you choose Window | Dockers | Color. Unlike with Uniform Fill, you don't need to have an object selected to access it.

The Color docker is organized into three areas—color viewers and color sliders, the same as discussed earlier on the Uniform Fill dialog, and fixed palettes (actually, they were never broken...). You can display each area by clicking one of three buttons at the top of the docker. Each area is geared toward specifying a color using its unique parameters, and to then applying that color to the fill and/or outline of a selected object. Here's how each of the three areas is used for specifying color:

- **Color sliders** You can mix the components of any color model you choose from the drop-down selector at top by dragging the sliders or entering percentages in the number fields. Notice that the sliders are in color and change dynamically,

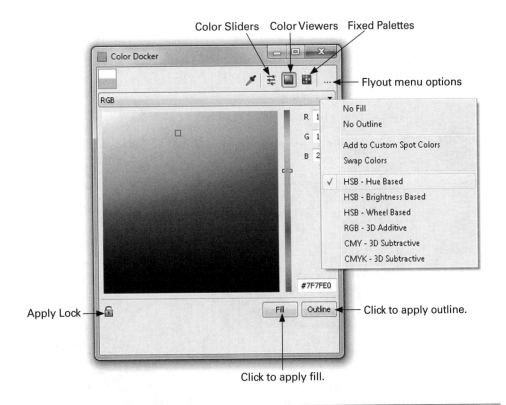

FIGURE 17-3   The Color docker is your one-stop shop for choosing by component values, by using a Color Model, and for choosing from custom predefined colors on the Palettes area.

instantly updating to show you how much of a component affects the overall color and the relationship between one component and the others.

- **Color viewers**   The color viewers (occasionally called *color pickers* in other programs) on the Color docker basically offer the same options as the color viewers on the Uniform Fill dialog; the Options button is simply located in a different place so the palette is more compact onscreen.

- **Fixed palettes**   Use this area to choose a color from a swatch collection from vendors such as Pantone, Trumatch, Focoltone, and others from the Palette selector. Use the flyout options menu to display a color by name; if you have Tooltips turned on (Tools | Options | Workspace | Display), the names of the swatches appear when you hover your cursor. The slider at the bottom of this docker is dimmed if you've loaded Uniform Colors or any user or custom palette. This slider is for creating a mathematically precise color tint of an industry-standard solid color, such as any swatches in the Pantone Fashion + Home Cotton collection. Solid colors can take tints, thus producing pastels, because the printer or a vendor of paints can mix white into this real-world, solid color according to numerical values. Therefore, you can use this tint slider with solid predefined colors, but not with process colors; *process colors* are created in the physical world through separate passes of C, M, Y, and K pigments, and as a consequence, it's impractical to tint the four components. However, CorelDRAW professionals make spot colors for designs by applying a tint to a solid. The technique works because a spot color always requires a separate printing plate.

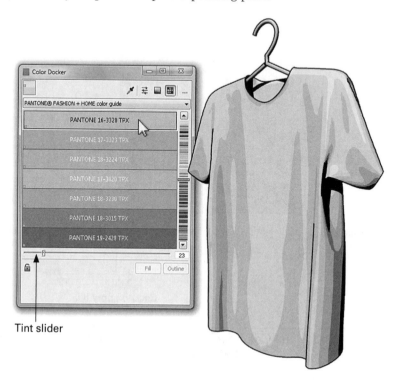

Tint slider

Solid Colors and Swatches

To set up a tint of a solid color quickly, you can click-hold a swatch, release the mouse button after the flyout appears, and then choose from 10-percent increments within the pop-up selector from solid (100%) to white (0%). You can click the tint on the flyout, and then click Fill or Outline to apply the tint. If you choose a color from any of the spot color collections, you can use the Tint slider to create a percentage of the color, because spot colors are considered to be solids, whereas process colors use a combination of pigments. In the following illustration, the Show Color Names option has been turned off by unchecking the option on the flyout menu. Doing this makes the swatches smaller, so you can preview more colors at one time.

Drag and drop swatch.   Click-hold to choose.

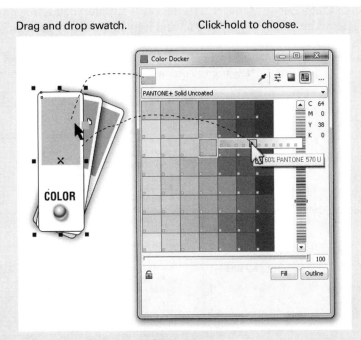

Swatches on the Color docker are "drag and drop," as is the New color in the New and Reference Colors box at top left. Alternatively, you can click the Fill, Outline, or both buttons in succession for "no miss" object coloring. You can click-drag a color onto an object, selected or unselected, to fill it instantly. If you have good skills with your mouse or other input device, you can set an outline color for an object by dragging and then dropping a color swatch on the edge of an object; even if the object has no outline attributes, the action of drag-dropping a color forces the object to take on a hairline-sized outline. If you miss the edge and the object itself while attempting to apply a color, CorelDRAW lets you know this by changing the cursor's appearance. If you release the mouse button over an empty area, this is the same action as redefining all object fill and/or outline properties, and you'll get an onscreen confirmation box about this action. You probably want to cancel such an action—you might grow bored if every new object you create is filled with Pale Avocado.

Using the Color Palette Manager Docker

The Color Palette Manager docker gives you the option to manage multiple palettes and palette colors. Sometimes you'll want to use a specific Color Palette, and this docker makes a chore into a breeze. To open the Color Palette Manager docker, choose Window |

Dockers | Color Palette Manager. The docker is structured as a tree directory so you can view palettes by folder as you browse, and it includes handy Palette command buttons.

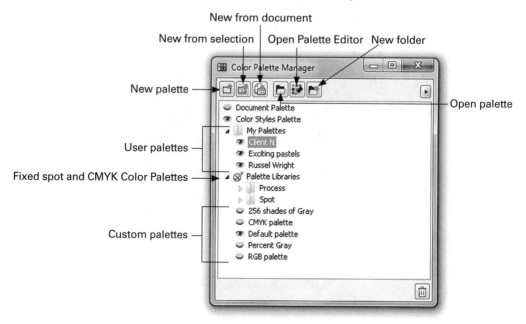

To make your own palettes and to work with this docker, which you'll use frequently, follow these example steps:

Tutorial   Accessing Color Palettes

1. Open the Color Palette Manager docker by choosing Window | Dockers | Color Palette Manager. To open a palette—which docks to the left of the default Color Palette in the workspace—click the eye icon from its closed appearance to an open eye. To close an open palette, click the eye from open to closed. You can float an open palette by dragging the top of the Color Palette strip into the workspace.
2. Create several objects (seven rectangles are fine) and then fill them with different colors using the (default) Color Palette wells. Just select an object with the Pick Tool, and then left-click a color well on the Color Palette.
3. Press CTRL + A to select all, and then click the Creates A New Palette From Selected Objects button on the top of the docker. CorelDRAW prompts you for a new palette name and a location in the Save Palette As dialog. Fill in the required information and then click Save. As a result, all seven colors now appear on a Color Palette to the left of the default in the workspace.

This is an invaluable method for saving colors you've spent a lot of time defining, and the palette can now be used on a new or existing document any time. If two objects share an identical color, the color is not duplicated on your palette.

4. To open a saved palette, click the Opens A Palette folder icon on the top of the Color Palette Manager docker.

Using the New Color Styles Docker

Corel engineers have worked on Color Styles so it integrates with the new Style Sheets features, and creating, modifying and editing not just colors, but *groups* of colors, and applying new colors to objects in a document is not only effortless, but also *fun*.

The Color Styles docker is opened by choosing Tools | Color Styles (CTRL + F6). Before the tutorials, it's a good idea to cover the layout and features on the Color Styles docker, as shown in Figure 17-4.

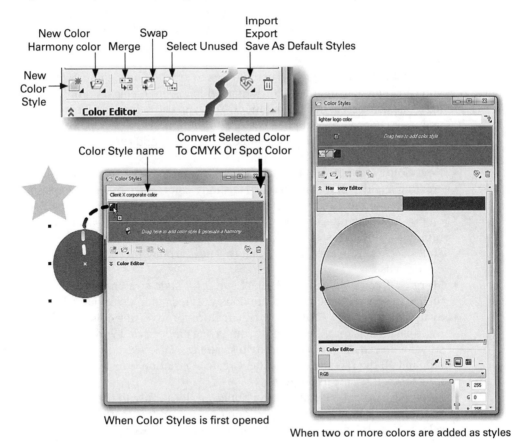

FIGURE 17-4 The Color Styles docker has commands for modifying saved colors and establishing a linked relationship between colors.

When Color Styles is first opened, there's not much to see; you need to populate the Styles and/or a Color Harmony folder before the Harmony Editor and Color Editor become visible and useful.

A *color style* can be thought of as a unique master color—equivalent to a style in a word processor: you define a style by dragging an object on the page that has a color you want to save into the Style area of the docker. Then the fun begins: you can apply this color to the fill of any object you then create, and you can also redefine the color, because it's a style and not a fixed set of color values. Here are what the options do:

- **Color Style name** Once you've added a color to the Styles list, you can type anything you like in the text field. This is a useful feature when you have two styles with similar colors. A color swatch in the top field of the Color Styles docker is considered a master color; if you select it, and then change the color in the Color Editor, every instance of this color in the current drawing changes. Fortunately, the Document Palette (covered later in this chapter) saves original colors so you aren't irrevocably ruining anything with Color Styles.
- **Convert Selected Color To CMYK Or Spot Color** This drop-down list lets you convert a selected color style in RGB color mode to printing color mode when a swatch is selected.
- **New Color Style** This drop-down offers to create a new color style (red) that you can change using the Color Editor, which is not displayed until you have at least one color style in the document. You can also select an object on the page and then choose New From Selected, and there is also a very powerful command, new for documents, which is covered a little later, and can add several styles and Harmony groups with just one click.
- **New Color Harmony** This drop-down is used to add a Harmony color while creating a folder that contains the Harmony color. Harmonies, as explained in the following section, are a relationship between two or more colors based first on hue and then on saturation. Users of previous versions of CorelDRAW will be reminded of the master/child hierarchy of color relationships in the older Color Styles docker. You'll see shortly that this new arrangement is a lot faster and easier to use.
- **Merge** If you hold SHIFT and select two color style swatches, this command moves the current color to the previously styled color, essentially deleting it.
- **Swap color styles** This is a terrific feature for inverting colors applied to multiple objects on the page. Say you have a circle styled with blue and rectangles styled with red. Shift-click these two swatches, click Swap, and the circle is now red, and all the rectangles are blue. Create a variation on a logo and school colors for a football poster in no time.
- **Selected Unused** Because color styles are local only to the current document, you might create some styles you don't need, and this feature is a quick way to select color styles not used in the document, and clicking the trash icon gets rid of them.

- **Import/Export/Save As Default Styles**   Again, color styles are set only for a single document, so if you created a fantastic combination of colors you want to use in a different document, click Export Style Sheet on the drop-down, save it with a name you'll remember, and then *make sure you check the Color Styles box* in the Export Style Sheet dialog. Importing the color styles to a new document is the reverse process of exporting, and if you want the current set of color styles to always be available in every document, choose Save As Default Styles.

Let's give this new Color Styles docker a workout in the following tutorial. You'll see how to create several different color variations of a logo to please even the fussiest client:

Tutorial   Recoloring a Logo with Color Styles

1. Open Breakfast To Go.cdr, a document containing a logo with several different colors but only a few strong hues. The objective here is to recolor the logo to a *different,* eye-pleasing color combination.
2. Choose Tools | Color Styles, and then click the New Color Style drop-down. Choose New From Document (callout 1 in Figure 17-5).
3. Make sure the Group Colors Styles Into Harmonies checkbox is checked and specify **5** groups. By doing this, you'll have control over every color aspect of the logo when you modify it. See callout 2 in Figure 17-5.
4. The wings in the logo are a linear Fountain Fill, and the gold color has its own color Harmony group (see callout 3). To dynamically modify this fountain fill, the last color in the fill needs to be in the same group. Drag the purple swatch to the right of the gold one.
   As a point of information before continuing, the Color Editor (see callout 4) will display two large colors and markers on the color wheel. When a marker is white, the color is selected and can be changed without changing other colors. When a marker is unselected, it can't be changed. If you click outside of the color wheel, all markers become active, and by dragging one around, the others change in proportion, and all colors within the Harmony are changed.
5. It's time for you to experiment! Click the top Color Harmony folder to select the gold and purple, and then in the color wheel, drag either of the selected marker handles around.
6. If and when you're feeling adventurous, click the second-from-top folder to select all the purples and blues in the logo, and then move any of the selected markers around the color wheel. Dragging toward the edge of the wheel saturates the colors, whereas dragging to the center removes color. And don't forget to experiment with the Brightness slider below the wheel. Use your artistic judgment and you'll experience a creative process illustrated in Figure 17-6.

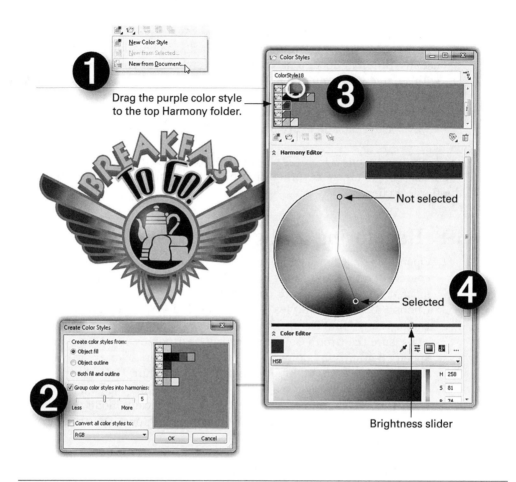

FIGURE 17-5 Create harmonies from a drawing so selective colors and color relationships can be changed.

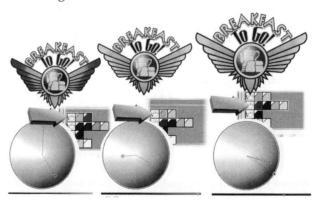

FIGURE 17-6 Modify colors as a collection, while leaving other colors alone; this is the Color Styles docker in action.

Color Gradients in Color Styles

The new Color Styles docker has done away with choosing child tints and shades of a master color. Now, to generate variations on a color, you use the Color Gradient feature in the New Color Style drop-down. The next steps cover a creative process: taking different colored boxes in an illustration and making them the same color. The first steps use the color harmonies technique explained in the previous tutorial, and then you'll conclude the assignment using the Color Gradient feature.

Tutorial # Styling a Drawing to a Unified Color Scheme

1. Open Boxes.cdr, and then press CTRL + F6 if the Color Styles docker isn't onscreen.
2. With the Pick Tool, marquee-select everything in the drawing. Then drag everything into the Drag Here To Add Color Style & Generate A Harmony area of the Color Styles docker. This is a different way to create new harmonies based on the document. The Create Color Styles dialog opens; save **4** groups, as shown here. Notice that the hues of the boxes are neatly arranged as Harmony groups.

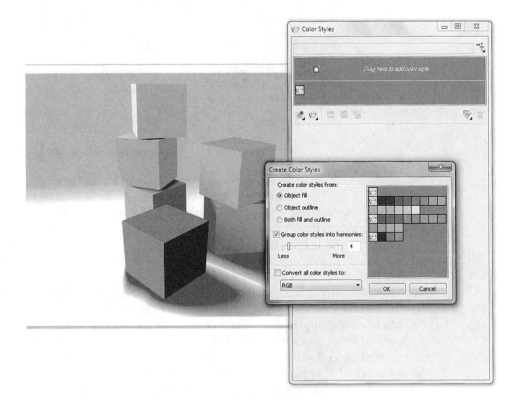

3. Click the Harmony folder to the left of all the golds and browns in the Color Harmony area of the docker. Then drag the group of markers in the color wheel to the cyan area of the wheel, and, if necessary, drag the brightness slider down a little until the gold boxes in the drawing look the same color as the turquoise ones at right.

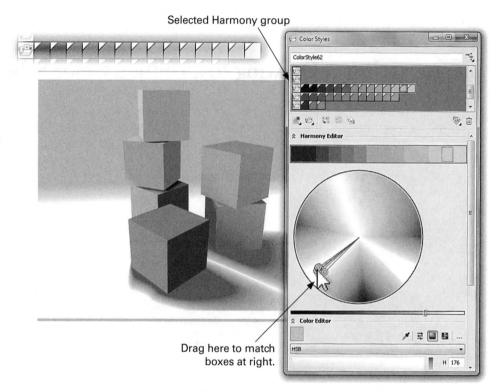

Selected Harmony group

Drag here to match boxes at right.

4. Click the last maroon swatch in the Color Harmony area, and then choose New Gradient from the New Color Harmony drop-down list. As shown in callout 1 in the following illustration, the New Gradient dialog appears, and here you can choose how many color swatches are created in the New Gradient group, whether they're all lighter, darker, or both compared to your selected swatch, and how much variation should exist between new colors. Enter **5** in the Number Of Colors box, choose Both (lighter and darker shades), and drag the Shade Similarity slider to about 26. You're only going to recolor three objects (the maroon box); if you had a more complex scene, you might want to generate several more shades. Click OK to make the entries a new gradient.

5. Select one of the maroon swatches you feel looks most like one of the faces of the maroon box in the drawing. Drag the swatch and drop it over this object, as shown in callout 2. Repeat this for the other two faces of the box. Guess what? The box is now composed of linked color styles and can be adjusted!

6. Click the Gradient group's folder on the Color Styles docker (*not* the original maroon Color Harmony group), and then drag the selected markers in the color wheel to the shade of turquoise appropriate for the drawing, marked as callouts 3 and 4 here.

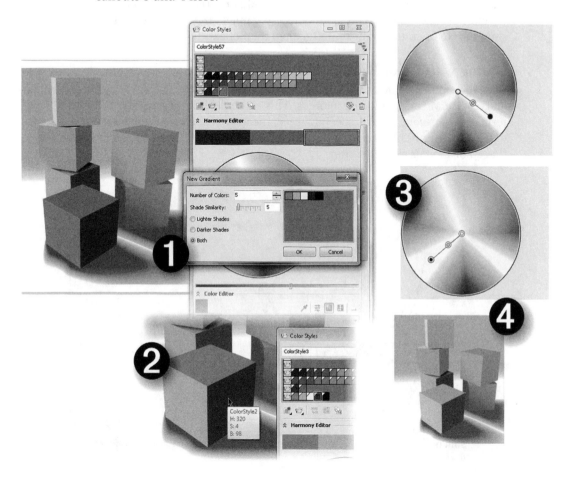

Now you know three ways to selectively recolor a drawing: by directly manipulating a color style, by adjusting a Color Harmony group, and by adjusting a Gradient group.

Moving from Color Models to Other Ways to Define Color

Although color models provide the designer with an intuitive device for picking colors, CorelDRAW offers alternative methods, in the form of the Color Mixer and Color Palettes—an extensive collection of swatches that simulate real-world ink, paint, and plastic colors on your monitor to match the colors manufacturers use from Pantone and other vendors. The following sections explore how to "mix it up" with the other tabs on the Uniform Fill dialog.

Using Color Mixers

Color Mixers provide ways to create as many coordinated colors as you need automatically. Any time you find yourself choosing a color in CorelDRAW's Color dialog, you have access to the Color Mixers. Mixers create colors using "color harmonies" and Color Blend tools. Select any object in your document and press SHIFT + F11 to open the Uniform Fill dialog; then click the Mixers tab.

Mixing with Color Harmonies

Click the Options button at the bottom of the Mixers tab dialog, shown in this illustration, and choose Mixers | Color Harmonies. This is the default mixing type for Mixers. The term *color harmony,* in this specific usage, means equal space is devoted to each color of the spectrum. Think of color harmonies as related to *organization* in the same way that color models show *structure.*

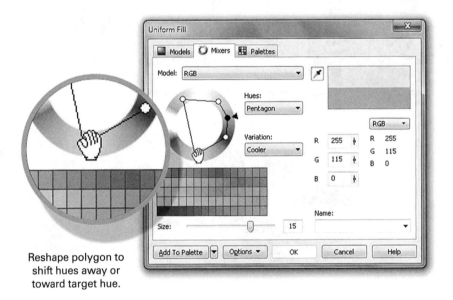

Reshape polygon to shift hues away or toward target hue.

The Color Harmonies mixer features a color wheel and control handles you drag to choose which Hue you want to make variations from and which other hues, if any, should be used to create variations. Remember, however, that the mixer is only a mixer; it does *not* generate a "Oh, these colors all work together well in a drawing" Color Palette.

Use the Model drop-down selector to choose a color model on which to base a collection of color variations you can save. Choose one of the configurations from the Hues drop-down list, and then click-drag to rotate the color wheel markers to alter the collection of swatches displayed at bottom left. Choose from Primary, Complementary, Triangle (1 and 2), Rectangle, or Pentagon hues to create color markers that move as you change the primary Hue marker around the color wheel; the related color markers range from a single point to five points. Use the Variation drop-down selector to choose among Cooler, Warmer, Lighter, Darker, and Less Saturated "children" of the target color you've defined on the color wheel. If you want a preference in your mix of a certain hue—and you've chosen a Triangle, Rectangle, or the Pentagon for the Hue variation—you can favor certain hues over others around the wheel. First choose the hue—drag the black triangle to your choice, and then drag any of the white circle color makers toward or away from their current location, distorting the polygon.

Here is a set of steps you can use to gain experience with the features of the Color Mixer's Color Harmonies mode.

Tutorial Experimenting with Color Harmonies

1. You might not want to mess up the default Color Palette in your workspace, so before exploring Mixers, create a new palette; click the menu options button on the default palette, as shown in this illustration, and then choose Palette | New. When prompted for a new palette name, name it "Test" or anything you'll remember later. A new blank palette appears to the left of the default Color Palette at the edge of the drawing window.

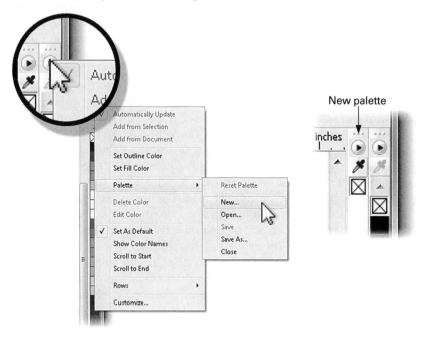

2. With an object selected on the page, open the Uniform Fill dialog (SHIFT + F11), click the Mixers tab, and choose Options | Mixers | Color Harmonies. Choose a color model from the Model drop-down menu.

3. Choose a Hue type—Rectangle is good for these steps. A four-pointed rectangle shape appears around the color wheel. Click-drag the black marker to change hue, and click-drag the white markers to reshape the rectangle; triangles and other multipoint harmonies can be reshaped, too. The result of making the rectangle wide and short is that the range of complementary colors to red (the selected color) becomes narrow; yellows, greens, and violets are eliminated from the Mixer swatches, in preference for cyans and blues.

4. Choose a Variation type to change the swatch collection below the color model, based on the color marker positions on the model. If you choose None from the Variation drop-down list, only one color per marker appears in the collection, and the Size slider is dimmed. In the case of the Rectangle harmony, four markers appear.

5. Choose a Variation other than None, and then choose a Size for your collection using the Size slider control. Choose up to 20 different variation colors per marker.

6. Work on this color collection using different Harmonies and Variations until you arrive at something you think you'll use in the future.

7. To save the collection now to the palette you created in Step 1, click the first color well (the color swatch), and then SHIFT-click the last color well to select them all. Alternatively, if you have some colors you feel are useless, CTRL-click only the valuable color wells. Highlighted color wells take on a bevel-edge highlight.

8. With your colors selected, click the down arrow to the right of the Add To Palette button, and then choose either the Document Palette—choose this one for this example—or a Color Styles Palette. You're not done yet; you've only chosen the palette's destination. Click the Add To Palette button, and your collection of colors is saved to the Document Palette.

9. To save the palette for keeps and not just to this document, click the arrow button at the upper left of the palette, and then choose Palette | Save As, and then save the palette as an XML document. It will become immediately available to display on the Window | Color Palettes list.

10. At any time, you can add a color directly to the custom palette by dragging a filled object into the saved palette, whether it is docked or not. Doing this saves the color of the outline as well as the fill color. You can also rearrange the order of colors by dragging from one position on the palette and then releasing the swatch when it's over its desired position.

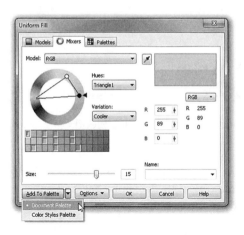

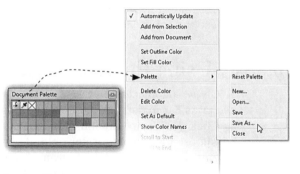

Drag a filled object over the palette to add its color.

Save selected color wells (swatches)
to the Document Palette.

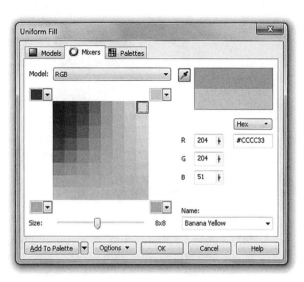

Mixing with Color Blend

The Color Blend Mixer (shown here) is the other mode of the Mixer module, where you define colors almost literally by mixing them, very much like when you create a multistage Fountain Fill. You can choose four different colors and then generate

a collection of up to 1,024 unique values, and then choose the ones you like to create your own Color Palette. All these color options are easier to sort mentally by task: when you want a specific color, you use the Models module. When you want a palette of colors based around your tastes, you use the Mixer module.

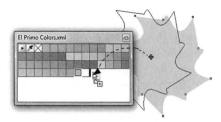

To access the Color Blend feature from within the main Uniform Fill dialog while you're on the Mixers tab, choose Options | Mixers | Color Blend.

Here's how to work the Color Blend feature to create a small collection and then to choose the colors you want to save as a palette.

Tutorial ## Using the Color Blend Mixer

1. Create an object, select it, and then double-click the Fill Color button on the Status Bar to open the Uniform Fill dialog.
2. Click the Mixers tab and then choose Options | Mixers | Color Blend.
3. Choose four colors for your blend by clicking each of the four color selectors in view and choosing a color from the palette displayed. You do not need to blend from four colors: you can choose the same color from two or more of the flyout palettes to hone in on a range of colors, making your decisions easier. Each time a selector is changed, the color field changes, as do the available colors from which to choose.
4. Choose a size for your collection using the Size slider control.
5. Save some of the more useful colors to a palette; let's use the palette you saved in the previous tutorial. Remember that if you've got some eye-pleasing colors in the collection, you don't *have* to save a huge, all-inclusive collection; you can create shades of your favorite colors by click-holding a Color Palette swatch so the color well flyout provides a variation. CTRL-click the color wells in the collection to select only, let's say, your favorite colors. See the following illustration.

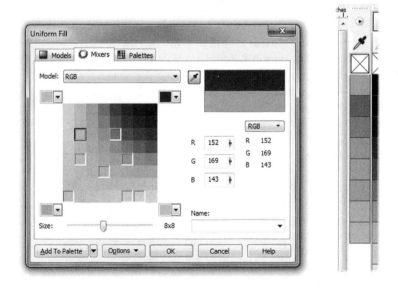

6. Choose a palette from the drop-down list, and then click the Add To Palette button. Your color blend collection is saved.

Using Fixed and Custom Palettes

A *fixed* palette is a collection of ink colors prepared by an ink manufacturer, such as a specific process or spot color. Because these color specialists have spent a good deal of time preparing combinations of inks and other pigments to match as closely as possible between your monitor's display and how the colors look on real-world packaging and other goods, you can't edit these colors as you can with Color Model colors and Mixers. However, if you choose a collection made up of one solid-ink color (not a process color) such as Pantone Solid Uncoated, you can specify a tint of this solid color (the Tint slider is below the color samples); the professional mixing the color for you simply adds white pigment. Fixed palettes are like small color catalogs. Manufacturers such as Pantone, Trumatch, and Focoltone have supplied color simulations for CorelDRAW users; you might use only one color collection, but you have a wide variety from which to choose, and these simulations are as faithful in the "What You See Is What Will Print" arena as technology can bring you today.

Using Fixed Palettes

Some of the palettes are for use in commercial print—they provide simulations for metallic inks and inks that will be printed to coated or uncoated stock (in English: glossy and matte finishes). Other palettes you'll find in this area of Uniform Fills are geared for the Web and not for print. The World Wide Web has color specifications, too. Using a specific Color Palette usually ensures that colors you use in a design fall within the capabilities of the reproduction or display technique used to show off your work.

To apply process color values (CMYK, usually, although Pantone Hexachrome fixed-palette inks use six values) to your work, the very first thing you do is talk with the commercial press operator. They might want to use substitution values (less expensive inks), or they might not even own the physical equipment to reproduce Hexachrome. You always work backward when your final output is print—you find out what can be reproduced on what budget, and then you choose your colors. Here's a short tutorial on how to specify a color from the Palettes list. Let's suppose you have a job that requires the use of a spot color. Here's how to proceed...

Tutorial   Choosing Predefined Colors for Print

1. With an object selected on the page, in the Uniform Fill dialog (press SHIFT + F11), click the Palettes tab.
2. Choose a palette from the Palette drop-down menu. Colors appear in the main selector window, and you can pick swatches by clicking them; their names appear in the Name list at bottom right. You can more quickly thumb through colors by choosing Options | Show Color Names; the selector window changes from swatches to larger color samples with the name in the center of the color. The vertical selector to the right of the selector window lets you navigate through the available colors *very* quickly.

Tip If your client has given you, for example, a Pantone number to use in a design, you can get to that value pronto by starting to type the color number in the Name field. CorelDRAW narrows down your selection as you continue to type. *Make sure, however, that you're choosing from the right catalog!* You don't want to use, for example, a process uncoated collection when the color you need is in the process *coated* collection.

3. Click the color you need.
4. If you've chosen a process color collection, the Tint slider is unavailable. However, if you've picked a Metallic, Pastel, or other *solid* color collection, choose a percentage value for your color using the Tint option. By default, tints of selected colors are set to 100 percent of the ink, but you can specify any value between 0 and 100 percent. However, choosing 0 for a Tint just changes the chosen color to white; printing white on white paper probably won't earn you big bucks with your client!
5. Click OK to apply the palette color or a tinted value of the color.

Information about the Palettes You Can Use for Printing Assignments

Here's a quick rundown on each of the commercial palettes you can choose in the Palettes tab of the Uniform Fill dialog:

- **SVG Colors** This collection was designed to address the need for standardized colors for Scalable Vector Graphics (SVG), an emerging technology that allows designers to post vector images as vector images (and not bitmaps) on web pages. These colors were agreed upon by the W3 Consortium.

Tip For a chart featuring user-friendly names for SVG colors, visit http://www.w3c.org/TR/SVG11/types.html#ColorKeywords

- **Pantone** Pantone dominates the publishing industry with its color-matching system. CorelDRAW X6 provides all of Pantone's color-matching simulations including coated, uncoated, and matte color versions for solids, as well as process and Hexachrome colors. CorelDRAW X6 also features Pantone's Metallic, Pastel, Solid-to-Process EURO, and Process-coated EURO palettes.
- **HKS (Hostmann, Kast, and Schmincke)** This palette collection uses CMY components that occasionally (depending on the color) don't require a black plate. The HKS collections use a Euroscale color space, ISO 12647:2 2002, the FOGRA standard. If you're a Westerner, you probably won't use this color collection. HKS palettes include HKS Colors, HKS E, HKS Z, HKS N, and HKS K.
- **Focoltone** This 750-color palette was designed from the ground up to be ICC-compliant. If your commercial printer supports Focoltone (an abbreviation for "Four-color tone"), if your client is insistent on color consistency between printed material and packaging, and if you, the designer, need some flexibility in choosing colors and tints, you might want to try this collection.

- **Trumatch**   The Trumatch process-color palette is made up of more than 2,000 printable colors. Trumatch has specifically customized its color-matching system to suit the digital color industry using the Computer Electronic Prepress System (CEPS). The palette has 40 tints and shades of each hue. Black is varied in 6-percent increments.
- **Web Safe**   The Web Safe Palette contains the 216 colors of the Web Safe color model. Colors are defined using the hexadecimal scheme; one of six shades of each color (red, green, and blue) is combined together to create each color in the palette.
- **DIC**   The DIC color-matching systems are widely used throughout Asia—Japan, in particular. Each system contains its own numbering system and collection of different process colors. The TOYO collection of colors has been developed using its own process ink colors, and as of 2008 is now a part of the DIC Corporation's colors. The DIC (Dainippon Ink and Chemicals, Inc.) brand of process color inks is divided into three categories: DIC, DIC Traditional, and DIC Part II.

Loading and Creating Custom Palettes

Through dialogs, the Color docker, or an open Color Palette, you can manage your color collections. The fastest way is to click the flyout arrow on a Color Palette and then choose Palette | Open from the pop-up menu. This displays the Open Palette dialog, where you can browse what's available. The pop-up menu also includes Save, Save As, Close, and New Palette commands.

The Palette Editor, shown here, is the ideal place to rework custom palettes. In this dialog you can create, save, edit, and manage new and existing palettes using convenient command buttons. While editing palette colors, you can also access CorelDraw's other color features.

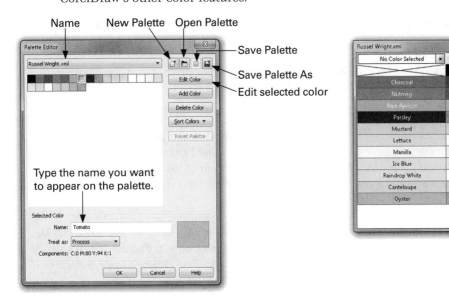

Refining and redefining your palettes is easy, fun, and often necessary to keep palettes for client colors up-to-date. Try these steps to appreciate the ease of this powerful dialog.

Tutorial   Editing Color Palettes

1. Open the Palette Editor; choose Tools | Palette Editor, or simply double-click a swatch on an open Color Palette to display the Editor.
2. To edit an existing palette color, click a color and then click Edit Color. The Select Color dialog opens to offer color models, Color Mixers, and Color Palettes, exactly like the Uniform Fill dialog.
3. To begin a new palette, click the New Palette button in the Palette Editor dialog to open the New Palette dialog. Enter a name and then click Save. Your new palette is automatically opened, but there are no colors yet.
4. To add colors, click Add Color, which takes you to the Select Color dialog. Define your new color—with the Mixer module, you can choose a whole color range in one fell swoop—then click the Add To Palette button. New colors are immediately added to your new palette.
5. Once your colors have been added, click Close to return to the Palette Editor dialog. In the Name box, here's where you get to name a new color. When you use the edited Color Palette, the color name appears on the Status Bar and in Tooltips pop-ups instead of the component values.
6. To remove a selected color, click Delete Color and confirm your action in the prompt that appears. To reorganize your palette colors, click Sort Colors and choose from Reverse Order, By Name, or By Hue, Brightness, Saturation, RGB Value, or HSB Value. You can also click-drag a color well (color swatch) to reorder swatches as they appear on the Color Palette.
7. To name or rename an existing color, select the color in the palette, highlight its current name in the Name box, and then enter a new name. Existing names are automatically overwritten once a new color is selected.
8. Use the Reset Palette button to restore your palette to its original state before any changes were made, or click OK to accept your changes and close the dialog.

There's one more way to make and save a user-defined palette: if you like the color of objects you have on the page, choose Window | Color Palettes | Create Palette From Selection (if you have objects selected in advance), or Create Palette From Document. This opens the Save Palette dialog, where you can name and save the colors you've used as a unique palette.

Tip You can quickly copy color properties between two objects (including groups) by right-click-dragging an object on top of a different object. Release the mouse button once the source object is in position, and then choose Copy Fill Here, or Copy Outline Here.

Color and Color Correction

Without defining a master color, creating relationships between parent and child colors, and without getting elaborate, there is another way to change colors in a CorelDRAW design. The Effects | Adjust menu has color and tone (brightness) corrections you can apply to an object—vector or bitmap—so you can modify all or parts of a design, and thus create variations on copies of your work. These changes are permanent; you should only use the commands on copies of your illustrations or have the Windows | Dockers | Undo docker handy in the workspace. These effects are mutually exclusive of one another, and depending on the color solution you seek, you might need to apply one and then a different one.

 Note Be sure every time you use the Effects commands to click Reset. All command palettes remember your last used settings.

- **Brightness/Contrast/Intensity**   This command displays a palette where you can compress or expand the range of tones between the lightest and darkest (Contrast), add or subtract illumination from the selected object (Brightness), and use Intensity as an inverse operator to Brightness to make an object's colors more pronounced—decrease brightness and then increase Intensity to see a working example of Intensity.
- **Color Balance**   Cyan is the additive color opposite of red, magenta is the opposite of green, and yellow is the color opposite of blue. Use this command palette to remove color casting in your selection in the three different tone areas. For example, suppose an image has several deep reds toward the top. You want to cool down only the deep reds, but not the medium reds. You put a check in the Shadows Range box, and then drag the Cyan-Red slider toward Cyan. Preserve Luminosity is an option when you want to shift the color in the selected object without changing its brightness. Color is linked to brightness, as you'll observe when using the HSV color model; when you change hue, you frequently also change brightness.
- **Gamma**   In video electronics, there is a "sag" (a nonlinearity) when plotting signal to brightness; it's a physical drop-off that visually affects the midtones in images and designs you work with. The relationship between brightness and signal is called *gamma*, and the practical (nontechnical) purpose for gamma adjustment is to open up or block midtones in a selected graphic or photo without impacting the lightest and darkest points in the brightnesses. Drag the Gamma slider to the right to increase the range of midtones, and drag it left to compress the midtone range.
- **Hue/Saturation/Lightness**   Use this command palette to shift certain hues to different ones, increase or decrease the richness of hues, and to increase or decrease the amount of white in the selection.
  When using any of the above commands, there is a pop-up menu that offers the other Effects menu items. If you've selected a bitmap, you can use any and all of the commands, but if you have a vector object selected, most commands are unavailable, except two.

- **Invert** This is a one-pop command with no options or command palette. It chromatically reverses color and tone areas. For example, deep red areas become light cyan.
- **Posterize** This command has one slider marked Levels. From a minimum of 2 to a maximum of 32, this effect moves all the colors in the selected object to a small, fixed range of colors. Although its use is perhaps best with photographs you want to make look like a rubber stamp art or a silk-screened poster, objects with Fountain Fills and Full Color Pattern Fills can take on an interesting look, too.

To get you comfortable with adjusting colors in a composition using the Effects menu, instead of using PHOTO-PAINT, let's try manifesting a minor miracle in CorelDRAW, using only a few steps. In a new document, import Hermes.jpg—an example of some elaborate jewelry the client's unhappy with. What else is new? He doesn't want any red in the photo, but wants to keep the gold hues. This is a job for Effects | Adjust | Hue/Saturation/Lightness, because you want to alter one predominant hue selectively, as follows:

Tutorial Changing Colors with Effects

1. Duplicate the image first and then move it to one side so you can compare your results with the original.
2. Choose Windows | Docker | Undo, so you can undo any effect at any time.
3. With the copy selected, choose Effects | Adjust | Hue/Saturation/Lightness.
4. Click Reset, as a matter of practice, to clear any previous settings. Click the Red button because you want to modify only the reds in the photo.
5. Drag the Hue slider to about 153 to the right. When you have the yellow hues in the After preview strip aligned with the red hues in the Before preview, click Preview.
6. Depending on the accuracy of your monitor, you might want to decrease the Saturation now to –22. Click Preview.
7. Drag the Lightness slider to –3, click Preview, and then try 0 again just to get a feel for lightening only one hue in a bitmap. Compare the graphic to its duplicate. For this example, let's consider the job well done, it's a startling transformation as you can sort of see in Figure 17-7. Click OK to Apply the filter.
8. The phone rings, it's the client, and they decide they like the original. On the Undo docker, click Duplicate to send the original back in steps to before you applied any adjustments. Sure, you could delete the original and use the duplicate, but then you wouldn't have learned how to use the Undo docker to save time! Charge the client extra for the time they don't know you saved on revisions.

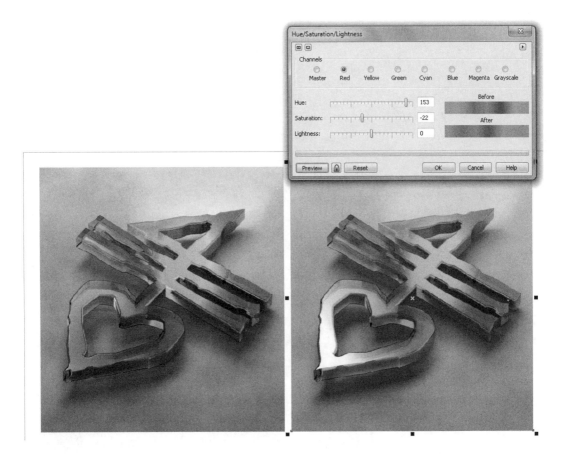

FIGURE 17-7   Change the colors of grouped objects selectively with the Effects | Adjust commands.

You've seen in this chapter that color is important; color sets a mood for an illustration, and the artistic use of color can actually remedy an illustration that lacks visual interest or complexity. And you now know how to define and save not only a color you need, but also an entire palette. This concludes the section on colors and fills; from here we travel to the land of very special effects—take what you've learned, take what you've drawn, and bend it, distort it, and, in general, make it a unique piece by learning how to sculpt vector shapes.

PART VI

Creating the Illusion of 3D Objects

18

Working with Perspective

The property of visual perspective was perhaps first expressed by Leon Battista Alberti, 15th-century architect, and later by Leonardo DaVinci. This artistic illusion is created in technical drawings to give an accurate sense of depth to 2D (two-dimensional) pieces. Perspective in drawings can be calculated today by CorelDRAW and other applications, and this chapter takes you through a definition of perspective, how to use CorelDRAW's Perspective effect, and how to feature the artistic quality of perspective in your work to produce lifelike illustrations. If you want your audience to be drawn *into* your work and not simply to stare at it, consider adding some perspective...so your *audience* will see it, too!

 Download and extract all the files from the Chapter18.zip archive to follow the tutorials in this chapter.

The Optical Principle of Perspective

We've all seen examples of *perspective;* for example, you make sure a train isn't coming, and then you stand on the tracks and look into the horizon. Apparently, the train tracks converge at the horizon. Naturally, the tracks don't *actually* converge, or it would be difficult to put a train on them. This is an optical illusion that demonstrates the very real optics of the human eye. Any object that has parallel sides (a milk carton, most tables) when viewed at an angle other than face-forward will look as though its parallel sides converge at a point somewhere in the distance. This point, whether you can see it on train tracks or imagine it by mentally extending the parallel lines, is called the *vanishing point,* and CorelDRAW's Perspective effect offers an onscreen marker for moving a shape's vanishing point when Effects | Add Perspective has been applied to an object or group of objects.

Depending on the angle at which you view an object—to use a cube as an example—you can see one, two, or three sides of the cube. When you draw a cube, face front, in CorelDRAW, you've drawn a square; there is no perspective, and it's not a very interesting. If you can see two faces of the cube, you're viewing from a perspective point; the object is said to have *one-point perspective.* Naturally, you can't see more than three sides of a cube at one time, but when you do see all three front-facing sides, this is called *two-point perspective.* It's visually intriguing to pose an object (or draw one) using two-point perspective; CorelDRAW helps you set up an object for two-point as well as one-point perspective.

What Is Normal?

Before getting into the wildly distorted perspectives you have available in CorelDRAW, let's understand what the human eye normally sees with respect to perspective. In your design work, you want to be able to draw an object in "normal" perspective. Learn how to do this, and you can increase and exaggerate perspective quite easily.

It's simple to calibrate and measure a camera lens. However, the *human eye* is in constant motion, and there's a brain behind the eyes that interprets and occasionally *mis*interprets the optical signals it receives. Three things primarily account for perspective when using your eye or your eye through a lens:

- **Distance of lens from subject**   When you copy a perspective setting to a new object in CorelDRAW, depending on the perspective, the object might grow or shrink in dimensions. Not to fret; this is covered later in this chapter—perspective *changes* the apparent distance of objects. Because you're drawing on a flat plane in a CorelDRAW document, the program scales objects according to their perspective to simulate depth in a composition.
- **Field of view**   There is no field of view setting in CorelDRAW's Perspective effect, but in the real world, this property affects how distorted an object looks and is related to focal length. Humans have anywhere from 140° to 180° field of view, but much of this is peripheral vision, not truly in focus, and the consensus is that we usually use about 40° normal field of view. To distort objects to simulate field of view, see Chapter 22 on Lens effects.
- **Focal length**   Focal length is the distance between a lens and the imaging surface, proportional to field of view. As one changes, so does the other. This property is the most responsible for the distorted or undistorted appearance of objects. It's generally conceded that humans have a focal length of 50–55mm. As this relates to CorelDRAW, to simulate short focal lengths (such as a fish-eye lens on a camera), the vanishing points for the Perspective effect are quite close to the object. As focal length increases, a telescopic effect is achieved, and the perspective of an object is lessened. For example, if you wanted to simulate a 500mm telescopic camera lens in CorelDRAW, the vanishing points for the perspective on the object would be clear off the page, probably in the parking lot somewhere.

This illustration of a child's toy block was rendered to a fairly accurate representation of what a normal human eye would see from a two-point perspective. The focal length is 50mm and the field of view is about 40°. The lines you see along the parallels of the block indicate the direction of the vanishing points: a normal lens on the child's block puts the vanishing points off this page.

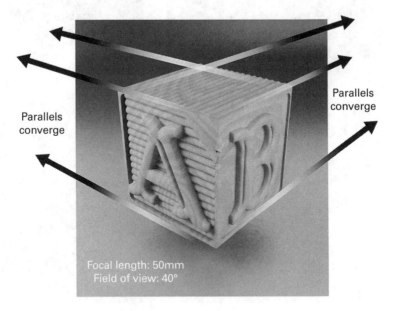

Parallels converge

Parallels converge

Focal length: 50mm
Field of view: 40°

Getting a Perspective on Perspective

Now that you understand what a "normal" lens does to perspective, let's take a look at a few abnormal (but artistic and creative) perspectives, beginning with no perspective and working our way up. In Figure 18-1, you can see at left an *isometric* view (also called an *orthographic* view) of the kid's block; regardless of the term, it's unrealistic because the parallels of the cube do not converge. Isometric views of objects are quickly accomplished in CorelDRAW by putting an object into Rotate/Skew mode (clicking once and then a second time), and then skewing the object by click-dragging a middle control handle. Isometric views are completely the province of computer graphics and geometry. They don't exist in the real world with human eyes, but they are useful in illustration to put equal emphasis on all visible sides of an object. For example, if you want your client to read the side panel of a proposed cereal box design but want the box posed to show more than one side, you'd use an isometric view (occasionally called *isometric perspective*). At right, you can see the same kid's block using a wide-angle perspective. In CorelDRAW, such an illustration is accomplished by putting the vanishing points outside of the drawing page. It's exaggerated mostly because the human eye does not have a field of view as large as 76°, that is, the view is not entirely in focus.

The following illustration goes way over the top; the vanishing points are quite close to the object, and the result is very dramatic, unrealistic, and unsuitable for presenting a product design. As you read through this chapter, you'll learn that there

Planes do not converge
on a vanishing point.

Planes eventually
converge in distance.

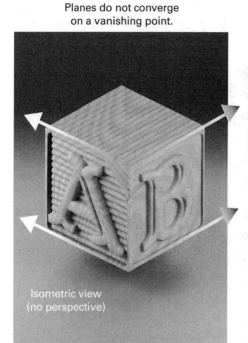
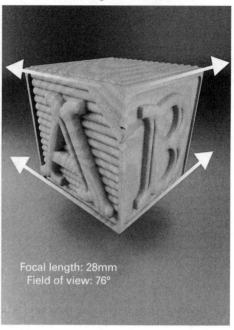

Isometric view
(no perspective)

Focal length: 28mm
Field of view: 76°

FIGURE 18-1 Examples of isometric views and a fairly wide-angle view of the same object.

are some occasions when you want a vanishing point on the drawing page and other occasions when you want perspective of the "normal" human-eye type.

Two-point perspective
Vanishing point

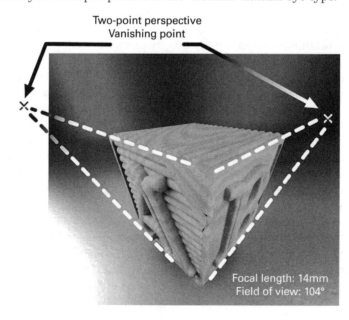

Focal length: 14mm
Field of view: 104°

Experiments in Perspective

It's a lot more fun and rewarding to experiment with the Perspective effect than it is to read about it. The operations are fairly simple and straightforward, and you'll probably get ideas for future illustrations just by playing with it! Single objects and object groups can be put in perspective; you can change the angle of a perspective shape (or group) by click-dragging any of the four control corners or by click-dragging the vanishing point(s), which changes two of the four control corners at once. Let's begin with a simple perspective, performed on an object that will immediately, visually give you a reference for what's going on: a 12 × 12-cell graph paper object. The Perspective effect displays subdivisions in red dotted lines on top of the object you're manipulating, which provides good visual feedback; with a graph paper object, you'll see exactly how the grid corresponds to the visual changes in the graph paper cells.

Tutorial   Creating One-Point Perspective

1. Press D, the keyboard shortcut for the Graph Paper Tool. On the Property Bar, set the number of columns to 12 and the number of rows to 12.
2. Hold CTRL while you click-drag to constrain the graph paper object to a square. Make the object fairly large, about 7" is good. Because the Perspective effect can appreciably shrink one or more sides of an object, it's a good design practice to create objects that are a little exaggerated in size.
3. Click a deep red swatch on the Color Palette to set the fill for all the cells, and then right-click over a pale yellow to set the outline color.
4. Choose Effects | Add Perspective, as shown here. Your object now has control handles around it, and your current tool has changed to the Shape Tool. The Shape Tool is used during Perspective creation. Additionally, if you intend to edit a Perspective effect while you're working on a different area of a design, all you need to do is choose the Shape Tool and then click an object that's in perspective.

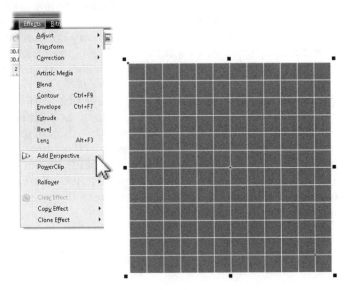

5. Click the top-right handle of the Perspective Effect box surrounding the Graph Paper object. Hold CTRL to constrain the movement of your cursor to the first direction in which you drag, and then drag down to about the second or third cell in the right column, as shown here. You've created a Perspective effect on the object, as you can see the cells align more or less with the effect's red-dotted overlay reference, and a vanishing point appears directly to the right.

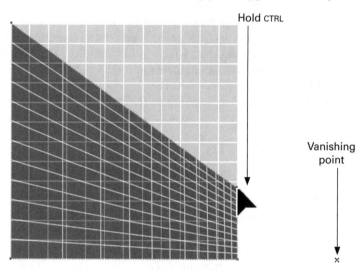

Hold CTRL

Vanishing point

6. Click-drag the vanishing point up and then down as long as this is an experiment and not playing for points. Notice what happens: you've defined one-point perspective—this is the right side of a hypothetical cube, and one-point perspectives have only one vanishing point. So the left side of the object is anchored; it doesn't change with the perspective change.

7. Click-drag the vanishing point left and right. The left side is still anchored, and what you're doing is making the hypothetical box's right side deeper and shallower, extending to and from an imaginary horizon on the page.

8. Save this document; you'll work with it in a moment, so don't close it. This is only the beginning of the experiment with suggesting depth in a 2D document!

There has to be a practical use for what you've just learned; adding one-point perspective to a graph paper object by itself is about as exciting as watching grass grow. In the following illustration, you can see the result of grouping some text with the graph paper object before applying the Perspective effect. It's a simple drawing and it certainly could use some embellishment, but the point here is that one-point perspective can establish a *ground plane* for a dimensional composition—a ground has been suggested in this illustration by the effect, the "scene" has depth, and the illustrator obviously can't read signs.

Working with Two-Point Perspective

Any 2D drawing can be made by the Perspective effect to look as though it extends into space, as you proved in the previous tutorial. However, it's time to up the stakes and create a *second* vanishing point. This second point will make this graph paper object look as though it occupies space, suggesting visually that the grid recedes away from the page, and that its depth is traveling in a direction. This tutorial is going to be fun; by the end of the following steps, you'll have created a great high-tech, sci-fi background you can use in several design situations.

Tutorial   Creating a 3D Ground Plane

1. With the graph-paper document you saved in the previous tutorial open, choose the Shape Tool and then click the object to reveal its Perspective effect control handles and the vanishing point you defined.

2. Click-drag the top-right control handle up and toward the center of the object, until you see a second vanishing point marker at about 12 o'clock on the page. You might want to zoom out to better see the second vanishing point because it is initially defined quite far away from the object. Use your mouse scroll wheel to zoom whenever you have a drawing or editing tool chosen; scrolling toward you zooms the window view out, and scrolling away from you zooms it in. Here, you can see how the graph paper object should look now. Notice also that because this two-point perspective is so extreme, the graph-paper outlines are actually curved to accommodate the severely distorted perspective. This is not an optical illusion (the lines are indeed curved now), but it does mimic the human eye's perception of parallel lines viewed at exceptionally wide angles.

3. Choose the Pick Tool, and with the graph paper object selected, click it to put it into Skew/Rotate transformation mode. Rotate the object about 45° counterclockwise—stop click-dragging when the Property Bar reports that you've rotated the object by about this amount. It would be difficult to change the orientation of the object by only changing the vanishing points' positions.

4. Choose the Rectangle Tool and then click-drag a rectangle to cover the graph paper object.

5. Choose the Fill Tool, and then click-drag from top to bottom on the object so the top is black, fading to white at the rectangle's bottom. Then choose a green from the Color Palette to fill the start color indicator of the fountain fill.

6. Choose the rectangle with the Pick Tool, and then press SHIFT + PAGE DOWN to put the rectangle on the back of the drawing page, behind the graph paper object.

7. Choose the graph paper object, and then right-click the white color well on the Color Palette. Then double-click the Outline Pen swatch on the Status Bar to open the Outline Pen dialog.

8. Left-click the No Fill swatch now while the graph paper object is selected to remove the fill.

9. Type **4** in the Width field, and then click OK to apply this width. You're done and your composition looks like the illustration here.

Vanishing point

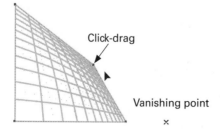

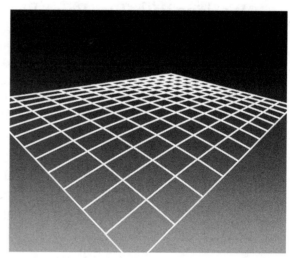

Vanishing point

Tip The outline properties of an object possessing the Perspective effect do not diminish in width along with the shape of the object. If you need outlines to follow a perspective, you need to first convert the outlines to objects: press CTRL+U, for example, to ungroup a graph paper object, and then choose Arrange | Convert Outline to Object (CTRL+SHIFT+Q).

Copying Perspective and Creating a 3D Scene

Like many of the features in CorelDRAW, a perspective can be copied from an object and applied to a different object using the options on the Property Bar. Being able to instantly copy and match perspective between objects in a composition can turn the entire drawing into a 3D event, as the following tutorial guides you through.

The commuter characters will make a nice part of a composition as you'll angle them using the Perspective effect in the steps to follow, but you can use an illustration of your own if you prefer. The idea is that these fellows are so self-absorbed they're going to miss the train pulling in behind them unless they look to the right a little. So you'll apply a perspective to one guy, copy the instance of the Perspective effect to the rest of the gang, and then embellish the composition a little to give the drawing true depth.

Tutorial Perspective Scenes via Copying

1. Open Commuters.cdr. Select the left guy on the page, and then choose Effects | Add Perspective.
2. Click the top-right control handle on the object, and then drag a little down. Then click-drag the bottom-right control handle, and drag up and to the right until the commuter is facing right in perspective, as shown in Figure 18-2. You will not see the vanishing points on the page because this perspective is not dramatic or severely distorted.
3. You can keep using the current tool, the Shape Tool; click the guy with his hat in his hand. Then choose Effects | Copy Effect | Perspective From. Click over the guy at left that has the perspective shown here, and the second object adopts the perspective of the first.

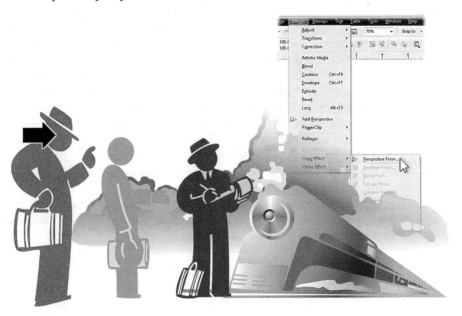

FIGURE 18-2 Create just enough perspective to give the shape some dimension.

4. Repeat Step 3 for the guy holding the writing pad.
5. Create a graph paper object, and then give it a deep red fill and a white outline. Put it to the back of the illustration.
6. Put the graph paper in perspective to make a ground plane. Next, drag the top-left control handle to the right, and then drag the top-right control handle to the left until you see a vanishing point just above the graph paper object. This object's perspective should be very distorted, suggesting a horizon at about the chest level of the characters.
7. Create a second graph paper object, and then choose Arrange | Ungroup, and then Arrange | Combine so the graph paper object is truly a single path.
8. Give it a medium to light blue fountain fill, and give its outline a white property exactly like you did with the first object in Step 5. Put it to the back of the drawing (SHIFT + PAGE DOWN).
9. Here are the simple steps to "grounding" the characters on the graph paper below them: click any of the fellows, and then choose the Drop Shadow Tool from the Effects group of tools on the Toolbox.
10. Choose Perspective Top Left from the Presets drop-down on the Property Bar. With your cursor, click-drag the black control marker for the shadow down and to the right until the shadow looks correct.

11. Repeat Step 9 with the two other commuters, select a guy, and then choose Effects | Copy Effect | Drop Shadow From, and click the first shadow (not the object casting the shadow) you defined. You can also add a shadow to the train and the cloud group of objects. Additionally, try moving the commuters up or down from their original position to increase the sense of depth in the scene. Your scene should look like the illustration shown here.

Tip Any object that has the Perspective effect can be quickly put into editing mode when the Pick Tool is the current tool by double-clicking the object.

Mirroring Perspective Control Handles

Occasionally in your design work, you'll need to add perspective or adjust the existing perspective of an object so the perspective is symmetrical. You accomplish this by holding CTRL + SHIFT while you click-drag a perspective control handle. Here's a creative example of the use of a symmetrical perspective; in a new document, import Bowling.png, and then follow these steps:

Tutorial   Building a Bowling Alley

1. With the Rectangle Tool, create a tall rectangle, about 1" wide and 5" high. Fill it with a light-brown color.

2. Choose the Pick Tool, and then drag and drop three copies, each to the right of the preceding one; drag right, tap the right mouse button while holding the left, and then release both buttons to drop the copy.

3. Group the four rectangles; after selecting them press CTRL + G, and then press SHIFT + PAGEDOWN to put them behind the imported PNG picture.

4. Choose Effects | Add Perspective.

5. While holding CTRL + SHIFT, click the bottom-right control node and then drag right. Strike! Here you can see that this technique is a convenient way to set up symmetrical perspective.

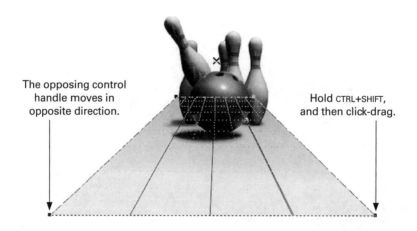

The opposing control handle moves in opposite direction.

Hold CTRL+SHIFT, and then click-drag.

Pre-visualizing Designs in Perspective

Often you'll design something, for instance, a pattern, and want to see what it will look like as a garment, gift wrap, or some other physical piece of art before you pay to have the design printed; this is called *pre-visualization* (preVis), and you can do this in CorelDRAW with the Perspective effect. In the following example, you'll create a simple gift-wrap pattern; then, using Perspective, you'll virtually wrap a package. The package is provided for you as an image on layers in a CorelDRAW document.

Let's use CorelDRAW's Artistic Media Tool to create the gift wrap for the present in the following steps. After completing the tutorial, you can use a design of your own with this file in the future.

Tutorial   Pre-visualizing a Design on a Product

1. After creating a new document (choose Landscape orientation), press CTRL + I to import A present.cpt. Just click at the upper left of the page to place it to size.
2. Open the Object Manager from the Tools menu. Expand the A present.cpt entry to reveal the two image layers.
3. Click the New Layer button at the bottom left of the docker. Doing this creates a new default named "Layer 2."
4. Click-drag the "Bow" entry on the Object Manager and place it on the Layer 2 title to move the bow image to the new layer.
5. Create a new layer, by default, named "Layer 3." Click-drag it to below Layer 2. This is where you'll be designing the gift wrap.

6. Choose the Artistic Media Tool from the Pen Tool group on the Toolbox. Then choose the Sprayer button on the Property Bar. You can use any preset you like; one of the festive Food presets is shown in the following illustration.

7. Create a rectangular area by scribbling up and down, like making several *W*s.

8. Choose Arrange | Break Artistic Media Apart (CTRL + K works, too). With the Pick Tool, delete the parent black path that's now visible. See Figure 18-3.

9. Choose Effects | Add Perspective. With the Shape Tool, drag, one at a time, the control handles for the effect to match the four corners of the face of the present, as shown here.

Create a new layer.

Move bitmap "Bow" to the new layer.

Create a new layer; sandwich it between Layers 1 and 2.

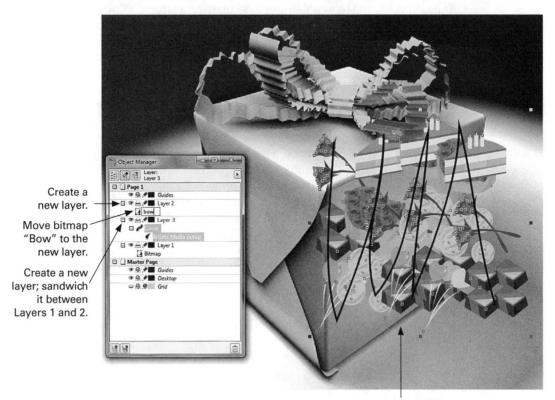

Arrange | Break Artistic Media Apart

FIGURE 18-3   Create a pattern with the Artistic Media Sprayer Tool.

10. Duplicate the pattern (press CTRL + D), and then use the Shape Tool to edit this duplicate (which also has the Perspective effect applied), so it matches the four corners of the top side of the present. Because the bow is on the top layer, you're actually adding the top pattern in perspective below the bow so it looks optically correct.

11. Repeat Step 10 to create the left panel of the pattern on the present.

12. The pattern shouldn't look totally opaque, but instead should take on a little of the shading on the blank present. The quickest way to apply transparency to the scores of objects that make up your Artistic Media stroke is to first turn it into a bitmap. First, let's check out the resolution of the present image so the conversion of the gift wrap pattern isn't unnecessarily larger than the present or bow images. After choosing the Pick Tool, click either the Bitmap or the Bow entry on the Object Manager list and then look at the Status Bar. The correct answer is 96 dpi.

13. Select one of the patterned sides and then choose Bitmaps | Convert To Bitmap. In the Convert To Bitmap dialog, choose 96 in the Resolution box, check the Transparent Background checkbox, and then click OK.

14. With the new bitmap selected, choose the Transparency tool on the Toolbox. On the Property Bar, choose Uniform Transparency type, Multiply style, and then play with the amount of transparency your eye tells you looks best and visually blends the pattern into the present. Repeat Steps 13 and 14 with the other two sides of the gift, be sure to include a card, and then send it to someone who deserves a gift.

This finished pre-visualization provides you and your client with a view of the goods you've designed, as they will appear from the customer's point of view, and perhaps this is the best "perspective" effect of all.

In this chapter, you've seen how to take a drawing, several objects, and even a complete design, and put a 3D spin on it. Perspective effects can help a client visualize what a design should look like when projected into real space, and at very least, the Perspective effect is a fun and quick method for embellishing a drawing that needs a "certain something" to lift if off the page. Chapter 19 takes you into a more complete visualization of 3D within a 2D drawing, as you explore the Extrude effect in CorelDRAW. Bring along what you know about vanishing points now, as well as an object or two that you want to add another dimension to—*literally*!

19
Extruding Objects

Although CorelDRAW is a 2D vector drawing application, the Extrude feature adds a simulated third dimension by adding objects that are shaded and in perspective. Depending on how you pose the object and light extruded objects, they can open up a whole new world of design opportunities. This chapter takes you through the rich feature set of the Extrude Tool, offers some creative possibilities for its use, and gets your head around the initial challenges of navigating 3D space in CorelDRAW.

 Download and extract all the files from the Chapter19.zip archive to follow the tutorials in this chapter.

How Extrude Works

CorelDRAW's Extrude effect examines the geometry of an object (a single or two or more combined paths). Then, with your input, it creates dynamic extensions to all path segments, whose appearance suggests that the added objects recede into the distance to a vanishing point. See Chapter 18 on perspective vanishing points. Figure 19-1 shows some finished artwork based on objects that are easy for you to draw in CorelDRAW. This figure is the result of knowing how to use the Extrude Tool and then being able to add an object here or there to complete a scene with shadows and a few 2D objects you create. By the end of this chapter, you'll know how to create a composition like this one and achieve predictable results with the Extrude Tool and its options. One thing to remember: even the most complex object you extrude probably won't convey a complete artistic idea. You'll need to use *other* CorelDRAW tools to create a scene you're happy with. For example, the train composition uses *several* extruded objects, and the tabletop was first created by extruding shapes, but then all the shadows you see were manually drawn on top of areas. The Extrude Tool can get you 75 percent of the way you want to go with a design, but you need to be imaginative to place the

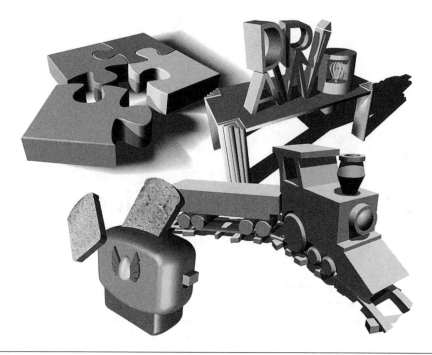

FIGURE 19-1 Imagine what an object looks like when projected into a third dimension, and then manually add what's missing from your complete idea.

extruded object in context, within a scene, to build a complete graphical idea. That's what the *rest* of this book is for!

When an Extrude effect is applied to an object, the original becomes a *control object*, and the Extrude effect objects become a dynamically linked group. Any editing you then perform on the properties of the control object, such as fills and edits to the outline of the control object, are immediately updated in the linked extrude group. The extrude group itself can also be modified in ways that increase the intricacy and photorealism of the effect; you can change the depth, color, lighting, and rotation of the Extrude effect.

Be aware that both lighting and the control object's geometry have an impact on how many extrude group objects are created. Although you don't usually need to concern yourself with how many objects are dynamically created to make an extrude, the sheer number of objects can slow down redraws of your page when you have, for example, hundreds of objects in the extrude group. When CorelDRAW creates an extrude group, it calculates lighting (when you *use* lighting, covered later in this chapter) and creates extrude group objects based on curved path segments in the control object. Next, you can see a star-shaped control object with lighting; the object has a Radial Fountain Fill, and it's an interesting design in Enhanced view. At right, the page is viewed in Wireframe, and 48 objects are grouped in the Extrude effect.

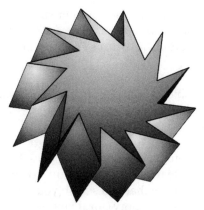

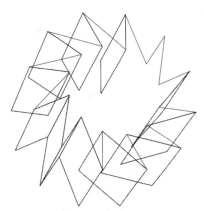

Extrude on straight path shape,
with lighting, Enhanced view

Wireframe view, 48 extrude
group objects

Here, a much more complex control object is used for an extrude. It not only is a compound path, but its path segments are curved. In Wireframe view, it's evident the Extrude group is composed of more objects than the star-shaped extrude. No lighting is used in the Extrude effect, which in turn limits the number of extrude group objects CorelDRAW has to create, and the design is fairly interesting.

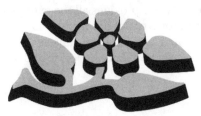

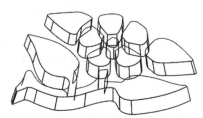

Extruded object
with flat fill

Wireframe view, 118 extrude
group objects

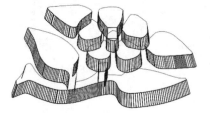

Extrude on curved path shape,
with lighting, Enhanced view

Wireframe view, 890 extrude
group objects

If lighting is now applied, you can see that the number of extrude control objects created to represent the curved paths with added lighting is an order of magnitude more. This *isn't* a warning to fellow Corellians to limit the intricacy of extrude objects you design, but rather a point to consider. If you own a video card with lots of RAM yet suddenly find you're getting slow screen redraws, consider going to a less refined view such as Normal or Draft via the View menu. Also consider simplifying an extruded object by replacing scores of objects used to simulate a Fountain Fill with *one* object that has a *single* Fountain Fill. CorelDRAW uses Fountain Fills for extrude objects on two occasions:

- When the control curve (the parent object) has a Fountain Fill and your color settings for the extrude shapes are set to Object Fill.
- When you use the Color Shading setting for extrude objects.

Either of these conditions can create not only a lot of extrude shapes, but also more complex fills than Uniform Color. As you learn to create elegant extrude objects, consider these two circumstances if the objects that you see on your monitor aren't printing (you might not have enough printer memory), or if your screen redraws are slower than you expect (you're commanding too many operations).

Choosing and Applying an Extrude Effect

The Extrude effect can be applied interactively using the Extrude Tool, which is located in the Toolbox with other effects tools, or you can choose from the Presets list to create a 3D object instantly.

While you're using this tool, the Property Bar provides all the extrude options for setting the effect's properties. Browse the Property Bar options as shown in Figure 19-2. Options are grouped into areas for saving your applied extrusions as Presets, controlling the shape, depth, vanishing point position, rotation, lighting, color, and bevel effects.

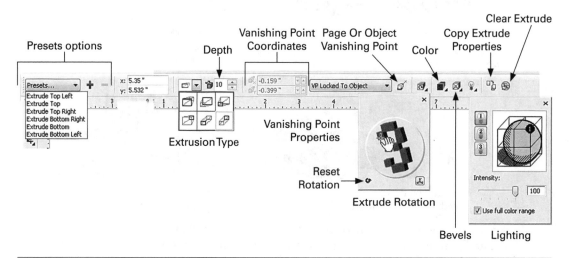

FIGURE 19-2 The Property Bar contains all the options for defining and saving the look of an extrude.

Note Almost all CorelDRAW users experience this: you've made only one copy of an object you've extruded, and now that you've extruded and rotated it, you want to save a copy of the object in its original form—not extruded and not distorted or rotated. *Do not* copy and paste the Control Curve; doing this does not return the object to its original orientation on the page. Instead, make a copy of the entire extrude group, double-click the group using the Pick Tool to display Extrude options on the Property Bar, click the Extrude Rotation button, click the Reset Rotation icon at bottom left, and then click the Clear Extrude button on the Property Bar. Your original shape now contains the same number of nodes, the same curve segments, and the same color.

Navigating the Markers

When you decide to extrude a shape manually, markers appear around the resulting object after you perform the first step in an extrude: you click-drag on the face of the object you want to be the control object. The markers offer you control over the position, depth, and vanishing point position of the 3D object. You'll be creating a 3D object by hand in the following tutorial, so familiarize yourself with the elements that surround a 3D extruded shape, as shown in Figure 19-3.

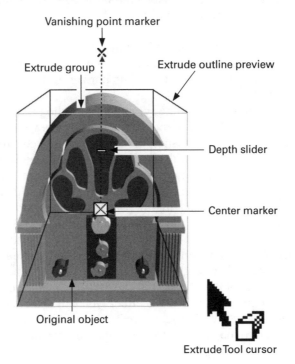

FIGURE 19-3 These control handles are used after an object is initially extruded to change the appearance of the extrude.

Alternatively, you can apply a Preset Extrude effect to get a 3D version of a shape in lightning time; however, you might want hands-on control over the creation of an Extrude effect. Follow this tutorial to get a handle on what some of the Property Bar options do to an Extrude effect; in no time, you'll be able to "sculpt" whatever you envision as a scene that has objects with depth.

Tutorial Going Deep with the Extrude Tool

1. Create an object to be the control object for the extrude. A rectangle produces results that make the relationship between the face of the object and the sides very clear, but not very artistic. Try a Star shape for more dramatic extrude results. Give the shape a fill (a Fountain Fill will produce a stunning effect), and give the outline a contrasting color such as white so you can visually track where the extrude objects are created.

2. Choose the Extrude Tool, and your cursor changes to the Extrude Tool cursor, which is hard to mistake for the Pick or Pen Tool. When held over your object, the cursor indicates a start extrude position by displaying a tiny shape with a direction line below the symbol of an extruded cube.

3. Drag from the center of your object outward in any direction, but don't release the mouse button. The control object now has markers and a wireframe preview of the front and back boundaries of the extrude; the front of the object is bound by a red outline, and the back of the 3D shape is bound by a blue outline. The preview indicates the length and direction of the Extrude effect and the X symbol you're dragging is the *vanishing point*. As discussed in Chapter 18, a vanishing point is a geometric indicator of where parallel lines on a surface would converge at the horizon if the surface were actually to extend to the horizon.

4. Drag the vanishing point X symbol around the page; not only does the preview outline change, but also, more importantly, the view on the 3D object also changes. When the vanishing point is above the control object, you're looking down on the object; similarly, you move your view to expose the side of an object in direct correlation to the position of the vanishing point.

5. As you use the Extrude Tool, you define both the direction of the 3D object and the depth. Try dragging the Depth slider toward and then away from the control object. Notice how you first make the extrude a shallow one and then a deeper one, all while the sides extend in the direction of the vanishing point. At any time from when you create the object by releasing the cursor, you can also set the object depth by using the Depth spin box on the Property Bar.

6. Click outside of the object, and the extrude operation is complete. However, because Extrude is a *dynamic* effect, you can change the appearance of the extrude at any time in the future by double-clicking either the extrude group or the control object with the Pick Tool to once again display the handles.

Using the Extrude Tool and Property Bar

Like other effects, extrusions can be set using the Property Bar. Using the Extrude Tool, you'll see several cursor states depending on where the cursor is. These states indicate what operation you can perform at any given point on the extrude group. Let's take a look at the different cursors and what they indicate in the following sections.

Extrude Tool States

The Extrude Tool cursor, shown here, changes appearance based on what it's hovering over in your document. When the cursor is held over an object that can be extruded, the cursor features a start symbol. If an object cannot be extruded, the cursor features the international "No" (⊘) symbol. Most shapes you draw with the pen tools except Artistic Media can be extruded. If you have your heart set on extruding Artistic Media strokes, you first need to break the strokes from the control path (CTRL + K); bitmaps cannot be extruded at all (but you can use the 3D Effects on the Bitmaps menu to make perspective and emboss effects). You can only extrude one object at a time: you'll get the "No can do" cursor if you select more than one object and then try to use the tool. Grouped objects can be successfully extruded; however, you can no longer ungroup them—you need to clear the extrude before you can select and edit only one of the group.

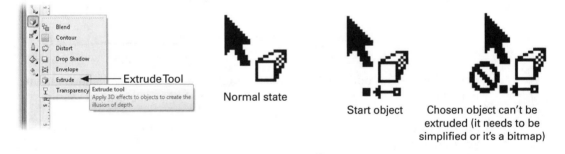

Normal state   Start object   Chosen object can't be extruded (it needs to be simplified or it's a bitmap)

Tip   Objects you want to extrude don't have to be filled. You can create interesting wireframes similar to those you'd see in a technical drawing by extruding objects that have an outline width but no fill.

Setting Extrusion Shape

The Extrusion Type selector, shown next, offers six different shape types with which you can control both the direction of the extrude and whether you need wide-angle, small perspective, or totally isometric (no perspective) 3D objects. Depending on the type you choose, your extrusion can extend toward the back or front relative to the control object. Choosing a front style causes the vanishing point to project from the front of your object; choosing a back style does the opposite. Because you're working with geometric solids, when you choose a back style, the direction of the extrude looks mirrored; although in Wireframe view, it's clear the object inverted itself, its back side projecting forward instead of into the distance. Icons in the selector indicate each shape type, with the darkened outline indicating your original object. Here are examples of the six different perspectives, which were created in order from the selector; see how the selector icons fairly represent each style.

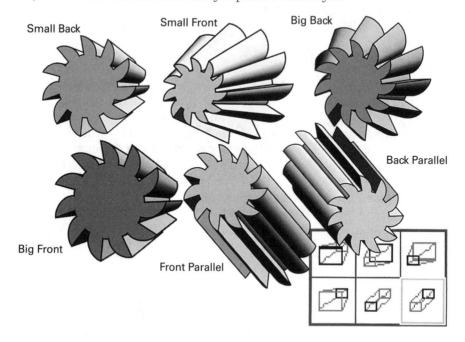

- **Small Back**   This option (the default setting) layers the extrusion and vanishing point behind your original object. Small Back is perhaps the most commonly applied extrusion type.
- **Small Front**   This option layers the extrusion and vanishing point in front of your original object.
- **Big Back**   This option layers the extrusion behind your original object, while placing the vanishing point in front.
- **Big Front**   This option layers the extrusion in front of your original object, while placing the vanishing point in back.
- **Back Parallel**   This option layers the extrusion behind your original object so the extruded surfaces appear parallel to the original surfaces. When you select this option, the vanishing point sets the depth of the extrusion, as the actual depth option is unavailable. No true vanishing point is used in this style.
- **Front Parallel**   This option layers the extrusion in front of your object so the extruded surfaces appear parallel to the original surfaces. When you select this option, the vanishing point sets the depth of the extrusion, as the actual depth option is unavailable. It's interesting to note that if you light a Back Parallel and a Front Parallel extrude with the same light setup, the two extrude groups appear to be lit differently.

Setting Extrude Depth

Extrude Depth is based on the distance between the control object and the vanishing point. You will get different appearances using the same Depth value but different styles, and you can set Extrude Depth as high as 99. Here, you can see a shallow and a deep extrude, using two different Depth values but the same Extrude style. You can control object depth manually by dragging the Depth slider on top of the object, or enter values in the Num box on the Property Bar (press ENTER after typing a value; the spin box controls update the object without your needing to press ENTER).

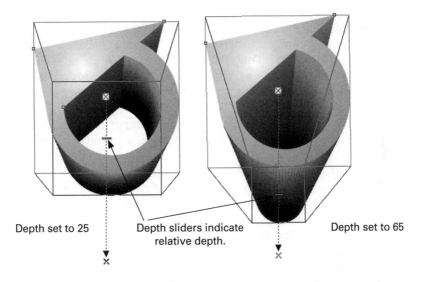

Depth set to 25   Depth sliders indicate relative depth.   Depth set to 65

Setting Vanishing Point Properties

The direction of the vanishing point determines only the point toward which objects diminish; it does not control whether the extruded portion extends from the front or back of the object.

 Note Vanishing points can be set on four of the six extrusion styles: Small Back, Big Back, Small Front, and Big Front. The sides of the extruded portions created in the Front Parallel or Back Parallel types never converge; these are *isometric* views, and, therefore, there is no horizon, so no vanishing point.

Using the Property Bar options shown here, you can lock an extrusion's vanishing point, copy vanishing points from an existing extrusion, and share vanishing points between extruded objects.

Vanishing Point Properties selector

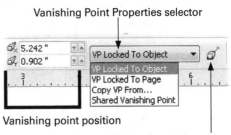

Vanishing point position

VP Object/VP Page (vanishing point relative page/object center) option

Here are the options for vanishing points; how they can be set and shared between different extruded objects:

- **Locking to the object** Choosing the VP Locked To Object option (the default setting) fixes the vanishing point to a position relative to the object, regardless of where the original extruded object is positioned.
- **Locking to the page** VP Locked To Page offers the option to tack the vanishing point to your page, forcing the extrusion to diminish toward a fixed page position, no matter where the original object is moved. Try this to see for yourself the effectiveness of this setting: lock the vanishing point of an extruded object to the page, and then move the object using the Pick Tool; you'll see that the sides of the extrude dynamically update to always show the object's correct perspective.
- **Copying VP From** This command doesn't define a vanishing point like the other drop-down choices do, but instead is used to copy an existing vanishing point. Copying a vanishing point lets you set up several extruded objects on a page, and in a few clicks, the objects all appear to be facing the same direction, at a common point of view from the audience's perspective. Immediately after you choose Copy VP From, your cursor changes to a vanishing point targeting cursor (a really, really large arrow), which you use to target any other extruded object on your document page, with the goal of copying its vanishing point position. For this command to be successful, you must have at least one other Extrude effect applied to an object and in view. After the vanishing point has been copied, the Property Bar indicates the object's vanishing point as VP Locked To object, and the vanishing point can now be moved as you rotate the extruded object.
- **Sharing Vanishing Points** Choosing Shared Vanishing Point lets you have several objects share the *same* vanishing point, but you must have applied at least an initial Extrude effect to your objects before attempting to use this command. Immediately after you choose this option, your cursor changes to a vanishing point targeting cursor, which signifies that you can now target any other extruded object for the purpose of creating a common vanishing point position for multiple objects. This option creates a similar effect to copying vanishing points, but the overall effect is that every object on the page is in the same scene. You move one object, and other objects reflect the change in perspective.

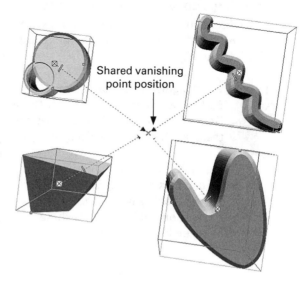

Shared vanishing point position

- **Setting a relative position for vanishing points**   The VP Object/VP Page option on the Property Bar is used to toggle the measurement state of object vanishing points between page and object. When the option is inactive (the button is not depressed), the vanishing point position boxes enable you to specify the vanishing point relative to your page origin—a value determined either by the lower-left corner, by default, or by the zero markers on your ruler origin. When the option is active (the button is depressed), the center of your currently selected object is used as the measurement value, which changes according to the object's page position. You will see this most noticeably if you have a depth on an object of more than 40 and you drag the object around the page with the Pick Tool. The extrude group actually changes to reflect different vanishing point views.

Setting 3D Rotation

Until now, the extrudes you've created and read about have been based on the control object facing you; this is a good beginning point in your 3D experience, but not always the most visually interesting of poses. You can rotate extruded objects; the extrude group follows and aligns perfectly with the control object, and you have two ways to perform 3D extrude rotations: via the Property Bar or via the control handles. Create an extrude group of objects and then let's begin with the precise, noninteractive method of rotation you access through the Property Bar when you've chosen the Extrude Tool and selected an object.

The Rotation pop-up menu offers a proxy box that you use by click-dragging on the "3" as shown next. As you drag, a very faint yellow line appears on the "3," indicating the current rotation of the object and the proposed new rotation once you release the mouse button. You might not always get the exact look you need using this technique because of the position of the object's vanishing point—your experience can be similar to levering an object seesaw-fashion when the pivot point (the fulcrum) is 15 miles away! To avoid imprecision, you can click the toggle button labeled in the illustration to move to a number field display of the X, Y, and Z rotational values (see the following Tip). The value fields have spin box controls that increase and decrease the values by 10; you probably want to enter values manually, because a single percent of rotation (from 0 to 100 percent, not degrees) can be quite significant, considering only 100 of them are in this pop-up box. If at any time you find you've gotten too deep in this 3D rotation stuff, clicking the "undo" curved arrow icon on the lower left of the selector, shown here, resets all rotation values to zero.

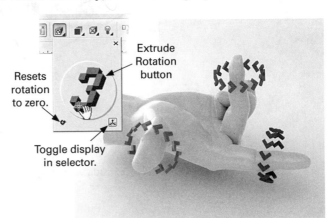

Resets rotation to zero.

Extrude Rotation button

Toggle display in selector.

Tip The Extrude Rotation values follow the right-hand coordinate system. If ever in doubt about which values correspond to which axes for rotation, face your palm upward, as in the illustration above, and then extend your forefinger to your right. Your forefinger is the *X* rotational axis, and positive values are measured in the direction your forefinger curls. Now point your middle finger straight up to indicate the positive motion along the *Y* axis. Point your thumb at yourself; you might want to do all this in a mirror to prevent cramps. *Z* motion travels toward you, and rotation along Z is counterclockwise, following the curl of your fingers.

Overall, the best teacher is experience, particularly with manipulating your view of a 3D object in CorelDRAW. Set aside some quality time, and you might even be pleasantly surprised by some of your errors!

Using the Rotation Tools

You don't have to use the Rotation pop-up box on the Property Bar to rotate an extruded object: you can define a degree of rotation along the *X, Y,* and *Z* axes of any object by click-dragging the object directly. To do some manual rotation, the object needs to be extruded and first put into Editing mode—you can double-click on the extrude group of objects with the Pick Tool to put the object into Editing mode, and then click a second time to expose the control handles shown here. Before you leap in, read on for an explanation of what the controls do and what you do with them to achieve the desired result.

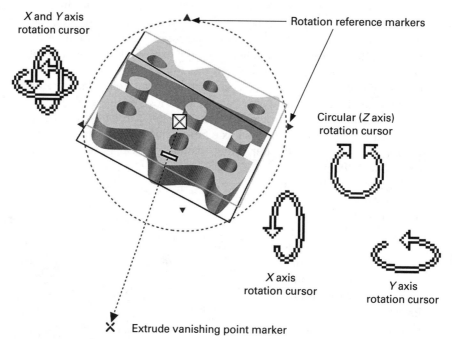

X and *Y* axis rotation cursor

Rotation reference markers

Circular (*Z* axis) rotation cursor

X axis rotation cursor

Y axis rotation cursor

✕ Extrude vanishing point marker

Note If either Back Parallel or Front Parallel is selected, the Extrude Rotation controls are unavailable; parallel extrusions have no vanishing point, so there's nothing to pivot with. Also, when the vanishing point is locked to the page, Extrude Rotation cannot be performed.

 Tip When an object is rotated, the vanishing point controls on the Property Bar cannot be used, mostly because mathematically, the vanishing point is nowhere near your drawing page! If you need to adjust an object's vanishing point, you must work backward; on the Extrude Rotation pop-up panel on the Property Bar, click the Reset Rotation icon. Then the vanishing point options and controls become active (and your object is no longer rotated).

Rotating an Extrude Effect

Because a rotated extrude graphically describes an object more completely than a face-front view, the following tutorial will come in handy when you've extruded an object that has some built-in visual interest. Extrude something interesting now, and let's take the manual rotation feature out for a spin.

Tutorial Putting a New Spin on an Extruded Object

1. With the Pick Tool, double-click the extrude group or the control object to expose the editing handles. Alternatively, you can use the Extrude Tool to select the object put it immediately into Editing mode.
2. Single-click the *extruded* portion a second time. The rotation markers appear, and circular guides surround the effect. The inside and outside areas of this circular area determine the tool's cursor state.
3. Move the cursor outside of the green dashed circle, and notice that it changes to the rotation cursor. This cursor is used to rotate the face of the object, the Z axis, counterclockwise and clockwise. Dragging right and down creates a clockwise rotation and left and up rotates the face of the object counterclockwise.
4. Move the cursor inside the green dashed circle area, and it changes to the X/Y axis rotation cursor. Using this cursor is a lot like using an onscreen trackball; you just drag in any direction to simultaneously rotate the X and Y axes of the extrude object. It's fun, you can see the vanishing point move to reflect the object's new aspect, and it's also not as precise as it could be when you only want to, for example, rotate the object along the top-to-bottom (Y) axis.
5. Release the mouse button for a moment and then hold CTRL. Then click-drag upward (downward is okay, too); you're now constraining rotation to the X axis of the object.
6. Release the mouse button again and then hold CTRL. Now click-drag left or right; you're constraining rotation to the Y axis of the object and not touching the X axis rotation.

7. When the amusement has worn thin or your task is accomplished, click a blank space on the document page outside of the rotational cursor area to deselect the effect. The cursor returns to the normal extrude cursor state. You've just completed manually rotating an extrude object.

Note After an Extrude effect has been rotated, you can still adjust the extrude depth of the effect.

Adding Lights

Adding lighting to an extruded object can spell the difference between an effect and a piece of artwork that truly attracts a viewer with its realistic appearance; many of the figures in this chapter use the Lighting option. To access the lighting controls, click the Extrude Lighting button on the Property Bar while selecting an Extrude effect, as shown here.

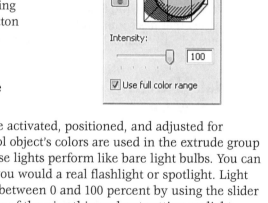

Extrude Lighting button

Active, positioned light

Light Sources

Intensity:

100

☑ Use full color range

Working with the Options in the Lighting Control Window

Three independent light sources can be activated, positioned, and adjusted for intensity and for whether all the control object's colors are used in the extrude group (the Use Full Color Range option). These lights perform like bare light bulbs. You can reposition them, but not aim them as you would a real flashlight or spotlight. Light intensity is set on a light-by-light basis between 0 and 100 percent by using the slider control when each light is selected. One of the nice things about setting up light intensity and position is that response is immediate—there is no Apply button and your object's light changes as you make changes in the control window.

When you first open the Extrude Lighting control window, all lights are inactive. To activate a light, click one of the three Light Source buttons—the numbering is for your reference; it's just a label. There is nothing special about light 3 versus light 1, for example, in any of its properties. Once you click a light button, a circle with the light's number inside appears in the front, upper-right position on a 3D grid surrounding a sphere, which represents the extrude object (see Figure 19-4). The lights themselves aren't visible on the drawing page, but the lighting effect you define displays highlights and shaded areas on your extrude object, particularly evident when the sides of the control object are curved. You can pose the light sources by adding them to the grid and then dragging them—there are over a dozen possible positions for lights; some of the positions can create very interesting "edge lighting" on your object.

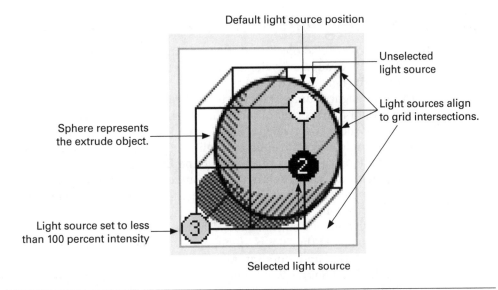

FIGURE 19-4 The 3D grid represents light positions relative to the selected extrude object.

Every time you activate a new light, it appears on the grid in the default position of front, top, right. This means if you click to activate two or three Light Source buttons in succession without first moving them, you'll stack them on top of each other and wind up with one extremely intense light source on the object. When this happens, drag the individual lights to reposition them at different points.

A *selected* light is shown as a black circle in the preview; unselected lights are shown as white circles. Lights set to brightness levels less than 100 percent appear in shades of gray. As these light sources are dragged around the 3D grid, they automatically snap to line-intersection points on the grid. You *can* position lights at the back-mid-center or back-center-bottom position—if you're *really* determined and have lots of time to spare—but lights in these positions will not contribute significantly to the shading of the extrude shape.

Note There is no option to set the color of lights; all lights cast white. If you want a spotlight effect, read Chapter 22 on Lens effects for techniques on shading objects with color.

Adding and Editing Extrude Lights

The following tutorial obliges you to put on your stagehand cap as you work the lights in a scene, adding them to the extrude object's properties and learning how to position them and turn the wattage up and down.

Tutorial Working with Extrude Light Options

1. Create a color-filled object and apply an Extrude effect to it.
2. Using the Extrude Tool, click the Extrude Lighting selector in the Property Bar to open the light source option.
3. Click the Light Source 1 button, and a light source symbol appears in the upper-right-front corner of the grid, shown as a black circle numbered *1*. The Intensity slider is activated. Light Source 1 is now active, and the colors of your Extrude effect are altered (brightened and possibly a little washed-out) to reflect the new light's contribution to the Extrude effect.
4. Drag the symbol representing Light Source 1 to a different position on the 3D grid; notice how the coloring of the effect changes in response to the new lighting position.
5. With Light Source 1 still selected, drag the Intensity slider to the left, approximately to the 50% position, and notice how the color of the object becomes darker and more saturated.
6. Click the Light Source 2 button to activate it. Notice that it appears in the same default position as the first light source, and the symbol representing Light Source 1 is gray, indicating that it is not selected and it is not at 100% intensity. When an unselected light is at 100% intensity, the symbol is white. Drag Light Source 2 to a different grid position—in classic scene lighting, a secondary light of, say, 50% of the main light's intensity is usually positioned directly opposite the main light to make objects look rounder, deeper, and overall more flattering with more visible detail than when using only one light source.
7. Click the activation buttons for Light Sources 1 and 2 to toggle them off, and the color of the extrude object returns to its original state. To finish editing lights, click anywhere outside the Extrude Lighting selector.

 Tip Occasionally in your design work, you might like the perspective you've created for the face of an extrude object, but you might not need the extruded side or the extrude group of objects. You can remove an Extrude effect from an object and keep its perspective and position on the page by clicking the extruded portion of the effect and choosing Effects | Clear Extrude. You can also use the Extrude Tool by clicking the Clear Extrude button in the Property Bar.

Controlling Light Properties

Two additional options available when you're using lighting have the following effects on your extruded objects:

- **Lighting intensity** As mentioned in the previous tutorial, the Intensity slider determines the brightness of each light. When a light is selected, you can set the range between 0 and 100%; higher values mean brighter lighting.
- **Full color range** Below the Intensity slider, you'll find the Use Full Color Range option, which directs your display to use the full *gamut* of colors when coloring the surfaces of your original object and its extruded portion. *Gamut* is the

expressible range of colors available to CorelDRAW, which depends on the color mode (see Chapter 17) of the original object and the extrusion. When working in CMYK process or RGB color, you might find the shading on an object to have too much contrast; the lighting might look too harsh and might create washed-out surfaces. The remedy then is to uncheck Use Full Color Range; the gamut of colors is then limited, and the dynamic range of available colors becomes narrower. You just might wind up seeing areas that are hidden in deeply shaded zones when Use Full Color Range is not checked.

Using a Narrow Gamut for Spot Colors in an Extrude

If your original shape and/or the extruded portion uses spot colors, the Use Full Color Range option might help you get where you want to go. Deselecting it has the effect of limiting the color variations caused by light sources to only those percentages of the spot colors defined in both your original object and its extruded portion. Unfortunately, deselecting this option limits color depth and diminishes the effects of the lighting you apply, but it results in a print-legal spot color tint, as opposed to the normal color space of RGB that you see onscreen. This means that if your objects are filled with spot color, you should consider unchecking the Use Full Color Range check box.

Setting Extrude Color

In addition to shading an extrude group using lighting, you can further embellish and draw out photorealistic qualities by using color options for the extrude. You might need to perform some technical illustration with extrude objects, and you might need cross-hatching in addition to lighting, for example. This is when you turn to the Color option on the Property Bar; you have three different ways to shade an extrude group: object fill color, solid color, or color shading (much like a Fountain Fill transition from one color to a different color).

Starting from left to right on the Color Control window, you see the various color modes you can use.

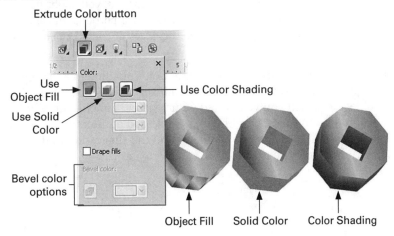

You can achieve effects that range from flat, technical illustrations to highly polished metallic surfaces—which actually can work on their own without your needing to light the object—and it all depends on the choices you make in the Color Control window:

- **Using an object's fill** The Use Object Fill option is the most straightforward to use, but it does not automatically create any sort of shading—if you choose to use the default object fill and the object is filled with a uniform color, it's usually a good idea to give the control object an outline width whose color contrasts with the object fill color. When Use Object Fill is selected, the Drape Fills option also becomes available (and is selected automatically). Drape Fills is discussed shortly; here is an example of a Fountain Fill control object, with and without Drape Fills.

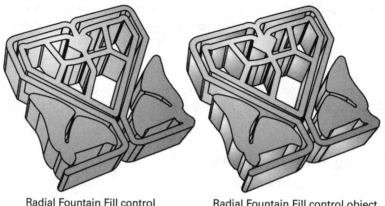

Radial Fountain Fill control object, Use Object Fill

Radial Fountain Fill control object, Use Object Fill, Drape Fills

- **Choosing your own solid fill** Choose Use Solid Color to set any uniform color to the extrude portion of your effect, regardless of the fill type currently applied to your object. The secondary color option becomes available only when Use Color Shading is selected.

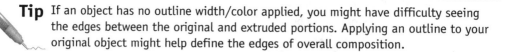

Tip If an object has no outline width/color applied, you might have difficulty seeing the edges between the original and extruded portions. Applying an outline to your original object might help define the edges of overall composition.

- **Using color shading** Choose Use Color Shading to add depth by using your object's color as the From color and black (by default) as the To color. If the object to which you've applied your Extrude effect is already filled with a Fountain Fill, Use Color Shading is selected automatically. Visual separation between the extrude group objects and the suggestion of depth is easy to create with Use Color Shading.

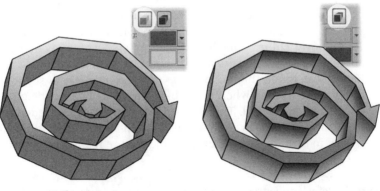

Extrude color applied with
Use Solid Color option

Extrude color applied with
Use Color Shading option

- **Draping your object's fill over the Extrude effect**   *Draping,* as used in
  CorelDRAW's Extrude effect, means, "treat each extrude group object's fill as a
  unique item." Say, for example, you have a patterned piece of cloth and you drape
  it over a coffee table: you will see discontinuity in the pattern as each angle of the
  folds of cloth travels in different directions in 3D space. Similarly, draping creates
  discontinuity in a Pattern and Fountain Fill that you apply to both the control
  object and the extrude group of objects, as shown in Figure 19-5. At right, with
  Drape Fills enabled, the polka dot shape (with some lighting applied) truly looks
  dimensional, even though the two-color bitmap fill doesn't change perspective
  (bitmap fills do not take on the rotation angle of extrude objects; they're always

Without Drape Fills
Pattern is continuous (looks hokey).

With Drape Fills
Pattern is discontinuous (looks realistic).

FIGURE 19-5   The Drape Fills options can make or break the realism you're trying
to illustrate.

face forward). At left, with Drape Fills turned off, the pattern proceeds across the object and the extrude group of objects in a continuous pattern, as though it's *projected* on the surface of the shape instead of *being* the surface of the shape.

- **Using bevel color** The Bevel Color option becomes available only if you've applied the Bevel effect to an extruded shape. Bevel options are located on the Bevels selector on the Property Bar (covered in the next section). This option is important to enable when your object and its child extrude group have a Fountain or Bitmap Pattern Fill. The effect of enabling Bevel Color does to the bevel edges what Drape Fills does to the extrude group—it breaks up the pattern continuity, which, in turn, makes the overall object more realistic in appearance.

 Tip To detach an Extrude effect, right-click the extrude group and choose Break Extrude Group Apart. This breaks the link between your original and its effect portion, making it a separate group that can be further broken down using the Ungroup command (CTRL+U). The result is the control object adopts the perspective of the Extrude effect; you can independently edit all objects for color and outline properties, and do some editing to manually increase the realism of your composition—some examples are shown at the end of this chapter. This is a *destructive* edit—be forewarned—and the only way to reverse the process is via the Undo docker or by pressing CTRL+Z.

Speak of the Bevel!

Bevels in the real world are the flattened edges where two planes meet on furniture to give it an ornamental look, to make the furniture safer for kids romping around the living room, and to make furniture more expensive. Similarly, the Bevel option in CorelDRAW's Extrude effect creates new objects, in perspective, that join the face and sides of an extrude object.

Bevel effects are built to put a cap on the front end of the control object. Therefore, if an extrude is defined using a style that projects from front to back, the bevel is created as a group of objects facing you. However, if you choose the Small Front style, the bevel goes to the back face of the object, and, without rotating the object, the bevel is hidden from view. Bevel shape is based on the angle and depth defined using the Bevel selector, shown here.

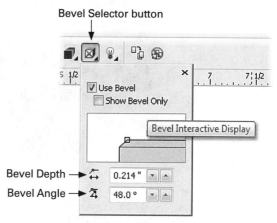

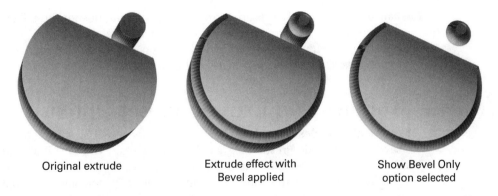

Original extrude

Extrude effect with
Bevel applied

Show Bevel Only
option selected

FIGURE 19-6   The shape of a bevel is determined by Bevel Depth and Bevel Angle.

- **Using bevels**   The Use Bevel option activates the Bevel effect and causes the remaining options in the control window to become available. Bevel effects can be used only after an Extrude effect has been applied.
- **Showing bevels only**   You might want not the extruded side but only the Bevel effect of an object to be visible; this is a quick and easy way to make a fancy engraved headline from Artistic Text. Click the Show Bevel Only check box, and the extrude for the selected object is hidden but can be restored at any future time by unchecking this box. You can rotate an object that has a Bevel effect, but the extrude parts are hidden.
- **Setting bevel shapes**   The Bevel Depth and Bevel Angle options can be defined by entering values in the corresponding fields on the Bevel pop-up on the Property Bar; you can also click-drag in the proxy window to define the angle and depth interactively. Bevel Depth can be set between 0.001 inch and 1.980 inches, but your results will just get silly looking after more than an inch or so of bevel. Bevel Angle may be set to a maximum of 89°. Shallow angles of less than 30° often provide the best visual results. At significant depths, you might get self-intersections in the bevel because control objects that have sharp curves along the path segments are difficult for the Bevel effect to reconcile mathematically. If you see a "bad" self-intersecting area, try reducing the Bevel Depth and/or changing the angle. Figure 19-6 shows the results of applying a Bevel effect with and without an Extrude effect involved.

Using Vector Extrude Presets

You might spend an hour or two creating the exact Extrude effect you've envisioned, and naturally it would be nice to save the parameters you've defined to later apply them to other objects. When the Extrude Tool is active, you have an area on the Property Bar for applying factory-designed Presets as well as for saving and ditching Presets. You use this area on the Property Bar exactly as you would with any other Preset list in CorelDRAW.

You can save and reapply Presets to any object that qualifies for the effect (in other words, no Artistic Media, bitmaps, or objects that have an incompatible effect already in place). If you've never used extrude Presets or any other Preset options before, do not pass "Go," collect your wits, and move on to the following tutorial.

Tutorial Working with Extrude Preset Options

1. If you've already designed an extrude group, make sure the object you're going to save as an extrude Preset looks good, because when you save it, CorelDRAW builds a full-color preview thumbnail.
2. If you're just starting and want to try out a factory Preset, select an object and then choose the Extrude Tool.
3. Using the Property Bar, choose an Extrude effect from the Presets list. The properties of the Extrude effect are immediately applied, and its properties are shown on the Property Bar.
4. To save an existing extrude as a Preset, select the extrude group (not the control object), and then click the Add Preset (+) button. The Save As dialog opens. Enter a name for your new Preset in the File Name box and then click Save and your extrude Preset is added to the Presets list.
5. To delete an extrude Preset, while no object is selected, choose the Preset from the Presets list and then click the Delete Preset button (–) on the Property Bar. The saved Preset is immediately deleted. However, there is no Undo command for this operation.

Using the Extrude Docker

If you're a longtime CorelDRAW user, you may have grown accustomed to applying Extrude effects using a docker; new users will probably find the editing methods and the options on the Property Bar to be more convenient to access, but the Extrude docker is available via Window | Dockers | Extrude. The Extrude docker is organized into five areas: Camera (referring to shape), Rotation, Light, Color, and Bevels, as shown here.

Although these options are organized differently from the Property Bar, all the options are there. Using the docker method for extruding objects lets you choose extrude settings before applying them.

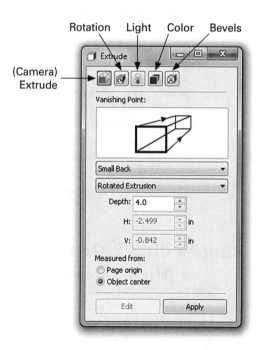

Copying and Cloning Extrude Effects

As with other effects in CorelDRAW, you can copy or clone from existing extrusions. Neither operation requires the Extrude Tool; both are accomplished by using menu commands.

When copying an Extrude effect, at least one Extrude effect must be in view, and at least one object must be selected. To copy an Extrude effect, choose Effects | Copy Effect | Extrude From. The cursor becomes a targeting cursor (the large right-facing arrow guy). Use this cursor to indicate to CorelDRAW the extrude portion of an existing Extrude effect to copy all applied extrude properties. If you're using the Extrude Tool, you can also copy the effect by clicking the Copy Extrude Properties button on the Property Bar and then clicking to target an existing extrusion.

Cloning an Extrude effect produces a slightly different result. When an effect is applied through cloning, the Master Clone effect object controls the new effect. Any changes made to the master are immediately applied to the clone. As part of the qualifying criteria for cloning an Extrude effect, you must have created at least one other Extrude effect and have this object in view. You must also have at least one object selected onscreen.

To clone an Extrude effect, choose Effects | Clone Effect | Extrude From. Your cursor becomes a targeting cursor. You then click the existing Extrude effect you want to clone by clicking directly on the extrude group portion of the effect.

Controlling Extrude Complexity Using Facet Size

When you apply the Use Color Shading option, the smooth curves and shading that are the visual result require complex calculations and produce a large number of extrude group objects to maintain curve smoothness. The smoother the curve and shading, the better the display and print quality.

When CorelDRAW creates an extrusion, the smoothness of curves and the number of objects used to create shaded extrusion fills are controlled by a value called a *facet*. Facet size can be increased or decreased to control curve smoothing and object count. This is what facet size is and does, so right now would be a good time to reveal where this option is *located*, right?

Click the Options button on the Standard Toolbar. Under Workspace | Edit, the option itself is named Minimum Extrude Facet Size, and it has a range between 0.001 inch and 36 inches—the default is 0.05 inch.

Controls complexity of curves,
with Use Color Shading applied

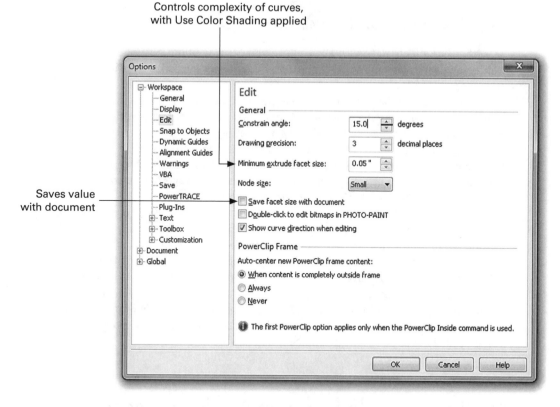

Saves value
with document

In Options, you can also choose Save Facet Size With Document to avoid the need to change the facet size each time your document is reopened. Higher facet values cause extrude curves to display and print less smoothly; lower values increase the smoothness of extruded curves but significantly increase display and printing times; here you can see that a Minimum Extrude Facet Size of 1" and a shape that has many curved segments and lighting needs to be rendered using a correspondingly high number of extrude facets.

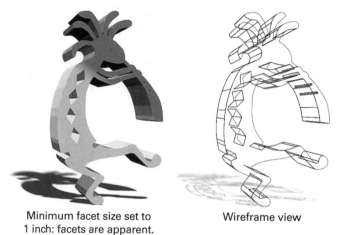

Minimum facet size set to
1 inch: facets are apparent.

Wireframe view

In this illustration, however, the Minimum Extrude Facet Size has been reduced to a fraction of an inch; the little cocopelli guy looks extruded, the curved edges look smooth, and the Wireframe view shows why.

Minimum facet size set to 0.001 inch:
facets are nearly invisible.

Wireframe view

Extruding shapes is something many artists who compete with you for jobs might not be able to offer, especially if they don't own CorelDRAW! However, it's probably not a career-enhancer to use the Extrude effect (or any other effect) as a substitute for your own talent as a designer. Use Extrude with good judgment. Use it when you're in a design rut and need that certain something to perk up a piece. But don't let yourself get branded as the Extrude King or Queen (it even *sounds* rude!).

As a bonus for completing this chapter, Extrude examples.cdr contains a page of base objects you can experiment with and get the same effects the author produced in Figure 19-7. Here you can see the file, and the following explanation of what was done and why will give you some ideas of your own based on the principles behind the novel use of the effect.

- The Artistic Text spelling out "DRAMATIC" is not a "straight" extrude, but instead it was created by extruding the first character and then rotating it. Then the Extrude effect was copied to every other character via the Copy Extrude From button on the Property Bar. Finally, the Rotation pop-up was used in Numerical Value mode to rotate the characters progressively by about 10° difference to create an arc of text instead of a somewhat flat and planar treatment of this flashy headline.
- The bottle takes advantage of the fact that an extrude doesn't have to face forward; the *side* of the rounded rectangle is exposed to view to represent the bottle; a circle was extruded to make the cap; and similarly, you see the extrude group edge more than you do the control object circle. When you extrude something, you're dealing with a 3D object, and it's up to you, the artist, to decide which side of the 3D shape is the most visually interesting. The label on the bottle was created by using the Perspective effect, covered in Chapter 18.

FIGURE 19-7 Create elements of a scene, and sometimes an entire scene, using the right object and the Extrude Tool and options.

- The little tin-roof hut is another example of using the extruded sides instead of the face of the extrude to convey an artistic idea. The roof is a squiggle created with the Bézier Pen Tool, and then the outline was converted to a shape (CTRL + SHIFT + Q) to extrude (you can't really extrude open paths). The shed itself is a compound shape, and the chimney is an extruded circle, rotated along its X axis so it's almost at a 90° angle to the roof.
- The glass cubes were made from extruded rectangles, but they were then simplified (CTRL + K), and the three faces hidden by the original extrude were drawn in by hand (using Snap To Objects for precision). The Extrude effect does not create back-facing facets. Then transparency was applied in Linear style, at different amounts to allow the back faces to show in certain areas and remain hidden in others.

The real lesson here is that the Extrude effect can sometimes be a jumping-in point for an idea and not necessarily the finished product. When you break the extrude group from the control object, you're free then to edit all the objects manually to arrive at *exactly* the design you had in mind.

Chapter 20 continues *The Official Guide* Effects Extravaganza, with Envelopes and Distortions the highlights. Learn to take an object or group of objects from being close to what you want to draw to *exactly* what it is you have in your head. Just rotate this page 180° counterclockwise along your local X axis.

PART VII

Creating Special Effects

20

Envelope and Distortion Effects

You've probably seen an effect in stores a dozen times: the words "Fresh Fish" are shaped in the silhouette of a fish. In CorelDRAW, this sort of transformation to conform objects to a different shape is done with the Envelope Tool. Also in CorelDRAW, there's the Distort Tool, a kissing cousin of the Envelope effect, which provides much more dramatic reshaping options and which makes quick work of adding a human touch to an otherwise perfect, yet sterile computer drawing.

Remember when you were a child and played with that putty that came in a plastic egg? This is the theme of this chapter. In it, you'll learn how to treat solid and stiff objects as though they had the flexibility of putty. In the process, you'll gather several practical and creative uses for the Envelope and Distort features ... and discover that work can be *fun*.

What Does an Envelope Do?

In CorelDRAW, you can start with a fresh envelope around an object, use presets, and copy a shape to use as an envelope of a different shape. Then, you edit the envelope until the shape suits your need. Envelopes are nondestructive; your original artwork can be restored at any time. The Property Bar has a Remove Envelope button when an enveloped object is selected with the Shape Tool. Once an envelope has been defined, you edit the envelope exactly as you would a path—you can drag on segments and nodes and change the node control points to your heart's content.

Here are two visual examples of the usefulness of the Envelope effect. In the top illustration, the Artistic Text object is enveloped, and the envelope is based on an existing shape seen at right. The bottom illustration shows the envelope control segments and nodes in the process of being edited. It's true: the CorelDRAW Envelope effect is just like playing with silly you-know-what!

Envelope shape copied from the object

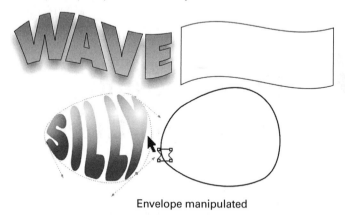

Envelope manipulated

Creating Envelope Effects

When creating Envelope effects, you can choose from three different methods:

- Shape your envelope from scratch by defining a default envelope and then manually reshaping it.
- Copy an envelope shape based on an object on the drawing page.
- Apply a preset.

Let's begin working with the first technique.

Using the Envelope Tool and Property Bar

Using the Envelope Tool, along with the Property Bar options, is the most intuitive way to apply envelopes. You'll find this tool in the Toolbox within the Interactive Tool group, with the Blend Tool on top.

With both the Envelope Tool and an object selected, the Property Bar displays the options shown here:

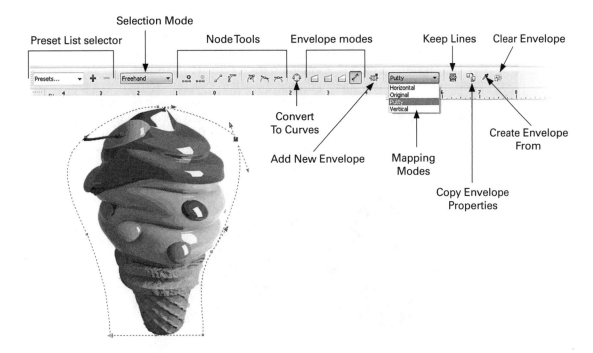

You'll get the best results from the Envelope effect if you follow a sequence of moves in CorelDRAW. Let's work through some basic maneuvers using the following steps.

Tutorial The Envelope, Please

1. Create or open an object (or group of objects) that you feel would make a good target for the Envelope effect, and then choose the Envelope Tool from the Toolbox. Notice that the Property Bar shows Envelope options. The more intricate the object, the more noticeable the effect will be. In general, don't choose a rectangular shape to which you want to apply a rectangular envelope; the effect would be more or less defeated.

2. Click the Envelope mode button that resembles a square with one corner higher than the other—the Straight Line Mode—and notice the markers surrounding your shape.

3. Drag one of the nodes on your object in any direction. Notice that the direction of movement is constrained, and the shape of your object changes shape to match the envelope as you release the mouse button.

4. Click the next mode button resembling a square with one curved side—Single Arc Mode. Drag any node in any direction, and notice the object shape changes, but this time you have some curvature going on with the edges of the envelope and the object(s) inside. Double Arc Mode provides more distortion, most noticeably when you drag a center envelope node instead of one of the four corner bounding nodes.

5. Notice that you can drag an envelope node to reshape the object, but the direction handles on either side of the node are fixed and won't budge. Click the Unconstrained Mode button, the rightmost Envelope mode on the Property Bar. Now try dragging nodes and then their direction handles. The following illustration shows the object group in its original state, and then, at right, it's been worked over a little in Unconstrained Mode ... it looks reminiscent of how your packages occasionally arrive on Mondays, doesn't it? In all seriousness, however, this is a prime example of the plasticity with which you can reshape objects through the Envelope feature. Nothing is hard and fixed in a CorelDRAW drawing and no changes are permanent.

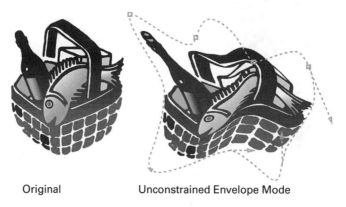

Original   Unconstrained Envelope Mode

You've applied a basic Envelope effect to your object, but the inherent shape of the object remains intact. Clicking the Clear Envelope button on the Property Bar removes the envelope, returning everything to normal.

Caution There is a limit, particularly with grouped objects in an Envelope, to how much you can reshape before the paths that make up an object begin to self-intersect. This is usually an unwanted effect, so the remedies are to take it easy on the extent of the envelope, ungroup the group, and apply similar Envelope effects to individual objects, or to use the Distort effect, shown later in this chapter.

Using the Envelope Docker

The Envelope docker provides an alternative to using the Envelope Tool method. This docker enables you to select options before they are actually applied. To open the Envelope docker, choose Effects | Envelope, or press CTRL + F7.

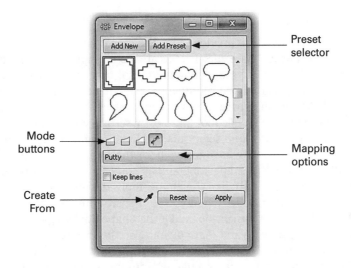

Mode buttons · Create From · Preset selector · Mapping options

---

Tip The main difference between using the Envelope Tool and the Envelope docker is that the docker is more visual—you have a good view of presets, but the set of editing tools on the docker is not comprehensive. The Envelope docker might be for a less experienced Corellian, whereas using the Property Bar with the Envelope Tool and the Shape Tool after an envelope has been created is the sport of designers who want hands-on, low-level control over the effect.

To apply the effect using the Envelope docker, follow these steps.

Tutorial Creating Envelopes via the Docker

1. Create or import an object, select it, and then open the Envelope docker (CTRL + F7).
2. Click the Add Preset button; notice how the Preset Selector window fills with thumbnails of the presets. Choose one (try the heart shape) by clicking the thumbnail; you can see a dashed outline preview surrounding your shape on the page. You *could* click Apply to apply the preset, but don't do that right now.
3. In any direction, drag a node on the envelope bounding box surrounding your object. Depending on the preset shape, you can also drag a direction handle—straight line presets don't have node direction handles, but curved shapes such as the heart do. Notice that the Apply button is now dimmed; when you edit a preset bounding box, CorelDRAW assumes you've accepted the preset shape, so there's no fussing with the Apply button.
4. The Reset button does not reset the preset shape; instead, it calls the last-used preset. If you want to clear the envelope now, notice that the Property Bar features the Clear Envelope button and other options as long as the Envelope Tool is selected and the docker is onscreen.

Envelope Tool Cursor States

By following either of the previous tutorials, you'll have noticed your cursor changes its look, as shown next. These *cursor states* are visual signals that you're about to edit the envelope in different ways, depending on what part of the envelope your cursor is over.

While you're shaping your envelope, the cursor becomes active. But when your cursor is held over envelope nodes or segments (the dotted lines surrounding your envelope shape), the Shape Tool takes over, letting you change the position and properties of the nodes and segments by click-dragging (see Figure 20-1).

You don't necessarily have to reach for the Envelope Tool to edit an enveloped shape. You can use the Shape Tool, and as you can see in Figure 20-1, the Envelope Tool's cursor looks exactly like the Shape Tool's default cursor when it's over an envelope segment or node. When you're repositioning or changing the property of envelope nodes, your cursor looks like the Shape Tool's reposition cursor, indicating the node can be moved, and that you can use the Property Bar's Envelope Node Tools to convert, for example, a Smooth Envelope node to a Cusp node. When held over an envelope segment, your cursor changes into the Shape Tool with a tiny curved-line symbol, indicating the segment can be edited. Using either cursor immediately alters your envelope, but editing envelope curves can be done only when the Unconstrained Envelope Node is selected.

Tip For speedy envelope editing, use the Pick Tool to double-click any object that has an envelope. The enveloped object is immediately available for editing, and the Pick Tool becomes the Envelope Tool. A single click with the Shape Tool also opens an enveloped object for editing.

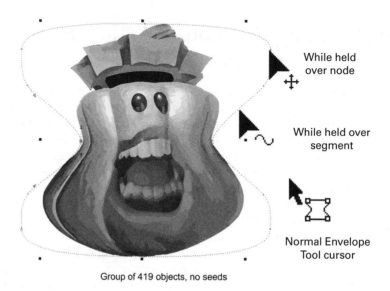

While held over node

While held over segment

Normal Envelope Tool cursor

Group of 419 objects, no seeds

FIGURE 20-1 The Envelope Tool has these three cursor states.

Choosing an Envelope Mode

The Envelope Mode you choose has no initial effect on the envelope you apply to an object; however, as you begin to move envelope nodes around, the mode of the envelope offers features or limitations, depending on what it is you want to accomplish. Depending on the mode, corner and segment nodes take on different properties, which result in different capabilities to edit the envelope, as shown in the illustration.

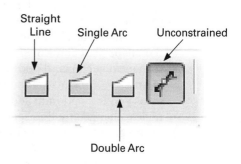

Straight Line — Single Arc — Unconstrained — Double Arc

Tip At any time while editing an envelope, you can change its mode just by clicking a button on the Property Bar. This capability gives you control over the overall shape you're trying to create. Any previous mode limitation is inherited with existing nodes, but nodes you've not changed inherit the new node property. For example, if your envelope is in Double Arc Mode and you drag a node to make a swooping arc, and then you click the Straight Line Mode button on the Property Bar, the arc remains an arc, but all the other nodes can now only be edited as connectors to straight lines.

These modes have the following effects during shaping operations:

- **Straight Line**   This mode (the default) causes envelope segments to be straight lines; in effect, you're manipulating an eight-point polygon when the envelope is in Straight Line Mode. Dragging an envelope node creates a different polygon shape, and this mode serves you well for imitating the shape of a traffic sign, a simple house shape, and other outlines you create with straight line segments. In this case, all node positioning is constrained to vertical and horizontal position changes.
- **Single Arc**   This mode sets the resulting envelope segments to curves and sets side nodes to Smooth nodes, and corner nodes to Cusp nodes; you can't change the angle of the Cusp for corner nodes directly, but you do change it when you reposition a side envelope node. Using this mode, dragging corner nodes creates a curved side on the envelope, whereas side nodes align with the path of the resulting curve. Node movement is constrained to vertical and horizontal movement, whereas side nodes can be moved independently of corner nodes.
- **Double Arc**   This mode creates the effect of sine-wave-shaped sides. Behind the scenes, corner points become Cusp nodes, and side nodes become Smooth nodes. However, the curve handles of side nodes remain stationary in relation to the nodes, causing the segments to take on a double-arc shape. The same vertical and horizontal constraint restrictions as with the previous modes apply. Side nodes may be moved independently of corner nodes, but they apply a similar curve effect, as with the Single Arc Mode.

- **Unconstrained** Unconstrained Mode gives you complete control over nodes, segments, and control handles for envelope elements; it's probably the mode of choice for ambitious enveloping-type artists. You can position either side or corner nodes as if they were ordinary vector path object nodes. In this mode, the Shape Tool and Envelope Tool give you unlimited flexibility (you can *severely* reshape objects), and nodes can be dragged in any direction to shape the envelope in any way. Unconstrained Mode also gives you the option to add or delete nodes, change any line segment states to straight or curved, or change the properties of nodes to Cusp, Smooth, or Symmetrical using Property Bar buttons for these tasks.

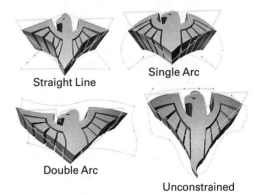

Shown here is a visual example of the four modes, with a faint outline overlay indicating the original shape of the extruded phoenix object.

Saving and Applying Envelope Presets

The Property Bar Preset List selector (shown in Figure 20-2) contains saved presets and options for applying, adding, and deleting preset envelope shapes.

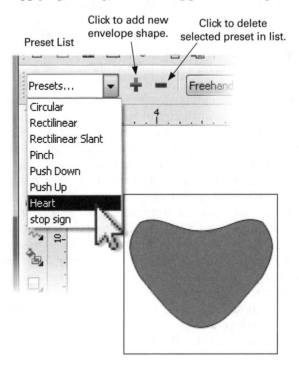

FIGURE 20-2   Use the Property Bar Preset List selector to access saved presets.

You can add a shape you've created as a new envelope shape, and delete presets from the list using the Add (+) and Delete (–) buttons. It's best to create an envelope shape from one single path (no sub-paths)—an object with a hole in it, for example, produces an envelope that's unusable except for abstract artwork. For hands-on, truly warped experience, follow these steps.

Tutorial Creating and Using an Envelope Preset

1. Create a simple closed path you think would make an interesting envelope; an egg shape would work well, for example.
2. Choose the Envelope Tool and notice that the Property Bar now features Envelope options.
3. To add the shape of your object to the Preset List selector, click the Add (+) button on the Property Bar. The Save As dialog opens with the Save As Type drop-down menu automatically listing preset files. Enter a name for your new preset. CorelDRAW automatically appends the name with the .PST file extension; then click Save to add it to the list.
4. To apply your new preset, create an object (it shouldn't look like your new preset envelope) or a group of objects, and then choose your new preset from the Preset List selector. The new envelope is applied.
5. To delete an envelope shape from the Preset List selector, make sure no objects are selected. It helps to switch to the Pick Tool, click an empty part of your document to deselect the current object and then back to the Envelope Tool. Then choose a saved preset from the Preset List selector.
6. With the preset selected, click the Delete Preset button, the minus (–) button. Confirm your delete action in the prompt dialog that appears and your preset is deleted.

Choosing Envelope Mapping Options

You have Envelope Mapping options both for the Envelope docker and while using the Envelope Tool and Property Bar options, which offer control over how the shape of an envelope changes your object's shape (see Figure 20-3). As you can see, Original and Putty Mapping provide almost identical results for this particular group of objects and the envelope shape used here, but Horizontal and Vertical Mapping give you the design opportunity to ignore the other envelope axis (Horizontal Mapping ignores the vertical aspect of the envelope, and vice versa). This option is useful when you want to limit distortion of an envelope but don't have the time (or need!) to create a unique envelope for several different design purposes.

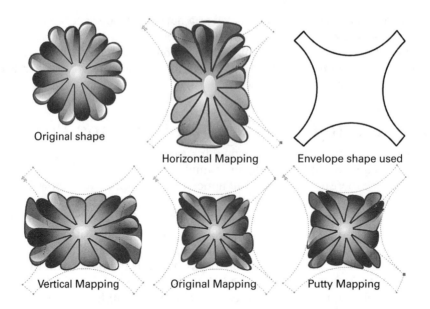

Original shape

Horizontal Mapping

Envelope shape used

Vertical Mapping

Original Mapping

Putty Mapping

FIGURE 20-3 This object group uses the same envelope but different Mapping options.

Mapping options give preference to the shape of your original object's node positions and path shapes. Four types are available: Putty (the default), Horizontal, Vertical, and Original, as shown here:

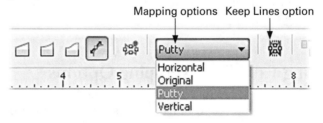

The four Envelope Mapping options, plus a special option for text and another to preserve lines, are worthy of explanation here:

- **Putty** This option (the default) distorts the shape of your object to match the envelope as closely as possible; the envelope's nodes are given priority over the nodes in your object being enveloped. The Putty option maps the envelope shape to your object and results in a smoothly mapped effect.

- **Horizontal**   This option maps the lines and node positions in your original object to match the horizontal shape of the envelope, without significantly altering the vertical shape of the original object.
- **Vertical**   This option maps the lines and node positions in your original object to the *vertical* shape of the envelope, with the horizontal shape mostly ignored.
- **Original**   This mapping type is similar to Putty. The main difference is that Original maps *only the outer shape* of your original object to the envelope shape. Corner nodes are mapped to the corner nodes of your original object's shape, while node positions and line shapes toward the inside of your object are mapped using an averaging value. The result can be less distortion. If Putty mode is too severe, try Original.
- **Keep Lines**   Using this option changes only the node positions in your object to match the envelope shape being applied, leaving any existing straight lines unaffected. If your object is already composed only of curved lines, choosing Keep Lines has no effect, as shown at right in Figure 20-4, which looks like Keep Lines has been turned off. While not selected (the default), all node positions and lines in your original object are reshaped to match the envelope shape—even if this means changing straight lines to curved lines.

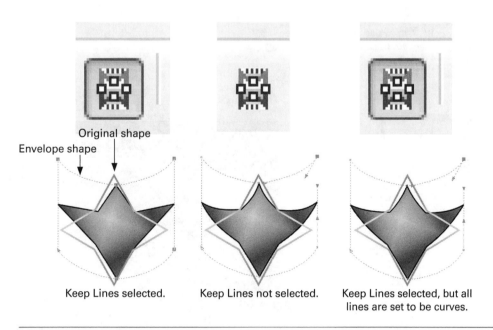

Original shape

Envelope shape

Keep Lines selected.   Keep Lines not selected.   Keep Lines selected, but all
                                                                 lines are set to be curves.

FIGURE 20-4   The Keep Lines option changes node positions but not any straight lines in the target object to match the envelope shape.

- **Text**   This option becomes available as the only mapping option when a Paragraph Text object frame is selected. Text mode applies an envelope to the *frame* properties of a Paragraph Text object; the actual text and line of text are not distorted. This feature presents a wonderful opportunity to walk through a tutorial.

In the next set of steps, you'll use the Violin.cdr file, which contains a silhouette drawing of a violin and a block of Paragraph Text attributed to Wikipedia. Your task is to fit the text inside the profile of the violin drawing. It's a class act, and this technique can be used for scores of designs. Especially music scores.

Tutorial   Creating a Text Envelope

1. In the Violin.cdr document, choose the violin object with the Envelope Tool.
2. On the Property Bar, click the + sign to the right of the Preset List selector. In the Save As dialog, save the custom envelope with an obvious name such as Violin.pst. Click Save to save and exit the dialog.
3. Select the block of Paragraph Text with the Envelope Tool. Click the Preset List selector and then choose Violin from the list.

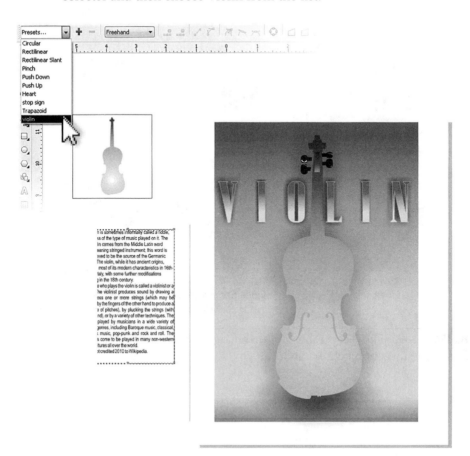

4. The edge of the newly enveloped text is going to look a little busy with the text offset margin and the envelope path around it; no big deal—choose the Pick Tool (the envelope outline disappears) and move the text to fit over the violin drawing.

5. The "fit" is not perfect because the Envelope effect is distorting the dimensions of the Paragraph Text block (but not the text itself) to match the proportions of the violin. Click-drag the object selection handles and adjust the text so it fits neatly within the violin drawing.

6. With the Text Tool, insert your cursor at the beginning of the paragraph, and then press ENTER to kick the text down so none of it is in the neck part of the violin, which looks awkward, reads terribly, and makes it hard to play the instrument. See Figure 20-5 as a reference for where your composition should be now.

7. Optionally, choose a more elegant typeface than Arial. Select the text with the Pick Tool, and then on the Property Bar, choose a font you have installed. In Figure 20-6, Bernard Fashion is used. End of exercise, pretty fancy graphic use of the Envelope Tool.

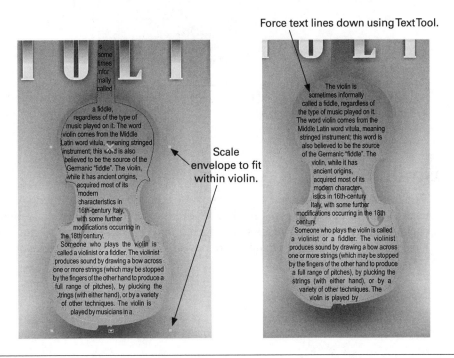

FIGURE 20-5 Perform a little manual editing to make the envelope text fit within the violin drawing.

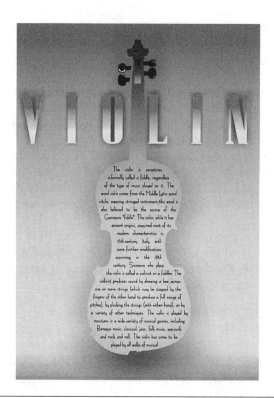

FIGURE 20-6 Create an elegant symbiosis of text as a graphic combined with a simple CorelDRAW drawing.

Constraining Single Arc Envelopes

Modifier keys offer valuable ways to constrain the shaping of an envelope while using *Single Arc* Mode. By holding key modifiers, you can quickly shape two sides concentrically or simultaneously. Hold SHIFT and drag any side or corner node to have the corresponding node on the opposite side move in the *opposite* direction.

Hold CTRL to move the corresponding node on the opposite side of the shape in the *same* direction and by an equal distance, as shown here with the star shape.

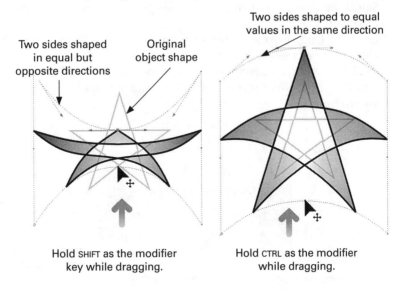

Two sides shaped to equal values in the same direction

Two sides shaped in equal but opposite directions

Original object shape

Hold SHIFT as the modifier key while dragging.

Hold CTRL as the modifier while dragging.

Using Envelope Shapes Between Objects

You can copy single-path objects—and even other envelopes—that already exist in your drawing and use them as envelopes. The commands for these operations are available from the Effects menu and by using the shortcut buttons on the Property Bar when the Envelope Tool is selected.

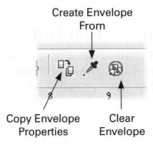

Create Envelope From

Copy Envelope Properties

Clear Envelope

Copying Properties from Other Envelopes

If you've taken the time to create an Envelope effect but you'll only use it a few times so it's not worth creating a preset, you can copy its properties to another object using the Copy Envelope Properties command. To copy an envelope's properties, try the following steps.

Tutorial Envelopes Based on Existing Envelopes

1. Select the object to which you wish to apply the envelope shape, and choose the Envelope Tool.
2. Click the Copy Envelope Properties button on the Property Bar. Your cursor changed to a targeting cursor.
3. Click to target the object with the applied Envelope effect you wish to copy. The Envelope effect is immediately copied and applied to the new object, as shown here:

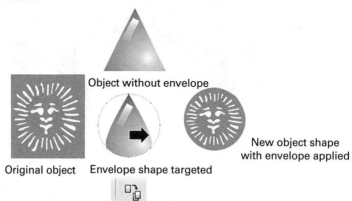

Object without envelope

Original object   Envelope shape targeted

New object shape
with envelope applied

Tip If the Envelope effect you need to copy from is on a different page of your document, try dragging a copy of the object onto the Desktop (the pasteboard outside the document page). You can copy envelope shapes from the Desktop.

Creating Envelopes from Objects

Creating envelope shapes from existing objects is another common operation that enables you to create and apply new envelope shapes based on the targeted object's shape. The steps are shown left to right here:

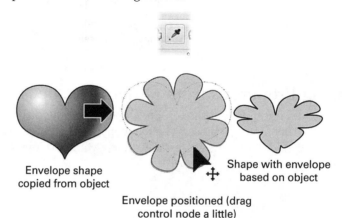

Envelope shape
copied from object

Envelope positioned (drag
control node a little)

Shape with envelope
based on object

Unlike the Copy Envelope Properties feature, copying a shape to apply to a different shape as an envelope requires an additional step. First, you target the object to be enveloped using the Envelope Tool. You click the Create Envelope From button on the Property Bar, click the source object, and then a preview of the envelope shape appears around the target object. It doesn't actually transform until you drag one of the control nodes just a little, or click an envelope path segment; then the target object transforms.

 Tip Envelopes you copy from a target envelope and from target objects produce more predictable results if these envelopes or objects have more than three or four control nodes along their edge. You can add control nodes with the Shape Tool; click a path segment and then press the + key on your num keypad.

Clearing an Envelope Shape

Removing an Envelope effect from an object is a quick operation. If you applied Envelope effects in succession, all shaping can be removed at once. To remove an Envelope effect, select the object bound to the Envelope effect, and choose the Envelope Tool. Click the Clear Envelope button.

 Tip The Clear Envelope command is also available by choosing Effects | Clear Envelope.

Tutorial Copying Envelopes with the Attributes Eyedropper Tool

You can copy applied effects (including Envelope effects) between one single object (not grouped objects) to another by using the Attributes Eyedropper Tool. To do this, choose the Attributes Eyedropper Tool and have both the objects in view. Got 'em? Follow these steps:

1. Choose the Attributes Eyedropper Tool from the Toolbox.
2. On the Property Bar, click the Effects button, click the Envelope check box in the list, and then click OK.

3. Click the object currently applied with the Envelope effect you want to copy using the Attributes Eyedropper Tool cursor to sample its properties.

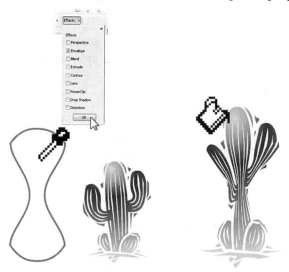

4. Click the object you want to apply the effect to.

 Tip You can apply *several* instances of an envelope, an envelope enveloping an envelope, and so on, if you need a truly gnarly effect. After you've sampled the envelope, click the cursor over the target shape three or four times until your laughter subsides.

Mastering Distortion Effects

Distortion effects apply complex math to the curve paths that make up your object. But artists don't need to know what's under the hood to take advantage of these wonderfully intricate equations to produce outstanding and very naturalistic artwork. The Distort Tool and options are also *dynamic,* which means they create distortion without ruining your original. Distortion properties can be edited at any time; your custom distortions can be saved as presets; and they can be cleared from your shape, just like envelopes.

Distortion effects also change your object without affecting its other properties such as outline width and fill. Using Distortion, the curve values and node properties are dramatically changed, and the more complex your object is to begin with, the more dramatic the Distortion effect will be. Adobe Illustrator users will feel right at home; although distortions are similar to Punk & Bloat, they go beyond this effect in variety and complexity, and when you're using CorelDRAW distortions, you can restore your objects at any time. Distortion effects are great for a number of illustration challenges, including organic-type effects. You can create flower shapes, zippers, swirly galaxies in space—not even the sky's the limit.

Using the Distort Tool and the Property Bar

Apply your distortions using the Distort Tool, shown next, which is found in the Toolbox grouped with other effects tools and is used together with these Property Bar options.

Property Bar options for distortion

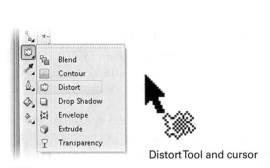

Distort Tool and cursor

You'll notice three distortion modes: Push And Pull, Zipper, and Twister. With each mode, a different set of parameters is available. Amplitude and Frequency values can be varied in combination with certain other options (covered next) controlled interactively or by setting values on the Property Bar. Let's first take a look at the Property Bar when one of the modes, Zipper distortion, is chosen. All three modes offer slightly different options; by reviewing Zipper Mode, you'll get a handle on many of the options.

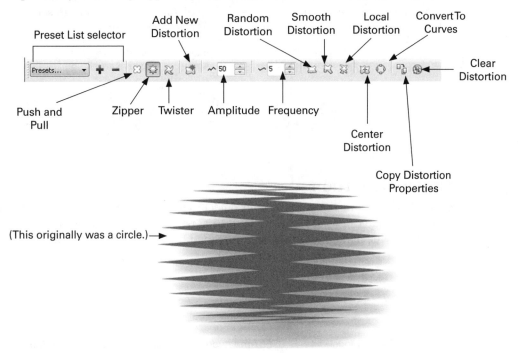

(This originally was a circle.)→

Choosing Distortion Modes

If you've tried using this Distortion effect, even just a little, you probably have a newfound appreciation for "steering" this effect—it's akin to slipping into a Ferrari right after your dad took the training wheels off your bike. However, the Distort Tool will grow on you, and the intimidation factor will dwindle.

During a distortion session, interactive markers provide much of the control over this effect. Interactive markers vary by the mode selected. The Distortion Modes are covered in the sections to follow in digestible, easy-to-assimilate, fun-size servings.

Push and Pull Distortion

Push And Pull distortions can inflate or deflate the slope of your shape's curves by amplitude. The *amplitude* value affects the extent of the effect, sloping the curves of paths from an object's original path, from shallow at low settings to severe at high settings.

Amplitude can be set from 200 to –200 percent. Negative values cause the effect to distort the path away from the center origin of the object, which creates the "push" condition of the distortion. Negative values (which you can also define interactively with the Distort Tool—it's fun and creatively therapeutic) can be used to illustrate flower petals, a cartoon splash into a pond, a thought balloon—all from beginning with a rectangle shape.

Positive amplitude values cause the effect to be distorted toward the object's center origin, the "pull" condition. Again, if you use a rectangle as the target shape, you can almost instantly produce anything from a diner sign from the 1950s, to a sleek, aerodynamic auto or airplane, to a nice 3D visualization of a TV tube viewed in perspective. At the amplitude of 0, there is no distortion. Here you can see the effects of both negative and positive Push And Pull amplitude settings.

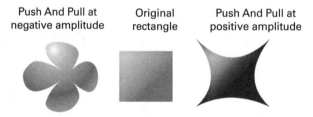

Push And Pull at negative amplitude   Original rectangle   Push And Pull at positive amplitude

Zipper Distortion

Zipper Mode distorts the paths in your object to resemble a zigzag or stitching pattern. Here, amplitude can be set between 0 and 100 percent and can be used together with a frequency value and options for Random, Smooth, or Local Distortion, as shown here:

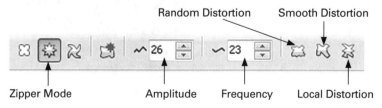

Random Distortion   Smooth Distortion

Zipper Mode   Amplitude   Frequency   Local Distortion

Interactive markers are made up of an outer marker controlling the amplitude and a slider controlling frequency, which enables you to set the number of zigzags within a given distance. Both can be set within a range of 0 to 100 percent. You can see the dramatic effects of various amplitude and frequency values while applying a Zipper distortion in the next illustration; all the zigzag shapes began life as straight lines. When beginning to work with the Distortion effects, you might prefer to use only the Property Bar to define an effect, but as you grow more comfortable with distortions, you'll surely want hands-on control by dragging the control handles directly with your cursor.

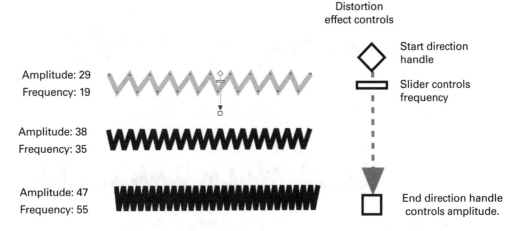

After the effect has been created, you can slant the zipper line by dragging the Start direction handle vertically, left, or right, as shown here:

Tip You can invert the direction of the zigzags on a line or closed shape by repositioning the control handles for the effect. For example, begin by placing the Start and End direction handles so they bisect the line that is affected. Then arrange the handles so both the Start and End direction handles are above the line; notice where the peaks and valleys are on the line. Now move the Start and End direction handles so they're below the affected line. You'll see that where there were peaks there are now valleys, and vice versa.

In addition to Amplitude and Frequency, three additional options are available for setting the shape and size of the zigzags. Each can be toggled on or off, so you can mix and match to create the following effects.

- **Random** Choosing the Random option causes the zigzag Zipper distortion on your object's path to vary randomly between the current Amplitude values and 0. This creates the appearance of nonrepeating frequency and varied wave size, creating an uncontrolled distortion appearance. In this illustration, you can see two examples of Random set at 25 and then at 74. Notice where the interactive frequency marker is on the controls just above each object. You can slide this control instead of entering values on the Property Bar.

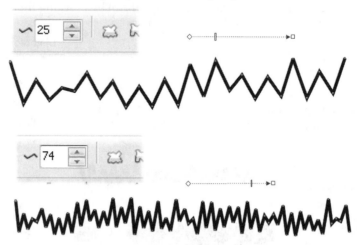

- **Smooth** When the Smooth option is selected, the cusps of the zigzag Zipper distortion become rounded, instead of the default sharp corners normally seen. This is a great option if you need to simulate sound-wave frequencies and equipment monitors in hospitals. The next illustration shows *constant* (Random is toggled off) Amplitude and variations in Frequency when the Smooth option is active.

Frequency = 48

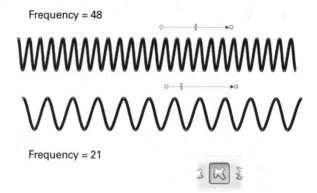

Frequency = 21

- **Local** Using the Local distortion option has the effect of varying the Amplitude value of your Distortion effect around the center origin. At the center of the Distortion effect, Amplitude is at its maximum value. Amplitude then tapers to 0 as the distortion emanates from the center origin of the effect. The results of applying the Local distortion option while the Frequency is varied are shown here:

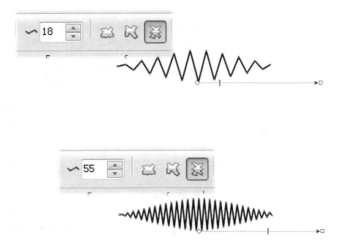

To bring all this Zipper talk down to a practical level, the following illustration shows two creative, commercial uses. At left, the Zipper distortion is used as a coupon border. The only finessing needed was to apply a dashed Outline Pen Style. At right, the diagram of a sewing pattern is gussied up a little by making the cut marks look as though real pinking shears were used.

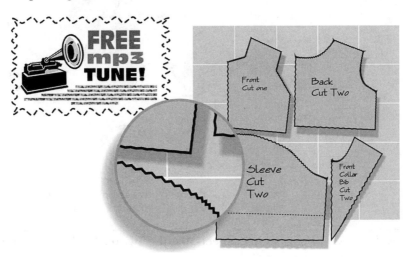

Twister Distortion

Twister distorts the outline paths and nodes of objects by rotating the outer areas around the center (which is largely undistorted), either clockwise or counterclockwise to achieve an effect much like a child's pinwheel toy. Twister options on the Property Bar include rotation direction, rotation amount, and degree of additional rotation.

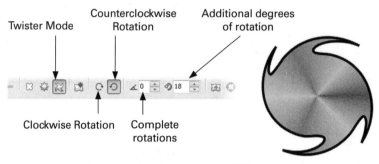

(This used to be a rectangle.)

Controlling a Twister distortion is simple; rotation can be clockwise or counterclockwise, but increasing the rotation really dramatizes the effect of this mode. Whole rotations can be set to a maximum of 9; additional rotations can be added up to 359°—nearly another full rotation. Figure 20-7 shows some of the widely differing effects that can result—it all depends on the number of rotations and the object used as the target for the effect.

 Note Objects applied with a Distortion effect can't be edited using the Shape Tool unless the effect is cleared. However, you can *convert* a distorted shape to curves (CTRL+Q) and then edit away to get the shape you need.

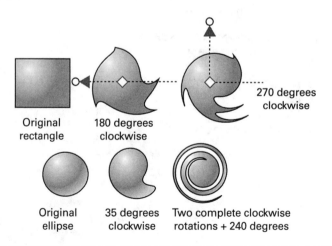

FIGURE 20-7   Using simple objects and the Twister Mode Distortion effect, create wild, organic shapes.

Getting Hands On with the Distort Tool Markers

The best way to shape a distortion is interactively by dragging directly on the Distort Tool markers with your cursor. Depending on which distortion mode you're using, these interactive markers serve different purposes.

There are different interactive markers, depending on which mode (Push And Pull, Zipper, or Twister) you've chosen, but basically you have a Start direction handle shaped like a diamond, which sets the center of the Distortion effect. The Start direction handle is connected to the End direction handle, which is used to define the direction of the effect and also the *amplitude* (with the Push And Pull and Zipper modes). Generally, interactive markers involve a center marker and at least one other, each joined by a directional guide. When Zipper distortion is being applied, a small extra slider appears between these two markers and controls the amount of *frequency* applied. In the case of Twister distortions, the outer marker serves as a handle for determining the degree angle and amount of rotation you apply to an object.

 Note To realign the center marker (the Start control handle) with the center of the distortion, click the Center Distortion button on the Property Bar while the Distort Tool and the distorted objects are selected. It's the button with the + symbol, to the left of the Convert To Curves button.

Changing Push And Pull Interactively

Push And Pull distortions are controlled using two markers: a diamond shape indicates the center of the distortion, and a square marker controls amplitude. The center marker can be moved around the object, but the amplitude marker movement is constrained to left or right movement. Dragging the amplitude marker left of center changes the negative amplitude values, causing the Push effect. Dragging it right of the center marker changes the positive values, causing the Pull effect. Figure 20-8 shows the effects of different marker positions.

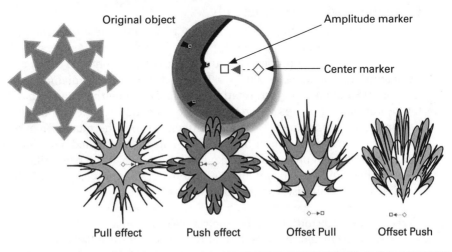

FIGURE 20-8   Push And Pull distortions are controlled by a diamond shape and a square marker onscreen.

Working with the Zipper Control Handles

Using Zipper distortion, the movable diamond marker represents the center origin, and the square marker to the right controls the amplitude value. Use the small rectangular slider on the dashed blue centerline to set frequency by moving it left or right. Dragging it right increases the frequency, adding more zigzag shapes to your object's path, while dragging it left does the opposite. You also have the opportunity with Zipper, unlike the fixed positions of the markers in Push And Pull mode, to move the amplitude handle to slant the zigs and zags in a specific direction.

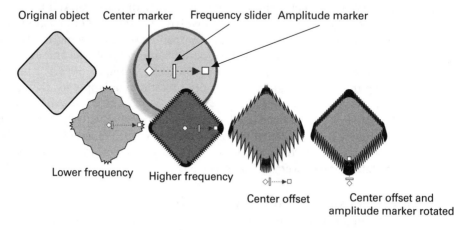

Tip Exactly as with Envelope effects, the Distortion effects can be copied using the Toolbox Attributes Eyedropper Tool. First, you put a check in the Distortion Box in the Effects drop-down list on the Property Bar. You then click over an object to "fill" the object with the Distortion effect you copied.

Changing Twister Interactively

Controlling Twister distortions by dragging with your cursor over the markers is the most productive (and fun) way to apply this distortion mode since one click-drag enables you to set two properties at once, both of which have a dramatic effect on the distortion. The markers during a Twister distortion are a diamond-shaped center marker and a circular-shaped rotation handle. Dragging the rotation handle around the center marker causes distortion based on the angle of the guide between the center and rotation markers and the number of times the rotation marker is dragged completely around the center marker. You'll also see a dashed blue line connecting the markers, which provides a quick visual reference of the beginning angle of the Twister effect and the current angle of distortion you define. Figure 20-9 shows examples of Twister distortions and positions of the markers.

Tip To copy a distortion to a new object, select an object with the Distort Tool, click the Copy Distortion Properties button on the Property Bar, and use the cursor to target an existing distortion.

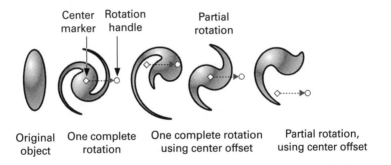

FIGURE 20-9   Use the control handles to create Twister distortions.

Using Distortion Presets

The Property Bar Preset List selector for Distortion effects gives you the power to apply, save, and delete saved distortions. Use the options on the Property Bar when the Distort Tool is chosen, exactly as you use the Preset List selector with other effects in CorelDRAW.

Exploring Distortion Presets

When the Distort Tool is the current tool selected, choosing a Preset from the list immediately applies a new Distortion effect to a selected object. If you've created a really awesome Distortion effect and you want to save the effect while the distorted shape in your document is selected, you can add it as a new Distortion Preset by clicking the Add button. The Delete button *permanently* removes a selected Distortion Preset from the list; therefore, think twice about ever clicking this button.

Between Distortion and Envelope effects covered in this chapter, you should be well on your way to massaging an object or object group from something close to what you like to *exactly* what you like and need. Remember, these are dynamic effects and, as such, you don't permanently change that shape you've worked on for hours. And if you need to exchange data with a client or coworker who doesn't own CorelDRAW:

- Take pity on them.
- Convert *a copy* of your effects work to curves (CTRL+Q), and then export the distorted or enveloped object to any number of file formats CorelDRAW supports. Effects are proprietary to CorelDRAW, but vector information can be used in other vector design programs and modeling programs or exported as typefaces—you name it.

Blends and Contours are the topic of the next chapter, each with their own use, and you can actually take what you know now about Distortion effects and apply a Contour to a distorted object. Will it look weird? Yep, and *interesting*. Just think of it as adding to weirdness, and building on your knowledge!

21 Blends and Contours

Although they're different effects, Blends and Contours share the common trait of creating many shapes based on control shapes. The additional shapes are dynamically linked to the control object, and the "in-between" objects will vary in size, color, and outline shape depending on how you set up the effect. Blends and Contours are terrific for shading flat color fills in a way that Fountain Fills sometimes cannot. Additionally, blend objects can be used to illustrate the transition between two objects of similar or completely dissimilar shape. This chapter takes you through the use of Blends and Contours, so you can add these effects to your bag of illustration tricks and create outstanding, intriguing work.

Blend and Contour Effects: Similarities with Distinctions

The Blend effects create a series of objects *between* objects in a number of steps you define—an object can be a closed path, a group of objects, and even a line (an open path). The properties of each step can be determined by the objects used in the blend; more on this later in this chapter. The Contour effect also creates additional objects in steps; however, only one object is used to produce a Contour. When you imagine a Contour effect, think of a shape surrounded by the same shape radiating outward (or inward) in a concentric pattern, like the circular waves produced when you drop a pebble in a still pond. The following sections explain the properties of the effects that you can manipulate, and then you can decide for yourself which effect to reach for when you need a complex graphic or a smooth, shaded fill in an illustration area.

Blending as Illustration Shading

If you've ever tried to add depth to a drawing and the Mesh Fill Tool is too hard and a Fountain Fill doesn't do the trick, the solution is to blend a large shape through transition objects to a smaller object inside the large one. By making, for example, the outer shape darker than the inner one, you can position a soft-edged highlight on an illustration of a shiny object. Similarly, a Contour effect can be used to create a highlight; however, the contour object should be symmetrical to achieve the highlight effect, such as an ellipse. You'll often see Blend effects used in illustration work for creating photorealistic illustrations, but regardless of whether the visual content of a drawing is real-life accurate or a whimsical cartoon, with Blend effects, you can add depth and suggest lighting and the type of material on an object. The left side of Figure 21-1 shows a decent drawing of a bottle, but you and other viewers detect that there's something missing from the illustration. At right, you can see the finished illustration in Enhanced view in CorelDRAW's drawing window after some Blend and Contour effects were added; a wireframe view, clearly showing the Blend and Contour steps, is shown at center. You'll see how to do this stuff later in this chapter.

Smooth shading and highlights accomplished by the artistic use of blends create a visual impression of strength, size, and other qualities that help the audience see very quickly, "Oh, that's a *porcelain bottle*! It looks really bright! And it probably contains

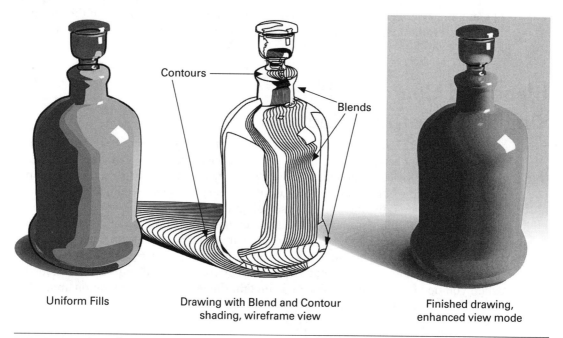

Contours

Blends

Uniform Fills

Drawing with Blend and Contour shading, wireframe view

Finished drawing, enhanced view mode

FIGURE 21-1 A drawing, especially a perspective drawing of an object, can appear flat until you add shading with **Blend** and **Contour** effects.

perfume that's too expensive..." Seriously, the more complexity you build into an object's fill, the more you tell your visual story, and the more readily the audience will pick up on that story and fill in *more* details. And before you know it, you've *sustained your audience's attention.*

Blends can also be used to create many similar objects very quickly; the trick is to blend between similar objects that are quite a distance apart on the page. The illustration here shows an example of two groups of objects blended to create a bar graph; the reference lines were blended from two identical lines. This is a graph with an even, upward progression. However, when you need to create similar blend objects that *don't* follow an even progression, you use the Break Apart (CTRL + K) command to break the relationship between the blend control objects and then ungroup the blend group. Finally, you edit the individual blend shapes to create a more random transition from object to object.

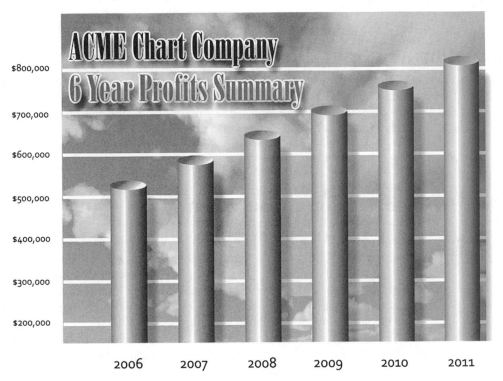

The Interactive Blend Tool and Property Bar

The Blend Tool is in the Toolbox at the top of the Interactive tool group. When you choose the Blend Tool, the Property Bar offers options (shown in Figure 21-2) for customizing the effect. By default, 20 intermediate steps are created between two blend control objects.

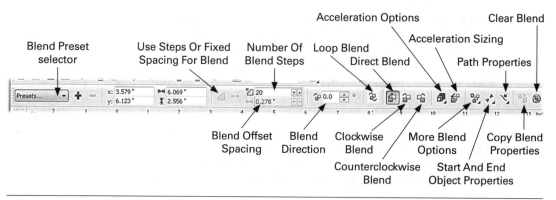

FIGURE 21-2   When you use the Interactive Blend Tool, the Property Bar has options to customize your Blend effects.

Creating a Simple Blend Effect

You might want to work with similar objects to create blends that look like repeats— rubberstamped copies of the original objects—but there's another creative use for the Blend Tool. You can morph totally dissimilar objects, and the resulting blend will probably contain some interesting and useful transitional shapes. Work through the following tutorial to experiment with a basic Blend effect between a star and an ellipse object.

Tutorial A Basic Blend Between Very Different Shapes

1. Choose the Star Tool; it's in the group on the Toolbox with the Polygon Tool. Click-drag a star that's about 1" in size at the top left of the drawing page. Fill it with yellow on the Color Palette, and give it a 4-point blue outline. First, choose 4 pts. from the Outline Width drop-down box on the Property Bar, and then right-click any blue color well on the Color Palette.
2. Choose the Ellipse Tool (F7), and then click-drag an ellipse at the top right of the page. Fill it with blue and give it a yellow outline, but keep the outline width at the default of .5 pts.
3. Choose the Blend Tool from the Toolbox. Your cursor changes and the Property Bar's options are all dimmed because a blend doesn't exist yet on the page.
4. Click inside the star and then drag until your cursor is inside the ellipse. Once you release the mouse button, a series of new objects appears, and the Property Bar comes to life with almost all options available.
5. Twenty steps is too many for this example: type **2** in the Steps field on the Property Bar, and then press ENTER As you can see in the following illustration, the blend shapes make an interesting progression; the outline color makes the transition from blue to yellow; the fill color transitions from yellow to blue;

and the intermediate shapes show two interesting stars in various stages of distortion as they become the ellipse. These intermediate star-like objects are actually a little difficult to make using the standard drawing tools!

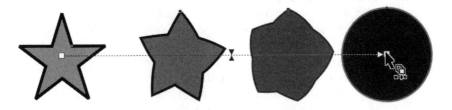

Tip To remove a Blend effect, click the blend portion of the effect to select it, and choose Effects | Clear Blend. Or while using the Blend Tool, click to select the Blend effect portion, and click the Clear Blend button on the Property Bar.

Looking at the Components of a Blend

The Blend effect you built in the previous tutorial creates a fun composition, but to build on your *knowledge*—to be able to create more complex blends—let's examine what really went on and the current properties of the objects on your page. A two-object blend includes several key components: the original objects become *control objects*; any changes made to either the star or the ellipse change the blend itself. The effect portion—called a *blend group*—and the *control objects* maintain a relationship as long as the blend exists.

Each of the interactive markers around a Blend effect corresponds to an option on the Property Bar. Figure 21-3 shows the various parts of a two-object blend.

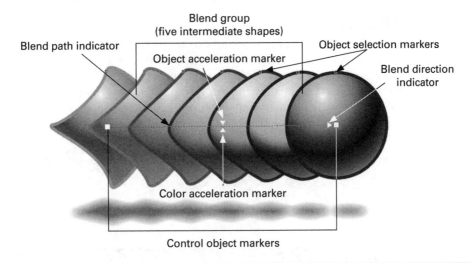

FIGURE 21-3 This blend between two shapes shows the interactive markers controlling the effect.

Editing a blend is a little more of a challenge than making dinner reservations, but significantly less challenging than brain surgery. With the Pick Tool, click the blend group to begin editing it using the Property Bar options. Single-clicking selects both the blend and its control objects. To select either control object, click only the control object itself. You'll see that the Status Bar tells you that a "Control *Whatever*" (Object, Curve, Rectangle) is selected, confirming that the correct object is selected for editing. Your cursor becomes a crosshair as you perform an operation. Similarly, when you want to adjust the acceleration, hover your cursor over the central color and object markers, the cursor becomes a crosshair, and you drag.

When you attempt to do something not allowed with the Blend Tool cursor (such as move an intermediate blend object), an international "no" symbol appears at the lower left of the cursor.

Editing Blend Effects

You can create a custom Blend effect by directly manipulating markers and objects with your cursor, setting specific values for options using the Property Bar, and occasionally by using a combination of the two interface elements. The following sections take you through the features you'll use most often; then it's on to useful but less frequently used options. Think of this as a journey from mildly amusing to wonderful and then on to totally bizarre effects as you progress through these sections.

Setting Blend Options

Options controlling a Blend effect can have an impact on each intermediate step of the blend itself. You can change the steps' value, rotation, color, and the acceleration of the blend objects, as well as save the effect you've custom-designed as a preset.

Controlling Blend Steps

The number of steps in the blend group can be set within a range of 1 to 999. To set a number of steps, enter a value in the Property Bar Blend Steps num box and then press ENTER. Notice that as you set higher step numbers, depending on the closeness of the blend control objects, they might overlap. This is an interesting effect, but if you need intermediate blend objects that don't touch one another, you can resize both blend control objects or move them farther apart from one another.

5-step blend effect

20-step blend effect

Specifying Blend Spacing

To set spacing values between Blend steps, use the Step option, which becomes available *only* if a blend has been applied to a path, as shown in Figure 21-4. This limitation is because the distance between the blend control objects must be fixed by the length of the path. Use the Blend Spacing option on the Property Bar; enter the value to a specific unit measure. CorelDRAW automatically calculates the number of objects required to fit the path's length. Blend Spacing works within a range of 0.010 inch to 10.00 inches, in increments of 0.010 inch. To learn how to blend objects along a path, see "Assigning a Blend Path," later in this chapter.

Rotating a Blend

You can rotate the objects in a blend group by fixed degree values using the Blend Direction option, shown next. Enter an angle value (based on degrees of rotation).

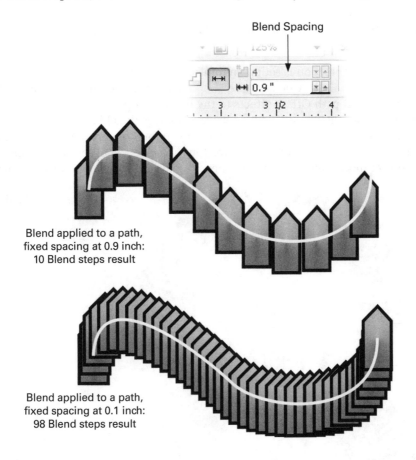

Blend Spacing

Blend applied to a path, fixed spacing at 0.9 inch: 10 Blend steps result

Blend applied to a path, fixed spacing at 0.1 inch: 98 Blend steps result

FIGURE 21-4   Fixed spacing between blend objects applied to a path can be controlled using the Blend Spacing feature on the Property Bar.

Positive values rotate the objects counterclockwise; negative values rotate them clockwise. With a rotation value specified, the last object in the blend group is rotated the full angle, with the intermediate steps rotated in even increments starting at 0° rotation—the rotation value of the Start blend control object. This is a handy feature for suggesting action or even an animation.

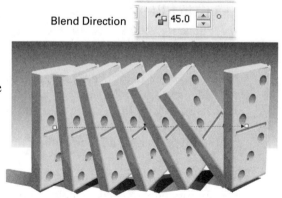

Blend Direction

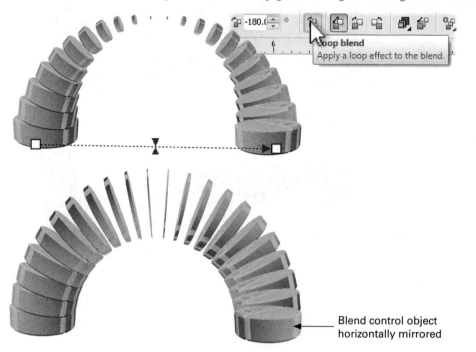

Last object in a blend group rotated 45°

Note Blends along a path cannot be rotated.

When Blend Direction is set to anything other than 0° on the Property Bar, the Loop Blend option is available. Choosing the Loop Blend option has the effect of applying both rotation and path Offset effects to the blend group. Looping a blend works in combination with the Blend Direction value, offsetting the objects from their original direction and rotating them simultaneously. If you then modify a blend control object, as done in the illustration here at bottom, you can achieve a different Loop effect, sort of like one of those children's toys that never really got the hang of walking down stairs.

Loop blend
Apply a loop effect to the blend.

Blend control object horizontally mirrored

Changing Color Rotation

By default, the object colors in your blend group are blended *directly* from one color to the next to create a smooth color transition. However, you can change this using either Blend Clockwise or Blend Counterclockwise on the Property Bar. Ideally, if you want, for example, a Rainbow effect, one control object should be red and the other filled with blue so the Blend Clockwise or Counterclockwise can cycle through the visible spectrum.

Acceleration Options

Acceleration increases or decreases the rate at which your blend group objects change shape; think of it as "preferring" one control object over the other—the technical term is *bias*. When a default Blend effect is applied, both of these settings are at the midpoint of the blend; the blend group objects change in color and size evenly between the two control objects. You change object and color acceleration rates simultaneously (the default) when the two options are linked, or make acceleration changes independently of one another by clicking the Unlink Acceleration option from the Object and Color Acceleration buttons on the Property Bar. In this illustration you can see linked acceleration to the right, and then, to the left control object.

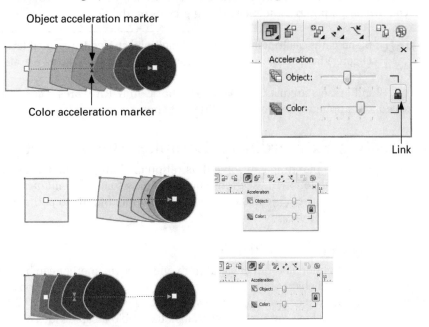

Moving either slider in this popout box to the left of the center position reduces (or slows) the acceleration from the start object toward the end object of the Blend effect. Moving either of the sliders to the right increases the acceleration of your blend group objects from the start object toward the end object of the Blend effect.

Interactive acceleration markers can also be used to adjust these values. While the two rates are unlinked, changing the Object Acceleration affects only the progression of shapes in the blend group.

 Tip Double-clicking either the interactive object or the color markers shown in the previous illustration is a quick way to unlink them from each other.

With Object Acceleration sliders unlinked, changing the Color Acceleration affects only the change in progression of the fill and outline colors between the two objects, leaving the blend group's shapes unchanged. Moving the sliders, or the interactive markers, left or right changes the acceleration. Changing the Color Acceleration also affects the width properties applied to outline paths of objects.

Using Blend Presets

It's taken up to now to learn how to change Blend steps, rotation, color, and acceleration rates of Blend effects; naturally, you want to be able to save an elegantly customized blend so you can apply it to other objects in the future. Saving your hard work as a preset is accomplished through the Blend Preset list when you have selected a blend; you can also tap into some nice *existing* presets on the list.

Note Blend paths, multipoint blends, and multiobject blends (covered later in this chapter) have to be created manually and cannot be saved as presets.

Blend presets are used the same as other CorelDRAW preset controls and can be saved and applied to two or more different shapes.

Creating Extraordinary, Complex Blend Effects

More advanced blending can solve illustration challenges when a standard, direct blend can't. The following sections show you how to create *multipoint blends,* how to *map* blend control object *nodes,* and how to apply blends to paths. Yes, this is the "good part" of this chapter!

Creating Compound Blends

A simple, straightforward direct blend from one object to another can be split so one or more of the child objects in the blend group becomes another control object. Once you have a "mezzanine" control object between the *original* control objects, you can reposition it on the page—which can make a blend look like Pablo Picasso's idea of a caterpillar—you can recolor the new control object, and you can also edit it with the Shape Tool.

You now have *two* different stages of blends within the Compound Blend object; a transition from the start point to the point you created, and then a transition between this point and the end point control object. There are two different ways to achieve the same goal when you want to add a transition control point within a simple blend:

- Double-click a blend group object. This method is imprecise, especially if there are more than ten Blend steps spaced tightly together.
- Click the More Blend Options pop-up button on the Properties Bar and choose Split. Your cursor turns into a targeting cursor, and you can now pick the exact child object in the blend that you want promoted to an intermediate control object.

Here is a visual of both processes:

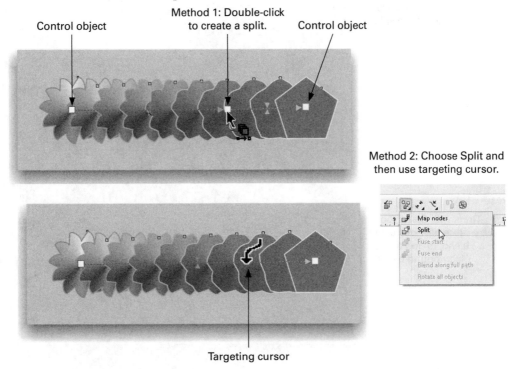

Control object

Method 1: Double-click to create a split.

Control object

Method 2: Choose Split and then use targeting cursor.

Targeting cursor

After you've created a split in a blend, you can edit the intermediate control object—change its fill, change the path with the Shape Tool, reposition it on the page, scale it, you name it. To perform edits on the new control object, deselect the compound path—choose the Pick Tool and click a blank area of the page—then select the new control object and perform your edits. As you can see in this illustration at top, splitting and then editing the new control object affects all the child group objects on either side of the control object.

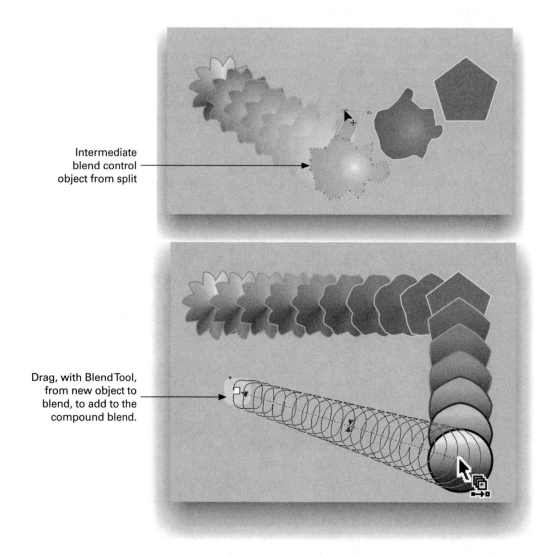

Intermediate blend control object from split

Drag, with Blend Tool, from new object to blend, to add to the compound blend.

You can split a blend in as many places as you have child blend objects. Alternatively, you can add a new shape to the blend by dragging from any new object you've created to any control object on the blend while using the Blend Tool. You'll achieve some wonderfully bizarre effects should you choose to blend between a new object and the middle of a compound blend, but it can be done. In the illustration at bottom, you can see a rounded-corner rectangle being blended to the end of a complex blend.

Fusing a Blend

Fusing, as the term applies to CorelDRAW Blends, is the opposite of splitting, and it applies to a complex blend made by adding an object to a direct blend. When you apply a fusing action to a blend, you remove a control object. The resulting blend adjusts to reflect the new lack of a control object and its properties. To remove an intermediate control object you created by double-clicking with the Shape Tool, you double-click this marker with the Blend Tool, and it disappears. To remove, for example, a control object that's part of a complex blend created by adding a control object, you can click the More Blend Options flyout button on the Properties bar and choose Fuse (Start or End), depending on which end of the blend you added a control object to.

Tip   Because a blend with child blend objects is more or less a blend within a blend, the markers between control objects and child objects also include acceleration marks for objects (their positions) and colors. You can make use of the acceleration markers with child objects to create phenomenally complex arrangements from blends, such as autumn leaves scattered on a sidewalk and a box of marbles someone carelessly dumped on the floor.

Mapping Control Object Nodes

When a blend is applied, the blend group is built from a series of intermediate objects between the control objects. When you use two completely different shapes as control objects, the chances are they won't have the same number of nodes connecting path segments; additionally, the position on the page of the first node you draw is usually arbitrary, depending on your style of drawing. By default, CorelDRAW blends two different objects using *node mapping*: the Blend effect makes an assumption that the blend should start with the first node on the start object, and end at the first node on the end object, and that all objects in the blend itself make the transition based on the same node position on the page as the start and end control objects.

Occasionally you might get a blend that looks like a parade of crumpled sheets of paper, or something similarly nasty—it's interesting, but not what you had in mind! Fortunately, you can match the nodes of your control objects in a few clicks. To map the nodes in a blend, click the More Blend Options button and click the Map Nodes button. The cursor becomes a targeting cursor, your signal to click the nodes you want matched. Node mapping is a two-step operation: click a node on the start blend control object (the operation temporarily increases the size of the nodes so

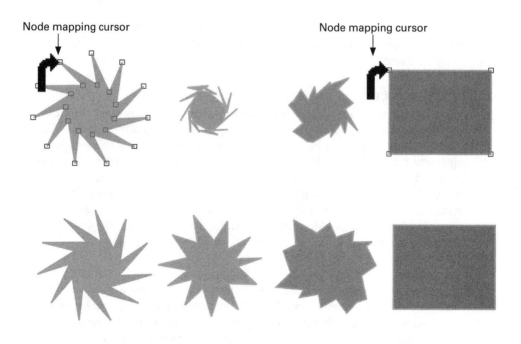

FIGURE 21-5 The blend is confused; you need to remove the kinks by node mapping the control objects to make a smoother blend transition.

you can easily tell what the targeting cursor wants you to do), and then click the corresponding node on the end blend control object (see Figure 21-5).

Note Node mapping is unavailable if a Blend effect has been split into a multipoint blend.

Assigning a Blend Path

Objects can be blended along a path: either a path you draw before the Blend operation, or by ALT + dragging from one object to another with the Blend Tool, with nothing selected on the page. Blend objects on a path can also be rotated, offset from the path, and set to fill the full path or only part of the path.

You can see in Figure 21-6 an example of the ALT + drag a path technique. If your path is a little shaky or otherwise imperfect, choose Show Path from the Path Properties pop-up on the Property Bar. Once you can see the path, you can edit it, just as you'd do with a drawn path, using the Shape Tool.

The following tutorial takes you through the more studied and precise approach to binding a blend to a path, again using the Path Properties pop-up.

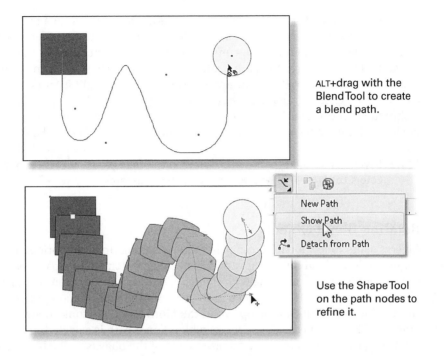

ALT+drag with the
Blend Tool to create
a blend path.

Use the Shape Tool
on the path nodes to
refine it.

FIGURE 21-6   Create a freehand path that the start and end objects blend across.

Tutorial Blending Objects Along a Path

1. With a Blend effect already created and an open or closed path in view on the page, choose the Blend Tool, and then click the blend group portion of your effect to select it, not the control objects on either end of the blend.
2. Click the Path Properties button and then choose New Path. Notice your cursor changes to a targeting cursor.
3. Click the open or closed path with this special cursor; the blend now follows the path you clicked. Notice also that the blend has changed position to align with the path exactly where it's positioned. The number 1 turning into number 2 illustration shows a Blend effect applied to a path.

Path targeting cursor

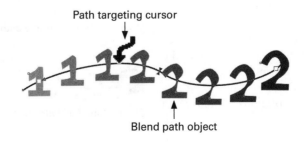

Blend path object

Choosing New Path while a Blend effect is already applied to a path lets you assign a new and different object as the blend path. To remove a Blend effect from a path, use the Detach From Path command. If the blend includes so many steps that the path is hidden—or if the path itself is not visible because it has no outline color applied—use the Show Path command to select and highlight it for editing. Show Path is also a good command for editing a path you created using the ALT + click-drag technique described earlier. Remember: as long as the path is visible (in any view mode), you can change its course by using the Shape Tool to edit the path's nodes.

> **Tip** If you don't want a path to be visible in the final effect, set its Fill and Outline Colors to None. This way you can edit the path later.

Rotating Blend Objects

Objects set to follow a path do so using their original, unaltered orientation by default. For example, a blend involving vertical lines when blended to a path results in the centers of the objects aligning with the path, but their orientation remains vertical. If you need your blend group objects to *align* with the orientation of the path itself, choose the Rotate All Objects option in the More Blend Options pop-up menu on the Property Bar, which is available when a blend on a path is selected.

Doing this applies rotation values to each of the objects in the blend group to align with the direction of the path. Here you can see 3D stars were created using the Star Tool in combination with the Extrude Tool; the Extrude effect was simplified (Arrange | Break Extrude Group Apart), and then the objects were grouped and duplicated to make a start and an end control object for the Blend effect. Clearly, the bottom Blend effect in Figure 21-7, where Rotate All Objects was used along an arc path, is more visually interesting.

Blend Along Full Path

If the path you've applied your Blend effect to is the right size and length to cover your blend completely, you may automatically set the blend group and control objects to cover the entire path. To do this, choose the Blend Along Full Path option from the More Blend Options pop-up. Using this option, you can move the center origins of the control objects in the blend to the first and last nodes of the path. The illustration here shows the effect when a blend is applied to an open path.

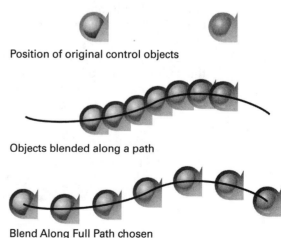

Position of original control objects

Objects blended along a path

Blend Along Full Path chosen

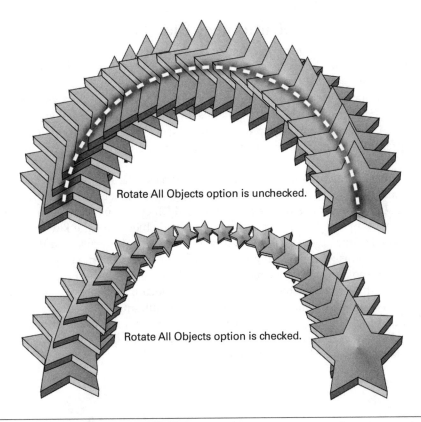

Rotate All Objects option is unchecked.

Rotate All Objects option is checked.

FIGURE 21-7   Use the Rotate All Objects option to put a new spin on your artwork.

Tip   Once a blend group is bound to a path, you can manually space the blend objects by click-dragging the start control object with the Pick Tool. This technique might not get you where you want to go 100 percent of the time, so you also can consider moving the end control object. However, this is a good feature for visualizing how you want spacing to occur in a blend.

Controlling Blend Object Path Alignment

When a blend follows a path, the point at which all objects align with the path is determined by their center origin. The *center origin* is where all objects are rotated during any default rotation. Controlling how a blend aligns to a path is one of those hidden features you won't find in any dialog or Property Bar. Instead, the center origin is moved manually using the Pick Tool, with object rotation and skew handles in view. By moving the center origin, you can control how the objects align to the path.

To perform this alignment operation, you click a blend control object to select it, click again to reveal the center origin and rotation handles, and then moves the center origin point. The blend moves in the opposite direction, and this trick is a very quick way to reshape and move a blend along a path with a minimum of steps.

Working with Multiobject Blends

Blending between *more* than two objects can produce an effect quite unlike splitting a blend, and it's just as easy to do. You click-drag between different objects on your document page. Each time you do this, a new blend group is created. The dynamic link is maintained between all objects in a multiobject blend, which means you can change control objects and the blends are instantly updated. Figure 21-8 shows two Blend effects applied to three different objects with the multiobject blend defined in different directions. The one at left is linear, and the one at right converges onto the circle object.

Each blend of a multiobject blend is considered a separate effect; each has its own control objects with defined start and end blend objects. You can change the start and end blend objects using the Start And End Object Properties pop-out menu commands on the Property Bar. The start and end blend objects are the key to making blends that change shape all over the place in very intriguing patterns. And the key to selecting blend groups within blend groups is to hold CTRL and then click a sub-group within the compound object. Then you can access the options on the Property Bar.

With a blend selected, you first need to locate the start or end blend objects—choose either the Show Start or Show End command. Choosing New Start changes the cursor to a targeting cursor, so you can then unlink the Blend effect from one object and target a different one. Doing this creates a new effect each time a different object is targeted. Choosing New End works similarly.

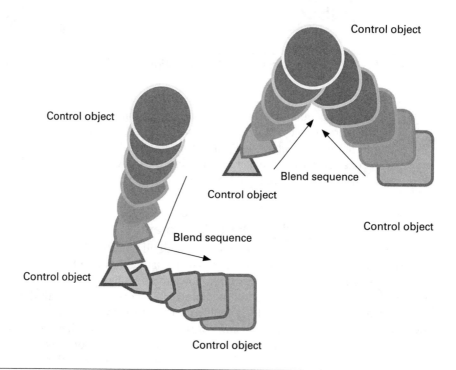

FIGURE 21-8 These three shapes are blended in different sequences.

After a blend has been made, you might need to dismantle it and break the link between the control objects. This is easily done, but keep in mind that it can't be reversed without using the Undo command (CTRL + Z). To dismantle a blend, choose the Pick Tool, right-click the blend group portion, and choose Break Blend Group Apart from the pop-up menu (or press CTRL + K). The control objects then become separate objects, leaving the blend intermediate objects grouped. To further dismantle the arrangement, select only the blend group by using the Pick Tool, and then choose Arrange | Ungroup (CTRL + U).

Copying and Cloning Blends

You can also copy or clone from existing blends. Neither command requires that you have the Interactive Blend Tool selected as you do this, and both operations are done through command menus.

To copy a blend, at least one blend must be in view, and at least two objects must be selected. To proceed, choose Effects | Copy Effect | Blend From. Your cursor then changes to a targeting cursor—click the blend portion of an existing blend to copy all its properties. The selected objects then adopt the Blend effect you targeted. This command can also be performed using the Blend Tool by clicking the Copy Blend Properties button on the Property Bar.

Cloning a Blend effect produces a slightly different result than copying the effect. When an effect is applied by cloning, the master clone effect object controls the new effect. Any changes made to the master are applied to the clone. However, any changes made to the clone override the properties of the master; any properties you've *left alone* with the clone still link to the master clone effect. To clone a Blend effect, you must have created at least one other Blend effect and have this in view. The options you have for cloning a Blend effect to a different existing blend group are essentially limited to the properties you can set and change on the Property Bar: for example, you can remap the nodes in a master blend and the clone's mapping changes, and you can change acceleration of objects and the colors.

To clone a blend, choose Effects | Clone Effect | Blend From. Your cursor becomes a targeting cursor used to target the existing blend to clone. Be sure to click directly on the blend group portion of the effect.

Using the Blend Docker

The Blend docker provides an alternative way to apply blends. Like all dockers in CorelDRAW, it's handy and a persistent interface element, and all the functions you can access on the Property Bar are located on this detachable palette. The Blend docker has been redesigned in version X6 so is options are clear and much quicker to use.

Choose Effects | Blend or choose Window | Dockers | Blend to open the docker in the drawing window. Blend options in the docker are organized into four docker areas: Steps, Acceleration, Color Blend, and More Options Blends, shown in Figure 21-9. Unlike with the options on the Property Bar, the Blend docker lets you choose all your blend options before applying them; no changes are made to the selected objects in your drawing until you click the Apply button.

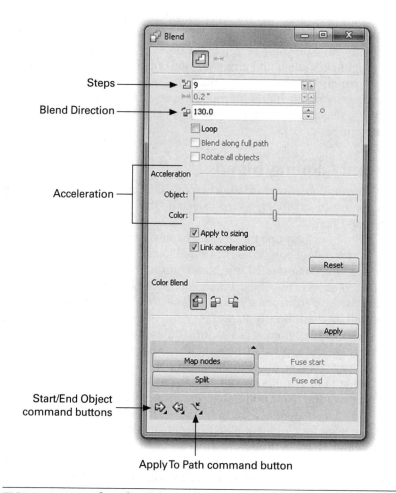

Steps

Blend Direction

Acceleration

Start/End Object
command buttons

Apply To Path command button

FIGURE 21-9 The Blend docker provides an alternative way to apply blends.

Tapping into Contour Effects

Contour effects instantly create perfect outlines of shapes or paths by the dozens or even hundreds. The result is similar to viewing a topographical or *contour* map, hence the name.

During a Contour effect, dynamically linked shapes are concentrically created outside or inside an object's path. CorelDRAW effectively calculates the shape of each Contour step and applies progressive outline and fill colors based on the original object's properties and selected contour options.

While a Contour effect is linked to an object, the object itself becomes a control object, and the new shapes created become the *contour group*. Changes made to the properties of the original immediately affect the linked group. While the contour group is selected, its properties can be edited at any time—without your having to begin the effect from scratch.

Exploring CorelDRAW's Contour Effects

First, let's see what Contour effects enable you to do. One of the more popular uses is to simulate depth.

Figure 21-10 shows two illustrations of climate zones in the Urals region of Russia. At left, Uniform Fills (solid colors) occupy the objects; at right, the same objects have Contour effects. In the Contour version, the control objects still use a uniform color, but the Contour effect uses different colors for the outermost and innermost objects. This is one of the uses of the Contour effect. As with blends, intermediate objects are generated from the beginning object; however, you don't have to draw the end—the inner object—it's part of the Contour effect function. Because many steps are used in the Contour effect, you see a smooth color transition in most of the objects. Also note that some of the objects have a low number of intermediate objects, producing banding, which can be useful in your design work. Just use a low number of steps when drawing a map of the Steppes.

The illustration here shows two versions of the Contour effect applied to text. At top, a two-step Contour effect runs inside the word "Opera," creating an engraved look. At bottom, 25 Contour steps are used outside the word to create a glowing effect; a duplicate of "Opera" with Linear Transparency was put on top of the design as an embellishment. You do not have to convert text to curves to apply a Contour effect.

2-step Contour effect inside text

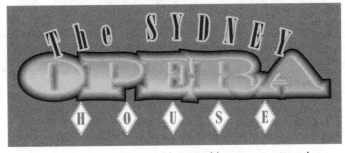

25-step Contour effect outside text with transparent overlay

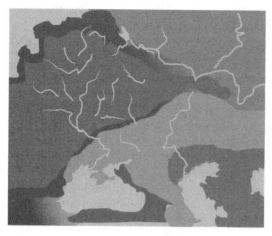
Original filled with solid colors

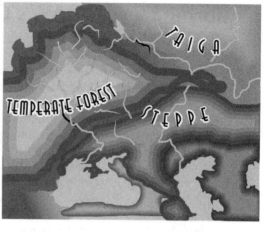
Finished artwork with Contour effects

FIGURE 21-10   Contour effects create a smooth color transition.

Using the Contour Tool and Property Bar

To apply Contour effects, you use the Contour Tool, shown in Figure 21-11, in combination with the Property Bar. You'll find the tool in the Toolbox, with other interactive tools: Blend, Drop Shadow, Envelope, Distort, Extrude, and Transparency.

While you're using the Contour Tool, the Property Bar displays options for customizing the effect. These options include Contour Presets, contour direction, steps and offset spacing, color rotation, outline and fill color, and buttons for copying and clearing the effect, as shown in Figure 21-11.

Let's dig right into using the Contour Tool's features.

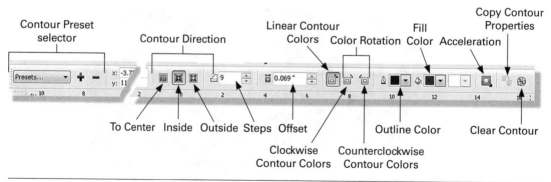

FIGURE 21-11   Use the Property Bar to make the fullest use of the Contour Tool.

Tutorial Applying a Contour Effect

1. Create an object (a polygon or star shape is a great seed shape for contours); apply a fill and (optionally) outline properties. If you'd like to go wild with this Contour tutorial, try filling the object with a Fountain Fill—Contours produce interesting results with Fountain Fills.
2. Choose the Contour Tool. Notice that your cursor changes and the Property Bar now displays Contour options.
3. Click the object and drag (click-drag) in the direction you want the contour to be applied. Dragging from the center outward creates Outside Contours; dragging in the opposite direction creates Inside Contours. The angle of the drag action has no effect on the contours themselves—only inward and outward count. Notice that as you drag, a silhouette of the final size of the Contour effect appears in inverted screen colors.
4. Release the mouse button, and your effect is finished and ready for customizing.

These steps created a contour in its default state. Adjusting the effect to suit your needs takes a little more work with the Property Bar options. The contours outside or inside the object can also be controlled using the interactive markers surrounding the effect. The next section explains the use of these markers, their purpose, and how to manipulate them.

Tip To remove a Contour effect, click the contour portion of the effect using either the Contour Tool or Pick Tool and choose Effects | Clear Contour, or click the Clear Contour button on the Property Bar.

Editing Contours Interactively

The easiest way to edit a Contour effect is to do it hands-on, using the Interactive Contour Tool to change the interactive markers in combination with adjusting Property Bar options. Use them to adjust the direction, spacing, and offset values of the effect.

The black diamond-shaped marker indicates which object is the effect's control object. The rectangle marker indicates the final object in the contour group, and its position sets the distance between the control object and the last object in the effect. A slider between these two enables you to adjust the spacing between the Contour steps interactively, which, in turn, sets the number of steps by dividing the difference. Figure 21-12 identifies the interactive markers and their purpose.

Note Different types of objects are eligible for Contour effects in CorelDRAW. You can apply contours to closed paths, compound paths (such as a doughnut shape), and grouped objects. Some groups, such as an extrude object, need to be broken apart (CTRL+K) and then regrouped for the Contour effect to work. These object types don't have to have a fill, but obviously they'd need an outline width, or you'd be applying a contour to an invisible object. Applying a Contour effect to a group applies the effect

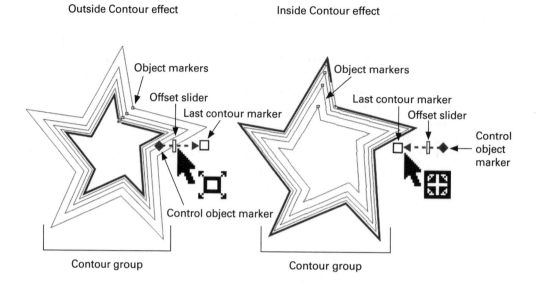

FIGURE 21-12 These two shapes have contours applied in opposite directions.

to the entire group. Depending on how a group is arranged, if objects overlap, the Contour effect "traces" the silhouette of the objects as though the two shapes were combined using the Weld operation. An object applied with the Contour effect is not eligible for other effects unless it's first grouped with its linked Contour effect object.

You'll also notice the Contour Tool cursor changes its appearance as you drag outside, inside, or to the centermost point of your selected object, as shown in Figure 21-13. While hovering over an object, the cursor also indicates whether the object is valid for the Contour effect.

Tip To quickly edit a contour, double-click the effect portion of an existing contour with the Pick Tool.

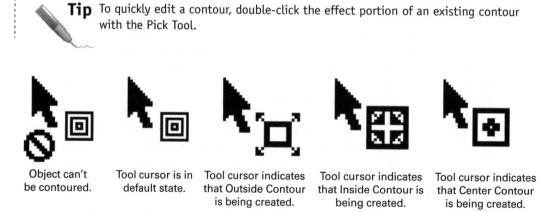

| Object can't be contoured. | Tool cursor is in default state. | Tool cursor indicates that Outside Contour is being created. | Tool cursor indicates that Inside Contour is being created. | Tool cursor indicates that Center Contour is being created. |

FIGURE 21-13 The Contour Tool cursor lets you know what's going on.

Choosing Contour Direction

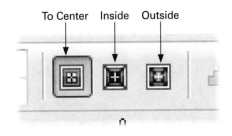

To Center   Inside   Outside

In addition to click-dragging a contour to set its direction, you can also use Property Bar options, shown here. Choosing To Center, Inside, or Outside causes the contours to be applied in the direction relative to the object's outline path. When Inside or Outside is selected, you can set the number of steps and the offset spacing between the steps by entering values in the Steps and Offset boxes on the Property Bar, and pressing ENTER.

Tip To separate an applied contour and break the dynamic link to the original object, right-click directly on the effect (objects), and then choose Break Contour Group Apart from the pop-up menu.

The effect's contour direction, spacing, and offset values affect one another. In the sections to follow, remember that when you change one parameter's values, a different parameter will probably auto-change.

Contour Inside

With the exception of the 47 clowns who can get out of a Volkswagen, there is a real-world and mathematical limit to how many steps you can use to create a shape within a shape. For contours, if the offset spacing value you enter in the Offset box (on the Property Bar) exceeds the number of steps the distance allows, the Steps value is automatically reduced to fit. Here you can see some results of applying Inside Contours to different objects; as you can see, compound paths produce quite elegant Contour steps. Remember: open paths are not eligible for Inside Contour effects; it can't be done mathematically, and it can't be done in CorelDRAW.

Contour Outside

Choosing Outside creates contours *around* your object, and yes, you can use an open path, as shown in the following illustration with outside contouring. It creates an interesting effect you can use for designing everything from neon signs to expensive paperclips.

The Steps value can be set as high as 999, and the Offset values travel within a range of 0.001 to 300 inches.

Open path

Contour To Center

The To Center direction creates the contour inside the selected object, but it does so using as many steps as mathematically possible. The number of steps depends on the Offset value (editing the number of steps is not available)—in any case, your object is filled with a contour. This is a terrific option for illustrating game mazes—with a little editing after making a contour of a bicycle or a flower in a pot, you could fill a book with games like you see on children's menus in restaurants. Here, the Offset value is the only parameter that can be changed; the number of steps is calculated automatically. This illustration shows contours applied using the To Center option; as with the Inside option, open paths cannot take a To Center contour.

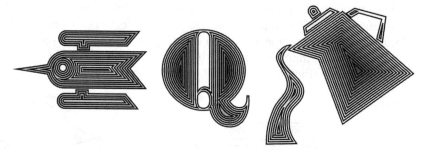

Setting Contour Colors

Controlling the progression of color between your original object and the colors of the Contour effect is key to creating great illustrations; CorelDRAW is a wonderful drawing program, but *you* are the artist! You can set color in several different ways, specify a *nonlinear color rotation,* control pen and fill colors, and even set Fountain Fill colors for individual Contour steps.

Color Rotation Options

A default contour creates fill and outline colors in a steady progression between the base object and the final contour (the end object if contours were blends). However, you can rotate these colors to create Rainbow Contours and other special effects. To do this, choose either Clockwise or Counterclockwise Contour Colors, as shown here, which has the effect of applying fill and outline colors based on color positions located around a color wheel—red, orange, yellow ... you get the idea!

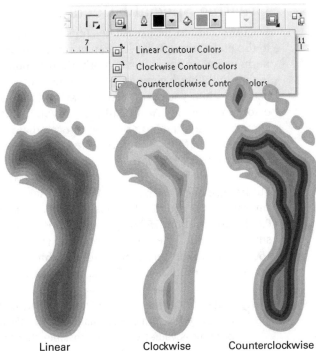

Outline Color

The Outline Color option, the pop-up mini palette directly to the right of the Color Rotation options on the Property Bar, sets the outline color of the last contour in the effect, meaning the colors change steadily from your original to the last contour object. If your object doesn't have an outline color applied,

| Linear | Clockwise | Counterclockwise |

this option still displays black as the default color, but no color will be applied to your contours. To set the outline color, click the Outline Color selector and choose a color.

Fill Color

If you want to wow your audience, definitely play with Fill Color to create significant changes along the steps of a contour. It's the mini-palette directly to the right of the Outline Color on the Property Bar. If an object doesn't have a fill, although you can set a contour color, the contour will not have a fill. This creates an interesting effect if you have outline width and colors applied to the base object, but with no fill and no outline set for the base object to which you want to apply a contour, it's an exercise in artistic futility. To set the fill color, click the Fill Color selector and choose a color.

Note Although base objects cannot have a transparency effect in place when you use the Interactive Contour Tool, you can do some interesting things if you first create a contour, break it apart (CTRL+K), and then apply the Transparency effect to the group of objects that used to be a dynamically editable contour. Try using Uniform transparency at about 90 percent in XOR mode on a group of 10 to 20 objects. Without a lot of preplanning, you can easily generate a color palette simply by experimenting (see Chapter 17).

Creating Special Effects with Contours

Because Contour intermediate steps travel concentrically from the control object to the end of the effect, you can accomplish certain things that would take hours or perhaps not be possible using other tools and effects. For example, a Blend effect is simply the wrong choice of tool when you want interior shading in an object, because when you scale an irregularly shaped object (such as the letter Q), it scales disproportionately. As a result, when you blend, say, a Q to a smaller Q you've centered inside the larger Q, the intermediate blend objects scale different areas disproportionately. Therefore, a key to creating smoothly shaded objects is to use a Contour effect with many steps and a small Offset value. Here's an example recipe: with the Artistic Text Tool, type the letter **Q** (uppercase), choose a bold font such as Futura, use black as the Fill Color, and make it about 200 points in height. With the Interactive Contour Tool, choose Inside on the Property Bar, set the Offset to about 0.001", create about 150 steps, and choose white as the Fill Color. The result is a very smoothly shaded piece of artwork that will print beautifully with no banding, because 150 intermediate steps from black to white within relatively small objects is just about the upper limit for laser printers and most inkjet printers.

 Tip *Grayscale images*—those composed only of shades of black—are usually written to an image file format such as BMP and TIFF as 8-bit-per-pixel images. Eight bits of brightness values yield 256 possible shades from black to white, and this number is a good one to remember when you want to create smooth transitions with the Blend and Contour effects. In theory, you should see no banding in contour steps if you use 254 steps between a white and a black object of small size on your page. The greater the distance between Blend and Contour effect objects, the greater the chance you'll need to increase the number of steps, but 254 is a good bench value to begin your work with if a smooth transition is your goal.

However, a smooth contour transition might not always be your artistic goal; by using no fill but only an outline width on objects, a small number of steps, and a relatively high Offset value, you can indeed design topographic maps, magnetic fields, and other illustrations in the technical vein. In Figure 21-14 you can see an object with the top edge suggesting a landscape—created by using the Roughen Brush. The contour objects are white lines, they have a high Offset value so they're clearly visible, and then the Effects | Add Perspective command was used to suggest Contour effects that have depth in the illustration. The text also has a Contour effect; a Linear Transparency was then added from top to bottom.

Fountain Fill Color

Contour effects also support the use of certain Lountain Fills in Linear, Radial, Conical, and Square modes. If you've applied a Fountain Fill to your original object, the Color Fill properties of the contour group are also applied with the same fill type. If you've contoured an object that has a Fountain Fill, use the Property Bar to set the last color in the Contour Fountain Fill; if the Fountain Fill uses multiple colors, the Contour Fountain Fill ignores the transition colors. If an object doesn't include a Fountain Fill, the color selector on the Property Bar is unavailable.

FIGURE 21-14   Make smoothly shaded Contour effects or make the effect obvious; the technique you choose depends on the illustration assignment.

Copying and Cloning Contour Effects

You can also copy and clone Contour effects to other objects, just as with blends, as discussed earlier. To perform either operation, the effect you want to copy or clone must be in view on your screen at the same time as the object to which you want to copy or clone the effect. To copy an existing Contour effect to your selected object while using the Interactive Contour Tool, click the Copy Contour button on the Property Bar, and then use the targeting cursor to click an existing Contour effect. You can also use the Eyedropper and Paintbucket tools (discussed earlier). While using the Pick Tool, choose Effects | Copy Effect | Contour From, and use the same targeting operation. To clone a Contour effect to a selected object, use the Pick Tool and choose Effects | Clone Effect | Contour From, and target the existing effect.

Controlling Contour Acceleration

Just like blends, Contour Acceleration options have the effect of either increasing or decreasing the rate at which the contour group objects change shape (and color) as they progress between the control object and the final object. You can choose Object Acceleration and Color Acceleration options on the Property Bar when a Counter effect object is selected in the drawing window. When a default contour is applied, both these settings are at a default midpoint—the contour objects change in color and size evenly. Change both acceleration rates simultaneously (the default) while the two options are linked, or change them individually by clicking the Unlink Acceleration option, shown here.

Click to unlink Object and
Color Acceleration sliders.

To access Acceleration options, click the Object And Color Acceleration button on the Property Bar, and adjust the slider controls and/or choose the Unlink option. Moving sliders to the left of the center position reduces (or slows) the acceleration rate between the control object and the final contour in the effect. Moving sliders right increases the acceleration. While the two acceleration options are unlinked, changing the object acceleration affects only the progression of shapes in the contour group. Figure 21-15 shows the effects of increasing and decreasing acceleration.

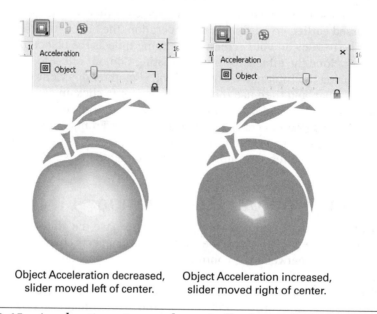

Object Acceleration decreased, slider moved left of center.   Object Acceleration increased, slider moved right of center.

FIGURE 21-15   Acceleration rates can dramatically change the look of an object that has a Contour effect.

When the Object Acceleration sliders are unlinked, changing the Color Acceleration affects only the change in progression of the fill and outline colors between the control object and the final contour in the effect, leaving the object shape acceleration unchanged. Moving the sliders (or interactive markers) left or right increases or decreases acceleration between the control object and the final contour.

Tip Changing the Color Acceleration also affects the color properties applied to outline paths of objects.

Using Contour Presets

Up to this point, you've learned about the effects of changing contour direction, steps, offsets, color rotation, and pen and fill colors of applied Contour effects. Next, it's only natural to save your efforts as presets to apply to other existing contours using the Presets options. Saving and loading a Preset is accomplished exactly the same way for all effects and other CorelDRAW presets accessed from the drop-down list on the Property Bar.

Using the Contour Docker

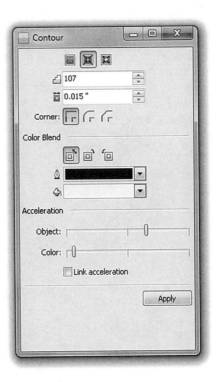

Although the Contour Tool is the most intuitive way of applying contours, you can still apply them using the old Contour docker as an alternative. The Contour docker has been redesigned in CorelDRAW X6 to offer you *all*, not just some, of the Property Bar options.

To open the Contour docker, shown next, choose Effects | Contour, or choose Window | Dockers | Contour (CTRL + F9). The docker's options are organized a little differently than on the Property Bar, but the same options are found here. One advantage to using the docker is that as with the Blend docker, you can choose all your options before applying them.

In this chapter, you've seen where to find the options for controlling and customizing Blend and Contour effects, so you know where things are, but like operating heavy machinery:

- You don't take prescription medicines an hour before beginning.
- You turn the key and the real fun begins!

Dig into Blend and Contour effects; add shading to simple objects to make workaday illustration work an inspiring endeavor and to reap the reward of the automation that's possible within CorelDRAW. You can knock off 20 signs an hour using these effects instead of only 2 or 3. Don't forget that you can break these effects into groups (CTRL + K), ungroup the objects (CTRL + U), and rearrange the objects to suit your specific assignment. Blends and Contours effects are one of the best ways to generate scores of similarly shaped objects, so fill your page with little drawings to make patterns, charts, you name it.

Chapter 22 continues with a survey of CorelDRAW effects, turning now to applying photographic qualities to your drawings through Transparency, Shadows, Glows, and Lens effects. Bring along some drawings you want to spruce up, and bring along your thinking cap. Specifically, your *Lens* cap.

You can groan now...

22

Lens Effects, Transparency, Shadows, Glows, and Bevels

When you feel a design needs something more than distortions, but less than a full-blown 3D extrude look, *elements* of photorealism can push a design in your intended direction. This chapter takes a look at automated and manual techniques you can use to add shadows, engravings, and reflections and highlights to a composition. You'll also learn to use the Lens Effects docker, a device for modifying both vector and bitmap artwork. Many looks that use transparency or a traditional fisheye lens distortion are easily accomplished with Lens Effects. The only hard part is deciding the type of effect that works best in your illustration!

 Download and extract all the files from the Chapter22.zip archive to follow the tutorials in this chapter.

What's Behind a Lens Effect

Looking at your drawings with a Lens effect object on top is like looking through a window or a magnifying glass. What you see through the Lens effect object is influenced by the *properties* of the glass. For example, tinted glass in the real world makes objects in the distance appear darker—this phenomenon can be easily simulated with the Lens effect set to Color Limit applied to a 50% black object.

A remarkable thing about Lens effects is that they work with a vector drawing or a bitmap—you get the same results regardless. One of the more popular uses of this feature is to partially overlap a shape with a Lens effect over a drawing area, to see affected and original areas at once. You can also freeze the Lens effect object, capturing whatever's underneath the lens, and then move the lens object around, retaining the original view within the object.

Using the Lens Docker

Later this chapter covers the Transparency Tool; this tool can create wonderful shading effects and its function slightly overlaps some of the Lens effect features; let's start with the easier of the two effects, which is called in sections to follow simply the *Lens*.

The only way to apply a Lens in CorelDRAW is through the Lens docker, opened by choosing Effects | Lens (ALT + F3). Figure 22-1 shows the Lens docker, whose options change depending on the function you choose. The way to operate the Lens docker is to first place an object—which becomes the lens object— over a *different* object (or several objects, vector or imported bitmaps), choose a Lens type from the drop-down menu, and then choose from different property options.

When an object is selected, the Lens docker preview window shows a thumbnail of the effect you're about to apply; with no objects targeted for the effect, the preview window features a graphic of a circle over a rectangle. Options are covered in later sections, but for now, there's no reason not to take the Lens docker out for a trial spin:

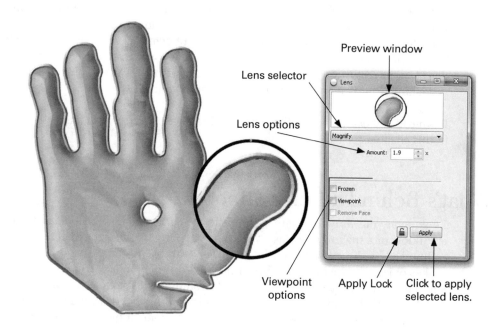

FIGURE 22-1 The Lens docker is where you customize effects to create the specific type of lens you need.

Tutorial   Working with a Lens Effect

1. Create a rectangle and then with the Interactive Fill Tool, click-drag to create a default Linear Fountain Fill from black to white. This rectangle will serve this demonstration; you'll most certainly get better effects using artwork of your own.
2. Create an ellipse and, with the Pick Tool, arrange the ellipse so it partially overlaps the rectangle to better see the creative possibilities of apply a Lens to the ellipse object.
3. With the ellipse selected, open the Lens docker (ALT + F3).
4. Choose Custom Color Map from the docker's selector drop-down list. Choose a deep blue from the From mini-palette and then choose a bright green from the To mini-palette.
5. Click the Apply button. The Lens effect has remapped deeper shades in the rectangle to blues and lighter shades to greens. But areas of the rectangle not covered by the ellipse are still a black to white Fountain Fill.
6. Move the ellipse around a little to see how the Lens effect changes only those areas of the rectangle that the ellipse covers.
7. With the ellipse partially eclipsing the rectangle, click the Frozen box to put a check in it and then click Apply.
8. Move the ellipse around. As you can see, its contents colors remain constant, even when you move the ellipse totally away from the rectangle.
9. Call your friends over and show them this effect. This is *fascinating* stuff!

Tip The Apply Lock on the Lens docker causes Lens effects to be applied immediately with no need to click the Apply button.

Exploring the Lens Effects

There are 11 different Lens types, and each has different properties you set using the docker controls. Each Lens type and its options are covered in detail so you can better judge your starting point when you want to dress up an illustration with a certain type of Lens effect. Because the figures are in black and white in this chapter, you might not discover a personal use for some of the effects types, so certain really interesting effects that benefit most from showing them in color are highlighted in this book's color section.

Brighten Lens Effect

Colors in objects seen through a Brighten Lens can appear brighter *or* darker, depending on the Rate you define in the number box. The Rate can be between 100 and –100; positive values brighten up underlying colors whereas negative values darken them, as shown next. Brighten is a handy effect when, for example, part of an illustration you've worked on for days looks under- or overexposed when you print it. The solution is to design an object to use as the Lens and place it directly on top, perfectly aligned with the area that prints poorly. Brighten can also be used for creative effects, as shown here to make the hat look more stylish.

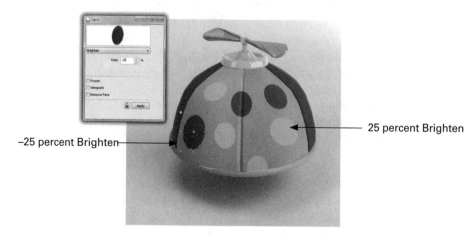

-25 percent Brighten

25 percent Brighten

Color Add Lens Effect

The Color Add Lens fills the lens object with the color you choose by clicking the Color drop-down mini-palette, then combining all underlying colors in an additive fashion (see additive color models in Chapter 17). For example, if you created an object with a red to blue Fountain Fill, and then put a red Color Add Lens object over it, the red areas will look unaffected at all rates whereas the blue areas will change to cyan. This effect is good for adding a tint to isolated areas of an illustration and imported bitmaps. Any color can be added within a range of 0 to 100 percent in increments of 5 percent. Higher values add more color; 0 adds no color at all.

Color Limit Lens Effect

The Color Limit Lens produces an effect that looks like the opposite effect produced by the Color Add Lens. Color Limit tints underlying areas and decreases brightness in all underlying areas *except* for the hues in the color you choose from the docker. This can be explained visually very easily.

Tutorial Deepening a Selected Color Area

1. In a new document (specify RGB color mode and use the sRGB profile found under Color Settings to avoid any attention boxes), import Test tubes.jpg and place it on the page at full size by clicking the cursor at the page's upper left corner.
2. With the Rectangle Tool, drag a horizontal strip about an inch tall through the test tube image.
3. Choose Window | Dockers | Lens.

4. With the rectangle selected, choose Color Limit from the Lens selector list, and then click the Color mini-palette flyout.

5. Click the eyedropper at the bottom left of the palette, and then click a red area on the left test tube. If the Apply button is locked, you'll immediately notice that the areas covering the green and blue test tubes with the Lens rectangle become a lot darker, but not the red tube. If the Apply button is unlocked, click Apply now to see the result.

6. Try increasing the rate to 100, and then try sampling green and then blue using the eyedropper. You'll see that the colors sampled from the image retain most of their color after applying the Color Limit Lens, whereas the contents of the other two tubes get a lot darker.

Color Limit can be quite useful, for example, to highlight an object in a composition by de-emphasizing all other objects, as shown here with colored test tubes.

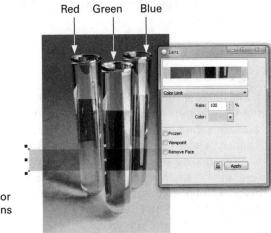

Custom Color Map Lens Effects

A Custom Color Map Lens object looks at the original colors in the underlying objects based on brightness values and then reproduces the design with the remapping colors you specifying on the Lens docker. Usually, you want to choose a deep From color and a light To color; this tints and colorizes a drawing or bitmap in a predictable way. You can also remap your drawing colors in untraditional ways; mapping options consist of three palette-mapping choices:

- **Direct Palette** Choosing this option offers two colors (From and To) and maps the colors found in your objects evenly between the brightness values of colors found directly between these two around the color wheel.
- **Forward Rainbow** This option has the same effect as Direct Palette, but in this case, each of the object colors is mapped to *all* colors between your two chosen colors in a clockwise rotation. For example, if you choose red as the From color and green as the To color, instead of a blend between these two colors throughout

your illustration, distinct areas of red, orange, yellow, and green are mapped with equal emphasis to the underlying design. Blue and purple are not included in the Color Map because on a color wheel, these hues don't appear between the chosen red and green in this example. If you want the entire spectrum of the rainbow, you'd choose red as the From color and violet (purple) as the To color.

- **Reverse Rainbow**   The Reverse Rainbow option has the effect of mapping the colors in your object to the RGB brightness values of all colors between your two chosen colors in a counterclockwise direction. If you choose this option after setting up Forward Rainbow colors, you'll get a chromatic inverse of Forward Rainbow color mapping, a highly solarized look, much like what developed physical film would look like it if you opened the back of the camera before rewinding the film.

Tip   To swap your selected From and To colors quickly in the Lens docker while applying Custom Color Map Lens effects, click the small button located between the From and To color selectors.

Fish Eye Lens Effect

A conventional camera "fish eye" lens has a very wide angle of view—famous architectural photographs feature 90 degrees of vision and more. CorelDRAW's Fish Eye Lens performs the virtual equivalent; you can produce exceptionally distorted artwork, which can be an interesting, if not an everyday, effect in commercial design. Fish Eye is controlled by setting the rate of distortion within a range of 1,000 to –1,000 percent. The effect is so dramatic at maximum settings that the object shapes viewed through this lens can become unrecognizable. At lower rates, the effect is subtle while retaining a sense of drama and dynamics.

Although Burger.cdr—the file you'll work with in a moment—is a good illustration, let's say the fictitious client, Mr. Beefbarn, wants to "accentuate" his sixteenth of a pound all-beef special by plumping up the illustration for the advertisement instead of the actual weight of his product. You can occasionally use an Envelope effect (see Chapter 20) to create a Fish Eye effect manually, but with groups of objects (the burger is made up of 138 objects, many of them simplified Blends), you always run the risk of unpredictably bent objects within a group. Instead, what you can do in a few mouse clicks is create a shape that roughly fits over only the burger in the drawing and then apply the Fish Eye.

`Tutorial` Changing Object Size with the Fish Eye Lens

1. Open Burger.cdr; with a Pen Tool, draw a shape that roughly matches the shape of the hamburger, just a little larger so the Lens effect works best. If you want to cut to the chase, creating an ellipse around the burger provides decent results.
2. On the Lens docker, with the object selected, choose Fish Eye. Set the Rate to 45%. If the Apply button is unlocked, click Apply now to see the results.

Try moving the lens object around a little if the illusion that the burger is almost twice its original size isn't perfect.

3. Let's say Mr. Beefbarn gets on a health food kick and wants you to design a leaner burger. You just crank the Fish Eye Lens effect to –90 and then click Apply. In one click and perhaps moving the lens object a little, today's health-conscious culture will buy the advertisement, if not the burger.

In Figure 22-2, you can see at left the result of an ellipse shape with the Fish Eye Lens type defined at a rate of 45%. The burger bulges toward the viewer, and Mr. Beefbarn is happy. At right a negative rate, –90%, is defined using the same lens object. Happy client, very little editing work.

Heat Map Lens Effect

The Heat Map Lens is similar to the Color Map effect except the colors are predetermined (there are no specific color options). The effect simulates "black body" physics: a hypothetical object (in space) absorbs all light, and the presumption in this hypothesis is that the body is warm. With the Heat Map Lens, colors in underlying objects on the warm side of the color wheel (red, orange, yellow) appear in shades of red or orange. Cool colors—green, blue, and violet—appear in shades of white, yellow, purple, blue, and light blue. By default, colors in the resulting composition tend to feature warmer over cooler colors, but you can offset the color mapping by using the Palette rotation spin box. This is an effect that you really need to experiment with on your own. When you use the Palette rotation spin box, values between 0 and 49 usually cause colors to appear warmer, and values between 50 and 100 cause colors to appear cooler.

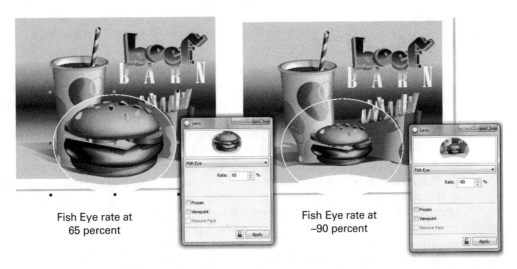

FIGURE 22-2   Two different Fish Eye Lens effects settings are used to bloat and pucker the underlying drawing area.

Invert Lens Effect

The Invert Lens applies color inversion to the colors of underlying objects. In this case, colors are directly mapped to colors found on the opposite side of a color wheel. Black areas change to white, light grays turn to dark grays, reds turn to greens, yellows turn to blues, and so on. To make a "day and night" composition follow these steps:

1. Open the Sundial.cdr image.
2. Put the black half-circle over the left half of the logo.
3. Choose Invert from the selector list on the Lens docker.

Magnify Lens Effect

The Magnify lens produces a straightforward and predictable effect, but it can make underlying objects larger *or* smaller, depending on the settings you enter for the Rate value. The Rate can be set within a range of 0.1 to 100, where values between 1 and 100 cause increased magnification and values less than 1 cause reduced magnification. The following illustration of the sports drink bottle shows one of scores of creative possibilities for putting a magnifying glass in a drawing. You can try this out for yourself by opening Swamp Water.cdr. Bitmaps are resolution dependent, so there is a limit to which you can magnify the image of the bottle. However, the text in this composition is pure native CorelDRAW vectors. Place the ellipse over the fine print in the image, and then magnify it 8× or even higher if you like, and the text remains crisp, legible, and, in this example, a little reminder about what it is you're actually drinking. In "Using Lens Options," later in this chapter, you'll learn about the Frozen, Viewpoint, and Remove Face options for the Lens effect.

Viewpoint

Tinted Grayscale Lens Effect

By default, the Tinted Grayscale Lens converts the colors of underlying objects to grayscale values, which is terrific if you're into black and white photography, but you can use any color you like, thus tinting photos and drawings just by choosing a color from the color selector. It would be silly to show you a figure here of a Grayscale Lens effect; you'll see the results yourself in your own work. Remember that digital images use the additive color model, so the lighter the lens color, the fainter the resulting composition will be. This might be an effect you want, however; try light grays and light warm browns to make new photographs look like they were taken in the 1940s.

Transparency Lens Effect

The Transparency Lens effect is a simplified version of the effects that can be achieved using the Transparency Tool on the Toolbox. Blending modes are unavailable and the object itself becomes transparent—not the underlying objects—to varying degrees, based on the rate you set on the Lens docker. The perk to using a Transparency Lens effect over the Transparency Tool is that you can freeze the effect and then move a partially transparent copy of the underlying area anywhere you like on the page.

Wireframe Lens Effect

The Wireframe Lens effect converts the color and outline properties of objects to specific colors; this effect is very useful for pointing out the technical details in an illustration. You can set the outline and fill colors of objects beneath the lens to any uniform color you choose using the color selectors. The fill and outline colors of your objects are replaced with the selected colors, while outline properties—such as applied widths and line styles—are ignored; Wireframe produces a fixed-width outline.

Using Lens Options

Only one option has been discussed so far with the Lens docker, the *types* of effects. You'll gain more control of your effects in a moment when the other options on the docker are explained in the following sections. Locking an effect, altering viewpoints, and controlling whether the page background is involved in an effect open extra doors to this docker.

Using the Frozen Option

The Frozen option causes the view seen through any Lens effect to remain constant—even if the lens object itself is moved. This gives you the option to apply and freeze the lens object view and use it for other purposes. Behind the scenes, some complex calculations are being performed. A Frozen Lens effect object can actually be ungrouped to reveal a set of objects based on the lens you've applied. If the effect is applied above a bitmap, the result is often a complete copy of the filtered image area, and it can be exported as a bitmap.

After choosing the Frozen option, the lens object can be ungrouped (CTRL + U). This action breaks the dynamic link between the lens object and the view of objects seen through it and converts the effect to a collection of ungrouped vector and/or bitmap objects. Each of the objects representing the complete effect becomes a separate object, including the lens object, the page background, and the objects within the lens view.

Walk through the following tutorial to see how the Wireframe Lens is used in combination with freezing a lens object so you can move and edit the lens object independent of the spanner illustration. Open Spanner.cdr now:

Tutorial Making a Frozen Treat

1. Choose the Polygon Tool (press Y) to make this a mechanical-looking composition. On the Property Bar, set the Points or Sides to **7**, and then hold CTRL and drag to create a symmetrical polygon about 2" wide.
2. With the Pick Tool, select the spanner group of objects and then right-click over black on the Color Palette. Wireframe doesn't work if the underlying objects have no outline, and ostensibly doing this action ruins the look of the illustration, but you're not done yet.
3. Put the polygon over any area of the spanner, and then on the Lens docker, choose Wireframe, set the Outline Color to white, and then set the Fill Color to blue, to create a blueprint-style Lens effect, which you can see in Figure 22-3. You can't change the Outline Width so the effect might look a little wimpy right now; just wait a few steps when you can dramatically enhance the Lens view.

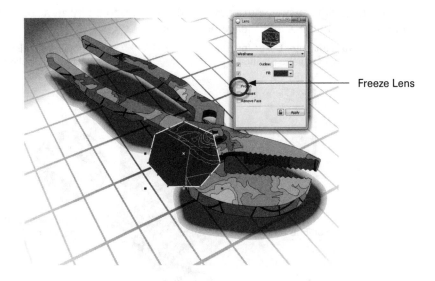

Freeze Lens

FIGURE 22-3   Freezing a lens object lets you move and edit it without affecting the underlying objects.

4. Click the Frozen checkbox. A Lens can be frozen and unfrozen (thawed?) and then moved; however, if you alter the contents of the frozen object, it is no longer a lens object—it becomes a group of objects.
5. On the Toolbox, click the Outline Pen, and then choose **2 pt** from the list.
6. Move the polygon around if you like. Notice also that by applying a 2-point outline to the frozen lens object, background areas such as the grid the spanner is resting on become visible. Everything under the Lens is now part of a group of vector objects—you can press CTRL + U now to ungroup the objects and individually recolor them if you like.

Changing a Lens Viewpoint

The Viewpoint option offers the chance to move a lens object but also to retain the view of the objects the lens was originally over. The Lens Viewpoint option lets you move a Lens and keep the view inside the Lens constant—like freezing a lens—but this option *keeps the effect dynamic*. When you check Lens Viewpoint on the docker, an Edit button appears. You then click-drag interactively to reposition the viewpoint of the lens effect either using your cursor (indicated onscreen by an *X*) or by entering numeric values in the X and Y page position boxes.

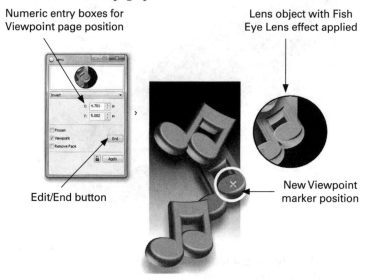

Numeric entry boxes for
Viewpoint page position

Lens object with Fish
Eye Lens effect applied

Edit/End button

New Viewpoint
marker position

Tip The view seen through a lens object is dependent on the object order on a layer—all objects layered below the lens object appear in the lens. When the Viewpoint is repositioned, you may find that an object might not appear visible. Arranging objects in back of the lens object causes them to be affected; arranging them in front of the lens object prevents the Lens effect from changing them.

The default Viewpoint position of a lens effect is always the center of your object, but you can move it anywhere you like. After moving it, click the End button and then the Apply button on the Lens docker to set the new position.

Using the Remove Face Option

Remove Face is available for only a few types of Lens effects and lets you specify whether or not other objects and the page background participate in the effect. By default, whenever a Lens effect is applied, the background—your page, which is usually white—is involved in the effect.

However, if the Lens you are using changes the colors—such as Custom Color Map—and you *don't* want your background to be changed within the view seen through the lens object, choosing this option leaves the background unaltered. The design idea is to remap only the objects under the Lens. Without Remove Face, a background on your drawing page is tinted, but after Remove Face is applied, the page background of your composition is unaffected by the tinting effect.

Clearing Things Up with the Transparency Tool

Transparency is an effect CorelDRAW users have leveraged for many years to illustrate scenes that have a very photorealistic look. The Transparency Tool is quite different than the Transparency Lens in how you use it and the effect you achieve. You can set directions for transparency such as linear and radial, and also various operators (styles of transparency) are available from the Property Bar that let you determine how a partially transparent object interacts with objects below it.

One thing is good to keep in mind when working with transparency in a design: this is the way you blend colors between objects. That's it; your work doesn't benefit from a totally transparent object—there has to be *some* influence from the object to which you apply transparency, and it's usually color. In a way, to think about transparency is to think about color blending.

One of the keys to accomplishing amazing artwork using the Transparency Tool is *the fill* that a semitransparent object has; in addition to Uniform Fills, Fountain and Pattern Fills can also take on transparency. You put fills and transparency together, and you're talking seriously sophisticated compositions! Another key lies in how you approach a drawing in which you plan to feature partially transparent objects. To illustrate with a real-world object, there will certainly be a few *nontransparent* objects in such a drawing, so don't overindulge in transparency when only certain parts of an illustration need the effect. In the illustration here, you can see what is today a fairly common button for a Web page; it suggests glass. At left, you can see a wireframe view; not many objects went into a fairly convincing drawing of a glass button.

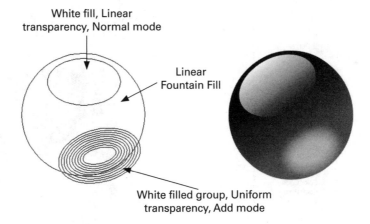

White fill, Linear
transparency, Normal mode

Linear
Fountain Fill

White filled group, Uniform
transparency, Add mode

Using the Transparency Tool and Property Bar

The Transparency effects discussed next are applied using the Transparency Tool located in the Toolbox and grouped with other interactive tools; the Contour Tool is on top.

Tip When creating a transparency, you can set whether the Fill and Outline properties of objects are included in a Transparency effect. Choose All, Fill, or Outline using Property Bar options.

When the Transparency Tool is selected, the Property Bar displays all options to control the Transparency effect. These options, as shown in Figure 22-4, are used together with any interactive markers surrounding the target object.

Often, the most rewarding way to discover and gain control over a feature in CorelDRAW or any program is to dive straight in. The following tutorial might seem a little challenging because an explanation of the Transparency options is provided on the fly, sort of like getting directions *while* you're driving, but you might want the power of transparencies at hand *right now*, as we all do with valuable stuff! Follow along here to create a fairly realistic composition of a child's marble; the Transparency effect will take care of the shading and the highlights. You can check out the Marble. cdr document to see and take apart the components at any time:

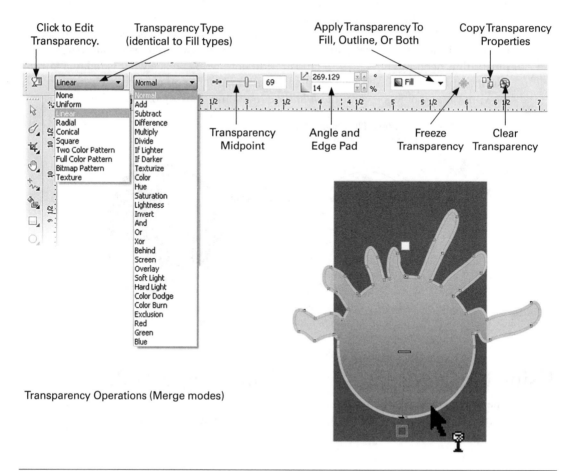

FIGURE 22-4 Use the Property Bar to customize a transparency object.

Tutorial   ## Creating a Dimensional Drawing Through Transparency

1. Create a circle (choose the Ellipse Tool and then hold CTRL while you drag). Give it a Bitmap Pattern Fill by first choosing the Fill Tool; choose Bitmap Pattern from the Fill Type selector on the Property Bar, and then choose the first pattern from the Fill drop-down on the Property Bar, to the right of the Fill Type selector.
2. Press CTRL + C and then CTRL + V to put a duplicate of the circle directly above the original. Click the black color well on the Color Palette to give this duplicate a uniform black fill.
3. Choose the Transparency Tool. Choose Radial as the Transparency type from the Property Bar, and then choose If Darker from the Operator list on the Property Bar.
4. Click-drag the interactive marker, the black one that shows the start of the radial transparency, and move it just a little toward 10 o'clock. Then click-drag the end marker (the white one) toward 4 o'clock until the shading that this semitransparent object lends to the underlying bitmap-filled object creates the appearance of light coming into the scene from 10 o'clock. This is a classic *key lighting* effect used by photographers, so the composition should look a little photorealistic now. Refer to the illustration here, because you were promised directions while you're driving, and this figure is a road map!
5. Create a small white circle, about a tenth the size of the circle. Fill it with white and then choose the Transparency Tool.
6. Set the Transparency type to Radial for the circle, and leave the Operator Merge mode at the default of Normal.
7. By default, the Radial Transparency produces the opposite effect from the one desired here: this object should serve as a highlight on the child's marble; on the Color Palette, drag the black color well onto the end marker of the transparency, and then drag white to the start marker.
8. Drag the end marker to just inside the circle object; doing this ensures that the object is 100 percent transparent at its edges, creating a perfect highlight object. Put it at the upper left of the marble drawing, and consider this a frenetic tutorial well done!

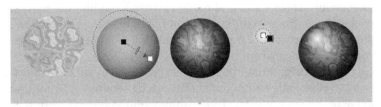

Step 1   Step 4   Result of Steps 1–4   Step 7   Finished marble
                                                                illustration

Setting Transparency Properties

If you have experience with CorelDRAW's Fill Tool, you're 99 percent of the way to mastering the Transparency Fill types with the Transparency Tool. Because transparency isn't the same as an object's fill, the following sections take you through some unique properties. There are wonderful design potentials you can leverage by choosing your Transparency type according to what you need to design.

Uniform Transparency

Uniform Transparency is the default for objects to which you assign this trait; the object will feature a flat and even Transparency value. The way this semitransparent object blends with underlying objects is completely predictable. For example, if you assign a red rectangle and then a blue rectangle with 50 percent (the default Transparency amount) and overlap them, yep, you'll see violet in the intersection.

Tip The Uniform Transparency type has no control markers over the object as other types do.

Fountain Fill Transparencies

Transparent objects that use any of the Fountain Fill direction types are an exceptionally powerful tool for illustration, as you'll see in a moment. What governs the degree of transparency at the start and end points are the control markers, not only their position relative to the object underneath but also *the brightness value* of the markers. Fountain Fill Transparencies are driven *by any of 256 shades, from black to white.* Let's use the Linear Transparency type; you understand this type and all the others (Radial, Conical, and so on) will become obvious. When you click-drag using Linear Transparency on an object, the start marker is white, indicating full opacity, and the end marker is black, indicating no opacity at all.

Here's Trick Number One in creating an elegant Fountain Fill Transparency: you can change the degree of opacity at the start and end points by using two methods and a combination of the two:

- Reposition the start and end markers. If you position the markers way outside of the object, the transition between full and no opacity will be gradual and the outermost parts of the transparent object will be neither completely opaque nor completely transparent if you do this.
- Change the brightness; the markers can have any of 256 shades of black. Let's say you have the start and end markers exactly where you want them; you like the angle of the Fountain Fill Transparency. But you don't want the end (the black marker) to be 100 percent transparent. You click-drag a deep shade of black from the Color Palette and then drop it onto the black end marker. The end of the transparency then becomes mostly but not 100 percent transparent.

Trick Number Two is to choose the transparency object's color to influence (usually to tint) the objects below the transparency object. Here's a visual example: some black Paragraph Text is on the bottom of the drawing page. On top of it is a rectangle. At left, the rectangle is filled with white and a Linear Fountain Fill Transparency is click-dragged from top to bottom. The text appears to be coming out of a fog. In the center, a 50 percent black fill is then applied to the rectangle and a different visual effect is achieved—the Paragraph Text still looks like it's in a haze, but more of it is legible toward the top. At right, black is the fill for the rectangle, and now the top of the text is as illegible as the white rectangle example, but a different artistic sense of drama has been achieved. You now know two different methods for shading with Transparency Fills of the Fountain type: change the control markers and change the color of the transparency object.

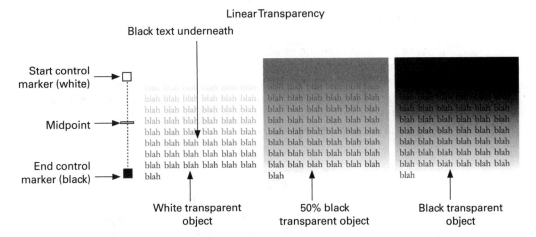

Property Bar Options for Transparency Effects

Some CorelDRAW users prefer the hand-on controls of interactive markers whereas others choose the precision offered by the Property Bar's numeric entry fields and sliders; let's look at what is available on the Property Bar when the Transparency Tool is selected along with a target object. In Figure 22-4, you saw the Midpoint slider, and the Angle and Edge Pad fields called out; here's what they do:

> **Tip** If no object is selected and you want to make any object partially transparent, the Transparency Tool is a selection tool in addition to controlling the interactive markers. With the tool selected, click once to select the object to which you want to apply transparency, and then click-drag to add and set the control markers.

- **Midpoint slider** This slider controls where the 50 percent point in a transparency is located. It does not indicate where an object is 50 percent transparent, but, instead, sets a relative 50 percent break point, because as mentioned earlier, you can set the start and end markers to any brightness value you like.

- **Angle**   When you click-drag, for example, a Linear Transparency, you might not get the angle exactly the way you'd like it. Use this box to set an exact angle for the transition. Ninety degrees runs a Linear Fountain Fill from transparent at bottom to opaque at top, and the angle measurement decreases as you travel clockwise.
- **Edge Pad**   Increases or decreases the "speed," the contrast of the Fountain Fill Transparency. The highest value is 49, at which the transition is so abrupt you could shave yourself with the edge between the start and end opacity amounts.

> **Tip**   By default, when you hold CTRL and drag a control marker for a Fountain-type Transparency, you constrain the angle you're setting in 30 degree increments. You can also straighten a crooked Fountain Fill Transparency you've manually defined by CTRL+click-dragging.

Here is a practical example of a Linear Transparency used in an illustration to imitate the "glass icon" reflective look. In this illustration, the folder design has been copied and then mirrored horizontally. Then the Linear Transparency is applied to the duplicate group of objects, from almost 100 percent opaque where it meets the original, to 100 percent transparent at the bottom. Transparency is not only good for simulating glass but also reflective objects.

Additional Fountain Transparency Types

You also have Radial, Conical, and Square Fountain Transparency types at hand when you design something you need to look more dimensional. The Radial Transparency effect is fantastic for making specular highlights—brilliant but soft-edged highlights you commonly see when sunlight hits a highly polished metal or smooth plastic object. A Conical Transparency is good to use when you need a pie-wedge-shaped area, and this, too, is good for simulating highlights and reflections. The Square Transparency type might not prove to be useful on a day-to-day basis, but it's very easy to create soft-edged highlights to use as window panes and other right-angle geometric areas you want to emphasize visually.

Before covering the Bitmap-type Transparency Fills—listed below the Fountain Fill Transparency types on the Property Bar drop-down list—let's take a detour in this documentation to explain *transparency operations*. Also called Merge modes and Blend modes, operations have an additional effect on all objects that have a Transparency effect. Operations can get you out of a design predicament when a transparent object doesn't seamlessly blend with objects below it.

Using Transparency Operations (Merge Modes)

The Property Bar has a list of *modes* for you to set how your transparency colors interact with the colors of underlying objects. These options further the visual complexity of semitransparent objects, and their use is for professional-level illustration work. For example, a red plastic drinking glass on a yellow tablecloth will show some orange through it due to the nature of colors that mix as light passes through it. However, the shadow cast by the nontransparent areas of the glass will not be the same shade of orange as the light we see through the glass, because light in the real world is subtractive and the shadow in such a scene would be a deep, muddy orange, almost brown. But you don't have to calculate light properties or material properties when you illustrate if you understand what the Transparency operations do, and then you choose the one appropriate one for your illustration.

The following definitions of Merge modes describe the effects you can expect; let's use "source" as the top object that takes the Transparency effect, the "target" is one or more objects below the transparency object that are overlapped by the transparency object, and the "result" is the color you see in your drawing in the overlapping areas:

- **Normal** Normal Merge mode is the default whenever a new transparency effect is applied to an object. Choosing Normal at 50 percent opacity usually produces predictable color blends between the source and target objects; for example, a pure yellow object at 50 percent Normal opacity over a pure red object yields orange as a result in overlapping areas. Similarly and in traditional physical painting, a white source object produces a *tint* result over a pure color object (a pastel color), whereas a black source object produces a *shade* of the target object's color (if you're shopping for house paints, the salesperson will love this jargon).
- **Add** The Add(itive) mode applies transparency in a similar fashion to Normal mode, except it whitens and brightens the result, seriously! In English, there's a subtle but distinct difference between "plus" and "added to"; similarly, Additive mode moves the combined result of the target and source object colors in a positive direction in brightness value. The artistic result is good for adding subtle shading to composition areas; this is something painters through the centuries could not do without the added step of applying pure white because inks and pigments use the real-world subtractive color model.
- **Subtract** This mode ignores the brightness value in the source object and is similar to mixing physical pigments. If you use Subtractive Transparency mode on green and red objects and overlap them with a target blue object, the result color will be black.

- **Difference**   Remember color opposites on the color wheel? This is what Difference mode performs; it moves the result color to the difference (on the color wheel) between the source and target colors. For example, a red Difference Transparency object over a yellow target object produces green areas. You'll see the Difference effect most clearly if you just put such an object over an empty area of the drawing page. A Red Difference object will cast cyan on the page as the result. This is a useful blending mode for creating dramatic lighting effects—for example, you can shine a Difference mode drawing of a shaft of theater spotlight on an object and get truly wonderful and bizarre lighting effects.

- **Multiply**   Multiply always produces a darker result color from merging the source and target objects. Its effect is similar to wood stain or repeatedly stroking a felt marker on paper. Several objects in Multiply mode, when overlapped, can produce black, and this is perhaps the best mode for artists to re-create real-world shadows cast on objects. If the source object's color is lighter than the target object, the result is no change.

- **Divide**   The Divide mode produces only a lighter result color if neither the target nor the source objects are black or white. Use this mode to bleach and produce highlights in a composition by using a light color for the transparency object such as 10 percent black. Also, if the source object is darker than the target object, no color change is the result.

- **If Lighter**   If the color of the source object is darker than the target, lighten the result according to how much lighter the source is than the target object. And if the color's lighter, the result is no change. This mode is useful for shading selective areas of a composition without affecting others, without reshaping the transparency object, and without the need for PowerClips.

- **If Darker**   Similar in effect to Multiply mode, If Darker calculates the result color based on whether areas in the target object are darker, in which case, a color combination is the result; if the area's the same color or lighter, there is no result color. It's particularly interesting to view the result when an If Lighter or an If Darker object is placed above a Fountain Filled target object. You will see clipping, a hard edge where the Fountain Fill reaches a specific value where the result color doesn't qualify to display a change.

- **Texturize**   This mode will not produce much of a change unless you fill the source object with a Bitmap or Pattern Fill. However, for example, if you fill the transparency object with a Bitmap Fill, the result is a shaded and patterned area. This mode removes the hue and saturation from the Bitmap Fill, leaving only brightness values, in effect, making your target object a shaded version of the original, sort of like merging a grayscale photograph over an object. This is a useful mode when you do not want the target object to influence the result colors with any distinct hues, and you can use this mode to build up texture and simulate real-world complexity quickly in your composition.

- **Hue**   The Hue Merge mode changes the result color to the hue of the target color, without affecting saturation or brightness in the result. This mode is useful for tinting compositions and the target object colors are ignored in the result.

- **Saturation**   The Saturation Merge mode can be used to remove color from the result; it's quite nice at making black-and-white photographs from color images. This mode ignores hue and brightness components in the result. Try using shades of black as the transparency object's fill. Highlighting saturated target and source objects produces no change in the result.

- **Lightness**   The target object's lightness values are calculated, ignoring hue and saturation. This is a great mode for brightening the result colors because the target object's colors are never changed, just the *lightness* (also called *value* and *brightness*).

- **Invert**   Creates a result color that is the chromatic inverse of the target color. You can occasionally reproduce the look of a color negative using this mode—it moves the result color to 180 degrees the opposite on the color wheel. Using Invert mode on the same colored target and source objects produces gray.

- **AND, OR, and XOR**   The AND function includes similarity between the source and target objects; for example, two red ellipses that overlap and both have the AND Transparency Merge mode appear not to be transparent at all but instead display 100 percent red where they overlap. This mode is useful when you want only a color result in overlapping areas because AND creates no change outside of the overlapping result area. The OR operator is an exclusive operator, it excludes stuff: this is a good mode for clipping a color change, thus limiting it to only areas where the target and source objects overlap. You'll see nothing outside the overlapping areas when the target object has the OR operator. XOR is a Boolean math statement, based on something called a *Truth Table* where certain conditions must be met to produce a result. However, you might not find this Transparency mode helpful unless you use more than two objects in a design area; if either or neither objects in an XOR operation are similar, you'll get no result color. This operation only works if there is one differently colored object in the color calculation operation.

- **Behind**   You need two objects that have Transparency for Behind mode to work. Wherever the target object on bottom contains Transparency, the top object with Behind mode assigned to it fills the transparent bottom areas with its source color. Therefore, the top object will appear invisible in areas where the bottom object has no Transparency. This mode is useful for filling in transparent areas of a photo in PNG or CPT file format.

- **Screen**   This mode always returns a lighter color, or the source object is invisible if it is darker than the base object or if it's black. Screen is similar to, but less intense an effect than, Add Merge mode; the effect looks like bleach applied to a colored garment.

- **Overlay**   This mode examines the brightness value of the base color. If the result of combining the source with the base is greater than 128 on a brightness scale of 256, the result is a screened area. If the result is not as light as 128, the area is color multiplied. Highlights and shadow areas are preserved in the base image when you use this mode. You almost always achieve a result that has more visual contrast than the original when you use Overlay.

- **Soft Light** This mode is akin to Overlay Merge mode, except instead of screening and multiplying areas, the result is lightening and darkening—a less intense effect.
- **Hard Light** Very similar to the screening and multiplying effect of the Overlay Merge mode, except highlight and shadow regions are *not* preserved. Use this mode if Overlay doesn't prove to be an intense enough effect for merging two color objects or images.
- **Color Dodge** The base colors are brightened, based on the colors used in the source object. Black produces no effect when used as a source color, whereas white can produce a near-white. The effect could be compared to adjusting the exposure of the base image by brightening and tinting the base image simultaneously, while reducing overall contrast.
- **Color Burn** The inverse effect of Color Dodge. White in the source object produces no effect above the base object; colors are reduced in exposure, increased in contrast, and black and darker shades of color in the source object appear to stain the base object.
- **Exclusion** Similar to the Difference Merge mode, but instead of subtracting either the source or the base color (whichever is brighter) to arrive at a darker color, Exclusion mode removes the color of the transparent areas in the resulting blend. When white is used in the source object, it inverts the underlying colors in the base object. Using black produces no effect.
- **Red, Green, and Blue** Each of these merge modes filters out a respective (RGB) channel, and the native color of the source object is ignored. This Transparency mode is useful for color correcting photographs you import to CorelDRAW; for example, if you put a Green Transparency mode object over a portrait, and then play with the amount of transparency on the Property Bar, you can sometimes correct for harsh indoor (particularly cheap fluorescent) lighting.

Creating Multistage Transparencies

You might find you need a transparency object that's more complex than the Fountain types offered on the Property Bar; for example, a lens flare can add photorealistic qualities to an illustration, and this type of effect doesn't appear on the Property Bar. CorelDRAW's Transparency Tool's power can be extended by building a Multistage Fountain Fill for an object, and then using the Transparency Tool in a Blend operation that hides certain colors in the Fountain Fill.

For example, if you wanted to create bands of transparency in an object, you drag shades of black from the Color Palette and drop them onto the marker connector, alternating with white markers. Remember, darker shades represent transparency, and lighter shades stand for opacity. You might want to reposition the new markers once you've added them; this is done by click-dragging with the Transparency Tool. If your drop point for a new marker isn't exactly over the marker connector (the blue dashed line), your cursor turns into an international "no can do" symbol.

Pattern and Texture Transparencies

Pattern and Texture transparencies can add texture to object fill areas below the object, creating intricate detail. The Transparency Type drop-down menu includes

Two Color Pattern, Full Color Pattern, and Bitmap Pattern Transparency types. With any of these selected for the Transparency type, the Start Transparency slider controls the percentage of transparency applied to brightness values in the chosen bitmap that are greater than 126 on a brightness scale of 0–255 (256 shades); the End Transparency slider controls the percentage of transparency applied to brightness values in the chosen bitmap that are less than 128.

Figure 22-5 shows Shirt.cdr, a file you should feel free to experiment with, along with the options on the Property Bar when the Transparency Tool is selected and the control handles are above the target object; you work with scale, rotate, and skew in addition to setting the center point for the Transparency exactly as you would rotate and scale an object in CorelDRAW. Clearly, CorelDRAW not only provides you with a robust feature set, but it also provides you with enough Hawaiian shirt patterns to last you several months of vacationing.

Using Transparency Freeze

Freezing a transparency object captures the composite of the object's properties combined with whatever was beneath the object before using the Freeze button on the Property Bar.

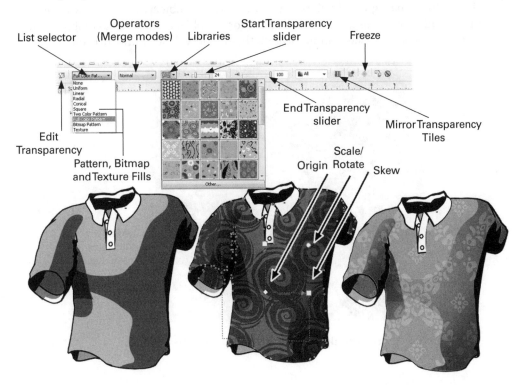

FIGURE 22-5   Use patterns as the basis for a transparency to add visual complexity, simulating a woven texture, a painted one, or other engraved and embossed effects.

Tip Deactivating the Freeze option (without ungrouping it) returns a transparent object to its current and active state. This means if you freeze the object, move it and then unfreeze it, its interior will display whatever is *currently* under it.

Using the Bevel Effect

The Effects | Bevel docker provides you with a way to make objects dimensional, but not as completely 3D as the Extrude Tool. The Bevel docker offers two different types of engraving effect: Emboss and Bevel. The Emboss effect is an automated routine that creates duplicates of an object, offsets them, and gives them different colors to create the effect of, for example, a seal crimped onto a piece of paper like notary publics used to do. Although you can manually create this Emboss effect, the Bevel docker creates a dynamic, linked group whose color and position can change when you define different light intensities and light angles.

Here are visual examples of the Emboss effect. If you choose to use Emboss, it's a good idea to create a background for the object, because either the highlight or the shadow object might not be visible against the page background. Usually, a color similar to the background will serve you well for the object color. You can use any fill, including Bitmaps and Fountain Fills, for the object you want to emboss, but the resulting emboss objects will not *feature* the fill, only solid (uniform) colors.

Original

Two offset duplicates create the effect.

Here you can see the Bevel docker and the options available while applying the Emboss effect.

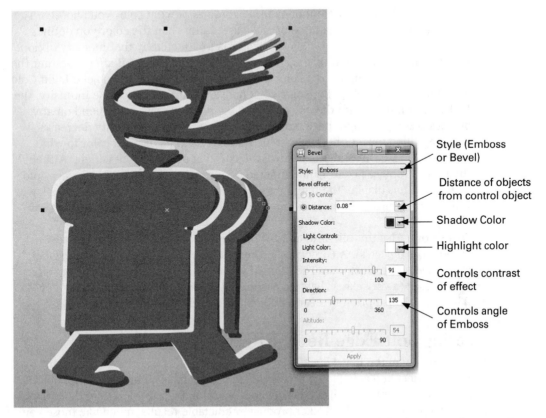

Style (Emboss or Bevel)

Distance of objects from control object

Shadow Color

Highlight color

Controls contrast of effect

Controls angle of Emboss

Here's a rundown of what the options do on the Bevel docker in Emboss mode:

- **Bevel Offset – Distance**   (The To Center option is only available in Bevel mode.) This combination num box and spin box is used to set the distance of the duplicate objects from the original. You don't gain anything visually by setting a high value for an object; rather, this box is used to set a relational distance, depending on the size of the object to which you apply the Emboss effect. For example, a 4" object looks nice and embossed if you use a 0.09" Distance setting, but the effect looks a little phony at greater distances. On the other hand, an 8" object will probably not look embossed with a 0.09" Distance setting—0.16", however, scales the effect proportionately to the object and the Emboss effect looks good. Use distance as a scaling factor. Also, distance does not auto-scale when you scale the control (parent) object. Therefore, if you need to resize an object, plan to redefine the Distance setting for the Emboss effect after you scale the parent object.
- **Shadow Color**   The color of the object has a direct influence on the color of the shadow object behind the control object. For example, if you create an Emboss effect with a blue object, the shadow object is a dark blue, even if you set the color to black. You can neutralize the shadow color by defining the color opposite of the control object; for example, if you have a cyan circle, set the Shadow Color

to red, the color complement of cyan. Regardless of what color you choose for the shadow object, the result color is always duller than the color you define, because—well, it's a *shadow*! Shadow color is unaffected by the Intensity option.

- **Light Color** This controls the color of the highlight object; it affects neither the control object's color, nor the color or brightness of the shadow object. Light Color at full intensity displays the color you choose, and as you decrease intensity, the Light Color blends with the object color—Light Color does not depend on any object's color you might have beneath the effect. As light intensity decreases, a bitmap-filled object's highlight color changes from its original color to white.

- **Intensity** Use this slider to control the contrast of the Emboss effect. Although the shadow object's color is not affected by intensity, the highlight object's color is. High values display the highlight object's color most faithfully, whereas lower Intensity settings dull the highlight color and move its hue toward the control object.

- **Direction** Use this slider to control the direction that light seems to cast on the emboss object(s). A Direction setting of 0° points the highlight at 3 o'clock, traveling counterclockwise. Therefore, if you need a highlight on an Emboss effect at 11 o'clock (a very classic lighting position), you'd set the Direction at about 160°.

- **Altitude** This option is reserved for the Bevel effect, covered next.

Creating Soft Edge Bevel Effects

The other mode on the Bevel docker, Soft Edge, performs many more calculations than the Emboss effect and actually creates a bitmap image, masked by the control object, which can be dynamically adjusted. The Shadow Color, Light Intensity (and Color), and Direction options on the docker produce predictable results, much like those you get when using Emboss mode, but because the Soft Edge effect is generated to bitmap format, the results look more detailed, refined, and almost photorealistic in appearance. In addition to having an Altitude slider in this mode, you have To Center as an available option in the Bevel Offset field. Here's what it does and how To Center works.

All Soft Edge bevels are produced from the edge of a shape traveling toward its center. If, for example, you've created a circle that's 3" across and then type a Distance offset value in the num box in any amount smaller than 1.5", you'll see a dimensional, sloping bevel created inside the circle, with a flat top in the shape of the circle in its center. If, however, you type in a value greater than 1.5", the center of the object bevels to a point, and the front face of the object is entirely lost. The reason this happens is that the Bevel effect travels toward the interior of the shape, and half of the 3" diameter of this circle is 1.5". Just keep in mind the size of the shape to which you apply a Bevel effect to gain total control over the effect. If, on the other hand, you intend for the sides of the bevel to come to a point, you don't need to set values in the Distance field; you choose To Center, click Apply, and CorelDRAW creates the maximum-width bevel, meeting at a point inside the shape. You can create interesting marine creatures such as a starfish by using the Polygon Tool to create the silhouette of a starfish, fill the object, and then choosing To Center auto-creates a very lifelike composition.

Here are two very different looks for the Bevel effect: at top the Distance is set for Offset, and at bottom To Center has been chosen.

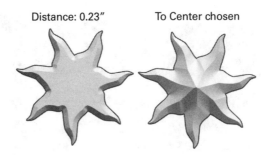

Distance: 0.23"   To Center chosen

Determining Altitude

Altitude determines the angle of the sun illuminating the Bevel effect ... if the sun were actually *involved* in creating the effect. Altitude is a simulation that does something a little different than Shadow and Light Color do to increase and decrease the contrast of the effect. At Altitude settings that approach 90°, you lessen the difference in brightness between the darkest and lightest areas in the Bevel effect. Think of a coin on the sidewalk at high noon; you can't really see the embossed famous person on the coin because the bulges and recesses on the coin are fairly evenly lit. It's the same with the Bevel Altitude setting; smaller Altitude amounts cast the hypothetical sun closer to the hypothetical horizon, and you get a lot more contrast on the bevel. If you want the Bevel effect to produce the greatest visual impact with your work, use a moderate Altitude value most of the time.

Using the Drop Shadow Effect

With the Drop Shadow Tool and the options available on the Property Bar when this tool is active, you can create both shadows and glows, based on the shape of the target object (or group of objects). Although this section walks you through several variations, basically you have three different types of effects at hand when you use the Drop Shadow Tool, as shown in Figure 22-6.

- **Drop shadows**   This shadow type creates the impression that you're viewing an object from the front and that the object is basically lit from the front. Drop shadows are a popular effect; however, they don't always bring out depth in a composition because the drop shadow suggests a face-front orientation of a scene—a viewpoint usually reserved for driver's license photos and wanted posters in the post office. However, drop shadows will indeed perk up a web page because the audience expects a face-front orientation—since we all tend to face the front of our monitors.
- **Cast shadows**   This effect is sometimes called a *perspective shadow* in CorelDRAW. The effect suggests a shadow casting on the ground and diminishing in size as it travels to a scene's vanishing point. It visually suggests that the audience is looking *into* a scene from a perspective point and is not looking *at* an object placed *on* a scene, as drop shadows tend to do.

Drop shadow   Perspective (cast) shadow   Glow

FIGURE 22-6 The Drop Shadow effect can have perspective and can be used to light up a scene, not simply to make things cast shadows.

- **Glows** All effects created with the Drop Shadow Tool are dynamically updated bitmaps, and as such, they can look soft as shadows do on overcast days; they can also be put into Merge modes. Therefore, you take a blurry bitmap, put it in Multiply Merge mode, and you have re-created a shadow. However, if you take that same blurry bitmap, give it a light color, and then put it in Normal or Add Merge mode, you have a Glow effect. This is part of what CorelDRAW does when you use a Glow preset, and you have a lot of manual control for creating a shady or glowing look that perfectly suits a piece of work.

Like other effects in CorelDRAW, drop shadows maintain a dynamic link; any changes to the control object automatically update the shadow. A shadow's look—its position, color, opacity, and feathering—can be customized, plus you can manipulate the angle, stretch, and fade properties of shadows and glows.

Using the Drop Shadow Tool and Property Bar

The Drop Shadow Tool is about as hard to use as click-dragging, and after you click-drag to create a custom shadow, you'll see a series of Property Bar options. The tool is found in the Toolbox with other interactive tools.

 Note A Drop Shadow effect is anchored to an object at a specific point. For example, after you click-drag to create a drop shadow, the shadow is apparently anchored to the object by the white marker, the beginning of the effect. However, if you drag to any of the other three sides of an object, the shadow snaps to these other areas. Shadows are anchored because you probably don't want your drop shadow to become detached from your object if you move the object. Losing your shadow is a privilege only to be enjoyed by vampires.

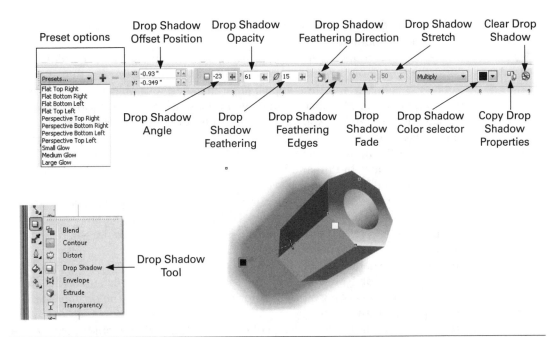

FIGURE 22-7   You might be a shadow of your former self after sifting through all the Drop Shadow options!

After an initial click-drag to add a drop shadow to an object, you'll notice the Property Bar lights up, and you now have a ton of options for refining what amounts to sort of a "default" Drop Shadow effect. Drop shadows can take one of two states: Flat (drop) or Perspective (cast). Depending on which state you use, the Property Bar options change. Figure 22-7 handsomely illustrates a look at the Property Bar when applying a Flat shadow.

Here's an introduction to shadow-making through a tutorial intended to familiarize you with the Property Bar options as well as with a little interactive editing. As with most of the effects in CorelDRAW, the onscreen markers for click-dragging to customize a shadow are very much like the markers for the Extrude Fountain Fill and other tool control handles.

Tutorial   Working the Property Bar and Shadow-Making Interactive Markers

1. Create an interesting object to which you want to apply a shadow, and finish applying its fill and outline properties. If you deselect it, this is okay—a click on the object with the Drop Shadow Tool selects it.
2. Choose the Drop Shadow Tool, and notice that your cursor changes to resemble the Pick Tool with a tiny Drop Shadow icon in its corner. If you don't do anything

with the tool, the only option on the Property Bar is the Presets drop-down selector at the moment.

3. Click-drag from roughly the center of the selected object; continue holding down the mouse button so you can see some of the mechanics of this effect. Notice that a preview outline appears that matches your object. This indicates the position of the new shadow once you release the mouse button. Notice also that a white marker has appeared in the center of the object, and that another marker has appeared under the cursor as you drag it. A slider control has also appeared at the midpoint of a dotted guideline joining the two markers.

4. Release the mouse button and boing!, a drop shadow appears. This is a default shadow, colored black, and it has default properties.

5. Drag the slider control on the guideline between the two square-shaped markers toward the center of your original object. This reduces the shadow's opacity, making it appear lighter and allowing the page background color—and any underlying objects—to become more visible.

6. To change the shadow color, click the color selector on the Property Bar and then select a color. Notice that the color is applied; you can do some wild stage-lighting stuff by choosing a bright color for the shadow, but the opacity of the shadow remains the same.

7. Drag the white marker to the edge of one side of the original object. Notice the shadow changes shape, and the marker snaps to the edge. This action changes a drop shadow to a perspective shadow.

8. Using Property Bar options, change the default Feathering value to 4, and then press ENTER. The shadow edges are now more defined. Increase this value to a setting of 35, and notice that the shadow edges become blurry; you've gone from a sunny day shadow to an overcast day shadow.

9. Click the Fade slider control and increase it to 80. Notice that the shadow now features a graduated color effect, with the darkest point closest to the original object becoming a lighter color as the effect progresses further away from your object. This is not only a photorealistic touch, but it also helps visually integrate a shadow into a scene containing several objects.

10. Click the Drop Shadow Stretch slider and increase it to 80. The shadow stretches further in the direction of the interactive marker and you've gone from high noon to almost dusk in only one step.

11. Click a blank space on the page to deselect the effect, or choose the Pick Tool, and you're done. Take a break and hang out in the shade for a while.

Tip To launch quickly into the editing state of an existing Drop Shadow effect while using the Pick Tool, click the shadow once to display Property Bar options, or double-click the shadow to make the Drop Shadow Tool the current tool.

Manually Adjusting a Drop Shadow Effect

After the Drop Shadow effect is applied, you'll notice the interactive markers that appear around your shape. You'll see a combination offset position and color marker joined by a dotted line featuring an Opacity slider. If you're new to interactive controls, this illustration identifies these markers and indicates their functions.

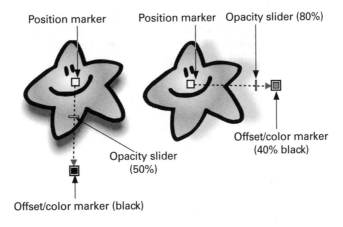

Position marker Position marker Opacity slider (80%)

Offset/color marker (40% black)

Opacity slider (50%)

Offset/color marker (black)

Tip To change a selected drop shadow's color, click-drag any color well from the onscreen Color Palette onto the shadow's color marker.

Shadows as Glow Effects

CorelDRAW's Drop Shadow effect is not limited to making shadows; if you think about it, a blurry bitmap can also represent a glow effect by using a different Merge mode and color.

By default, whenever a new shadow is created, black is automatically the applied color. You can reverse this effect by applying light-colored shadows to dark-colored objects arranged on a dark page background or in front of a darker-colored object. Here you can see a black Compound path (the cartoon light bulb) on top of a Radial Fountain-Filled rectangle (black is the end color and 30 percent black is the start color at center) with a light-colored shadow effect applied. The result is a credible glow effect; there are also Glow Presets on the Property Bar when you use the Drop Shadow Tool to give you a jump-start on creating glows.

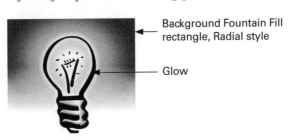

Background Fountain Fill rectangle, Radial style

Glow

This chapter has shown a lot of nonspecial effects; effects that aren't supposed to "wow" your audience, but rather PowerClips, shadows, and bevels speak of a quiet elegance that strikes the viewer on a subliminal level. It's well worth your time to become proficient with these effects for future times when you need a touch of photorealism in a drawing, something that strikes the audience without hitting them over the head.

This concludes the special effects portion of *The Official Guide* but if you turn the page, you'll be entering an arena of graphics that look so real, they're picture-perfect. You're going to get into digital imagery and what CorelDRAW and Corel PHOTO-PAINT offer in the way of photo-retouching features. Bring along a snapshot of the kids.

PART VIII

The Bitmap Part of Corel Graphics Suite

23

Bitmap Boot Camp:
Working with Photographs

You'll occasionally want to set aside the Bézier Pen Tool and the Fountain Fill. Your layout for a brochure, for example, is all done, and now you want to add a photograph of your product. The good news is that CorelDRAW can import just about any bitmap file you have. Photos from your camera, a scan of a photo, a painting you created in PHOTO-PAINT, or an image you snagged off your client's website—you can crop, rotate, and perform enhancements on it within CorelDRAW. This chapter takes you first through the structure of *pixel-based images* (bitmaps). You'll learn how you can get them to print well, what you can and cannot do with them, special properties, and the difference between this type of graphic and the one you're more accustomed to: vector artwork. Then you'll work with some photographed and created bitmap images to learn how to do some necessary—and fantastic—image editing and enhancing.

Putting a photo into a CorelDRAW document isn't very rewarding unless it's a really *good* photo, and you feel confident it will print well. This chapter delivers the goods on the whats, whys, and whens for bitmap importing, finessing, and integration to make your documents come alive and communicate.

 Download and extract all the files from the Chapter23.zip archive to follow the tutorials in this chapter.

The Properties of a Pixel-Based Image

We all tend to take a photograph with our megapixel camera, copy the image to hard disk as a JPEG, e-mail it, and that's the end of the story. We don't question the *structure* of a digital image at all.

However, if you want to do something with a digital image, such as incorporate it into a flyer, crop it, resize it, or put something else into it within a CorelDRAW composition, this is the beginning of the story of pixel-based images and their manipulation that you should heed. Without a cursory understanding of how pixel-based images are structured, you won't be able to do as many things successfully as you'd like to do with them in CorelDRAW. Therefore, the following sections dig a little into what goes into a pixel-based image, so you can get more out of them as covered in the rest of this chapter.

Pixel Artwork vs. Vector Artwork

Although there are two fundamentally different types of graphics you can work with on a personal computer—vector graphics and pixel graphics—actually 100 percent of what you see onscreen is a *pixel-based graphic*. Your computer monitor has no easy way to display vectors as vectors, so even when you work with paths in CorelDRAW, what you're seeing onscreen is a pixel-based representation that CorelDRAW draws to your screen on-the-fly. So it's a good and appropriate time to think more about pixels as an art form and as a tool.

Vector artwork, the kind of art you create in CorelDRAW, is *resolution independent,* a term you hear a lot, particularly if you're around programmers. Resolution independent means that the art you create in CorelDRAW can be scaled up and down, rotated and distorted every which way, and it still retains focus and its structural integrity. Vector artwork can be boiled down to a direction a path travels in, the width of its outline, its fill color—regardless of how complex you make a drawing, it can be explained and saved to file in math terms. And because math can be divided and multiplied without discarding the values you put into an equation, scaling a vector drawing doesn't change its core values. For example, $150 \times 2 = 300$ is an equation that results in twice the 150 value, but the 150 value isn't really altered to produce a result of 300.

Pixel-based graphics, on the other hand, are *resolution dependent.* This means a finite number of pixels go into what you see onscreen, and they cannot be increased or decreased without making a visible, fundamental change to the structure of such a graphic. Pixel-based images aren't truly as flexible as vector artwork, and until you understand the term *resolution,* it's quite possible to damage a pixel-based image irrevocably. You could throw a digital photo out of focus or add artifacting (explained in a moment). However, the positives of pixel images outweigh any negatives: Although taking a snapshot is easy, drawing something that looks exactly like a photograph, using vectors, is quite hard. Pixel-based images can have depth of field, exposure, a source of scene lighting, and other properties; although many talented artists have created CorelDRAW pieces that look almost like a photograph, many of us cannot invest the time or have the sheer talent to "make photographs" using CorelDRAW. Fortunately, this chapter shows you the easy way to make your CorelDRAW more photographic in nature: you just import a *photograph!*

Artifacts and Anti-aliasing

It's possible to take resolution-dependent bitmap images and make them larger, artificially increasing the size (and the saved file size) of the final image. However, you cannot add *detail* to an existing photograph by enlarging it: when a computer application is told to add pixels to an image, it has no real way of telling what color pixels should be added to the photograph. Not CorelDRAW, not Adobe Photoshop, there's no application (except those phony forensic computers you see on TV shows) that can intelligently, artistically, or accurately add, for example, detail to a photo of a mailbox so the address instantly becomes crisp and legible.

What you get when you perform any "make this photo larger" command is "fake resolution"; the program averages pixel colors neighboring the original pixels to create more, similarly colored pixels. This can often lead to *artifacting,* what we commonly describe as "there's some junk in the upper left of this photo near my aunt's face." Artifacting can be introduced to a digital photograph at any stage of photography: your camera didn't write the file correctly, the image became corrupted when you copied it to your hard drive, and or you tried to enlarge a resolution-dependent image. The cure for the last reason is don't resample important images; instead, print a copy of the image at its original size and see how it looks. From there, increase its size, check for visible artifacts in your print, and if there's visible corruption, go back to your original or seriously consider reshooting the image.

One of the methods CorelDRAW, PHOTO-PAINT, and other programs that can import bitmaps use to lessen and occasionally eliminate visible artifacting from resampling a photo is called *anti-aliasing,* and you have some control over this method, discussed later in this chapter. Anti-aliasing is a math calculation that performs averaging in a resulting photo that's been altered in areas where there is visual ambiguity (some of the pesky pixels are traveling under an alias). For example, suppose you could photograph a checkerboard plane that extends from your feet way out to the horizon. You look down toward your feet and clearly see black squares and white squares. You look at the horizon, and you do not see clear edges of the black and white squares: actually you'll see a lot of gray, as your mind blends black and white together because your eyes don't have photoreceptors fine enough to resolve the very distant black and white squares. Similarly, our computers cannot reconcile black and white areas in a digital image that are smaller than the size of the pixels in the image, so when you resample the image, they create—inaccurately—little black and white squares where they shouldn't be. The inaccuracy means the black and white squares are traveling as an *alias* and presenting themselves falsely.

Anti-aliasing comes to the designer's rescue by *averaging* pixel colors when you resample such a checkerboard photo, or any photo. The anti-aliasing technique examines, in this example, areas that include both a white square and a black one, understands that both colors can't be assigned to only one pixel, and so writes a blend of colors—gray—to the new pixel color value. At left in this illustration, you

(continued)

can see some unwanted patterning toward the horizon—this image was not anti-aliased when it was resampled to produce a larger image. At right, the same image was resampled using anti-aliasing; at 1:1 viewing, you can see the smooth transition as the checkerboard extends into the distance—and the close-up shows the result of good anti-aliasing (some applications anti-alias poorly)—gray is substituted for black and white when it's a tossup for a single pixel color.

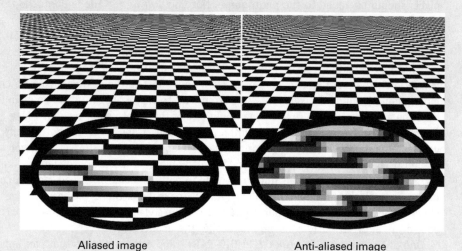

Aliased image   Anti-aliased image

Bytemaps and Pixels

Programmers and users alike are accustomed to calling a pixel-based image a *bitmap*. However, the term "bitmap" is a little like the term "dial phone." Telephones haven't had dials in nearly two decades, and similarly, a bitmap—literally a map of bits of information—is inadequate to describe a pixel-based image, but "bitmap" is used as the term for non-vector graphics in this chapter anyway. We're comfortable with the term; the term is described in the next paragraph; and "bitmap" is shorter to write than "pixel-based image."

Let's say you have onscreen a JPEG fresh off your camera. What are you seeing? Of course, you're probably seeing a friend or relative, but what you're *really* seeing is a finite number of placeholders for color—the number of placeholders for color is so large that your mind integrates the placeholders into a familiar image. That's the "map" part of the term "bitmap"; this map could also be called a *mesh*, a *grid*, or a *canvas*. All the bitmap images you take with a camera or paint in a paint program are composed of information units all lined up in a grid. You don't *see* the grid (or the *map* part of a bitmap); it's only a figurative thing, intangible—it's the *structure* for the visual information. The finer the grid, the less likely you are to see the individual color elements, instead of your mind blending the elements into a photograph. The "bit" part of the term "bitmap" is actually a *byte* of color information: a bit of information can only have two possible values (usually on or off); the graphics that artists work with today have a byte (8 bits) of information (sometimes more) per color channel with which to express a color value. The term "bitmap" was coined in the days when a monitor could truly only display a color or no color, thus the term "bitmap"; and the term has stuck with us for more than 30 years.

To extend this explanation further, this unit of information lodged in a map is called a *pixel,* short for *pic*ture *el*ement, the smallest unit of color you can see in a bitmap image. A pixel is only *a placeholder for a color value;* it is *not* a unit of measurement, and it doesn't even have to be square (digital movie cameras take rectangular-proportioned movie pixels), and it has no fixed size. Other things a pixel is *not* include:

- **A dot**   Even professionals lapse into describing the resolution of a digital image in terms of dots per inch once in a while. This is okay if they're using the term "dot" as slang to mean a pixel, but this jargon is confusing. Printers print dots of toner and other pigment onto a surface (usually paper); a 1,200 dpi printer, for example, renders 1,200 dots of toner per inch of paper, but it is not rendering 1,200 pixels per inch of toner! In fact, a 1,200 dpi laser printer is incapable of rendering 1,200 pixels per inch (ppi). A pixel is *not* a dot of toner or ink, nor is a dot of ink equal to a pixel—pixels alone have no size.

- **A screen phosphor or LED**   Pixels that make up an image do not usually correspond 1:1 to whatever the elements on your monitor are made of. With high-quality images, there are many more pixels per inch than there are light units (phosphors, LEDs, and so on) on your screen. This is why CorelDRAW and paint programs such as PHOTO-PAINT and Adobe Photoshop offer zoom tools, so you can get a better look at image areas, mapping small amounts of pixels to your screen, which has a finite number of light-emitting elements. As resolution is discussed later in this chapter, it's good to know that the most frequently used resolution for web graphics is 96 ppi (pixels per inch). Therefore, if the resolution of an image is also 96 ppi, this means that when you view it at 100 percent viewing resolution, what your screen's light-emitting elements are mapping corresponds 1:1 to the image resolution. You're viewing a bitmap graphic exactly as the creator of the bitmap intended it.

- **Any sort of ratio**   The measurement commonly used in bitmap evaluation is *pixels per inch,* which is a ratio, like mph is a ratio—miles (one unit) per hour (a different unit). A pixel is a unit, but not a ratio. Therefore, if someone says they have an image that's 640 by 480 pixels, they've told you how many pixels are in the image, but not its resolution and not its size. A pixel is a unit and needs to be contextualized—for example, 120 pixels per inch or 300 pixels per centimeter—before the unit becomes meaningful and useful to a printer or designer. If you told friends you were driving your car down the Autobahn at "200 miles," they probably wouldn't be impressed because you haven't contextualized this unit into something meaningful such as a measurement. But "200 miles per hour" tells your friends something—that they probably don't want to ride with you!

Color Depth

In addition to being color value placeholders, pixels also have "depth," not "depth" as you'd measure a swimming pool, but rather a color "density." For example, GIF images have a maximum color depth of 256 unique values; grayscale images have a brightness depth of 256 shades.

Because 256 unique colors can't truly express the beauty we capture with a digital camera (even dull scenes can contain tens of thousands of unique colors), programmers decided early on in the digital imaging game to structure high-quality images into components, the most common structure being red, green, and blue, like your computer monitor is based on the RGB color model. These three components are usually called *color channels*: by adding the brightness values of these three channels together, you get the composite view of digital photos and other bitmaps. Channels are a very efficient method for storing bitmap color information—in contrast, GIF images store image colors as explicit color table values, and this is one of the reasons why GIF images are limited to 256 unique colors. By assigning the red, green, and blue color channels in a bitmap image an 8-bit per channel color capability, this equals 2^8, meaning the red, green, and blue channels can each have one of 256 possible brightness values with which to contribute color to the RGB composite image. Eight bits per channel times three color channels adds up to 24-bit images—BMP, PNG, TIFF, TGA (Targa), and Photoshop PSD being the most common file formats that can hold this color information. So 24-bit images have a maximum unique color capability of 16.7 million colors.

However, color depth doesn't stop at 24-bit (8 bits per channel); although most affordable monitors today can only display 24-bit image depth, camera manufacturers anticipate that this will change soon, with the increasing popularity of high dynamic range (HDR) displays and higher-definition monitors. Today, many of the middle-range digital cameras can write photos to the Raw file format, whose specifics vary from manufacturer to manufacturer as do the file extensions. Happily, CorelDRAW can import most digital camera Raw files. *Raw files* (as covered later in this chapter) are "unprocessed film": they contain exposure settings, f-stops, and other camera data, but they also provide a lot of flexibility and leeway when you import such an image. CorelDRAW has a little utility called Camera Raw Lab where you can color-correct, change image exposure—all after the photo was taken. You can do this because Raw images can contain 16 bits per color channel, to offer a 48-bit image—more than 281 trillion possible colors ... indeed this would require a very large crayon box.

Consider it a given that because CorelDRAW can handle such mega-information and has some very good processing tools for imported bitmap images, the compositions you create using bitmaps along with vector designs will print splendidly. Now it's time to discuss image resolution as it relates to outputting your work.

Resolution and Resolution-Dependent Images

As mentioned earlier, resolution is expressed as a fraction, a ratio between units (pixels) and space (inches, usually). As you'll see later in Table 23-1, a few image file types such as PSD and TIFF can store image resolution information, and this is good.

For example, let's say you need to inkjet-print a brochure, and the front page needs a photograph. A photograph of insufficient resolution is going to print lousily, pure and simple. However, if the photographer saved the digital photo to PSD, TIFF, PNG, or Raw camera file format (and knows about image resolution), you can import the image and know before you print whether the image needs to be resized or not (resizing is covered later in this chapter). The rule is that an image's resolution should be in the neighborhood of your printer's resolution. Therefore, let's say that you've imported a photo and you know (by looking at the Bitmap page of Object Properties, covered in detail later in this chapter) that it's 4" wide, 3" tall, and 250 pixels per inch in resolution. Your next move is to check the printer manufacturer's documentation: although manufacturers tend to tap dance around specific printer resolutions, a good working guide is that an inkjet prints about one-third of the stated overall resolution on the box. Image resolution for day-to-day printing, without giving yourself a headache over empirical values, should be anywhere between 240 to 300 pixels per inch.

There is a way to tell the resolution of image file formats that cannot hold resolution information, so don't worry if you have a bunch of JPEG images you want to use in a composition you need to inkjet-print. As you progress through this chapter, working tutorial files will demonstrate what you want to do and when.

Resolution vs. Image Size

Another digital-image reality that makes many designers pull their hair out is that image resolution is inversely proportional to dimensions: this is another cold and hard fact about bitmap resolution. When you make an image larger in dimensions, its resolution decreases. Now, viewing resolution and image resolution display the same thing onscreen, but changing *viewing resolution*—zooming in and out of an image—is nondestructive, whereas changing *image resolution* is destructive editing and often irreversible. Here's an example that demonstrates the resolution-dependence properties of bitmaps. Figure 23-1 shows a desktop icon; it's 128 × 128 pixels, and the largely adopted resolution convention is that screen pixels are 96 per inch. At 1:1 viewing resolution, this icon looks fine, but when you zoom into it to 10:1 viewing resolution, it begins to look coarse. The same thing would be visible if you actually were to change the resolution of the image. Bitmap images are resolution dependent; the pixels you capture of a scene with a camera can't be added to later to increase detail—no application can guess what the extra detail and extra pixels would be. At right in Figure 23-1, you can see an extreme enlargement of the icon, and the pixels are so clearly visible that you can't make out what the design is!

The lesson here is that to take advantage of the unique property of bitmap images—that they accurate portray a photographic scene—you need to take a photo that is high resolution—3,264 pixels × 2,448 pixels is average for an 8-megapixel camera, a little larger than 10 × 8 at 300 ppi. CorelDRAW can resize an image; for example, this same 8-megapixel image could also be expressed as 20 × 15 at 163 ppi without changing any visual information. CorelDRAW can also resample an image, and this is the *destructive* type of editing; you change pixels when you resample, so generally it's a good idea to resize and only resample as a last resort when adding photos to a CorelDRAW composition.

128×128-pixel icon
viewed at 1:1, 96 ppi
resolution

128×128-pixel icon
viewed at 10:1, 96 ppi
resolution

128×128-pixel icon
viewed at 20:1. Pixels
are clearly visible.

FIGURE 23-1   With resolution-dependent bitmaps, the larger the image, the fewer pixels per inch.

Importing Bitmaps into a Document

As a CorelDRAW user, you have at your fingertips a vast collection of bitmap import filter selections. Although Import commands are discussed in Chapter 3, some of the Import options apply specifically to bitmaps and are explained here; you'll definitely find them useful if your work requires photographs and graphics from the Web. Table 23-1 does not list the bitmap types CorelDRAW can import the way that the Files Of Type drop-down list does in the Import dialog. Although it's terrific to have a billion different file types available for import, particularly if you have legacy file formats, you probably only use a handful of image types in everyday work. Therefore, the table lists the most common file types first; more exotic and legacy file formats appear toward the bottom of this table. The asterisk after the file extension indicates that a file type can retain resolution information; this is a capability—it doesn't necessarily mean the person who saved the file actually saved resolution information.

If you intend to print a CorelDRAW composition you've created that features a bitmap photo or painting, Step 1 is to set up the color management of the document. You can access settings for your document's color profile through Tools | Color Management | Color Settings.

TABLE 23-1   CorelDRAW's Importable Bitmap Formats

Bitmap Type	File Extension
Adobe Photoshop	PSD*
JPEG and JPEG 2000 bitmaps	JPG*, JP2, JFF, and JTF
Adobe Portable Document File	PDF
TIFF bitmap	TIF*
Portable Network Graphic	PNG*
Targa bitmap	TGA* (Enhanced mode, export only)
Raw image file format	CRW, CR2 (Canon); MRW (Minolta); NEF (Nikon); ORF (Olympus); DNG (Adobe); PTX (Pentax); ARW, SRF, SR2 (Sony), MRW, THM, RAF, DCR, KDC, PEF, RAW, MOS, SRW, NRW, RW2
Corel PHOTO-PAINT	CPT*
CompuServe bitmap	GIF
GIF Animation	GIF
Windows bitmap	BMP (DIB, RLE)
CALS compressed bitmap	CAL
Computer graphics metafile	CGM
Corel (and Micrografx) Picture Publisher	PP4
Gem Paint file	GEM
GIMP image	XCF*
Lotus Pic	PIC
Macintosh PICT	PCT
MACPaint bitmap	MAC
OS/2 bitmap	BMP
Painter 5/6	RIF*
PC Paintbrush bitmap	PCX*
Scitex CT bitmap	SCT, CT
Windows Icon Resource	ICO, EXE, DLL
WordPerfect graphic bitmap	WPG

The following steps aren't a tutorial but rather a checklist, a workflow based on your need to bring a copy of a photo into a CorelDRAW composition.

1. After launching CorelDRAW, press CTRL + N (File | New) if you've set up your copy not to show the Create A New Document After Launch.

2. Define the Color Settings after you've specified page size, resolution, and other parameters. Your *color settings*—the color space within which everything on the page "resides"—is not an "Oh, yes! I know the answer!" sort of conclusion or decision you make lightly. Generally, you're safe choosing sRGB IEC6 1966-2.1 because many digital cameras and scanners use this color profile. If, however, after importing a photo, the photo looks dull or lacks contrast, then the color space of the photo doesn't match the color settings of your CorelDRAW document. You can change this later; let's continue the workflow here...

3. Before importing a photo, choose Tools | Color Management | Default Settings. Check both the Warn On Color Profile Mismatch and the Warn On Missing Color Profile boxes. Do this both in the Import and the Paste section. You're all set to import a photo now.

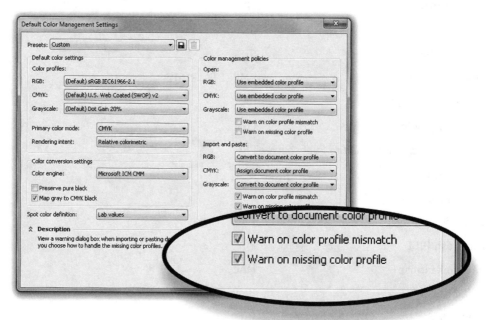

4. When you choose File | Import (or press CTRL + I), you then have the opportunity to scale an image before placing it on the page. More experienced users might want to simply drag an image file into the workspace when CorelDRAW is not maximized. Using either technique, when you import an image, if it has a color profile that doesn't match your current document—or has no color profile at all—you'll get an alert box where you have the opportunity to choose the color space for the imported image.

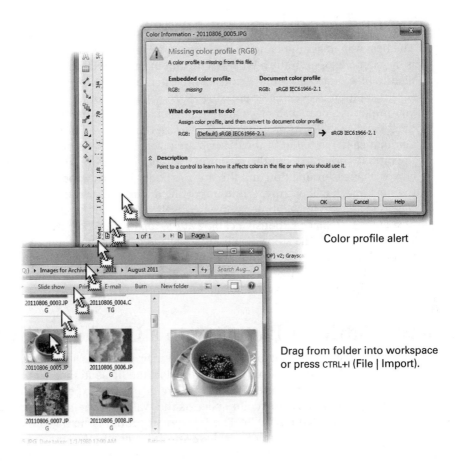

Color profile alert

Drag from folder into workspace
or press CTRL+I (File | Import).

5. Generally, you'll want to choose the same color space as the document's color space. However, if you set up your document incorrectly—for example, your client specified Adobe RGB, you had soap in your ears and thought they said "sRGB"—import the photo using the Adobe RGB choice from the drop-down list. Then choose Tools | Color Management | Document Settings, and choose Adobe RGB from the RGB drop-down list in the Edit Document Settings area.

Because the method of dragging an image file into the workspace doesn't afford scaling options, you might want to stick with CTRL + I for importing. File | Import also gives you the chance to filter for the file types you seek in a windows folder, and there are other options you're given in the Import dialog (discussed in Chapter 24). Choose your bitmap format from the Files Of Type menu.

After the Import dialog closes, your cursor changes to an import cursor that has two functions: with it you specify the upper-left corner of your new bitmap using a single-click, which, in turn, imports the image onto a document page at its original size—whatever dimensions, by whatever its original saved resolution. Pressing ENTER instead of using a mouse click imports the image to the center of the page.

Placing and Modifying an Image

The best way to get the hang of inserting an image into a CorelDRAW composition is by example: open Wally's Wheel's.cdr, and in the tutorial to follow you'll place a picture of an auto and then perform a little manual cropping.

In addition to clicking or pressing ENTER with a cursor that's loaded with an image you import, you can also place and proportionately scale the imported image by click-dragging diagonally After you specify the size this way, the bitmap is imported and automatically resized to fit the defined area closely with the original *proportions* of the bitmap preserved, but the resolution will not be the original's. As you drag, the cursor changes orientation and the image's bounding box appears, showing the space the new image will occupy. While importing during either operation, the original filename and the image dimensions are displayed beside the cursor. Your goal in the next steps is to place Expensive car.jpg at the top of the 5" × 7" riser card layout. As you work through the steps, you'll note that the document's color space isn't the same as the JPEG image, but you already know how to correct this. The native dimensions of the JPEG are also larger than the CorelDRAW page layout, which affords the perfect opportunity to try out this importing and scaling stuff.

| Tutorial | **Putting a Picture into a Car Advertisement**

1. Click the Import icon on the Standard Bar or press CTRL + I to import the Expensive car.jpg. Locate it on your hard drive, select the file, and then click Import.

2. You'll now see the attention box that tells you the Expensive car.jpg is not tagged with the same color space as the Wally's Wheels.cdr file. Click Convert The Embedded Profile To The Document Profile radio button, and then click OK. There is often a noticeable color difference in the image you view on the page when you choose to ignore the color profile (the first option in this attention box), instead of allowing CorelDRAW to convert it to the document's color space. Another good reason not to ignore a color profile is that if you send this file to a commercial printer with two different color spaces in the document, the commercial printer is not likely to thank you for the time and paper the two of you have wasted. One document requires one color profile for all of its contents.

3. Begin your click as close as possible to the top-left point on the rulers, and then drag down and to the right; don't release the mouse button yet. When you believe you're very close to the right edge of the layout, look at the cursor. If the dimensions it reports are close to 5 inches, you're good to release the mouse button. In the illustration here, if you can read the cursor, it reports a height and width of 4.997 inches, which is close enough for government work. Move your pointing device up and down on the page just a fractional amount until you're close to 5", and then release the mouse button.

Begin click-drag here. ─────

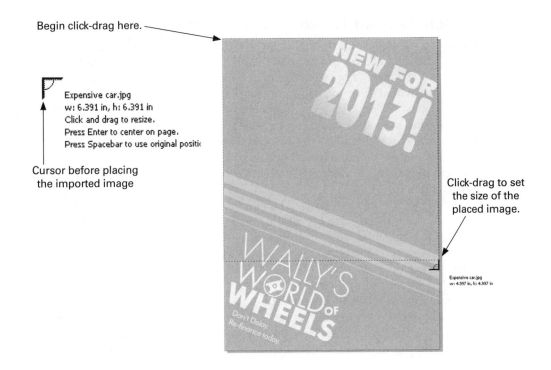

Expensive car.jpg
w: 6.391 in, h: 6.391 in
Click and drag to resize.
Press Enter to center on page.
Press Spacebar to use original positic

Cursor before placing
the imported image

Click-drag to set
the size of the
placed image.

Expensive car.jpg
w: 4.997 in, h: 4.997 in

4. If you want this image (or one in your own assignment) to be *exactly* 5" wide, now choose Arrange | Transformations | Size. Click the top-left checkbox below the Proportional checkbox to set the direction in which the image should be scaled, and then type **5** in the W field, press ENTER, and you've accomplished precision placement and scaling.

5. Save this file to disk and keep it open for the sections to follow.

Tip Bitmap images can't be edited at the pixel level directly in CorelDRAW. For example, if your cousin Flossie's mascara is a little runny in the photo, this is an isolated photo problem area, and you need to use a bitmap-editing application to make the makeup look better. Not to worry, Flossie: you can open PHOTO-PAINT by clicking the Edit Bitmap button on the Property Bar or by right-clicking the bitmap and then choosing to edit it from the context menu. See Chapters 25 and 26 for details on editing techniques using PHOTO-PAINT.

Switching from Resizing to Resampling

If you had right-clicked over the Expensive Car.jpg image in the Import dialog box earlier, and then chosen Properties | Details, Windows would have told you the image is 1,700 × 1,700 pixels at a resolution of 266-pixels/per inch. Any bitmap's resolution can be discovered this way, within the Import box, and anywhere in Windows where you can open a folder. However, if you click the image as placed now, the Status Bar tells you that Expensive car.jpg on Layer 1 is currently 340-pixels/inch in resolution. The reason why is that *image resolution is inversely proportional to image dimensions*— you make one smaller and the other one becomes larger, as discussed earlier. This is a function of resizing; by default, CorelDRAW doesn't change the number of pixels in an imported photo.

However, it might be requested by an imaging service bureau or commercial printer that an image placed in a CorelDRAW file be of a specific resolution—many services that make full-color business cards, for example, want 300 ppi images in files and often reject or charge extra for processing fees if an image is of higher resolution. When you change the number of pixels in an image, this is not called resizing; instead it's called *resampling,* and you're basically altering the visual content of the copy of the image in your CorelDRAW document.

Let's pretend that this auto advertisement needs to be sent to a commercial printer with the image at exactly 300 ppi. Follow these brief steps to prep this file for proper printing.

Tutorial   Resampling a Photo

1. Select the image with the Pick Tool.
2. Choose Bitmap | Resample.
3. With Identical Values is checked, type **300** in either the Horizontal or the Vertical Resolution field.
4. Check Anti-aliased (which makes the reduction of the image smooth and basically undetectable from the original image), check Maintain Aspect Ratio, but do *not* check Maintain Original Size. If you maintained the original size of the image, no resampling would take place; instead, the image would be resized. Compare the before and after file size in this dialog box; this not only provides you with an estimate of how large you saved CorelDRAW file size will be, but it's also intellectual reassurance that you're down-sampling the photo and not simply resizing it. Click OK and you're finished. Keep the file open because the layout isn't done. Yet.

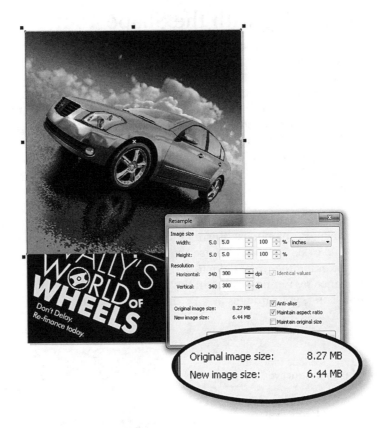

Nonrectangular Cropping in a Jiffy

This mock advertisement clearly is designed on the diagonal, but the car image—like most bitmap images—is rectangular, somewhat spoiling the look of the ad as it's currently placed. This isn't a big design challenge; it's an opportunity to explore CorelDRAW's features. CorelDRAW offers a Crop Tool on the Toolbox, which performs *destructive* editing. No, it doesn't paint a moustache or blacken a front tooth on your portrait photos, but it does *permanently* remove areas of a bitmap (and vector objects) that lie outside of the crop you define. It's useful, but unnecessary for this assignment when you learn how to use the Shape Tool.

CorelDRAW considers any placed bitmap image to be an object that has four control nodes, one at each corner of the rectangle. Moreover, these control nodes can be moved (inward because there's nothing outside the boundary of a bitmap) to change the shape of a bitmap without removing areas of the bitmap—CorelDRAW simply hides them for you. Work through the following steps to hide a triangular area of the Expensive Car-placed jpeg image and complete the design.

Tutorial Cropping with the Shape Tool

1. With the Pick Tool, select the image and then press CTRL + PAGEDOWN to put the image behind the text at top.
2. Choose the Shape Tool from the Toolbox.
3. Click the image to reveal the control nodes.
4. One approach to removing the slice of the image that's covering Wally's name is to hold CTRL (to constrain the direction in which you'll drag the node) and then click-drag the bottom-left control node way up to about the 5" tick on the vertical ruler so you can see the underlying stripes first. Then, while holding CTRL, drag the control node down so it meets the bottom of the top diagonal stripe in the design. Then perform the same action on the bottom-right control node.
5. Nodes can be nudged: try saying that three times fast! You can use your up and down keyboard arrow keys to nudge a selected image control node up or down. If you choose this method, it offers precision and you don't have to hold CTRL. You can also use the Super Nudge option and hold SHIFT while keystroking the up and down arrow keys. You can quickly set the Nudge Distance by typing a value in the field on the Property Bar. By default, if you hold SHIFT, your nudges are 2× the value you set.

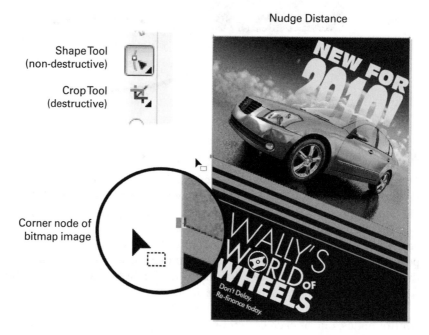

Importing Nonstandard Bitmaps

With kind permission from Nicky Elliott, a small version of her Monkey Pants Media poster has been provided for you, Monkey Pants Media.psd, so you can get hand-on experience importing and performing a minor edit with a bitmap type that CorelDRAW handles well. Adobe Photoshop and Corel PHOTO-PAINT both can write image files that contain layers; you'll see the advantages to using a layered bitmap image shortly, tutorial-style. When you choose File | Import and then choose PSD, PHOTO-PAINT's CPT, and even Corel Painter's RIF file format, any layers in these file types are imported and nested within an entry on a CorelDRAW layer. You can un-nest the layers, move them, or delete them, and one of the most useful properties of layered image files is that the file's creator probably did so to include partially transparent areas within the bitmap composition.

Let's say Ms. Elliott wants a change made to the background of the Monkey Pants poster, that she'd prefer a more dramatic treatment than the medium-blue solid color. Here's how to import and edit a layered bitmap image:

Tutorial   Working with Layered Bitmaps

1. Create a new document. Standard letter size is fine—the Monkey Pants Media .psd file is 8" × 10" at 96 ppi resolution, so it comfortably fits inside standard letter size at its original 100 percent size.
2. Click the Import button on the Standard Bar, and then in the Import dialog box, scout down Monkey Pants Media.psd on your hard drive. Select it, and then click Import.
3. With the cursor loaded and ready to place a copy of the file, press ENTER to place the file at full size, centered on the page.
4. Choose Tools | Object Manager. Click the + icon to the left of the imported image title to open its nest of layers.

5. Click the Background layer item on the list to select it in the document window. This was a thoughtfully prepared file; the layers were named in Photoshop. In your own work, you might not be so fortunate if the creator of the layered file didn't name the layers. Therefore, always check out what's selected in the drawing window before proceeding.
6. You're sure the blue background is selected? Then click the trash icon to delete this layer.

7. Choose the Rectangle Tool from the toolbox, and then drag a rectangle of about the size as the Background layer you deleted.

8. On the Object Manager, click-drag the Monkey Pants Media.psd entry to above the Rectangle entry. This puts the remaining two nested layers above the rectangle.

9. Choose the Interactive Fill Tool from the Toolbox. Click to select the rectangle, and then choose Radial as the style of fill from the Property Bar.

10. Click the inner color marker on the Radial Fountain Fill, and then click a light gray swatch on the Color Palette. Click the outer color marker, and then click a darker gray on the Color Palette.

Fill Tool,
Radial style

11. The logo layer could use some visual separation from the background. CorelDRAW native effects can be applied to nontransparent areas of imported bitmap layers: choose the Drop Shadow Tool from the Toolbox, click the Logo layer in the Object Manager to select it, and then choose Large Glow from the Presets drop-down on the Property Bar.

12. Large Glow, at its default settings, will not provide much of an effect. So you *change* the default settings: click the outer color marker, and then choose Black from the Shadow Color pop-up on the Property Bar. Then set the Shadow Opacity (also on the Property Bar) to almost **100%** opaque. Finally, set the Shadow Feathering to only about **10**. Figure 23-2 shows a dramatic transformation of the poster—and because the imported bitmap layers can be edited separately, you could even reposition the Monkey Pants logo on the CorelDRAW page.

Drop
Shadow
Tool

FIGURE 23-2   Combine CorelDRAW objects in a layered bitmap file to edit
layouts extensively.

Working with Raw Images

Camera Raw is the new generation of high-fidelity imaging: it's affordable; most
cameras you *don't* buy at a drugstore can write a Raw file format; and as with any
comparatively new technology, there's a small learning curve, which we'll tackle in
this section.

A Raw image is similar to an unprocessed physical piece of camera film; although
it contains a lot of data about exposure, light temperature, f-stop, lens, and other
conditions, the Raw image does *not* have locked data about pixel colors. Raw offers
the ultimate in flexibility—if the light was too low or the wrong temperature, you can
adjust for these and other flaws through CorelDRAW's Camera Raw Lab. The Camera
Raw Lab appears after you choose to import a Raw camera image; a Raw image cannot
be placed in a CorelDRAW composition before it passes through the Lab (even if you
choose not to do anything to the image). Depending on your camera settings, you'll
most likely be working with a 48-bit image, 16 bits per channel; this offers a color
space of several trillion unique colors and is part of the reason why Raw images can
be adjusted to make dramatic lighting changes while retaining high image fidelity.

Working with the Camera Raw Lab

Working with the Camera Raw Lab in CorelDRAW is an experience you won't want to miss. If you don't have a Raw image handy, or if your camera cannot take Raw file format images, a small DNG file is in the zip archive you downloaded for this chapter.

Because no two manufacturers could agree on a file extension, a Raw image could have .CRW, .DNG, or any of over a dozen other file extensions. The good news is that CorelDRAW doesn't care about the file extension—you just choose All File formats (*.*) from the drop-down list in the Import dialog, and then navigate to the location of a Raw image, in the following example, Catch of The Day.dng. The *better* news is that CorelDRAW can import Raw images from a *three-page list* of manufacturers—just short of photos on a View-Master reel, you're assured that CorelDRAW can import most Raw files.

Let's dig right into the features and options available to you when you import a Raw image; follow these steps and guidelines to import the image, and then perform minor processing enhancements. There's nothing truly wrong with the image, but this tutorial is instead an opportunity to gain hands-on experience with the Camera Raw Lab features.

Tutorial Raw Image Color Correction

1. Choose File | Import, or click the Import button on the Property Bar.
2. Choose All File Formats (*.), and then choose Catch of The Day.dng from the folder you downloaded the file to. Click Import or press ENTER.
3. The Camera Raw Lab interface appears. The very first thing to do is to check the properties of this unprocessed photograph. The Properties tab tells the day and date of the photo, the camera, whether flash was used, aperture, and ISO-equivalent film speed. If you're familiar at all with cameras, the info shown here will give you a clue to what, if anything, needs adjusting in the image. For example, the photo has a very shallow depth of field, and isn't truly an "out of focus" picture: at ISO 50, at an f-stop of 2.2, and a shutter speed of 1/25th of a second, the Properties tab confirms this. Also, because a flash wasn't used, when you get to the Color tab, you can rule out Flash as a choice from the White Balance options.

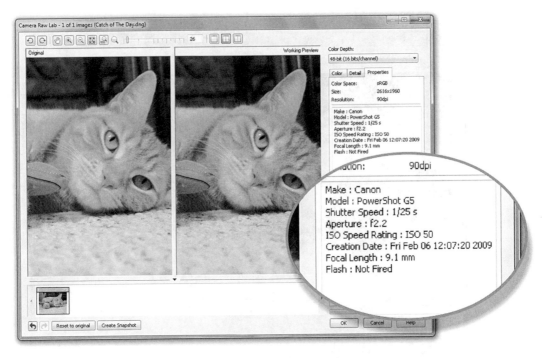

4. The Detail tab has a slider for sharpening the image as well as sliders for reducing Luminance Noise and overall Color Noise. This photo doesn't require these enhancements. The Hints area at the bottom of the tab is a handy context-sensitive reminder of what each slider does, and before you take your next Raw image, it's good practice to "get it right in the camera." You get less noise in a photo generally if you set your camera to slower ISO speeds. The ISO of 50 in this example image produces very little visible noise (similar to *grain* in traditional physical film), but an ISO setting of, say, 400, for the camera that took this photo would, indeed, have required noise reduction using the Detail sliders.

5. Click the Color tab; here's where the fun begins. Follow the callout letters in Figure 23-3 to guide you through which features do what.

   - The *A* area is for rotating the Raw image before placing the copy into your CorelDRAW document. Raw camera data can also include portrait and landscape orientation, so you might never need to use these buttons if your camera saved orientation info.

   - *B* marks your navigation tools for previewing the image. From left to right, you have tools for panning the window (you click-drag when your cursor is inside the preview window), zoom in and out, Fit To Window, 100% (1:1) viewing resolution, and finally there's a slider to zoom your current view in and out.

   - *C* marks the Split Pane view so you can compare the original image to any corrections you make.

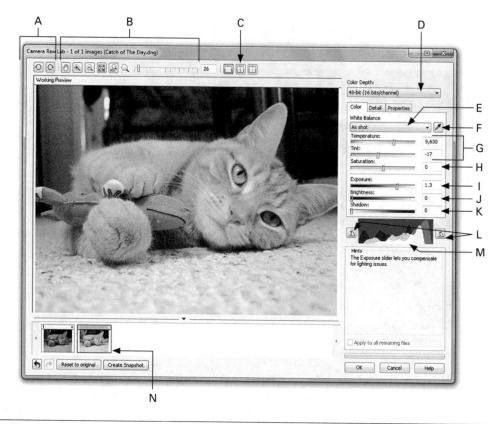

FIGURE 23-3 Use the Raw Lab to color- and tone-correct high-quality digital images.

- *D* marks Color Depth. You'd be ill-advised to change this from 48-bit because only a high-depth image can be adjusted extensively without taking on banding and color clipping (explained shortly). The only reason you'd choose 24-bit from the selector list is if the image were flawless and you wanted to get down to work by placing it in your document and saving space on your hard disk.
- *E* marks the White Balance selector. You have many choices that influence the color casting of the Raw image. Ideally, you want the placed image to be casting neutral; the grays in the image contain no hues, and the photo looks neither too warm nor too cold. You have selections such as Tungsten, Cloudy, and other lighting conditions that influence the color cast of images. As Shot is the default setting, and this image appears to be fine As Shot.
- *F* is the White Balance Eyedropper Tool, which is used to define a completely neutral area in the preview window to better set and possibly neutralize color casting. The cursor for this tool gives you an RGB readout of the current area in the preview photo; this is the true color over a pixel, and not the

"ideally neutral color." You click over an area you believe *should* contain equal amounts of red, green, and blue components (R:64, G:64, B:64, for example), and this action remaps the image to reflect the color casting in the image based on where you clicked. Although it's a useful tool, you might not have a photo that contains a perfectly white or a perfectly neutral gray area; if this is the case, don't use this tool.

- *G* marks color Temperature and Tint, perhaps the least intuitive of Raw digital image properties. The values in the Raw Lab's color Temperature controls run from low at the left of the slider (cools down warm images) to high at right (warms cool images). The temperature controls, specifically values you enter in the numeric field, are *not* degrees of Kelvin; they are correction values only for you to refer to and compare with other settings and other images. However, it *is* correct to *think* of color temperature in general as measured in degrees Kelvin. You might want to "uncorrect" a perfect image to make it warmer or colder. The Tint slider is the color complement of the color Temperature control; a neutral temperature displays a band on the Tint slider from magenta at left to green at right. You always use Tint after you've set Temperature because Tint varies according to temperature.

- *H* is the Saturation control, which is mostly self-explanatory—it's used to compensate for dull photographs (you increase Saturation) or for overly colorful images (you desaturate by dragging to the left with the slider).

- *I* marks the Exposure control. Exposure is not the same as, for example, the brightness/contrast controls on a TV set or the Levels command in image-editing applications. Exposure is the *total light that falls on a scene,* and it's set when you take a picture by setting the ISO value. Therefore, it's always a good idea to double-check the info on the Properties tab: if the ISO is a low value and the picture looks dark or muddy, then Exposure is probably the Color option that needs adjusting.

- *J* marks Brightness, which you should play with only after setting the best Exposure. If you drag the Brightness slider to the right with this image, you'll see that the upper ranges of the image become brighter, but not the shadow areas. So you use this slider to bring out detail in the midranges in an image without ruining the deeper tones.

- *K* is the Shadow slider, and this option is used only to make deeper areas more pronounced without affecting the midtones and highlights. Shadows might also be called *contrast*; dragging the slider to the right does indeed create a difference between the lighter and darker areas of the overall image.

- *L* marks both the Shadow and Highlights clipping regions. These two buttons that frame the histogram (*M*) display a bright red color overlay in the preview window in areas where the brightest brights have fallen out of range (they can't be accurately displayed onscreen, and they can't be accurately printed), and the deepest shadows display a green-tinted overlay. If you see a tint in areas, this means the Shadow, the Exposure, or the Saturation adjustments you've made are too intense. The solution is to choose lesser values for any of these options until the tint disappears in the preview window.

- *M* is the histogram of the current photograph. A *histogram* is a visual representation of how many pixels of what color are located at what brightness in the image. A well-toned image has a lot of color pixels in the mid-region of the histogram—this is where the most visual detail is apparent in digital photographs. If the histogram shows too many pixels—for example, in the lower regions in this example, you see a hump in the histogram curve toward the left—it means your image needs less Shadow or more Exposure.
- *N* is the area where you can create Snapshots. When you arrive at a good exposure for an image you want to copy into a page, click the Create Snapshot button and a thumbnail appears at bottom left. Snapshots are not saved—they are for comparison purposes—and ultimately, you choose one you'll import.

6. Once you've made your adjustments, you click OK, and you're then presented with a loaded cursor for placing and scaling the imported image, as discussed earlier in this chapter.

 Tip To import more than one digital image at a time, hold SHIFT while clicking to select contiguous files, or hold CTRL while clicking to select noncontiguous files in the Import dialog. As multiple files are imported, the cursor indicates the file information for each image being placed.

An Everyday Bitmap-Oriented Workflow

In addition to CorelDRAW's capabilities to import, resize, resample, and develop Raw images, you also have many of PHOTO-PAINT's effects right within CorelDRAW to filter imported images. And CorelDRAW has an Image Adjustment Lab for enhancing Raw file format images. Once you're finished working on a composition, whether it's vector, bitmap, or a combination of these two elements, you probably want to pop a copy of your work off to a friend or a client. The following sections take you through these four stages of CorelDRAW design work; in the process, you'll grow quite comfortable with all this "bitmap stuff" and appreciate CorelDRAW's power to bring different media together for both your import and export needs.

Creating a Catalog Cover

Lux, a fictitious candle manufacturer, needs a new catalog cover for 2013. As to be expected, they have no money to take a new picture for the cover, but they've heard that your copy of CorelDRAW ships with some really cool filters that might put a new spin on an old image. Follow along in the next sections' steps to take a tour of the Image Adjustment Lab, the Bitmap effects CorelDRAW offers, and as a grand finale, you'll breeze through the Export options for the JPEG file format so you can send a comp to the fictitious client.

Working in the Image Adjustment Lab

For "normal" photographs—photos in JPEG, TIFF, and file formats other than Camera Raw— the Bitmaps menu in CorelDRAW offers a fairly comprehensive Image Adjustment Lab to make practically every *global* adjustment (but not pixel-editing adjustments) you'll find in PHOTO-PAINT. The Image Adjustment Lab makes it easy to photo-correct imported bitmaps and to integrate them into a composition without ever leaving CorelDRAW; better still, the features are almost identical to those in the Camera Raw Lab.

Let's work through the mock assignment now: first, you'll import and place an image in the layout that's been designed for you.

Tutorial   Adjusting a PNG Image in the Lab

1. Open LUM catalog.cdr. Choose the Object Manager docker (Tools | Object Manager). Click the "Put The Photo On This Layer" title on the Object docker to make it the current layer (the background layer with the text is locked).

2. Choose File | Import (CTRL + I), and then choose LUM candles.png from the location where you downloaded it. Click Import.

3. Your cursor is loaded with the image now, and it's much larger than the place reserved for it within the layout, so you'll scale the image as you place it. First, make sure Snap To Guidelines is checked on the Snap To list on the Standard Bar. Click an insertion point at the top left of the guides intersection and then drag down until the right edge of the image meets the right guide. You've scaled and placed the image now, as shown in the illustration here.

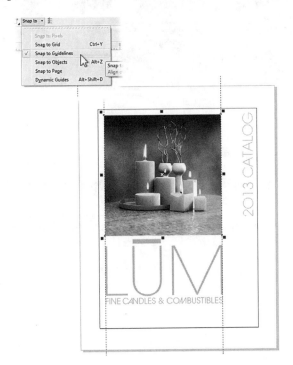

4. With the photo selected, choose Bitmaps | Image Adjustment Lab.
5. In Figure 23-4, you'll see many of the same navigation controls as you did in the Camera Raw Lab, but with slightly different features for color and tone adjustments. Select the Split Pane view now to make the adjustments easier to compare to the original photo. Always shoot for tone correction for exposure, and then work on the color if necessary.
   - *A* marks Auto Adjust, a one-step routine that adds contrast to an image; let's skip this feature—automated routines don't give "one off" assignments the custom attention they need, and you don't learn anything from automated routines.

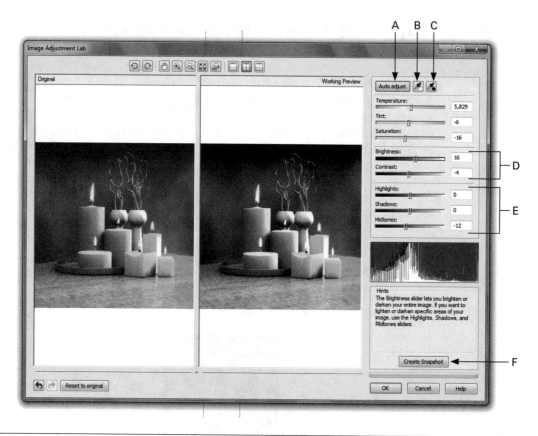

FIGURE 23-4   Color and tone correction can be performed on photographs with CorelDRAW.

- *B* marks the White Point Eyedropper Tool, used to define in the preview window the lightest area that should be in the picture. Click in the center of one of the candle flames (presumably the whitest white in the image) to see if the Lab adjusts the other tones and snaps up the image.
- *C* marks the Black Point Eyedropper Tool, which redefines the darkest point in the image based on where you click in the preview window. This step is optional; hover your cursor over the top left of the background in the image. Your cursor will tell you that the background toward the top is almost black with a little red tossed in. Click this point with the Eyedropper Tool; your artistic judgment might tell you that the preview pane at right shows a better, snappier image. If you disagree, click the Reverse To Last Operation arrow button at bottom left.
- *D* marks the Brightness and Contrast sliders. They basically do what you'd expect, but brightness and contrast don't always make an image better. Skip these controls for this assignment.
- *E* marks the area the professionals use to snap up a photo: Leave the Highlights slider alone in this assignment; this brightens the brighter areas in the image without affecting the midtones or shadow areas. However, do drag the Midtones slider up to 10 or 12 to open up the darker regions to provide image detail without messing up the Shadows region, which is fine as is.

6. Finally, click the Create Snapshot button (*F*). This creates an entry on the Undo docker in case you want to reverse a correction after exiting the Lab. Click OK and your adjusted image is now placed in the layout. Keep the file open, and now is also a good time to Save (press CTRL + S).

Creating Alterations with Photo Effects

If you need to do something dramatic to a photo, such as bowing the image so it looks as though a fish-eye lens was used, these options are available:

- Put an object over the photo, and then use Lens effects, covered in Chapter 22. You might not get exactly the effect you want with a Lens; therefore, the advantage to this method is that the change isn't made directly to the photo—a Lens effect can be deleted at any time, restoring the normal appearance of objects beneath it.
- Use the effects on the bottom of the Bitmaps menu, as you'll do in the following tutorial.

Effects you apply via the Bitmaps menu are permanent changes; the bad news is that you can only choose to Undo an applied effect right after you've made one if you don't like it. The good news is that all effects are applied only to an image you've imported—your original photo is safely tucked away somewhere on your hard disk.

Effects filters in CorelDRAW are divided into categories, and you'll only be using two from the Color Transform and Art Strokes categories in this assignment. You should feel free and set aside some time to experiment with the various filters on an image you believe has the potential to look more interesting after a little Distortion or Trace Contour filtering.

It's important to understand that any filter you apply to a photo removes original image information and occasionally supplies altered image information. Therefore, you need to make a creative and qualitative judgment as to whether an image looks "better" after applying one or more filters. There is no such thing as "instant art"; you yourself need to use your artistic taste when applying a filter to change the original image's data, and don't dismiss the possibility that an original image might look better and be more appropriate than a filtered one in a paying assignment.

Usually, there are two occasions when you might want to reach for the Bitmaps menu's filters:

- When a photography session isn't possible to provide a new photo for a new catalog or brochure. You or the client have to use an older photo, but you want it to look a little different than last year's photo.
- When a photo is visually boring. Not a bad photo, but just an uninspired photograph whose composition, geometry, and colors are very staid and simple. The LUX candle image isn't a bad image; its problems in this example are that it was used last year and the geometry in the scene is exceptionally simple and looks like any still photo of a bunch of cylinders.

To use a Bitmaps effect, you first need to select an imported bitmap. The bitmap has to be either an 8-bit (Grayscale mode, for example) or 24-bit image in either RGB or CMYK color mode. Raw images you import—if they are higher than 24-bit—need to be changed to a *bit depth* that the effects can work with. In English, if the Effects menus and submenus are dimmed, choose Bitmaps | Mode and then convert the selected image to RGB 24-bit, and life is good. Working with an effect is easy and intuitive: specific effects have different options and sliders, but to use an effect, you work in three key areas of the dialog that appears when you choose one:

- **The Preview button**   Even at an effect's default settings, you need to click Preview to see what the effect will look like on the page.
- **Reset**   Clicking this button removes all changes you've made to the sliders and other controls for all effects.
- **Apply**   Click OK to apply the effect using the options you've defined; the dialog then closes.

- **The controls**   To customize an effect, you drag sliders, enter values in number boxes, and/or drag other controls such as the direction of an effect. Once you've made changes to the effect's values, click Preview to update the page preview, and when you're satisfied with the customized effect, you click Apply.

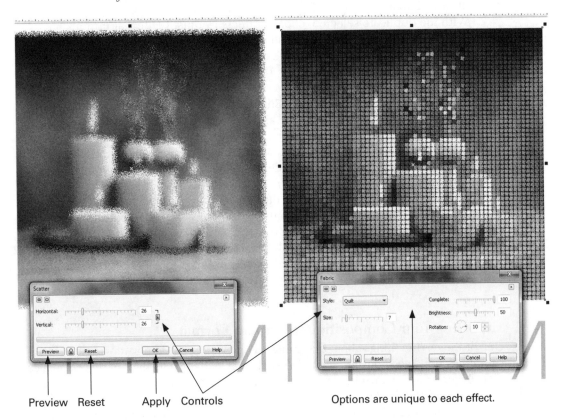

Preview   Reset   Apply   Controls   Options are unique to each effect.

In the following steps, you're going to kick out all the stops and combine two effects to create a unique stylized version of the candles image. You'll duplicate the image, apply two different filters to the two images, and then use CorelDRAW's Transparency effect to combine the two filtered images. You don't *have* to do this in your own work if one effect filter does the job, but these steps show you that you *can*.

Tutorial Filtering a Photo

1. With the Pick Tool, click-drag the candles image to the right and then tap the right mouse button before releasing both buttons to drop a copy of it to the right of the original.
2. With the duplicate selected, choose Effects | Adjust | Hue/Saturation/ Lightness. Drag the Saturation slider all the way to the left to make a grayscale version of the image and then click OK to apply. You do this to prepare the duplicate image for a filter effect; this command could also be done in the Image Adjustment Lab.
3. Choose Bitmap | Contour | Find Edges. In the Find Edges box, click the Solid button, click Preview, utter some amazement at how neat the outline version of the image looks, and then click OK to apply the effect.
4. Select the original image. Choose Bitmaps | Art Strokes |Crayon. Drag the Size slider to 20, move the Outline slider to 0, click Preview, and then click Apply.
5. With the Pick Tool, drag the duplicate over so it's aligned on top of the original. The guides should help snap the duplicate into perfect alignment.
6. Choose the Transparency Tool from the toolbox. Select the top duplicate image, and then on the Property bar, set the Transparency type to Uniform (from the drop-down list). First try the If Lighter operation from the drop-down list. Divide and Texturize operations also produce an interesting effect—it's your call here but 50% Uniform Transparency seems to work best.

Exporting Your Composition to Bitmap Format

One of the terrific things about designing using a computer application is that you can repurpose a good design. A good design such as the front cover of this catalog can yield several different uses from only one investment in time—and from knowing how to export the design.

Although CorelDRAW is a vector drawing program, it can create a bitmap copy of photographs, a bitmap from photos combined with vectors, and it can also export vector art only—text, graphics, anything is fair game. When vectors are copied out of CorelDRAW as bitmaps, a process called *rasterizing* is performed; CorelDRAW examines the vector artwork at the size and resolution you specify and then uses anti-aliasing (unless you specify no anti-aliasing) to create a bitmap that looks as good as what you see onscreen in your CorelDRAW document.

Let's say you want to feature the front cover of this company on your website. This narrows your export choices down to GIF, PNG, and JPEG. Let's briefly run through exporting the composition to JPEG now (exporting bitmaps is covered in detail in Chapter 24).

Saving a Bitmap Copy of
Your CorelDRAW Composition

1. In the Object Manager, unlock the layer titled "This One's Locked" by clicking on the pencil icon to remove the red slash mark. With the Pick Tool, drag a marquee from outside the top left of the design to the bottom right. Doing this is simply good practice for exporting designs: if there had been a hidden object or one outside of your workspace view, CorelDRAW's Export filter will not include it in the bitmap version it's going to render.

2. Click the Export button on the Property Bar.

3. In the Export dialog, choose JPG-JPEG Bitmaps as the Save As Type from the drop-down list. Check the Selected Only check box, type a name in the File Name field, use the directory pane to choose a location for the export, and then click Export.

4. You have the option to select a preset export for JPEGs by choosing from the Preset list at top right, but this doesn't teach you anything. First, set the color mode to RGB—JPEGs are increasingly used today for commercial printing, but it's the wrong color mode for the Web and e-mail attachments.

5. For starters, set the Quality to 80% (the High setting). Choose the Hand Tool and use your mouse scroll wheel to zoom in or out of the preview window. To produce a smaller file, choose **50%** (Medium) quality—which is reported at the bottom left of the dialog. This image shows some JPEG artifacting (noise and corruption) at 50% but not very much at 80%.

6. Check the Color Profile. Doing this costs about half a K of file size, but today's web browsers, such as Safari, Firefox, and Internet Explorer 9, have color management features. This means what you see on your monitor (if it's calibrated) will appear on the Web with colors as expected.

7. Check Optimize to save on a few K of exported image.

8. Choose Pixels as the unit, and then choose **96** as the Resolution for export. The resolution is meaningless for screen documents, but 96 provides you with a benchmark by which you can calculate the absolute height and width of the exported image—in pixels. The layout's original size is a little large for the Web and for the reading pane in mail readers such as MS Outlook; type **700** in the Height field to reduce both the height and width of the export.

9. The estimated download time shown at bottom left is calculated based on a hypothetical Internet connection you specify by selecting from the drop-down list toward the bottom center of the dialog. By default, it's set to fast dial-up, which represents an estimated 75 percent (and shrinking) of the United States, but Europe and many other countries are almost entirely on

broadband in 2012. ISDN (dial-up) essentially plays to the lowest common denominator—it's the worst speed you can use to estimate how your audience receives your image files. Therefore, 6.2 seconds—and almost certainly less time for most audiences—is acceptable. Click OK and your work is exported to JPEG file format.

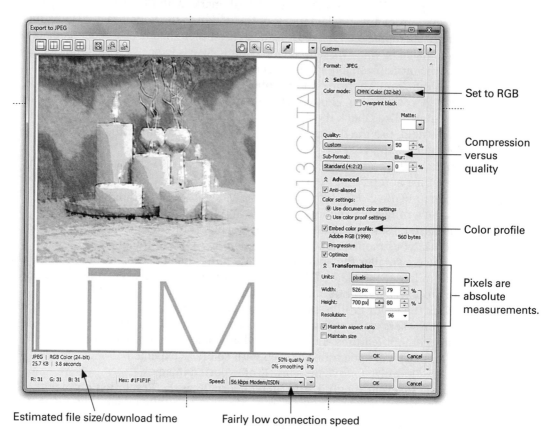

Set to RGB

Compression versus quality

Color profile

Pixels are absolute measurements.

Estimated file size/download time   Fairly low connection speed

If you're feeling a little jazzed after reading this chapter, get a friend to pat you on your back, because you deserve it. You've taken a serious detour in your "CorelDRAW is a drawing program" education and vaulted right into the arena of design professionals who integrate photos and vector artwork on a daily basis. You now know how to scale an image, to check to see whether its resolution is sufficient to pull a good print, to color-correct both Raw images and regular ones, and how to export your work so friends you'd like to send an e-mail attachment to can see it without necessarily owning CorelDRAW—and the composition is Web-worthy, to boot.

This is not the complete story of CorelDRAW and bitmaps. You'll want to do things as special as you do with vectors, so Chapter 24 covers more advanced bitmap-editing techniques, converting bitmap art to vector, and working with transparency to better integrate bitmap and vector objects in a composition. Read on and see how to create exactly the effect you need for tomorrow's assignment at work.

24

Advanced Photography Techniques with CorelDRAW

Because people seldom photograph an object or a scene with exactly the elements they want in a composition, the field of retouching has thrived since the day a professional had something to sell using a photograph! This is why professionals trim photographs, and so can you, using the CorelDRAW features covered in this chapter. As objects, photographic areas that have been carefully cut out can be composited with other photos and vector shapes to add a whole new dimension to your posters, flyers, and fine art. Additionally in this chapter, Corel PowerTRACE, part of CorelDRAW, is demonstrated; you'll learn how to create a vector copy of a bitmap so you can scale and rotate it, edit it, and never lose details or resolution as bitmap images are prone to do.

Download and extract all the files from the Chapter24.zip archive to follow the tutorials in this chapter.

Cropping a Placed Photograph

You can perform two types of cropping on placed photos: destructive (permanent) and nondestructive (you can undo what you've done). The Crop Tool on the Toolbox performs destructive cropping. Unless you press CTRL + Z to undo a crop you don't like, you're stuck with your crop, and no exterior areas beyond the cropped image remain that you can expose later. To crop a photo involves several steps:

1. You define the area you want to crop by click-diagonal-dragging the Crop Tool from one corner to the opposite corner.
2. You can redefine the crop by click-dragging the resulting bounding-box markers. The corner markers scale the proposed crop area proportionately, while the center markers are used to resize the proposed crop area disproportionately.
3. You can rotate the crop box, if, for example, you need to straighten a horizon. To do this, make a crop, then click inside the crop to put the crop into Rotate mode. You then drag on a corner double-headed arrow marker to rotate the crop. This doesn't rotate the photo itself, but rather the crop area.
4. You double-click inside the crop area to finish the crop. Figure 24-1 shows the elements you work with onscreen to crop a bitmap image.

Tip To see the resolution of a placed bitmap image quickly, with the bitmap selected, look at the Status Bar, which names the file and tells you its color mode and its current resolution. The rule is: as you increase bitmap dimensions, resolution decreases proportionately.

FIGURE 24-1   The Crop Tool eliminates the exterior image areas of your defined crop area.

Nondestructive Cropping

In a nutshell, if you want to hide an area of a photo and not delete it as you do with the Crop Tool, you use the Shape Tool. Try this out with the Macaw.jpg image by following the steps here.

Tutorial   Using the Shape Tool to Crop

1. Create a new (default-sized) document with landscape orientation. Place the image of the Amazon Macaws in a new document by clicking the Import button on the Property Bar and then selecting the image from the location you downloaded it to. With the loaded cursor, click-diagonal-drag to place the image so it fills most of the page.
2. Choose the Shape Tool. Notice that the photo, which is still selected, now has control node markers at each corner. These markers behave and operate exactly like control nodes for vector shapes.
3. Just for the fun of it, click a node to select it, and then drag it toward the center of the image. This is not what the pros call an "expert crop," but you've just learned something that will come in handy in your future work. When you drag a node inside of the outside dimensions of a placed photo, the two sides that meet at this node hide areas of the photograph. Press CTRL + z to undo this, and now perform a more practical crop.
4. Click-drag so you've marquee-selected two neighboring nodes; they can make up a horizontal or vertical edge of the photo. For this experiment, it makes no difference.
5. Use the keyboard arrows to nudge the nodes toward the center of the image. Hold SHIFT to super-nudge the nodes if you like. This is how you can nondestructively crop a placed photo; nudge the nodes in the opposite direction now—you've hidden and then unhidden one dimension of the photograph.
6. With two nodes selected, hold CTRL and then drag the nodes toward the center of the photo. The CTRL key constrains movement so the edge you're cropping remains parallel to the dragging page.

Masking Through Nondestructive Cropping

Go to the head of the class if you've already discovered that you can *add* control nodes to a placed photograph with the Shape Tool! CorelDRAW "sees" a bitmap as an object that has a fill—specifically a bitmap fill. Therefore, this object can be shaped and reshaped by adding nodes and also by changing the segment property between nodes. The following sections take you through some advanced bitmap editing to trim around a photograph so it becomes a floating object in a composition.

Trimming Away Unwanted Image Areas

What you'll learn in this section goes way beyond the simple cropping of an image. You're going to trim the background away from an image of a bust of classical composer Johann Sebastian Bach, put a new background behind the bust, and by the end of this section, you'll have designed a concert poster. There are two nondestructive methods for removing the background from a photo's subject, and both techniques are described in this section. The elements of the poster have already been created for you, and shortly you'll see how to make a design with elements in front of and behind each other, just like you do with vector shapes, but using *photographs*.

To begin this poster design (call it the overture), you need to create a new document (portrait orientation, default page size) and import the image of Bach—a little smaller than the page size, but he can be scaled at a later time when needed. Then you use the Shape Tool to trim the background.

Tutorial Background Removal, Technique 1

1. Click the Import button on the Property Bar, and then in the Import dialog, locate JS Bach.tif, select him, and then click Import.
2. Your cursor is loaded with the image: click-drag, and then release the mouse when the cursor reports that the height for the placed image is about 9 inches.

Click-diagonal drag to size and place.

JS Bach.tif
w: 6.34 in, h: 8.942 in

3. Choose the Shape Tool. Begin by clicking the top-right node of the image, and then click-drag it toward the center of the image until the top and right edges touch the bust of Bach, as shown here. Clearly, you're not going to get where you want to go with only four control nodes because the geometry of the bust is far from perfectly rectangular. This is okay; you'll add nodes to the outline of the image in the following step.

Click-drag

4. With the Shape Tool, click a point on the outline of the photo where you want to change the direction of the line; Bach's powdered wig near his forehead is a prime area. Now, either double-click the segment, press the keyboard plus (+) key, or click the Add Node button on the Property Bar to add a node. While you're in the vicinity of Bach's forehead, several additional points are needed. A quick way to add points in-between existing points is to click a point repeatedly and press the + key.

5. Click-drag points so they visually coincide with the vertices of Bach's wig. It's okay if the lines between the nodes hide areas you want exposed.

6. Click a straight line segment that should curve away from the photo. Then click the To Curve button on the Property Bar. The segment can now curve; click-drag the segment away from the photo, as shown here, until you can see Bach's locks. You can also right-click a segment and choose To Curve from the pop-up menu.

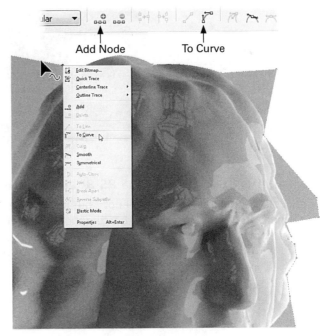

Add Node   To Curve

7. That's it; all it takes now is about 10 minutes of your time to work around the profile of the bust, hiding areas and creating curve segments where needed. Yes, it's a lot of work; so is putting on a tuxedo or gown to go and collect an industry award for outstanding design work (*prompt, hint, encouragement!*).

A good thing to do once you've trimmed away the non-essential Bach, because the default color of the page is white, is to put a colored vector shape behind your work to check your edge work. Make a rectangle, fill it with a dark color, and then press SHIFT + PAGE DOWN to put the rectangle to the back.

If you'd like to confirm the fact that the editing you performed is nondestructive, take the Shape Tool and marquee-select several control nodes. Then drag them away from the center of the photo, as shown here. Then press CTRL + Z to undo this nondestructive *and unwanted* edit!

Boolean Operations as a Trimming Technique

It takes an equal amount of effort, but it might be easier to visualize the nondestructive photo-trimming process by drawing the outline of the image object you want to isolate and then use the Shaping commands to slice out the area you want to use. If you have Bach trimmed now, you don't have to follow this tutorial, but *do* read the steps because you might find this technique easier than editing the control nodes.

Tutorial   Background Removal, Technique 2

1. Using the Pen Tool with which you're the most comfortable and experienced, draw a silhouette around the object you want to isolate in the photo, as shown here. It usually helps if you choose a contrasting outline color as you progress; you right-click, in this example, on white on the Color Palette after you've begun tracing. Choosing outline and fill colors *after* you've begun drawing a shape avoids triggering the attention box asking whether all new objects should get a white outline.

2. After you've closed the shape, choose Arrange | Shaping | Shaping to display the docker for performing an Intersect Boolean operation. You could use the Property Bar Shaping buttons to perform this operation, but the Property Bar Shaping buttons, by default, leave a copy of the target and source objects after the operation, a minor hassle to clean up later.
3. Select the object you just drew. Choose Intersect from the drop-down selector, and then uncheck both "Leave Original" boxes if they are checked. Click Intersect With, click the region of the photograph that is outside of the white outline you just drew, and you're home free, as shown in Figure 24-2.

Compositions with Mixed Media

Creating the poster is going to be fun—you're going to go beyond arranging and moving both bitmap and vector objects to laying out a finished art composition. What you'll see in the Concert poster.cdr file are two image objects: the background night image is locked on the bottom layer, and the gold title is an *alpha-channel masked image,* something covered a little later in this chapter.

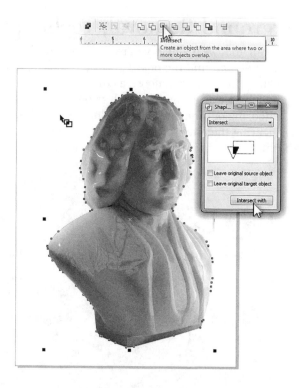

FIGURE 24-2   Use the Intersect Shaping command to remove all regions of the photo outside of the shape you drew.

Work through the following steps to duplicate your Bach trimming work to the concert poster document (an unlocked layer is active, so duplicating takes only one step). Then you'll add a vector shape to the composition to create an air of elegance ... it's a piece of *chorale* sheet music, actually, not an *air.*

Tutorial Composing a Design Using Vector and Image Shapes

1. Open Concert poster.cdr, and then choose Window | Tile Vertically so you have a view of both your Bach work and the tutorial .CDR file.
2. Hold CTRL and then drag your trimmed bust of Bach into the Concert poster window, as shown in Figure 24-3. This duplicates your work; it doesn't move it. You can save and then close your Bach image as a CDR file now.

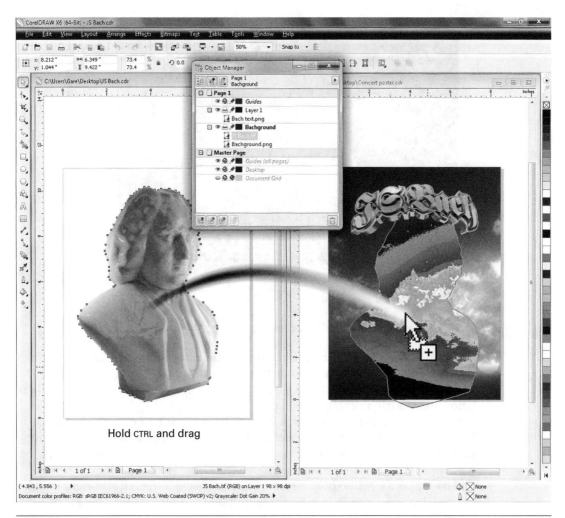

FIGURE 24-3 Duplicate your work in the Concert poster.cdr window.

3. Click the Import button on the Property Bar, and then choose the Bach 4 part Chorale.cdr file from your hard drive. Click Import; your cursor is now loaded with the imported file. You can click anywhere to place it at its original size, but, for this example, click-drag beginning about ¾" from the left edge of the page until the legend at the bottom right of the cursor reads approximately **w: 7.5 in**.

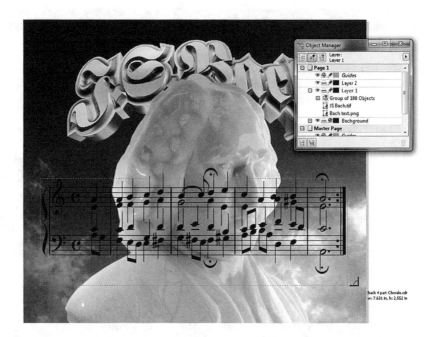

4. With the music notes selected, click the white color well on the Color Palette.

5. Choose Window | Dockers | Object Manager. Click-drag the title "Group of 100 Objects" (the music notes), and then release the mouse button when the title is below the "JS Bach.tif" object.

6. Let's make the music sort of swell behind its composer. Choose the Envelope Tool from the Effects group on the Toolbox. You're working in Putty mode by default, a good place to start; now, let's customize the envelope for a specific distortion. With the Shape Tool, marquee-select the middle nodes on the top and bottom lines; while holding SHIFT, marquee-select the left and right middle nodes. Then click the Delete Nodes button on the Property Bar; see top left, Figure 24-4.

7. Click the left side of the Envelope bounding box, and then right-click and choose To Line from the pop-up menu. Then perform the same edit on the right side. The top and bottom default property for Putty mode envelopes is curved segments—they need no editing. See middle left in Figure 24-4.

8. With the Shape Tool, one at a time, click the control nodes that bound the music notes, and then drag the top ones up a little and the bottom ones down a little. Then click-drag the bottom line up and the top line down. Use your artistic eye and Figure 24-4 to guide you. Bach's compositions are stirring; the music notes should visually reflect this.

9. A time and place for this concert would help sell it; read Chapter 13 if you haven't done so already for good text-composition techniques. As you can see in Figure 24-5, the completed poster looks handsome, and most of its visual success is because you now know how to isolate an important subject from a fairly boring background.

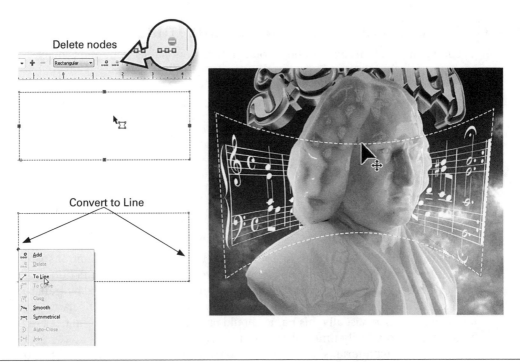

FIGURE 24-4   Shape the music so it appears to extend around the bust toward the audience.

FIGURE 24-5   When you can move image objects around on a page as easily as vector shapes, new design opportunities open up for you.

Working with Alpha Channels and Image Transparency

The following sections explain how you can trim your subject out of an image background, why certain file types are imported with transparency, and what transparency really means in your CorelDRAW work. More features than you might imagine are available for working with bitmaps directly in CorelDRAW; for *exceptionally* tricky image editing assignments, Chapters 25 and 26 cover Corel PHOTO-PAINT.

Working with Partial Transparency

Both Alpha Channel transparency and Image Layer transparency offer more than simply 100 percent opaque or 100 percent transparent areas. With 24-bit images, you can have 256 levels of opacity in any area of the image, and this leads to some fascinating visual effects that you can create. You'll work shortly with an image that has semitransparent areas, but right now, it's time to learn how to *build* semitransparent areas into an image that has none but should have them. Bob's Beer, a fictitious micro-brewery, has an image of a bottle in PNG file format that is surrounded by transparency. Let's say Bob wants the bottle to sit in front of a background that has his name repeated far too many times. Visually, his name should partially show through the neck of the bottle where there's only tinted glass and no beer.

   The following tutorial shows you how to trim away the top quarter of the bottle, the most transparent part. Then you'll see how to make this area only partially opaque so some of the background shows through. And to top it off, you'll see how to build a cast shadow from the bottle onto the "ground" in the composition.

Tutorial   Creating a Photorealistic Glass Effect

1. Open Bob's Background.cdr, and then click the Import button and choose Bob's Beer.png; it's a domestic beer, but you'll import it anyway. Click Import and then with the loaded cursor, click-diagonal-drag until the bottle is placed in the image as shown here.

2. With a Pen Tool (the Bézier Pen works fine in this example), create a shape that fits in the top part of the glass, from the fill line to the bottle's lip, staying slightly inside the neck of the beer bottle so the edge is not part of the trimming operation you'll perform in a moment. You should fill the shape after creating it to better see what you're doing in the following steps—any color is fine.

3. Select the shape but not the bottle. Choose Arrange | Shaping | Shaping to display the Shaping docker. Choose Intersect from the selector drop-down list, and then check Leave Original Target Object(s). Click the Intersect With button, and then click the bottle. The shape is deleted because it's the source object, and you didn't choose to leave it. Apparently the bottle has not changed, but there is a perfect cutout duplicate of the top of the bottle resting on top of an unchanged bottle; you're halfway there—you need to trim away part of the bottle using the new intersect shape now.

4. Click the spot formerly occupied by your drawn object to select the product of the intersect operation in step 3 (don't worry; it's hard to see that it's a separate object). Choose Trim from the Shaping docker's drop-down list, check Leave Original Source Object(s), and uncheck Leave Original Target Object(s). Click the Trim button and then click the bottle, and the beer bottle is now actually two separate pieces. See the following illustration for the docker settings for steps 3 and 4. Now it's on to transparency.

Separate object (not obvious)

5. Select the top part shape, and then choose the Transparency Tool from the Effects group of tools on the Toolbox. Choose Uniform from the selector drop-down on the Property Bar, and then drag the Opacity slider on the Property Bar to about 50%. As you can see here, your editing work resulted in quite

a convincing illustration. You can see Bob's logo in the background peeking through semitransparent glass; the background is even tinted a little from the green of the object on top of it.

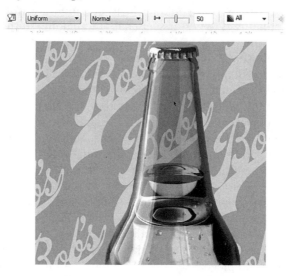

6. Here's the *pièce de résistance*: with the bottle selected and not the semitransparent piece, choose the Drop Shadow Tool. Click toward the bottom of the bottle image to define an anchor for the shadow and then drag up and to the right.

7. Click-drag the end marker of the shadow so the shadow ends closer to the bottle. Then, because the bottle should be casting a deep green (not black) shadow, click the Shadow Color flyout on the Property Bar, and then from the Color Palette, choose a deep green.

8. Well, oops. The area you trimmed in step 4 is not part of the shadow—there's a hole in the shadow where there should be a lighter green, because a shadow cast by green glass through beer would be a little darker than a shadow cast through green glass alone. No problem; you draw a fill shape for the missing part of the shadow as shown here, fill the shape with green, and then give it about 50 to 60% Uniform transparency.

Blending Photos with Transparency

You'll learn in Chapter 25 how to use PHOTO-PAINT to mask the exterior of an object in a photo. For the moment, let's imagine that the Tree.png file you'll work with in the following steps was created by masking everything except the tree in the photo, and then you saved it as a PNG file with transparency using PHOTO-PAINT.

You know now that an image can have transparent areas, and you know that you can use CorelDRAW's Transparency Tool to make any object on a page partially transparent. The steps that follow show you how to perform surreal, completely professional photo retouching with two images you graft onto one another with only one CorelDRAW tool.

Tutorial   Creating a Transition Between Two Images

1. Press CTRL + N to create a new file; accept the default standard letter page size and define it as Portrait orientation.
2. Import ThumbsUp.jpg. JPEG images do not retain resolution information, so you need to click-drag the loaded cursor after clicking Import to scale the imported image to the 11" height of the page.

3. Import Tree.png. PNG files can (in some cases) retain image resolution information, so all you need to do is click the loaded cursor on the page.

4. With the Pick Tool, position the tree so its trunk fits over the thumb in the underlying photo.

5. Choose the Transparency Tool from the Effects group of tools on the Toolbox.

6. Click-drag downward, starting from around the thumbnail area in the underlying photo to just above the trunk on the tree. You should see the amazing transformation between the guy's thumb and the trunk of the tree. If the beginning and end points for this Linear transparency aren't perfect, you can adjust the start and end point with the Transparency Tool cursor.

7. Unfortunately, the guy's thumb doesn't taper toward the top like the tree trunk does; some of the thumb is visible, ruining the special effect. Choose the Bézier Pen Tool from the Toolbox, and then draw a closed shape whose right edge matches the contour of the tree trunk's left side. Fill it with the same color as the background of the thumb photo—choose the Color Eyedropper Tool from the Toolbox, click over the background and then click the paint bucket cursor on the shape you drew. See Figure 24-6 for the exact location of this edit in the photo.

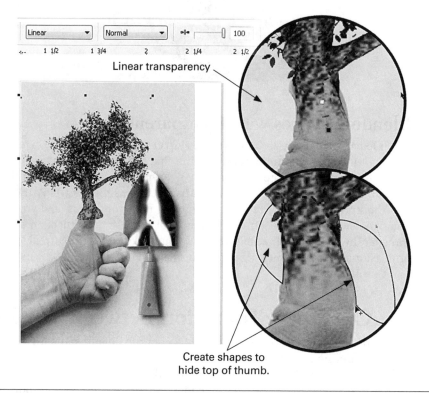

FIGURE 24-6 Create a blend between two photos to present unique and visually arresting imagery.

8. Perform Step 7 on the right side of the thumb, after drawing a second shape.

9. Remove the outline of both shapes (select them both) by right-clicking the No Fill color well on the Color Palette.

10. With both shapes selected, press CTRL + PAGEDOWN to put them behind the tree, yet in front of the thumb photo.

11. Read Chapter 13 on working with text because this image would make a terrific magazine cover.

Bitmaps to Vector Art: Using PowerTRACE

You can export both vector art and bitmaps to bitmap file format, but once in a while, you'll need to go the other way: taking a bitmap and making vector art from it. Many design professionals are faced daily with clients who want to use their logo for a truck sign or a high-resolution print ad, when all they can provide the designer is a really pathetic GIF copy from their web page.

Fortunately, designers don't have to reconstruct logos by hand—Corel PowerTRACE is a highly accurate utility that often produces a vector equivalent of a placed bitmap that requires no hand-tweaking afterward. What PowerTRACE does is simple: it creates a vector version of the selected bitmap. *How* PowerTRACE does this is not easy to explain, but if you understand the "how," you'll be better prepared to choose the right option before making a vector copy of an imported bitmap. In a nutshell, PowerTRACE examines the bitmap based on the criteria you specify in the dialog and then seeks edges in the bitmaps that show a clear and marked difference in color and/or brightness between neighboring pixels. PowerTRACE then creates a vector line at this neighboring region, continues to create a closed path (with the Centerline option chosen, it creates open paths), and fills the path with the closest color match to the pixels inside the area it creates. The following sections take you through the operation of PowerTRACE and offer suggestions on settings and when and why you'd use this handy feature.

Bitmap Conversions for Logo Alterations

Sometimes you'll want to use PowerTRACE to rework an existing logo that's in bitmap format. Suppose SilverSpoon.png, a good, clean graphic, is the logo for a caterer that was bought out yesterday by Phil Greasy, and Phil likes the logo but wants the name changed to... you guessed it. You use settings for PowerTRACE to make a vector conversion of the logo covered in the following section, but this is a prime example of "knowing your fonts" (covered in Chapter 13). Many times it's a futile endeavor to trace typography in a logo: it's much easier and provides cleaner results just to recast the text using the same or a similar font.

Pretouching: Use PHOTO-PAINT for Cleanup Before Tracing

The Silver Spoon logo you're going to have PowerTRACE convert so you can alter the logo for the new owner is a detailed and complex one. The logo has four or five areas that you need to assist PowerTRACE with by manually editing the logo before auto-tracing it. Your own artistic eye is hooked up to your brain, and it can discern the edge between the black outline around "Silver" and the black background checkerboard. PowerTRACE, on the other hand, doesn't have eyes and doesn't have a brain (these features are expected in CorelDRAW X37). Therefore, you will make life a lot easier for yourself if you use Corel PHOTO-PAINT to erase the areas—working to the outside of the outline around "Silver"—so there is a gap and so PowerTRACE can create separate objects for the word "Silver" and the checkerboard background.

This logo is probably the hardest one you'll encounter professionally to use PowerTRACE on for clean-up work and alterations. If you succeed at this fictitious example, your paying gigs will be a charm. These are really quite easy steps, and shortly you'll see how little sweat you have to break to alter the logo dramatically:

Tutorial Working Between CorelDRAW and PHOTO-PAINT

1. In a new document in CorelDRAW, import the Silver Spoon.png image. Click the loaded cursor to place the bitmap at its original size.
2. Click Edit Bitmap on the Property Bar. In a moment, PHOTO-PAINT loads with Silver Spoon.PNG displayed in a document window.
3. Choose the Eraser Tool from PHOTO-PAINT's Toolbox. On PHOTO-PAINT's Property Bar, type **10** in the Size field to set the diameter of the Eraser Tool. Leave the Feather amount at its default value. Doing this gives you a small, hard tool for erasing areas to the default white background color.
4. The bottom right of the S, the dot over the i, the upper left of the l, the top and bottom left of the e where it touches the outline of the spoon, and the bottom and right portions of the r all touch what you can see as black background areas. Refer to the following illustration, and carefully erase areas outside of these characters, creating a white gutter between background elements touching the black border around the letters in "Silver".

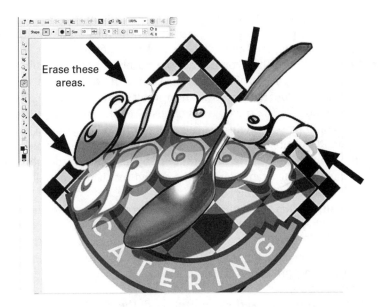

Erase these areas.

5. When you're finished, choose File | Exit or press ALT + F4 to close PHOTO-PAINT. Click Yes to save changes, PHOTO-PAINT closes, and you're returned to CorelDRAW with your edits made to the copy of the logo you imported.

6. With the bitmap selected, click Trace Bitmap (the button on the Property Bar when a bitmap is selected), and then choose Outline Trace | High Quality Image. It's not time to trace yet, but it's time to *explore your options* before tracing.

PowerTRACE Options

After you import and select the bitmap, you have the option to QuickTrace the bitmap, or to get more specific about the final traced object's quality and fidelity. This logo has no dithering and no aliased edges. Therefore, the PowerTRACE can be set for less smoothing and greater precision. As you can see here, the logo has no transparent background, but because you'll trace it, you can automatically delete its white background, a little perk for your client.

- **Trace Type**   You can choose Outline or Centerline from this drop-down. Outline is the method that produces objects based on areas of similar color in the bitmap. Centerline is a good option when your source bitmap is calligraphy or a technical drawing; this option generates open paths to which you can assign different widths and styles after the trace is placed on the page.

- **Type Of Image**   This is a convenience based on what many people call different types of bitmap art. Depending on your choice—from Line Art to High Quality Image—PowerTRACE renders a few objects or hundreds. You can customize a Type Of Image setting by altering other settings, and you can also use an "inappropriate" Type Of Image setting for your imported image. No two images are alike, and you might be surprised at the hi-fi rendering of a piece of clipart you trace using the Line Art Type Of Image setting, for example.

- **Colors** On this tab, you can set the number of unique colors PowerTRACE evaluates, from 1 (which renders a stencil of your original) to a varying maximum of unique colors, which you can limit by typing in a value. You can specify the color mode for the trace; you'd choose CMYK, for example, if you needed a trace that could be sent as an EPS file to a commercial printer. Generally, your best bet is the RGB color mode. You can also sort the colors to be used by how frequently they appear in the original bitmap or by similarity. Additionally, if you intend to replace a color when you edit the traced result, you can do so by clicking a color well and then clicking Edit.

- **Settings** This tab is used to define how tightly and accurately you want PowerTRACE to render the bitmap as vector object.

- **Detail** You set the overall complexity of the trace with this slider. Higher values instruct PowerTRACE to evaluate the bitmap carefully, whereas lower Detail settings can produce a stylized, posterized trace with fewer colors and much fewer groups of objects.

- **Smoothing** This setting controls both the number of nodes along paths and, to a lesser extent, the number of objects the trace yields. A higher smoothing value is good when your bitmap import is a GIF image that contains a lot of noise, dithered colors, and jagged edges.

- **Corner Smoothness** Use this setting depending on the visual content of your imported bitmap. For example, a photo of a sphere probably doesn't require any corner smoothness. However, a photo of a bird's feather will certainly have a lot of abrupt color and geometry changes—you'd want to use a very low Corner Smoothness setting to represent accurately the sharp turns and corners that make up a feather.

- **Remove Background** Usually you'll want to check this box. When an imported image such as this logo is floating in a background of white, Remove Background doesn't make the background a huge white rectangle. Optionally, any color can be removed from the final trace by clicking the Specify Color button and then using the Eyedropper to choose a color from the preview window.

- **Merge Adjacent Objects Of The Same Color** This option makes one object instead of several if the bitmap contains areas of almost identical color in neighboring regions.

- **Remove Object Overlap** Most of the time, you'll want to leave this box unchecked. If you do choose to enable Remove Object Overlap, there might be visible gaps between the resulting grouped vector shapes, making it hard to put a solid background behind your trace without the background color or texture peeking through. This option must be chosen before you can use Group Objects By Color.

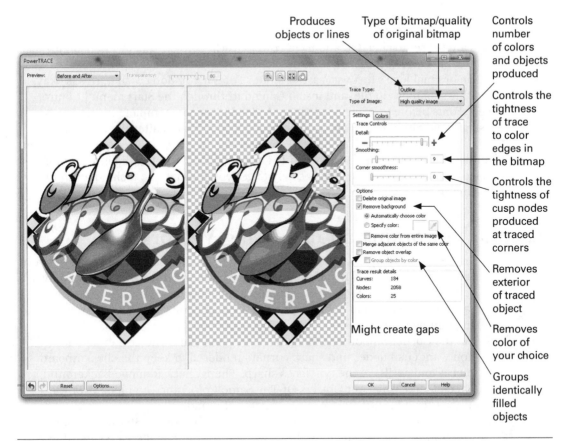

FIGURE 24-7   Use the features and settings in PowerTRACE to create an optimized group of vector objects based on the bitmap.

- **Group Objects By Color**   This is a handy feature that automatically groups identically colored objects after you click OK to make the trace. You can then choose a different color and apply it to the entire group, delete an entire group of objects identically filled, and you don't have dozens of objects that can be accidentally moved lying all over the page.
- **Trace Results Details**   This area on the dialog predicts how many objects (Curves), how many nodes, and how many different colors are produced. As a guideline, if the results show more than 200 objects will be created, think twice. It's a large number of objects to edit, and the resulting trace will possibly be a challenge to work with.

Let's put all this knowledge into practice in the next section.

Performing a Trace

You're almost set to click OK and have PowerTRACE convert the Silver Spoon.jpg logo into a set of vector objects.

The original logo's text was cast in Motter Fem; if you don't own it, this is okay. Open this chapter's zip file, and install Candid.ttf through the Start menu | Control Panel | Fonts before you begin the tutorial. Candid is not a complete typeface; it's missing punctuation marks and numbers, and it was created after the Candy font by URW. It's very close in look to Motter Fem, and Candy is a great packaging design font you might seriously consider purchasing for your collection—Candid is an author-cobbled knockoff whose purpose is solely to get you through the techniques in the following steps.

Tutorial Reworking a Logo Using Vectors

1. In the PowerTRACE box, set the Detail all the way to the right lower setting to ignore details such as the "Catering" text because the text is made up of only a few pixels in character width. Set Smoothing to about 25%; the logo is already fairly smooth and will not benefit from the averaging PowerTRACE would make in defining paths.

2. Set the Corner Smoothens to the far left on the slider (no corner smoothing). You want cusp nodes and sharp corners rendered to keep the checkerboard pieces and serifs on the typefaces sharp. Then, check Remove Background, check Merge Adjacent Objects Of The Same Color, and then look over the Trace Curve Results field just as a matter of practice.

3. Click the Color tab and then set the Number Of Colors to **30**—there really aren't more colors than 30 in the image; more colors will create superfluous additional objects. These settings should yield less than 200 separate objects, so click OK.

4. Move the objects away from the bitmap original; you want to keep the original on the page for reference. Ungroup the group of objects, and then delete what's left of the word "Silver." This will leave a hole in the background in a few places.

5. With the Text Tool, type **Greasy**, and then apply Candid from the Font selector drop-down on the Property Bar.

6. Apply a white fill to the text, and then press ALT + ENTER to display the Object Properties docker. Click the Outline button and then set the outline to **8** points and check Behind Fill; this makes the apparent outline width 4 points, but areas are filled in within the characters to give the text a bold look.

7. Choose the Envelope Tool from the Effects group on the Toolbox, and then perform the same steps as you did earlier with the music notes in the Bach composition. Use the Shape Tool to massage the text to look arced like the original text. If your design now looks like the one shown next, you're in good shape with only a step or two to go.

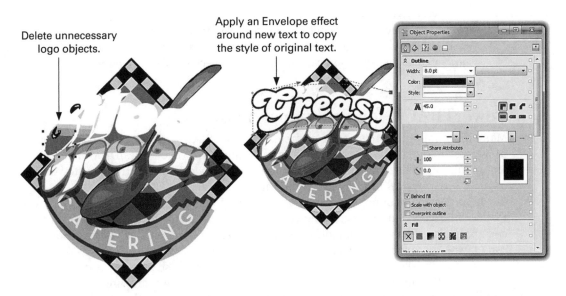

Delete unnecessary logo objects.

Apply an Envelope effect around new text to copy the style of original text.

8. Create rectangles that match the color of the missing checkerboard in the logo, rotate them to the correct diamond-shaped orientation as the original logo, position them accordingly for your patchwork, and then send them to the back of the page by pressing SHIFT + PAGEDOWN.

9. With the Shape Tool, edit the characters in the word "catering" to make them look more refined. At small image sizes, CorelDRAW does its best to render approximations of small text, but the images often need a little human intervention!

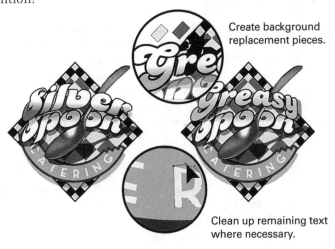

Create background replacement pieces.

Clean up remaining text where necessary.

10. You can embellish the revised logo by adding a drop shadow to the new owner's name, as it appears in the original logo, and you can smooth out the posterized edges on the spoon by overlaying an object that uses a Fountain Fill with the same colors. But, as you can see here, the new logo is pretty faithful to the original, and with the help of PowerTRACE, it took ten steps. Think of how many steps and lost nights of sleep you'd have without an auto-tracing utility.

Tip To get superfluous objects out of a finished PowerTRACE very quickly, use Edit | Find And Replace | Find Objects, and set the criteria for the search to specific unwanted colors. Then you can delete all the selected objects at once.

PowerTRACE for Traditional Artists

Many different types of users are attracted to CorelDRAW. Logo and other graphics designers are one category of visual communicators. However, CorelDRAW's tracing feature also appeals to artists who come to the digital world of illustration after years of work with physical pens, pencils, and inks.

If you have a scanner, and have, for example, a pen and ink cartoon, PowerTRACE makes child's play out of re-creating your cartoon as scalable vector art, to which you can apply color fills with a smoothness and precision that enhances your cartoons and can elevate them to the status of Fine Art. Seriously!

Cartoon sneaker drawing.png is a fairly high-resolution scan to get you started with a specific workflow you can adopt with scans of your own drawings. One important issue is removing pencil or other marks on the physical paper before you scan; use a kneaded eraser, and even if the paper doesn't come completely clean, the following steps show you a novel way to use PowerTRACE to remove stray marks.

Here's how to create a digital cartoon suitable for exporting as either vector or bitmap art to any size you need; this is a perk you don't have when working with only physical tools.

Tutorial Digi-tooning

1. In a new document, select Landscape orientation, click the Import button on the Standard Bar, and then choose Cartoon sneaker drawing.png. Place it by click-dragging the loaded cursor so it fills the page.
2. Click Trace Bitmap, and then choose Outline Trace | Line Art. You'll receive an attention box that the bitmap size is too large and that, if you choose not to resize the bitmap, the trace process might be on the slow side. This is your artistic call: if you want the pen strokes to look extremely faithful to the author's original cartoon, click Keep Original Size. If you're in a hurry, click Reduce Bitmap.
3. In the PowerTRACE window, choose a medium amount of detail, about 25% Smoothing, no Corner Smoothness (see illus on next page), check Remove Background, and then click the Colors tab. Set the number of colors to **2**. Doing this generates almost entirely black objects with the exception of one or two

areas that are totally enclosed, which should produce a white fill inside a black object. Check Delete Original Image, click OK, and you'll see that the pencil marks that are not entirely a black color disappear from the trace.

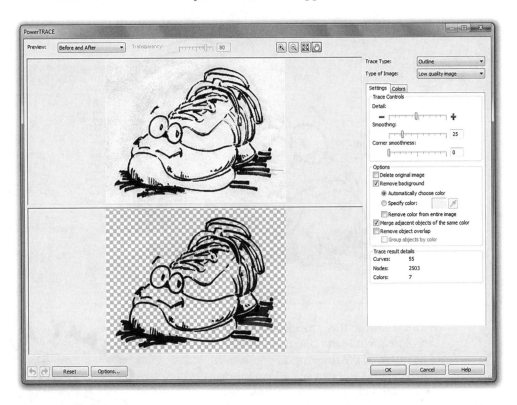

4. Delete the bitmap; you'll need to move the grouped objects first.
5. Choose Tools | Object Manager. Create a new layer and then drag its title on the list to below Layer 1. You can rename these layers **Coloring** and **Trace** by clicking to select the name and then clicking a second time to open the title for editing—type anything you like in the field. Lock the tracing layer.
6. Using the Pen Tool you're most comfortable with for creating free-form shapes, create objects that represent the different areas of the cartoon you'd like to color in. For example, the treads of the sneaker would look good in several different shades of warm gray. The solution would be to use the Mesh Fill on this object you draw—see Chapter 15 for thorough documentation of object fills.

The top of the sneaker could be an interesting Linear Fountain Fill, traversing from deep orange at bottom to a bright yellow at top. Another great thing about coloring your work digitally is that you never have to decide on a final color.

Linear Fountain Fill

Mesh Fill

7. You continue this process until you've "colored inside the lines" and filled as much of the drawing as you see fit artistically. You can see a logo mockup here for a children's footwear store. Clearly the drawing has an organic sense about it, the opposite of the sterile and flawless "computer art" we see occasionally, and yet this is CorelDRAW computer art, with a little ingenuity added to create a symbiosis between the physical and traditional elements.

You can take a look at how this drawing was completed if you open Sneaky kids finished.cdr.

This chapter has shown you how to work with bitmaps in almost the same way as you work with vector art in CorelDRAW. Both vectors and bitmaps can happily coexist in a single document. You can shuffle and rearrange objects as if they were made of the same digital materials, and you do need bitmaps in your work when you're trying to convey any sense of photorealism. Your next stop in Chapter 25 is to get some hands-on education with PHOTO-PAINT as you work directly on bitmap photographs and illustrations. You'll see shortly that editing bitmaps and drawing with vectors can be a seamless creative process when you put the power of the Corel Graphics Suite to its best use.

25

An Introduction to Corel PHOTO-PAINT

Photography tells a different story than the vector graphics you create in CorelDRAW. Although vector drawings can look crisp, powerful, and brilliant in coloring, photographs typically mirror more of a literal, human story. Digital images deliver emotional content through soft tones, an intricate latticework of highlights and shadows, and all the photorealistic qualities that portray the world as we're accustomed to seeing it. Understandably, the tools you use to edit a digital photo or other bitmap image are different than those you use to edit paths in CorelDRAW. This is where PHOTO-PAINT enters the creative scene to round out your creative toolset.

This chapter introduces you to the fundamentals of *bitmap images:* how you measure bitmaps, how to crop them to suit a specific output need, and ultimately how to make your original photo look better than when it came from the camera.

Download and extract all the files from the Chapter25.zip archive to follow the tutorials in this chapter.

The Building Block of Digital Photos: The Pixel

The term "pixel" is funny-sounding, and although the word is used occasionally in a humorous context in conversations, seldom is a helpful explanation or definition of a pixel given when you need to alter a digital photograph. A *pixel*—an abbreviation for *pic*ture *el*ement—is the smallest recognizable unit of color in a digital photograph.

It is *not* a linear unit of measurement; a pixel doesn't have to be square in proportions; and it's not any specific color. Now that what a pixel *isn't* has been covered, read on to learn what a pixel *is,* and how understanding its properties will help you work with PHOTO-PAINT's tools and features to make photo-retouching go as quickly as your CorelDRAW work.

Pixels and Resolution

A pixel is *a unit of color*; as such, it has no fixed size you can measure the same way as you'd measure the length of a 2 by 4 (which is usually 2" by 4"). If you were to discuss a pixel with a friend or coworker, it would be hard to do so without any sort of context because these units of color cannot exist unless they're within a background, which is usually called the *paper* or the *canvas.* The *paper* in PHOTO-PAINT is an imaginary grid into which you assign units of colors with the Paint Tool or the Fill Tool. When you open a digital photograph, the paper is predefined by the digital camera's capability; the *resolution* of your photographs is of a fixed size.

 Note The term "bitmap" was derived from the imaginary grid on an image's canvas—a *map*—and the amount of color information placed on this map, expressed as a *bit* of digital information. Usually, there is more than one bit of information held by a pixel, more often a *byte* of information (8 × a single bit), but somehow the phrase "bitmap" stuck as one of the names for pixel-based images.

Resolution is expressed as a fraction, a ratio: how many *pixels per inch* expresses image resolution in the same way that *miles per hour* expresses speed. This resolution is often called *dots per inch (dpi)* due to the visual similarity of dots of ink on a printed page and the pixels of color seen on a monitor. Bitmap images are also called *resolution-dependent* images because once a photo has been taken or a paper size defined for a PHOTO-PAINT painting, you cannot change the resolution without distorting the visual content of the picture. Here's an example that shows the use of resolution when you press CTRL + N or choose File | New.

1. In the Create A New Image dialog box, you're offered a Preset Destination of PHOTO-PAINT Default size, which, as you can see here, is 5 inches in width by 7 inches in height. However, this is not a *complete* description of how large in real world units this default paper size is. How many *pixels* will be created per inch? Pixels are the units of color for the document, so without knowing the resolution, the size of the paper is as meaningful as how many grapefruits per inch will fit on the page! Fortunately, below the Height and Width fields, you're offered the Resolution, which is set to the default of 72 dpi.

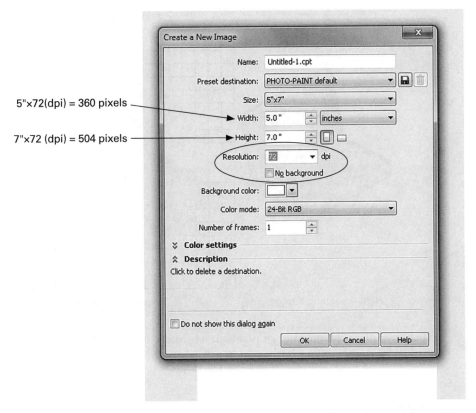

5"x72(dpi) = 360 pixels

7"x72 (dpi) = 504 pixels

2. Aha! Now you can discover the number of pixels in the new document. This can be important for website work, because a fixed screen resolution with the audience is always presumed, and, therefore, images are always measured in absolute number of pixels in width and height for graphics. In this example, 504 pixels wide might make a good logo on the first page of a website; the majority of people who visit websites run a screen resolution of 1024×768 or higher, so this default paper size is about half the width of an audience's monitor width.

Image Resolution

Any PHOTO-PAINT document resolution can be great for web graphics, but *not* so good for printing. The reason why is the finite number of pixels in the resolution-dependent bitmap image. Figure 25-1 shows, at left, a CorelDRAW illustration of a child's paint box. In this book, the drawing looks crisp around the edges, and smooth in its transitions from neighboring tones. It was a graphic suitable for printing as a

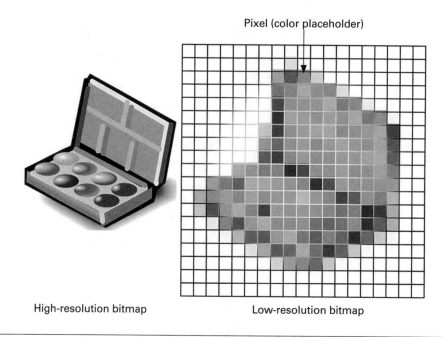

Pixel (color placeholder)

High-resolution bitmap   Low-resolution bitmap

FIGURE 25-1 The number of pixels in a bitmap, combined with the image's resolution, determines whether an image is suitable for printing.

bitmap because it was exported at a high resolution (300 dots per inch) for printing in this book. However, at right is an illustration of the same paint box, with the imaginary bitmap grid shown, but it was exported at desktop icon size (about 19 by 19 pixels) and the loss of image detail is evident at its resolution of 72 pixels per inch.

Resolution, Pixel Count, and Printing

It's a frequently asked question, and one whose answer is not a precise one: what is the resolution I need for a photograph to make a good print?

Scanning a physical photograph doesn't provide the best sampling of color pixels to produce a terrific photograph, but it does ensure that you have a sufficient number of pixels (an image's *pixel count*) to then print the scanned photo.

The most direct way to acquire a photo and manipulate it in PHOTO-PAINT is by using a digital camera. Today's digital cameras are capable of taking full frame pictures that can be printed to inkjet printers at 12" by 18" in high quality. Digital cameras measure the number of pixels in width and height of the picture's frame in megapixels (Mpx): a million pixels equal a megapixel. For example, the Nikon D90 can take 12.3 megapixels—its sensor array captures 4288 along one dimension and 2848 pixels along the other: $4288 \times 2848 = 12.2$ (plus a fractional amount of) pixels.

Depending on the make and model of your digital camera (price plays a deciding factor here), you can take images that can be printed that vary in maximum print size. The following table provides the maximum printable dimensions for different megapixel-capable cameras:

Camera	Maximum Print Size
12.3 Mpx	12"h×18"w
10.1 Mpx	10.8"h×16.2"w
9 Mpx	10.2"h×15.3"w
6 Mpx	8.3"h×12.5"w

These are not hard-and-fast dimensions but instead are guidelines for print output for two reasons:

- The dots that inkjet printers render are imprecise. They are more like *splats* than dots as the print head sprays color onto the page.
- There is some flexibility when printing to home inkjet printers because *image dimensions are inversely proportional to image resolution*.

The math for calculating maximum resolution goes like this: most affordable inkjet printers offer a high-quality resolution of about 720 dpi. The documentation might claim that the printer offers "enhanced resolution of 1440 dpi" but usually this enhancement is only rendered in one direction, height or width, depending on your print layout. The true resolution is always the lower number when two are offered in the inkjet printer's documentation, for instance 720 divided by 3 is 240 dpi. Manufacturers of inkjet printers, makers of inks, and other printing experts agree that the ideal resolution for printing—in dots per inch—requires about 1/3rd this number—in pixels per inch—for the image to be printed.

The good news is that you can change the resolution of an image, thereby changing its real-world dimensions, without changing the pixel count—which tends to sharpen an image when it's made smaller but blurs it when enlarged. For example, a photo that is 3 inches by 3 inches at 300 pixels per inch is *exactly equal* to the image at 6 inches by 6 inches at a resolution of 150 ppi. Both images have the same number of pixels, but the print dimensions and resolution have been changed.

Let's walk through an example on how to determine a photo's resolution and then adjust it for printing.

Tutorial   Resizing a Photograph

1. In PHOTO-PAINT, open CRW_6115.jpg, a photo that has been (mal)adjusted to demonstrate a technique in this chapter.
2. Let's say you need to print this photo at inkjet high quality. This means at least 240 pixels/inch are required. To check the resolution of the current foreground document, with the Object Pick Tool, right-click over the document and then choose Document Properties from the context menu.

> **Tip** To display rulers around the edges of a document, press CTRL+SHIFT+R. To hide rules, press CTRL+SHIFT+R again to toggle them off. If the rulers don't display the units you need, right-click over either ruler and then choose Ruler Setup from the context menu.

3. Well, oops. This photo is a nice 8" by 11", but it's of insufficient resolution to print at the required 240 ppi, as shown here. It *can* print with high quality and great image fidelity, but the physical output dimensions need to be decreased to *increase* the resolution.

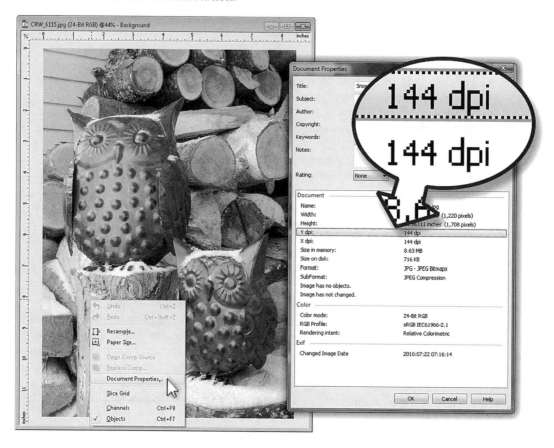

4. Right-click over the photo and then choose Resample from the context menu. The Resample (Image menu item) box does more than resample an image; it can also *resize* an image, and the two terms are very different. Resizing is the action of decreasing or increasing image resolution, affecting image

dimensions inversely, and the result is an image that has the same number of pixels. *Resampling* (covered in this chapter) involves changing the number of pixels in the image. Original pixel colors are moved around the grid, some are duplicated, some removed, and the resulting color pixels are a new color based on an average of neighboring original color pixels. Resampling changes original image data and occasionally blurs or creates unwanted harsh edges in image areas.

5. Click to check the Maintain Original Size box, make sure the Maintain Aspect Ratio Box is checked, and then type **7** in the Height field, as shown in Figure 25-2. Because the photo was doctored for this example, the photo is now a perfect 7" by 5", smaller than its original dimensions. As you can see, as the dimensions decreased, its resolution increased and is now more than adequate in resolution for inkjet printing. Save the file if you like owls, and then print it to see what image resolution does for digital images: it *improves* them.

FIGURE 25-2 As image resolution decreases, image dimensions increase.

Note There is a little disagreement in the imaging community over screen resolution: whether it should be measured at 72 pixels per inch or 96, the standard that Microsoft put forth with Windows 95. The answer to this disagreement is: when you're measuring pixels for screen display, *it makes absolutely no difference*. Screen resolution, regardless of how you measure it, is of a fixed size, so a 300-pixel-wide bitmap might look larger or smaller depending on the screen resolution you use for display, but nothing changes the number of pixels in width, nor the total pixel count of a bitmap when you display it on your monitor.

Scanning Photos into PHOTO-PAINT

There are two common reasons why you'd want to acquire an image by scanning instead of using a digital camera:

- The picture wasn't originally taken with a digital camera. There were very few digital cameras in 1924, so your great grandmother's photo probably only exists as a print or, if you're extremely lucky, as a film negative.
- The picture is a drawing. You want to use Corel PowerTRACE to clean up a logo or other graphic.

In either event, scanning images is very simple using PHOTO-PAINT as the host for the resulting bitmap. Follow these steps:

1. Make sure the scanner is plugged in, turned on, and connected to your computer directly or through a network. Don't laugh; these are the first things the manufacturer's tech support asks you for $5/minute.
2. Make sure your computer recognizes the scanner. Your scanner came with an installation disk that has drivers that Windows needs to read to be able to create a handshake between the two pieces of hardware. Go to the manufacturer's website and download and then install the most current drivers if you put the install disk in a safe place you've forgotten about.
3. Make sure the imaging surface (the platen) on the scanner is clean, place your image on the platen, making sure the image isn't crooked facing the rectangular edges of the platen, and then launch PHOTO-PAINT.
4. Choose File | Acquire Image | Select Source. If you scanner doesn't show up under Select Source, first be sure that it's turned on. If it still doesn't appear, your scanner might be an older scanner that needs updated software from the manufacturer. Choose your device from the list and then click Select. If you have several devices hooked up to your computer via

USB, FireWire, or other connection protocol, choose your scanner. It's possible that an entry that begins with "WIA" (Windows Interface Application) is a scanning choice. Don't choose the WIA connection if you have a different choice; WIA is a generic driver and, as such, you can only access the most basic of features on your scanner.

5. Choose File | Acquire Image | Acquire. The UI for your scanner appears on top of PHOTO-PAINT's UI. Different scanners have different interfaces, but the common elements are a preview window in which you can crop the image you want scanned to a bitmap file and dimensions and resolution fields. Usually, you click the Preview button to refresh the preview, updating your view to the scanner's current contents on its platen.

6. Choose your color mode for scanning. RGB is generally the best choice because you can always convert an acquired image to grayscale or other color mode directly in PHOTO-PAINT. Only choose Grayscale if you're scanning a black-and-white photo—aged photos that look like a black and white can contain valuable image data in sepia areas, so color scan heirloom photos. If given the option to scan in bitmap, fax, or 1 bit per pixel, *don't*. This mode should be reserved for documents, faxes, and other material that requires absolutely no image fidelity.

7. Use the interface controls to drag an area of the platen that contains your document. Don't crop too closely to what you want scanned.

8. Set the scanning percentage to 1:1 (100%) so a scanned inch actually equals an inch at the resolution you'll set in Step 10.

9. Check the height and width of the highlighted, cropped area on the platen. Many scanners do not offer onscreen rulers; there should be fields onscreen, as shown in Figure 25-3. If you need to increase the dimensions, adjust the value in the Percentage field.

10. Set the resolution of the scan. As mentioned earlier in this chapter, if your intended output is 1:1 scale and the printer is a personal inkjet, set the scanning resolution to 240 ppi (often labeled "dpi"). However, if your scan is destined for a desktop publishing document done at a commercial printer, set the resolution to *at least* 266 ppi. Many commercials printers ask for 300 ppi.

11. Click Scan and wait a little while as the samples of the image are streamed to your computer.

12. When the scan is completed, your scanner's interface disappears and Untitled-1.cpt appears in PHOTO-PAINT's workspace. Save the image to hard disk (CTRL+S); in the Save An Image To Disk dialog box, name the file and choose a file type to save the image as from the Save As Type drop-down list. PHOTO-PAINT's native *.CPT file format is fine, except in business situations where you need to share documents. The CPT file format can only be opened in CorelDRAW and PHOTO-PAINT. TIFF and PNG file formats are almost universally understood by applications other than Corel's—the TIFF format can retain image resolution information; PNG as written by PHOTO-PAINT saves files at the default screen resolution of 72 ppi, but the files are often smaller than uncompressed TIFFs. Do not save as JPEG—it compresses images by discarding visual detail it thinks is unimportant (but you might not).

FIGURE 25-3 Good scans for retouching rival the saved file size of photos taken with digital cameras, anywhere from 6 to 35MB.

Resampling and Resizing Photos

There will be times when you absolutely *have* to upscale a photo; you might not have a better image and you can't retake the scene or person's portrait. When you increase the number of pixels in a photo, you're not increasing image detail—all the details in the scene were captured when you took the photo. PHOTO-PAINT adds pixels by duplicating existing pixel colors, and then averaging the colors a little to make a smooth photo transition between neighboring pixels in the resampled photo *if* you leave Anti-alias checked in the Resample box.

How much larger you can make a photo before the individual pixels become apparent depends on the visual content of the photo. Pictures of intricate machinery and images of lots of differently colored small objects such as leaves do not upsample nearly as well as, say, a photo of soft clouds on an overcast day. If you need to make a photo 150 percent of its original size, usually you can get away with this with no additional steps.

However, if, for example, you need to print a picture from the Web that's only 300-pixels wide, you have two things going for you in this endeavor:

- Inkjet printers tend to smooth out small rough areas in a digital image because ink spreads on the printed page, blending flaws together. Don't count on this factor; it's an assistant, but a small one.
- PHOTO-PAINT can sharpen edges in the resampled photo while keeping large areas of similar colors smooth in appearance.

Tip PHOTO-PAINT has several sharpening filters under Effects | Sharpen. PHOTO-PAINT's Help system provides a good general explanation of the Sharpen filters; launch any of them and then click Help in the Filter box. Generally, when in doubt, choose Unsharp Mask to add some crispness to resampled photos. It provides very good sharpening without an overwhelming number of options you need to learn. Click the Preview button in any of the Filter dialogs to toggle the effect on and off within the document window for comparison.

Figure 25-4 shows a small JPEG photograph; let's pretend for the purposes of working through a tutorial that you own this condo and want to time-share it. And you want to print postcard-size images to hand out in addition to your website's image.

350-pixels wide   Zoom to 800%

FIGURE 25-4   Unless some corrective steps are taken, this small photo would print with huge, clearly visible color pixels.

Tip   The Zoom Tool (Z) affords you the opportunity to get in very close to an image area to view and edit. However, if you're not familiar with resolution-dependent bitmap editing, a zoomed-in view of a photo might look coarse and your instinct might be to soften the image. Periodically check the document title bar: after the name of the file, there's an "@" symbol followed by your current viewing resolution. If the zoom factor is greater than 100 percent, this document is not displaying as your audience will see it. To quickly zoom a document to 1:1, 100 percent viewing resolution, double-click the Zoom Tool on the Toolbox.

The following set of steps are a "worst-case" scenario—you will almost certainly be able to enlarge photos so they are printworthy by resampling up to 150 percent or so, and not the *gross* sort of enlargement and image corrections shown in these steps. However, as you'll soon see, the High Pass effect you use does indeed enhance a copy of the small JPEG photo to a usable state.

Tutorial   Making a Thumbnail Image Suitable for Printing

1. Open Hollywood-5203.jpg in PHOTO-PAINT. With the Object Pick Tool, right-click over the image and then choose Resample from the context menu.
2. In the Width field, type **7**, and then click an insertion point in the Resolution | Horizontal field. Make sure the Maintain Aspect Ratio and Anti-alias check boxes are checked, and then type **240** in the box. Click OK to resample the photo.

3. At 100 percent viewing resolution, clearly the photo needs a little edge sharpening without sharpening the larger smooth areas of the photo. Press CTRL + F7 if the Objects docker isn't docked to the window or isn't visible. You're going to duplicate this image and put the copy on top of the original. This is an unusual thing to do, and *to be able to do*, but PHOTO-PAINT has advanced image-editing features that let you change and merge image areas (called *objects*) so the pixels in objects can have different colors but are aligned to the imaginary grid in the document identically.

4. With the Object Pick tool, drag the thumbnail labeled Background on top of the New Object button on the Object docker, and then release the mouse button. Doing this duplicates the image, creating the new object directly on top of the original.

Drag Background thumbnail
on top of New Object button.

The result is a duplicated object.

5. Click the Object 1 thumbnail on the Object list to select it—you want to edit this, not the Background object.

6. Choose Effects | Sharpen | High Pass. Wherever sharp transitions between pixel colors appear in the photo, edge details are retained and strengthened. Wherever there is little color difference between neighboring pixels (called *low-frequency* areas), the visual information is filtered out, leaving a neutral gray. The higher the Percentage you specify (use **100** in this example), the less original color is retained. The greater the Radius (use about **12** in this example),

the greater the distance this filter examines neighboring pixels, to filter out areas of little detail difference. Click OK to apply these settings.

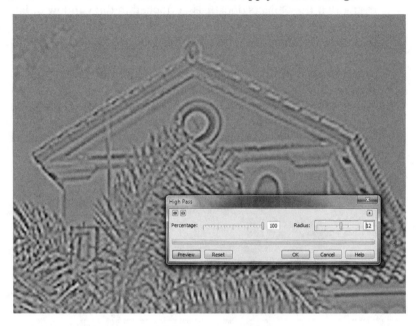

7. Beyond the strong edges in Object 1, this object doesn't look as though it will contribute much to enhancing this enlarged image, but the correct answer is, "Yes, it will!" Merge modes are covered in the transparency section of Chapter 22, but for now here's a simple explanation of why Overlay mode turns this largely gray object into a perfect "lens" to sharpen the underlying Background photo. The brightness values in a photo (the tones, not the colors) are usually calculated on a scale from 0 to 255, 255 representing the brightest area (pure white has a brightness of 255). Overlay Merge mode can be thought of as a filter: Overlay Merge mode objects that have a brightness greater than 128 lighten (bleach, screen) objects under them, whereas brightness pixel values less than 128 darken (multiply) the underlying pixels. The High Pass filter made most of the pixels in this object neutral gray—which has no effect in Overlay mode on the underlying pixels. However, the *edge details* in Object 1 are darker and lighter than the underlying, corresponding background areas. Choose Overlay from the Merge Mode drop-down list.

8. Objects do not have to be 100 percent opaque. This Overlay Merge mode object contributes a little too strongly to the overall picture; click the Transparency combo box at the top right of the Objects docker to reveal the slider and then drag the slider left to about 29%, or whatever value looks best in the document window.

9. You can choose to save this file right now as a PHOTO-PAINT (CPT) or Adobe Photoshop (PSD) document and the objects will retain their order using these special image file formats. And you can now print the composition. However, if you'd like to standardize the image so it can be saved to practically any file format (PNG, JPEG, TIFF, and others) and thus shared with most other computer users, with the Object Pick tool, right-click either object on the Objects docker, and then choose Combine | Combine All Objects With Background.

As you can see in Figure 25-5, without the High Pass copy of the image in Overlay mode, at left the pixels dominate the image in visual importance. At right, however, with the duplicate object you filtered and merged with the original, it's a fairly photogenic image ... given you enlarge it to almost *23 times* its original file size!

Without High Pass object   High Pass object in Overlay mode

FIGURE 25-5   Use PHOTO-PAINT filters and objects to strengthen and smooth image areas selectively.

Automation: Recording Your Cropping and Resampling

It's almost a foregone conclusion that if you work at a small- to medium-size business, you have dozens if not hundreds of photos that need some sort of alterations and uniformity so they'll be consistent in size when you make a catalogue or web page. Cropping is a separate process from resizing photos in PHOTO-PAINT, but the good news is that if your collection of photos are even remotely similar in subject matter, you can record your cropping and resampling moves, and then play this recorded script back on an entire folder of images. No errors, no recalculations, and you might have a free hand to eat your sandwich as you work through lunch.

Evaluating a Crop Area for a Collection of Photos

PHOTO-PAINT's Crop Tool does only one thing perfectly well: it eliminates areas of a picture outside the crop rectangle you drag before double-clicking or pressing ENTER to finalize the crop. Before finalizing, you are free to reposition, reset, and move the crop rectangle. The Crop Tool resizes an image area, and depending on whether you've chosen Custom on the Property Bar, the Crop Tool can possibly resample an image, and you might not be happy with a photo that was resampled to be *larger* than the original. Therefore, if you want to enlarge or decrease the number of pixels in the finished version, perform the additional step of resampling *before* saving a copy of the photo.

The imaginary company in the tutorial to follow specializes in exotic minerals—no common quartz or hematite to be found on their website—and the photographer took seven pictures whose visual content is more or less all in the same position from photo to photo. Your mission is to crop out the bottom pedestal and place card in all the photos to favor the mineral itself and to reduce the size of all the pictures, all sized to exactly the same dimensions, so the collection of minerals can be featured on a web page. Because Windows 7 can display large thumbnails of common image file formats such as PNG, it's easy to preview the contents of an entire folder of images, so you can to better see which individual photo needs the most height or width to then apply a suitable crop for all the images.

Figure 25-6 is a view of the folder of mineral pictures as seen from the File | Open box in PHOTO-PAINT, with Extra Large Thumbnails chosen in the dialog box. The overlay of the dotted line shows that the Fliakite.png image requires the greatest width of all the files—this is something you can detect by eye. Therefore, when you begin the tutorial, you begin by choosing Fliakite.png as the image you'll record your cropping and resampling edits on.

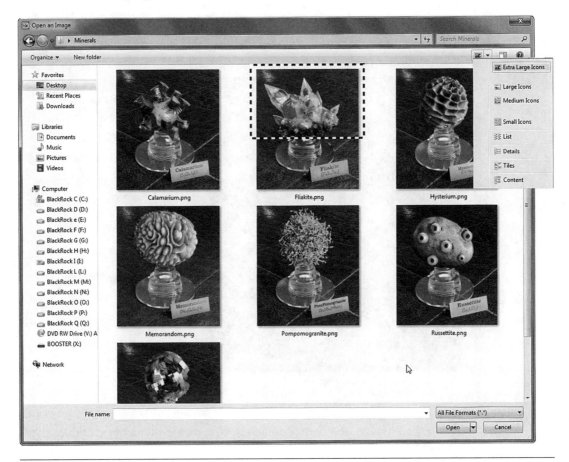

FIGURE 25-6   Out of the many images you need to resample and crop, choose the one that requires the loosest cropping as the basis for your automation recording.

Tutorial Recording Your Edits

The following set of steps guides you simultaneously through recording and editing the resampling and cropping process. Playing the saved recording back on a folder is very simple and covered in a following section. If you have a real-world need to crop and resample scores of images, and your boss or client wanted them yesterday, you're going to have your solution and the images completed sooner than anyone might imagine! Locate the images you downloaded at the beginning of this chapter: put only the mineral PNG files in a unique folder.

1. Choose Windows | Dockers | Recorder (CTRL + F3).
2. Choose File | Open (CTRL + O), and then open Fliakite.png from the folder to which you copied the seven PNG files.
3. Click the red button on the Recorder docker; you're recording now. Choose the Crop Tool from the Toolbar.
4. Drag a rectangle around the top of the image, excluding the glass pedestal from your crop.

Crop Tool

5. Press ENTER to finalize the crop (double-clicking inside the document does the same thing).
6. Press O (for the Object Pick Tool), and then right-click over the image and choose Resample.

7. Three or possibly four thumbnails across a conservatively sized web page of 800-pixels wide means the width to resample this image should be about 200 pixels. Choose Pixels from the Image Size Units drop-down list, and then type **200** in the Width field. The Height will automatically scale down in proportion.

8. Because you're not measuring in real-world units but instead in number of pixels, you don't have to specify 72 or 96 dpi for the resampled image. On the Web, a screen pixel is an absolute, unchangeable size. Additionally, if you change the dpi setting now, you'll need to go back and respecify the Width as **200** because you've changed the resolution value. If the percentage field reads 32%, you're good to go—click OK to apply.

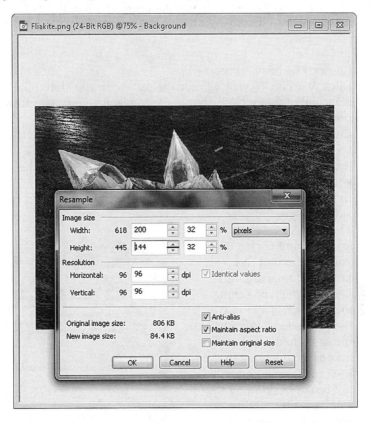

9. Double-click the Zoom Tool to move your view to 100%. The resampled image could use just a touch of Effect | Sharpen | Sharpen, a good choice for extremely small images. Set the Edge Level to about **26%**; this is the degree of sharpening with emphasis on neighboring pixels that have dissimilar colors. Set the Threshold to **0** (zero)—the lower the value, the more pronounced the sharpening effect. Click OK to apply the filter.

10. Click the square Stop button on the Recorder docker.

11. Click the Save button on the Recorder docker, name the script, and let PHOTO-PAINT save the script to the default location because you'll never find it again if you create a custom location.

Note The Save icon on the Recorder and other dockers is of a floppy disk. Floppy disks used to store digital media before DVDs, CDs, air travel, and horses were invented.

12. You can close the Fliakite file without saving changes. In the following section, you'll run the recorded script on this image and save it, so your work that's not done yet will be automatically done for you in a moment.

The Fun Part: Playing Back Your Script

The following steps will seem anticlimactic; the bulk of the work you have ahead of you is accomplished merely by filling out a few fields in the File | Batch Process box and clicking Play.

1. Choose File | Batch Process.
2. Click Add File. Navigate to the dialog where you stored the mineral images. Select all of them; click on one file to place your cursor inside the file box, press CTRL + A to select all, and then click Import.
3. Click Add Script. Look at the path to where PHOTO-PAINT default saves scripts at the top of the box. The location is under your *user account*/Appdata/ Roaming/Corel ... if you lose a file in the future. Click the name of the script you saved in the previous tutorial, and then click Open.
4. In the Options field, click the On Completion drop-down list and then choose Save As New Type.
5. The Save To Folder is an important choice if you want to find the processed images later! Because you'll be saving to JPEG, it's okay to save the processed images to the same folder as the originals, which are in the PNG file format and will not be overwritten by the batch process.

6. You probably want the JPEG file type for the resampled photos if this is a web site display. Click the Save As Type drop-down list and then choose JPG-JPEG Bitmaps.
7. Click Play. Done!

Back in CorelDRAW, the Extrude Tool is used for a fancy website banner. As you can see here, when you select the multiple files for import into CorelDRAW from the destination folder to which you saved your batch processing, you can simply click the page to place the images, one at a time, at 100 percent their size, and in no time either you look like a miracle worker to your boss, or if you're self-employed, you can look in your bathroom mirror and say, "Darn, I'm good!" (this is a PG book).

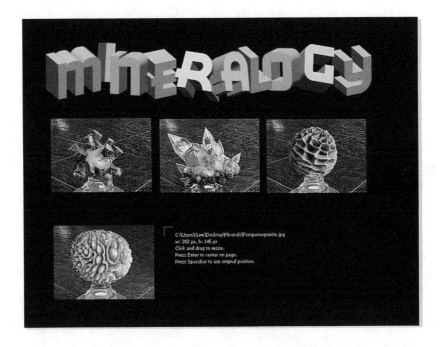

Flipping Images ... with a Twist

Let's cover one more common imaging need before Chapter 26 and advanced imaging. A problem can occur when you try to accomplish something seemingly as simple as mirroring a photograph. This is going to be your first step into the league of the pros with invisible image retouching.

Many objects that you photograph in the real world, as well as portrait photography of people, are bilaterally symmetrical—when you look in the mirror, you recognize yourself because even though your image is horizontally flipped, the right and left side of your face looks pretty much the same. This reality usually allows us to flip a photograph when you need, for example, your subject looking to the right instead of the left. The fly in the ointment, however, is when your subject is wearing a garment that has text on it; similarly, when a building in the background has text, or there's only one shirt pocket on a garment—these flipped images have something in them that's clearly wrong to the audience.

The following steps venture into the area of PHOTO-PAINT objects; how you can lift an area, copy it to a new object, and then flip the background but not the new object—which, in this example, is the text on a child's T-shirt. Retouching is not this simple, you will have a little edgework to clean up before considering the task completed, but with some guidance, you'll learn a technique now that you can apply to a number of different retouching needs down the road:

1. Open Two Kids.tif in PHOTO-PAINT. On the Objects docker, you need to convert this "normal" bitmap image into an object-capable one so the objects can be flipped independent of one another. Click the From Background icon at the right of the thumbnail, as shown here, and the name of the item now changes to "Object 1." Once a photo is an object, you can perform many PHOTO-PAINT feats not possible with a standard JPEG or other image file

Click to turn a background
into an object.

2. Choose the Freehand Mask Tool from the Toolbox; if it's not visible, click-hold on the second from top icon on the Toolbox (usually the Rectangle Mask Tool) to reveal the entire group of Masking tools, and then choose the Freehand Tool.

3. On the Property Bar, set the Feathering value to about **6** pixels. Feathering softens a selection, so inside and outside the edge of a selection mask some pixels are *partially* selected. This might sound strange to have an area partially selected (like an egg being partially broken), but the effect ensures smooth and seamless retouching work.

4. Drag around the word "Julian" on (Julian's) T-shirt to select it; double-click when you're done and the image area is now available for editing. If you don't include the entire name on your first try, click the Additive Selection button on the Property Bar and use the Freehand Mask Tool to add to the existing mask.

5. Right-click inside the dashed indicator lines for the mask area, and then choose Object: Copy Selection from the context menu, as shown in Figure 25-7. On the Objects docker, you'll now see a new thumbnail at the top of the list of objects, titled "Object 2."

Tip Pressing CTRL+SHIFT+H reveals and hides an object marquee onscreen. Pressing CTRL+H alternately hides and shows mask marquees, *not* the same thing as the dotted lines running around objects.

---

6. Click the Object 1 entry in the Objects list to make it the current editing object. Then, choose Object | Flip | Horizontally. And yes, it will look strange to have "Julian" floating above the other kid's chest!
7. Click the Object 2 entry on the Objects docker, choose Lightness Merge mode from the drop-down list—a good mode for making underlying areas fade away only if the top affecting object has lighter corresponding pixels—and then move the object over Julian's chest at the left of the image with the Object Pick Tool.

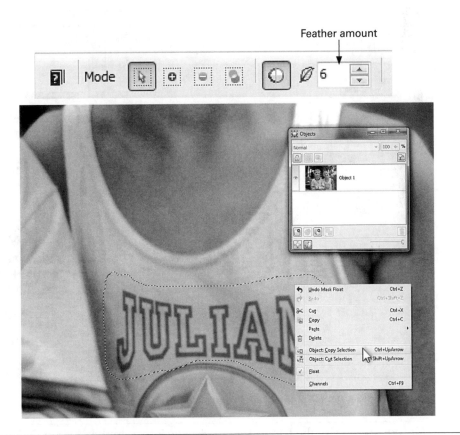

FIGURE 25-7 Copy the image area that you don't want to flip to a new object in the document.

8. Evaluate the composition for a moment. What needs to be done now is to remove some of the backward text on Object 1 to keep it from showing through. A straight paint color won't do the job because the image area has varying tones of color from the texture of the T-shirt. Choose the Clone Tool from the group that contains the Red-Eye Removal Tool.

9. The Clone Tool picks up an image area you define by right-clicking and then applies the image area to a different area when you drag, based on the diameter and hardness you set for the tool. On the Property Bar, choose Medium Soft Clone from the drop-down list.

10. Click Object 1 to choose it for editing, and then hide Object 2 by clicking the visibility (the eye) icon to the left of its thumbnail.

11. Right-click with the Clone Tool just below the name on Julian's T-shirt; see Figure 25-8. You're choosing a sampling area that's close in tone and color to the area you want to hide.

Clone Tool   Hide Object   Active object

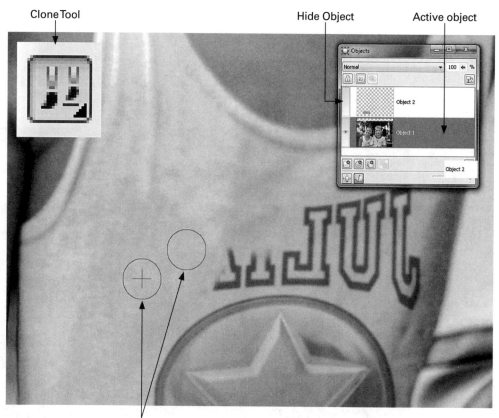

Right-click to set sample point... then stroke over area to be retouched.

FIGURE 25-8 Use the Clone Tool to visually integrate the areas in Objects 2 and 1.

12. Drag, ever-so-slowly, slightly, and carefully over the backward lettering on the T-shirt to get a feel for the Clone Tool. When you release the mouse button, the sampling point for the Clone Tool snaps back to its original position. Therefore, release the mouse button when you see that the traveling sampling point is getting mighty close to an undesired area for sampling. Work from the outside inward, resampling frequently to match the original tones of the light shirt. Periodically, unhide Object 2 to see how much work you need to do, and what areas are not necessary to clone away.

13. When you think you're finished cloning, restore the visibility of Object 2. You might be done, but you might want to refine the edges of Object 2 with the Eraser Tool. If so...

14. Click Object 2 to select it for editing. Choose the Eraser Tool, and then on the Property Bar, choose a soft tip from the Presets drop-down list, and set the size to about **35** pixels in diameter.

15. Zoom into the editing area, and then drag over any areas whose brightness doesn't match the edge of the object. The work in progress and the illusion shown here looks pretty convincing.

Eraser Tool

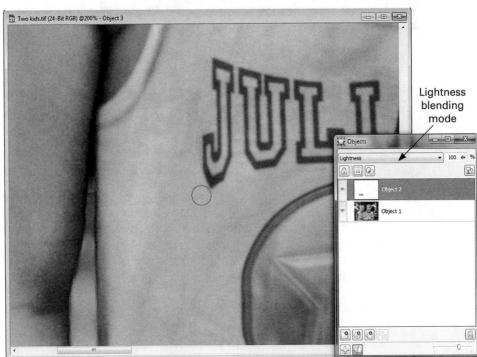

Lightness blending mode

16. Optionally, you can standardize this image's data by combining all objects—as you did in the Hollywood condo example. Right-click over either object title on the Objects docker and then choose Combine | Combine All Objects With Background.

Consider what you've learned in this chapter: you now know how to repeat actions on an entire folder of images; you can scale, crop, and flip pictures; and you have a basic handle on all the sophisticated editing you can perform using transparency, objects, and merge modes. But the biggest payoff is an ironic one: a good photo retoucher's work should go unnoticed!

Bring what you've learned into Chapter 26 now, for more invisible mending, and a technique or two that will definitely get your work noticed. Special effects and advanced retouching techniques lie ahead.

26

PHOTO-PAINT Effects and Advanced Editing

Chapter 25 got you off the ground with some basic photo-editing techniques; this chapter approaches a lot more ambitious editing of images, yet it stays within the realm of common tasks for professionals that you've seen and would like to re-create. Removing backgrounds, combining areas of different photos into a seamless composition, and creating animated GIFs are on the menu today. Along the way, you'll discover and learn to use some of the most important tools and features in PHOTO-PAINT, and by the end of this chapter, you'll be able to do a lot more than simply re-create the images in the following tutorials. You'll make the techniques, and anything you work on in the future, truly *your own*.

 Note Download and extract all the files from the Chapter26.zip archive to follow the tutorials in this chapter. This folder has a subfolder "Gallery," with finished examples of the tutorial files for this chapter.

Turning a Snapshot into a Photograph

If you've ever worked in a large manufacturing company as a designer, you already know that the person who takes the picture of a new product has tunnel vision. They pay attention to focus, and perhaps even lighting the product—and pay *no* attention to a cluttered and inappropriate background! And your boss is no help because he's conditioned by watching YouTube, "Oh, you can just Photoshop this, can't you? Takes two secs!"

Nope: you own Corel PHOTO-PAINT and you're going to learn how to PHOTO-PAINT this sorry photograph into something that looks terrific in that brochure that was due yesterday.

Objects and the Path Tool

Open Labeling machine.cpt in PHOTO-PAINT now: clearly, all that's missing is a coffee cup and a deck of playing cards to *totally* ruin the visual importance of the Market Up® 8500 labeling machine. When photographing a product, either you highlight it within a compatible setting (in this example, next to retail packages or a shopping cart) or you go very minimalist and shoot against a pastel seamless sheet of paper. The purpose of this section is to show how you use PHOTO-PAINT to lift only the labeling machine off the background and then replace the background with something stylish yet neutral in content so the machine is the hero of the photo.

Because the silhouette of a machine, or a box, or anything with clearly defined geometry is a hard edge, the best and quickest tool to use in PHOTO-PAINT for extracting the image area is the Path Tool. The Path Tool operates almost identically to the Bezier Pen Tool in CorelDRAW. When you use the tool, the Property Bar displays options that you'll feel right at home with, and the paths you draw have special properties in this bitmap editing program. Paths you can create include:

- **Stroke a path**   Once a path is selected, you can choose any of the Brush tools (Paint, Effect, Image Sprayer, and even the Eraser Tool), and then choose Object | Edit Path | Brushstroke From Path. If you're new to PHOTO-PAINT, this action is fraught with peril, so don't just leap into this command. You probably want to create a new object on which to stroke the path before doing anything permanent to a photo: choose Window | Dockers | Objects, and then click the New Object button. You also make sure the size of the brush and the preset for the brush, along with the color (if any), are the ones you want. By stroking a path onto an object—paths do not belong to any specific object—you're free to experiment and can delete the object if you mess up.
- **Mask From Path**   This is the command you use in the steps to follow. A selected area of an object or the background of a photo can be made—called a *mask*—based on the shape of a path. The mask allows edits only within the interior of the shape; you can fill (see the next item here) and also delete the interior of an object, leaving transparency. If you want to work on the exterior areas defined by a mask, press CTRL + SHIFT + I to invert the areas so the exterior is subject to changes while the interior of the shape is protected from changes.
- **Fill a path**   You can fill the interior of a path by first defining a mask based on the shape of the path; to do this, with the Pen Tool selected on the Toolbar (so you can see options on the Property Bar), you click the Mask From Path button, and then mosey on over to Edit | Fill. In the Edit Fill & Transparency dialog, click the type of fill you want, and then click Edit to use and customize the presets available.

Tip Regardless of how you create a mask, to remove it, the keyboard shortcut is CTRL+R.

Here's the game plan: in the following steps, you convert the image background to an object. Then use the Path Tool to work around the edge of the labeling machine, closing the path around the machine. Next create a mask from the path, choose the Object | Create | Copy (or Cut) Selection, and then delete the original background. Let's begin:

Tutorial Using Paths as Masks

1. Open Labeling machine.cpt in PHOTO-PAINT. Then choose Window | Dockers | Objects (CTRL + F7 is the shortcut).
2. Click the Background icon to the right of the Background item on the Objects Docker list. This is a shortcut to Object | Create | From Background, and the title of the image is now "Object 1."
3. Drag the document window edge outward a little. You'll notice a white area surrounding the image—this is the background to the composition, and Object 1 is now floating above it. If you like, increase the size of the thumbnail for Object 1 by dragging the slider to the bottom right of the Objects docker to the right.

Document background
Entire photo is a floating object.
Click to turn a background into an object.

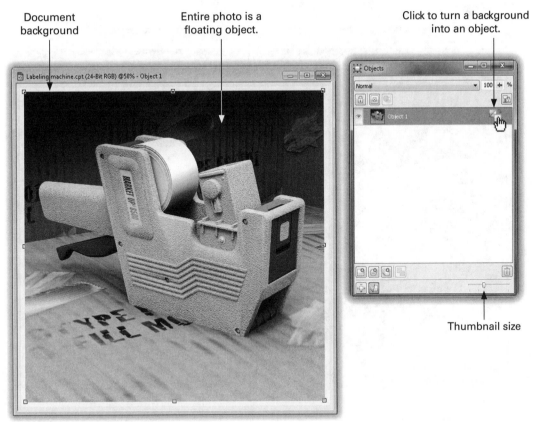

Thumbnail size

4. Press ALT + F10 to display the Paths docker. You're going to draw a path around the labeling machine now.

5. Choose the Path Tool from the group of Shape tools in the Toolbox. Before you begin, if you're not experienced with CorelDRAW's Shape and Bezier Tools, the Path Tool is used to both draw paths and edit them. Figure 26-1 shows what the Property Bar in PHOTO-PAINT looks like when the Path Tool is active. The callouts in this figure pertain only to this chapter's example. The other tools have familiar icons that perform the same functions as those on the Property Bar in CorelDRAW when using the Pen tools.

6. Traveling clockwise, click to place a control point toward the top left of the outline of the labeling machine; you can start anywhere you like along the edge, but this tutorial would become a little oblique if we don't use a common reference point.

7. The next node to be placed is at the end of a curve: to build a curved path between node 1 and node 2, click + drag after you define the point, exactly as you would using the Bezier Tool in CorelDRAW.

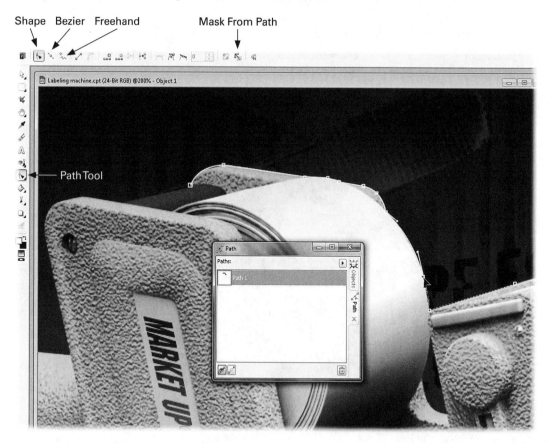

FIGURE 26-1 The features on the Property Bar when using the Path Tool to refine the paths you create.

8. At some point, you might need to zoom or pan your view of the document. If you choose to press H as a shortcut to the Pan Tool, then press SPACEBAR to return to the last-used tool, there's a good chance you won't be able to extend the path

Begin Path and Create Node   **Extend Current Path**   **Close Path**

you're drawing because you've switched tools. Make sure to click the last node on your path; the cursor features a "+" sign, which means you can extend the path now. The illustration here shows the three cursor states for the Path Tool. As you pan your view and change tools, do not try to extend the path when your cursor looks like the Create Node cursor. If you use the document scroll bars for changing your view, you haven't switched tools and you're cool to continue drawing the path.

9. Draw a tight path all the way around the outline of the labeling machine, and finally click at your start point to close the path. Right now is a good time to zoom into various areas to make sure the path is faithful to the edge of the machine. If there's a misplaced node or curve segment, with the Path Tool selected, choose the Shape Tool on the Property Bar, click the node and move it, or click the node to display its control handles and then drag a control handle to steer the curve segment so it fits the edge of the machine.

10. Click the Mask From Path button on the Property Bar now. The interior of your path is now selected.

11. Choose Object | Create: Copy Selection (CTRL + UP ARROW) to duplicate the contents within the mask. Usually it's better to duplicate something by copying it than by cutting it. On the Objects docker, click the Object 1 entry—the original image—to make sure it's the chosen object (the title will be highlighted in a foreground Windows color) and the Delete button (the old-fashioned metal trash can). Now you have only the labeling machine as an object in the document, and it's surrounded by a checkerboard pattern indicating that there are no pixels surrounding it.

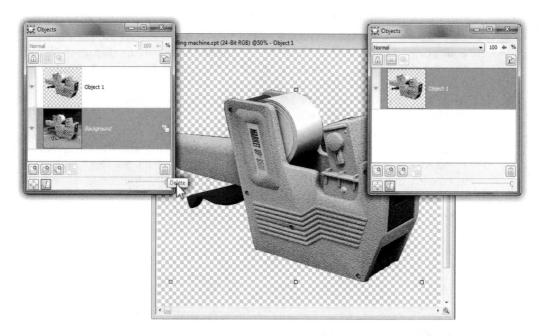

12. Take a break, keep the document open, and press CTRL + S to save your work up to this point.

> **Tip** You can name an entry on the Objects docker anything you like; you don't have to accept the default name. To rename an entry, click the name to select it, then click the selected name to open it for editing, and then type anything you please.

Replacing the Background

Because the labeling machine is supposed to be the primary focus of the image, a new background can be quite simple—you just add a hint of detail to make the overall scene look consistent in its photorealism. In the next steps, you add a gradient to a new object behind the machine, distort the object a little to add three-dimensional perspective, and apply a little texture to keep the Fountain Fill object from looking too perfect.

Here's how to set up and edit a new background for the scene:

Tutorial Putting a Background Behind an Object

1. Hide or delete the path in the document by clicking either the Show/Hide Path button at the bottom of the Paths docker, or click the Delete button.
2. On the Objects docker, click the New Object button. A new entry appears on the docker, labeled "Object 2," and it appears above the machine in the order of objects in the document.
3. Drag the title "Object 2" to below "Object 1" on the Objects docker. You'll see the little hand turn into a little clenched hand as you perform this action.

Drag Object 2 below Object 1.

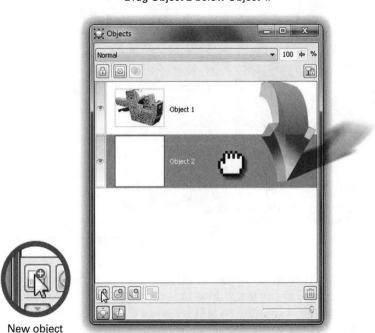

New object

4. Click the "Object 2" title to make sure it's the current editing layer. Choose the Fill Tool from the Toolbox, and then drag from top to bottom in the document window.
5. Right now, you might not have the Fountain Fill traveling from the ideal color to an ideal color. The Fill Tool uses the current foreground and background colors on the Toolbox to create a Linear Fountain Fill. Double-click the top color marker (node), and then in the Node Color dialog, on the Models tab, choose R: **148**, G: **148**, and B: **148**. Click OK to apply the color. Double-click

the bottom node marker, and set its color to R: 204, G: 204, and B: 204. Click OK to apply the color and close the box.

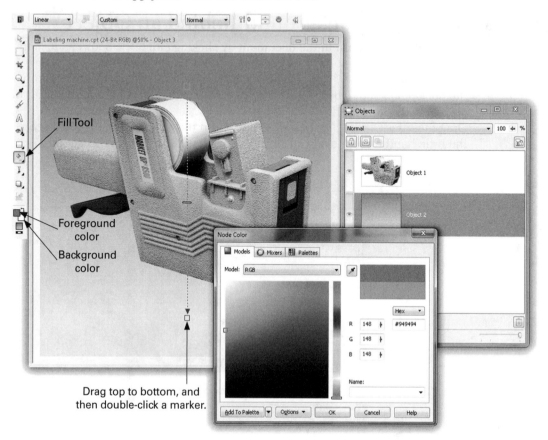

Fill Tool

Foreground color

Background color

Drag top to bottom, and then double-click a marker.

6. Eventually in this tutorial, you'll use the Mesh Warp effect to bend the background to suggest a floor in the composition. To do this, you first need to shrink Object 2 a little so you can drag the handles of the Mesh Warp past the edges of the object. Choose the Pick Tool, click the Scale button, and then click the Maintain Ratio button so the object scales proportionately. Zoom out of the document if you can't see the four handles at each corner of the object (you can scroll toward you with the mouse wheel to do this); drag the corner handle toward the center of the background art until it's just a little wider than the labeling machine, and then drag toward the center of the background art object to move it back so it's centered relative to the document window.

Scale

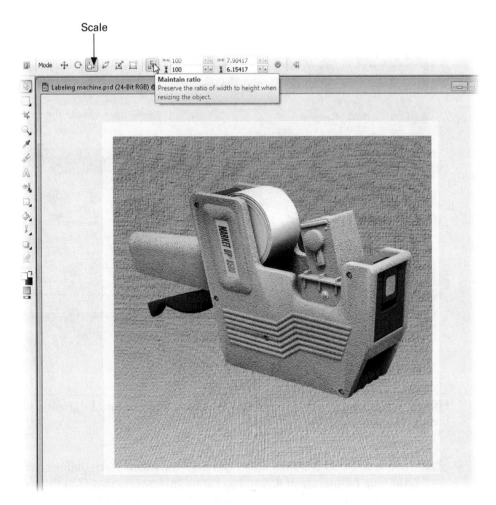

7. Choose Effects | Texture | Canvas. In the Canvas dialog, set the Transparency to about **66%** so the Fountain Fill isn't completely hidden by the effect, and then set the Emboss value to about **115%** for a visible, yet not overwhelming, effect; see Figure 26-2. Experiment with the X and Y Offset values to determine where the texture details appear on the background; click Preview before you click OK to apply the texture.

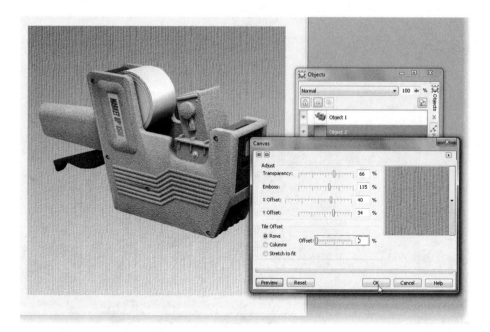

FIGURE 26-2 Apply a subtle Texture effect to the Fountain Fill to add visual business to the background object.

8. Choose Effects | Distort | Mesh Warp. In the Mesh Warp dialog, at a default Gridlines frequency of **4**, you have nine intersections within the warp lines that you drag to reshape the selected object. The idea is to mold the canvas object so its bottom sweeps toward the audience, creating the illusion that the labeling machine is resting on a plane that sweeps up and back off the top of the document window. First, drag the bottom-right intersection to the right; doing this warps the middle-right intersection in an unpleasant way, bulging the right side too much. Drag the middle-right intersection to the left until the right vertical warp line describes an arc toward the bottom. Then drag the top-right intersection to further smoothen the arc that the right vertical mesh line describes.
9. Perform Step 8 on the left vertical mesh line, mirroring it in its direction. Click OK to apply the effect.
10. With the Pick Tool, click the Scale button on the Property Bar and then increase the size of the object until you cannot see a blank background in the composition.
11. Save your work but keep the file open.

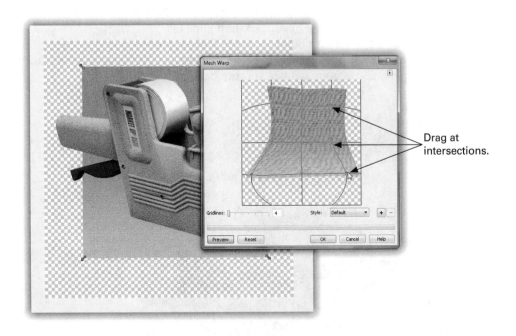

Drag at intersections.

FIGURE 26-3   Apply the Mesh Warp effect by dragging on the intersections to reshape an object.

Adding a Shadow

What's missing now is a visual element that binds the machine to its new background: a drop shadow. Frequently, a shadow can be painted into a composition, and you really only need to suggest the shape of the shadow—audiences anticipate the presence of a drop shadow, but usually don't notice whether the shape is authentic.

In the following steps, you'll add an object between the background and machine objects, do a little painting to represent the shadow, blur it to make it look more believable, and then use the Multiply Merge mode before combining all the objects to make your blurry painted shadow look more dense in the composition.

Tutorial   Painting Detail into the Picture

1. Click the Object 2 title on the Objects docker, and then click the Add Object button. Doing this forces PHOTO-PAINT to create a new object directly above the current object, sparing you the need to reorder objects by dragging their entries on the docker.
2. Choose the Paint Tool on the Toolbox. On the Property Bar, choose the Art Brush category thumbnail, and to its right, choose Loaded Cover from the drop-down list. It doesn't make much difference which brush you choose because you'll soon blur your strokes, but this particular variation is nice because it adds a little grain when you use it.

3. Double-click the Foreground color icon on the Toolbox to display the foreground color mixer. Choose black and then click OK.

4. Make a few strokes beneath the machine, as shown in this illustration. Notice how your strokes appear to go behind the labeling machine because it's the top object, above your strokes and the background object.

5. Click the Merge Mode drop-down list while the shadow object is the current editing object, and then choose Multiply. Then drag the Opacity slider to about 75%.

6. Choose Effects | Blur | Gaussian Blur; there are several effects for applying a blur to an object, but Gaussian produces the most intense and pronounced. You'll see that Gaussian Blur leaves what looks like a diffuse shadow beneath the labeling machine. Set the Radius for Gaussian Blur to about **35** pixels and then click OK to apply it. Press CTRL + S to save your work one final time.

7. You can consider your retouching work finished, or you can "standardize" the CPT file so a copy can be shared as a JPEG image. PHOTO-PAINT object files can't be shared with friends and clients who don't own PHOTO-PAINT. On the Objects docker, over any of the object titles, right-click and then choose Combine | Combine All Objects With Background.

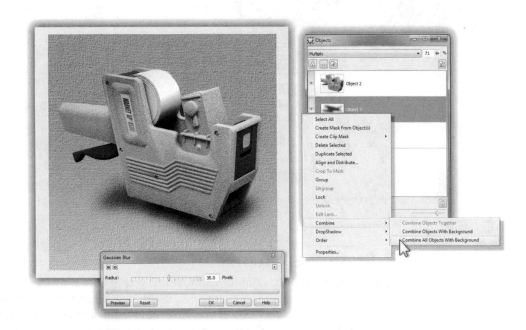

8. Choose File | Save As and then click the Save As Type drop-down list and pick JPG-JPEG Bitmaps. Select a file location, and then click OK. In the Export As JPEG dialog, click the Quality drop-down list, choose Highest, and then click OK. Then e-mail your work to your fictitious client, and they'll be astounded and send you a large fictitious check. Take it to a fictitious bank and cash it right away.

Creating a Fantasy Composition

It would be hard to miss some of the extraordinary ads on the Web that feature smaller-than-life people in settings: swimmers in a drinking glass, ant-sized folks exploring a kitchen drawer—you get the picture. This section takes you through the steps involved in getting a fellow ice-skating into a scene of a miniature turtle pond;

he won't care that the water might not be frozen, it's all in good fun and you'll use PHOTO-PAINT's features to make it a *believable* fantasy. Here are the two images you'll visually integrate.

Using the Brush Mask Tool

Shortly, you'll use PHOTO-PAINT's Cutout Lab to assist you in trimming the skating fellow from his skating rink background. However, it will give you a better idea of how much the gentleman needs scaling down if you first remove most of the background manually—doing so also gives you the opportunity to experience the Brush Mask Tool in PHOTO-PAINT. The Brush Mask is an intuitive and easy-to-use selection tool; wherever you stroke in an image becomes subject to editing, while the exterior areas are not available for editing. In the steps to follow, the editing is simple—you move the selected area, the skater, to a new object in the image, and then drag him over to the turtle pond image.

Tutorial Stroking to Select an Area

1. Open Skating Claus.cpt and Rink.png. Arrange the windows so both are in full view.
2. Click the title bar of the skater image to make it the foreground document, and then choose the Brush Mask Tool from the Mask tools group just below the Object Pick Tool on the toolbox.

3. Click the Nib Shape drop-down list and then click the 100-pixel diameter hard nib. Then increase the size of the nib by typing **133** in the size box, or you can use the elevator buttons to the right of the box to enlarge the nib size.

4. Stroke around the image so the skater is entirely selected. If your work doesn't produce a marquee, check Mask | Marquee Visible to make it appear. If you've gone a little too far, click the Subtractive Mode button on the Property Bar and stroke over the areas of excess in your selection. Figure 26-4 shows you what your screen should look like.

5. Right-click inside the selection border and then choose Object: Copy Selection. Note that the Toolbox has automatically chosen the Object Pick Tool for you now. You'll see selection box handles now at the edges of the new object.

FIGURE 26-4   Every area you stroke over can be selected.

6. With the Object Pick Tool cursor, drag the object from the Skating Claus.cpt document window into the Rink.png image window.

7. Close the Skating Claus.cpt document without saving it.
8. Save the Rink.png file as **Rink FINAL** in PHOTO-PAINT's native CPT file format. Keep the image open in PHOTO-PAINT, and use the Object Pick Tool to increase the window's size so you can see the entire fellow in the composition.

 Note If you are uncertain about the exact areas you've selected with the Brush Mask Tool, you can preview the area by using the Mask | Mask Overlay view of your work. By default, the red tint is covering areas that are not selected by your Brush Mask work.

Working in the Cutout Lab

PHOTO-PAINT's Cutout Lab is sort of an advanced Mask Tool; it provides you with a complete workspace for tracing around the edge of an area you want to integrate with other document objects. However, unlike the other mask tools, the Cutout Lab automatically refines edges that are fuzzy, such as the soft edges of our Santa's cap and bag, as well as producing crisp edges in clearly defined areas. In the steps to follow, you'll enter the Cutout Lab and cook up a beautifully refined selection of Santa for the composition.

Tutorial   Cutting a Complex Selection

1. If you don't have the Objects docker open right now, press CTRL + F7.
2. Click the Object 1 entry on the Objects Docker list, and then choose Image |
   Cutout Lab. You can quickly navigate your way around by using the scroll
   wheel on your mouse to zoom in (push the wheel away from you) or to zoom
   out (pull the wheel toward you). You can also use the shortcut key H to access
   the Hand Tool, and then press SPACEBAR to return to using the previous tool.
3. Zoom into Santa's hat. Choose the Highlighter Tool, set the Nib size to **13**
   pixels in this example, and then choose Black Matte for the moment from the
   Background drop-down list so you can clearly see the edge of the object.
4. This is the key technique for telling PHOTO-PAINT where to refine the edge
   of the selection you create: you straddle the edge of your subject—you want
   to leave a little of the Highlighter *both inside and outside* the area you define as
   the edge of your object. Then PHOTO-PAINT works on the edge for you later,
   producing refined edges in both soft and sharply contrasting areas where you've
   stroked. Work counterclockwise in this example: start at the cap, stroke along the
   edge, and if you make a mistake, click the Eraser Tool and erase the stroke, and
   then continue with the Highlight Tool. Figure 26-5 shows the work in progress.

FIGURE 26-5   Use the Highlighter Tool to trace an outline of the intended selection.

5. Continue tracing at the edge of Santa until you've completely outlined him in the Highlighter color. When you get to the ropes Santa's holding his bag with, completely highlight them. Also, when you arrive at the point where the skate meets a boot, highlight around the negative space—the area through which you can see the background.

6. Click the Background button and then choose None, so you can clearly see Santa's trousers separated from the background. Click the Inside Fill Tool, and then click *inside* your highlighter boundary. This tells PHOTO-PAINT to leave everything that's default blue alone.

7. Click Preview. Your Cutout Lab should look like the illustration shown here. If some area is *grossly* missing, you need to choose the Highlighter tool again. The moment you click-drag in the window, the preview goes away and you're left with your current highlighting work. You will need to fill the highlighted areas again if you do this, and then click Preview. Let's assume you took your time, and after clicking Preview, the cutout Lab did pretty well. Your next step is to zoom into the edges and check for any areas that need refining. Check out the ropes Santa is holding to his sack first.

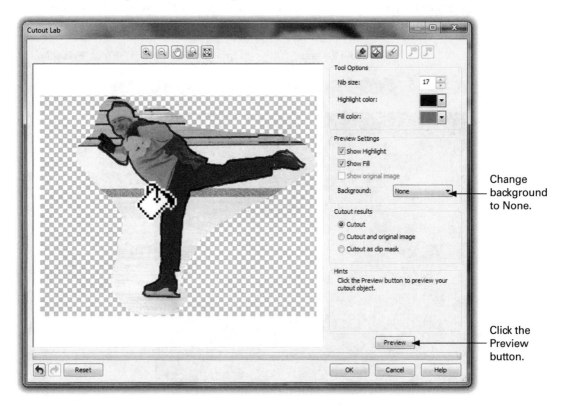

8. Learn to leverage the power of the Background drop-down list. First, change the Background to gray so you can clearly see contrast around the ropes. If areas outside the ropes need removing, click the Remove Detail tool, and use it as you would an eraser or a Brush tool. Stroke around the areas that shouldn't

show and the tool gently and smoothly hides these areas. If you're missing an area of the rope, click the Add Detail Tool and stroke over the missing areas. You might need to unhide areas and then hide them again, working between the Add and Remove Detail tools.

9. When you arrive at the hat area, switch to black as the background color: always use a background that provides color contrast with the edge of your subject, as shown here.

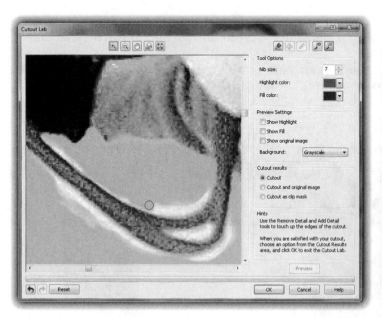
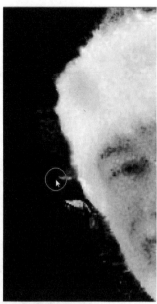

10. Pan around the entire silhouette of Santa, and *only* when you've corrected all the edge work, click OK, and Cutout Lab makes a *permanent* change to the object. Only Edit | Undo can restore the object.

11. Press CTRL + S; keep the file open.

Final Edits

Although you have a pretty good view in Cutout Lab of how the edge work looks compared with the gray, black, and other background views, the proof is in the pudding. Now you need to check out and perhaps correct a few areas now that you can see Santa against the turtle pond picture. Santa also needs to be scaled down, by almost half his current dimensions, but there's an important reason to do this *last*. When you erase part of an object—by using the Cutout Lab, the Eraser Tool, or other device—you aren't changing the resolution of the object. However, when you *scale* an object, you're removing or adding pixels to the entire object; pixel colors shift as part of any bitmap scaling; and frequently editing becomes obvious if you later try to edit a scaled object.

So first, in the following tutorial you'll erase any stray areas that weren't remove in Cutout Lab, and *then* scale Santa to fit in his new skating rink as a final edit.

Tutorial Erasing and Scaling the Object

1. You'll want to turn off the Object Marquee elements over the image; you don't really need these indicators now. Press CTRL + SHIFT + H. Choose the Eraser Tool from the Toolbox. In this example, the default soft 10-pixel diameter tip works well. When you erase in an image that is a background-only image (such as a JPEG), you erase to the current background color. However, when you erase object areas, they erase to transparent.

2. Zoom into the skate area, where the color of the skate is nearly the same as the ice in the original photo—there is probably an area or two that the Cutout Lab didn't catch.

3. Take your time; erasures are destructive—meaning permanent! Slowly stroke around the outside edge of the skate, as shown here, if this proves to be an unwanted area.

4. Work this way: zoom in or out of the object using the mouse wheel. As you erase and finish an area, press H to toggle to the Hand Tool and move your view. If an area needs attention, press SPACEBAR to return to the last-used tool (the Eraser), do your work, and then press SPACEBAR again to access the Hand Tool. Work around Santa's perimeter, and then press CTRL + S when you're done.

5. Scaling an object proportionately can be done one of two different ways: by using the percentage spin boxes when Scale Transform (and Maintain Ratio) are active on the Property Bar, or by directly click-dragging the object control handles. When you click the down button for Scale Percentage, you get live feedback, but the exact amount of scaling needs to be determined by watching what's happening in the document. Santa is currently a little more than 20" tall, and he needs to be about 12", which is about 60 percent of the original height. You *could* type **60** in the percentage box, but this value can't really be discovered, so let's use the control handles surrounding Santa, instead, for immediate visual feedback. Using the Pick Tool, zoom out so you can see all of Santa, and then drag the document window edges away from the document center to reveal all the control handles around the object.

6. Click the Scale Transform button on the Property Bar, then hold SHIFT to scale from the center inward, and then drag a corner control handle until you judge that Santa is comfortably scaled to fit into the composition. If necessary, begin by pressing CTRL + SHIFT + R to display rulers, and then stop shrinking Santa when you see that he's about 12" tall.

7. You might feel Santa needs a little rotating counterclockwise to look more appropriate—*balanced,* literally and compositionally—within the document. Click the object with the Pick Tool while Santa is selected to put the object into Rotate/Skew mode, and then drag a corner rotation handle just a little in a counterclockwise direction. Figure 26-6 shows the composition nearing completion.

8. Press CTRL + S, and leave the document open.

FIGURE 26-6   Use the Transform controls on the Property Bar for moving, scaling, and rotating an object.

Adding a Reflection

Santa Claus hasn't quite come to town in the composition—notice that the turtle is casting a reflection, and Mr. Claus should, too. Fortunately, Santa was photographed at about the same camera height as used with the rest of the scene, and so a copy of the object can be successfully mirrored and superimposed below him. The next tutorial shows how to scale a copy of the object disproportionately and mirror it horizontally using only the object control handles. Then you'll add transparency so the copy fades out at the bottom of the composition, and finally you'll learn how to blur the copy a little so it looks appropriate but is a little hard for the audience to examine closely for trickery.

Putting someone *in* a scene and not simply on top of one is the distinction between photo retouching and just another humorous picture. Here's how to add a reflection that serves as a binding element to tie all the components of the composition seamlessly together:

Tutorial Santa Needs to Do Some Personal Reflecting

1. The fastest way to duplicate an object so it occupies the same position in a document is to drag its title on the Objects docker so it's on top of the New Object button (just like in Photoshop ... okay, delete this aside). Click the Santa object entry on the docker, so it's the currently selected object, and then drag. The new object is the top entry on the Objects docker now. Click the bottom object entry, Object 1, to make it the current active object.

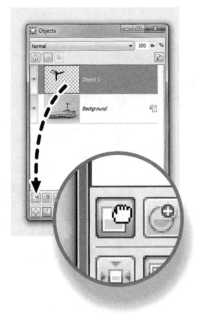

New Object button

2. With the Pick Tool, click the duplicate Santa in the document window to make sure you can see the object control handles. Then click-drag the top, center handle so Santa mirrors his original horizontally with disproportionate scaling—exactly as you perform in CorelDRAW, going way past the object's original bottom point, and releasing the mouse button when Santa's original top point lies at the bottom of his right skate blade.

Drag middle handle to scale disproportionately.

3. Click directly on the duplicate object now and move it down so both of Santa's ankles are in about the same location in the composition.
4. Choose the Object Transparency Tool from the Effects tool group on the Toolbox.

5. Beginning at Santa's ankle region, click-drag down to about the duplicate's head area. By default, you've created a Linear style transparency, with opaque regions traveling to transparent regions from top to bottom, almost exactly the way you'd see a real reflection when viewed in perspective.

Object Transparency Tool

Drag down: Black=opaque, White=transparent

6. Choose Effects | Blur | Motion Blur. This type of PHOTO-PAINT blur filter comes in handy in a variety of design situations because it can emphasize the direction of a blur, which can often lend a more photorealistic quality to blurry areas than Gaussian Blur does. Set the direction to about **34** degrees, adding much more horizontal blurring than vertical in this example. Then set the distance to about **35** pixels—distance is relative to the overall size of your images when doing editing outside of this tutorial. Click the Sample Nearest Edge Pixel so transparent areas outside of this object take the Motion Blur effect using the nontransparent object pixels toward its edge. Finally, click Preview, and if the document looks good, click OK to apply the effect.

7. You'll have a little clean-up work to do with Object 2 in the document, because not only is the ankle area visible, but also it's blurred now. With the Eraser Tool, stroke over areas that are visible outside of Object 3's leg area.

8. You can choose File | Save As, and choose the JPEG file format now so the completed composition can be shared as an e-mail attachment.

In the Gallery folder, in the zip file you downloaded, is the completed version of the preceding tutorials. Compare your version with the author's, and then have a good laugh because you did much better than he did!

Creating an Animated GIF

No tour of PHOTO-PAINT would be complete without a tutorial on how to build an animated GIF. Although GIF files are giving way to Flash and other video file formats, GIFs are universally supported by Internet browsers—they don't require your audience to go fetch a browser plug-in. GIF animations can make terrific banner ads for websites, and the following sections take you through some CorelDRAW and PHOTO-PAINT moves to create a sample animation.

Playing with a Paper Airplane

When you design an animation, you follow a checklist as you do when gathering resources for any composition. The example in this section is a paper airplane that has already been drawn for you as a CDR file. Let's pretend that a travel agent wants you to put a web banner on her site advertising that children under 12 fly free this month only, or some similar offer. The concept is to fly a paper airplane across a sky, with a tag attached that spells out the offer.

The sky photo has been provided for you in the zip archive for this chapter, but the paper airplane CorelDRAW illustration is blank—it needs something written on the tag—so it's off to CorelDRAW to begin the next tutorial. The tag is intentionally blank: feel free to work with the file, take it apart and learn from it, and use it as a part of your own composition with a different slogan written on it. Let's begin:

Tutorial Adding Text and Exporting a CorelDRAW Drawing

1. Open Paper Airplane.cdr in CorelDRAW and then zoom into the tag area.
2. With the Text Tool, type **Kids Fly Free** (or whatever you like) over the tag area. You can put a line break after **Kids** to avoid running over the tag's hole in this area.
3. With the text selected using the Pick Tool, choose a contrasting color for the text, such as bright yellow, by clicking the color well on the Color Palette.
4. On the Property Bar, choose a light-hearted typeface such as Comic Sans MS, Bold. Scale the text up or down so it nearly fits inside the tag area.
5. Choose the Envelope Tool from the Effects group of tools on the Toolbox, and then distort the text a little, as shown in Figure 26-7. The drawing is at an angle to an imaginary camera, so the text shouldn't be perfectly parallel to the screen.
6. Select all the objects and then click the Export button on the Standard Bar. In the Export dialog, choose PNG-Portable Network Graphics (*.PNG) from the Save As Type drop-down list. Make **Paper Airplane.png** the name for the file, choose a hard drive location for the bitmap file, and then click Export.

FIGURE 26-7   Don't export with the text you've added looking too perfect!

7. In the Export dialog, make sure the Export Resolution is **96** dpi or the airplane will be far too large for the GIF animation; see the following Note. Check the Transparency check box if it's not checked, and finally, look to see it the export file width is 513 pixels—choose Transformation | Units and select Pixels if it's not set this way. Click OK to export, and after CorelDRAW makes a bitmap copy of the illustration, you're finished and can close CorelDRAW and launch PHOTO-PAINT.

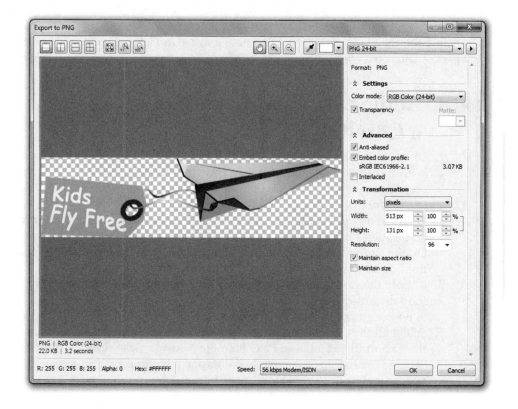

Note You didn't have to set a lot of options in the Export dialog because the CorelDRAW file was carefully set up and the airplane scaled to a predetermined size that made the tutorial work easily. When exporting drawings to be used as bitmap versions in PHOTO-PAINT, you begin your drawing with a new file in CorelDRAW whose resolution is 96 dpi, the same as your screen and the same resolution as graphics you see in your Internet browser. In the Create A New Document dialog, type **96** in the Rendering Resolution field and you're good to go. Then you set the Units in CorelDRAW to Pixels by choosing Pixels from the Units drop-down on the Property Bar. Keep in mind that GIF animations have to be small in dimensions. For example, the airplane is about 500-pixels wide because the composition you'll make is about that width. When you draw a foreground object, you keep it to the width you want it to be, measured in pixels, for your final composition. Then, exporting the drawing to the correct pixel width and height is a simple and nearly automatic process. Measuring is a pain, so when you set up your document for web export, it's a pain you only have to experience once when you begin a new drawing.

Animation: Defining Frames and Basic Setup

You'll move procedurally, and this means "not at breakneck speed," through the next sections; you need to build each frame of a GIF animation one at a time—PHOTO-PAINT doesn't perform "tweening" to auto-create intermediate animation frames. First on your To Do list is to import the background image, Sky.jpg, and turn the document into a movie. Then you open, and keep open, the imported paper airplane file, and then copy it several times into the movie document. By changing its position in each frame you add to the movie via the Movie docker, you create an animation of the airplane traveling from left to right, thus creating an *animation cycle* that plays indefinitely on a web page. You create six animation frames as the airplane travels from camera left to an exit at camera right, with a pause in the middle of the frame so audiences can clearly read the text.

Let's get moving!

Tutorial Building a GIF Animation: Part 1

1. In PHOTO-PAINT, press CTRL+O and then choose Sky.jpg from your hard drive.
2. Choose Movie | Create From Document. Open the Movie docker by choosing Window | Dockers | Movie. Note that currently there is one frame on the Movie docker list, and it's set to a 200-millisecond duration. Duration can be changed, and you'll do so a little later; a millisecond is a tenth of a second, about the duration of a 16th note in music (at an average tempo of 60 beats per minute), also evaluated as the minimum time it takes for a human to recognize a picture.
3. Open Paper Airplane.png. Because you exported this PNG file with Transparency, it's floating against a transparent background and is easy to animate against the sky image.

4. Click the title bar of what PHOTO-PAINT is now calling Sky.avi to make it the foreground document. Click the Insert Frames button at the lower left. In the Insert Frames dialog, type **5** in the Inset frames box, click After Frame 1 (this is not critical, but just a good practice), and click the Copy Current Frame button and then OK.

5. Let Figure 26-8 be your visual reference for the rest of this chapter. What you're going to do is to create frames as they exist in time as the airplane animates across the screen. The Objects docker isn't going to be of help; it won't show you what's going on in the document at any point in time, but the Movie docker will. First, click the First Frame button on the Movie docker. Your document is now at the first point in time for the GIF animation you'll build, and at this time there's nothing in the foreground. CTRL + click-drag the airplane in the Paper Airplane window into the Sky.avi window to copy (not move) the airplane object on top of the sky. You have not really added the airplane to a "normal" document—it's a movie document, and although the Objects docker shows the airplane object, it exists only in Frame 1 *in time,* not in any other frames.

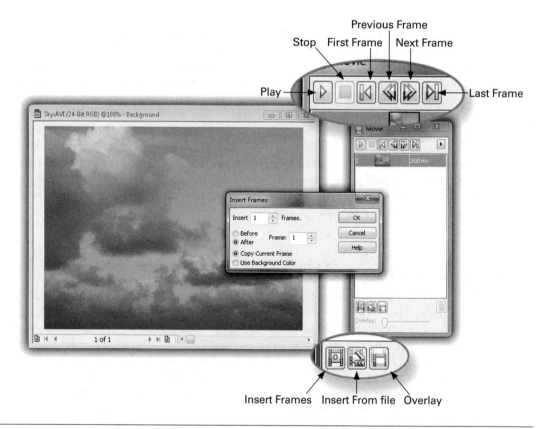

FIGURE 26-8 The Movie docker features DVD player–like controls for advancing and rewinding to the exact frame you want to build or edit.

6. Drag the window edges away from the center of the document so you can see white surrounding the composition, and can move Object 1, the airplane, to put it in position for an entrance, camera left. First, click Previous Frame to return to the original frame in the image stack.

7. With the Pick Tool, move the airplane mostly out of the frame, just so its nose is sticking out. Your four-arrowhead cursor should be slightly in the white border area as you move the airplane out of frame, vertically centered.

8. You're going to turn Frame 1 into an honest-to-gosh movie frame that features the nose of the airplane for a duration of 200 ms. Right-click over the Object 1 title on the Objects docker, and then choose Combine | Combine Objects With Background. The Objects docker now shows only the background in the Sky. avi file, and evidently you cannot move the airplane more to the right for Frame 2. Fortunately, that's not how you animate a GIF file—this is why you have five more frames on the Movie docker. Yes, Frame 1 has the nose of an airplane so the background sky has been altered, *but only in Frame 1*, as shown in Figure 26-9. Frame 2 *has* no airplane; let's add one now.

FIGURE 26-9 Add copies of the paper airplane and then combine the airplane with the background in a current frame.

9. Click the Next Frame button on the Movie docker; you'll see that the nose of the airplane isn't in this frame, because at Frame 2 in time, it's not there. CTRL + click-drag the airplane from the Paper Airplane.png document window into the Sky.avi window.

10. It's not critical here, but when you want to move objects in time in PHOTO-PAINT, use the Overlay feature on the Movie docker to display a combination of the frame and the next frame at once in the document window. In traditional animation, this is known as *onion skinning,* a term you might not be familiar with.

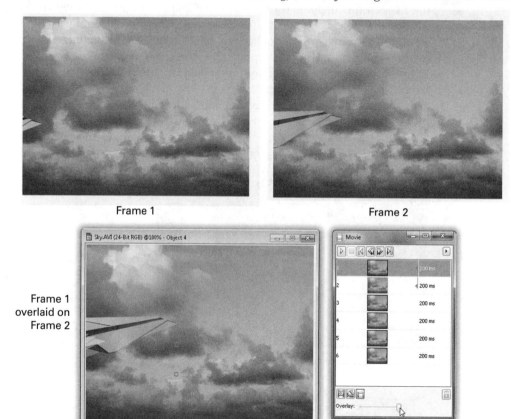

Frame 1   Frame 2

Frame 1
overlaid on
Frame 2

11. First click the Overlay button on the Movie docker to activate the slider. Click the First Frame button and automatically Frames 1 and 2 are bracketed, and you see a blend of both frames in the document window. Drag the Overlay Amount slider to adjust how much of Frame 1 intrudes on Frame 2.

12. Using the Pick Tool, drag the airplane until it more or less aligns vertically with the nose of the plane in the overlaid Frame 1. You can progress the plane to camera right so you can almost see the tail of the plane, but not the message tag.

13. When you think the airplane has moved enough to suit Frame 2, check the Movie docker to make sure that the second frame in your animation is selected. If necessary, press the Next Frame button to select Frame 2. You can double-click the frame title (or the thumbnail) to go to a specific frame; you're not limited to using the Next and Previous Frame buttons. Then do what you did in Step 8: flatten the copy of the airplane against the copy of the sky.

Take a well-deserved break, but don't save the file and don't close it. This movie file is a special file format that cannot be saved as a CPT file. It's PHOTO-PAINT's presumption that when you save the file, you're saving a movie ... but the movie's *not finished* yet. But this *tutorial* is. And there's much more ahead.

Caution It's a good idea, just before combining the plane object with any background frame, to double-check which frame is the current one. You can easily see this on the bottom of the document window. In fact, the document window has advance and rewind controls you can use instead of the Movie docker's buttons. Remember, an object doesn't belong to any frame—it's a floating element within the context of the animation and only "belongs" to a frame after you choose Combine | Combine Objects With Background, which you access by right-clicking the thumbnail on the Objects docker, by right-clicking in the document window, or via the Object main menu.

Finishing the Animation

You have four frames remaining that don't contain the plane. You don't need a repetition of the preceding tutorial steps to finish animating the plane: you use the Next Frame button to advance to the following frame—the plane's missing frame—and then CTRL+click-drag a new copy in from the PNG document, position it, and then combine the plane with the frame's background. The last frame, Frame 6, should show only the extreme tail of the plane's message tag. Once you've done that, it's fun to click Play and see what you've whipped up!

The following steps take you through timing; as mentioned earlier, the frame where you get a good view of the message you typed on the tag needs to be set for a longer duration. Follow these steps to put the finishing touches on the animation, and then you'll see how to export it to GIF file format.

Tutorial Exporting an Animation: Part 2

1. Now that the frames all have content in them and there are not objects in the composition but only backgrounds, go to the frame that's centered with the text easy to read, probably Frame 3 or 4. Double-click an entry on the Movie docker and you're sure to get it in two.

2. Click the 200ms title for this frame to select it for editing, then type **800**. Press ENTER and PHOTO-PAINT automatically tags "ms" at the end and you're all set. Four-fifths of a second is plenty of time for the audience to see the message. Also, this GIF continuously loops (coming up next), adding more time for the "sell" sandwiched in-between the light entertainment.

3. Choose File | Save. Choose GIF-GIF Animation (*.gif) as the file format you want from the Save As Type drop-down list. Choose a file location, give the file an appropriate name, and then click OK to go to a couple more dialog boxes where you specify color depth and the means by which certain colors are averaged to produce a relatively small file size.

4. In the Convert To Paletted dialog, you set the type of dithering and color palette used in your animation frames. You'll see that many options are dimmed on the Options and the other tabs. This is because you're exporting a special animated file, not a still image. GIFs can be stills or animations. You're best off with either Uniform Colors or Image Palette as the Palette choice; GIFs have a maximum of 256 unique colors, and these colors help preserve the delicate shading of the cloud photo and some of the Fountain Fills used in the CorelDRAW airplane drawing.

5. Jarvis, Stucki, and Floyd-Steinberg are all types of diffusion dithering. They evaluate the most predominant colors in the animation and attempt to represent these colors accurately, while letting less frequently used colors degrade by scattering similarly colored pixels around in the frame to represent, or "fake," the colors the process eliminates. The other choices are Ordered Dithering, which looks like a pattern weave and is usually inappropriate for photographic GIF animations. None is the other choice; don't use this unless your animation uses uniform-colored geometric shapes. When no dithering is used on photographic images, the result looks like a bad poster print made by silk-screening. Click OK to proceed to the next and final dialog.

6. In the GIF 89 (that's its proper name) Animation Options dialog, choose Automatic for the Page Size, because we intended all along for this slightly larger than usual GIF animation to be presented using the frame size of the sky image. You could make the dimensions smaller by unchecking the Automatic box and typing in custom values in your own work to make the animation smaller in both file size and dimensions. In the Color Options dialog, PHOTO-PAINT calculates in this example animation that only 236 of the 256 possible colors are necessary, saving a little on the file size of the animation. The evaluation is based on the Dithering and Palette preferences you set in the previous dialog box. You can decrease the number by using the spin controls or by typing in a value; then click Preview to see if fewer colors are acceptable or make your animation look hideous.

7. Click the Loop Frames check box to make the animation start over again after the last frame. You can choose Loop Forever, or set a number of times for the animation to loop. It's usually a good idea to set it to Loop Forever; if a visitor to your web page is distracted, for example, and your animation plays only five times before stopping, your audience misses the show unless they know how to reload a web page—but probably won't bother.

8. For sure check Save Difference Between Frames Only! This helps reduce the saved file size because only the pixels that change from frame to frame are rewritten with each successive frame.

9. There is nothing on the Frame Settings tab that applies to this example animation, but here is what you might want to choose from in your own animation work: Transparency is actually assigned to a single color in your animation, and this option makes that color invisible. This option is great for composing a web page with a colored background you want to "float" an animation against, but the paper airplane doesn't need this option because we want the entire background area visible. Palette, Use Local/Use Global is a strategy for making your animation a little higher in quality at the same or slightly smaller in file size. Global means that one palette is used to dither down colors in the entire animation, whereas Local means PHOTO-PAINT's rendering engine examines each frame for the most predominant colors while dithering down. Frame Delay I is your last chance to speed up or slow down frames, and How To Dispose is an option for clearing a single frame before the following frame loads. Dispose options are only relevant for experienced users who want to do something tricky or startling with how an animation plays. Your airplane animation doesn't fit into this category of special effects. You've created a highly interesting animation; let's leave the options at that. Click OK, and then drag the GIF file into an Internet browser window to watch it play!

Kids fly Free.gif is the completed animation file in the Gallery folder in the zip archive you downloaded.

You owe yourself a big pat on the back (don't try this by yourself) for getting through this chapter. Imagine: you now not only have quite a few advanced image-retouching tricks tucked under your belt, but you also now know how to make a visually rich GIF animation with a moving object that loops continuously. This is a *lot* better than learning how to make a GIF animation that blinks static text on and off like "My First Website 101." Now that you know how to make, save, and change movie frames, you have weeks, if not years, of experimenting to be done with new ideas and different animation objects of your own. And you can save an animation to AVI and QuickTime in addition to GIF file format—you can choose these from the File | Export menu, not File | Save As.

Chapter 27 moves from the screen to the printed page. Come learn how to ensure the best possible render to a home printer and a commercial printer with CorelDRAW's features.

PART IX

Thinking Outside
of the Toolbox

27
Printing: Professional Output

Print is alive and well in 2012 in almost every enterprise. Outputting your work so your clients can hold it in their hands is just as much an art as designing a piece in CorelDRAW. This chapter takes you through *professional* output—CorelDRAW's features that extend *beyond* the now-familiar File | Print command—and what it takes from CorelDRAW, and you, to make every dot of ink on a page look exactly like every pixel you designed on the screen.

CorelDRAW's print engine is organized into several well-defined and easy-to-understand areas for setting printer hardware parameters, previewing your print selection, and using various other options to enhance your finished printed work. In this chapter, you'll learn to set options from beginner to advanced levels in these areas.

Printing a Document to a Personal Printer

Let's suppose that you want to print a "one of," perhaps to show to your boss or coworkers as a proof of concept, or for personal pleasure, or to see if everything is arranged on the page correctly before packing off a copy to a commercial press. If your artwork is for black and white (you used no color, but only shades of black in the design), you might print to a laser printer. Laser printers don't really have any color-critical settings, so you're probably as ready to go as you'd be if you were printing a text document. If you're printing to an inkjet, most of today's inkjet circuitry does an automatic conversion from RGB color space and the color ink space (usually CMYK, although many affordable printers use six inks), and again, you really don't have to jump through any hoops if you've designed a document that uses RGB, LAB, or CMYK color spaces to define the colors you filled objects with.

Here's a tutorial that covers the basics for outputting your work to a personal printer. Before you begin, on the Object Manager docker, make sure the layers you want to print are visible and that printing is enabled for the layers; a tiny red international "no" appears on layer properties that are disabled—click the "no" symbol to enable the layer property.

Tutorial   Printing Single- and Multiple-Page Documents

1. Open the document you want to print, and then choose File | Print (CTRL + P), or click the Print button on the Standard Toolbar. Any of these actions opens the Print dialog, shown here. Pay attention to the orientation of the page with respect to the *orientation of the paper* as it will print. The Page drop-down offers to match the orientation of the page or to use the Printer default orientation settings. Changing the orientation doesn't change your document—only the way it prints.

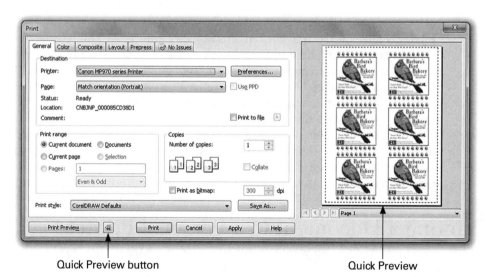

Quick Preview button   Quick Preview

2. On the General tab, choose your printer from the Printer drop-down menu, and then click Preferences to set any printer properties such as the print material page size, orientation, and so on. Keep in mind that any special features specific to your printer might override any CorelDRAW-specific features, in particular, color management (discussed later in this chapter). In general, it's *not* a good idea to have a color management feature enabled on your printer when CorelDRAW color manages the document. Two color management systems contend with each other, and what you see onscreen will *not* be what you get in print.

3. Click the Quick Preview button to expand the dialog to show a preview window if you'd like to check the document for position on the printable page. A dashed line appears in the preview window, indicating document areas that are close to or that go over the printable page margin. If you see this, you might want to cancel the print operation and rework your page. Alternatively, you can click the Layout tab and then check Fit To Page, although doing this scales the objects in your document, so forget about the business cards aligning perfectly to that micro-perforated paper.

4. If you have more than one document open in CorelDRAW, you can choose which document to print by clicking the Documents radio button in the Print Range area; make certain that all documents you want to print have the same portrait or landscape orientation before printing, or you're inviting a headache. In a multi-page CorelDRAW document, choose the page(s) you want to print from the Print Range area, and then enter the print quantity in the Number Of Copies box.

5. Before you click Print, check to see whether there are any Issues on the Issues tab. If the tab reads "No Issues," proceed to Step 6 and collect $200. However, if there's an issue, you should address it (or them) first. Issues come in two varieties: showstoppers, indicated by a triangular traffic sign with an exclamation mark, and trivial stuff, indicated by an info (*i*) icon. A common example of trivial stuff is printing blank pages; the Issues tab will inform you, and you can easily correct this by changing the Pages value in the Print Range area on the General tab. Showstoppers require careful reading of the explanation provided on the Issues tab; the remarks and explanations are quite clear—such as attempting to print a low-resolution image to a high-resolution printer—and your best bet is to cancel the print and read the rest of this chapter first ... and save paper and ink. Here's what the Issues icons look like:

Life is good: click Print.

Minor inconvenience: check Print Range.

Possible showstopper: read the info, and then consider canceling the print.

6. Click Print, go get your favorite refreshment, wait a moment, and then get your printout.

The Quick Preview deserves a little more coverage here. After clicking the Quick Preview button, you're shown a preview window and page browsing controls. While you're previewing, a right-click offers invaluable commands from the pop-up menu to Show Image, Preview Color, Preview Separations, and to toggle the view of Rulers. When you want to print a multi-page CorelDRAW file, you can quickly turn pages in Quick Preview to make sure you're printing within page boundaries and that all the pages contain what it is you want to print. To print the preview page at the current settings, choose Print This Sheet Now from the pop-up menu, as shown here.

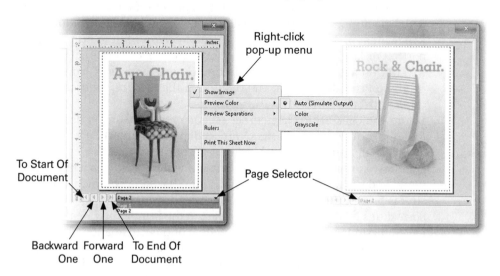

Setting Print Options

The tabbed areas of the Print dialog more or less follow from left to right a progression from personal printing options to more ambitious endeavors such as printing separations for process *color composite* (commercial) printing. Some of the areas on the tabs are device dependent and appear only after CorelDRAW evaluates your printer's capabilities; the option Use PPD (PostScript Printing Description), for example, is dimmed on the General tab until you've chosen a printer that is PostScript capable. This is why selecting your printing device must be your first step in printing from CorelDRAW. Depending on the printer defined, you'll see tabbed areas for General, Layout, Separations (or Composite), Prepress, PostScript, and Issues.

Setting General Options

The General tab of the Print dialog, shown here, offers control over some of the most common printing options.

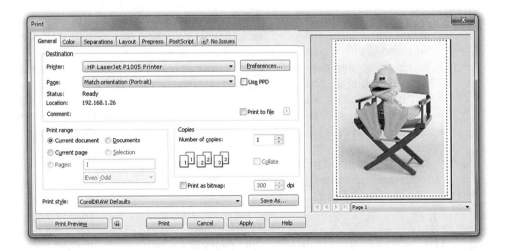

Here's a description of what each option on the General tab controls:

- **Destination** This area displays feedback provided by the printer driver used with your selected printer. It shows the Printer name, Status, Location (local port or on a network), and Comment information. Direct, network, or spooler printers are indicated according to their connection status. If CorelDRAW cannot find a printer connected directly or remotely (through a network) to your computer, you'll need to pay a visit to the Windows Start menu | Devices and Printers, and then choose to Add A Printer. The good news is that this is a wizard-style process and that Windows ships with just about every conceivable print driver for popular makes and models. You might be prompted for a specific print driver, so it's a good idea to have the manufacturer's disk handy or to download the latest drivers from their website. Clicking the Preferences button provides control over printer-specific properties and output material sizes. Choosing Use PPD lets you assign a PostScript Printer Description file; checking this box displays the Open PPD dialog, where you locate and then select an appropriate PPD file. Unless you're already familiar with what Print To File does, don't check this box in your everyday printing; see "Saving a Print File" later in this chapter.

- **Print Range**   This area contains options to select pages from the file you have maximized in the drawing window—or from *any* document you have open in CorelDRAW; the document can be minimized, and you can print it as long as it's open. Choose Current Page to print the page currently in view in your CorelDRAW document, or enter specific page numbers in the Pages box. If you go into the Print command with one or more objects selected in your document, the Selection option becomes available, so you can print *only* your selection; this is quite handy for printing only a part of your document without rearranging or hiding objects or for changing your document before printing. If you have more than one document open, choosing the Documents option displays a list of the open documents, so you can choose which document to print. Choose Even and/or Odd from the drop-down menu to print only certain pages. By default, both Even and Odd pages are printed.
- **Copies**   This area has two options for setting the Number Of Copies to print, either collated or not. When Collate is chosen, a picture appears indicating the effect of collating. Collating is a great timesaver when you want to publish a multi-page presentation and don't need the hassle of reordering pages as they come out of the printer.

Tip   To print contiguous (consecutive) pages of a document, in the Print Range area's Pages box, enter the page numbers separated by a hyphen (for example, type **6-8** to print pages 6, 7, and 8). To print noncontiguous pages, for example, pages 6, 8, and 16, type commas between specific page numbers—**6, 8, 16** in this example. You can also combine these two conventions to print both contiguous and noncontiguous pages by separating each entry by a comma. For example, entering **6-8, 10-13, 16** will print pages 6, 7, 8, 10, 11, 12, 13, and 16.

Using Print Styles

Print Styles remove the repetitive task of setting up the same (or similar) printing parameters by letting you choose to save all the selected options in the Print dialog in one tidy Print Style file. If your printing options have already been saved as a style, open the Print Style drop-down menu on the General tab of the Print dialog, and choose the style from the list.

To create a style that includes all the settings you have currently selected, follow these steps:

1. On the General tab, click Save As to open the Save Settings As dialog, shown next. As you can see, this dialog includes a Settings To Include tree directory listing the categorized print options and check boxes according to current settings.

2. Click to select the options you want to save with your new style, enter a
   unique name for your style, and then click Save to store the settings, after
   which they are available from the Print Style drop-down list.

Saving a Print File

Print To File goes back to the days of DOS, and today you'd be hard-pressed to use
this option more than twice in your career. However, Print To File is supported in
CorelDRAW, and you might want to generate this huge, text-based PostScript file for a
couple of reasons:

- If you're handing the document over to a third party to print because you don't
  have a specific printer hooked up to your computer, and you don't want them
  editing the document in any way. Print To File files are text-based printing
  instructions; they contain no graphics as graphics, so they are nearly impossible
  to edit using a graphics application.
- If (and this is a *big* "if") someone has specifically requested a Print To File
  document because they like the intellectual challenge of decoding the PostScript
  printing instructions to reconstruct the graphic using Ghostscript or a similar
  PostScript deciphering program.

Throughout the history of PC printing, Print To File has served a valuable purpose. It enables someone who doesn't own CorelDRAW to print your CorelDRAW file; a dozen years ago, high-resolution printers such as Linotronics imagesetter devices were the only game in town when you wanted coffee table–book printing quality. If a service bureau that owned the device didn't own CorelDRAW, you printed to file. Today there are alternatives to making a CorelDRAW document portable for a service bureau to render, but if Print To File is a client's mandate, here are the steps you need to take:

1. Choose the Print To File check box on the General tab of the Print dialog, and then choose from four options in the adjacent flyout menu. Choose For Mac if the file is to be printed from a Macintosh system; you need to define a PostScript printer first, or this option is dimmed. Choose Single File (the default), Pages To Separate Files, or Plates To Separate Files to set how the files are prepared. Single File creates one, usually huge, print file for the entire printout. Pages To Separate Files creates separate files for each page. The Plates To Separate Files option creates a single file to represent each page *and* each of the color separations you've chosen to print if your printing destination is to CMYK process color printing.
2. Click Print to start creating the print files, and the Print To File dialog opens, where you choose a destination for the PRN (for non-PostScript printers) or PS (for PostScript printers) file.

You then copy the PRN or PS file to removable media and take it to the party who will print the file; alternatively, many service bureaus offer FTP upload sites·for getting files to them. Traditionally, before artists use Print To File, they have a target device's print driver installed—this is done just like you install a printer in Windows, except you're only installing a *device driver* and *not* the physical printer itself. Service bureaus like to provide you with their print drivers because if you write a Print To File using an incompatible driver, you're left with a job the service bureau can't print, and you've wasted time and hard disk space.

Also, if the CorelDRAW file you print to file contains fonts, you either need to convert all text to curves (which significantly increases the saved PRN or PS file's size), or you need to include the typefaces on the disk you give to the service bureau, which is a thorny legal issue. Users give service bureaus digital typefaces all the time, but according to most font licenses, this isn't legal. On the other hand, you cannot depend on a service bureau or commercial press house to have exactly the same font as the one you used—if a high-resolution printer reads a Print To File and cannot find the typeface on its operating system, chances are you'll get a beautiful high-resolution print that uses Courier instead of your typeface.

In short, before you send out work for printing:

- Find a service bureau that owns CorelDRAW and save yourself some headaches.
- Failing that, find a service bureau that accepts Acrobat PDF documents (more on this later in this chapter).
- Export a copy of your CorelDRAW to Illustrator file format. It might not export perfectly, and certain CorelDRAW-specific effects will not translate, but Windows and especially Macintosh service bureaus are likely to own a copy of Illustrator.
- Use Print To File.

Using the Color Tab Settings

When outputting to color, to streamline the process, all options relating to color can be found on this single tabbed menu. The following sections document color-related operations.

Print Composite/Print Separations

At the top of this tab is the area where you choose to print color separations (covered later in this chapter), or to print a composite—which is the standard way most users print color documents to a home inkjet printer. If you choose separations, the composite tab in the Print box changes to Separations options and vice versa.

Document/Proof Settings

Your either/or choice by clicking one of these buttons determines whether your printer uses your current document color settings—found under Tools | Color Management—or disregards color settings you've made in the file and uses the settings you pick in the Print dialog.

Color Conversions Performed By

This drop-down list gives you a way to convert the color space of the document using CorelDRAW's features, or to let your printer handle the conversion from your monitor's color space to the slightly smaller and duller color space of physical pigments. If you're undecided, it's a safe bet to let CorelDRAW handle the conversion if your printer is an inkjet and not a PostScript printer. When a Postscript printer is defined, the alternative option to CorelDRAW is the currently selected PostScript printer. PostScript is PostScript, so the specific make and model of the printer is not relevant.

Output Colors As

When you're printing to a personal, non-PostScript device such as an inkjet, your options are only RGB and Grayscale, which is fair enough: laser printers can only reproduce grayscale halftones, and inkjets usually use the RGB color space to then convert colors to the CMYK color space. When a PostScript device is defined, your options are:

- **Native**   CorelDRAW handles the reconciliation between any different color models you've used when filling objects and the colors in any imported bitmap image.
- **RGB**   The file is sent to the printer using the RGB color model. This option is appropriate when you're printing a composite image (not separations) and you're lucky enough to own a color PostScript printer.
- **CMYK**   This is a good mode to use when you want to proof your work and get a good idea of what your colors will print like when sending a file to a commercial printer (composite printing). Similarly, if you're printing separations, CorelDRAW forces all colors in your document into the CMYK color space using the Rendering Intent you've selected
- **Grayscale**   Choosing this mode sends all color information to the printer as percentages of black. When choosing this option, you also see a Convert Spot Colors To Grayscale option, something you might not want to choose if you want a plate to print of your spot colors.
- **Convert Spot Colors To CMYK**   If for some reason your budget doesn't allow a spot color, clicking this check box forces any spot color plates to be rendered as CMYK process color equivalents. Forget about color fidelity and accuracy, but the option is available.

Correct Colors Using

When printing to a non-PostScript device, you have the option to choose to correct colors to the color profile of a specific printer or to choose from the list of available ICC color profiles installed on your computer.

Tip   You might be surprised at the lush colors you can render to a home inkjet printer by choosing sRGB IEC6 1966-2.1 as the color correction option instead of relying on your printer's color correction. sRGB is a widely used color space for today's consumer-level scanners and printing devices.

When you've defined a PostScript printer as your target device, you can choose from several presets defined from many different imagesetting manufacturers or choose a predefined color space, the same ones as if you were using a non-PostScript printer.

Rendering Intent

You have four options for how CorelDRAW handles the conversion of one color space to another. See Chapter 17 for thorough documentation on color conversion and choosing the best Rendering Intent to suit a specific document.

Choosing a Layout

Options on the Layout tab control how the page is laid out on the printing material you've loaded into your rendering device. Although the options are set to defaults for the most common print tasks, you can customize options in each area.

Setting Image Position and Size

Image Position And Size options control the position of each page's layout. These settings override settings you've defined in Printer Properties (your system's printing preferences, which aren't related to CorelDRAW). The following options are available:

- **As In Document**   This option (the default) leaves the current layout unchanged.
- **Fit To Page**   Choose this to enlarge or reduce your page layout to fit exactly within the printable area for your selected output material size. Understand that choosing this option ignores any precise measurements you've created in your file. For example, if you've labored on a fancy spine design for a presentation booklet that's 12" high, CorelDRAW scales the design for print to the maximum dimension of your media, such as an 8½ × 11" sheet of paper. If you run into this problem, hang on and check out the Print Tiled Pages option covered shortly.
- **Reposition Images To**   Choose this option to change the position of images as they print relative to how they're arranged on your CorelDRAW page. The default setting of Reposition Images To automatically moves images to the Center of Page. However, you can align images to the top, left, right, and bottom corners of the printing material page size—a convenient way to save paper and make trimming a printed piece easier. Using this option, you can also individually specify the position of images on each page of a multi-page document differently by choosing a document page number from the Settings For Page menu. Use the Position, Size, and Scale Factor boxes to enter specific values. Unlocking the horizontal/vertical lock by clicking the nearby lock icon gives you the opportunity to set the horizontal and/or vertical Scale Factor separately for nonproportional scaling, although you might not want a distorted print.
- **Imposition Layout**   *Imposition* is the orientation and position of multiple pages to create a book signature—pages are ordered and rotated so a commercial press can print a large page, and then the pages can be trimmed and bound so the book looks like a finished product. If you intend to print to high-resolution output, this option must be set exactly according to the specifications given to you by the printing service or other vendor you are using. It's always wise to talk with press operators (or their boss) before an expensive print job because the owners of the press know the characteristics of it better than you do. Clicking the Edit button opens a preview feature, where you can customize the imposition requirements, and you can rotate pages, move gutters, and even reorder pages at the last minute.

However, Imposition Layout is also an important feature even if you're home printing a single copy of a booklet from your inkjet printer. Here you can see a layout defined from a four-page CorelDRAW document; a template was *not* used to set up the file, and yet by choosing from the Imposition Layout drop-down, you ensure that the pages will, indeed, be printed in book fashion.

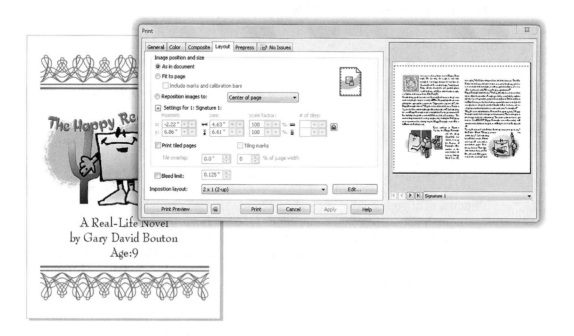

Tiling Your Printed Document

Often you need to print a piece that is much larger than the maximum output size of a personal printer: a bake sale banner, for example, or other display that exceeds even the output dimensions of today's wide-format inkjet printers. This need calls for using the Print Tiled Pages option. After printing, you get a utility blade, a metal ruler, some adhesive, and a cutting surface, and you're in business. The options for setting how each tile is printed are as follows:

- **Print Tiled Pages**   Choose this option to print pages in portions. Once selected, the # (Number) Of Tiles, Tiling Marks (you want to use Tile Overlap if you use this, to avoid showing the marks in your finished project), and Tile Overlap options are available. The # Of Tiles option lets you print your document in vertical or horizontal tiles, up to 24 portions for each. Setting the Tile Overlap option gives you control over how much image portion is repeated around the edges of each tile, based on unit measure or a percentage of the original page width. By default, Tile Overlap is set to 0 inches.

- **Tiling Marks** Choose this to have crop-style marks print around your tiles, making it easier to realign the tile pages when you put the tiles together.
- **Tile Overlap** This option adds an extra printed portion around each tile to make it easier to align the tiles for your large sign. Overlap can be set from 0 through 2.125 inches.
- **% Of Page Width** Use this to specify the tile overlap as a percentage of the page size between 0 and 25 percent.
- **Bleed Limit** Choosing this check box lets you use a portion of the area surrounding your document page. For example, if certain objects overlap the page border of a document, this option lets you print a portion outside the limits of the page. Bleed Limit can be set within a range of 0 to 40 inches, the default of which is a standard 0.125 inch.

The illustration here shows dashed lines (which would not be in the finished banner) where the single sheets tile in the bake sale banner, only one of scores of options for tiling a print when your budget prohibits extra-extra-large-format prints.

Printing Separations

If you know what color separations are and you work at a commercial printer, this next section is for you. If you *hire* a commercial printer when you have a color job, and only have a working understanding of process color and separations, read on to learn a little more, but *don't* provide a commercial press operator with your own color separations! CorelDRAW creates terrific color separation work, but you really need to output to a high-resolution (expensive, you don't buy them at a department store) imagesetting device that can render to film or other reproduction medium. You need to know as much about the printing characteristics of a printer as you do about color separations to prepare your own job for printing presses—for example, trapping margin of error, undercolor removal, ink characteristics, and other factors. You probably wouldn't practice brain surgery on yourself—similarly, don't do your own separations ("seps") if you're inexperienced in the field of standard web-offset printing.

If you're a silk screener or know a commercial press inside-out, when Print Separations is selected on the Color tab of the Print dialog, you have control over how each ink color prints.

Choosing Separation Options

Here is the rundown on your color separation options, as shown in the dialog in Figure 27-1:

- **Print Separations In Color** This option is available only if the printer you've defined is a color printer such as a personal inkjet, which prints a simulation of a coated printing plate, each plate reproduced in its respective color. This option

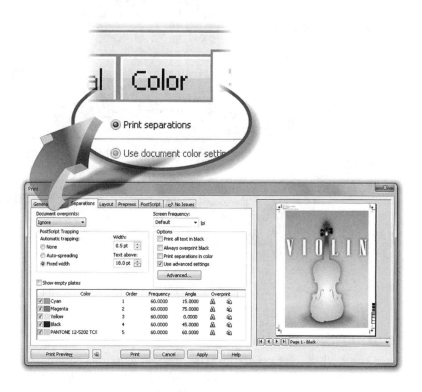

FIGURE 27-1 Use the Separations tab options to specify ink colors and trapping preferences.

is sometimes used for printing progressive proofs, checking registration, and checking color accuracy. Understand that if you use this option on a personal inkjet printer, you'll print several pages, each containing a single color; this could use a lot of ink, particularly if your CorelDRAW is dense with colored objects! Printing separations in color results in a good test for separations, but it's nothing you would want to frame and hang in the den later.

- **Convert Spot Colors To CMYK**   This option is important, but it's on the Color tab, *not* Separations. Choosing this option is often a wise choice in non-color-critical printing, when you can't afford to print a fifth plate using a spot color. This option converts non-CMYK colors such as fixed-palette, spot-ink colored objects to the closest process color equivalent when printing. You can usually get away with this if your spot color *is not* a special ink, such as a metallic. Letting CorelDRAW convert a metallic, fluorescent, or other specialty spot ink to process dulls the final print job; the results will look amateurish at best.
- **Show Empty Plates**   While unchecked (the default), this option causes pages without any objects to be skipped during printing to avoid printing blank pages. To include the blank pages, check this option. This can save you time, for example, if you only have a spot color on one page but not others in a multi-page document.

Frequency and Angle and Overprint Options

When separations are selected to print, the ink colors used in your document are listed at the bottom of the Separations tab. Each ink includes options for choosing if and how it will print. You see a series of columns that show how each ink color is set to print, with its color reference, ink color name, screen frequency, screen angle, and overprint options. The inks ultimately print in order from top to bottom as you see them on the list.

Don't change the frequency or line angle unless you're a professional—the default values are standard among the printing community. To change the frequency and/or angle of a specific ink color, first check the Use Advanced Settings check box, and then click directly on the value and then enter a new value. To change overprinting properties of a specific ink color, click directly on the overprint symbols for text and/or graphic objects to toggle their state. The following list explains what each of these options controls:

- **Order**   Use the selector for each ink to set the order in which separations are printed based on the number of available ink colors.
- **Frequency**   This option sets the output resolution in *lines per inch (lpi);* high-resolution imagesetters that speak PostScript organize dots for printing into lines. A typical line frequency for high-quality printing is 150 lpi, which results in color process prints of 2,500 dots per inch and higher. In comparison, a home laser printer, the 1,200 dpi variety, is only capable of rendering 80 lines per inch—you would not get magazine-quality prints using 80 lpi for color separations. Screen frequency values are automatically set to the default values of the imagesetter or printer selected on the General tab. Screen frequency values are also controlled by settings in the Advanced Separations Settings dialog.

- **Angle**   This option sets the angle at which the rows of resolution dots align. When separating process color inks, the following standard default screen angles are set automatically: Cyan = 15°, Magenta = 75°, Yellow = 0°, and Black = 45°. When separating fixed palette ink colors such as Pantone, Toyo, DIC, and so on, all colors are set to the default 45° value. You occasionally need to check the Issues tab when custom inks are used for spot-color plates to ensure that the spot plate is not at the same or even similar angle to the process plate screen angles. Change the angle if necessary; an incompatible spot-color screen angle can result in moiré patterning in your print, an effect similar to laying a screen window on top of another one at a certain angle.
- **Overprint**   Click directly on the symbols for text (the *A* symbol) and/or objects (the page symbol) to set whether text and/or objects for each ink are printed. Both states toggle on or off when clicked, and a gray overscore above the icons confirm your alterations

Note   If you've used two (or more) spot-ink colors in your document, these inks will separate at the default 45°. Consult with your print vendor for the correct screening angles for overlapping fixed-palette, spot-ink colors.

The Use Advanced Settings option is always dimmed unless you have a PostScript printer selected. When it's enabled, advanced settings override settings on the Separations tab. Clicking the Advanced button displays the Advanced Separations Settings dialog, shown here.

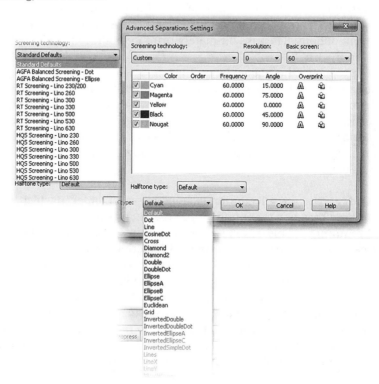

Here's what the options in this dialog control:

- **Screening Technology**   This selector drop-down contains scripts for specific printing technologies such as Agfa and Linotronic imagesetter devices. When Standard Defaults is used as the Screening Technology, other options are set according to settings for your specific printer driver, accessed through Preferences on the General tab.
- **Resolution**   This displays the output resolution of your printed material, the default value of which is set according to the Screening Technology selected. A service bureau or your print vendor knows the specifics.
- **Basic Screen**   This option sets the resolution as measured in lines per inch of the screens rendered in your output material. Check with your print vendor for the exact setting needed. If you need to adjust this value manually, you do it right here.
- **Halftone Type**   The Halftone Type selector is used to set the shape of the actual dots that compose the screens in the final output. Using this drop-down menu, you can choose such shapes as the default (Dot), Line, Diamond, Elliptical, Euclidean, Lines, Grid, Microwaves, Rhomboid, and Star. If you're just getting into commercial printing, anything other than a dot halftone shape is either used because the print press pulls better prints, or because you really know what you're doing and want to create an effect in the finished print job. Microwaves, for example, is a special effect that sounds interesting, but you would have to have already seen the effect on a printed sample before choosing it, and then you do a short run to see whether the example produces the same effect in your own piece. On the other hand, Elliptical and Star shapes can be used to sharpen the output of a print and, therefore, are more enhancers than effects.

Setting Trapping Options

Trapping involves either spreading or overprinting portions of colored objects to avoid printing inaccuracies, the most common one being paper white showing at the edge between two color objects. Overprinting causes one ink color to print over another, resulting in two layers of ink—it's a technique used to work around imprecise ink alignment. You can set the overprinting of fills and outlines applied to objects directly in your document; you cancel out of the Print dialog and return to the open document. Then with the Pick Tool, right-click one or more objects, and choose Overprint Fill or Overprint Outline from the pop-up menu options.

Overprinting can be set in three ways: directly in your document for each object, on the Separations tab, or using automated trapping. Where options have been set manually in your document or for each ink color, overprinting operates on a three-level hierarchy, which creates a condition where one overprinting setting overrides another one as follows:

1. When printing, the objects in the drawing are first examined for any selected fill and/or outline overprinting properties. Applying overprint properties directly to an object in a drawing overrides all other overprinting functions unless Document Overprints is set to Ignore.

2. Next, ink color overprinting options are examined. If no objects have overprinting properties applied, and if Always Overprint Black is checked, the black ink overprints objects beneath it. If text or graphic objects are set to overprint for any of the inks, then *they* overprint the items beneath.

3. Finally, the trapping options you have chosen on the Separations tab of the Print dialog are examined. If no other options are set, the automatic settings are used.

Automatic trapping and overprinting options on the Separations tab have the following effects on how colors in your document are printed:

- **Preserve Document Overprints**   This option (enabled by default) preserves the overprint options applied directly to your drawing objects, regardless of the settings selected elsewhere. Your other option, Ignore (on the drop-down list), lets you work with the settings on the Separations tab, and any custom overprinting you've applied directly to objects in your document is ignored.

- **Always Overprint Black**   When this option is selected, all objects that have color tints between 95 and 100 percent black overprint underlying ink colors. It's useful for designs that have a lot of black text, but can muddy pages you print that have a lot of delicate art and graphics work. Use Tools | Options | Global | Printing to adjust the amount of black from its default of 95 percent.

- **Auto-Spreading**   This option causes CorelDRAW's print engine automatically to create an overprinting outline of identical ink color around objects where they overlap other ink colors. When the option is selected, you can set the maximum width of the spread within a range of 0 to 10 points (0.5 point is the default, a little wider than a hairline). Automatic width values vary according to the difference between the color being overprinted and the underlying color. Choose Fixed Width to set the Auto-Spreading width of the outline to a constant width regardless of this color difference. When Auto-Spreading is selected, choosing the Text Above option makes CorelDRAW ignore text sizes below a certain size; small text is often distorted by the spread effect. Choose a size between 0 and 200 points; the default is 18 points. Auto-Spreading requires three conditions in order to work:
  - The object has no outline applied.
  - It's filled with a Uniform Fill.
  - It has not already been set to overprint.

In-RIP Trapping Settings

If your output device is equipped with its own In-RIP trapping software, you can use this option. The term *RIP* stands for *raster image processor*, the process of converting mathematical chunks of information to a map of where dots of ink go on the page to represent what you see onscreen. Many high-end imagesetters are equipped with internal software with which certain In-RIP trapping makes the whole trapping process faster and more efficient.

This option is dimmed unless the output device defined on the General tab is PostScript compatible, PostScript 3 is selected on the PostScript tab, and Print Separations is *disabled* on the Color tab. With the feature enabled, on the Composite tab, click the PostScript Level 3 In-RIP Trapping box, and then click the Settings button to open the In-RIP Trapping Settings dialog, shown here.

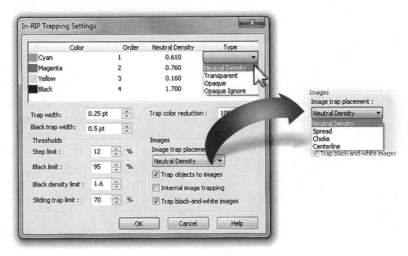

Here you'll find an ink listing similar to the one on the Separations tab, plus other options for setting these items:

- **Neutral Density**   This is a value based on an ink color's CMYK equivalents, ranging from 0.001 to 10.000. Default values often work, or the value can be set according to advice from your print vendor. Most third-party ink swatches list the neutral density values for each ink color.
- **Type**   You choose the type for an individual ink by clicking its type in the top list to reveal an options drop-down. Although Neutral Density is the default for Image Trap Placement, this option becomes available when you have a specialty ink defined for a spot plate, such as a spot varnish. You can choose from Neutral Density, Transparent, Opaque, or Opaque Ignore. Opaque is often used for heavy nontransparent inks such as metallic inks to prevent the trapping of underlying colors while still allowing trapping along the ink's edges. Opaque Ignore is used for heavy nontransparent inks to prevent trapping of underlying color *and* along the ink's edges.
- **Trap Width**   This option controls the width of the overlap value, where due to imprecise printing tolerances and ink impurities, a plate's ink might spread. This used to be known as "choking" (choking compensates for spreading); the term has fallen into disuse.
- **Black Trap Width**   This option controls the distance that inks spread into solid black, or the distance between black ink edges and underlying inks. It is used when the amount of black ink reaches the percentage specified in the Black Limit field (in the Thresholds area).

- **Trap Color Reduction**   Use this option to prevent certain butt-aligned colors (areas on different plates that meet one another) from creating a trap that is darker than both colors combined. Values less than 100 percent lighten the color of the trap.
- **Step Limit**   This option controls the degree to which components of butt-aligned color must vary before a trap is created, usually set between 8 and 20 percent. Lower percentages increase sensitivity to color differences and create larger traps.
- **Black Limit**   This value controls the minimum amount of black ink required before the value entered in the Black Trap Width field is applied.
- **Black Density Limit**   This option controls the Neutral Density value at, or above, the value at which the In-RIP feature considers it solid black. To treat a dark spot-color as black, enter its Neutral Density value in this field.
- **Sliding Trap Limit**   This value sets the percentage difference between the Neutral Density of butt-aligned colors at which the trap is moved from the darker side of the color edge toward the centerline. Use this option when colors have similar Neutral Densities to prevent abrupt shifts in trap color along a Fountain Fill edge, for example.
- **Trap Objects To Images**   Choosing this option lets you create traps between vectors and bitmaps.
- **Image Trap Placement**   This option sets where the trap falls when trapping vector objects to bitmap objects to either Neutral Density, Spread, Choke, or Centerline in this option's drop-down list. Neutral Density applies the same trapping rules used elsewhere in the printed document. Using this option to trap a vector to a bitmap can cause uneven edges because the trap moves from one side of the edge to the other. Spread produces a trap in areas where bitmaps meet vector objects. Choke causes vector objects to overlap the bitmap (the bitmap is choked). Centerline creates a trap that straddles the edge between vectors and bitmaps.
- **Internal Image Trapping**   This option creates traps *within* the area of a bitmap, which is useful when very high contrast and posterized images are part of a design.
- **Trap Black-And-White Images**   Choosing this option performs trapping between vectors and black-and-white (monochrome) bitmaps.

Setting Prepress Options

The term *prepress* is used to describe the preparing of film for various printing processes. Choosing the Prepress tab displays all options controlling how your printing material is produced and which information is included on the page, as shown here:

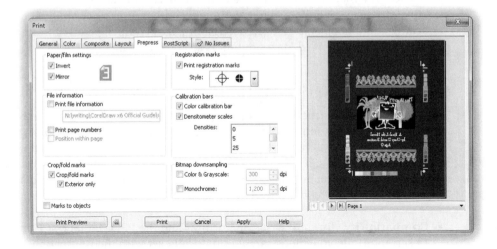

Here's what the options on the Prepress tab offer:

- **Paper/Film Settings**   These two options specify negative/positive printing and on which side of the film the light-sensitive emulsion layer appears. Choose Invert to cause your output to print in reverse; choose Mirror to cause the image to print backward. Ask the press operator or service bureau which way their imagesetter is set up for film.
- **Print File Information**   A Job Name/Slug Line text box is printed on each separation, to better visually identify each printed sheet. The path and filename of your document is used by default, but you can enter your own information. Choose Print Page Numbers to print page numbers as defined in your CorelDRAW document; choose Position Within Page to print this information *inside* the page boundaries—outside is the default.
- **Crop/Fold Marks**   Crop marks help locate your document's page corners; fold marks indicate folds for a specific layout. Choose Crop/Fold Marks to print these markings. With this selected, you can also choose Exterior Only to cause the marks to print only outside the page boundaries on your printing material, which produces a more polished final presentation. Both options are selected by default.
- **Registration Marks and Styles**   Registration marks help to align each separation plate; the film print is used to make the plate, and the plates need to be precisely aligned when your piece is printed, or you get a "Sunday Funny Pages" finished output. Choosing Print Registration Marks (selected by default) includes these marks on your output. Use the Style selector to specify a specific mark shape; the selector includes a preview of both positive and negative versions.
- **Calibration Bars and Densitometer Scales**   These two options enable you to include color calibration bars and densitometer scales outside the page boundaries of your printed material. Calibration bars are useful for evaluating color density accuracy by printing a selection of grayscale shades that may be used for measuring the density—or blackness value—of film or paper output.

- **Marks To Objects** Choosing this option causes whichever prepress marks are currently selected to be included with your output to print around the entire arrangement of objects on each document page. These appear regardless of whether the Crop/Fold Marks option is selected to print.

Choosing PostScript Options

None of the above information on separations and advanced trapping features is meaningful if your chosen output is not to a PostScript device. If you don't currently see the PostScript tab, shown in Figure 27-2, you need to define a different print driver. Options on this tab area offer control over PostScript options that use a specific type of page description language, Level 2, Level 3, the type of device, and so on.

You set the following options on the PostScript tab:

- **Compatibility** In most cases, the printer and the PPD (PostScript Printing Description) file you choose are automatically set with the Compatibility option, which determines which PostScript features the output device is capable of handling. Older printers may be limited to PostScript Level 1 or 2 technology; most new models are compatible with Level 3. If you're unsure which to choose, check out the manufacturer's FAQ area on their website or the physical printer documentation.
- **Conform To DSC** Document Structuring Convention (DSC) is a special file format for PostScript documents. It includes a number of comments that provide information for *postprocessors.* Postprocessors can shuffle the order of pages, print two or more pages on a side, and perform other tasks often needlessly performed by humans.

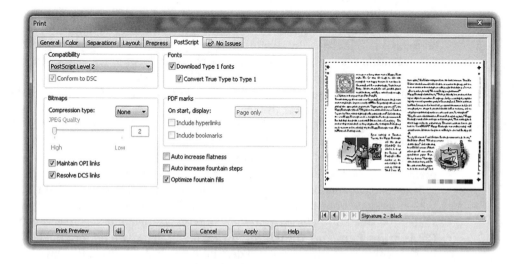

FIGURE 27-2 Use these options to control how PostScript options are made, but only after you've defined a PostScript printer as your output device.

- **Bitmaps**   Selecting Level 2 or 3 PostScript-compatible printers offers you the option of using the Use JPEG Compression option to reduce printing time if you have bitmap images in your document. When this option is selected, the Quality Factor slider is available for setting the quality of the bitmaps being printed. Keep in mind that JPEG is a *lossy* compression standard, some of the original image information is discarded, quality is compromised, and at high compression settings, a photograph can take on visual noise. You might want to alternatively choose LZW or Run-Length Encoded (RLE) compression, both of which are lossless, unlike JPEG.
- **Maintain OPI Links**   This option preserves links to server-based bitmap images, provided you have imported temporary low-resolution versions using the Open Prepress Interface (OPI) option when you created your CorelDRAW document. Using OPI, you can store high-resolution bitmap images in a printer's memory, and work temporarily with an imported low-resolution version. When your document is printed, the lower-resolution version is swapped with the higher-resolution version. By default, this option is selected.
- **Resolve DCS Links**   Desktop Color Separation (DCS) technology is similar to OPI; you use placeholders in your document that have links to digitally separated images for use in process or multi-ink printing. When this option is enabled, the linked images automatically replace the placeholder images at print time. By default, this option is selected. If this option is not selected, a prompt appears while the document is being printed, so you can relink the files manually.
- **Fonts**   PostScript printing devices can print both Type 1 and TrueType fonts. Type 1 fonts are often preferred because the font data is written in PostScript language. CorelDRAW's options let you control which fonts are used during printing. It's more reliable to download the fonts to the printing device; this speeds printing and produces better-looking text. To enable this feature, select Download Type 1 Fonts. If this option is disabled, fonts are printed as curves, which can take a lot of printing time when you have a lot of text on a page. When you select the Download Type 1 Fonts option, the Convert True Type To Type 1 option becomes available (and selected by default).
- **PDF Marks**   If your document is being prepared for printing as a composite to an Adobe PDF distiller, these options become available. You can specify how your PDF file initially displays when viewed in Adobe Acrobat Reader or a third-party reader by using options in the On Start, Display selector. Choose Page Only, Full Screen, or Thumbnail view. You can also choose whether to Include Hyperlinks and/or Include Bookmarks in the resulting PDF file. If you're preparing a PDF to send to a service bureau for high-resolution output, don't use hyperlinks; they mess up the appearance of your printed piece, and let's get real—how does your intended audience click a piece of paper to visit a website?
- **Auto Increase Flatness**   This option lets you simplify the printing of curves by decreasing the number of straight vector lines that describe the curve. This option can be used as a last resort if you run into problems printing highly complex shapes in your CorelDRAW document, usually a printer memory problem, as in *not enough* memory.

- **Auto Increase Fountain Steps**   This option makes the print engine examine your document for opportunities to increase the number of fountain steps in an effort to avoid Fountain Fill banding. *Banding* is the visible effect of not having enough sequential steps in a Fountain Fill; you see bands of gradually changing color instead of a smooth transition from one object area to another. Increasing the number of steps that describe a Fountain Fill causes Fountain Fills to appear smoother, but it also increases printing complexity and output time.
- **Optimize Fountain Fills**   This option works as the reverse of the previous option by setting the print engine to *decrease* the number of fountain steps set for objects in your document to the number of steps your printer is capable of reproducing.

CorelDRAW's Printing Issues Tab

The process of verifying that every last detail in your document will print as expected is often called *preflight,* and the good news is that the Issues tab is your flight attendant. CorelDRAW checks out the contents of your document and the printing options you've selected and then compares them to the capabilities of your selected printer and your selected output material. Printing snafus are found automatically and flagged by warning symbols as shown in the second illustration in this chapter. Figure 27-3 shows the Issues tab, which is divided into two sections; with Print Preview turned on, it's both documented and visually obvious what this proposed print has going against it.

The top half of the Issues tab lists the preflight issues detected with a brief explanation. The bottom half explains the causes, identifies the exact problems, and offers suggestions and recommendations for correcting them.

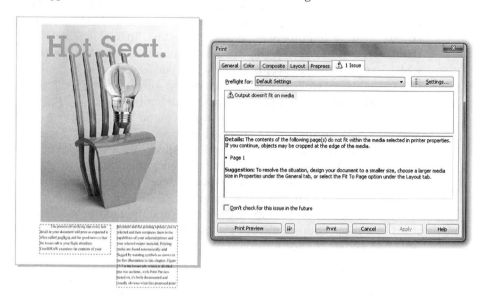

FIGURE 27-3   If CorelDRAW detects printing problems, they'll be explained on the tab.

The Issues feature will not prevent you from printing your document. If you want, you can deactivate the feature by selecting the found issue in the upper portion of the tab and choosing Don't Check For This Issue In The Future at the bottom of the tab. This disables the detection of the issue in the Preflight Settings dialog. Clicking the Settings button opens this dialog, which also lets you save and load current settings for future use.

Previewing Your Printed Document

CorelDRAW's Print Preview feature provides a very good way of viewing your document and performing minor touchups, and it's fully integrated with CorelDRAW's print engine. To open the Print Preview feature, click the Print Preview button from within the Print dialog. Print Preview also is available in the File menu.

Print Preview (see Figure 27-4) is a separate application window and includes its own command menus, toolbars, Property Bar, Status Bar, and Toolbox. When Print

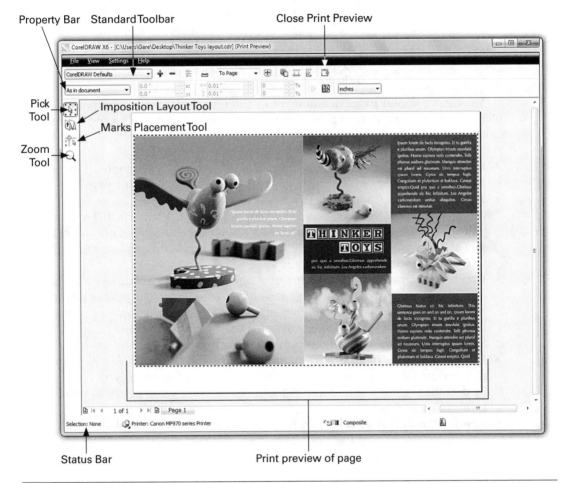

FIGURE 27-4   Print Preview is a program within a program, with its own interface, tools, shortcuts, and commands.

Preview is open, CorelDRAW is still open in the background. You'll also find that nearly all of the options that can be set while viewing your document in the Print Preview window are available, except they provide a higher level of control.

Browsing and Viewing Previews

The first thing you'll want to do in Print Preview is examine how your printed pages will look. Across the bottom of the Print Preview window, you'll find page controls, shown next, so you can browse each printed page. Use the arrow buttons to move forward or backward in the sequence, or click a page tab to display a specific page. As you do this, you'll discover each printed page is represented—including individual ink separation pages for each page in your document when you're printing separations.

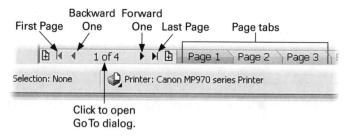

You can view your pages in a number of different ways based on output mode, color, and object type. To change view modes, choose one of the following from the View menu:

- **Show Image**   Choosing this lets you hide the display of page contents to speed screen redraw times when you've got a lot of objects on a specific page.
- **Preview Colors**   Choose this to access three basic previewing states. Auto (Simulate Output) shows each page's color according to your selected options and your printer's capabilities. If your chosen printer driver does not print in color, you see only grayscale color on your pages. To override this, choose either Color or Grayscale, which forces a specific view.
- **Preview Separations**   Choose Preview Separations to access three basic states. Auto (Simulate Output) displays separations according to your printer driver and selected print options. If separations are not selected to print, only a composite is shown, and vice versa. You can override this by choosing either Composite or Separations to force a specific separation display state.
- **Printable Area**   This varies from printer to printer; the *printable area* is the physical area that the printer can render onto a page. Choose this option (selected by default) to show a dotted line representing the maximum extent to which the printer can render.
- **Render PostScript Fills**   Use this option to have PostScript fills display as they will print. Deactivating this option can free up system resources when viewing documents where you used a lot of PostScript-filled objects.

- **Show Current Tile**   This option highlights individual tiles as you hover your cursor over them when previewing, and it's useful when printing large documents in sections onto small output material (*tile printing,* covered earlier in this chapter). To use tile printing from within Print Preview, choose Settings | Layout to open the Print Options dialog to the Layout tab, and then click to activate the Print Tiled Pages option.

Print Preview Tools and the Property Bar

The key to using Print Preview to its fullest is learning where all the options are located, what each tool does, and what print properties are available while using each. There are four tools on the Toolbox—the Pick Tool, Imposition Layout Tool, Marks Placement Tool, and Zoom Tool—each of which is discussed in the sections to follow. The Standard Toolbar, shown next, contains printing options, viewing options, and shortcuts you can use to open print-related dialogs.

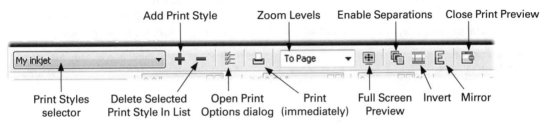

First is the Print Styles selector, which is used to choose all printing options according to a saved set of print parameters. As with other CorelDRAW Preset features, you can select, save, delete, or modify Print Styles in the selector. Choose an existing Print Style, use the current unsaved settings on the current print job, or choose Browse to show the Open dialog so you can work with a saved Print Style. To delete a selected Print Style, click the Delete (–) button. To save a Print Style, click the Add (+) button (or use the F12 shortcut) to open the Save Settings As dialog. Use the Settings To Include options to specify which print options to save with your new style, and click Save to add the Print Style to the selector.

The remaining options on the Standard Toolbar have the following functions, many of which are covered earlier in this chapter:

- **Open Print Options dialog**   This option opens the Print Options dialog.
- **Print button**   This option immediately sends the document to the printer using the current options. Use CTRL + P as a shortcut.
- **Zoom Levels**   Select a predefined Zoom Level from the list to change the view magnification level.
- **Full Screen Preview button**   This option is self-explanatory. Press ESC to return to Print Preview. You can also use CTRL + U as a shortcut.

- **Enable Color Separations button** This option sends the printing of color separations to the output device using the color selected on the Separations tab of the Print Options dialog.
- **Invert button** This option inverts the printed image to print in reverse. This is for film using an imagesetting device, but can also provide an amusing special effect (and use a lot of ink!).
- **Mirror button** This option flips the printed document to print backward to set emulsion orientation on imagesetting devices. You can also use this to print to T-shirt transfers.
- **Close Print Preview button** Pressing this (or using the ALT + C shortcut) returns you to the current CorelDRAW document.

Pick Tool Property Bar Options

The Pick Tool in Print Preview is used in much the same way that it's used in the drawing window; with it, you select and move (by click-dragging) whole pages. While the Pick Tool and objects on a page are selected, the Property Bar features a variety of printing options, shortcuts, position settings, and tool settings, as shown here:

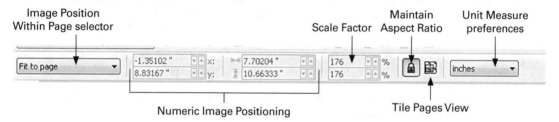

Many of these options are for positioning and scaling the contents of whole pages in relation to the printed output page size that your printer is currently set to use. You can click-drag to move whole pages or enter numeric values in Property Bar boxes. Click-dragging the page object control handles lets you scale the objects interactively.

Imposition Layout Tool Property Bar Options

The Imposition Layout Tool provides control over the print layout. Only certain imagesetters are capable of printing multiple pages in signature formats, so it's best to check with the person doing your print job before making changes using the Imposition options.

When the Imposition Layout Tool is selected, the preview is changed to display imposition-specific properties. This tool has four separate editing states, each of which is chosen on the Edit Settings selector. Options accessible on the Property Bar while Edit Basic Settings is selected, shown next, give you control over imposition layout options. Choosing Edit Page Placements, Edit Basic Settings, or Edit Margins from this selector displays a set of imposition options for each state.

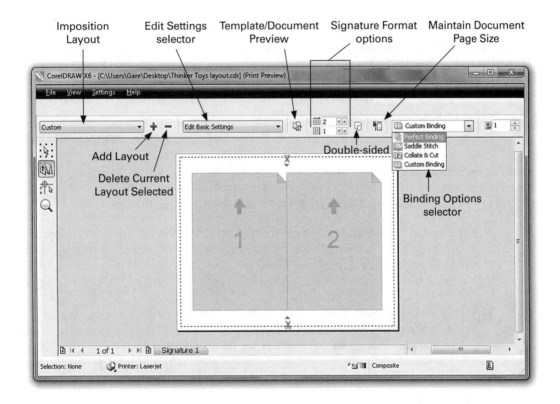

Marks Placement Tool Property Bar Options

The Marks Placement Tool lets you alter the position of crop and fold marks, registration marks, color calibration bars, printing information, and Density Scale positions. When the Marks Placement Tool is selected, the Property Bar features options for positioning and printing certain mark types, as shown here.

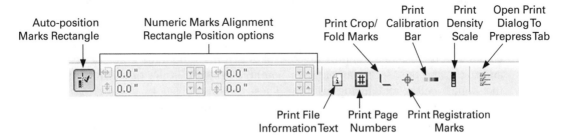

To view or position crop and fold marks, click-drag the top, bottom, or sides of the rectangle defining their position or enter values in the Property Bar boxes. To change the position of other marks you have selected to print with your document page, click them one at a time and then change the values on the Property Bar num boxes.

Zoom Tool Property Bar Options

The Zoom Tool in the Print Preview window is used much the same way as the Zoom Tool in CorelDRAW, so you can increase or decrease the view of your Print Preview. Many of the Zoom Tool's functions are performed interactively or by using hot keys. While the Zoom Tool is selected, the Property Bar features all Zoom options and magnification commands, as shown here:

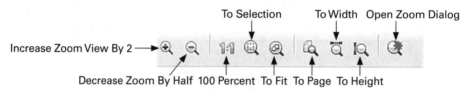

You can also change Zoom settings by choosing View | Zoom (CTRL + Z) to open the Zoom dialog to choose among all Zoom Tool functions. Use shortcuts to change your view magnification while using Print Preview's Zoom Tool: Zoom Out using F3, Zoom To Page using SHIFT + F4, Zoom To Selection using SHIFT + F2, and Zoom To Fit using F4.

> **Tip** Print Preview doesn't have an Undo command; to reset options quickly, close and then reopen Print Preview. Click the Close button on the Standard Toolbar to return to either your CorelDRAW document or the Print Options dialog.

Setting Printing Preferences

Once you're familiar with the ocean of printing options, what your output device is capable of, and what you want from a specific print job, Printing Preferences can be your one-stop shop for most of the items covered in this chapter. Choose Settings | Printing Preferences (CTRL + F is the shortcut) while in the Print Preview window to open the Printing Preferences dialog, shown in Figure 27-5. Preferences are subdivided into General, Driver Compatibility, and Preflight options. To change any of the options, click a Setting title; a drop-down selector appears, and then you make your change.

General Printing Preferences

Options on the General tab provide control over fonts, crop mark color, driver banding, and so on, and they set parameters for potential preflight issues or warning dialogs that appear before and during printing. These options are set, by default, to the highest fault tolerance for most printing jobs; 99 percent of the time your prints come out fine if you don't change the settings. Here's a list explaining the most common states:

- **Spot Color Separations Warning**   This option lets you control the warning state while printing color separations. The warning can be set to appear if more than one, two, three, or any spot colors are used in the document being printed.
- **Preview Color Default**   This option sets the initial color display of your printed document when the Print Preview window is first opened. Choose Auto (Simulate Output), Color, or Grayscale.

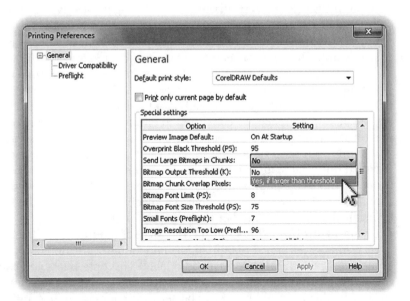

FIGURE 27-5   The Printing Preferences dialog offers comprehensive control over output settings.

- **Preview Separations Default**   This option sets the initial color display of your separations when the Print Preview window is first opened. Choose Auto (Simulate Output) or Composite.
- **Preview Image Default**   This controls whether your document image is automatically set to show when the Print Preview window first opens. Choose On At Startup (the default) or Off At Startup.
- **Overprint Black Threshold (PS)**   During overprinting, CorelDRAW sets a default value for overprinting black objects only if they contain a uniform fill of 95 percent or more black. The Overprint Black Threshold setting can be changed using this option, so you can further customize the global overprinting function. The threshold limit can be set between 0 and 100 percent black.
- **Send Large Bitmaps In Chunks**   This option works in combination with the Bitmap Output Threshold setting and can be set to the default Yes, If Larger Than Threshold (referring to the Bitmap Threshold value), or No.
- **Bitmap Output Threshold (K)**   When printing to non-PostScript printers, this option lets you set a limit on the size of bitmaps, as measured in kilobytes, sent to the printing device. By default, this value is set to the maximum, but you can set it to specific values within a range of 0 to 4,096 (the default). This is a good option to change if your non-PostScript printer doesn't have a lot of memory and you're pulling prints that are unfinished due to lack of RAM for processing the image.

- **Bitmap Chunk Overlap Pixels** If a printing device has insufficient memory or another technical problem processing very large bitmap images, you can have CorelDRAW tile sections of such a bitmap. The Overlap value is used to prevent seams from showing between "chunks" of the large image. When you're printing to non-PostScript printers, this option lets you define the number of overlap pixels within a range of 0 to 48 pixels. The default is 32 pixels.

- **Bitmap Font Limit (PS)** Usually, font sizes set below the Bitmap Font Size Threshold preference are converted to bitmap and stored in a PostScript printer's internal memory. This can be a time-consuming operation that usually increases the time your document takes to print. You can limit the number of fonts to which this occurs, forcing the printer to store only a given number of fonts per document. The default setting here is 8, but it can be set anywhere within a range of 0 to 100. Unless your document is a specimen sheet of all the fonts you have installed, 8 is a good number to set this option to.

- **Bitmap Font Size Threshold (PS)** Most of the time CorelDRAW converts very small sizes of text to bitmap format when printing to PostScript printers, such as 4-point legal type on a bottle label. This option lets you control how this is done, based on the size of the font's characters. The default Bitmap Font Size Threshold is 75 pixels, but it can be set within a range of 0 to 1,000 pixels. The actual point size converted to bitmap varies according to the resolution used when printing a document. The threshold limit determines exactly which font sizes are affected. For example, the equivalent font size of 75 pixels when printing to a printer resolution of 300 dpi is roughly 18 points, whereas at 600 dpi, it's about 9 points. The higher the resolution, the lower the point size affected. A number of provisions determine whether these controls apply, including whether the font has been scaled or skewed, and whether Envelope effects, Fountain or Texture Fills, or print scaling options such as Fit To Page have been chosen.

- **Composite Crop Marks (PS)** This feature is useful for setting the pen color of crop marks either to print in black only or to all plates, making the crop marks print to every color plate during process color-separation printing.

- **PostScript 2 Stroke Adjust (PS)** The PostScript Level 2 language has a provision particularly useful for graphics programs such as CorelDRAW. PostScript 2 Stroke Adjust produces strokes of uniform thickness to compensate for uneven line widths due to the conversion of *vector* artwork to *raster* printed graphics, which is what all printers do. The PostScript 2 Stroke Adjust option *should not* be used for older printers that are not compatible with PostScript Level 2 or Level 3 technology. Most recently manufactured printing devices are, at least, PostScript Level 2–compatible. If you are not sure what level your printing device is, leave this setting as Off or consult the documents that came with the device.

- **Many Fonts** This controls a warning that appears if the document you're printing includes more than ten different fonts. If you're new to CorelDRAW and are experimenting with all the cool fonts that came on the CD, your file can easily exceed this limit. If your printer's memory and/or your system resources are capable of handling large numbers of different fonts, consider increasing this value. The Many Fonts warning option can be set within a range of 1 to 50 fonts. Tangentially related to this option is a creative design issue: very few professionals use more than ten different typefaces in a design; five can express an idea using text quite well in most situations.

- **Small Fonts**   This controls a warning that appears if the document you're printing includes fonts below a 7-point size threshold by default. The Small Fonts warning option can be set between 3 and 18 points. Resolution plays an important part in rendering small point-size typefaces, as does the design of the characters within the font. For example, a 1,200 dpi laser printer can render 4-point Helvetica quite legibly, less so with a serif typeface such as Times Roman because the serifs at this size are about equal to insect parts. Choose a simple sans serif font for extremely small font sizes. Do not expect a perfect rendering of a very small typeface because the dots of ink or toner cartridge can only render a finite number of dots to represent small text.
- **Render To Bitmap Resolution**   This option, by default, is set to Automatic, which causes bitmaps to be output at the same resolution as vector objects and text in your document. To specify the resolution of bitmaps to be printed at lower or higher resolutions than the rest of the document, choose specific settings within a range of 150 to 600 dpi.

Driver Compatibility

The Driver Compatibility area, shown in Figure 27-6, provides control over specific driver features for *non-PostScript* printers. Choose a Printer from the drop-down menu, and then choose specific options in the dialog to make changes. Clicking Apply saves and associates your changes with the selected driver.

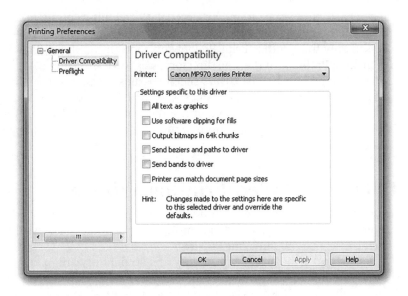

FIGURE 27-6   Use the Driver Compatibility options to specify how non-PostScript printers handle specific object types.

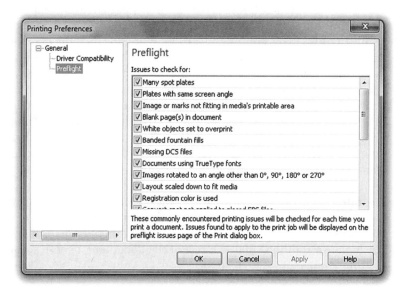

FIGURE 27-7 Preflight options let you control how and when detected printing issues appear.

Printing Issues Warning Options

You can customize issues found by CorelDRAW' s built-in preflight feature using options on the Preflight tab of the Printing Preferences dialog (CTRL + F), which can be accessed only from within Print Preview by choosing Settings | Printing Preferences and clicking Preflight in the tree directory, as shown in Figure 27-7.

This comprehensive list covers specific issues ranging from mismatched layout sizes to spot colors with similar names. Use the check box options in the list to activate or deactivate each option, or use the Don't Check For This Issue In The Future option, located at the bottom of the Issues tab of the Print Options dialog when an issue is discovered.

Corel's Double-Sided Printing Wizard

You can create booklets and other double-sided printed documents on your personal printer by using the Double-Sided Printing Wizard. You can access this feature by pressing CTRL + D while in Print Preview.

This wizard is fairly self-explanatory and straightforward to use. When a driver is set to use the duplex printing feature, the Manual Double-Sided Printing dialog displays when CorelDRAW's print engine starts to print, asking whether you want to print on both sides of a printed page. For specific page-insertion directions, you'll find an option that prints an instruction sheet to show you which way you should reinsert the sheet of paper after printing the first side.

Using the Collect For Output Wizard

CorelDRAW provides a wizard that collects all the information, fonts, and files required to display and print your documents correctly if you don't own an imagesetter or other high-end output device and need to send your document to press.

Corel has a service bureau affiliate program, and service bureaus approved by Corel can provide you with a profile to prepare your document with the Collect For Output Wizard. This profile can also contain special instructions that a service bureau needs you to follow before sending your files. Check with your vendor to see whether it is a Corel Approved Service Bureau (CASB).

To launch the wizard, choose File | Collect For Output. From there, the wizard guides you through a series of question-and-answer pages that gathers the information you need to upload or put on a disk to deliver to a printer or service bureau. When you finish the process, all necessary files are copied to a folder you define, and optional documents specifying your required output are included, depending on your wizard option choices. Figure 27-8 shows the succession of wizard dialogs from the beginning to the end of the process. At the end, CorelDRAW offers a final screen with a summary; click Finish.

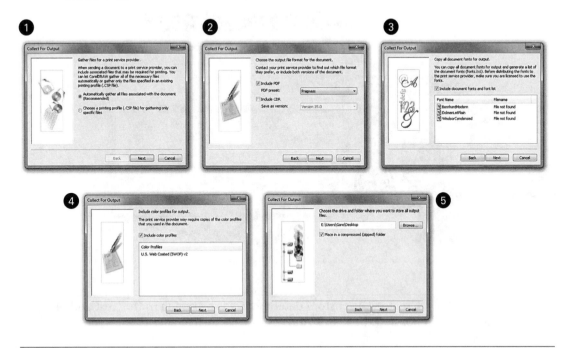

FIGURE 27-8   The Collect For Output Wizard helps prepare files for sending to a service bureau.

Print Merge

Print Merge gives you the design and business opportunities to merge database information with specific fields of your CorelDRAW documents at print time, so you can print personalized documents with only a click or two. If you create mailing labels, short runs targeted at a specific audience, and marketing documents, this feature is invaluable. By creating special fields, you can merge specific database information into your document and set properties such as color, font style, and so on. This feature also lets you use ODBC Data Sources from database management systems that use Structured Query Language (SQL) as a standard.

Follow these steps when you need to create a Print Merge:

1. Choose File | Print Merge | Create/Load Merge Fields. Choosing this command opens the Print Merge Wizard, and you either create a database from scratch or choose an existing one.
2. If you need to create a custom merge document, choose the Create New Text option and then click Next. Create fields for your custom database by entering unique names in the Text Field and/or Numeric Field, shown in Figure 27-9, and then click the Add button. As you build your field list, you can change the order of the fields by clicking to highlight a field in the Field Name list,

FIGURE 27-9 Create your custom database fields by typing in the Text and/or Numeric Field box and then click Add.

and then clicking the Move Up and Move Down buttons. You can also edit the fields you've created by using the Rename and Delete buttons to change or remove a selected field. Choose the Incremental Field Data option while a field is selected in the list to number each entry in the field automatically. If you need numeric data, enter the value in the Numeric Field; when this option is used, new fields display, letting you specify the numeric sequence of your data and formatting. You can also choose the Continually Increment The Numeric Field box to save time making your field entries. Once your list is created, click Next to proceed.

3. The next page of the wizard, shown in Figure 27-10, gets you right into building your database by entering values to build sets of field entries. To begin a new entry, click the New button, and then fill in the fields with the appropriate data; click the spreadsheet-like box to highlight it, and then type your entry. You can quickly revise an entire field by highlighting it and then pressing DELETE or BACKSPACE. To delete an entire record, make sure it is the only one with a check to the left of it, and then click the Delete button. Browse your database entries using the navigation buttons, or search for specific entries by clicking the Find button. Once your database is complete, click Next to proceed.

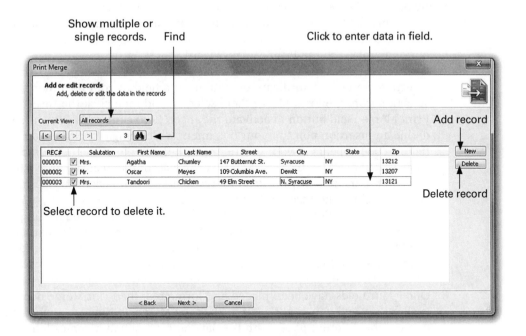

FIGURE 27-10 Use this page of the wizard to begin building your field entry sets.

4. The final wizard page is where you save your database to reuse and update in the future. Choose the Save Data Settings As box, and then browse your hard drive for a location to save the file in one of these formats: Windows Rich Text Format, Plain Text, or File With A Comma Used As A Delimiter (CSV Files). You probably also want to save the Incremental field data to make looking up a record easier in the future. Click Finish to exit the wizard and automatically open the Print Merge Toolbar, shown here:

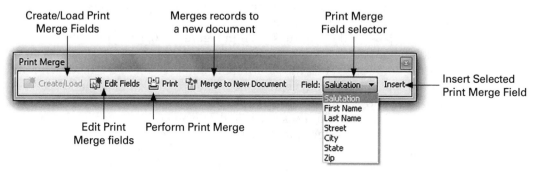

5. By default, the toolbar opens with your newly created database open and the individual fields it includes listed in the Print Merge Field selector. To load your fields from a different database, click the Create/Load Print Merge Fields button to relaunch the Print Merge Wizard.

6. By inserting fields, you're creating a link from entries in your database to insertion points in your document. To insert a field in your document, make a selection from the Print Merge Field selector, and then click the Insert Selected Print Merge Field button to activate the Insert Tool cursor. Use the cursor to define an insertion point in your document with a single click. As you insert a field, a code appears in your document with the name of the field bracketed, such as < Street Address >. Repeat your insertion procedure for each field you want to include in your Print Merge operation, or deactivate the Insert Tool by clicking the Insert Selected Print Merge Field button.

7. The Print Merge fields can be formatted as Artistic Text, so you can apply any properties associated with Artistic Text to the field text to format it as you would like it to appear when printed. This includes color, alignment, font, size, style, and so on. Fields can be inserted as stand-alone text objects, inserted into Paragraph Text, or simply typed using the same code format.

8. Once your fields have been placed and formatted, the Print Merge document is all set up, and you might want to click the Merge To New Document button to proof the different pages with the data entered. When it comes to merging your printed document with the Print Merge feature, you must use the Print button *on the Print Merge Toolbar,* not CTRL + P. Alternatively, choose File | Print Merge | Perform Merge. Doing so immediately opens the Print dialog, where you proceed with printing using your print option selections.

9. To edit Print Merge fields and records, click the Edit Fields button on the Print Merge Toolbar, or choose File | Print Merge | Edit Merge Fields. This opens the Print Merge Wizard, where you begin the process again or choose an existing database to edit. Choosing Import Text From A File Or An ODBC Data Source in the wizard causes the next page to offer options for choosing a data file (in TXT, CSV, or RTF format), or an ODBC Data Source. Use the File option to open an existing database file containing the information you want to merge. Use the ODBC Data Source option and the Select ODBC Data Source button to open an existing data source.

This chapter has shown you where the print options are for both PostScript and non-PostScript output, how to check for errors and correct them before you send your CorelDRAW file to an output device, and how to make your work portable so someone with more expensive equipment than mere mortals own can print your work to magazine quality. But this is only part of the story of CorelDRAW output. Take a trip to the following chapter, where output for the Web is explored; you'll want to post companion pieces up on your website in addition to printed material. Regardless of whether you put dots of ink on a page or broadcast pixels to a screen 10,000 miles away, today it's called *publishing* your work.

28 Basic HTML Page Layout and Publishing

Whether it's for personal pleasure or selling your wares, the Web is your connection between your ideas and your business and social contacts. It's far less expensive than other publication media such as television and print, and the really great thing about it is it's *hot*. You don't have to be a rocket scientist to get media up on your website using CorelDRAW, and once you've designed a piece for print, it's practically ready to go on the Web. Create once, publish many times!

In this chapter, you learn about the many tools and features at your disposal in CorelDRAW for optimizing your work for the Web and about how to create special web graphics such as rollover buttons that turn your art into *interactive* art.

 Note Download and extract all the files from the Chapter28.zip archive to follow the tutorials in this chapter.

Web Page Navigation Buttons and Hotspots

What makes the Web a *web* are the links that connect pages to other pages. The World Wide Web is engineered by connecting *this* bit of this page to that bit of *that* page on the same site—or on any other website in the world. The engine that performs all this interconnecting magic is actually the text-based *hyperlink*. Although text-based hyperlinks are the foundation of the Web, text links are about as attractive as a foundation, and the links themselves often are just a bunch of letters and numbers that mean something to a computer, but mean nothing to a human.

However, if you put a graphic *face* on a link—perhaps one that changes as a visitor hovers over or clicks it—you have a web page that speaks well of your artistic skills. You also get a chance to provide nonverbal communication, the sort that plays to a worldwide audience, many of whom might not speak your native tongue. With a graphic, you can clearly point out that Area *X* is a link and not part of your text message. Using a graphic also gives you the opportunity to provide a visual clue about where the link goes. How about the humble shopping cart icon? A great many people in this world now know that clicking a shopping cart button takes them to a page that has to do with buying something. That's a pretty all-encompassing message using only a few pixels.

Creating and applying attractive, well-thought-out navigational aids to a web page are a must in the competitive online marketplace. The following sections take a look at how you can use CorelDRAW's tools in combination with your input and ingenuity to create web pages worth a thousand words.

CorelDRAW's Internet Toolbar

You'll find that several web tools and resources are located throughout CorelDRAW, but the *central* location for many of these resources is the Internet Toolbar. Here's a look at the toolbar; you choose Window | Toolbars | Internet or right-click any visible toolbar, and then choose Internet from the pop-up menu. The buttons on this toolbar are dimmed unless you have an object or two on the current drawing page; now is a good time to create a few button-shaped graphics for tutorial steps you can follow a little later.

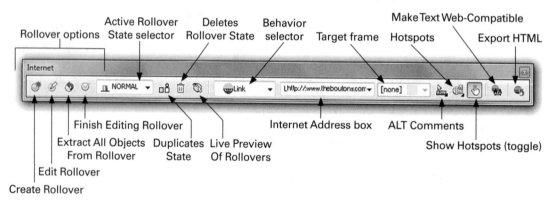

From the Internet Toolbar, you can apply web-specific properties to objects, such as hyperlinks, rollover effects, and image maps. *Hyperlinks* are links to existing web pages (or to bookmark links applied to objects in your CorelDRAW document). *Rollovers* are objects that can change their appearance and perform an event in response to a visitor's cursor action over the object. *Image maps* are objects that have one or more linked areas to web page destinations. Rollovers are unique object types (that this chapter shows you how to make); however, hyperlinks can be applied to *any* single object or to specific characters in a Paragraph Text object.

Caution Arial, Verdana, Times New Roman, and several other typefaces are Web-compatible; when CorelDRAW exports one of these fonts, it appears as editable text in the audience's browser. Be sure to click the Make Text Web-Compatible button before exporting your HTML, or CorelDRAW will export the text as a bitmap graphic when you get to the Images tab while exporting. See "Web Text Options" later in this chapter.

The Internet Toolbar provides a convenient hub for applying nearly all web object properties. Many of these properties can also be found and applied elsewhere in CorelDRAW, but it's more convenient to use the toolbar. Making your graphics actually perform the duties you've assigned to them (by applying web properties) requires that a matching piece of HTML code is added to the web page HTML. CorelDRAW writes this code for you when you export your Corel document. You *will* need to provide the HTML along with the graphic to your client or to the webmaster to make the interactive graphics you've created do what they're supposed to do. In the sections to follow, you learn what options are available, and where they are.

Creating Rollover Buttons

Almost any object you draw can be made into a rollover that reacts to cursor actions, so you can liven up your published document with simple animated effects and hyperlinks. *Cursor actions* are events such as when a user holds or passes a cursor over the object or clicks the object by using a mouse.

When you're creating rollovers, you can define three basic states: Normal, Over, and Down. The *Normal state* sets how an object appears in its "static" state—when the cursor is not over or clicked on the object on the web page. The *Over state* sets the appearance of the object whenever a cursor is over it. The *Down state* sets how the object appears when being clicked, when the visitor's mouse button is clicked on an object. By varying what the graphic looks like in these states, you can create interesting visual effects and give your users meaningful feedback related to their cursor movement.

This is fun stuff and deserves a tutorial. The following steps show how to make a region interactive when an object (or group of objects) is displayed on a web page. Although the button reacts to cursor actions when you've completed the tutorial, the actions will not link to anything; linking a button is covered later in this chapter—let's concentrate on the *art* for the button first. Suppose you want a button that tells the visitor that something is for sale: a button with a $ symbol plays in several countries, or use a currency symbol of your preference in this example. To continue the concept here, the action a visitor takes is to click to buy the item; therefore, when visitors hover their cursor over and/or click the button, the button should change to a different look. In this example, it changes its text from a $ symbol to an official-looking "SOLD" message. Yep, as ambitious as this might seem, all you need to do is to follow these steps...

Tutorial Creating Different Looks for Rollover States

1. Create a button object, make it as fancy as you like (Effects | Bevel works well), but keep the size of the button to approximately the size you'd want it on your web page—under an inch is fine for this example. Then with the Text Tool type **$** and give the symbol a fill color that contrasts with the button color.

2. Select all the objects (CTRL + A), and then click the Create Rollover button on the Internet Toolbar to let CorelDRAW know this is going to be a rollover button once you've finished, as shown here.

3. With the object now defined as a rollover object, all the states on the Active Rollover State selector display the same group of objects you selected ... and it's time to create a change now. Click the Edit Rollover button to enter the editing state, as shown here, and then choose Over from the selector list.

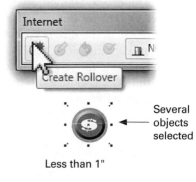

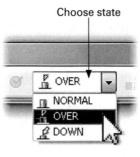

Several objects selected

Less than 1"

Choose state

4. Edit your button; in the illustration here, the embossed circle has actually been replaced with a polygon object. You *can* replace objects, change the fill, do just about anything you like because this editing state is not a "normal" page view in CorelDRAW's drawing window. Some tricky stuff is going on behind the scenes, and if you choose to delete a shape and replace it now, you haven't really deleted it. You remove an object from a state's *view,* in this case from the Over state, but in the Normal state, all your original objects are still there. Similarly, delete the $ and then with the Text Tool type **SOLD** in an interesting font.

Replacement objects

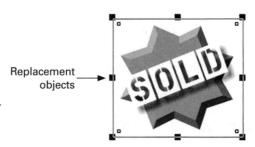

5. For the sake of testing all these features, let's suppose that the Over state, the SOLD button, is also good for the Down state, the state that occurs when the visitor clicks the button. By default, the Normal state is assigned to all three available states when you first made the collection of objects a rollover button. First, click the Active Rollover State selector and choose Down; a view of the Normal state object appears.

6. Trash the contents of the Down state by clicking the Deletes Rollover State trashcan button.

7. Choose Over from the Active Rollover State selector, and then click the Duplicates State button. The Over state now duplicates the following unassigned state (Down).

8. You're finished! Click the Finish Editing Rollover button (shown here), and save this file to CDR file format.

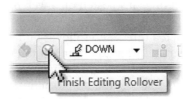

9. Oh, *yeah*; you want to see your creation *in action*! CorelDRAW previews your interactive button right on the drawing page. Click the Live Preview Of Rollovers button; before you move your cursor over the button, it should look like it did when you set it to Normal—your original group of objects. Move your cursor over the button, and it should show the Over state, as it will in the Down state (when you click the button) because you duplicated Over to Down in the tutorial. After previewing the effect, click the Live Preview Of Rollovers icon again to deactivate the live preview, because live drawings can get a little disconcerting.

Look at rollover.cdr and take it apart to better see the wealth of creative possibilities in your own work. This setup has three different states, and when you click the button, it changes shape and sort of squishes away from you. Just about any edit you can perform on objects, including totally replacing them, can be used for a rollover button.

The Internet Toolbar also has other rollover-related commands for objects, as follows:

- **Edit Rollover**   This was covered earlier, but you should know that even after you think you're finished, rollovers can be edited a week or a year from now.
- **Extract All Objects From Rollover**   This is a *destructive* edit! Think about this command twice before you undo all your rollover work. Depending on the replacement objects you've built into a rollover, use this button to view and edit everything CorelDRAW has hidden while the document was a rollover. The objects are stacked on top of each other, so you have to change the stack order or drag them apart to see them.

Tip   Rollover buttons can't be edited while the Live Preview Of Rollovers option is on. To edit any button, first disable this option by clicking the button. You can turn on Live Preview again when you finish editing the button.

- **Duplicates State**   Covered briefly in the tutorial, this button is used to copy the Normal state to Over and Down states if you have deleted them using the command button, discussed next.

- **Deletes Rollover State**   This button deserves a little more quality time: while editing any rollover state, you can delete the object(s) representing it by clicking this button. After a state has been deleted, no object represents it, so the rollover state appears blank. If needed, use the Duplicates State button to create an exact copy of the Normal state back into a blank state to avoid having to re-create the object(s) used for this state. If you've deleted a state, be sure to set the Active Rollover State selector list back to Normal, or your button will be blank when someone clicks it once it's posted on a web page.

You've just created a three-step rollover button! It is an interesting graphic effect, and sometimes you might want to use it just the way it is—a sort of graphic hide-and-seek game. Most of the time, however, you'll want something additional to happen; you want the action of clicking the link to activate a hyperlink and the user to be taken to the link's destination. The destination can be a bookmark location on the current page, like the top or bottom of the page, or the destination might be another web page or URL location altogether. How to make the rollover or any other element do something is presented in the following section.

Setting Internet Object Behavior

While any individual object or rollover state is selected, you can set its behavior as a web object to either a URL or an Internet bookmark using options on the Behavior selector on the Internet Toolbar, shown here.

Adding URL Behavior

You can apply hyperlinks to any object using this option. For example, Corel's URL is http://www.corel.com. Internet addresses must be preceded with the correct Internet protocol prefix (such as *http://*, *https://*, or *ftp://*). For example, if you're linking to www.corel.com, the format must be http://www.corel.com. You can also use a "mailto" protocol to link to an e-mail address, such as by entering **mailto:*someone@ somewhere.com***. This is a great way to get, for example, a potential client to write to you. By default, the *http://* protocol is automatically added to precede your URL, but you can edit it as needed.

To set a URL as the behavior for your web object, click to select the object, and use the Behavior selector on the Internet Toolbar to specify the URL. With this option selected, type the actual URL in the Internet Address box, pressing ENTER to apply the address link. Once a URL has been applied, the Internet Toolbar displays other options. Here are the URL-specific things you can define:

- **Target Frame**   Use this option to specify an optional browser window location for the new page to open into. Unless you specify differently using this drop-down, the page called by the assigned URL address opens in the current browser window, replacing the page that contained the link. This produces the same results as the Default [None] setting in the Target Frame list. Choosing the _blank option from the list causes a new web browser window to open to display the linked page. If your web page uses frames for its display, you can specify where in the frameset the new content will open. Choosing _self opens the new URL in the same frame where the web object is located. The _top option opens the new URL in the full body of the window, and all frames are replaced with a single frame containing the new document. The _parent option opens the new document in the current frame's Parent frameset. You can also enter custom frame names by typing them in the Target Frame combo box.

Note Frame-based web pages cannot be searched by most search engines such as Google, and onscreen readers for the visually impaired cannot read the contents of frames. Think very carefully if you choose a frame-based web document, and consider the audience you might lose and annoy.

- **ALT Comments**   Use this option to add ALT (alternative) text to your web object. ALT text is a text description that is displayed either until the web object downloads or while your web user's cursor is held over the object. It is both polite and professional to add meaningful ALT comments text to all graphics for accessibility reasons. Because page-reading software usually prefaces the reading of ALT text with an announcement of what kind of object the ALT text belongs to, such as a graphic or a hyperlink, don't repeat the link URL or enter the words "graphic" or "link." Instead describe the function or content the link leads to, for example, "Home Page," or "CorelDRAW Forums," or "send e-mail to this terrific guy or gal." If you don't enter ALT comments for an URL, reading software will probably read or spell out the URL to your visitor; this is not a considerate way to treat visitors to your site.
- **Hotspots**   A hotspot in a graphic can be a great way to create one graphic and yet tag several different areas to different links. Once you've entered a link for an object, click this icon to choose whether an object's shape or its bounding box defines the clickable area. Choose either Object Shape or Bounding Box Of Object in the selector, as shown next. You can choose the Cross-hatch and Background

colors if the currently set colors are difficult to distinguish from other colors in your document. These don't show on your published web page; they're only a visual convenience while you work in CorelDRAW.

- **Show Hotspot** This option in the middle of the toolbar can be toggled on or off, and it can activate or deactivate the display of the crosshatch pattern, which indicates hotspots applied to web objects, shown here.

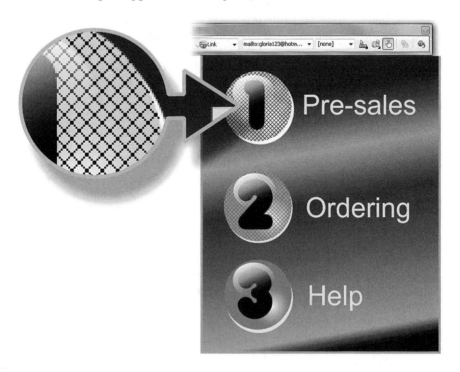

Adding Bookmark Behavior

Assigning a bookmark to a graphic object is a method you can use to provide a convenient way for users to navigate between web pages on your site. For example, you could use a bookmark if you wanted your audience to be able to click a button or other link and return to the first page of your site from another page in your site. This is a two-step process. In the first part of the process, you define a fixed location to which one or more URL links can point. The fixed location is an anchor or bookmarked object. The second step in the process would be to create a button or text link elsewhere that points to the object's bookmark. Let's walk through the process.

Tutorial   # Creating Bookmark Links

1. Select an object that you want to serve as the anchor or bookmark, for example, a graphic at the top of your first page. The object that is bookmarked *must be a graphic, not text.*
2. From the Behavior selector list on the Internet Toolbar, choose Bookmark.
3. In the Internet Bookmark box, enter a descriptive name for the bookmark, such as **home_page** or **bottom_of_page_4,** and press ENTER, as shown in Figure 28-1. In compliance with web server file-naming conventions, you can use mixed-case names for bookmarks, but not spaces. If you need a space, use a hyphen or underscore instead.
4. Select another object or button or piece of Paragraph Text on the same page or on another page in your document. This is the object that when clicked will take your user to the object you previously bookmarked.
5. From the Behavior selector list on the Internet Toolbar, choose Link.

FIGURE 28-1   A bookmark object can be on any page of a multi-page document you want to publish as a website.

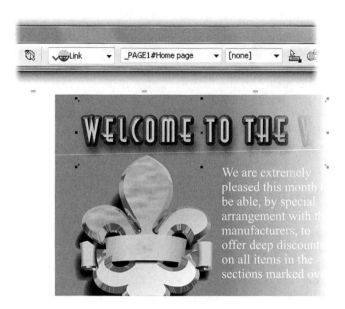

FIGURE 28-2 Use the target for the bookmark you find on the Internet Address drop-down selector.

6. From the Internet Address drop-down list, choose the Bookmark name you gave to the object in Step 3. For example, if **home_page** was the bookmark name you used, you would see an entry like this: _PAGE1#Home_page, as shown in Figure 28-2.

You can also enter a fully qualified URL in the Internet Address field to link to the bookmark. The URL would take the form of the web page's address, followed by a pound (#) sign and then the bookmark name. For example, a website's home page is usually named index.html. So a bookmark named "picture" on the index.html page would be typed in as **http://www.mysite/index.html#picture**.

> **Tip** If you are not familiar with how to write valid HTML hyperlinks and link anchor names or IDs (called *bookmarks* in CorelDRAW), consult your favorite HTML manual or the World Wide Web Consortium (W3C) page on Links and Anchors at http://www.w3.org/TR/html4/struct/links.html#h-12.2.1.

Web Properties and the Object Properties Docker

You can use the Object Properties docker, shown in Figure 28-3, as an alternative to using the Internet Toolbar. Although you can apply many of the same settings from this docker, you can't create rollovers from here. To open the Object Properties docker

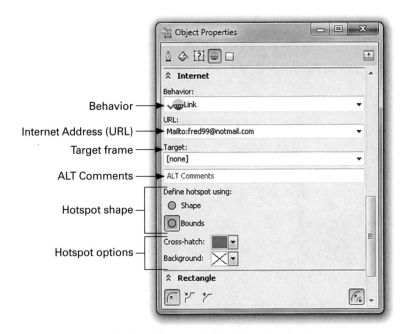

Behavior

Internet Address (URL)

Target frame

ALT Comments

Hotspot shape

Hotspot options

FIGURE 28-3   The Object Properties docker provides an alternative way of applying common Internet properties to objects.

to display web object properties for a selected object, press ALT + ENTER or choose Object Properties from the right-click context menu. With the Object Properties docker open, click the Internet (Globe icon) tab.

Using the Links and Bookmarks Docker

Use the Links and Bookmarks docker to view, name, and apply preexisting bookmarks to objects. To open this docker, shown in Figure 28-4, choose Window | Dockers | Links And Bookmarks.

Purely for convenience, this docker automatically lists the currently applied bookmarks and includes commands for linking, selecting, and deleting existing bookmark links. The bookmarks themselves can only be created using the Bookmarks option from the Behavior selector on the Internet Toolbar. You will find this docker most useful if you are trying to find a particular bookmarked graphic in a multi-page document that contains a lot of bookmarked items.

To find a bookmark in your document, open the Links And Bookmarks docker, and then double-click an entry in the Name column. You're automatically taken to the page, and the bookmarked object is selected.

To create a link to any web page, first select the object to contain the link, click the New Link button, and then type the web address in the open field in the Name list.

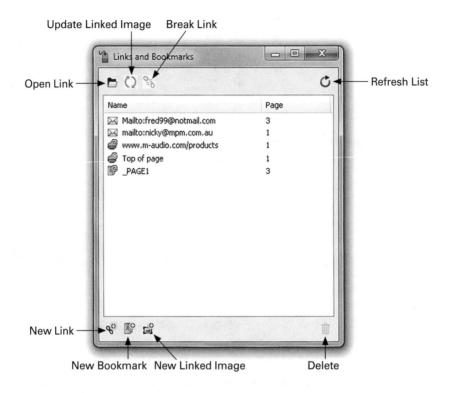

Update Linked Image   Break Link

Open Link

Refresh List

New Link

New Bookmark   New Linked Image   Delete

FIGURE 28-4   The Links And Bookmarks docker provides a convenient way to manage bookmarks applied to objects.

Applying a Page Background

If the background of your web page design calls for something other than white, you'll need to apply a unique background color or tiling pattern. Page background is applied using the Page Setup pane of the Options dialog (CTRL + J), shown in Figure 28-5. To access this dialog quickly, click to expand the listing under Document, and then click Background in the tree directory to view the available options.

Although it might seem logical to create a separate background object for your page and to apply your background properties to it, this can cause problems when it comes time to export your page. The background should be chosen in this dialog as being No Background (the default), a solid color, or a saved bitmap.

Choose Solid to access the color selector for choosing a uniform color. Choose Bitmap and click the Browse button to select a bitmap image as the tiling background.

While Bitmap is selected and a bitmap file has been specified, the Source and Bitmap Size options in the dialog become available. The Source option lets you link to and embed the bitmap with your document, but it has no bearing on how exported web pages are created. The Bitmap Size options let you use either Default Size (the inherent size of the original bitmap) or a Custom Size as the size. By default, the Print And Export Background option is selected, and should remain selected to be included as one of your web page elements.

FIGURE 28-5   Use these options to apply color or tiling bitmap backgrounds to your web document pages.

Publishing Web Documents

The Publish To The Web command is used to export your CorelDRAW document to web page file format. To access this command, choose File | Export HTML or click the Export HTML button on the Internet Toolbar. Both open the same Export HTML dialog, shown in Figure 28-6, which has options for you to set exactly how your web page content is exported. The tabbed dialog looks like and is arranged similarly to CorelDRAW's Print dialog.

Here, you'll find everything you need to save your web page and images. You can also use options to upload your page and the image content to a web server. The dialog itself is divided into six option areas ranging from General to Issues. You can also view a detailed summary of the exported content and any web export preflight issues that CorelDRAW detects. Once CorelDRAW has exported the site, you can preview it by dragging the .HTM files into an open browser window. The sections that follow provide a close look at all the options available.

Setting General Options

Use the General tab to set options such as the destination folder for your exported files. You can specify a separate subfolder for your graphics or remove the default subfolder name (images\) to have the graphics saved in the same folder as your HTML document. To give the graphics subfolder the same name as the HTML document, select Use HTML Name For Image Sub-Folder.

As for the HTML Layout Method area, the best choice for the majority of users is the HTML Table (Most Compatible) method. If you're using the export filter only to export the HTML code for an image map (rather than for an entire web page), you should select Single Image With Image Map.

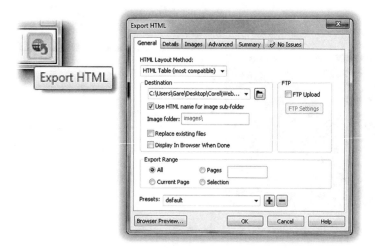

FIGURE 28-6 You can use these options to totally control how your page content is exported.

Examining Web Page Details

The Details tab, shown next, provides information regarding exactly what you selected for export and what the exported file(s) are named. If you want, you can apply unique page titles and/or HTML filenames to your exported web pages by clicking the existing fields and typing in the current names.

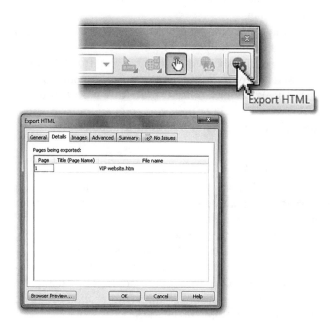

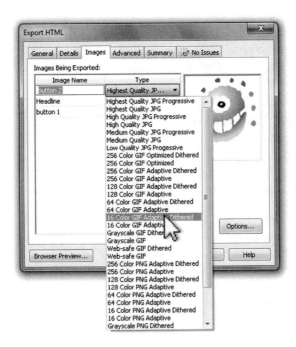

FIGURE 28-7   The listing shown in this tab provides you with invaluable details and options on how each of your web images will be exported.

Reviewing Web Images

The Images tab, shown in Figure 28-7, provides a detailed list of the images that will be exported and their default filenames. For a thumbnail preview of each image, click the Image Name. To change the export format for an image, click the field adjacent to the Image Name under the Type heading.

To change the settings used for each type of exported image, click and then choose from the Type drop-down list. This tab is where you choose an export format for GIFs, JPEGs, and PNGs.

Setting Advanced HTML Options

The Advanced tab provides options for maintaining links you may have made to external files, including JavaScript in your HTML output, and for adding cascading style sheets (CSS) information in your web page. If you're using rollovers, be sure to choose the JavaScript option.

Browsing the Web Page Export Summary

The Summary tab, shown next, provides information on the total size of your web page and how long it will take users to download your page at various modem speeds.

The information is then itemized
for each HTML page and image,
so you can see if something in
particular (such as a large image)
might cause an unnecessarily
long download time.

Preflight Web Issues

The Issues tab, shown in
Figure 28-8—where an object from
the web page has been flagged—
detects and displays potential
HTML export problems by using
a series of preflight conditions.
Preflight issues are found and
displayed according to the options
set throughout the Preflight
Settings dialog, most commonly
regarding issues surrounding text

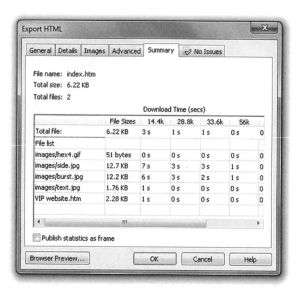

compatibility and image links. The top portion of the dialog tab lists any found issues,
and the bottom portion offers suggestions for correcting the problems. Images should
be RGB for the Web.

FIGURE 28-8   Use the Issues tab to troubleshoot problems and resolve them
before exporting.

To change the issues the preflight feature detects, click the Settings button to open the Preflight Settings dialog, and then click to expand the tree directory under Issues To Check For. You can also use options in this dialog to Add (+) saved preflight issue sets or to Delete (−) existing issue sets in the list. HTML preflight rules are a function only of the web document HTML that you are exporting. If you have, for example, more than three issues flagged, make a mental note of the problems, cancel out of the Export HTML dialog, and then manually correct the issues in your drawing.

Setting Web Publishing Preferences

CorelDRAW gives you control over your personal web publishing preferences by letting you set Publish To The Web options. These options enable you to predetermine many of the settings used when your documents are exported to HTML format, as described earlier. To access these options, open the Options dialog (CTRL + J), click to expand the tree directory under Document, and click Export HTML, shown here.

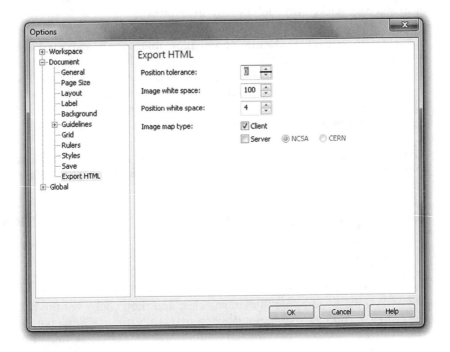

When this Options page has been chosen, you'll see three options for setting conditions under which object position and white space are handled when your web page is exported, as well as an option for image maps:

- **Position Tolerance**   Here you can specify the number of pixels that text objects can be nudged to avoid creating very thin rows or narrow columns when the page is converted to HTML during export. Position Tolerance can be set within a range of 0 (the default) to 100. Increasing this value adds extra space.

- **Image White Space**   Here you specify the number of pixels an empty cell may contain before being merged with an adjacent cell to avoid unnecessary splitting of graphic images.
- **Position White Space**   This option controls the amount of white space to be added to simplify your exported HTML document.
- **Image Map Type**   Choosing Client for the Image Map is the best option because client image maps provide faster interaction with your user than do server image maps. Only use Server if your provider specifically requests it.

Exporting Images for the Web

Although you can specify PNG, GIF, and JPEG file formats for images in your HTML page, you don't have access to nearly the variety of compression types or transparency options unless you pass your images through File | Export For Web. This process is separate from Export HTML. To create images that feature transparency so they "float" against a page background, follow this procedure:

1. Export your HTML document and allow images to be exported to the Images folder CorelDRAW creates.
2. Export images you'd like to treat as special elements—such as PNGs and GIFs with transparent backgrounds—using File | Export For Web.
3. Save these files and then replace the ones in the Images folder with your new files, using the same filenames as the ones in the Images folder.

Then create a graphic you'd like to appear on a web page against a background, and follow the steps in this tutorial to learn how to export the graphic with transparency:

Tutorial   Exporting a Graphic with Transparency

1. Select the graphic on the page with the Pick Tool. If the graphic has a background, don't select the background and you'll save a step.
2. Choose File | Export For Web.
3. In the Export For Web dialog box, choose GIF from the Format drop-down list.
4. Click the Eyedropper Tool to select it, and then click over the background in the GIF preview pane, not the one marked "Original" at its bottom.
5. Click the Makes The Selected Color Transparent button; in a moment, you'll see the preview of the graphic with a checkerboard background indicating the transparent areas of your intended export.
6. Because GIF images can drop out only one color and not a range of colors, if the background of your document isn't black, consider using one of the Matte colors, selected from the Matte mini-palette. If, for example, your web page is solid blue, choose Solid Blue. Doing this has nothing to do with the background color you selected to drop out, but instead has to do with fringing. You choose a compatible background color from the Matte colors to disguise aliased edges around your graphic.

7. Set the unique number of colors for the export. By default, it's 256, but to save transfer time, many simple graphics look fine using 128 or even 32 colors. You specify the number of colors from the Number Of Colors drop-down below the preview of the Color Palette, or you can type a value in the box.

8. If you need to resize the graphic, use the Percentage boxes in the Transformation field of this dialog. But *think twice about this:* your HTML page *won't display the image properly* if you're replacing, for example, a 400 × 300-pixel GIF CorelDRAW just exported to the Images folder with a new graphic that's 375 × 285 pixels.

9. Click Save As, and after you're done, replace the original exported image with this one, renaming the file to match the original filename. See Figure 28-9 to locate the features used in this tutorial.

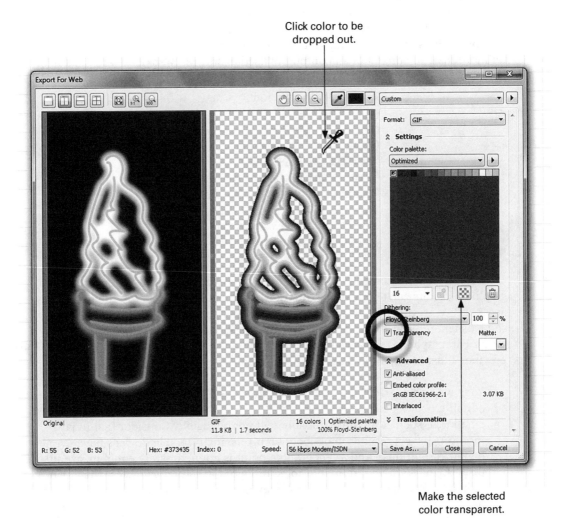

FIGURE 28-9   Export at the file size and with the options you need using Export For Web.

Swapping graphics in an HTML page has to be done with precision. The filename, the file type, and image dimensions have to be identical, because the image dimensions are written into the HTML code. And very few artists want to edit to backward correct an HTML document!

Web Text Options

Recently, web fonts have become a popular, slightly nonstandard way to use any font that can be embedded in a document on a web page. Unfortunately, the method to embed web fonts is outside of this chapter's scope and *standard* W3C-compliant typeface used on web pages is this chapter's topic.

There is no true "default" font for the Web—font display is dependent on the HTML, the web browser your visitors use, and the fonts that are installed on their system. Over the years, though, Microsoft has quietly provided your system—and tens of millions of others—with system fonts that you can be basically assured reside on more than 90 percent of all computers used to surf the Web. Here are the current "web-safe" typefaces:

Arial is a web-safe font.

Comic Sans MS is a web-safe font.

Courier New is a web-safe font.

Georgia is a web-safe font.

Impact is a web-safe font.

Lucida Sans is a web-safe font.

Palatino Linotype is a web-safe font.

Tahoma is a web-safe font.

Times New Roman is a web-safe font.

Trebuchet is a web-safe font.

Verdana is a web-safe font.

On the Web, it's considered discourteous to post long sections of text as bitmap graphics: visitors can't copy or bookmark the text, and it violates the rules of accessibility—text-to-speech readers can't decipher text-as-graphics and indexing services ignore what might be valuable information to you. Therefore, when you create Paragraph Text for a web page, you should use one of the typefaces listed in the previous illustration, for at least two more important reasons:

- Your web page loads slower with text displayed as a graphic instead of as editable text.
- Small text, such as 8 point, probably will not be legible. Consider that today's monitors have a resolution of about 96 pixels/inch (mobile devices have even higher resolutions), and a typographic point is approximately equal in size to one pixel. Eight-point text, then, has to be rendered to screen using less than 11 pixels in height. That's the size of the font previews on CorelDRAW's Fonts drop-down list, and many of the fancier fonts are not legible at this size as bitmap renders.

Figure 28-11 is an example of a web page layout, and as you can see, the text for the business hours is small and formatted as Paragraph Text. This text needs to be

FIGURE 28-10 Text that uses a distinctive typeface has to be exported as a bitmap to retain its look on the Web.

exported as text and not as a bitmap. On the other hand, the name of the fictitious spa, and the elegant headlines above business hours, can be exported as bitmap graphics, especially if the designer wants to retain the style of the typeface.

Follow these steps with any web page layout you have that contains text to learn how to make the document conform to web standards for text:

Tutorial Formatting Text for the Web

1. Format any text you want to be editable text on the web page using the fonts listed earlier.
2. The first thing to do is to check to see that any text you want displayed as text on the web page is Paragraph Text. Select any text in question with the Pick Tool, and then choose Text from the menu. If the command Convert To Paragraph Text is available, choose this command. If it's not available, the text is already Paragraph Text; it's easy to spot on the page because there is a nonprinting frame around Paragraph Text.

3. Conversely, any headlines or other ornate large, short text entries should be Artistic Text. If you don't already have the Make Text Web Compatible button pressed, then with the Pick Tool, select any text that's Paragraph Text but needs to be Artistic Text, and then choose Text | Convert To Artistic Text.
4. Choose Window | Toolbars | Internet. Select a Paragraph Text block, and then click the Make Text Web Compatible button. Do this again for any remaining Paragraph Text blocks.
5. If there is nothing left to link on your web page, click Export HTML.

You will not see Paragraph Text change in any way on your CorelDRAW page; the Make Text Web Compatible button is a toggle—you can select tagged text and then turn off its Web compatibility, and this compatibility is just an instruction on how CorelDRAW writes the HTML. You need to look at the finished HTML page in a web browser—*on a computer other than your own*—to truly see how the Web-compatible Paragraph Text looks. Because web browsers examine your installed fonts, you have no other way to see the text as the rest of the world sees it unless you go through the unpleasant process of temporarily uninstalling several typefaces from your own computer.

Use ALT Tags

The ALT Comments button on the Internet Toolbar—popularly known as *ALT tags*—is used to provide descriptive information about a graphic for those in your web audience who either are surfing with graphics disabled (it's a fast way to perform text searches), or have a visual impairment. It's good "Netiquette" to label graphics on a web page with an ALT tag, particularly if your logo is a graphic and it's the only time it's seen on a web page. Applying ALT tags takes only a second, and here's an example: the fictitious Spa-Di-Dah Health Club's logo is a special typeface and, therefore, has to go out to the Web as a bitmap graphic. Here, the logo is selected, the ALT Comment button is clicked, and a description of the graphic is typed in.

SVG: Export as Vector Objects

The Scalable Vector Graphic (SVG) is a web object CorelDRAW can both import and export. Since 1999, the SVG file format has been under development by the World Wide Web Consortium (W3C). SVG is based on the text-based Extended Markup Language (XML) for describing two-dimensional vector graphics. Most current web browsers can directly render an SVG web page element to screen.

One of the most useful properties of an SVG graphic is that it is scalable, with no loss of image detail. This means you can post a graphic, for example, of directions as a map, and if the SVG file is coded properly into a page, a visitor to your site can enlarge or decrease the size of the map to find exactly where a location is. Also, SVG files are small because they are text-based, and if a friend or client doesn't own CorelDRAW, SVG is an ideal medium for sharing graphics, a good alternative to the PDF file format.

Open Map.cdr in CorelDRAW now, and follow these steps to see how to export a graphic to the Scalable Vector Graphic file format:

Tutorial Exporting Vectors as Vectors for the Web

1. Select the graphic with the Pick Tool or press CTRL + A to select all.
2. Choose File | Export (or click the Export button on the Standard Toolbar). Choose SVE Scalable Vector Graphic (*.SVG), pick a filename and location, and then click Export.
3. Choose SVG 1.1 from the Compatibility drop-down, unless your site absolutely needs to conform to the older standard, perhaps for an enterprise intranet. Choose Unicode UTF 8 as the encoding method. This produces a smaller file than UTF 16 because it encodes words to 8 bits, eliminating some multilingual parameters used in non-Latin text.
4. In the Export Text area, you can choose to export any text in the selected objects As Text or As Curves. If you chose UTF 8, you should export as curves, if you've used non-Latin characters such as those available in fonts such as Arial and Georgia—Chinese and Greek glyphs are present in Unicode fonts. Choose to embed fonts if you're using a typeface that's not Web-compatible.
5. In the Styling Options list box, you can choose to embed a style sheet (a cascading style sheet, CSS) internally or externally with the exported SVG file. If you choose an external style sheet, it's linked to the graphic and can help a Webmaster embed the graphic in a web page.
6. You can also make the SVG part of a rollover button if you check the Link Externally box in the JavaScript area.
7. You can create smooth Fountain Fill steps by increasing the value using the Fountain Steps box. Doing this increases the saved file size, however.
8. Choose the dimensions at which you want the SVG graphic to display in a browser window. It makes no sense, in this example, to make it a small graphic, so a width of 900 pixels is chosen.
9. Export Bitmap is only a relevant field in this export box if objects you've selected cannot be interpreted as vectors. Choose this option if you've used drop shadows, mesh fills, texture fills, and any effect such as Lens effects.

You can embed or export the bitmaps as linked files. Embedding the bitmaps makes the SVG file much larger; if you choose to do this, JPEG—a highly compressed image file type—is probably a smarter choice than PNG.

10. Click OK to export the SVG file. If you have Firefox, Safari, Opera, or Internet Explorer version 9 or better, try dragging the SVG file into an open browser window to see the results. Also, it's safe to continue even if there are preflight issues on the Issues tab. For example, if you use non-RGB colors, Corel converts them automatically. And IDs are of no concern with the accuracy of an SVG file export.

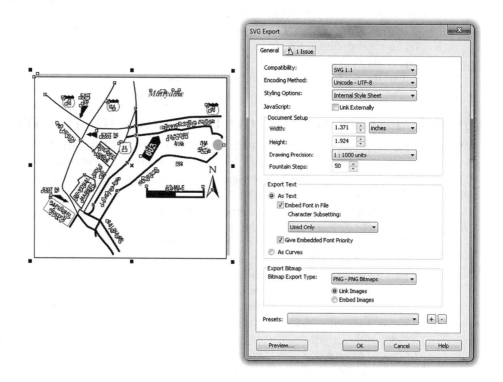

Exploring SWF Files

There has been some confusion in recent years over mobile devices and the general decision not to support Flash, an Adobe product that has been used on the Web to play exceptionally compressed, but high-quality video. A Shockwave file (a file with the SWF extension) is not a Flash file, not strictly speaking. A Shockwave file can contain bitmap images but usually does not. There are two types of SWF files: animations and still images. CorelDRAW can export only still SWF files, but the overall attractive thing about SWF artwork is that it can be scaled with no loss in image quality, and you might find that an SWF piece of artwork might be smaller than the same size graphic exported as an SVG file.

There are some fill and outline properties CorelDRAW can add to objects that the Shockwave format doesn't support. Like SVG files, if an SWF file can't write a vector, a bitmap copy of the graphic is included in the exported file. Exporting bitmaps within an SWF file defeats the purpose of this compact vector-enabled file type, so a review of what can export as vector objects, and what cannot, is a good thing to do here.

Objects and Fills that SWF Supports

The good news is that everything that an SWF file can handle, CorelDRAW can create. The following list describes what you should and shouldn't use when making a drawing destined for SWF export:

- **Outline properties** Standard SWF export supports outline width and color, but only rounded line caps and joins; CorelDRAW's export filter can convert straight end caps to rounded if you choose High Quality-Optimized from the Presets drop-down list. The Export dialog box also offers to convert only dashed outlines to be compatible with SWF.
- **Fill Properties** SWF renders Uniform Color Fills, plus Linear and Radial Fountain Fills. A gradient can contain up to eight color transitions (color stops).
- **Transparency** If you apply transparency to a gradient-filled shape, you are limited to the Uniform Transparency type. However, when a shape is filled with a flat (solid) color, you can use Linear and Radial Transparency types.
- **Text** You can use any typeface you have installed, as long as you uncheck Text As Text before exporting so the text is converted to curves. A visitor's computer must have the same font you do installed to read text as text.
- **Bitmaps** Photos and digital paintings can be exported to a Shockwave file, but they cannot be as efficiently compressed as vector shapes. It's a good idea to make a copy of high-resolution images at the size you intend to use, in JPEG file format.
- **Effects** All effects—Contours, Blends, and Envelopes—applied to shapes can be exported; using these effects is a good workaround to certain types of Fountain Fills that don't work as Shockwave vector objects.

Exporting a Static Shockwave Vector Design

Open Solutions Graphic.cdr in CorelDRAW now. Here's the procedure and your options for exporting an SWF file:

Tutorial Making a Single-frame SWF File

1. Select all the objects using the diagonal-drag, marquee technique around the objects. They are on different layers, so CTRL + A doesn't work here.
2. Click the Export button on the Standard toolbar, and then choose SWF-Adobe Flash (.SWF) from the Save As Type drop-down list. Choose a location for the saved file and name it, and then click Export.

3. On the General tab, shown here, Bitmap Settings are only of relevance when objects have fills that the export engine cannot recognize. In your own exporting adventures, use JPEG with no or 10 percent compression to preserve the appearance of vector objects that have texture or other nonacceptable fills.

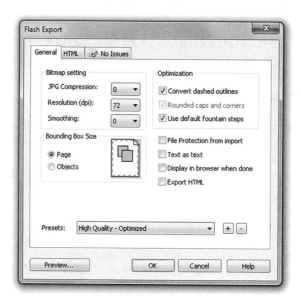

4. Click Objects in the Bounding Box Size area; you have the objects already selected in Step 1, so this option is the smart one.
5. Check Convert Dashed Outlines just as a matter of practice. Use Default Fountain Steps is a handy option if your objects only have subtle fills or fewer than eight color transitions. Unchecking this box can create larger files, but unchecking this box can produce smaller files with visible banding.
6. The HTML tab really only contains one item of interest: Image Size. If you want to export this graphic at any size, select the size using the spin boxes or by typing a specific value here.
7. If the Issues tab reports that there are non-RGB colors in the selection, dismiss it. Click OK to export the graphic as a Flash media object.
8. Some older web browsers require JavaScript to display an SWF file directly on the Web, but if you have a copy of Firefox or IE 9 or later, you can drag the SWF file into its browser pane and you'll see the graphic full-screen. Also, Adobe's Flash Player 10.*x* displays the file if you've downloaded the player; chances are good some application has already fetched it for you and made the file association. Double-clicking the file icon might bring up Flash Player.

This chapter has shown you how to take just about any media on a CorelDRAW page, be it a drawing, a photo, or text, and make your design compatible as a web page. With links, your web page connects you to a community and keeps you connected with business associates, friends, and potential customers you haven't even met yet.

Index